PLAS

PITT LATIN AMERICAN SERIES

PITT LATIN AMERICAN SERIES
Cole Blasier, Editor

AUTHORITARIANISM AND CORPORATISM IN LATIN AMERICA

AUTHORITARIANISM
and
CORPORATISM
in Latin America

JAMES M. MALLOY, Editor

UNIVERSITY OF PITTSBURGH PRESS

Library of Congress Cataloging in Publication Data

Main entry under title:

Authoritarianism and corporatism in Latin
America.

(Pitt Latin American series)
"Outgrowth of a conference . . . held at the
University of Pittsburgh in April 1974."
Bibliography: p. 529
Includes index.
1. Latin America—Politics and government—
1948–   —Congresses. 2. Corporate State—
Latin America—Congresses. 3. Authoritarianism
—Congresses. I. Malloy, James M.
JL958.A9 1976   320.9'8'003   76-6669
ISBN 0-8229-3328-4
ISBN 0-8229-5275-0 pbk.

Contents

Preface

Periodically social scientists find it necessary to rethink and reevaluate the conceptual tools they use to analyze the substantive problems of the societies they observe. During the past several years such a process of reevaluation has been going on among analysts concerned with problems of political economy in the context of Latin America. This process has been spurred on in part by the appearance in the region during the 1960s of a number of "modernizing-authoritarian" regimes and the discovery by social scientists that most of our concepts and theories were inadequate tools with which to analyze these regimes. Thus, there developed a renewed interest in "authoritarianism," both as a specific type of regime and as a political approach to the problems of economic development and modernization.

In attempting to come to grips with the phenomenon of modernizing-authoritarian regimes, many analysts began to point out that the standard theoretical frameworks applied to Latin America, while useful, did not provide sufficient help to analyze a number of crucial dimensions of the contemporary political economy of the region. Specifically, they were inadequate to analyze the important role of the state in Latin America or to deal with the complex process by which the interactions between the state and organized societal groupings have been structured and restructured over time. In approaching these issues many scholars have suggested that the concept of "corporatism" provides a more useful theoretical perspective to study the relationships between state and society in Latin America.

These intellectual developments have set off a generalized debate among Latin American specialists regarding the theoretical and conceptual perspectives through which the substantive problems of the region are approached. Increasingly the debate has centered around the question of the use or abuse of the concepts of authoritarianism and corporatism. This book tries to contribute to this debate. In my view, the debate is an important attempt to deal with crucial issues and cannot be passed off simply as reflecting the propensity of social scientists periodically to indulge themselves in intellectual faddishness.

This book is the outgrowth of a conference on authoritarianism and corporatism in Latin America held at the University of Pittsburgh in April 1974. For three days a group of twenty Latin American specialists met to present papers and to debate the issues raised by the papers. Over the next year the participants exchanged various revised drafts of their papers for further criticism and discussion. The chapters by Evelyn P. Stevens and Henry A. Dietz were solicited by the editor subsequent to the conference. While we sought to develop a coherent and integrated volume of papers, uniformity of views was neither sought nor achieved; each author assumes responsibility for the views set forth in his or her chapter.

As editor of the volume my thanks go first to the contributors, both for the excellence of their papers and for their willingness to make an editor's lot easier by meeting a very tight schedule of deadlines. I would also like to acknowledge the generous financial support of the University of Pittsburgh's Center for International Studies, which made the conference possible, and the unflagging cooperation of the center's director, Carl Beck. My thanks also go to Cole Blasier, Carmelo Mesa-Lago, and the staff of the University of Pittsburgh's Center for Latin American Studies for their invaluable help in planning the conference. I would also like to thank Alfred Stepan and Ronald Newton, who attended the conference and made numerous contributions to our discussions.

I think all the participants at the conference would agree that our meetings benefited immensely from the active participation of an outstanding group of graduate students specializing in Latin American studies at the University of Pittsburgh. Thanks and recognition are owed to Luis Abugattas, Helen Douglass, Silvio Duncan Baretta, German Garrido, Judith Ludvick, Mark B. Rosenberg, and Mitchell Seligson.

I owe special thanks to Helen Douglass and Mark Rosenberg for their tireless help in organizing the conference and the volume and for the important contributions they made to my two papers. My thanks also go to Linda Perkins, who helped in numerous ways to prepare the papers for presentation to the publisher. Finally, I would like to thank Beth Luey for the excellence with which she carried out the grueling job of copy editing the entire manuscript.

I

Introduction

JAMES M. MALLOY

1

Authoritarianism and Corporatism in Latin America: The Modal Pattern

For the foreseeable future at least, "modernizing authoritarian" regimes will remain a part of political life in Latin America. This fact has forced a rethinking of much of the conventional wisdom regarding the area, be it based on Marxist or liberal democratic theoretical foundations. The recent experiences of Brazil, Argentina, and Peru, and the discovery that behind the façade, Mexico is really an authoritarian system, have led many to suggest that the region is generating a "new path" to development which, if it is to be understood, demands the fashioning of new conceptual approaches to the analysis not only of these regimes but of the region as a whole.[1] Central to this rethinking is the recognition that authoritarian regimes are not historically doomed to extinction as societies modernize and develop but are potentially viable (if unpleasant) modes of organizing a society's developmental efforts. Indeed, one author has persuasively argued that authoritarian regimes of a certain type are actually a product of high levels of modernization in the Latin American context.[2] Whichever is the case, it is now generally agreed that authoritarian systems constitute a regime type which must be understood in its own terms and within which it is possible to delineate a number of subtypes.

While the significance of the concept of authoritarianism as a regime type has been largely accepted, there remains some confusion regarding the delineation of subtypes, particularly when one comes to grips with authoritarian regimes that are self-consciously oriented toward the development and modernization of their respective societies. Thus, the terms bureaucratic authoritarianism, populist authoritarianism, and military populism have all recently been offered as ways of talking about specific modernizing authoritarian regimes in the area—with Juan Perón and Getúlio Vargas representing populist authoritarianism, Peru

3

since 1968 military populism, and Brazil since 1964 bureaucratic authoritarianism.[3] These distinctions are undoubtedly useful in that they point out significant differences among these regimes in terms of the role of charismatic leadership, group coalitions supporting regimes, and differences in policy emphasis and developmental strategies. These, in turn, have been effectively traced to the varying levels of development achieved by the different countries when the specific regimes appeared.

Despite the important differences unearthed by this approach, others have pointed out an overarching similarity in structure and organizational principles among the regimes just mentioned and other authoritarian systems such as Mexico's. The critical point of similarity is that each of these regimes is characterized by strong and relatively autonomous governmental structures that seek to impose on the society a system of interest representation based on enforced limited pluralism. These regimes try to eliminate spontaneous interest articulation and establish a limited number of authoritatively recognized groups that interact with the governmental apparatus in defined and regularized ways. Moreover, the recognized groups in this type of regime are organized in vertical functional categories rather than horizontal class categories and are obliged to interact with the state through the designated leaders of authoritatively sanctioned interest associations. This mode of organizing state and society has aptly been termed "corporatism."[4] Viewed from this perspective, the conceptual problem in the Latin American context can be broken down to three levels of analysis: (1) a general level of regime-type authoritarianism of which there can be many variants, running from an old-fashioned caudillo such as Anastasio Somoza to a sophisticated regime such as Brazil's; (2) an overarching subtype "corporatism" which is defined in terms of structural and organizational principles; and (3) a series of subtypes within corporatism (those noted above) defined in terms of the roles of leaders, supporting coalitions, and policy strategies. Thus, corporatism can be seen as a major authoritarian theme upon which there can be different variations.

Among those who address themselves to these questions there is considerable disagreement as to the factors, both regional and country-specific, that account for the emergence of corporatist authoritarian regimes. Some authors stress a Hispanic-Catholic tradition that has long lain dormant in the region and is presently asserting itself.[5] Others go a step further and point to a persistent de facto mode of group formation and conflict always present in the region behind the façade of previous liberal democratic constitutional forms.[6] From either of these two perspectives, one might say that the emergence of an authoritarian corporate regime in a given country represents less a breakdown of democracy into authoritarianism than a break-out from a grafted liberal democratic structure of an underlying mode of political organization. Be that as it may, others who recognize the significance of these two factors rightly point out that they alone cannot account for the emergence of authoritarian corporate regimes and particularly their orientation toward the promotion of development and modernization.[7]

For these authors, the problem must be placed in its developmental focus. To do this, one must take into account the level of development achieved by specific countries and the international context of development impinging on the region as a whole and on specific countries. Those who approach the question from this more complex and historically specific developmental context have pointed to two important processes that are closely linked to the emergence of authoritarian corporate regimes. First, they point to the crucial fact that the region as a whole and countries within it began to develop later than the advanced industrial states; therefore, the nations of Latin America confront the process from different vantage points and different perspectives. One critical aspect of this lateness is the fact that all of the nations of the region are based on economies that are to one degree or another dependent on and influenced by the more advanced industrial states. In brief, the first factor of significance is the phenomenon of "delayed dependent development."[8] The second factor is connected with the fact that throughout a large part of the region the most significant political movements that have sought to promote reform and change since the 1920s and 1930s were based, in some fashion or other, on an orientation generally called "populism."[9] The term is no doubt vague and embraces a variety of political movements. Most agree, however, that the phenomenon of populism has been critical in the region. Thus, besides the Hispanic tradition and de facto modes of group conflict, two processes rooted in the region's twentieth-century developmental experiences are closely linked to the emergence of corporatist authoritarianism. These are the phenomena of delayed dependent development and populism.

Delayed Dependent Development

The contemporary trend toward authoritarian corporatist regimes in Latin America must be viewed against the backdrop of the region's previous pattern of economic development, which is best described as delayed dependent capitalist development. In this chapter, then, authoritarian corporatist regimes are seen as responses to a general crisis of public authority brought about by the multiple effects of delayed dependent development. More specifically, the problem to which these regimes have responded has been that of integrating a multiplicity of societal interests into a decision-making structure that guarantees a minimum of political stability and allows decision makers to launch development-oriented policies. By and large, formally democratic regimes have been unable in the Latin American context simultaneously to integrate societal actors and to sponsor development, thus leading to the predisposition in many countries to adopt authoritarian corporatist solutions.

In this chapter, we will examine in broad terms the major sequences in the region's development pattern with the aim of linking the phenomena of delayed dependent development, populism, corporatism, and authoritarianism. Particular attention will be paid to the phenomenon of populism, which from the 1930s on was the most significant type of political movement in the entire region and, in my view, is the most important direct link between delayed dependent development and corporatist authoritarianism. In brief, the argument of this chapter is that populism was a general regional response to the first crisis of delayed dependent development. In both orientation and practice, populism was at least implicitly corporatist but left open the question of whether it would establish corporatist structures within a formally democratic or authoritarian framework. Both variations were attempted at various times in different countries. By and large, however, not only did populist elites fail to resolve the underlying crisis, but because of internal contradictions within the movements, in most cases they actually exacerbated the situation. They thereby contributed to an environment which tended to give rise to the more blatant authoritarian corporatist regimes we see in the region today.

The phenomena of delayed development and external dependence in Latin America have been examined at length by numerous scholars. In brief, this pattern of development took place during the end of the nineteenth and the beginning of the twentieth century in response to stimuli emanating from the more industrialized capitalist states of Western Europe and the United States. As a result, the various nations of the region were integrated into an international capitalist market system where they functioned mainly as suppliers of raw materials and consumers of manufactured goods. For the most part, economic growth and modernization in the region were the results of an outward-oriented growth model which overemphasized development of the export sectors of the local economies.

The outward-oriented growth model had numerous secondary effects on the nations of the region. In the first instance, the local economies became increasingly dependent on an international market structure over which they had little or no control. In addition, internal development was extremely unbalanced, which in turn led to a local situation of structural dualism: The nations of the region experienced a differentiation into a relatively modern urbanized sphere based on the export sector and a more traditionally organized and more backward agricultural sphere. The former dominated and exploited the latter, thereby recapitulating within the countries of the region the phenomenon of the dependency of a more backward periphery on a more advanced center. Thus, by the 1920s, a major characteristic of the region was an interlocking hierarchy of dependency structures descending from the advanced industrial center, through the various states of Latin America, and into the most backward regions of the various nations.

Development during this period did not eliminate previous societal patterns in the region but added onto them more modern, externally derived patterns, creating the general Latin American phenomenon that Charles Anderson has labeled the "living museum."[10] Internally, the countries of the area were cleft along myriad lines of division and potential conflict that cut along regional, racial, cultural, caste, and class lines. Internally, these powerful centrifugal tendencies were held in check by a powerful local elite of landed, export, and commercial interests—often referred to as the oligarchy—that was able to assert its hegemony through control of the state. The key to this pattern of elite control was a de facto internal structure of vertically organized patron-client networks based on an internal hierarchy of dependency and dominance that pervaded the nations of the region. These vertically ordered patron-client networks, as Julio Cotler has shown for Peru, ran from the local center to the local periphery, cutting across class, caste, and regional lines, thereby fostering highly particularistic orientations and vitiating mobilization along horizontal lines of class or caste.[11] Particularism, along with the multiple lines of cleavage, fostered a columnar social structure which has been excellently described by scholars such as Kalman Silvert and Ronald C. Newton.[12] Thus, in one sense, the various nations of the region manifested the invertebrate social structure that José Ortega y Gasset described in Spain.[13]

The tendency for this type of society to fly apart was held in check somewhat by a hegemonic elite in effective control of authority and the interlocking clientelistic nets descending from national elites down into intermediary and local subelites. Internally interconnected points of dependence created a vertically structured system of interdependence which tended to hold the parts of the system together.

A central social grouping to appear during the first stage of export-based development was a new urban middle class. As a product of delayed export-based development rather than autonomous industrial development, the Latin American middle class differed markedly from

the middle class in the industrial center. In the main, it was a class of
liberal professionals and public and private white-collar employees who
were dependent in the sense that they did not control hard sources of
wealth but lived off wages, salaries, and fees. A large sector of the
middle class depended on public employment, a phenomenon often
referred to as premature bureaucratization: the tendency of the formal
governmental apparatus to expand faster than underlying socioeconomic structures. This pattern of premature bureaucratization fostered consumption patterns which in later years outstripped the local
economies' ability to sustain them.[14] In any event, the new dependent
urban middle class was destined to become a critical political actor
from the 1930s on and the human base that spawned populism.

Finally, delayed dependent development significantly affected the
position of formal governmental structures or "the state." By the late
1920s, most Latin American state structures vis-à-vis both internal and
external actors were characterized by low levels of autonomy and
relative weakness. In other words, the general situation of dependence
translated into the specific dependence of the state upon a limited
number of internal and external actors. The growing need for financial
resources to support expanding public employment owing to the incorporation of sectors of the urban middle class into the public bureaucracy increased even further the state's dependence on a limited
number of internal and external sources of revenue. Thus, governments
in the region were subjected to heavy pressure from the local elite as
well as from external private and public interests who were able in the
main to shape local public policy to reflect their interests. Again from
the 1930s on, a critical political issue was to be the power, effectiveness, and autonomy of the various central state structures of Latin
America.

The Emergence of Populism

The 1930s and 1940s are an important watershed in Latin American
history. The worldwide depression hit the region with particular
ferocity, bowling over the props of the area's export-based economies
and causing widespread internal dislocation. The disruption of international trading structures threw the bulk of the Latin American states
back on their own resources; the relative economic isolation of the
1930s was reinforced in the 1940s by World War II. Economic depression, sociopolitical disruptions, and relative isolation forced a general
rethinking of the region's internal structures and their links to international structures.

Central to the rethinking of Latin America's position was a generalized rejection of the "liberal" concepts of political economy that had been previously dominant and a significant rise in nationalist sentiment expressed as a generalized desire for autonomous national development of individual societies. Nationalism and developmentalism became, and were to remain, dominant ideological themes throughout the region.

The problem, of course, was to give concrete substance to the sentiments of nationalism and developmentalism. Although a variety of groups from left to right vied for power and the capacity to redefine individual societies, the most significant alternative political expression to emerge during the period was populism. Populism is a general and somewhat amorphous concept that embraces a wide-ranging spectrum of political movements and programs. Nonetheless, there is sufficient similarity in terms of group composition among these movements and enough thematic consistency behind their programs to justify considering them *as of a piece.*[15]

In retrospect, it is evident that populism was a specific and indigenous regional response to a general crisis which emerged from the exhaustion of a particular phase of delayed dependent development: namely, the exhaustion of the primary-product, outward-oriented growth model. The inability to sustain this model in the face of the global crisis of a stage of international capitalism reflected itself in Latin America in a general crisis of authority of the internal oligarchic power structures that had previously held sway. The hallmark of this "hegemonic" crisis was the disaffection of large sectors of the middle class from the system of which they had been the bedrock of support.[16] With the collapse of oligarchic authority, sectors of the middle class were thrust to the forefront of the political struggle. However, these disaffected elements of the middle class could not independently carry out basic structural transformations, and to buttress their position they had to seek allies in other social strata. Populism became the guise within which change-oriented segments of the middle class sought to construct multiclass coalitions powerful enough to gain control of the state and underwrite programs of structural transformation. Populism in Latin America was and remains largely the ideological product of the highly bureaucratized and largely dependent Latin American middle class which found its previously secure position threatened by the multiple effects of the exhaustion of the export-oriented growth model.

Populist movements varied widely from the highly personalized style of Perón and Vargas, who both constructed movements and ideologies from positions of formal power, to the more organized movements such as the Alianza Popular Revolucionaria Americana (APRA) in Peru, Acción Democrática (AD) in Venezuela, and the Movimiento Nacionalista Revolucionario (MNR) in Bolivia, which constructed organizations and ideologies as a means to assault the bastions of formal power. The biographies and relative "success" of these movements varied considerably; but in all cases populism left a deep imprint, both in terms of its concrete impact on the respective systems of political economy and as a potent ideological legacy. Populist rhetoric has played a major role in structuring political debate in Latin America since the 1930s, and in one manner or another all political forces from left to right have been forced to structure their behavior in response to the populist challenge. For good or ill, populism has, since its inception, been the major political force in Latin America.

Rhetoric and self-designation notwithstanding, Latin American populism was never revolutionary in the sense of advocating a radical break with the past and a total overhaul of existing structures. On the contrary, in both theory and practice it was and remains a reformist attempt at limited structural transformations aimed at adapting to new exigencies, while at the same time maintaining basic continuity with past cultural traditions. Populist political doctrine proceeded from a diagnosis of the ills of Latin America which anticipated many later theoretical formulations, including those of Raul Prebisch of the United Nations Economic Commission for Latin America, and many aspects of the contemporary theory of "dependence."[17]

For the populists, the central problems of Latin America were economic underdevelopment and deformed economic structures. A central dilemma was the lack of internal "integration" owing to the dichotomy between a modern sector and what the populists called a semifeudal agrarian sector. In the Indo-American countries such as Peru and Bolivia, populists also stressed a lack of geographical and cultural integration reinforced by dualism. These internal structural problems were due to the structure of the international system—for example, imperialism, particularly that of the United States—and the way the international structures penetrated local economies, transforming them into semicolonial appendages. The mechanism of imperial penetration was the local oligarchy, which identified its interests with those of the imperial powers, thereby becoming agents who plundered the local economy for the benefit of their foreign allies.

The local oligarchy was a nonnational class that aided the imperial center to exploit the nation as a whole. Thus, the problem was not, as the Marxists would have it, the internal exploitation of class by class, but the global exploitation of the "nation" by the "antination." The nation was made up of all the groups other than the oligarchy (at a minimum, the middle class, workers, and peasants) who, because they were equally exploited, shared a common set of interests. The task, therefore, was not to form a class-based party to establish the rule of one exploited class, but to form a broad multiclass movement to unseat the oligarchy and install leadership that would represent the entire nation.

The chief declared goals of the populists were: (1) to assert national economic independence, for example, anti-imperialism; (2) to break local semifeudal structures so as to liberate human and material resources for economic development; and (3) to promote social justice for all sectors of the nation. The central agency charged with achieving these goals was the state; central themes for the populists were state, nation, development, and social justice. The task of the multiclass movement was to seize the state and use it to promote the other goals. Populism was oriented to a system in which the state would control national resources to assure their local reinvestment and equitable distribution.

Populism was therefore "statist," but it was not socialist: Indeed, populism rejected in rhetoric both socialism and capitalism and advocated a third route to development which was unique to each nation. While populism was rhetorically anti-imperialist and anticapitalist, most populist ideologies argued that its backward, semifeudal condition made the nation's attempt to break completely with internal and external structures both impossible and foolhardy. Rather, the task was to expand state power so as to reform and regulate internal and external structures and achieve an evolutionary process of controlled economic development. In terms of political economy, populism advocated a system of "neomercantilism" or what some would call "state capitalism."

Another populist theme was that of "integral" development, an organizational principle to achieve maximum sociopolitical harmony. Having rejected Marxian principles of class analysis and the "egotistical individualism" of liberalism, and having assumed a community of interests among all groups of the nation, populism projected the possibility of achieving development with a minimum of social conflict. The key to achieving this goal was to construct society around a set of principles that would foster interdependence and cooperation.

The profound impact of the populist vision can be seen not only in those countries where populists came to power, but also in the fact that during this period most Latin American nations either amended or rewrote their constitutions in terms that heavily reflected populist concepts. The process of constitutional revision was so general that some have referred to the period as the "era of social constitutionalism."[18] These ideas were so widespread that one could argue that there developed, particularly among the middle classes of Latin America, a general consensus around the image of reform preferred by the populists.[19] The problem, of course, was to put the image into practice. Latin American politics since the 1930s can be interpreted in part as a struggle to realize the reformist image of populism. When the Cuban Revolution transcended this reformist image and created an alternative radical revolutionary image, a sense of urgency was added which created among many groups, including sectors of the elite and the military, a belief that something resembling populist reform had to be implemented if more radical solutions were to be avoided.

Looking back at populism from this vantage point, in terms of ideological formulations, constitutional principles, and the kinds of practices implemented by populist governments such as those of Vargas, Perón, and the Mexican Partido Revolucionario Institucional (PRI) (the Mexican Revolution anticipated populism and was a major symbol for most populists), the MNR, and others, it is now evident that populism was and is based on an implicit *corporatist* image of sociopolitical organization. With the exception of Vargas, the populist preference for a corporatist solution to the pressures of modernization was seldom stated explicitly, but there seems little gainsaying that populism has always shown a high affinity for corporatist principles of organizing the relations between state and society.[20] The real issue has been whether it would be a more or less democratic corporatist solution or a more or less authoritarian solution.

Populism advocated a pluralistic coalition to achieve reform and therefore sought to mobilize the working class and to some degree the peasants. But it is important to keep in mind that populism was primarily a middle-class phenomenon. Populist doctrine was also founded on the notion that because of economic backwardness and structural deformity, the mass of workers and peasants were themselves underdeveloped and hence ill prepared to define either their own interests or those of the nation. Populists saw the mass of workers and peasants as "human capital" to be freed from semifeudal fetters and more rationally organized as a productive force.[21] Another theme was that the workers and peasants had to be "capacitated" (educated) to play their future role. In short, populism has always looked at the masses of workers and peasants as backward groups whose main role was to follow the lead of the populist elite, that is, the progressive sectors of the middle class. From its inception, populism has been infused with an elitist orientation in which the masses tended to be viewed as objects to be manipulated and controlled (for their own good) and were to remain the passive recipients of paternalistic social policies formulated by the elite. Whatever else it was, populist ideology was at its base nationalist, statist, and elitist.

The Impact of Populism

While populism was a multifaceted phenomenon whose impact varied throughout the region, a number of generalizations hold for most of Latin America from the 1930s to the 1960s. These can be related either to the direct impact of populist governments or to the indirect effect of populist orientations on public policy and/or the need of status-quo elites to respond to the challenge of populist movements.

Populism rejected classical liberal political economy and argued that one of the key problems of the region was the inability of the states of Latin America to limit the influence of external actors and to direct local economic activity so as to promote broad-based economic development. This inability was rooted in the weakness and low autonomy of the state, which in turn was rooted in external economic dependence and local oligarchic control. Thus, populist elites sought to control the state and use it to undermine the power of the local oligarchy, restructure external economic relations, and intervene in the economy to overcome the outward-oriented export model by stimulating economic diversification, mainly through policies of import substitution. In a sense, the real problem was to seize the state and create a base so as to render it capable of acting as an autonomous factor shaping both its internal and external environment rather than as a more or less passive instrumentality reflecting the push and pull of environmental stimuli and pressures.

In coping with this problem, populist regimes sought to expand the support base for more effective and directive governmental decision-making by mobilizing broad popular support, not on the basis of "class," but on the basis of "citizenship," that is, the nation (concretized in the state) versus the antination. Throughout the region, populism directly contributed to a significant increase in both the breadth and the tempo of political mobilization, drawing large sectors of hitherto excluded social groups (organized labor, marginal urban residents, peasants, etc.) directly into the political arena. To use E. E. Schattschneider's image, one impact of populism was to expand significantly the scope of political conflict.[22]

In its first phases, then, by emphasizing mobilization, populism was oriented to the inclusion of a very broad set of actors into the political game. The purpose of this "inclusionary" approach was to underpin the power of populist regimes and increase the autonomy of the state. However, to make the state an effective regulatory instrumentality, central authorities had to achieve a degree of independence not only from traditional foci of pressure but from those mobilized by the populists as well. Populist regimes therefore sought not only to mobilize a broad popular base but also to control that base and structure the relationships of its support groups to the state.

The objective need to control and structure the mobilization process fed directly into the elitist and statist tendency implicit in the populist leadership's orientation, which in some cases (Perón and Vargas, for example) mutated quickly into an openly authoritarian governmental style. Populist regimes attempted to structure and control their support base by a combination of three factors. In the first instance, they offered symbolic gratification in the form of charismatic leadership styles, new symbols of dignity (Perón's *descamisados*), nationalist rhetoric, and significant nationalistic acts such as the expropriation of foreign corporations. Populist regimes also offered their supporters material gratification in the form of increased wages and salaries, expansion of public employment, expansion of public services, etc. Finally, populist regimes sought to fashion centrally controlled organizational structures to link their support groups directly into the state structures. The bulk of these organizations were formed on sectoral and functional criteria, thereby fragmenting support groups into parallel primary organizational structures joined at the top by interlocking sectoral elites.[23] The success of populist organizational efforts varied considerably, but they all manifested a clear predilection for corporatist organizational principles; in the case of Vargas, the corporatist bias was made explicit in the constitution of the Estado Nôvo.

A central problem hampering the ability of most populist regimes to maintain control over their own followings was the inherent contradiction between the populist goal of stimulating state-sponsored economic development and the tactic of mobilizing a mass base by increasing the levels of popular consumption. The tension between policies fostering development and those increasing consumption in an environment of relative scarcity was manifested most directly in the problem of inflation, which was chronic in most countries of the Latin American region from the 1940s on.

Political mobilization concomitant with a rise in nationalism and increases in levels of popular consumption had two further impacts: the introduction of new principles of legitimacy, and the creation of serious strains on the limited economic resources of most countries in the region. By the 1940s, the principles of a nationalist-oriented welfare statism had become so deeply implanted that even status-quo regimes at least had to pay lip service to them. The problem of meeting an increase in range and intensity of material demands, manifested most directly in chronic inflation, created serious problems of social control which plagued populist as well as nonpopulist regimes. A combination of the inability to unseat traditional elites as well as to control their own followers brought numerous populist experiments to untimely and often violent ends.

By the 1950s, populism had had a profound impact on the area. It had (1) weakened the power of the traditional elites; (2) stimulated import substitution growth, which increased the relevance of local industrialists and organized labor; and (3) stimulated a general increase in political mobilization and popular consumption. The last factor in particular tended to outstrip both the rate of growth and the control capacity of public institutions, contributing thereby to a general tendency in the direction of praetorian politics.[24]

An important aspect of the praetorianization of Latin American politics during this period was the fact that although the formal state apparatuses in the region grew markedly, this was accompanied not by an increase in the power and efficiency of the states but rather by the reverse. The continuing reality of dependence was a critical factor in the development of states that were formally large and powerful but in practice weak. Another factor was a kind of de facto disaggregation of the state as various particularistic interest blocs in a sense captured relevant pieces of the state which they manipulated to their own benefit.[25] This de facto parceling out of bits of the state was particularly evident in the politics of social security policy. As some analysts have shown, the many funds tended to become the fiefdoms of the interests they served and were used in a manner that actually reinforced socioeconomic inequality even as social security spending fed inflation.[26] Thus, instead of an assertion of the autonomous power of the state apparatus to regulate its internal and external environment, this period saw an increase in the size of the state but a decrease in autonomy, power, and efficiency of governmental apparatuses.

Despite these developments, the pressures generated in the 1930s and 1940s were to a large extent contained during the 1950s and 1960s despite recurrent predictions of violent revolutionary upheavals that would sweep the continent. Anderson has effectively argued that containment was achieved because of the flexibility of established elites who adapted to the new situation by allowing proven power contenders into the political game as long as they did not seek to unseat established power groups.[27] In short, the period saw a kind of de facto politics of informal and nonstructured inclusion which expanded the participants in the political game without any significant restructuring of the game. This process (which Cotler described in Peru and labeled segmental incorporation) had numerous effects, including an increase in particularism, reinforcement of columnar social organization, and expansion of clientelistic politics.[28]

The ability to maintain a politics of inclusion by co-optation of specific power contenders was a direct function of resources available to meet demands which, of course, varied widely in the region. The ability to generate resources was in turn tied to the previous nature and degree of external dependence, and the ability to generate horizontal growth based on import substitution—capacities which fluctuated widely. Variations on these factors were important variables accounting for the political patterns in different countries during the 1950s and 1960s. But even in countries with more diversified export sectors and a large capacity for import substitution, the ability to generate resources and maintain a politics of segmental incorporation was not unlimited. By the mid-1960s it became evident that even in nations such as Brazil and Argentina there were both internal and external structural limits on import substitution growth and that instead of diminishing external dependence, import substitution resulted in new and more onerous forms of dependence.

By the mid-1960s, a new structural crisis developed with the exhaustion of import substitution growth and the reality of even more pervasive external economic penetration by multinational corporations that assert control over local manufacturing activities. This time the crisis took place against a backdrop of an accumulated public legitimation of nationalism and developmentalism, and societies characterized by high rates of political mobilization. One might also add the existence of revolutionary Cuba, which acted as a specter of what might come if matters were left to drift. In this situation, increased praetorian politicization in a context of large but weak and disarticulated states rendered a civil solution to the accumulated problems and bottlenecks all but impossible.

Thus, acting under the guise of doctrines of national security and national developmentalism, military organizations in several Latin states seized formal power. Again, the effectiveness of these regimes has varied, but in all cases the orientation to state-sponsored rapid industrial development has been paramount. To achieve this general goal, two subsidiary goals have loomed large. First has been a concerted attempt to increase the power and autonomy of the formal state and establish it as the primary regulator and arbiter of political economy. Related to this has been a conscious decision to favor some power contenders and their interests over others. This has given rise to what Guillermo O'Donnell has called the politics of "exclusion," or the forcing of previous players out of the political game.[29] Given the fact that few groups would leave voluntarily, the perceived need to exclude has generated a move to blatant authoritarianism which consciously seeks to control political participation through a combination of state-imposed structural controls and, when necessary, violent repression. Although the apparent mix of included and excluded varies from system to system (Peru versus Brazil, for example), the structural mechanisms of organizing and controlling participation are more than ever explicitly corporatist in principle and practice. Thus, in confronting this second crisis of delayed dependent development, a large part of Latin America has moved from the implicit and at least potentially democratic corporatism of the populists to the present blatant authoritarian corporatism of the soldiers and technocrats.

NOTES

1. Philippe C. Schmitter, "Paths to Political Development in Latin America," in *Changing Latin America: New Interpretations of Its Politics and Society*, ed. Douglas A. Chalmers (New York: Academy of Political Science, 1972), pp. 83–108.

2. Guillermo A. O'Donnell, *Modernization and Bureaucratic-Authoritarianism: Studies in South American Politics* (Berkeley: University of California, Institute of International Studies, 1973).

3. These types are developed by O'Donnell in *Modernization and Bureaucratic-Authoritarianism*.

4. The concept of corporatism has recently been used by a number of scholars when discussing Latin American politics. For an overview of several such usages see Frederick B. Pike, ed., "The New Corporatism: Social and Political Structures in the Iberian World," *Review of Politics*, 36, no. 1 (special edition, January 1974). For an exhaustive operational definition, see especially Philippe C. Schmitter, "Still the Century of Corporatism?" in the same issue, pp. 85–131.

5. See, for example, Howard J. Wiarda, "Toward a Framework for the Study of Political Change in the Iberic-Latin Tradition: The Corporative Model," *World Politics*, 25 (January 1973):206–36.

6. Ronald C. Newton, "On 'Functional Groups,' 'Fragmentation,' and 'Pluralism' in Spanish American Political Society," *Hispanic American Historical Review*, 50 (February 1970):1–29.

7. Among the more salient proponents of this viewpoint are Schmitter, "Still the Century of Corporatism?" and O'Donnell, *Modernization and Bureaucratic-Authoritarianism*.

8. See James D. Cockroft, André Gunder Frank, and Dale L. Johnson, eds., *Dependence and Underdevelopment* (Garden City, N.Y.: Doubleday and Company, 1972); Susanne Bodenheimer, "Dependency and Imperialism," and Theotonio dos Santos, "The Structure of Dependence," both in *Readings in U.S. Imperialism*, ed. K. T. Fann and Donald C. Hodges (Boston: Sargent, 1971), pp. 155–82, 225–36; and Helio Jaguaribe, *Political Development: A General Theory and a Latin American Case Study* (New York: Harper and Row, 1973), pp. 470–78.

9. See Torcuato di Tella, "Populism and Reform in Latin America," in *Obstacles to Change in Latin America*, ed. Claudio Veliz (New York: Oxford University Press, 1970), pp. 47–74; James Malloy, "Populismo militar en el Perú y Bolivia: antecedentes y posibilidades," *Estudios Andinos*, 2, no. 2 (1971–1972):114–34; Alistair Hennessy, "América Latina," in *Populismo*, ed. Ghita Ionesui and Ernest Gellner (Buenos Aires: Amorrotu, 1969); Ronald C. Newton, "Natural Corporatism and the

Passing of Populism in Spanish America," *Review of Politics*, 36, no. 1 (January 1974):34–51; and Jaguaribe, *Political Development*, pp. 440–54.

10. Charles W. Anderson, *Politics and Economic Change in Latin America* (Princeton: D. Van Nostrand Co., 1967).

11. Julio Cotler, "The Mechanics of Internal Domination and Social Change in Peru," in *Masses in Latin America*, ed. Irving Louis Horowitz (New York: Oxford University Press, 1970), pp. 407–45.

12. See Kalman Silvert, "The Costs of Anti-Nationalism: Argentina," in *Expectant Peoples*, ed. idem (New York: Random House, 1963), pp. 347–72; and Newton, "On Functional Groups."

13. José Ortega y Gasset, *Invertebrate Spain* (New York: W. W. Norton and Company, 1937).

14. The phenomenon of premature bureaucratization has recently been linked to a more general process labeled "premature modernization." One author has argued that this process, which involves the diffusion of modern values to economically less developed societies, is a major impediment to further economic development. See Alejandro Portes, "Modernity and Development: A Critique," *Studies in Comparative International Development*, 8, no. 3 (Fall 1973):247–79.

15. See n. 9.

16. The literature on this period in Latin America is voluminous. One of the best studies of this "hegemonic crisis" in a single country is Julio Cotler, "Political Crisis and Military Populism in Peru," *Studies in Comparative International Development*, 6, no. 5 (1970–1971):95–113.

17. See n. 8.

18. For an exhaustive compendium of constitutional changes adopted in this period, see Academia de Ciencias Economicas, *Las clausulas económica-sociales en las constituciones de América*, 2 vols. (Buenos Aires: Editorial Losada, 1947–1948).

19. One should remember, for example, that Fidel Castro mobilized broad middle-class support by returning to the Cuban populist constitution of 1940.

20. The constitution of the Brazilian Estado Nôvo decreed in 1937 was explicitly based on corporatist principles.

21. The following statement of MNR leader Víctor Paz Estenssoro is a good example: "It is a general law that the men of the oppressed class are never the ones who achieve gains for their own class, and this for a simple reason: those of the oppressed class do not have the economic means to even raise themselves culturally and develop their personality, let alone be able to make a great reform or a revolution" (*Discursos parlamentarios* [La Paz, Bolivia, 1955], pp. 316–17, my translation).

22. E. E. Schattschneider, *The Semi-Sovereign People* (New York: Holt, Rinehart and Winston, 1960).

23. See chapters 7, 8, 10, and 14 in this volume.

24. Samuel Huntington, *Political Order in Changing Societies* (New Haven: Yale University Press, 1968).

25. Eldon Kenworthy, "Coalitions in the Political Development of Latin America," in *The Study of Coalition Behavior*, ed. Sven Groennings et al. (New York: Holt, Rinehart and Winston, 1970), pp. 103–33.

26. Carmelo Mesa-Lago has conducted extensive research on social security in Latin America. See his "Social Security Stratification and Inequality in Chile" (Pittsburgh: University of Pittsburgh, Center for Latin American Studies, 1973); "Social Security Stratification and Inequality in Mexico" (Santa Monica: Fourth

International Congress of Mexican Studies, October 1973); and "La estratificación de la seguridad social y el efecto de desigualidad en América Latina: el caso peruano," *Estudios Andinos*, no. 8 (1973):17–48.
  27. Anderson, *Politics and Economic Change.*
  28. Cotler, "Mechanics of Internal Domination."
  29. O'Donnell, *Modernization and Bureaucratic-Authoritarianism.*

Authoritarianism, Corporatism, and the State

DOUGLAS A. CHALMERS

2

The Politicized State in Latin America

In the last decade there have once again been major changes in the political institutions of many Latin American countries. This time they brought a wave of military-dominated authoritarian regimes, beginning with the Brazilian coup of 1964, touching in various ways Argentina, Peru, Panama, Ecuador, Bolivia, and Uruguay, and culminating in the bloody replacement of Allende's Popular Unity government in Chile in 1973 with a military dictatorship.

Before the breadth of this wave became obvious, two sets of hopes and expectations reigned concerning the political future of Latin America. Some assumed that economic progress and social development would gradually but surely bring some form of liberal democracy in their wake. After the Cuban Revolution, others expected that the contradictions of Latin American society, exacerbated by dependence on foreign powers and international economic structures, would lead to a socialist revolution and some form of popular democracy. Now, as the military regimes set aside liberal democratic institutions and preempt or suppress revolutions, observers have begun to discuss the possibility that "authoritarian-corporatist" regimes might emerge as a dominant form.[1]

There is another more obvious possibility, however. Change may continue. The enduring quality of Latin American politics in this century may not be a particular form of regime, but rather the fact of change and the quality of politics in any regime which has only a short history and the prospect of a brief future. It is always possible that the cycles of varied types of regimes have come to an end. But the turmoil in Argentina, the prospect of "decompression" in Brazil, and the experimentation in Peru all suggest that the present regimes are not likely to be more fixed than their predecessors.

Most Latin American countries have, in this century, experienced several types of political institutions, with shifting combinations of

23

democratic and authoritarian, federal and centralized, populist and conservative characteristics. These regimes have usually replaced each other dramatically and rapidly in the midst of crisis and confrontation. Venezuela, to take only one example, experienced several decades of strongly authoritarian rule at the beginning of the century, a rather more liberal rule during the late 1930s and early 1940s, a brief period of populist democratic government under the Acción Democrática party after a military coup, almost a decade of a strongly authoritarian rule under a military dictator, and, after his overthrow, a competitive regime with generally liberal democratic political institutions for almost two decades. The sequence, frequency, and violence of these changes varies from country to country, but the twentieth-century history of most Latin American countries includes such shifts.

The repeated transformations imply that political institutions are considered tentative and are viewed instrumentally, not as permanent fixtures. Many problems which might be resolved by reference to a fixed set of procedures or laws are likely to be dealt with purely politically, subject to resolution only through a clash of forces. Policy-making institutions are themselves subject to active political questioning and conflict, and their reconstruction is viewed not so much as a violation of basic principles (as it would in the United States) but as the outcome of a particularly important confrontation.

This politicization and changeability of regimes must always qualify interpretations of the significance of new types of regimes, even when they come in waves. It is true that from the 1964 military coup in Brazil to the 1973 coup in Chile, the trend has been overwhelmingly toward military-dominated, authoritarian regimes. This recent wave, in fact, has been consistently authoritarian despite the diverse ideological inclinations of the generals involved and the varying political conditions from which they emerged. But before interpreting this trend as indicative of basic characteristics of Latin American society or its position in the world, it must be remembered that the newly established authoritarian regimes are no more firmly rooted in the habits and expectations of the people than were their predecessors. The legitimacy of the new organizations and institutions is not yet taken for granted. The new leaders will not return to the preceding regime (a step few revolutionaries of any kind can suggest seriously), but reigning elites (as well as the opposition) talk about new basic reforms and continually discuss experiments with new structures. The tentativeness of these regimes, like all of those which preceded them, is part of the politicized quality of the state in Latin America; and this, rather than any particular form of regime, is in this century the dominant structural characteristic of politics in the region.

In this chapter, the characteristics of the politicized state will be discussed and its significance for other aspects of politics in the region will be explored. Faced with periodically changing regimes, the normal reaction of observers has been to ask why and under what conditions a more fully institutionalized regime might emerge. In the short run, however, it is more important to understand the operation of the current sort of politics. The various forms of "instability" need clarification, and the characteristics of Latin American politics which are said to be distinctive to the area need interpretation in the light of these changes. In particular, the analysis of the politicized state can throw light on the meaning of the apparent trend to authoritarianism.

The Politicized State

Observers have often noted the absence of effective legitimation for Latin American political institutions.[2] When the established rules and procedures of policy-making are not buttressed by respected tradition and broadly accepted ideology, the chances are great that effective influence will by-pass such rules and procedures and that they will be altered frequently to accommodate new patterns of power. Rather than a process in which certain key steps are protected from scrutiny and evaluation by a legitimating myth, it is a politicized process in which at every crisis, and to some extent for every decision, the actors are called on to determine the way in which the system will operate. The possibility of exerting effective influence outside established procedures means that the policy-making process is potentially created anew for each decision. The structure and interests of the groups involved, the arena in which they confront each other, and the manner in which the conflict is resolved take shape in the course of the encounter itself and are not given over at some point to a mechanical counting of heads or to the negotiation of a settlement among a specific set of legitimate "final" participants. The action that is finally taken must be justified in terms of its political consequences for shaping society and the political process itself, rather than becoming the "postpolitical" public policy of formally constituted authority. In an institutionalized regime there is a constant tendency to establish a fixed and recognized set of legitimate participants, set arenas for action, and rules for decision. In the politicized state, a premium is placed on redefining the groups, classes, and interests involved, the way in which they should encounter each other, and the way in which the outcome is determined.

An issue emerging, for example, as a conflict among government, labor unions, and organized business over salary adjustment to inflation may shift drastically as it is redefined as a problem of the economic requirements of long-term growth and the distribution of its burdens or, perhaps, as a question of the regime's stability or relations with multinational corporations and the International Monetary Fund. Shifts like these redefine not only the issues involved, but the actors and the arenas in which they confront each other. What began as an issue to be settled by negotiation among organized interest groups may shift to a confrontation of government technicians and economists versus the "tribunes of the people" in churches, radical movements, and community groups, and then at some stage become a major confrontation between ideological blocs, represented by parties. Many tactics become routinized, but there is always the possibility of finding a technique, a definition of the situation, or an appeal which will create a totally new situation. A president may ostentatiously bring the military into the negotiations, an economics minister might make an unusually provocative speech at the rally of a populist political movement, or new organizations of economic planning or international financing might be set up, bringing new participants to the foreground.

Politics in all countries, under all degrees of institutionalization, experience some of this fluidity. The difference between a politicized and an institutionalized state, however, is that the latter conducts politics of this sort as a prelude to a decision-making process (such as voting in Congress or in a cabinet) which is routinized and as much as possible freed from the possibilities of reordering the conceptual world in which it takes place, and concentrates on the mechanical application of some device (such as vote-counting). In the politicized state, on the other hand, such a mechanism, if it exists, is in effect only one of the instruments shaping the outcome. A vote in Congress may be a significant step in that process, but the process is politicized to the end. A resolution only comes with a broad agreement, combined with a threat of intimidation, some satisfaction of ambitions, and a conviction that the outcome is the best possible for the country at that moment. In short, the politicized state is one in which there is a sense that "everything is possible." In countries like the United States, such feelings can be associated only with moments of crisis, such as those which occurred during the height of the civil rights, student, and peace movements in the late 1960s. This example may be misleading, however, because it suggests not only possibilities and changing realities, but also euphoric revolutionaries on the one hand and frightening violence on the other. Politicized moments are traumatic in highly institutionalized countries such as the United States. In the politicized states of Latin America, the reality is much less euphoric, much less intoxicating, and, in compensation, usually much less violent. Romantic revolutionaries always find periods of politicization to be liberating, but the prospect of constant "liberation" from settled rules requires more fortitude and creativity than enthusiasm.

The discussion above is something of an "ideal-type" characterization, exaggerating the open politicization of the process. In reality, of course, the independent strength of procedural norms for handling major decisions and crises varies from country to country in Latin America, and from time to time. The institutional framework was very strong during the three hundred years of colonial rule (suggesting, incidentally, that the situation is not ingrained in the "Latin American character"). There have been a few relatively enduring regimes in this century, but recent upheavals in the two supposed bastions of constitutional democracy, Uruguay and Chile, show that the fragility is widespread in this period. Chile had the strongest, most institutionalized commitment to elections and parliamentary authority before 1973. It was strong enough to convince Salvador Allende, the constitutionally elected Socialist president, that adherence to the constitution would lend him additional support beyond the numbers of his followers. But such support was not strong enough to prevent the coup of September 1973. In most other cases, constitutional arguments gave way more easily to political arguments—at times with the help of provisions in the constitutions themselves that suspend their action in emergencies, or with calls on the military to step in to guard the security of the nation. The weakness of popular commitment to the constitutional procedures is indicated generally by the ease with which elites and masses have parted with elections, parties, and parliaments in the wake of recent military coups.

Since this politicization yields recurring changes in government, it is related to what has long been called political instability in Latin America. Most discussions of instability are concerned with why it occurs and how to overcome it, treating it as a pathological condition which threatens disaster if not cured. This medical analogy is, however, misleading if it implies that a country cannot survive for long without settling on a single set of strong political institutions, or if it implies that society cannot be economically, culturally, and intellectually productive until it does. If the long experience with such cycles of change in Latin America is not convincing, then one might offer the examples of modern France and Italy. The assumption that instability destroys society is not often made with regard to France, not very often with regard to Italy, but rather frequently with regard to Latin America.[3]

"Political instability," in any case, is too ambiguous a term to be useful in an analysis of the politicized state, embracing as it does two very different patterns of behavior. It applies not only to the reconstruction of regimes every ten or twenty years which is associated with politicization, but also to the less significant, more frequent, and very different changes of cabinets and chief executives through recurring no-confidence votes or frequent palace revolts. The replacement of a semicorporatist populist dictatorship with a competitive democratic one in Brazil in 1945 and the destruction of democratic institutions in favor of military dictatorship in Chile in 1973 are clearly more significant upheavals than the replacement of a premier in France in the Fourth Republic or a successful barracks revolt in early twentieth-century Ecuador. The changes of regime which are the focus here are not social revolutions, but the reconstruction of the political system goes far beyond a mere change of top personnel.

Cabinet crises and palace coups are in one way the direct opposite of a regime change. The musical chairs of *ministeriables* and generals are often part of a well-understood "game" whose rules and boundaries, although treated cynically, are accepted.[4] There may be some empirical tendency for the two forms of "instability" to occur together in the same country, but the phenomena are very different. The regime change and the attendant politicization are distinguished precisely by the lack of any "well-understood rules."

A failure to distinguish the various forms of instability can be very misleading with respect to implications for the decisiveness of governments. During periods of ministerial musical chairs and repeated palace coups, "immobilism" may be the norm. "Immobilism" is hardly the word, however, for a sequence involving a strong populist leader such as Getúlio Vargas in Brazil, a presidential system under Juscelino Kubitschek with a strong thrust toward industrialization, and the present development-minded and repressive military. The "musical chairs" may indicate a blockage in the system, but changes of regime indicate an effort, successful or unsuccessful, at unblocking and driving forward. The tendency to confuse the two patterns may come from excessive attention to the moments of breakdown in politicized states, in which a case can be made (and always is by the new elites) that the old regime was too weak. A longer perspective, however, gives a different picture.[5]

The transformations of regimes in Latin America are, however, not usually revolutionary in their consequences for society. Despite the visible upheavals and the drastic changes in political institutions, the policy impact and associated social changes are closer to a particularly active session of the U.S. Congress than a social revolution. In a few cases the breakdown of a regime led to revolutionary change. In Mexico after 1910 this happened because of the depth of the breakdown and the long period before stabilization. It happened, too, in Cuba after 1959 because of the particular domestic and especially international situation of the new regime. It has been persuasively argued that a revolutionary process was underway in Chile during Allende's Popular Unity government (although not always under its direction) and that the military coup of 1973 can be meaningfully interpreted as counter-revolutionary. In the majority of cases of regime change, however, the resulting alterations are not so great as to touch the basic structures of society, nor does the "revolutionary process" (often cited by conservative elites as justification for a coup) amount to much more than a few "anarchic" popular actions and a division among the political elites involving an ambitious segment appealing for popular support through radical rhetoric.

Given the politicized nature of the policy-making process, the likelihood of radical rhetoric is very high, since the effort to reconstruct the meaning of the situation and the consciousness of the actors stimulates "basic" justifications and rationalizations for new steps and structures. But the process is not one of continual radical change.[6] The process of regime change is meaningful, but its significance is closer to that of a rather special and sometimes spectacular policy-making process, not a process of social dissolution and reconstruction.

The degree of violence in a politicized, regime-changing country is often grossly exaggerated. Political conflict without controlling procedures is described as "praetorianism" in which the groups in society confront each other "nakedly" without the moderating influence of mediating institutions and legal restraints.[7] The picture of the politicized society emerges as something close to a Hobbesian war of all against all. Other scholars have noticed, however, that change in Latin America has often been relatively free of violence. At times the picture is drawn of a rather polite quadrille of "power contenders."[8] The innumerable deaths in Chile, the persecutions and terrorism in Brazil, and the political gangsterism in Argentina have destroyed the notion that such systems are always peaceful, but it is important to realize the obvious: The absence of violence is not always the result of law; it lies in various inhibitions, from rational calculation to moral conviction, which restrain the actors. The politicized encounter always has the "ultimate" threat of violence, but then so does the application of law. Political power may flow "from the barrel of a gun," but it also comes from the effective use of material resources to pay off supporters, from organizational skills, from the ability to win personal trust, from words and actions which convince influential people that one is capable of leading the country in the "right direction." The tendency to see nothing between civil war and orderly bargaining seems to be endemic among many scholars. In fact between those two extremes lies most of politics. It is because most conflict in Latin America is neither orderly bargaining nor violent confrontation that it must be called "politi-cized."

Politicization: Some Associated Characteristics

While the absence of an institutionalized regime is the most impor-tant characteristic of the politicized state in Latin America, other factors fit into the pattern, in both democratic and authoritarian phases. First of all, there is no ideological conflict over the "right" regime. The lack of an institutionalized regime reflects a generally instrumental view of political institutions rather than division of politi-cal groups according to ideologically founded beliefs about the correct structure of the polity. Ideological politics surely exists, but it focuses on socioeconomic issues and state-society relations, not on political forms. The great European debates over democratic versus artistocratic forms of representation and popular participation which followed in the wake of the English and French revolutions were echoed in the Latin American political struggles of the last century. But now, in Latin America as elsewhere, competing ideological positions all appear to assume the desirability of some form of mass politics. Differences concerning expansion of the suffrage, forms of elections, types of group representation, and forms of decision-making reflect historically spe-cific short- and medium-range interests of the groups involved, and are likely to change when the circumstances change. Groups may consis-tently identify some political value—egalitarianism, law and order, state action for development—but these are not consistently identified with regime form. Parties on the left and right will demand honest elections and expanded franchises when out of power and strong in popular sympathies of potential voters, and a far more authoritarian mode when they are strong at the top. Advocacy of regime form in general terms varies, too, with the commitment of the group in question to the international bloc identified by those regimes: advocacy of U.S. institu-tions at one time, Sovietlike ones at another, and some indigenous authoritarianism or populism when a "third position" is needed. For better or for worse, this pragmatic use of political justifications for one or another regime form gives greater importance to political goals than to the forms of politics. This is probably becoming a general, worldwide phenomenon as the Cold War fades, although it is somewhat obscured for those of us living in a well-institutionalized regime, where the ideological justification of the regime remains a system necessity.[9]

Politicization contributes to, and is reinforced by, the central role of the state in Latin American society. The state is a beneficiary of a tradition which awards the top representatives a greater responsibility for the welfare of the community than they have in liberal societies. Officials are expected to take the initiative in social and economic affairs, and their decisions, whether crassly self-interested or generously community-oriented, are accepted as part of the social process since the political structures are more central to social life. The state is central, not because it commands an exceptionally large share of the GNP or employs an overly large proportion of the working population (figures which are large and increasing, though not particularly striking on a world scale), but rather because it has a share in so many decisions.

The ability of the government to exploit the intertwining of state and society to unite the nation in great collective efforts is severely limited by the many rivalries and entrenched interests which are imbedded in every town and government agency and by the capacity of some major interests to mobilize massive resources when they feel threatened. Nevertheless, the penetration of the state into society affords political leaders many opportunities for making marginal changes in patronage and benefits.

The control and manipulation of the state apparatus are therefore a major element in the political struggle. The effort to manipulate it in such a way as to promote the power and goals of one group over another is a major part of the political game. Being "in power" is very important because it gives the leader wide patronage and the authority to establish government programs to benefit existing supporters and attract new ones. He can rewrite electoral laws and modify decision-making institutions to favor government supporters more than in institutionalized systems. The preeminence of the role of the state makes these manipulations more important because their social impact is great.

Political leaders are driven to build their political support in ways which ensure the largest possible base (not a "minimum winning coalition"). The chief executive who comes to office through constitutional means in an institutionalized regime is limited in his manipulation of the governmental apparatus by the legal norms which define his role, but at the same time he is protected from early "irregular" overthrow by those same provisions. In some parliamentary regimes the premier is subject to sudden overthrow by a vote of no confidence, but in most constitutional regimes, either constitutionally or by the device of party discipline, a chief executive has a certain amount of time in which to carry out his program without fear of sudden deposition. In the politicized state the chief executive must constantly build and rebuild his political support to meet the threat of attempts to overthrow him. His support must be exceptionally broad and flexible.

"Building a majority" is meaningless without a single, binding, quantifiable measure of what a majority is, such as votes in Congress or in an election. Since there is no such binding rule, the chief executive is compelled to build a "maximum winning coalition" to protect himself. There is a strong inclination to expand his support as much as possible, and a strong tendency for his supporters to jump on the bandwagon of an apparently successful opponent. During moments of calm it appears that everyone is a government supporter; in a crisis, no one is. The Brazilian military, for example, met with very slight resistance when they came to power in 1964 despite probably correct assumptions that prior to their move political support was at least evenly divided between the government and the opposition. Castro's march out of the Sierra Maestra, after the initial struggles, took on the character of a triumphal parade through a disintegrating regime rather than the civil war which might have been predicted by the disposition of forces a few weeks earlier.

One consequence of these support-building patterns is the blurring of the division between the administrative and party-electoral lines of action.[10] A leader must establish organizational control over enough of the right kinds of resources and be able to employ them effectively in a showdown, or otherwise demonstrate their potential power. Making use of the great flexibility provided by the instrumental character of the legal restrictions, the executive builds support by establishing links with a variety of hierarchies, including political parties but necessarily extending beyond to local chiefs, the church, the major administrative units, the interest groups (often through linking them directly into administrative structures), and, of course, the military. The support a leader secures through partisan-electoral bases is not distinguishable from the support he receives from the various administrative and institutional hierarchies. This is "bureaucratic politics" with a vengeance. Not only do agencies and departments acquire distinctive interests and outlooks, but the manipulation of bureaucratic lines of authority is crucial for retaining power.[11] Cultivating the loyalty of factions within every accessible institution and organization is crucial to political survival. In the struggle for power, the incumbent has the advantage of being able to manipulate the lines of authority directly. The challenger cannot build totally new counterorganizations outside the state but rather must find some way of "cutting into" the hierarchical lines of loyalty and authority and taking over or rebuilding them. Leaders in all states try to build such networks of loyalty to secure personal power beyond the limited power given by the role of chief executive.[12] In the politicized state, such "personal power" is all there is, and it is necessary for survival.

The fluidity of group structure makes analysis of group politics, coalitions, and alliances rather imprecise. Such terms imply stable units which are linked together. Any major actor, however, is likely to have several potential spokesmen and be strongly factionalized by the competition, active or latent, for control. Alliances are like networks among the factions. The military, for example, rarely acts politically as a unit, except in moments of crisis. It is divided into factions which contend for influence (and external allies). "Swing men" at key switching points (major commands and high staff positions) decide to move with one or another group, bringing along their followers or dependents, and rapidly shifting the apparent support or opposition of "the military" for the government in power.[13]   The military does have the capacity to act as a unit—perhaps more than other groups—when the conflict situation is defined as a military one, or the military as an institution is under attack. Even in the Chilean crisis of 1973, however, when the lines were sharply drawn around political alternatives and the atmosphere of armed confrontation was intense, there were apparently significant elements of the military who defied their military superiors in order to defend the Allende regime.

The same sorts of pressures undermine the most "objectively" defined interest group, with unions, business organizations, rural unions, and others strained by the factional fighting which tends to fall along the lines of opposition and support of the government. In cases of severe conflict which is publicly defined as being along class lines or around a particular interest which sharply differentiates groups according to opposing interests, a measure of "interest-group solidarity" may hold. But in the long sweep, the pressure of politicization and the strain toward establishing the vertical links necessary for maintaining or winning power, the lines are likely to be blurred and to be constantly shifting.

The resulting pattern of vertical relationships among political groups and institutions fits badly into conventional political analysis, and terms like "clientelism" and "corporatism" have become common. The establishment of controls from the top over the requisite political resources, and the anxiety from below to find a place in the complex vertical links of political power, yield a variety of structures familiar enough to observers, but difficult to place within the pluralist or class approach to politics. The importance of personal, informal ties has been noted by many observers, and the term "clientelism" has been commonly used to describe these ties. "Clientelism" can be defined as a pattern of relationships in which goods and services are exchanged between people of unequal status.[14]   A patron-client formation emerges when one patron establishes many of these dyadic, particularistic ties, establishing thereby a highly dependent following. The systematic use of the term to describe systems of national politics has been hampered by the difficulty of handling the great diversity in content and stability of ties which constitutes the following of a major national leader.[15] But it is clear that the term catches something of the common relationship in parliamentary factions, the cliques in ministries or the military, the relationships between national and regional leaders in party "machines," and the personal clients of parliamentary deputies. The particularistic clientelistic ties are clearly of great importance in the politicized state, often constituting the only links which hold together combinations of political forces that participate in major confrontations.

The vertical patterns of dependency have a much more formal aspect, too. Despite the tentative character of political institutions and the lack of a fundamental legitimating sentiment for the legal structure of the state, the legal status of groups and their formal relationships with the government are extremely important, and the subject of constant political struggle. As the framework within which factional conflict is conducted, the legal status of a labor syndicate or a trade association expresses at least part of the exchange of support and services. In periods of strong authoritarianism, the legal structure expresses the strong controls on interest groups, which typically fall most heavily on mass organizations such as labor unions. The formal ties are not limited, however, to periods of maximum control. Even in democratic phases the struggle for political support is often carried out by manipulating union recognition or granting a particular set of industries privileged access to government financing. Buttressed by the importance of the state and by the attention given to the building of strong vertical ties, the struggle over the legal status of all sorts of groups is crucial in the political process. Added to this is the apparently long-standing tendency in Latin American and Iberian history to place great importance on the status awarded by official recognition.[16]

The term *corporatist* has come into use to describe some of these formal relationships, and in particular to emphasize the patterns of vertical dependency which are involved. The term has great attractiveness for those wishing to describe a distinctive Latin American tradition, since it has played an important role in Catholic social thought, which may be plausibly considered part of the Latin American heritage. The term is highly ambiguous, however, and causes confusion. In its ideological formulation, "corporatism" often refers to a general system of interest representation in which specified groups are awarded a monopoly status with regard to their clientele and, in one form or another, brought into official recognition as the central bases for decision-making, replacing the parliaments built on liberal, individualistic representation. But complete official organization of all major groups in society and "functional parliaments" are absent or marginal in Latin America. The vertical dependencies, even when buttressed by legal forms such as I have been describing, deal with groups one by one, varying considerably in form. In other words, one might call these "corporatist" if one acknowledged that the term referred, not to the organization of a whole system, but to a set of relationships with some groups and not others. Clientelistic patterns and sometimes rather autonomous bargaining relationships almost always persist side by side with the "corporatist" relationships, no matter how all-pervasive the government tries to make them.

Corporatism is also highly ambiguous in the sense that some use the term to refer to government control—using the fascist experiments of interwar Europe as their model—while others refer to a kind of autonomy of the groups involved, resting on the conservative, often Catholic tradition which owed much to the notion of the medieval guilds. The power relationships among government, groups, and clients vary greatly, from group to group and from time to time—particularly from regime to regime. Corporatism is useful in pointing out the importance of the legal status of groups in the politicized state, but its ambiguity may lead to more confusion than insight.[17]

Authoritarianism and the Politicized State

An understanding of the politicized character of the state in much of Latin America provides useful perspectives on the question of whether the wave of authoritarian regimes in the region has the potential of becoming permanent. The temptation is strong to consider this wave a decisive step in Latin American history. The intellectual mood is one of lost faith in the inevitable march of democracy and a general loss of confidence in the models presented by the United States and Western Europe. Further, renewed appreciation of ethnic diversity and cultural relativism suggests the need to consider alternative paths to development.[18]

Authoritarianism has been defined as a political pattern distinct from the liberal democracy of the first world or the popular democracy (or "totalitarianism") of the second, and thus fits the requirements.[19] Authoritarian forms are claimed to be more natural to Latin America, either because of the propensities of the Latin tradition, or because of the dynamics of late development and economic dependence. After years of "experimentation" with "alien" forms, the new wave of regimes may better express the underlying reality. Culturally speaking, there is a plausible argument that Latin America has a distinct heritage.

Despite the fact that its origins lie in Europe, it is from the southern branch of the family, so to speak, and the conditions of its evolution have been different (colonization by a declining, nonfeudal power, long-term isolation, etc.). Cultural relativism has opened up like an accordion in the intellectual perspective of the 1970s, and Latin American authoritarian regimes seem to fit logically into the new perspective.

It is sobering to remember, however, that each wave of regimes since World War II (at least) has brought analyses which seemed to show that the most recent type of regime was likely to endure because of its fit with underlying conditions. In the late 1950s, when a number of military rulers were overthrown—the "twilight of the tyrants"—scholars were demonstrating that economic and social modernization was producing the differentiated and integrated modern society which would provide the basis for stable, pluralist democracy. Shortly thereafter, the emergence of a socialist revolution in Cuba and its echoes in the programs and actions of numerous popular and guerrilla movements in the region were the stimulus for analyses that class tensions, national and international, would inevitably produce violent or peaceful revolutions which could be stabilized only by some form of socialist regime. Now we have a new set of regimes and a new set of projections.

Armed with skepticism born of sensitivity to the long history of regime changes in the region, one can begin to notice that many of the elements which seem "naturally authoritarian" are in fact more closely associated with the conditions of politicization that we have described, or with tendencies in the state and society which have been shown to be compatible with many types of regimes. Juan Linz's influential definition of an authoritarian regime, developed in the course of an effort to classify Franco's regime in Spain, has perhaps encouraged a belief in the affinity of the Latin American states with authoritarianism. Despite his intention to describe a solidly entrenched, institutionalized regime, a bit of stretching may make defining characteristics applicable to the politicized state.

Linz defines authoritarian regimes as those with "limited, not responsible pluralism, without elaborate or guiding ideology (but with distinctive mentalities), without intensive nor extensive mobilization (except at some point in their development), and in which a leader (or occasionally a small group) exercises power within formally ill-defined limits, but actually quite predictable ones." Some of these characteristics, without further specification, are ambiguous enough to cover both authoritarian regimes and aspects of the politicized state no matter what sort of regime is currently established. The "ill-defined limits" on the power of the leader fits both the patrimonial ruler of the authoritarian regime and the relatively more insecure leader in a politi-

cized state who is expected to show innovative strategies, within limits.
"Limited pluralism" can refer to the rather precise and strongly enforced limits placed on the "corporatist" interest groups in a well-
entrenched authoritarian regime, and it can also apply to the elements
of vertical dependency which evolve in the fluid, changing struggle to
secure maximum support in a policized situation. The "limits" on relatively autonomous interest-group formation is present in both aspects,
but in quite different ways.[20]

Authoritarianism is obviously compatible with the politicized state,
but so are democratic types of institutions. Our definitions of "democratic" (and it is significant that the term "stable" is often linked with
"democratic" as if they were part of the same concept) often rule out the
politicized situations that have been described here. Democratic regimes
are supposed to have procedural frameworks, consensual rules of the
game, and pluralist competition among relatively autonomous and freely
forming interest groups. Such a definition implies, clearly, a high degree
of institutionalization. If we accept that usage, however, then we have
no way to talk about the regimes that occupy the periods between the
authoritarian ones in Latin American countries. We need a way of
talking about "politicized democracy." Sometimes such a condition is
suggested by referring to Argentine politics under the Radical party
prior to 1930 and Brazilian politics between 1945 and 1964 as "experiments in democracy." The authoritarianism of the current period then
perhaps should be called "experiments in authoritarianism."[21]

One of the consequences of an attempt to understand the dynamics
of changing regimes such as those in Latin America is a profound
skepticism concerning the many theories which suggest a high correlation—even a necessary connection—between types of regimes and the
modernization of the state and society. Some popular theories suggest
that democracy is a necessary outcome of the process of differentiation
and integration that goes on. More popular now, it seems, is a notion
that some form of authoritarianism is the necessary outcome of trends
involving the increasing concentration of power in the hands of the
state and the increasing fragility of highly interdependent social and
political institutions which need to be defended against the erratic
disruption of anarchic students and other pathological extremists. Skepticism is fueled by observing that through a period of very significant
changes, Latin American countries have nevertheless experienced many
sorts of regimes. Despite a growth in the proportion of the GNP
handled by the state, despite considerable sophistication in state control of dissent, despite increased interdependence within societies, the
trends toward one government or another are not overwhelming.

The fact, made obvious by the many changes of regime but clear from a little reflection, is that the evolution of the state and society merely sets a context for the particular regime institutions. The modernization of the state apparatus excludes some forms—the recruitment of completely amateur politicians or instant recall of leaders, perhaps—but the prevalent notions that modernization makes the state so strong as to be irresistibly authoritarian, or so fragile as to be necessarily authoritarian, simply cannot stand up to serious scrutiny.

The imposition of military-dominated authoritarian regimes in Latin America over the last decade has been the product, not of general characteristics of state, society, and culture in the area, but of particular historical crises and the choices men made during those crises. The long-term survival or entrenchment of those authoritarian regimes will depend first of all on the persistence of the factors which brought about those choices, the strength of the impulse toward making the choice, and the success of the authoritarian rulers in carrying out their goals. Only in the very long run will it also depend on the cultural traditions and the nature of the state. In politicized, regime-changing countries such as those in most of Latin America, the important questions about the future of authoritarian (or any other) regimes will be those which can only be answered by attention to the specific historical situation.

Despite the apparent wholesale acceptance of authoritarian institutions and the difficult problems which appear to require a "firm hand," there are reasons to be cautious about predicting that they are bound to endure. First, one may note that the evidence of the strength of the swing to authoritarianism lies in the *number* of countries which have taken that route rather that the intensity of their commitment. The fact that many countries—Brazil, Argentina, Peru, Panama, Ecuador, Bolivia, Uruguay, and Chile—have adopted some form of authoritarian regime indicates more about the role of models in the region's experiments with political institutions than about the strength of the need to adopt authoritarian institutions in each country.

The current wave of military regimes sometimes appears overwhelming, but few are institutionalized sufficiently to withstand future challenges from within or outside. Any of them might be overthrown by a significant decline in economic fortunes, by the impact of trends indicated by the overthrow of authoritarian regimes in Portugal and Greece, or by significant splits among the elites over policies for greater equalization of the burdens and benefits of economic growth. Of the current crop of military regimes in Latin America, Argentina has already provided an example of a military government which was unable to establish itself firmly, despite a self-conscious attempt by General Juan Carlos Onganía to establish a link with the "Iberian tradition."

One of the sources for the expectation that authoritarian regimes are here to stay in Latin America is the deeply held assumption that authoritarian regimes are more durable than democratic ones.[22] The latter are considered highly fragile, and authoritarian ones, almost impregnable. It is obvious, however, that at least in Latin America authoritarian regimes collapse as often as democratic ones do. The process of collapse is different, and when history is written from the perspective of the politician skilled in parliamentary maneuver and electoral politics it may seem that authoritarian regimes are much more solid. But a staff official skilled at intrigue may see it differently. Revolutionaries are likely to talk as though repression were directed at them and the authoritarian regime's greater capacity for repression reduced their chances of success. But stimulating "fascism" in order to expose the weakness of the ruling class is a major revolutionary strategy. Probably the single most important historical fact which has led to the feeling that authoritarian regimes are irreversible is the fact that it took World War II to unseat Hitler and Mussolini. Aside from all the problems that raises about the particular situation in Germany and Italy, it is not clear that these two cases out of thousands have much to do with the durability of the Latin American military authoritarian regimes, which are very different.

The most important arguments about the staying power of authoritarian regimes in Latin America deal with the need for strong governments at this particular historical juncture to counteract tensions which arise from rapid economic growth and social change. Perhaps the argument which has been most persuasive, not only among observers, but for the actors themselves, has been that economic growth requires high rates of investment, which demands high rates of saving, which in turn demands considerable sacrifice. The only source of such savings, whether as taxes, inflation, or profits, is the people. The natural reaction to unequal sacrifice by workers and peasants who bear the major portion of the burden, it is said, is to revolt. Strong government is necessary to prevent chaos and maintain discipline through difficult times.[23] Other arguments suggest that strong government is necessary to combat the agitators and rabble-rousers who thrive in moments of transition and change, capitalizing on widespread insecurity.

Each one of these and other arguments, of course, has a radical and a conservative version. The conservative presumably accepts the arguments, perhaps sadly, and applauds the measures strong government takes to counteract the dangers of unrest. The radical, on the other hand, condemns the argument as the logic of the dominant class and argues that unrest shows signs of the need for much more fundamental change. Many radicals on the left are, of course, merely arguing for a transformation that would change the class that carries out the repression, but in the end they accept the necessity for present sacrifice and therefore the repression that goes with it.

Such arguments cannot serve as the basis for a prediction of long-term authoritarian regimes for two reasons. First, the superiority of authoritarian regimes in containing these "excessive" demands is by no means obvious, and second, the long-term projection of such "pressures of development" is impossible. On the first point, it is clear that there are many ways to bring about restraints on excessive demands. It is worth noting that the history of social institutions in societies with liberal democratic political institutions shows as much inequality as that of authoritarian regimes, and probably more. It has long been a theme of critical theorists that the institutions of liberal democracy justify and rationalize the inequality which is found in society. The notions about adjusting mass expectations to available resources are at least as much an argument for democratic institutions as they are for authoritarian ones. People will often accept much deprivation when they have had a say in allocating burdens. Whether the result is the consequence of the mystification of the people (as the radical would maintain) or the rational acceptance of a reasonable set of social results (as the moderate would maintain) is interesting, but not relevant here. The relevant point is that authoritarian institutions are not the only ones which can adjust demand to supply in the context of a development policy. The image of the authoritarian leaders "holding down the lid" is common and seems to fit the show of force and the decisiveness of the authoritarian leaders. But it is show. They can hold the "lid" when they can satisfy their political clientele. The authoritarian regime does that differently than a democratic one, but it has no inherent superiority. Such superiority, if it exists at all, deals only with the suppression by force of particular armed movements or riotous demonstrations. It is not clear at all that this is the main problem.[24]

The second problem with the arguments about the necessity for long-term authoritarianism is that it is impossible to project the degree of the tensions produced by development. Much of the analysis on this point argues that the recent signs of unrest show a rising curve of tension, or at least one which will not subside. The rationale for this projection in the future may rest on a fundamentally Marxian notion that Latin America finds itself in a late capitalist stage (perhaps with international complications) in which the capacity of the bourgeoisie to repress peacefully the legitimate demands of the working class is inevitably diminishing, and therefore inevitably coming to rely more and more on force. Anti-Marxists tend to reject this completely and posit instead a rising curve of satisfaction and consequently greater consensus, the end of ideology, and (perhaps) the inevitability of democracy. Both projections seem to me to overstrain greatly our capacity for understanding social processes and to simplify the relationship between social structure and political demands so drastically as to render them highly suspect. Clearly trends are not all positive in Latin America, but just as clearly things are not going steadily downhill. And whatever the trends in popular satisfactions are, it is obvious that the relation of popular demands to alienation and political action fluctuates. And a fluctuating curve cannot provide the rationale for a constant repression generated, presumably, by a constant authoritarian regime. It does, in fact, seem to suggest far more a continuing trend of changing regimes, adapting to the changing circumstances.

It would be naive to believe that authoritarian regimes will collapse because they always have. It is risky to put one's faith in the notion that what goes down must come up. But one must be careful not to leap to conclusions on the basis of vague similarities and general propositions about the presumed needs and characteristics of authoritarian regimes.

Politicization and Depoliticization

The politicized quality of the state, with the associated changes of regime and tentative quality of political institutions, can be as enduring and stable a characteristic of a society as any institutionalized regime. Such continuous "turmoil" is often treated as a malady, but it does not necessarily imply weakness or violence. Both of the latter may and probably will occur in cycles of regime change, but so do weakness and violence appear in countries with institutionalized regimes such as the United States. Politicized states may range from those marked by continuous civil war to those in which deliberate adaptive stages deal successfully with a series of problems. Similarly, institutionalized states may range from vacillating weakness to stable and effective government.

The costs and benefits of institutionalization are thus not foregone conclusions. The politicized state may be a realistic response to changing conditions, in which political action continually focuses on questions of the shape and consequences of basic political institutions. Every arrangement is open to question, since their appropriateness for achieving political goals is constantly being reevaluated, and the goals themselves are changing as the society changes.

Depoliticization, or institutionalization, means closing off certain areas from political contention through a structure of power so overwhelming that it precludes fundamental questioning for long periods of time, or through agreement or apathy so profound that the questions are never raised. Depoliticization would mean establishing a framework which would specify the right to rule of certain kinds of elites and, to a greater or lesser extent, reinforce certain characteristics of social structure over others.

Asking why Latin America is so unstable puts the question the wrong way. It tends to assume that some correct form of regime for achieving most social goals is both known and attainable. It continues the myth that the basic questions about political structures have been answered by the Western liberal democracies (or, perhaps by the Socialist bloc) and that these answers are applicable to Latin America. These are untenable assumptions because of the very legitimate doubts about both the effectiveness of the established models and their exportability. There is no ground for believing that any single set of institutions is best for all societies, or even that one set of institutions is best for any one group in society in all places. It is an old dream of liberal thinkers that there are sets of procedures which are neutral with regard to their political consequences, that it is possible to set up a political system like a game, where everyone has an equal chance to win. There are probably times in history when one kind of institutional reform would be desirable for popular welfare no matter what the particular conditions. Such was probably the case during the struggle for universal suffrage and free representation of interests against the pretensions of aristocrats to rule in the name of the community. Now, however, few would defend the proposition that further broadening of the suffrage or further freedom of organization would in all cases increase the general welfare. Few would argue that such measures would increase the neutrality of the political process. Such goals are advocated for specific purposes at specific times.

It is similarly impossible to argue, I believe, that more democratic or more authoritarian political institutions would necessarily benefit workers, businessmen, peasants, landowners, students, lawyers, economists, or any group within society. The lack of firm commitment to ideological positions regarding political institutions that was mentioned before appears to me a totally rational response to the facts. At least as political institutions are presently classified and defined, they have lost their links with social groups. The models that have been held out to Latin America by the more settled countries of the world, sometimes diffidently, sometimes insistently and even arrogantly, have been seized upon but, in the end, used rather than worshiped, and rightly so.

The politicized state in Latin America and the changing regimes that go with it are obviously not necessarily permanent features of the region. Perhaps some new way of defining and structuring regimes will emerge that will be perceived as providing a better chance for a very large majority of the population, and therefore will be accepted definitively in the fashions that various forms of mass politics have been in the last two centuries. More likely, a measure of stabilization may occur in one country or another through the imposition of a reasonably efficient and effectively repressive regime which, perhaps after some particularly violent episode, may convince the citizens that the costs of change are greater than the costs of an entrenched system. After such a civil war the Spanish system under General Francisco Franco and the Mexican system beginning with Plutarco Calles and Lázaro Cárdenas have managed a measure of institutionalization. For most of Latin America, however, the politicized state appears likely to remain for the foreseeable future.

NOTES

1. Some recent examples of this last trend include Philippe C. Schmitter, "Paths to Political Development in Latin America," in *Changing Latin America*, ed. Douglas A. Chalmers (New York: Academy of Political Science, 1972); and several articles in both Frederick B. Pike and Thomas Stritch, eds., *The New Corporatism* (Notre Dame: University of Notre Dame Press, 1974), and Howard J. Wiarda, ed., *Politics and Social Change in Latin America: The Distinct Tradition* (Amherst: University of Massachusetts Press, 1974).

2. The "lack of legitimacy" theme has a long history and many approaches. It is analyzed as a failure to replace Iberian colonial legitimacy formulas because of the "inappropriateness" of the Western constitutional models in some writing. See, for example, Martin C. Needler, *Latin American Politics in Perspective* (Princeton: Van Nostrand, 1963). It appears as largely the result of the failure of any class to assume real ascendancy in, for example, Irving Louis Horowitz, "Political Legitimacy and the Institutionalization of Crisis in Latin America," *Comparative Political Studies*, 1 (April 1968):45. In Samuel P. Huntington, *Political Order in Changing Societies* (New Haven: Yale University Press, 1968), the lack of legitimacy appears as the product of social tensions stemming from rapid modernization.

3. Although the diagnosis that the ills of developing countries are rooted in instability is very widespread, it is most explicit in Huntington, *Political Order*.

4. Emphasis on the regularity and institutionalization of instability is perhaps most common in treatments of France. See, for example, Nathan Leites, *On the Game of Politics in France* (Stanford: Stanford University Press, 1959), or Philip Williams, "Crisis as an Institution," in his *Crisis and Compromise*, 3d ed. (London: Longmans, 1964). For Latin America, Charles W. Anderson, *Politics and Economic Change in Latin America* (Princeton: Van Nostrand, 1967), chap. 4, is the most relevant.

5. Endings appear to be much more interesting than beginnings, or even transitions. The writings on the end of democracy in Europe in the interwar period, to take one example, are full of drama and spectacular attempts at theoretical analysis. The literature on the founding of new democratic regimes after World War II tends to be dry, descriptive, and tentative.

6. Albert O. Hirschman, *Journeys Toward Progress* (New York: Twentieth

Century Fund, 1963) makes some insightful comments about the relationships of rhetoric about "fundamental solutions" and policy-making, which he seems to ascribe to cultural traits, but in a politicized state appear to be functional.

7. See Huntington, *Political Order*.

8. See Anderson, *Politics and Economic Change*.

9. The Cold War stimulated an elaborate rigidification of ideological positions about political forms. These positions were held by nations and probably undermined the identification of such an ideology with classes or other groups. In practice, the sorts of regimes supported abroad by the United States or the Soviet Union soon showed a weakening of rigid attachment to political forms in favor of pragmatic considerations, and by now there are few firm principles left. This may be the real arena for the "end of ideology."

10. See Douglas A. Chalmers, "Parties and Society in Latin America," *Studies in Comparative International Development*, 7 (Summer 1972):102–29.

11. Studies of "bureaucratic politics" in the United States tend to confine themselves to asking how organizational interests affect particular decisions. See, for example, Morton H. Halperin, *Bureaucratic Politics and Foreign Policy* (Washington: The Brookings Institution, 1974). Such studies will become more interesting when they consider how organizational structures can be manipulated, and how variations in organizational structure affect policy outcomes in a systematic way.

12. This was the major theme in Richard Neustadt, *Presidential Power* (New York: John Wiley and Sons, 1960).

13. See particularly the analyses of Alfred Stepan, *The Military in Politics: Changing Patterns in Brazil* (Princeton: Princeton University Press, 1971), and Ronald Schneider, *The Political System of Brazil* (New York: Columbia University Press, 1971), for analyses of such switching and factionalism in the Brazilian case.

14. A considerable literature on clientelism has been produced in recent years. For some basic definitions and early application, see John Duncan Powell, "Peasant Society and Clientelistic Politics," *American Political Science Review*, 64 (June 1970):411–26, and James C. Scott, "Patron-Client Politics and Political Change in Southeast Asia," *American Political Science Review*, 65 (March 1972):91–114.

15. For a very useful critique of the concept which points to this difficulty among others, see Robert R. Kaufman, "The Patron-Client Concept and Macro-Politics: Prospects and Problems," *Comparative Studies in Society and History*, 16 (June 1974):284–308.

16. See particularly Ronald C. Newton, "On 'Functional Groups,' 'Fragmentation,' and 'Pluralism' in Spanish American Political Society," *Hispanic American Historical Review*, 50 (February 1970):1–29, and also several of the articles in Pike and Stritch, *The New Corporatism*.

17. Philippe Schmitter, in "Still the Century of Corporatism?" in Pike and Stritch, *The New Corporatism*, pp. 85–131, strives to reduce the confusion by offering two types of corporatism, state and societal, relevant to the dimension of relative power of government and interest group. Whether it is applicable only to whole systems or if it can be applied to a relationship between one group and the government remains uncertain. On the varied intentions of corporatist theories, see Ralph H. Bowen, *German Theories of the Corporative State* (New York: Columbia University Press, 1947), and Matthew H. Elbow, *French Corporative Theory* (New York: Columbia University Press, 1953).

18. The clearest identification of the possibility of a "third way" was that of Philippe C. Schmitter, "Paths to Political Development."

19. In particular, Juan Linz, "An Authoritarian Regime: Spain," in *Cleavages,*

Ideologies and Party Systems, ed. Erik Allardt and Y. Littunen (Helsinki: Transactions of the Westermarck Society, 1964).

20. For the definition of "authoritarianism," see Linz, "An Authoritarian Regime: Spain," p. 297. Linz has developed and refined his typology further in later publications. See his contribution to *Handbook of Political Science*, ed. Fred Greenstein and Nelson Polsby (Boston: Addison Wesley Publishing Co., 1975). Susan Purcell refers to Brazil prior to 1964 as "authoritarianism without an apex" in her review article, "Authoritarianism," *Comparative Politics*, 5 (January 1973):301—12. Separating out authoritarianism and politicization will help to clarify this sort of difficulty.

21. Note the title of Thomas Skidmore's basic work on Brazil, *Politics in Brazil 1930—1964: An Experiment in Democracy* (New York: Oxford University Press, 1967). See also Juan Linz's interesting analysis of the possibilities of overcoming such an experimental stage in "The Future of an Authoritarian Situation or the Institutionalization of an Authoritarian Regime: The Case of Brazil," in *Authoritarian Brazil*, ed. Alfred Stepan (New Haven: Yale University Press, 1973), pp. 233—54. Another interesting analysis of the possibilities of institutionalization of authoritarian regimes can be found in Robert R. Kaufman, *Transitions to Stable Authoritarian-Corporate Regimes: The Chilean Case?* (Beverly Hills: Sage Professional Papers in Comparative Politics, 1976).

22. The language we use reflects this assumption. Democratic regimes "collapse," but authoritarian ones must be "overthrown." Democratic regimes must be "built," while authoritarian ones can be "imposed."

23. Guillermo O'Donnell presents the most sophisticated version of this argument in *Modernization and Bureaucratic-Authoritarianism* (Berkeley: Institute of International Studies, 1973). He is specifically arguing against the notion that development produces democracy and suggests instead that it produces authoritarian regimes, with Brazil and Argentina as his major examples.

24. A large and apparently growing number of people see the major threat to order as being not anomie or lack of cooperation, but rather violence. Such an emphasis on part of the problem marks much conservative thinking and justifies authoritarianism as the only regime with the type of military repressive capability appropriate to that particular task. Although Huntington's *Political Order* does in fact define institutionalization and order in more general terms, the description of the raw and violent confrontations in their absence leads to a decided impression of the importance of authoritarianism.

GUILLERMO A. O'DONNELL

3

Corporatism and the Question of the State

The central thesis of this chapter is that "corporatism" should be understood as a set of structures which link society with the state. Therefore, any examination of the actual operation and social impacts of corporatism must consider it with systematic reference to some of the main characteristics of the state and society it helps to link. In the final analysis, the study of corporatism is part of the broader problem of interrelationships between state and society. This means that the concept of corporatism is useful when it is limited to certain linking structures between state and society. However, if the concept is "stretched" to a global characterization of state or society, or to a general and unchanging attribute of certain countries, or further still, if it is postulated as an "alternative paradigm" to resolve the present crisis in conceptualizations of Latin American politics and society, then I fear it will become another contribution to the tower of Babel we are making of the social sciences.[1] Even at the risk of making such a contribution of my own, I have felt it worthwhile to discuss the level of generality and the approach under which I think it most appropriate to use the concept of corporatism.

Since the discussion will be somewhat complex, it may be useful to begin at the end and briefly present the main arguments to be developed. Later I will formulate them more stringently and some of their interconnections will appear, but for the moment they can be synthesized as follows:

1. In spite of old ideological continuities, corporatism in Latin America, as an operating set of societal structures, is a relatively recent phenomenon. It arose alongside the urbanization and industrialization processes started in the world economic crisis of the 1930s.

2. In its patterns of functioning and social impacts, Latin American corporatism displays crucial differences from the corporatism observed by some authors in the "developed" countries. Moreover, even within

47

Latin America, changes have occurred that force us to distinguish between past and present forms of corporatism. In particular, it will be useful to distinguish here between the corporatism of the populist periods and that arising with a new type of state, the "bureaucratic-authoritarian." At the same time, such a state is intimately related to patterns of growth (which I will call *profundización*, "deepening") of a type of late, dependent, uneven, but also extensively industrialized, capitalism. Consequently, without forgetting that at a very abstract level different cases may be considered as generic instances of corporatism, the present analysis will adopt a level of specificity that will enable us to locate a certain type of corporatism as a function of the type of state and socioeconomic structure in which corporatism is one of the linking structures.

3. This work focuses upon corporatism in the bureaucratic-authoritarian state. This is "bifrontal" corporatism, in that it contains two components which must be carefully differentiated. The first of these is *estatizante* ("statizing"); it consists of the conquest and subordination by the state of organizations of civil society. The other is *privatista* ("privatist"); it entails the opening of institutional areas of the state to the representation of organized interests of civil society. Therefore, the institutional setting in which corporatization appears differs greatly from one case to the other. In the former it occurs by means of the "statization" of organizations of civil society; in the latter, through the partial "privatization" of a state's institutions. Bifrontal corporatization (that is, statizing *and* privatist) tends to appear in situations of authoritarian domination. In contrast, the corporatism of political democracies in the central capitalist countries (the United States and Western Europe) is basically privatist.

4. Besides being bifrontal, corporatism is "segmentary." Its actual functioning and social impacts differ systematically according to cleavages largely determined by social class. Statizing corporatization tends to function effectively when crystallized in the statization of the class organizations of the popular sector, especially the trade unions. Among other things, this guarantees that the representation of interests of the popular sector in the privatized state areas remains subject to restrictions absent from other cases—such as those of the central capitalist countries—where class organizations have much greater autonomy from the state.

5. The bifrontal and segmentary character of this corporatism entails that the main link established with the popular sector is one of control. This can be seen as a "penetration" of the state into one of its most problematic boundaries with civil society. On the other hand, one of the components of privatizing corporatism is the representation of

interests vis-à-vis the state, especially of the dominant classes and sectors of civil society. However, a degree of mutual control also exists at this level and can be seen as complex interpenetrations between those sectors and classes, and the state. This mutual control expresses an alliance subject to significant tensions; the state exercises control over the dominant sectors by less direct and much less coercive means than those applied to the popular sector.

6. Corporatism is not a static phenomenon. It changes from country to country, and along time within countries. These variations arise, above all, from the differences and changes in the type of state which corporatism helps to link with civil society. And, as suggested by its "segmentary" attribute, neither is corporatism a homogeneous phenomenon: Its impacts are not distributed evenly throughout society. However, some of the literature stresses the corporatist content of various ideologies and legislation, almost to the exclusion of the historicostructural factors that will be used here. This easily leads to the error of postulating fundamentally unchanging and homogeneous characteristics for Latin American corporatism. The origins of those ideologies can be traced at least as far back as the early Middle Ages, though there they corresponded to a nonindustrial society in which the modern state had not yet arisen. Since that time, the continuation of a hierarchical view of society, based upon the functional representation of segments of civil society and denying class divisions (or the formal existence of legislation based on this view) undoubtedly has facilitated changing and nonhomogeneous (segmentary) historical expressions of corporatism in Latin America. But such ideological and legislative continuities must not prevent us from perceiving changes and differences in the effective modes of functioning and the impact of concrete instances of corporatism.

It is time to specify the content of the term with which we are dealing. I will consider "corporatist" those structures through which functional, nonterritorially based organizations officially represent "private" interests before the state, formally subject for their existence and their right of representation to authorization or acceptance by the state, and where such right is reserved to the formal leaders of those organizations, forbidding and excluding other legitimate channels of access to the state for the rest of its members. This generic definition includes both statizing and privatist corporatization and, moreover, allows us to begin to differentiate corporatism from other patterns of linkage between state and society.[2] However, in itself, this first conceptual approximation does not free us from the level of analysis which considers corporatism as a phenomenon that can be studied without reference to social and historical context. It is worth repeating, therefore, that this chapter is concerned with the particular type of corporatism that corresponds to the bureaucratic-authoritarian state. This corporatism shares, of course, the generic characteristics already mentioned. However, at a more specific level, which will allow us to differentiate this variety of corporatism from those corresponding to other types of state, the one with which we are concerned here has two additional characteristics: its bifrontal and segmentary condition, already mentioned, and its existence within a framework of political and economic exclusion of the popular sector. On the basis of these attributes, which do not pertain to its formal characteristics or to its ideological expressions, the corporatism of the bureaucratic-authoritarian state can be differentiated not only from that associated with the constitutional democracies of the central capitalist countries, but also from that existing under populism.

If it is convenient to consider corporatism as a set of structures linking state and society, we must look at both of these to discern the coordinates that situate our subject analytically. The problem arises not only from the enormous amount of material to be covered, but also from difficulties in the conceptualization of the state. As a partial solution to this problem, the next two sections will examine some conceptual problems and will offer a basic survey of certain historico-structural factors. Then, in the fourth and fifth sections, we can begin to examine the statizing and privatist components of the corporatism that corresponds to the bureaucratic-authoritarian state, as well as the factors that determine its segmentary character.

Some Theoretical Coordinates of Corporatism

The Chilean tragedy closed a decade, begun with the Brazilian coup of 1964, that witnessed the frustration of reformist and revolutionary hopes that the countries of Latin America could move rapidly toward more humane forms of existence. Whatever our evaluation of what happened, it is obvious that today we must take account of very different realities than those foreseen by the numerous intellectual currents which echoed these hopes. It seems urgent to revise our instruments of analysis in order to record and begin to explain the changes which have taken place, and even to recognize some of the aspects which have been seriously ignored. One of these is the state itself, understood here as the set of organizations and relationships pertaining to the "public" sphere within a delimited territory, which claims from the population of this territory conformity with the expressed content of its commands and supports this claim with superior control of the means of physical violence.[3] One problem is that, in spite of recent valuable contributions, much remains to be rethought and investigated concerning the concept of the state, a theme which was ignored or explicitly denied by much of the dominant political analysis until a short time ago. Here I can only refer briefly to this problem.

The principal currents of Anglo-Saxon academic literature, especially North American, have been influenced until recently by factors which have led scholars not only to ignore, but even to deny the existence of, the problems I will stress here. Among these factors are a historical experience in which the role of the state was, although not insignificant, less visible in the formation of nations and in the emergence of industrial capitalism;[4] the tendency to see social change as a movement along a traditional-modern continuum, which helped to focus many studies on polar situations of "underdevelopment" (these are the most "destatized," since what is at stake is the establishment of effective command over a territory); and the tendency of many scholars to view their own countries as the epitome of a consensually accepted social rationality or "development," in which there is no place for the fundamental elements of coercion and ideological control, which are contained more or less openly in all systems of domination, including the modern state. This viewpoint has shown itself in different manners in the literature: in "pluralism,"[5] which sees politics in terms of a market analogy, as a scenario which passively registers adjustments between groups and in which it is therefore impossible to attribute to the state an independent initiative to explain decisions adopted invoking its coercive force; and in structural functionalism[6] and systems analysis,[7] which conceive of politics as the aspect of internal integration or the achievement of goals for a social totality about which is postulated an intrinsic homogeneity of interests.

Studies most directly focused upon comparative politics and "political development" either have been strongly influenced by some of the conceptions just mentioned, or, especially in the case of those based on quantitative data, have postulated a mechanical progression of political factors as dependent variables of economic and social "development."[8] On the other hand, intellectual currents inspired by Marxist thought have until recently been dominated by a conception that has led to similar conclusions.[9] For a long time the official line of the Communist parties saw the capitalist state as the direct expression of the interests of the bourgeoisie, with the result that they also denied the possibility of independent initiative by the state apart from the bourgeoisie. They thus joined other intellectual currents in suppressing the problem of the state as both concept and concrete reality.

Such brief references cannot avoid being excessively general, ignoring nuances and subtleties within these currents. Nevertheless, the point I would like to stress remains valid: With all their differences, these currents share a common viewpoint that I will call "societalist." That is, they deny or ignore the specificity of the problem of the state as a societal factor endowed with varying, but rarely insignificant, capabilities for autonomous impulse or initiative. By denying or ignoring such specificity, they make of the state a dependent or instrumental variable of civil society, which is consequently seen as the crucial explanatory key to the nature and dynamism of the societal whole.

In fact, over the last decade, new contributions have overcome these mistakes and have begun to open the way to investigations which will allow us in the future to reformulate and specify the problem of the state. Examination of these contributions must be left for another time. Here it is only necessary to comment that a simple reaction to the obvious failings of societalism can lead to a "politicism" or "statism" which involves a no less erroneous oversimplification, only in the opposite direction. For example, two of the most important books on comparative politics published in the United States during the last decade conclude that the accumulation of power is the alpha and omega of "political development."[10] First, the satisfaction of other values appears subordinated to the accumulation of power; and second, a state, (supposedly) capable of ruling sovereignly over society, is granted a disproportionate weight in the causation of observed and recommended social changes. Moreover, politicism tends to approve any accumulation of power, without asking by whom, for whom, and at whose expense such power is exercised. This contains a message analogous to that of most societalisms in the sense that it legitimates existing domination, although the lack of "integration" and "consensus" of the "underdeveloped" nations shifts the reference of that legitimation from society toward any consolidation of political power which appears capable of exercising effective control.[11]

Having pointed out the components of autonomy and domination, the analysis must shift toward examining characteristics of and changes in specific historical situations. This seems to be the most promising method, though we still do not know how to "reaggregate" such studies analytically in order to formulate general theoretical propositions.

In the pages that follow, I present an initial summary of some of the themes I am trying to advance. The reflections in this section were necessary to dispense partially with some problems in conceptualizing the state. Another reason for these comments is that the oscillations between societalism and politicism also appear in studies directly relevant to the theme of corporatism in Latin America. In particular, the current interest in "authoritarianism" in the region can channel itself in either direction: Authoritarianism can merely mask economic domination;[12] or the term "authoritarian" added to "regime" or "state" can lead to a view which postulates a political power, autonomous of civil society, which appears correlatively disarticulated and devoid of the capacity for any initiative or causal import. In this way, we risk losing sight of the dynamic of civil society itself and of its location in the international context.[13] This in turn has repercussions concerning the concept of corporatism, in that a "sovereign" view of the state implies postulating a society which is almost entirely subordinated, and a corporatism homogeneous (that is, nonsegmentary) in its impacts and modalities of functioning. The vision of corporatism as a mechanism of social equilibrium and integration is part of the ideology which makes absolute the relative autonomy of the state and presents it as the impartial guardian of the "common good." In this sense, the politicist interpretation of the authoritarian state tends to be too credulous with regard to ideological denials of the profoundly unequal and conflictive nature of Latin American societies, which, as we shall see, corporatism helps to crystallize.

These comments were intended to clear the way for a presentation of the social and state coordinates that specify a particular type of corporatism, which corresponds to the bureaucratic-authoritarian state. From there I will make some comparative references to other types of corporatism. The general coordinates are typical or modal aspects which result from contrapuntal interactions between changes in the socioeconomic structure, on the one hand, and the emergence and social impacts of the bureaucratic-authoritarian state, on the other. The result is an analytical creation, a "constructed type"[14] that does not seek to describe completely or exactly any of the cases attributed to it, though they approximate to it sufficiently to be included in a category which reveals common general patterns.[15] The cases of that type—which correspond, at a lower level of generality, to a certain type of corporatism—are Brazil, undoubtedly the "purest" example; Mexico, which differs in its historical emergence as a bureaucratic-authoritarian state and in the role of its armed forces, but which is notably similar in present structure and ways of functioning; and Argentina, which between 1966 and 1970 experienced a process which can only be understood as an attempt to consolidate the form of the state and the socioeconomic patterns of this type. The present political misfortunes of Argentina continue to express these tendencies though they are specified by characteristics whose examination must be left for another occasion. Chile and Uruguay are also examples of this type, although they lack the consolidation of domination which occurred in Brazil and Mexico, and certain limitations (many of them as a result of their small domestic markets) make less certain the achievement of socioeconomic transformations toward which Brazil and Mexico have advanced and over which Argentina has stumbled. Other Latin American countries are not cases of the bureaucratic-authoritarian state and do not share the corresponding form of corporatism. The most striking typological and genetic similarities appear in southern and eastern Europe, subject today or in the near past to political tendencies and processes of socioeconomic change similar to those discussed here. This emphasizes that our topic is "Latin American" only in a trivial sense; the pertinent historical context is provided by the political economy of nations that were originally exporters of primary materials and were industrialized late, but extensively, in a position of dependency upon the great centers of world capitalism.

The Emergence of the Bureaucratic-Authoritarian State

What are the main coordinates of the type of corporatism we want to analyze? They belong basically to two intimately related processes. The first comprises changes in the economy, mainly directed toward a high degree of vertical integration and property concentration in industry and the productive structure in general, basically benefiting large organizations, both public and private, national and foreign. I will call this process the *profundización*, "deepening," of a capitalism far removed from the archetypal situations of "underdevelopment" which nevertheless does not follow the patterns of growth of the central economies.

The second process I will call the "expansion" of a new type of state, the bureaucratic-authoritarian. This state is more (1) comprehensive, in the range of activities it controls or directly manages; (2) dynamic, in its rates of growth compared to those of society as a whole; (3) penetrating, through its subordination of various "private" areas of civil society; (4) repressive, in the extension and efficacy of the coercion it applies; (5) bureaucratic, in the formalization and differentiation of its own structures; and (6) technocratic, in the growing weight of teams of *técnicos* expert in the application of "efficientist" techniques of formal rationality. Furthermore, the bureaucratic-authoritarian state is closely linked to international capital, although this relationship is subject to tensions that will be examined later.

The contributions of Alexander Gerschenkron and Barrington Moore have begun to show the consequences of differences in the tempo of emergence and transformation of capitalism in several countries, especially in commercialization of agriculture and in advances toward vertical integration of industry.[16] Among other consequences, it is important to point out:

1. the more dynamic and visible role of the state in comparison with the Anglo-Saxon countries

2. the difficulties of growth experienced by the national bourgeoisie without the active tutelage of a state that carries out entrepreneurial activities and is "interventionist" to a degree unknown in the classic cases of capitalist development

3. the tendency toward the appearance of highly bureaucratized and expansive patterns of political authoritarianism

4. the "statist" content of dominant ideologies of societal organization and economic growth

5. the tendency to institutionalize mechanisms of control of the popular sector, including at some point the statizing corporatization of its organizations

These characteristics correspond generically to cases such as Germany, Italy, and Japan, whose incorporation into the central economies occurred by means of authoritarian patterns culminating in variants of fascism. The countries that concern us here are later examples of this same tendency,[17] although they were originally incorporated into the world market under very different conditions from those of the countries which followed the "fascist route" discussed by Barrington Moore.[18] Some of the consequences of this later tempo are additional to, and partially modify, the general characteristics indicated in the cases of Germany, Italy, and Japan. In Latin America, the demands of the popular sector for economic and political participation emerged much earlier, and the composition of the dominant classes is not the same. In these later cases, international capital plays a decisive role, completely unknown in the earlier ones. It reflects and helps to cause the enormous difficulties experienced by these economies in the internal generation of technology, capital goods, and even the currency which would allow them to "close" the cycle of capital accumulation in their own markets. In these cases, moreover, international capital is not simply juxtaposed to the state and the national bourgeoisie; on the contrary, it has a crucial influence in the very determination of the characteristics of the state and of the national bourgeoisie. Those bourgeois sectors which control the largest and most dynamic of the locally owned companies also tend to be those most closely linked and subordinated to international capital. The state tends to assume authoritarian forms which are—like fascism—"modern," expansive, and highly bureaucratized. But it has complex links with an international capital which is the most dynamic private element in its own economy, and this generates consequences that force us to differentiate it from the fascist state in which that external element was much less important with respect to the dominant local classes.

In order to understand the bifrontal and segmentary character of the corporatism corresponding to the bureaucratic-authoritarian state, we must focus not only on the expansion of the state but also on the conditions that preceded its emergence. These conditions can be summarized in two parallel but related processes: the massive praetorianization of Latin American societies, or the increasing randomization of their social relations; and social changes which stimulated the emergence and hypertrophic growth of complex public and private organizations.[19] The former process resulted from the increasing incapacity of preexisting institutional frameworks to regulate the behavior of diverse sectors of civil society. This expressed itself in growing levels of conflict, in the rapid political activation of the popular sector,[20] in the articulation by this sector of goals and leaders increasingly autonomous vis-à-vis the state and the dominant classes, and in the limited capacity of the state to extract and allocate resources. Although from other points of view they were different, the periods previous to the emergence of the bureaucratic-authoritarian state in Brazil, Uruguay, Chile, and Argentina had one important similarity: In all of them, the state increasingly lost the capacity to control its allies and adversaries, and its evident crisis left it at the mercy of the most powerful sectors, both internal and external, operating on their societies. Correlatively, the economic situation was characterized by erratic and declining growth rates, decreasing investment, flight of capital, sharp intersectoral changes of income, recurrent balance-of-payments crises, high inflation, and other phenomena which in part expressed and in part fueled the political crisis. To varying degrees (which must be seen in relation to the intensity of repression applied afterwards), the situation came to be seen as a "threat" to the capitalist systems and international affiliations of these countries. This feeling tended to be shared by middle sectors which, reacting in typical fashion, opted for "order and security" as a response to the political activation of the popular sector. All this led to the formation of political alliances oriented toward consolidating some type of domination that could control society effectively. During the praetorian period, society had devastated the state, but, perhaps because of this, proposed solutions tended to veer in the opposite direction.

The situation before the emergence of the bureaucratic-authoritarian state has been characterized as a "social impasse."[21] The term is descriptive, because no sector was able to establish a stable domination, and the norm was the creation of coalitions which, although unable to impose their own preferences, were able to prevent other sectors from imposing theirs. However, it is possible to detect changes taking place beneath the surface of this "impasse." Even with the inconveniences imposed by political and economic instability, and in degrees which depended upon the size of the internal market of each country, industrialization continued, mainly stimulated by local branches of international corporations. As a result, the number of branches of multinational companies which produced and distributed in Latin American markets rapidly increased. Moreover, these affiliates tended to grow more rapidly than the domestic economies, than their own sectors, and even than the most dynamic locally owned companies. [22] Not only did they create new activities and absorb an important part of the most dynamic and profitable of those already existing, but as a consequence of their orientation toward the internal market, they generated numerous backward and forward linkages with other stages of their own productive activities. This was the basis of real systems of economic power, centered upon branches of multinational companies, with local capitalists at their peripheries dependent on the multinationals for a good part of their sales, capitalization, and technology.

All of this implies the rapid growth of complex organizations that the weak state of the praetorian period had little possibility of controlling. At a different level, these changes involved another organization whose relative weight also grew, the armed forces. The "communist threat," acute political conflicts, and recurrent economic crises led the internal and external dominant sectors to see the armed forces as the last bulwark against social disintegration. Foreign aid programs and the pressures of diverse local sectors coincided with the aspiration of the armed forces to separate themselves from the praetorian state and from politicians, as part of the redefinition of their role in achieving "development" and eliminating "subversion" as prerequisites to "national security." [23] As a corollary, nothing could be attained without the emergence of a strong state, which could only be brought about by the armed forces' putting a quick end to the praetorian period.

The branches of multinational corporations and various sectors of the national bourgeoisie did not suffer economically from praetorianism. However, together with the armed forces and a large part of the middle class, they agreed on the necessity of ending it abruptly before the situation became uncontrollable and threatened to modify fundamentally the capitalist structures of their societies. One main concern was to eliminate the uncertainties generated by the continually changing situations imposed by praetorianism. The growing political activation of the popular sector encouraged the view that "excessive" and "premature" demands for political and economic participation were the principal cause of such uncertainties and of the risks of "subversion" they seemed to entail. This predetermined one of the fundamental characteristics of the bureaucratic-authoritarian state: its attempt at the political exclusion of the popular sector and its allies as the first foundation of "order" and "social peace."

It also predetermined the direction to be taken to reconstitute the mechanisms of capital accumulation. The economic growth of the praetorian period was far too erratic and its benefits, although not insignificant, were too sporadic. Presupposing—necessarily, given the composition of the coalition that imposed the bureaucratic-authoritarian state—the continuity of the capitalist structures of Latin American societies, the only possible points of equilibrium seemed to require rapid advancement toward the vertical integration of industry, the exportation of industrial goods, the proliferation of modern services, the rapid improvement of the physical infrastructure, and the diversification of the consumption of the high-income sectors.[24] All this would require huge investments oriented toward long-term benefits. Therefore, it was necessary to count upon sustained and important influxes of international capital and to eliminate the uncertainties which blocked public and private plans in the medium and long term. This would not only guarantee a high average rate of profit but also make it stable and predictable, to the benefit of the big organizations capable of "deepening" a productive structure which had been seriously weakened by the erratic processes of praetorianization.

Although this project emerged from the right, it was in no way conservative. On the contrary, it entailed the rapid introduction of profound changes at almost all levels of society. In fact, it implied nothing less than a capitalist revolution, although it did not follow the classical model. In its early stages, it grew from a state debilitated by praetorianism and from a national bourgeoisie which had been increasingly subordinated to international capital. International capital appeared as the main dynamic agent to bring about new investment and alleviate the restrictions imposed by balance-of-payments crises. The deepening could not be accomplished without a particularly decisive and visible role for international capital. But the problem was far from simple, because the uncertainties and apparent "risks" associated with praetorianism had made international investors wary, and their confidence had to be regained in order to attract capital in a quantity and continuity sufficient for a real advance toward that deepening.[25]

This problem had eminently political implications: In order to "solve" the economic problem, it was indispensable that a new state capable of imposing a drastic reorganization of society should emerge and expand. I have already commented that, after the praetorian period, the productive structure could not be "deepened" without imposing an "order" that would entail a high degree of stability and predictability in social relations. This could not, of course, be just any order. Its content emanated from the social imbalances that had been accentuated in the praetorian period. Thus, some of its principal aspects were to rid the market of "inefficient" producers (generally local capitalists), a heritage of the first stages of industrialization; to put an end to "excessive" or "premature" demands for political and economic participation by the popular sector; to eliminate elections and political parties which had transmitted these demands; to "discipline" the work force in its direct relations with employers; and to subordinate class organizations, above all trade unions, which could provide a base of support for the resurgence of new leadership and demands. The attainment of these goals would lead to the stabilization of social relations, which would encourage domestic and foreign investment. This not only implied immediate "social peace"; it signified, much more relevantly, the imposition of a new domination which could plausibly guarantee its continuity and thus support the socioeconomic decisions necessary to carry out the deepening. The reduction of social uncertainty via the stabilization of the new "order" had to be plausibly guaranteed for the future so that the bureaucratic-authoritarian state and the deepening would not be merely a passing phase, as happened in Argentina, in the reemergence of praetorianism.

It would seem that the need to reduce social uncertainty objectively increases with the degree of complexity of the society. This is one cause of the privatist type of corporatism in the central capitalist countries. At least this is the way it tends to be perceived, especially by those in control of massive organizational resources whose utilization is normally based upon highly routinized norms according to medium- or long-range planning. However, the specific ways in which a highly complex society is stabilized can vary from relatively gradual processes of political incorporation to the drastic exercise of coercion to exclude previously incorporated sectors. In those cases which concern us here, the economic crisis, the political activation of the popular sector, and the fears of the dominant classes determined the course chosen. If economic changes suggested the importance that the largest and most modern productive organizations were to have, then what has just been said points to a new type of state, a "strong" state in much more than the obvious sense of its increased coercive capacity. It had to be an *expansive* state, not only to impose the great social transformations implied in the deepening, but also to guarantee for the future the consolidation of the new "order," without which deepening could not advance very far. Statizing corporatism is a fundamental aspect of that "guarantee."

The state to which we refer is not of the traditional authoritarian type, which rules over a politically inert population; nor is it of the populist type, which activates, although in a controlled fashion, the popular sector. As I have argued elsewhere, bureaucratic-authoritarianism is a system of political and economic exclusion of the popular sector. Its central characteristic is that it emerges after a substantial degree of industrialization has been achieved, and also after, and to a large extent as a consequence of, substantial political activation of the popular sector. In this sense, its principal task—and one of the bonds of the alliance which supports its emergence and expansion—is to eliminate that activation. This is achieved by abolishing the channels of political access to the state of the popular sector and its allies, and by capturing and controlling the organizational bases of that activation. One of the mechanisms of control that links the state asymmetrically to the popular sector is the statizing corporatization of the trade unions. We will return to this point, but for the moment it should be mentioned that if this aspect of exclusion is not taken into consideration, then little can be understood about the functioning and real impacts of corporatism under the bureaucratic-authoritarian state.

As Marx pointed out, the economically dominant sectors may be unable to control the state directly, but they need the state to put the rest of society "in its place" in order to guarantee their own survival and expansion. Whoever controls, in whatever manner, the means of physical coercion and obtains the acquiescence of most middle sectors of society, can seize hold of the state and offer that guarantee. The result contradicts any simplistic view of the relationship between state and bourgeoisie, creating possibilities for the former to acquire an important degree of autonomy, in respect not only to the rest of society, but also to the bourgeoisie itself. But the Latin American cases have important differences from the European Bonapartism of the nineteenth century. In the first place, the Latin American bourgeoisie is not the "conquering bourgeoisie" of the earlier developed capitalist countries.[26] Neither is it the national bourgeoisie of cases of later development such as Germany and Japan. In contrast with the first case, the bourgeoisies of Germany, Japan, and the Latin American countries mentioned here had to enter into complex coalitions with the traditionally dominant agrarian classes and from the beginning align themselves subordinately to an authoritarian and "interventionist" state. In Latin American countries, moreover, the state and the national bourgeoisie must come to grips within their own territory with international investors who possess tremendous advantages in the control of economic and technological resources.

On the other hand, only the armed forces can put an end to the praetorian period, and only they possess the coercive means to force the exclusion of the popular sector and its political allies. Because of the "right" this power confers upon them, they occupy the highest government positions and open the way to civilian technocrats. Moreover, they acquire an impulse of their own which soon sours the tune they would have played if they had remained merely the "instruments" of the great economic interests. The alliance with these interests is woven around the deepening and its political requisite, the exclusion of the popular sector. Between these allies and the popular sector are broad sectors—employees, small and medium businessmen—who fluctuate between their initial support for the termination of praetorianism and the discovery that the new domination and the new "efficientist" and "rationalizing" patterns of economic growth are not oriented toward their benefit. Their positions oscillate in accordance with the increased opportunities for consumption that may follow the first years of "cleaning the market" (as in Brazil), or the uncertain radicalization which results (as in Argentina) from the inability or lack of time for the new system to begin rechanneling part of the economic growth toward these sectors.[27]

In order to stabilize and reorganize the postpraetorian society and, above all, to guarantee plausibly the continuity of the new domination, state institutions must also be "put in shape." Their expansion consists in the differentiation and technocratization of the state.[28] At the same time, bureaucratic interests are generated. These feed state expansion which, while a necessary condition for the deepening of the economy, is also a partial obstacle to it. There is here an important element of bureaucratic pathology, but there is also an objective need, even though it runs counter to the strictly economic rationality of the situation. The expansive impulse of the state quickly puts on the ideological cloak of "nationalism." This reflects an important aspect of reality: Not even the most consolidated of these systems could operate freely an economic system which would excessively bias accumulation in favor of international capital. Because international capital possesses so many resources—capital, technology, access to external markets, and influence over international institutions—it is an indispensable member of the coalition. But because it has these advantages, its growth in the domestic market must be limited to prevent it from absorbing all the dynamic and national components of the capitalism the new state is to protect.

We have here a fundamental tension which decisively influences the characteristics of the bureaucratic-authoritarian state. This is partly the result of an alliance of mutual dependence, rooted in the deepening process, between the state and international capital. Without the latter there would be no deepening and the new state would rapidly collapse. At the same time, international capital could not operate without the political guarantee of a state capable of "reorganizing" and controlling society. On the other hand, the alliance is filled with tensions resulting from the political impossibility of what is economically rational or, conversely, from the economic irrationalities imposed by the survival of the new system of domination. Because it includes so dynamic and indispensable a role for international capital, the process of making these types of capitalism politically viable makes their operation much more difficult than it was under European Bonapartism. The latter, after all, was not faced with the gigantic task of economically limiting and ideologically blurring the role of its international allies without "discouraging" them.

These are fundamental tensions of the situation we are examining. They affect the mutual interpenetrations and controls at the privatist level of corporatism, which the state opens to this ally. But it must also be stressed that these tensions contribute to some aspects of the expansion of the bureaucratic-authoritarian state, in that they lead to limitation of and vigilance over the internal growth of its indispensable ally. The bureaucratic-authoritarian state is not merely an "interventionist" one which increases the regulation of "private initiative." It is, especially after sustained investment by international capitalism, an "entrepreneurial" state which, accentuating a previous tendency, takes over the direct exploitation of diverse productive and service activities, differentiating itself into public enterprises, decentralized organisms, and the like. In this way arises what some authors have called a "state bourgeoisie": functionary-businessmen who remove diverse productive activities from private capital, absorb an important portion of accumulation, and together contribute so that the state grows more than would have been necessary in strictly economic terms.[29]

This combination of a growing state and international capital, in which each element depends on and is limited by the other, is a relationship between economics and politics which is only beginning to be explored. The state's links with its indispensable but conflicting ally, although very different from its links with the popular sector, express the resulting ambiguities. However, before considering these limits under the rubric of privatist corporatism, we must quickly examine other topics.

From this tension arise factors which convert the state—international capital duo into a trio, a *ménage à trois* in which a new partner, although weaker than the other two, comes to play a very important role, making the coalition even more complex and opening up new possibilities of autonomy for the state. This new element is, of course, the national bourgeoisie. Its companies tend to be closely linked to international capital, and also to have a long history as suppliers, concessionaires, or coparticipants in the state's activities. This is the national bourgeoisie of the deepening stage of this type of capitalism. In spite of the announcements of its death or nonexistence, it has survived, though at the cost of subordination to the state and international capital and abandonment of all possibility of leading the new patterns of economic growth and political domination. It is a viable national bourgeoisie only if it finds a state which shelters it to a degree unknown in previous cases of capitalist development. Without such protection it would disappear, or at least remain in its own market in a totally peripheral position with respect to international capital, working only in branches the latter had disregarded, negotiating from a position of growing weakness, and losing the possibility of sharing in the new patterns of accumulation.

In order to gain a place in the new alliance, the national bourgeoisie uses "nationalistic" arguments which are echoed in the ideology of military men and technocrats, and which reflect the fundamental tension between the two principal allies. This mitigates polar tendencies between a state capitalism that would excessively "discourage" international capital and a totally internationalized economy that would put an end to the political viability of the new domination. The *ménage à trois* is not a fiction. The bureaucratic-authoritarian state, as well as expanding its own entrepreneurial activities, shares with the national bourgeoisie "strategic" products and services that could only be exploited by them; areas in which international capital could only participate in association with a national partner, public or private; and diverse "controls" of foreign investment and forms of association which international capital would accept only because they provide protection from political risks which its allies otherwise would have generated. That this bourgeoisie tends to be the most closely linked to international capital does not exclude the possibility of conflicting interests. Thus, the national bourgeoisie seeks positions of power from which it can negotiate its relationship with international capital and, if possible, exclude it from the direct exploitation of some highly profitable activities.[30] On the other hand, the bourgeoisie is disposed to abandon to their fate the sectors of national business which, because they are smaller companies or in stagnant branches of the economy, have no option but a policy of survival, at the periphery of the trio, in conditions much more orthodoxly competitive.[31]

Only the state can open these opportunities to the national bourgeoisie in the face of international capital. To survive, the bourgeoisie requires much more than the erection of customs and trade barriers. It needs active state protection against competitors who have overcome these barriers and operate in the national bourgeoisie's own market.

Here lies the paradox of a bourgeoisie that becomes highly politicized when, in contrast to its "classical" ancestors, it has lost all possibility of leading the economic and political process. As is to be expected, this is reflected on the ideological plane. The myth of the "economic miracles" of this capitalism is not so much nationalist as statist; more precisely, it is "national-statist."[32] Its goal is the expansion of the bureaucratic-authoritarian state and the growth of the national and private component of the national bourgeoisie which that state has practically reinvented. To this end, a rhetoric of national-statist "grandeur" emerges, which contrasts with the much more privatist ideas articulated by international capital. These differences reflect the very real tensions I have pointed out.

To recapitulate, the resulting direction is toward capitalist growth based upon the exclusion of a previously activated popular sector. This direction is national-statist but has an indispensable axis in international capital, in which the national bourgeoisie recovers its importance because of its decisive political and ideological contribution to the viability of the new domination, despite its economic subordination. This entails a notable expansion of the state and, at the same time, a more "advanced" level of dependency. The apparent paradoxes implied by these terms, as well as the difficulty of expressing them verbally, indicates how primary and tentative are the concepts with which we must deal in order to take into account historical realities for which we have not been prepared by other experiences or the conceptions they have inspired. However, they may serve to put into perspective the theme of bifrontal and segmentary corporatism with which I will now deal.

The "Statizing" Element of Corporatism

Recall that I conceive of corporatism as a bifrontal and segmentary set of linking structures between state and society. The bifrontalism results from two simultaneous yet distinct components: the "statization" of organizations in civil society and the "privatization" of some institutional areas of the state.

Corporatism interests me as an effective social reality, not as a point of departure for the study of corporatist ideologies. The latter is a valid topic, but it does not appear to be the most fruitful way of beginning on our theme. In the first place, the finite invariant content of these ideologies tends to hide those historical transformations of the corporatism that now exist socially. Second, its vision of class equilibrium and integration clashes with the segmentary character of a phenomenon that presupposes and contributes to the formation of numerous structural inequalities. Third, most of the ideological postulates of corporatism imply a degree of class integration which—except to an extent in fascist Italy and Salazar's Portugal—was never formally attained: that is, the integration of all classes, or of all the organized sectors of society, in "public" institutions that are components of the state itself. Perhaps this is most clearly expressed in the idea of the great corporatist "chambers," which comprise the whole of society and are a component part of the state. This idea replaces "liberal" (territorial and individual) and "class" principles of representation.[33] In no case did the real functioning of these structures correspond to that postulated by the ideology or its legal-formal design. On the contrary, these structures showed clearly the segmentary character they shared with the Latin American cases in which we are interested.[34]

It should be pointed out that statizing corporatism involves something very different from what the ideology claims. It is a way of connecting these groups—especially the trade unions—into the state directly and at a subordinate level, without any pretense at "integrating" them with other classes or organizations. With regard to privatist corporatism, the formal similarity is greater, since in the state areas open to civil society, diverse sectors can appear "represented," including the trade unions. However, this opening of the state does not, as corporatist ideology would have it, include all classes and their activities. Moreover, the formal role tends to be that of advisor to the state and not actual participant in public decision-making. The presence of organized interests on advisory planning commissions or on regulatory boards or councils resembles, but is not the same as, that architectural vision of global class integration and of fusion of classes in a state of which they are a constituent. The *formal* similarities with the images delineated by this ideology may have been great in some European cases. But Latin American corporatism has never been more than a very fragmentary reproduction of those images, even with regard to present-day legislation. Neither the statizing corporatization of class organizations nor the opening to civil society of some institutional areas of the state amounts to more than distorted fragments of the global architectural vision of the ideology. This is one important reason why it is very hazardous to use these ideologies as the axis of an analysis to deduce social reality. These ideologies hide the detectable historical changes in Latin American corporatism, as well as the bifrontal and segmentary character of the corporatism which corresponds to the bureaucratic-authoritarian state.[35]

In particular, examination of these ideologies can hardly answer the questions that interest us: What is this type of corporatism? How has it varied through time and from country to country? How can these variations be explained? Another way to answer these questions would be to look at formal legal norms. This type of analysis can also be instructive, but it cannot tell us much about problems like: What part of that legislation is really applied? How can patterns of application differ from one social class or sector to another?[36] It should be obvious that only at the level implied by these and the previous questions can we begin to explore the real social import of this phenomenon.

It is well known that Latin American society has never been pluralist (at least in the Anglo-Saxon sense), that the role of political parties and of parliament has been very different from that presupposed by the model of constitutional democracy, and that "vertical" relationships between diverse social sectors have greatly complicated the expression of "horizontal" class cleavages.[37] However, the manifestation of these characteristics has been changing significantly. By some simplification, we can distinguish a first stage in which clientelism is the principal form of articulation of the society and of linkage between the society and the state. Clients and patrons are connected by means of social relationships in which lower-level patrons are grouped in a clientelistic fashion around others of a higher level. The highest level is the state, the point of convergence for confederations of patrons. When this is the principal pattern of linkage, the society tends to be little differentiated and political activation of the population is low.[38] Patron-client relationships are interpersonal links, not mediated by formal or bureaucratic organizations; they tend to contain a small number of people; their base is territorial, although narrow because of its interpersonal character; and they are multifunctional, although the low level of differentiation of society restricts the number of available roles. These characteristics come together with the result that political life generally "passes over" a politically inert population—except for eruptions of protest without stable organizational bases—and consists fundamentally of unstable coalitions of patrons. The state, although usually authoritarian and projecting an image of strength as the "patron of patrons," scarcely penetrates civil society. It is restricted to working through coalitions of patrons which effectively control the territory. Also, the entry of clients into multifunctional vertical structures with a narrow territorial base atomizes the popular sector and hinders the emergence of cleavages and solidarities other than regional ones or direct conflicts with the patron. The state is more a nominal entity than an effective commander of the territory, while classes are dispersed around clientelistic systems. This corresponds to the period of oligarchic domination in Latin America, within the framework of an agrarian society in which capitalist relations have penetrated to a limited extent and in which the formation of a national market has not been completed.

Clientelism did not decline abruptly, nor has it completely disappeared. However, as the principal pattern of vertical articulation between classes and of linkage with the state, it was displaced by something which, in contrast, has no territorial base, is not in principle multifunctional, can include multitudes, entails a high degree of bureaucratization and formalization of social relations, and corresponds to an active penetration of the state into diverse sectors of civil society. This is corporatism. Clientelism declined in favor of corporatism for reasons by no means accidental: the processes of internal migration which accompanied the commercialization of agriculture and the launching of industrialization. With this, the social conditions of oligarchic hegemony disappeared, and clientelism began to be displaced as the main means by which civil society articulated its relations between classes and linked itself to the state.

There is not enough space here to summarize either the immense changes that occurred with the launching of industrialization or the way it corresponded with the phenomenon of populism.[39] The state consolidated a new alliance which would now include the sectors created by urbanization, industrialization, and the growth of state institutions. One of the fundamental problems lay in incorporating the popular sector economically and politically, using it to break the domination of the oligarchy, but also controlling it to prevent the emergence of autonomous organizational bases, leaders, and goals that might carry its political activation beyond the limits acceptable to the new bourgeois and state-based sectors. There can be little doubt that populism implied transcendent changes in the organization and politicization of the urban popular sector, just as the parallel processes of expansion of the internal market initially improved its economic position.

However, populism was also corporatist: The social incorporation and political activation it permitted and, in its early moments, fomented, were carefully controlled, especially by the imposition of vertical relationships subordinating the unions to the state. Among other things, quite a few of these unions were created by the populist rulers, who reserved the right to grant or deprive them of recognition, to supervise the handling of their funds, to influence the selection of their leaders, and to decide upon the right of representation before the state and the employers. This did not make the popular sector, the working class, or the unions mere instruments of populism, but it did mark them with a degree of political, economic, and ideological subordination that differentiates their history from earlier capitalist experiences. This corporatism was not a new type of state or society, but rather a new way of "organizing" the popular sector by means of its subordinate association with the populist state, which facilitated its controlled social incorporation and political activation in a period of rapid urbanization and industrialization. Because of this, whatever may have been its affinities with existing ideologies, as an effective social reality, corporatism has not "always existed." On the contrary, it emerged together with, and as a consequence of, the processes to which I just alluded. Populism, in spite of its corporatization of the popular sector, entailed a crucial increase in its political and economic weight. It also implied a substantial improvement in the direct relations between the bourgeoisie and the unionized layers of the popular sector. Together with the complex process of redistribution of power that occurred under populism, those relationships changed. Above all, the recognition of the unions' right to represent the working class before the bourgeoisie, the codification of the right to strike (at least in principle), and important improvements in the statutes regulating security of employment all emerged together with corporatization. Especially in the great urban concentrations, the paternalistic sovereignty of the capitalist in "his" business was weakened by the role that the populist state—corporatist but also activist and "protective"—granted to the workers' representation by the union.

Later, the initial impulse of industrialization and growth of the internal market lessened and gave way to the crises already mentioned, and the populist state began to crumble, opening the way for mass praetorianism. The weakened state could do little to contain the growing activation of the popular sector. Likewise, the reduced capability of the state to mediate conflicts among classes, together with the economic crises, led the bourgeoisie increasingly to resent the rights labor had inherited from the previous period. Praetorianism implied, among other things, an activation of the popular sector sustained by a loosening of the corporatist controls populism had imposed on it; or, what amounts to the same thing, based on, and expressed in, a clear tendency toward the autonomy of the popular sector with respect to the state and the dominant classes. This is one of the main causes of the drastic defensive reaction that led to the implantation of the bureaucratic-authoritarian state.

Thus—and this must be emphasized because it differentiates the corporatism of the bureaucratic-authoritarian state from that of the populist state—the bureaucratic-authoritarian state is not a system of controlled incorporation. It is a system of *exclusion* of the popular sector.[40] It is not a case of heteronymously activating the popular sector, as under populism, or of increasing its consumption, or of using it to recompose the dominant coalition, or of increasing its weight vis-à-vis the state and the dominant classes. On the contrary, it is a case of guaranteeing an "order" and an accumulation that require post-poning the economic demands of the popular sector, depoliticizing it, and subordinating or destroying the class organizations that had become more autonomous during the praetorian period. Clientelism corresponds to the political inertia and atomization of the popular sector; populism incorporates and heteronymously activates it. But in the bureaucratic-authoritarian state there is an attempt to create a new situation of depoliticization, inertia, and atomization, in the context of a high degree of activation, urbanization, and industrialization. The state is not the same as in previous periods; nor, apart from the continuity of ideology and legislation, is the type of corporatism by which it is linked to the popular sector, controlling and penetrating it.

Under conditions of erratic growth and a high level of demand for economic and popular participation, the tendency toward autonomy of the popular sector and the new and much more "threatening" alliances this would permit appeared as the major obstacle to the stability of social relations and the redistribution of resources required for the deepening of capitalism. Therefore, with regard to the popular sector, the bureaucratic-authoritarian state has the fundamental task of *control*. That control is in part repression, which in these cases was used abundantly. However, this control is also *prevention*, in that it eliminates the conditions which could permit the reappearance of demands, leaders, and organization of the popular sector against its political exclusion and the new patterns of accumulation. Although both components coexist, one can discern a sequence in which the emphasis falls first on outright repression and then later, if and when the new system has achieved some degree of consolidation, on the implantation of such preventive mechanisms. The functioning of these mechanisms permits the stability and the *predictability of future stability* of the social relations required by the new pattern of economic growth.[41] Such preventive mechanisms imply, among other things, the repression of popular leaders emerging "from below"; the co-opting of those who have nevertheless in some way managed to "filter" through; the capacity to abolish and repress organizations which could be won over by "rebel" leaders; and the generation of anticipated reactions by means of severe sanctions against those who would break away from the required subordination.[42] The statizing corporatization of the popular sector is the most efficient mechanism for the exercise of this preventive control.[43] Under the bureaucratic-authoritarian state, corporatism is the main mechanism linking the state to the popular sector in order to guarantee its exclusion.[44]

The expansion of the bureaucratic-authoritarian state includes its control of the part of civil society composed of the popular sector, so

as to guarantee the viability of the new domination and of the new
pattern of economic growth. This imposition of control reverses the
tendency of the praetorian period. Though it may resemble the corporatism of the populist period in the formal operation of its mechanisms, the two are separated by the crucial difference between the
exclusion and the controlled activation of the popular sector.

Moreover, the corporatism of the bureaucratic-authoritarian state
corresponds to a significant weakening of the working class in its direct
social relations with the bourgeoisie. Gone are the initially benevolent
populist state and the weakened and erratic state of the praetorian
period. In their place, the bureaucratic-authoritarian state expands in
conquering fashion over the organizations of the popular sector. This is
part of a generalized defensive reaction oriented toward deactivating
and "putting in its place" a popular sector—and within it, especially, a
working class—that appears as the dynamic channel for "subversion"
and as the main impediment to the reconstitution and stability of the
new patterns of capital accumulation. The price of the partial but
important victory won by the popular sector during the populist period
was its corporatization. For the bureaucratic-authoritarian state,
statizing corporatism is one of the most important means of defeating
and excluding the popular sector. This defeat, accompanied by concomitant changes—typically the abolition or severe curtailment of the
right to strike and the modification of legislation governing workers'
dismissal—weakens the popular sector, not only in relation to the state,
but also in relation to the bourgeoisie in general. Here the bourgeoisie
finds one of the bonds that cement its alliance with the state.

Under bureaucratic authoritarianism, the statizing corporatization of
the class organizations of the popular sector is the principal linkage that
stabilizes and guarantees for the future the exclusion of the popular
sector and its weakening in direct relations with the dominant classes of
civil society. However, this theme of statizing corporatization includes
other aspects. In particular, we cannot ignore that in the most expansive and consolidated bureaucratic-authoritarian states, the state seems
also to have subordinated some business organizations. Their existence
may have come to depend formally on the state, perhaps in relation to
their financing, and in almost all cases their leaders express an acute
feeling of impotence in trying to influence public policy.[45] This theme
is important because it can lead to "statist" conclusions that are as
obvious as they are erroneous. The reasoning that can lead to such
conclusions is along the following lines: (1) In country X both the
employers' associations and the trade unions are subordinated to the
state, and their leaders express similar feelings of incapacity for initiative; (2) these organizations are the institutional expressions of the
bourgeoisie and of the working class; therefore, (3) in country X the

working class and the bourgeoisie—and almost certainly the rest of society—are equally subordinated to a highly autonomous state. I will argue that although (1) and (2) may be empirically true, (3) contains a non sequitur, because it ignores a much broader and mutually dynamic set of linkages between the bureaucratic-authoritarian state and the bourgeoisie.

Basically, through statizing corporatization, the bureaucratic-authoritarian state deprives the popular sector of almost all its organizational resources. This is not so with the bourgeoisie, which retains important organizational resources and numerous informal channels of access to the state. Moreover, the relative efficacy of these channels tends to increase as a consequence of the exclusion of the popular sector. These affirmations can be clarified by some brief references to diverse channels of access to the state.

1. The most obvious channel is the electoral one. Before the rise of the bureaucratic-authoritarian state, the popular sector had a certain weight here which, although not corresponding to its numbers, determined that its preferences would be attended to in some way. The elimination of this channel had a lot to do with the diagnosis that it had an excessive propensity to give voice to "irresponsible" or "premature" demands, antagonistic to "social stability" and capital accumulation.

2. A second channel results from the control of permanently functioning organizations, significantly autonomous from the state and other social sectors, that can formulate demands on behalf of a certain sector, elaborate and diffuse information, create and finance leading cadres, and, in general, have its "own weight" in conflicts and coalitions oriented toward influencing decisions invoking the power of the state. This cannot be done if the state imposes controls that make it impossible to formulate and support demands sustained by resources that could oppose the state and other sectors. This is precisely what statizing corporatization avoids: The leaders of organizations rely more on the state for their positions than on those they "represent"; the content, diffusion, and form of presentation of demands are severely limited (either expressly or through the "lesson" given in other cases by the use of severe sanctions); the management of economic resources, including the possibility of acquiring them, the legal existence of the organization, and its right to invoke representation of its members will depend on the state. Little remains here of a class organization. Rather, its role is reversed, and it becomes a bulwark of the state on one of its conflictive frontiers with civil society.

3. Another means of political access is the promotion of protest actions of sufficient importance to call attention to certain problems and eventually transmit the content of the demanded "solution."[46] The classic behavior in this category is, of course, to refuse to work.

Protest tends to be "expensive." It entails the risk of sanctions and requires the continued support of the sectors it mobilizes. It also suffers from diminishing returns: Escalating levels of protest (and of the consequent risks involved) are required to produce the same results. In the cases analyzed here, one of the first decisions of the new state was to limit the right to strike, prohibiting it directly or subjecting it to such requirements as to produce the same result. This is one of the main means of controlling the popular sector: to make difficult and to raise the costs of its most institutionalized means of protest. Other forms of protest come up against another aspect of state expansion—its greatly increased capacity for repression, and its willingness to use it.

4. Another important access channel is the result of informal relations between public functionaries and sectors of civil society. I will come back to this point later, but it is worth mentioning here that this channel tends to be much more open to the bourgeoisie and the higher layers of the middle class than to the popular sector.

This brief list permits an approximate answer to the question of the real impact of statizing corporatization on different social classes. Statizing corporatization implies stripping the popular sector of practically all its organizational resources. In the bureaucratic-authoritarian state, this is part of processes that tightly close other access channels. In effect, the effort to deactivate the popular sector includes repression and prohibitions directed against the movements and political parties that could invoke its interests; the closing or stringent control of the electoral system derives from the "necessity," upon which the state and bourgeoisie agree, of not obstructing the new social "order"; the increased disposition and capacity for repression, together with the corporatization of the unions, makes the use of the strike and other forms of protest very costly; and the totality of these measures, added to others regulating the work situation, also weaken the popular sector in its direct relations with the bourgeoisie.

What is the impact of statizing corporatization under the bureaucratic-authoritarian state with respect to the national bourgeoisie and international capital? The most extreme hypothesis is that such corporatization has occurred in a large number of entrepreneurial organizations, which is of course much less likely than in the case of trade unions. Even in this extreme case, which in Latin America is approximated only by Brazil, and to some extent by Mexico, it is important to note the following:

1. The corporatized associations tend to be national organizations which speak for highly aggregated interests, rather than associations of specific business interests.[47]

2. The corporatized associations tend to belong to the national

bourgeoisie, neither acting for, nor representing, the branches of multinational corporations.[48]

3. As these associations are corporatized, others tend to emerge, tolerated by the state, more active and better financed than the earlier ones, which remain limited to ceremonial functions or post facto comments on public policy.[49]

4. Above all, besides the organizations that escape corporatization, the firms themselves remain as a permanent base of important resources that can be mobilized by the bourgeoisie.

These points vary from one case to another, but it seems valid to affirm that the eventual corporatization of business associations does not deprive the bourgeoisie of much of the organizational resources it controls. Rather, in conquering these associations, the state converts them into shells whose substance is transferred to other organizations, which the bourgeoisie continues to control with an important degree of autonomy vis-à-vis the state. In the bureaucratic-authoritarian state, this strongly contrasts with the impact of statizing corporatization of the popular sector, which cannot count upon alternative permanent organizations and moreover finds itself subject to the constant threat of severe repression against any attempt to create them.

In order to evaluate these differential impacts, the indirect consequences of other aspects of the bureaucratic-authoritarian state and its linkages with society must be taken into account. First, the consequences of the closure of the electoral system are very different for the bourgeoisie than for the popular sector. This is especially true after the praetorian period and the political activation of the popular sector, which partly found expression through that channel. Second, there remains a broad area of informal links between public functionaries and the bourgeoisie. These links originate in personal relationships and in alliances of interests at the level of groups of companies or of branches of the economy with the "corresponding" state functionaries or institutions.[50] Third, though this does not directly refer to linkages with the bureaucratic-authoritarian state, the weakening of the popular sector also occurs at the level of its direct relations with a bourgeoisie which in this way consolidates its class domination. Fourth, there also remain linkages in the area of privatist corporatism. I will deal with these in the next section.

While I have been able to say something fairly concrete about the impacts of the corporatization of unions, I must end on a more ambiguous note concerning the corporatization of business organizations. Suffice it to say for the moment that the non sequitur mentioned earlier can only arise through a confusion of the area of the highly formalized and aggregated interests of some business organizations with the entirety of linkages between the state and the bourgeoisie. Of course, to avoid an error does not mean that we must now swing to the other extreme, toward a societalist non sequitur, that all this conceals a bourgeoisie which is omnipotent over the bureaucratic-authoritarian state. In fact, if our analysis is not too erroneous, what we should find in the linkages between the state and the bourgeoisie are the reverberations of a tense alliance which unravels itself in the context of the mutual dependence of the state and international capital, of the political and ideological legitimation contributed by the national bourgeoisie, and of the exclusion of the popular sector. These aspects were outlined earlier and will reappear in the discussion of privatist corporatism.

The "Privatist" Element of Corporatism

A summary is convenient at this point. We have examined the state's corporatization of class organizations, both of the popular sector and of the bourgeoisie. This implies a movement *from the state toward the society*, through which the former conquers or subordinates institutions of the latter. However, corporatism is also *an advance of "private" sectors toward the state*, through which some areas of the state are opened to the "representation of interests" from civil society. This is the privatist aspect of corporatism. In other words, the theme we have analyzed thus far implies a penetration of the state into civil society; the situations we will now consider are, in contrast, channels of complex *interpenetrations* between the state and the dominant sectors of civil society. I am not referring to informal relationships, but to the public institutionalization of links between state and society, constituted by commissions, boards, councils, and other centralized or decentralized state institutions in which one finds the bourgeoisie (and, at times, workers) "represented" by those directly designated by the state or proposed by their class organizations.

In a general sense, these are areas of partial privatization of some of the state's structures and activities. They are points of contact, publicly established between the state and sectors of civil society, which invoke the "legitimate representation" of certain functional, nonterritorial interests. At this level, the phenomenon is characteristic of the general category of complex capitalist economies in which tendencies to "adjust" mutually the behavior of public and private sectors appear. One reason for this is that the big organizations which control these sectors tend to require medium- and long-range planning, and all control resources capable of significantly affecting the future value of variables whose predictability is necessary for the attainment of their goals.[51] It is at this level of privatist corporatism that, in tacit recognition of their mutual limits of relative autonomy, the state and the oligopolized structure of complex and industrialized modern capitalisms join together, interpenetrating and mutually guaranteeing the predictability of their future behavior.

I have already pointed out that this is the only type of corporatism existing in the central capitalist countries and that the bifrontal corporatism that interests me here includes this privatist component as well as the statizing one already analyzed. I should add that this bifrontal character is not the result of the mere juxtaposition of the two components. On the contrary, the real functioning and impacts of privatist corporatism remain conditioned by the presence or absence of the statizing component. Contrasting the bureaucratic-authoritarian state with the constitutional democracies of contemporary central capitalism one can see two differences at the level of the privatist corporatization of institutional state areas. First, the relative weight of one of the sectors—the popular one—and its capacity to define goals and to formulate and support demands through autonomous control of resources is much lower because of the statizing corporatization which has been forced upon it. Second, this is reinforced by the fact that the general context which characterizes the bureaucratic-authoritarian state also includes the closure of the electoral system and the severe curtailment of the right to strike and other forms of protest. One consequence is that the presence of the popular sector in corporatized state areas tends to be manifested, not by leaders who have emerged from that sector, but by "functionaries" who, in order to maintain their positions, depend as much on the benevolence of the state as on those they "represent." Another consequence is that because channels of access in principle more appropriate to the popular sector are closed, in contrast with constitutional democracies, privatizing corporatization monopolizes the institutionalized channels for the "representation of interests" of civil society before the state. This monopoly is consolidated through linkages in which the number and patterns of organization of the popular sector tend to have less weight. Of course, this does not mean that the "representatives" of the corporatized unions cannot obtain the satisfaction of some demands, or that the state's privatized areas cannot be utilized to hand out differential benefits to some layers or organizations of the popular sector. However, what still stands is that in the bureaucratic-authoritarian state, statizing corporatization and the general context of exclusion fundamentally restrict the weight of "representation" assigned to the popular sector in the privatized state areas.

This is only preliminary to the examination of privatist corporatism. Its most complex and important dimension is that of the linkages it establishes between the state and the bourgeoisie. Here we again face a point that does not lend itself to simplification. On the one hand, the economically dominant sectors have in these areas an important mechanism of control *over the state*, as much by way of "agreements" in which the state commits future decisions, as by the opportunities they offer for less visible processes of co-optation of functionaries and of "colonization" of entire agencies. But, on the other hand, this opening of some of the state's institutional areas is a more or less successful attempt (depending on the particular case and period) at control of the principal allies of the dominant coalition. This component of corporatization is part of the attempt to "reorganize" and stabilize society. It includes the limitation and control of pluralism, including legitimated interests and the right to represent them; the exchange of information with a stable set of "representatives" who are the leaders of organizations through which social sectors must express themselves; the commitment of powerful private sectors to the support of public policies so as to reduce obstacles to their adoption and implementation; and the conversion by all possible means of the behavior of "private" actors and the treatment of issues relating to institutionalized areas of the state itself into a small number of private spokesmen who lack, or cannot express, fundamental objections to the existing patterns of domination and economic growth. In other words, though these areas are the principal institutionalized means of representation of civil society before the bureaucratic-authoritarian state—and in this sense are a "penetration" of civil society into the state—they are also a mechanism of state control, not only with respect to the popular sector (which is subject to the very different mechanisms of statizing corporatization) but with respect to its own principal allies. At the same time, the institutionalization of these linkages—which in principle makes them more visible and controllable than those of informal relationships—decreases the possibility of successful attempts by these allies informally to "colonize" the state.[52]   Of course, the state always retains non-corporatized spheres in which decisions can be enforced through the state's claim of universal validity for its commands over the territory and its superior control of the means of physical violence.[53] The resultant complexities express the alliance and the tensions between the state and the economically dominant sectors in a complex capitalist society. However, in the bureaucratic-authoritarian state, those complexities increase because of the unusually weighty presence of international capital. On the one hand, the state must economically attract and politically guarantee this capital and, on the other, it must limit its growth and protect the national bourgeoisie and its own economic activities from it.

This aspect of corporatism is even more ambiguous than the statized one. In the latter, we found a strongly asymmetrical relationship of domination. In privatist corporatism, there is a wide range of much more symmetrical linkages, true interpenetrations between the state and the external and internal dominant sectors, in which they "meet," constantly renegotiating and exploring the limits of their alliance. The intricacies, variations, and tensions of these adjustments are little known. This lack of information is particularly regrettable if, as is likely, the direction of resultant control tends to vary not only from one case and period to another, but also in accordance with the type of issue at stake.

Some Conclusions and Generalizations

We lack adequate theorization of the linkages between state and society. These, in turn, are aspects of the wider problem of the interrelationships between the political and the social, in which we must begin by reexamining the problem of the state itself. The intellectual currents that prevailed until recently all denied or ignored that any such problem exists. While this is beginning to be overcome, there is the danger of swinging toward a "statist" or "politicist" view, as erroneous as the previous "societalism." Moreover, to postulate the generic problem of the relative autonomy of the state vis-à-vis society, or to list diverse aspects of its domination, is only to pose a problem and in no way to resolve it.

There is no "relative autonomy" of "the" state in relation to "the" society. At this level we can only utter trivialities or smuggle in incorrectly generalized conclusions based on the observation of some aspect of the relationships between them. We must begin by specifying which state and which society we are speaking about. In order to do this, it would be useful to construct typologies which are neither so detailed as to make each case a type by itself nor so general that each type includes substantial differences.

Although this does not exhaust all the relevant factors, a focus upon historically oriented political economy may permit us to place ourselves at a useful level of analysis. This may allow us to identify, on the one hand, changes in factors central to the evolution of the economy and, on the other, equally central aspects for the characterization and dynamism of the state. Although there is no perfect fit, it is possible to distinguish correspondences, mutual influences, or "affinities" acting contrapuntally among these factors. I have mentioned one such instance: the correspondence between the deepening of capitalism in some Latin American countries and the emergence and expansion of a bureaucratic-authoritarian state. The interaction of these processes led to a new articulation of political, economic, and social relations which could be summarized thus: (1) the exclusion of a previously politically activated popular sector; (2) the reconstitution of mechanisms of capital accumulation in favor of large public and private organizations; (3) the emergence of a new coalition whose principal members are state personnel (especially the military and civilian technocrats), international capital, and the segments of the local bourgeoisie which control the largest and most dynamic national business; and (4) the expansion of a state with a greater capacity to guarantee the exclusion of the popular sector and, in general, to control the society, oriented toward its stabilization and predictability, appropriate to the new patterns of accumulation. None of this is specifically Latin American. On the one hand, there are similarities with European cases, both past and present, that have also been subjected to deepening processes of a retarded, dependent, uneven, but nevertheless extensively industrialized, capitalism. On the other hand, there are important contrasts with cases, both in Latin America and elsewhere, that have not "advanced" to the same stage as those countries mentioned in this chapter, which have been industrialized under a socialist economy, or which, by reason of exceptional circumstances (for example, oil) have massive economic resources directly controlled by the state that may modify the general conditions examined here.[54] In other words, the theme of this essay is a referent historically situated by a certain type of capitalism, not by geographic proximities or cultural areas.

The new patterns of domination—more specifically, the characteristics and social impacts of the bureaucratic-authoritarian state—are intimately related to the deepening of the type of capitalism under discussion. This does not prevent important internal tensions in the alliance which carries it through. However, these tensions must be examined together with the mutual dependence of the principal allies and from the broader perspective of their common interest in excluding the popular sector, drastically limiting its opportunities for political access, and "delaying" its economic participation in favor of the new patterns of accumulation.

Given the mass praetorianism of the period which preceded its emergence and the complexity of the society subject to the deepening, the expansion of the bureaucratic-authoritarian state is a necessary condition for guaranteeing the consolidation and reproduction of mechanisms of capital accumulation strongly biased in favor of the most complex and "modern" economic units—both public and private. The state's economic expansion extends, however, beyond that required by strictly economic considerations, partly because of bureaucratic impulse, but especially because of the crucial political need to retain national bases in a capitalism being deepened with the help of a protagonist such as international capital.

As part of its expansion, the bureaucratic-authoritarian state advances over society like a conqueror, increasing its effective control. Various means are utilized in this advance—some as obvious as the suppression of electoral channels, repression, and ideological manipulation. Others aim at the corporatization of class organizations, especially those of the popular sector which, moreover, is almost totally stripped of alternative resources. On the other hand, the corporatization of business organizations deprives the bourgeoisie of organizational resources to a much smaller extent and allows it to retain effective alternative access to the state. This is the area of statizing corporatization, whose main role is that of principal institutionalized link between the bureaucratic-authoritarian state and the popular sector, to consolidate popular exclusion and to prevent successful challenges of the state's authority.

This "conquering state" is also a "porous state," open at numerous interstices—informal and institutionalized—to links which contain bidirectional processes of control and influence, especially with the dominant classes of civil society. The privatist plane of corporatism is the resultant of the institutionalized areas through which the state publicly opens itself to these interpenetrations. These two components of corporatism show it as bifrontal and segmentary, since its statizing component affects, above all, the popular sector, and its privatist component opens the state to interpenetrations with, above all, international capital and the national bourgeoisie. This expresses the differences in the modes of linkage with the state between those who have been excluded from, and those who are—although not without tensions—part of, the ruling alliance. Briefly, the statizing corporatization of the class organizations of the popular sector is the principal institutional means for the exclusion and preventive penetration of the bureaucratic-authoritarian state, which crystallizes the heteronomy of the organizational resources and leaders of that sector. The privatist corporatization of some institutions of the state itself is the main institutional channel for the representation of interests and for the mutual control between the state and the dominant classes of civil society.

Under the bureaucratic-authoritarian state, statizing corporatization of the popular sector occurs within a framework of policies—the closing of other access channels, the modification of labor legislation, the abolition of the right to strike—which help to consolidate the exclusion of the popular sector. This sector is therefore weakened, not only in the face of the state, but also in relation to the dominant classes. This is a central requirement for the stabilization of social relations and for the consolidation of the new patterns of accumulation in which the alliance which sustains the bureaucratic-authoritarian state is cemented. The deepening of capitalism undertaken by this alliance requires the political deactivation of the popular sector and the guarantee of its future control by the state and its class allies. Because the popular sector had experienced a period of strong activation, its forced exclusion divorces these societies from democratic-constitutional patterns and directs them toward authoritarian forms. During the first stage, naked repression prevails, oriented to the destruction of the organizational bases and leadership of that political activation. Later on, the preventive and less visible controls of statizing corporatization are emphasized.

Perhaps now some of the initial affirmations of this chapter are clear. In particular, we have seen that the phenomenon of corporatism must, first, be differentiated into its various components and, second, be related to other linkages between state and society. The mode of functioning and real impacts of any type of corporatism are a function of, and in turn indicate, the type of state which it helps to link with civil society. Therefore, beyond ideological and formal similarities, the exclusion of the popular sector is enough to differentiate the functioning and real impacts of bureacratic-authoritarian corporatism from that existing under populism. On the other hand, its bifrontal character separates it even more clearly from the solely privatist corporatism of the political democracies of the central capitalist countries.

Like the others, the bureaucratic-authoritarian state neither floats sovereignly over civil society, nor acts as the "agent" of the economically dominant sectors, nor serves as the passive scenario established for adjustments among "groups." It is a much more complex phenomenon that we could only examine briefly here. In the cases with which we are concerned, such complexity is even greater, since the political viability of the deepening of a historical type of capitalism causes the bureaucratic-authoritarian state to expand as a direct economic agent and as custodian of a national bourgeoisie which may be—in conjunction with its economic weakness, on the one hand, and its political and ideological importance, on the other—the most vivid indication of the original characteristics of these cases.

Returning to a qualification made at the beginning, although today the Mexican case—even considering the peculiarities resulting from the PRI—can be included in the category I have delineated here, what I said about the praetorian period which preceded the emergence of the bureaucratic-authoritarian state does not apply to Mexico. This may be a consequence of the fact that the elective affinities between the state and the stage of deepening of capitalism that the Mexican case shares with the rest are even stronger than I have argued here. This is only one of the questions implied by the initial speculations about the tempo of the appearance of certain contrapuntally related factors, which future studies can perhaps answer. For this to be possible, it will be necessary in the meantime to redeem conceptually one of these factors, the state, at a level which permits the detection of its changes through time, together with its differential modes of linkage with diverse social classes and sectors at each stage. Corporatism is only a chapter, though certainly an important one, in the study of those modes.

I insist again that each type of corporatism is a function of the type of state of which it is *one* in the set of structures or modes of linkage with civil society. In turn, each type of state results from complex interactions with certain characteristics and processes of change in civil society. The corporatism of the bureaucratic-authoritarian state must be understood within these coordinates. From these result its bifrontal condition—statizing and privatist—and its segmentary condition—the summary of the differential impact which the statizing and privatist components entail for the allies of the bureaucratic-authoritarian state and for those which it excludes. Corporatism—especially, but not only, statizing corporatism—is a fairly recent addition to the manifold mechanisms of class domination. The fact that the emergence and expansion of an authoritarian state are necessary to impose it should not lead us to forget this fundamental fact.

NOTES

This chapter was translated from Spanish by Richard Gillespie and Anthony Powell. I wish to express my gratitude to those who have criticized and commented upon this essay in its various stages of preparation. Among the many to whom I am indebted, I must mention David Collier, Atilio Boron, John S. Fitch, Jean-Noel Grau, Lila Milutin, Elizabeth Jelin, Alfred Stepan, Marcelo Cavarozzi, Oscar Oszlak, and Philippe Schmitter. With Oszlak and Schmitter, I gave a seminar on "The State and Public Policy in Latin America," sponsored by the Centro de Investigaciones Administracion Publico, Instituto Di Tella, and the Social Science Research Council, at the Instituto de Desarrollo Economico y Social, Buenos Aires, from June to August 1974, which greatly contributed to this work. I wrote this essay in the very congenial environment provided by the Institute for Advanced Study at Princeton.

1. See Giovani Sartori, "Concept Misformation in Comparative Politics," *American Political Science Review*, 64, no. 4 (December 1970):1033−53.

2. This definition owes much to that proposed by Philippe Schmitter in "Still the Century of Corporatism?", *Review of Politics*, 36, no. 1 (January 1974):85−131. Also see James Malloy, "Authoritarianism, Corporatism, and Mobilization in Peru," *Review of Politics*, 36, no. 1 (January 1974):52−84. My

interpretations and conclusions are somewhat different from those of these two authors.

3. This definition is an "analytic minimum," just sufficient to distinguish the state from other phenomena. In more specific analyses, it will be necessary to add other, more variable characteristics.

4. The differences in the weight and role of the state in the historical formation of a territorially based political unit and in the implantation of a market which covers that territory are fundamental topics for a comparative theory of political economy. It is worth consulting the pioneer work of Joseph Nettl, "The State as a Conceptual Variable," World Politics, 20, no. 4 (July 1968):559–92. Investigations being carried out by Charles Tilly and his associates offer an important analysis of the formation of national states in Western Europe, which differ substantially from the strongly "destatized" and much more gradualist view of change presented in the greater part of the literature on "political development." See especially Charles Tilly, "Postscript: Western Statemaking and Theories of Political Transformation," in his Formation of National States in Western Europe (Princeton: Princeton University Press, 1975). Barrington Moore's Social Origins of Dictatorship and Democracy (Boston: Beacon Press, 1966) continues to be invaluable on this topic, as do the recent contributions of Immanuel Wallerstein, The Modern World System (New York: Academic Press, 1974), and Perry Anderson, Passages from Antiquity to Feudalism (London: NLB Editions, 1974).

5. See especially the work of Arthur F. Bentley and its influential reformulation by David Truman in The Governmental Process (New York: Alfred Knopf, 1961).

6. See Talcott Parsons, "The Political Aspects of Social Structure and Process," in Varieties of Political Theory, ed. David Easton (Englewood Cliffs, N.J.: Prentice-Hall, 1966), pp. 71–112.

7. See Karl Deutsch, The Nerves of Government (Glencoe, Ill.: Free Press, 1963).

8. The works that have best reflected this point of view are those of Seymour M. Lipset, including Political Man (New York: Doubleday, 1960).

9. See, for example, Nicos Poulantzas, Hegemonia y dominacion en el estado moderno, Pasado y Presente no. 48 (Cordoba, 1973), esp. pp. 11–105; and Oscar Oszlak, "Capitalismo del estado: alternativa o transicion?" Latin American Seminar on Public Enterprises and Their Relations with the Central Government (Caracas, November 1974), mimeograph.

10. I refer to Samuel Huntington, Political Order in Changing Societies (New Haven: Yale University Press, 1968), and Leonard Binder et al., Crisis and Sequences of Political Development (Princeton: Princeton University Press, 1971).

11. On this point, I rely on the excellent critique published by Mark Kesselman, "Order or Movement: The Literature of Political Development as Ideology," World Politics, 26, no. 1 (October 1973):139–54.

12. This is the case of certain simplistic versions of the problem of dependency, which postulate a mechanical and unilateral causation on the part of "external" dominating factors. This, of course, implies once again stifling the problem of the Latin American state, authoritarian or not, so that it appears as the agent or the immediate consolidation of domination exercised by "external" factors. This, I hasten to add, is not an objection that can be validly opposed to other works concerned with dependency, which were much richer and more subtle conceptualizations.

13. One of the better empirical investigations carried out recently is Susan Kaufman Purcell, "Decision-making in an Authoritarian Regime: Theoretical Impli-

cations from a Mexican Case Study," *World Politics*, 26, no. 4 (October 1973): 28–54. See also chapter 7 in this volume.

14. See John McKinney, *Constructive Typology and Social Theory* (New York: Appleton Century Crofts, 1966).

15. In this essay I can only refer in a very general way to the specifics of the cases included in the "type."

16. Alexander Gerschenkron, *Economic Backwardness in Historical Perspective* (Cambridge, Mass.: Harvard University Press, 1962); Moore, *Social Origins*; David Collier, "Timing of Economic Growth and Regime Characteristics," *Comparative Politics* (forthcoming), presents an interesting statistical treatment of these problems of timing in Latin America.

17. Albert Hirschman considers these as cases of "late-late" industrialization, in contrast with the "late" cases discussed by Gerschenkron in *Economic Backwardness*. See Hirschman, "The Political Economy of Import-Substituting Industrialization in Latin America," in his *Bias for Hope* (New Haven: Yale University Press, 1971), pp. 85–123.

18. The Latin American countries to which I am referring here, as well as most Eastern European countries, were originally incorporated into the world market as exporters of raw materials. This was not the case with the countries which followed the "fascist route." Although "late" in relation to England, the United States, and France, these soon joined the nucleus of industrial capitalism to which the Latin American and Eastern European countries remained linked as exporters of primary materials. From this spring the sequential (and dependent) characteristics of industrialization, as well as the historical roots of differences in the formation and articulation of classes, and in the role and type of authoritarianism in the countries which interest us here, in contrast to those following either the "democratic" or "fascist routes" in Europe. For more discussion of this topic see my "Reflexiones sobre las tendencias generales de cambio en el Estado burocratico-autoritario," presented at the Conferencia sobre Historia y Ciencias Sociales, University of Campinas, Brazil, June 1975.

19. In this section I update the analysis presented in *Modernization and Bureaucratic-Authoritarianism* (Berkeley: University of California, Institute of International Studies, 1973). See also Guillermo O'Donnell and Delfina Linck, *Dependencia y autonomia* (Buenos Aires: Amorrortu Editores, 1973), chap. 3. A good analysis of these themes, with special attention to changes in the kinds of authoritarianism and corporatism, can be found in chapter 1 of this volume. For the more specifically political aspects of "authoritarian regimes," see Juan Linz, "An Authoritarian Regime: Spain," in *Mass Politics*, ed. Erik Allardt and Stein Rokkan (New York: Free Press, 1970), pp. 251–83; and idem, "Totalitarian and Authoritarian Regimes," in Fred I. Greenstein and Nelson W. Polsby, eds., *Handbook of Political Science* (Reading, Mass.: Addison Wesley, 1975). See also Huntington, *Political Order*.

The concept of increasing randomization has been proposed by David Apter as characteristic of the uncertainty and fragmentation of social relations of situations of high modernization (*Choice and the Politics of Allocation* [New Haven: Yale University Press, 1971]).

20. O'Donnell, *Modernization*, esp. chaps. 2 and 3.

21. See Torcuato Di Tella, *Clases sociales y poder politico* (Buenos Aires: Editorial Paidos, 1974); and Charles Anderson, *Politics and Economic Change in Latin America* (New York: Van Nostrand, 1967).

22. Although insufficient, the available information on the period prior to the

emergence of the bureaucratic-authoritarian state points in this direction. See O'Donnell and Linck, *Dependencia*. For the Argentine case see also Pablo Gerchunoff and Juan Llach, "Capitalismo industrial, desarrollo asociado y distribucion del ingreso entre los dos gobiernos peronistas, 1950—1972," *Desarrollo Economico*, 15, no. 57 (April—June 1975):3—54.

23. Regarding the armed forces and their role in implanting the bureaucratic-authoritarian state, see Guillermo O'Donnell, "Modernizacion y golpes militares (teoria, comparacion y el caso argentino)," *Desarrollo Economico*, no. 47 (October—December 1972):519—66.

24. For a more detailed treatment, see O'Donnell, "Reflexiones."

25. We are dealing here not only with an objective need for those types of capitalism to be "deepened," but also with the subjective perception of that need on the part of the functionaries who carried out the economic policy in the initial period of the bureaucratic-authoritarian states.

26. Charles Moraze, *El Apogeo de la Burguesia* (Barcelona: Editorial Labor, 1965).

27. See O'Donnell, "Reflexiones," with regard to the bifurcations in the recent history of the bureaucratic-authoritarian state and changing relations with international capital and the national bourgeoisie.

28. This is one of the numerous aspects which urgently require research. For Brazil, see Celso Lafer, "El sistema político brasileño; algunas características y perspectivas," *Desarrollo Economico*, 14, no. 56 (January—March 1975):641—76.

29. A term utilized, although not identically, by Fernando H. Cardoso in Fernando H. Cardoso and Enzo Faletto, *Dependencia y desarrollo en America Latina* (Mexico: Siglo XXI, 1969); Nicos Poulantzas, *Poder politico y clases sociales* (Mexico: Siglo XXI, 1972); Charles Bettelheim, and Paul Sweezy in Oscar Oszlak, "Capitalismo de estado."

30. The blocking of direct access to certain activities does not stop international capital from playing an important role as a supplier of inputs, capital goods, and technology to the national (private and state) companies that carry out such activities.

31. The dominant coalition includes a fourth member: the national and international sector dedicated to export activities (mostly primary products). Although it has lost its former primacy, this sector controls a large portion of the export income, and in some cases it also controls food prices in the domestic market. The variations from one country to another in the composition of this sector are too great to be analyzed here. However, although its interests in general are contrary to those of the urban sector as a whole (and thus also to international capital operating in industry and services), it tends to agree with international capital in a more "privatist" or "anti-interventionist" point of view than that of existing economic policy. This is especially evident in the way in which a large portion of export incomes is appropriated to finance state expansion. An interesting study of the relative dynamism of the principal allies is Peter McDonough, "Political Consequences of Economic Concentration in Brazil" (Ann Arbor: University of Michigan, 1974), mimeograph. See also O'Donnell and Linck, *Dependencia*, chap. 3 and sources cited for the Argentine case.

32. This is a seldom explored topic. See Bolivar Lamounier, "Ideologias em regimes autoritarios," *Estudos CEBRAP*, 7 (1974):67—92; and Fernando H. Cardoso, *Autoritarismo e democratizacao* (Rio de Janeiro: Paz e Terra, 1975), pp. 187—222.

33. State and society are fused in this ideology because these chambers appear

to be a fundamental part of the state itself, while the legitimated social relations appear to be essentially "public." The full manifestation of this ideology is found in texts of Mussolini which contributed to the generation of theories on "totalitarianism." These theories are currently discredited because—like some culturalist interpretations of Latin American "corporatism" and "authoritarianism"—they are little concerned with confronting the architectural design of the ideology with its actual patterns of functioning and social impact.

34. A useful introduction to the pertinent bibliography on Italian fascism can be found in Renzo de Felice, *Le interpretazioni del fascismo* (Bari: Laterza, 1969).

35. Perhaps the most articulate recent expression of an approach centered upon the ideological and juristic-formal aspects of corporatism is to be found in Howard Wiarda, "Toward a Framework for the Study of Political Change in the Iberic-Latin Tradition: The Corporative Model," *World Politics*, 25, no. 1 (January 1973): 206–36; and "Corporatism and Development in the Iberic-Latin World: Persistent Strains and New Variations," *Review of Politics*, 36, no. 1 (January 1973):3–33. This viewpoint leads (in my view, inevitably) to already criticized conclusions.

36. The first stages of an interesting project of recompilation and evaluation of the legal and institutional characteristics of corporatism in Latin America are found in chapter 15 of this volume.

37. In spite of its brevity, an exemplary work is Richard Morse, "The Heritage of Latin America," *The Founding of New Societies*, ed. Louis Hartz (New York: Harcourt, Brace and World, 1964), pp. 123–77. See also chapters 2 and 5 in this volume. Also relevant are James Kurth, "Patrimonial Authority, Delayed Development and Mediterranean Politics," and William Glade, "The State in Mediterranean Politics," papers presented at the annual convention of the American Political Science Association, New Orleans, 1973.

38. By this term I understand, with admitted vagueness, the mode of relationship or linkage between state and dominant classes, on the one hand, and the popular sector (urban and rural) on the other, which embraces the greater part of social relations between one and the other.

39. This is not the occasion to discuss populism except in respects directly connected with the theme of this chapter. On populism, see especially Francisco Weffort, "Classes populares e desenvolvimiento social. Contribucao ao estudo do 'populismo,' " (Santiago de Chile: ILPES-CEPAL, 1968), mimeograph; Fernando H. Cardoso and Enzo Faletto, *Dependencia y desarrollo en America Latina* (Mexico: Siglo XXI, 1969); Torcuato di Tella, *Clases sociales*; Helio Jaguaribe, *Crisis y alternativas de America Latina: reforma o revolucion* (Buenos Aires: Editorial Paidos, 1973); O'Donnell, *Modernization*; and idem, "Populismo," *Diccionario de ciencias sociales* (Paris: UNESCO, forthcoming).

40. In an important forthcoming book, Alfred Stepan distinguishes between "including" and "excluding" corporatism. These correspond approximately to the populist and bureaucratic-authoritarian periods. I prefer to use "inclusion-exclusion" as characteristics of types of states which manifest themselves, inter alia, in the modalities of functioning and impacts of their corporatism.

41. This guarantee of the future predictability of the "order" attained through bureaucratic authoritarianism (and therefore of the domination it contributes to impose) is fundamental in attracting foreign capital. For an elaboration of this argument and an examination of the contrast between Brazil and Argentina, see O'Donnell, "Reflexiones."

42. An excellent study of the effectiveness of repressive and, above all, preventive control can be found in chapter 10 of this volume. See also Marcus Maria

Figuereido and Peter McDonough, "Repression and Institutionalization in Brazil" (Ann Arbor: University of Michigan, 1974), mimeograph; and Kenneth Erickson, "Labor in the Political Process in Brazil: Corporatism in a Modernizing Nation" (doctoral dissertation, Columbia University, 1970).

43. Philippe Schmitter has rightly insisted upon the fundamental preventive role of corporatism in "Corporatist Interest Representation and Public Policy-Making in Portugal" (1973), mimeograph. He points out that "the role and consequences of corporatism must be evaluated not so much in terms of what it openly and positively attains as in terms of what it negatively and surreptitiously prevents from occurring."

44. Although I have referred to the urban sector, it is worth noting that when the level of political activation in the agrarian popular sector is low, clientelism tends to prevail; but when it increases significantly, or seems imminent, it is replaced by corporative types of control. The present Peruvian case demonstrates this clearly, as does the study of Dominican rural communities by Kenneth Sharpe in chapter 11 of this volume.

45. The most important work which draws attention to the corporatization of entrepreneurial associations in Latin America is that of Philippe Schmitter, *Interest Conflict and Political Change in Brazil* (Stanford: Stanford University Press, 1971).

46. Albert Hirschman, in *Journeys Toward Progress* (New York: The Twentieth Century Fund, 1963), presented a convincing argument concerning the use of protest to call attention to certain problems and, eventually, to transmit the content of the preferred solution.

47. In contrast with the unions, the entrepreneurial associations that have been corporatized are those which attempt to represent highly aggregated interests, not those formed for the representation of local interests or by branches or subbranches of a certain activity. I am tempted to propose a "postulate of the maximum efficiency of the minimum possible aggregation of interests," according to which, in order to obtain decisions from the state, it is useful to formulate demands which are as specific as possible and are directed toward the lowest level of the state with decision-making capacity to resolve the demands. National entrepreneurial associations, or those which for some reason must articulate a wide variety of interests, tend to direct their demands to high-level persons (ministers or those just below) who cannot easily resolve them by themselves. Therefore, these associations tend to fulfill a ceremonial role or one of general comment on the outlines of existing social and economic policies. The periods of scarce activity, when these associations are little more than a ceremonial façade, may be indicative not of state domination of the bourgeoisie, but rather of a situation in which both the extensive access to the state that the bourgeoisie enjoys and its general agreement with existing policy render unnecessary any other role for these associations.

48. Cf. Schmitter, *Interest Conflict and Political Change.*

49. Schmitter, personal communication, July 1974, What has been indicated in other paragraphs, modified by the specifics of the PRI case, is also applicable to Mexico. See Ricardo Cinta, "Burguesia nacional y desarrollo," and Julio Labastida del Campo, "Los grupos dominantes frente a las alternativas de Cambio," both in *El perfil de Mexico en 1980* (Mexico: Siglo XXI, 1972), vol. 3, pp. 165–99 and 99–164.

50. See Fernando H. Cardoso, *Estado y sociedad en America Latina* (Buenos Aires: Ediciones Nueva Vision, 1973), about "bureaucratic rings" as a mode of linkage between segments of the state and dominant sectors of civil society. See also O'Donnell, *Modernization*, regarding informal coalitions between actors situated at the top of complex public and private organizations.

51. See Andrew Shonfield, *Modern Capitalism* (New York: Oxford University Press, 1965), and Nicos Poulantzas, *Poder Politico.*

52. Between 1966 and 1970, I conducted interviews with government personnel in Argentina. Among military officers it was frequently said that the corporatization of state institutions was a good way of "bringing to light" and exercising vigilance over the opportunities of access enjoyed by big capital. The latter was seen as an ally but also as excessively aggressive (and successful) in its attempts to co-opt public functionaries. I do not wish to allude solely to situations which would be considered as cases of "corruption," but to more subtle relationships surrounding future career prospects in "private activity," compensations of social status, contacts coming from the same social class, and similar situations.

53. The privatization of some state institutions tends to be accompanied by the creation of new decision-making centers—centralized, multifunctional and polysectoral—which attempt, with varying degrees of success, to compensate for the state fragmentation promoted, among other factors, by the privatizing aspect of corporatism. Celso Lafer, "Sistemo politico brasileño," is particularly illuminating on this point.

54. I must refer here to what might appear as an important omission—the contemporary Peruvian case. In previous works, I have argued that the Peruvian case was closer to the "populist" category, on the basis of its processes of antioligarchical conflict, its extension of industry, and its controlled politicization of the popular sector. This case, however, has differential characteristics from those of previous populist experiences which have generated an important literature focused on the main patterns of social impacts and the functioning of its state and its corporatism. See especially Julio Cotler, "Bases del corporativismo en el Peru," *Sociedad y Politica*, no. 2 (1972); and "Crisis politica y populismo militar en el Peru," *Estudios Internacionales*, 12 (January—March 1970); Anibal Quijano, *Nacionalismo, neoimperialismo y militarismo en el Peru* (Buenos Aires: Ediciones Periferia, 1971); James Malloy, "Authoritarianism"; Alfred Stepan in his forthcoming book; and Abraham Lowenthal, ed., *The Peruvian Experiment: Continuity and Change Under Military Rule* (Princeton: Princeton University Press, forthcoming).

SIMON SCHWARTZMAN

4

Back to Weber: Corporatism and Patrimonialism in the Seventies

A New Old Problem

New problems often bring old answers, and this is all the more true when the problems are not as new as they seemed at first glance. This is certainly the case for today's strong, centralized political regimes in Latin America and the rediscovery of corporatism and patrimonialism as conceptual keys to their understanding.

For about twenty years after the Second World War, representative democracy seemed to bloom in Latin America, in spite of a few stubborn spots. In the late fifties, Juscelino Kubitschek dreamed of a new Marshall Plan for Latin America and launched his Operacao Panamericana, followed later by John Kennedy's Alliance for Progress. The Latin American Free Trade Association seemed to be in the making; there was hope for democracy, development, and integration. This was a time of promise not only for Latin America, of course. The old European empires were disappearing and giving birth to dozens of young new nations in Africa and Asia. In academia, Rostowian theories of continuous development emerged at several levels; David Lerner, Karl Deutsch, Gino Germani, and Gabriel Almond all taught us how societies develop from tradition to modernity, from isolation to communication, from reduced to expanded political participation, from political underdevelopment to political maturity, from national isolationism to international integration.[1]

Now in the seventies it is as if all this has started to crumble: Democracies have given way to dictatorships, participation to repression, economic development to stagnation, integration to new forms of isolation. As democratic regimes fell one after another throughout Africa and Latin America, so did the theories of continuous progress

89

and well-being that were used to explain and predict the future of these countries. It is important to notice that these theories had certainly been challenged all along by countertheories which denied the idea of a continuous and well-integrated process of progress and change. But both evolutionary and revolutionary theorists shared optimisim, a belief in historical progress and the future well-being of mankind and every one of its nations. Revolutionary theorists, of course, would deny the notion of political development as a progressive increase in political institutionalization; instead, they would think in terms of increasing class awareness and class conflict. For a while, the failure of the democratic regimes in the new world seemed to give credibility to the theories of conflictive and revolutionary development. But slowly it became clear that the new authoritarian regimes were more stable than expected, and that the closing of the political arena usually meant, not a corresponding increase in political conflict and radicalization, but an overall reduction of political participation and political concern.

In short, the new problem faced by social and political theorists is the failure of the Latin American countries to comply with the evolutionary pattern of Western Europe,[2] either attaining their type of bargaining democracy or creating the socialist and revolutionary regimes that one would "naturally" have expected in Europe if the growing demands of the working class had not been met. This is, of course, an old question—How and in what sense is Latin America different from Europe and the United States?

Corporatism and patrimonialism, sometimes apart and sometimes together, seem to be good, old, solid answers to this old question. When properly used, these terms can help to free the political analyses of Latin America from the bias produced by the Western European and North American experience, and at the same time lead to the recovery of a well-established tradition of historical analysis overshadowed for some time by the liberal and revolutionary optimistic tradition. Improperly used, however, they can have precisely the opposite effect: to increase ethnocentrism and bias and bring us back to the same mistakes and misunderstandings which helped to put these concepts in the limbo of social thought for so long.

Essentially, the difference between the proper and the improper use of these concepts lies in whether they are applied to a structural feature of these societies and its process or, on the contrary, to a more or less fixed cultural or historical trait or character and its permanence. A common criticism of modernization theories is that they tended to imply a very simplified model of unidirectional change, from tradition to modernity, or a dichotomous view of societies, according to the classic distinction between "community" and "society." Valid as this criticism may be, one should notice that the use of concepts like "patrimonialism" or "corporatism" could mean the substitution of a continuum or a dichotomy, that is, a variable, for a single and static concept, that is, a constant.

Returning to a founding father of the social sciences such as Max Weber has great advantages and some pitfalls. The main advantages are probably that it helps us to recover a broad conceptual frame in which our discussion belongs, or should belong, and also that it links us with a solid and well-proved intellectual tradition. The main danger is that it can lead us very rapidly into an endless debate about the "proper" understanding and interpretation of the author's concepts and ideas, which may turn a concern with theoretical relevance into a task of literary exegesis. In this chapter, I will be presenting a very personal interpretation of Weber which is not necessarily the "correct" one, but which can nevertheless help to point the way through the present problems of political change in the nonwestern context.

Corporatism

In a recent paper, James M. Malloy gave a comprehensive description of what he calls "corporatist theory," or the corporatist's prescription for the organization of society (in this sense, I would rather call it "corporatist ideology").[3] The picture that emerges from his description is the ideal of a harmonious, well-regulated, nonconflictive society, based on moral principles and well-defined norms which are issued and maintained by the public authority, the state. According to this ideology, there should be some intragroup autonomy and self-regulation, but the very existence of groups and their relationships with each other are granted and regulated by the state. A corporatist state can be more or less authoritarian, in the sense that these grants of autonomy and the regulation of inter- and intragroup activities can be more or less strict; but it is the state that legitimates and enfranchises group and individual participation in public affairs. This is exactly the opposite of the ideology that stems from the Western European tradition, in which society and its groups legitimate the power of the state.

Thus, the difference between the Western and the corporatist tradition seems at first to belong to the cultural or ideological realm, as alternative sources of legitimation for the exercise of political power and political participation. Since Max Weber, at least, we have known that the source of legitimation of a power relationship is very important when one is interested in the motivations, values, ideologies, organizational projects, and everything else related to this basic normative component. However, it is reasonable to assume that a given type of legitimation does not happen by chance, but tends to emerge in relatively well-defined contexts and historical circumstances. Consideration of these structural contexts and historical circumstances allows us to move from the phenomenology of a political ideology to theories that try to establish causal relationships of some kind. There is thus an empirical proposition that gives the foundation and explains the different types of legitimation of political activities in the two contexts. Broadly, this proposition says that in corporatist regimes, the state is stronger than civil society; while in Western European, noncorporative regimes, civil society is stronger than the state.

To say that the state is "stronger than society" is to say that the group which controls the state apparatus is able to impose its will upon other, private sectors of society, thanks to its control of extractive resources, military manpower, or communication networks. This strength is bound to have consequences at several levels: first, in the allocation of scarce resources; second, in the decisions about who can and cannot participate in political decisions; and finally, in the very ideology which gives the central government the right to grant legitimacy to actors in the political arena.

The type of corporatism we have been discussing does not encompass all the possible connotations of the term, which often implies the notion of autonomous, self-contained, and strongly institutionalized professional groups, the "corporations." The relative autonomy of the corporations is certainly one of the central issues in understanding this kind of regime, but it will be left aside for the moment. However, it is important to remember that, as Malloy puts it,

> in the corporatist scheme the principle is that groups are to be relatively autonomous in intra-group decisions but the groups exist by virtue of recognition and to that extent are dependent on the state. If they have semi-sovereign qualities in their spheres, it is because the state confers them upon them and then assumes the role of regulating inter-group relations.[4]

When this relationship of superordination is established in principle, we are talking about an ideology, a "scheme" or a "theory" in the sense of an ideal type. What is more important, however, is to establish if and to what extent this is an empirical fact in a given context, and then try to see if it has the consequences that one would expect from the conceptual model.

If we assume that this is the case for a great number of Latin American countries, including Mexico, Peru, and Brazil, the next problem is to determine whether the distinction between "the state" and "civil society" really has any meaning, and to evaluate whether the state is really "stronger" than society. This is where the concept of patrimonialism enters the picture.

It is useful to summarize what we already know about corporatism before moving to the next concept.

First, "corporatism" refers to the way social groups are organized and relate to each other and to the state. The expression belongs to the same group of concepts as "interest-group politics," class-oriented politics, and so on. In other words, it refers to a mode of *political participation*. It should be distinguished from concepts like patrimonialism or bureaucratic centralism, which refer to the way power is distributed and used in society (concepts of the same level are, for instance, feudalism, polyarchy, plutocracy).

Second, there are four important components in the concept of corporatism: (1) the rights of association and public action performed by the corporations tend to be granted by the state; (2) corporations tend to enjoy a fairly high degree of autonomy in internal matters; (3) the boundaries between corporations tend to be sharply defined and difficult to cross; and (4) corporations tend to be defined in terms of functional (professional) status dimensions, rather than according to geographical or ethnic dimensions, as in the status or castelike systems.

Third, empirically, contemporary corporatist systems tend to emerge in contexts of strong, centralized, politically dominant state structures, of a bureaucratic-patrimonial kind. These structures are in themselves organized along corporatist lines, which use the state apparatus as their property, their patrimony.

I believe that this gives a fairly good picture of what corporatism is about, but a number of important questions are left open. These include the question of the emergence and permanence of corporatist-like systems of political participation and their relationship with the better-known classlike or interest-group systems. This is where consideration of the Weberian concept of patrimonialism and the discussion related to it becomes central.

Patrimonialism: Concepts

To Weber, patrimonialism was a type of traditional domination, and this often leads those who try to apply this concept to contemporary non-Western countries right back into the traditional-modern dichotomy. I would contend, however, that the "traditional" aspect is not what is more important in Weber's conceptualization. Let us see how Weber himself put it:

The roots of patriarchal domination grow out of the master's authority over his household. Such personal authority has in common with *impersonally* oriented bureaucratic domination stability and an "everyday character." Moreover, both ultimately find their inner support in the subjects' compliance with the norms. But under bureaucratic domination these norms are established rationally, appeal to the sense of abstract legality, and presuppose technical training; under patriarchal domination the norms derive from tradition; the belief in the inviolability of that which has existed from time out of mind.[5]

Later on, he talks about patrimonial political structures:

We shall speak of a *patrimonial state* when the prince organizes his political power over extrapatrimonial areas and political subjects—which is not discretionary and not enforced by physical coercion—just like the exercise of his patriarchal power. The majority of all great continental empires had a fairly strong patrimonial character until and even after the beginning of modern times.[6]

Finally, he distinguishes patrimonialism from the other type of traditional domination, feudalism:

The structure of feudal relationships can be contrasted with the wide realm of discretion and the related instability of power positions under pure patrimonialism. Occidental feudalism (*Lehensfeudalitat*) is a marginal case of patrimonialism that tends towards stereotyped and fixed relationships between lord and vassal. As the household with its patriarchal domestic communism evolves, in the age of the capitalist bourgeoisie, into the associated enterprise based on contract and specified individual rights, so the large patrimonial estate leads to the equally contractual allegiance of the feudatory relationship in the age of knightly militarism.[7]

Besides "discretion" and "instability," there is another important difference between the two forms of traditional domination, which is related to how power is exerted:

In the association of "estates," the lord rules with the aid of an autonomous "aristocracy" and hence shares its domination with it; the lord who personally administers is supported either by members of his household or by plebeians. These are propertyless strata having no social honor of their own; materially, they are completely chained to him and are not backed up by any competing power of their own. All forms of patriarchal and patrimonial domination, Sultanist despotism, and bureaucratic states belong to this latter type. The bureaucratic state order is especially important; in its most rational development, it is precisely characteristic of the modern state.[8]

There are a number of theoretical clues to be followed from these passages. Let us consider legitimation versus discretion, absolute power versus contract, traditional versus modern patterns of dominance, the problems of rationality, and the possible outgrowths of traditional patrimonialism. Several of these alternatives overlap, but discussing them will help us to approach some very essential questions of contemporary political theory.

Legitimation and Discretion

While in the second quotation Weber speaks of patrimonialism as a form of domination "which is not discretionary and not enforced by physical coercion," in the third he mentions the "realm of discretion and the related instability of power positions under pure patrimonialism." Are these contradictory?

By definition, patrimonial power includes an element of tradition (which makes it a type of traditional domination) and an element of discretion, which has at least two components. First, it may just be part of the tradition that the ruler can rule as he pleases. But, second, what differentiates the feudal from the patrimonial ruler is that the latter exerts unchecked leadership, while the first rules only within the limits defined by the independent powers of the estates, as suggested in the fourth quotation from Weber.

Discretion is thus a necessary component of patrimonialism, but its amount and what it means in terms of power instability and the need for physical coercion are empirical matters which depend on historical circumstances. It might be argued that the difference between the second and the third quotation has to do with the fact that in the second Weber is talking about the patrimonial *state*, while in the third he is talking about prepolitical forms of domination. In the *patrimonial state*, political power would be exerted upon *extrapatrimonial* areas, upon subjects who would retain relatively high levels of independence and autonomy. An element of contract would thus exist between the center of patrimonial power and its political subjects, in a way which is quite similar to the feudal type of political domination. It is difficult to understand how such a political arrangement could still be called "patrimonial," if it is essentially based on nonpatrimonial relationships. On the other hand, it is reasonably easy to conceive of the existence of large, territorially based political systems with very limited autonomy for political subjects—a truly patrimonial state with great leeway for discretion based on physical coercion or legitimacy. It is precisely the existence of these political systems which makes the rediscovery of patrimonialism so important.

We seem to be facing, if not a contradiction, at least a serious theoretical difficulty. As a matter of fact, if the third quotation stands for Weber's ideas, two possible developments may arise from primitive patrimonialism. It may evolve into "the associated enterprise based on contract and specified social rights," that is, capitalism and rational-legal political domination. Or it may evolve into traditional patrimonialism, which later breaks into a myriad of feudal relationships, which can in turn evolve into the modern, capitalist state. *There is no place, in this perspective, for understanding the origins and social basis of modern, bureaucratic domination.* As we shall see later, the Weberian concern with the increase and spread of bureaucratic power stemmed from an analysis of the degradation of the rational-legal, "bourgeois" political regimes. It thus becomes extremely difficult to understand, in this perspective, the modern, bureaucratized political regimes which did not pass through the phases of advanced capitalism and rational-legal political domination.

Pure Power Versus Contract

The line of continuity that Weber traces between patrimonial and bureaucratic domination (which leads him to speak, sometimes, of "bureaucratic patrimonialism") should be seen in contrast with the similarities between capitalism and feudalism. What the first two have in common is that they are both cases of unquestionable power, even if organized and maintained by entirely different systems of norms and values. The last two are similar at the opposite end of exactly the same dimension: They are both cases of contractual relationships of relatively autonomous units.

Are the latter more "political" than the former? Only if by "political" we understand necessarily the presence of independent actors in interplay. In this sense a completely totalitarian and absolutist regime would be "apolitical," since it would not have room for a process of political bargaining and conflict. This definition of politics might be useful in some contexts, but it should not be confused with an empirical theory of state formation which relates the creation of large, territorially based states with the emergence of contractual or bargaining politics of some kind. This is sometimes the case, but very often it is not.

Traditional and Modern Patterns

What joins patrimonialism and feudalism at one end, and capitalism and bureaucratic domination at the other, is the dimension of tradition versus modernity. The Weberian notion of tradition can here be kept to a minimum: "the belief in the everyday routine as an inviolable norm of conduct."[9] At the other extreme, modernity is related with norms based on "the belief in the validity of legal statute and functional 'competence' based on the rationally created *rules.*"[10] Weber is obviously working with two dimensions, and we may as well place them in a canonic fourfold diagram (figure 1).

Power Relationship

		Absolute	Contractual
	Traditional	Patrimonialism	Feudalism
Normative System			
	Modern	Bureaucratic Domination	Legal-Rational Domination

FIGURE 1. Weber's Typology of Political Domination

Modernity and Contract

The Weberian characterization of rational-legal political domination is too well known to be repeated here. What is important in this context is less its definition than the explanation of its origin. A couple of quotations taken more or less at random from Weber make his perspective clear:

> Bureaucratic organization has usually come into power on the basis of a leveling of economic and social differences. . . . Bureaucracy inevitably accompanies modern *mass democracy*, in contrast to the self-government of small homogeneous units. This results from its characteristic principle: the abstract regularity of the exercise of authority, which is a result of the demand for "equality before the law" in the personal and functional sense—hence, of the horror of "privilege," and the principled rejection of doing business "from case to case."[11]

> Just as the Italians and after them the English masterly developed the modern capitalist forms of economic organization, so the Byzantines, later the Italians, then the territorial states of the absolute age, the French revolutionary centralization and finally, surpassing all of them, the Germans perfected the rational, functional and specialized bureaucratic organization of all forms of domination from factory to army and public administration. For the time being the Germans have been outdone only in the techniques of party organization, specially by the Americans.[12]

The basic problem seems to be the following: How essential to the Weberian notion of a modern (that is, a "rational, functional and specialized") bureaucratic organization is the presence of an underlying social contract?

One could continue for a long while tracking Weber's ideas on this.

Basically, it seems that modern bureaucratic domination emerges as an outcome of two conflicting forces: increasing centralization of power and increasing mass participation in politics. In his analysis of Weber's theories on the emergence of legal rationality, Reinhard Bendix shows that "in Western Europe patrimonial power eventually promoted the formal rationality of law and administration, and this conflicts with the tendency of patrimonial rulers to promote substantive justice and personal favoritism."[13]

This is explained as, among other things, a consequence of the central government's need to restrain the power pretensions of vassals and officeholders. This was done by establishing a "centrally-controlled officialdom," and "in the struggle against the entrenched position of the state, patrimonial rulers were frequently supported by the rising bourgeoisie."[14]

Modern rational-legal political domination is thus a child of Western European patrimonialism and an emergent bourgeoisie; it is mostly contractual, it is very efficient, and most suited to modern capitalism.

What about modern, rational domination, without the contractual component? We should refer here to the Weberian distinction between formal and substantive rationality. Formal rationality is tantamount to legal rationality, in the sense that a set of rules, or "laws," defines what should and should not be done by a bureaucrat in a given circumstance. In a broader sense, these rules are a way of implementing the social contract that limits the arbitrary power of the officeholders: " 'Equality before the law' and the demand for legal guarantees against arbitrariness demand a formal and rational 'objectivity' of administration, as opposed to the personally free discretion flowing from the 'grace' of the old patrimonial domination."[15]

So, one opposite of formal rationality is "free discretion," which is the old-style patrimonialism; but it has another opposite, which is substantive rationality, a kind of rationality which is concerned with maximizing a given set of goals without any regard for formal rules and regulations. Weber relates the development of this demand for substantive justice to the emergence of public opinion and its instruments, the plebiscitarian democracy so feared by Alexis de Tocqueville. Indeed, the emergence of the "propertyless masses" in public life can endanger a well-functioning political system based on agreed-upon and strictly defined norms of behavior for the civil servants. There is, however, another determinant of substantive rationality which is also indicated by Weber: "raison d'état" as defined by the holders of political power. The combination of a central government only ruled by its "raison d'état" and a passive and instrumental "propertyless" mass is the definition of a modern, patrimonial-bureaucratic regime. The combination of the same normless political power with an active and mobilized "propertyless" periphery is what later became known as fascism.

Bendix in effect stresses that Weber was as concerned as de Tocqueville about the totalitarian possibilities of mass democracy and universal bureaucratization, and he could conceive of a future society in which the social contract, as defined by the "right-granting laws," would cease to exist. As Bendix writes, "In such a situation, the entire body of norms consists exclusively of 'regulations.' . . . All private interests enjoy protection . . . only as the obverse aspect of the effectiveness of these regulations. . . . All forms of law become absorbed within 'administration' and become part and parcel of 'government.' "[16]

As rational-legal domination can degenerate into bureaucratic totalitarianism, so is it possible for this type of bureaucracy to subsist with its "rational," but not necessarily its "legal," component. This is, in a word, the theoretical link that is missing, the basis for rationality in the absence of contractualism. Bendix, for instance, does not think that it is possible:

> An ideally functioning bureaucracy in [Weber's] sense is the most efficient method of solving large-scale organizational tasks. But this is true only *if* these tasks involve more or less stable norms and hence the effort to maintain the rule of law and achieve an equitable administration of affairs. These conditions are absent where the tasks are assigned by an omnipotent and revolutionary authority.[17]

In other words, the predominance of substantive over formal rationality would tend to lead from rational-legal to charismatic domination, which is inherently changing and unstable.

We shall see that one could argue with Bendix about the necessity of this reversal to charismatic leadership, as well as the limits of rationality and governmental efficiency and stability in a context of absolute authority. What is certain, however, is that we are not facing a return to traditional power relationships. In this sense, the use of the term "patrimonialism" as applied to modern societies can be very misleading. Indeed, bureaucratic domination seems to be the modern version of traditional, large-scale patrimonialism—and this is where the political problems of contemporary developed and underdeveloped countries meet.

Patrimonialism: Processes

We already have an important theoretical point, namely, that the problems and issues of a modern, underdeveloped, "patrimonialistic" regime should be considered in terms of its system of bureaucratic domination, rather than in terms of some eventually surviving traditional patterns of behavior and values. It is still more important to consider that thinking in terms of patrimonialism and bureaucratic domination does not simply lead to identifying a given structure and its set of problems and alternatives; it should also lead to the explanation of historical processes, an explanation that should be better than those provided by the "modern-traditional" continuum, if it is to stand.

The basic issue in the analyses of the historical formation and development of patrimonial states is the relationships between central power and the centrifugal tendency of officeholders and private entrepreneurs. Richard M. Morse, who in 1961 was already using the concept of patrimonialism to understand Latin American politics, gives a good summary of the problems a ruler has to cope with in this type of regime:

> The patrimonial ruler is ever alert to forestall the growth of an independent landed aristocracy enjoying inherited privileges. He awards benefices, or prebends, as a remuneration for services; income accruing from benefices is an attribute of the office, not of the incumbent as a person. Characteristic ways for maintaining the ruler's authority intact are: limiting the tenure of royal officials, forbidding officials to acquire family and economic ties in their jurisdictions, using inspectors and spies.[18]

This general problem of patrimonial power acquires very precise contours as we look into a specific context. For instance, I have tried to show elsewhere that, in the case of Brazil, it is possible to think of the relationships between the central, patrimonial-bureaucratic regime and the other areas of the country exactly in those terms.[19] What comes out of this analysis is not the simple description of a patrimonial power, but propositions about the relationships between the political center, Rio, and the economic and military "peripheries" (São Paulo and Rio Grande do Sul), and a line of analysis that is proving much more fruitful for the understanding of Brazilian political history than the usual modernization framework could. Some of these propositions deal exactly with the way in which the system of political participation is organized and behaves. We can deal with this question more specifically as we reintroduce the concept of "corporatism."

Patrimonialism and Political Participation

Here again it is important to look back to Weber and his distinction between class and status groups. "Class" is used to refer to people who share the same "typical chance for a supply of goods, external living conditions, and personal life experiences," in terms of their economic power. " 'Class situation' is, in this sense, ultimately 'market situation.' " And, later on: "In contrast to the purely economically deterined 'class situation' we wish to designate as 'status situation' every typical component of the life fate of men that is determined by a specific, positive or negative, social estimation of *honor*. . . . Stratification by status goes hand in hand with a monopolization of ideal and material goods or opportunities."[20]

Both class and status situations often lead to political participation, which tends to be organized as political parties. Parties are based on class or status situations, or both. One central issue of contemporary political analysis is the determination of how much of the political action of individuals and parties is determined by status and class situations, and still more important, how much they are aimed at consolidating or destroying the forced inequalities of the market or the privileges of status. The bourgeois political revolution is a movement that breaks the monopolies of goods and opportunities based on ascribed status and puts into its place a stratification system which refers directly to the market. The system of political participation is characterized by the unabashed use of power to acquire better market positions and to consolidate them into political "rights" (that is, rights that are enjoyed independently from the market).

In general, there is a sociological axiom that says that positions of privilege, once acquired, tend to be subtracted from the market and transformed into ascribed, status-based monopolies; while there is always a tendency to take underprivileged positions out of the status system and put them into the market. A version of this axiom, which is at first glance unrelated to Weber, is E. E. Schattschneider's proposition that "the most important strategy of politics is concerned with the scope of conflict."[21] The tendency of the underdog is to widen the scope of political conflict, bring more actors into the arena, and thus change the power relationships. The top dog, on the contrary, tends to monopolize the arena for those already enfranchised to participate in the conflict. The struggle of monopoly versus open market has to do with both the functional quality of the participants and their sheer number. In the extreme market situation, issues are never kept within functional or professional boundaries, and there is universal enfranchisement. Politics is territorially based; specific issues are translated into broad political questions; and each gets his share according to his economic power and capacity for political maneuvering. At the other extreme, monopoly prevails; power positions are so established that there is little room for conflict; and when conflict occurs, it tends to be circumscribed and privatized by functional groups. This is the typical corporative mode of political organization and participation.

There are thus two ways by which a monopolistic, status-based corporatist system can be established. One is through the development of self-sufficient, strongly organized professional groups that are able to impose themselves and their own rules of trade and privilege upon the rest of society. This is the type of corporation one thinks of when one considers the medieval guilds or, today, some particularly strong professional groups. The other way is through grants of social and economic rights and monopolies by the state. Both systems can have the same ideological frame of reference, in terms of an organic integration of functional groups; but it makes a big difference whether this integration results from several entrenched status positions or from a powerful and (sometimes) benevolent central state.

Contemporary corporatism tends to be of the second type, and this has had a series of important consequences. First, no contemporary state was really able to develop a full-fledged corporatist system that could take the place of traditional class or interest-group politics in the Western-liberal regimes. I have suggested in another place the term "political co-optation" to describe the dominant side of the system of political participation created in Brazil since the Second World War.[22] One type of political co-optation in Brazil was represented by the Labor party and the bureaucratic structures of the Ministry of Labor and Social Welfare. One could consider this a type of corporatism, since it linked a whole section of society to the state and granted special social and economic rights to the workers, outside the market. But this system was controlled from above and had little participation from below. Co-optation systems lie midway between corporatism and open, interest-group politics. When they are effective, they tend to reduce political conflict to undisputed monopolies of privilege. By the same token, this type of political structure lacks internal consistency and strength.

Second, and related to the above, is the fact that political life tends to be very dependent upon the state and its central figure. Morse stated this idea very well in two of his five propositions about Latin American political life: "The Latin American peoples still appear willing to alienate, rather than delegate, power to their chosen or accepted leaders. . . . Society is perceived in Latin America as composed of parts which relate through a patrimonial and symbolic center rather than directly to one another."[23]

Lest one think that these are traits of the Latin American political culture (and as such forever established and impossible to change), one should recall that Bendix had made exactly the same point about czarist Russia and communist Germany several years before.[24] "State-less" England and the United States[25] allowed for open, competitive, and self-regulating class conflict and politics. In contrast, countries with a strong, centralized, patrimonially based structure tend to inhibit the emergence of autonomous political groups, not to allow for established patterns of political conflict through direct bargaining, but, on the contrary, to stimulate bilateral relationships between the central state and social groups of dependency, subordination, and the search for grants of privilege.

Third, corporatism does emerge in contemporary centralized states, *but not quite where one would expect it.* The absence of an arena of political participation, that is, of an open political "market," leads to a widespread search for status privileges throughout society. Corporations are not to be found among privileged economic groups or organized as ostensive political institutions. Rather, corporatist tendencies are to be looked for in the educational system, the multiplication of formally defined professional privileges and prerogatives, and self-serving sections of the civilian and military public bureaucracy. One should again quote Weber:

> The development of the diploma from universities, and business and engi-neering colleges, and the universal clamor for the creation of educational certificates in all fields make for the formation of a privileged stratum in bureaus and in offices. Such certificates support their holder's claims for . . . a "respectable" remuneration rather than remuneration for work done, claims for assured advancement and old-age insurance, and, above all, claims to monopolize socially and economically advantageous positions.[26]

Democracy, Rationality, and Bureaucratic Patrimonialism

We can conclude with the scenario of the supposedly emerging bureaucratic, patrimonialistic, and corporatist society. Society is sharply divided into well-defined status groups based on functional differentiations, educational credentials, or monopolistic control of property. These status groups tend to be strongly organized along corporatist lines that define their own internal rules of behavior and access, and are structured according to the legal-bureaucratic model. Government belongs to one or two corporations of this kind, the military and the "technocrats." Political activities outside the well-defined rules of intercorporation behavior are minimal or nonexistent.

Is this scenario likely to occur? One can only say that it is well within the range of possibility. Weber himself was very concerned with this problem. As Bendix says, "Universal bureaucratization was for

Weber the symbol of a cultural transformation that would affect all phases of modern society. If this development ran its full course it would result in a new despotism more rigid even than the ancient Egyptian dynasties because it would have a technically efficient administration at its disposal."[27] This scenario of a bureaucratic and corporatist nightmare haunts contemporary political science, and it is almost certain that any ingenious suggestion to avoid it would be fallacious. We can finish this discussion, however, with a few perspectives on the relationship between this scenario and the ideals of freedom, democracy, and rationality.

One of the most important conceptual clues to this question is provided by Albert O. Hirschman's *Exit, Voice and Loyalty*.[28] He establishes a link between the freedom of members to influence the behavior of an organization and the level of efficiency on which it operates. There are two ways of acquiring influence: exit, the typical market mechanism by which a customer (or employee, or supporter of a political party) changes allegiance; and voice, the political mechanism of influence and protest. The relationships between voice and exit are complex and are elegantly spelled out by Hirschman. What is important here is that voice is more likely to be used and is more effective when there is no possibility of exit; that is, in situations of economic or organizational monopoly. Without exit or voice—that is, without freedom—centralized bureaucracy cannot work efficiently in the long run and must resort to systems of double government (the administration and the party, or the administration and the security apparatus) or to the expediency of recurring cultural revolutions and declarations of national emergency in order to recover from systematic stagnation and routine.[29]

The alternative to these systems of double government and constant mobilization is the establishment of new forms of self-government and internal democracy in corporations and within the new patrimonial-bureaucratic state. It may just be that, in the long run, Weber was right, in that a system of large-scale political domination is inherently unstable if it does not have an underlying contract, right-granting laws, and, accordingly, freedom to participate and to influence—and the feelings of dignity and self-respect that accompany the effective exercise of opinion, the right of association, and the achievement of the intended goals.

Thus, the theoretical challenge is to give up the traditional modes of political organization which are apparently limited to an already old-fashioned Western European tradition, without giving up the ideals of freedom and individual rights, and in doing so, to combine political concern with theoretical relevance; to help draw a new social contract based on a proper consideration of the political reality of our times, and not on its rejection. As this concern spreads in academia, it may be that corporatism and patrimonialism in their new robes will cease to be simply bad terms to designate an unpleasant situation and become conceptual tools to start dealing with the new monster—before it devours us.

NOTES

This is a revised version of a paper presented to the Conference on Authoritarianism and Corporatism held at the University of Pittsburgh in April 1974, which I attended with support from the Ford Foundation. I am grateful for the comments and profound criticisms of Peter McDonough, Helen E. Douglass, and Fernando Uricochea. They bear no responsibility for this text, however, since I could not incorporate their comments as fully as they deserved.

1. See Dean C. Tipps, "Modernization Theory and the Study of National Societies: A Critical Perspective," *Comparative Studies in Society and History*, 15, no. 2 (March 1973):199—226, for a comprehensive ideological and conceptual criticism of the modernization theories. An earlier important reference is Reinhard Bendix, "Tradition and Modernity Reconsidered," *Comparative Studies in Society and History*, 9, no. 3:292—346.

2. It would be difficult to pinpoint what is meant here by "Western Europe"; it would exclude, for instance, the Iberian countries and Greece, as well as Italy; it would certainly include England.

3. James M. Malloy, "Authoritarianism, Corporatism and Mobilization in Peru," in *The New Corporatism: Social-Political Structures in the Iberian World*, ed. Frederick B. Pike and Thomas Stritch (Notre Dame: University of Notre Dame Press, 1974), pp. 52—84. See also, in this same volume, the important article by Philippe C. Schmitter, "Still the Century of Corporatism?", pp. 85—131, which only came to my attention after the completion of this text.

4. Malloy, "Authoritarianism, Corporatism, and Mobilization," p. 58.

5. Max Weber, *Economy and Society* (New York: Bedminster Press, 1968), p. 1007.

6. Ibid., p. 1013.

7. Ibid., p. 1070.

8. Max Weber, "Politics as a Vocation," in *From Max Weber: Essays in Sociology*, ed. H. H. Gerth and C. W. Mills (New York: Oxford University Press, 1958), p. 82.

9. Weber, "The Social Psychology of the World Religions," in *Essays*, p. 296.

10. Weber, "Politics as a Vocation," in *Essays*, p. 79.

11. Weber, *Economy and Society*, p. 983.

12. Ibid., p. 1400.

13. Reinhard Bendix, *Max Weber—An Intellectual Portrait* (New York: Doubleday, 1962), p. 405. This is a kind of historical analysis that some will find surprising in the supposedly "ahistorical" Weber. I am intentionally leaving aside the usual discussions of Weber's methodology, which often are an obstacle to seeing his substantive contributions to the understanding of society. Those interested in the issues of the relationships between ideal types, historical causation, models of

developmental sequence, and the like, I refer to the discussion presented by Bendix in "Tradition and Modernity Reconsidered," pp. 314 ff.

14. Bendix, *Max Weber*, p. 406.

15. Weber, "Bureaucracy," in *Essays*, p. 220.

16. Bendix, *Max Weber*, p. 463.

17. Ibid., p. 467.

18. Richard M. Morse, "The Heritage of Latin America," in *The Founding of New Societies*, ed. Louis Hartz (New York: Harcourt, Brace & World, Inc., 1964), p. 157.

19. Simon Schwartzman, "Regional Contrasts Within a Continental Scale Nation: Brazil," in *Building States and Nations*, ed. S. Rokkan and S. M. Eisenstadt, vol. 2 (Los Angeles: Sage Publications, 1973); see also Simon Schwartzman, *São Paulo e o estado nacional* (São Paulo: Difusão Européia do Livro, 1975).

20. Weber, "Politics as a Vocation," in *Essays*, pp. 180–95. See also Bendix, *Max Weber*, pp. 85–87.

21. E. E. Schattschneider, *The Semi-Sovereign People* (New York: Holt, Rinehart and Winston, 1960), p. 3.

22. S. Schwartzman, "Representacão e cooptacão politica no Brasil," *Dados*, 7 (1970):9–41.

23. Morse, "Heritage of Latin America," pp. 173, 176.

24. R. Bendix, *Work and Authority in Industry: Ideologies of Management in the Course of Industrialization* (New York: Wiley & Sons, 1956).

25. For the notion of "stateless" societies, see J. P. Nettl, "The State as a Conceptual Variable," *World Politics*, 20, no. 4 (1968):559–92.

26. Weber, "Bureaucracy," in *Essays*, p. 241.

27. R. Bendix, *Max Weber*, p. 459.

28. Albert O. Hirschman, *Exit, Voice and Loyalty* (Cambridge: Harvard University Press, 1970).

29. See especially the sections on "the structures of controls over economic enterprises," "the manipulation of controls over economic enterprises," and "the 'contact with the masses'" of chapter 6 in Bendix's *Work and Authority in Industry* for an analysis of these mechanisms at work in East Germany at a particularly troubled time.

Comparative and Case Studies

ROBERT R. KAUFMAN

5

Corporatism, Clientelism, and Partisan Conflict: A Study of Seven Latin American Countries

In the sixteen years since a noted Latin Americanist commended the subject to a "new generation of graduate students," the study of Latin American political parties has never really gotten off the ground.[1] With a few exceptions,[2] work on the topic has been confined to voting behavior studies, to some monographic descriptions of individual parties or party systems, and to a handful of articles which lament the fact that so little has been done in the way of systematic comparative research. With the passage of time, moreover, interest in the topic itself has come to be regarded as a bit old-fashioned, the product of somewhat strained attempts to apply general development theory—with its strong emphasis on the importance of parties—to the Latin American context.

One reason for this trend (or rather, for the lack of one) is the enormous difficulty of coming to grips analytically with such a complex, multidimensional phenomenon. Certainly the confusing and rapidly changing array of Latin American parties and party systems does not readily yield to comparative definition or typology. Yet without at least some relatively abstract conceptual categories, the few configurative descriptions of parties that one does find in assorted books and journals tend to overwhelm us in an avalanche of detail, often inhibiting rather than facilitating the simplification necessary for comparative analysis. This study is designed in part to provide a small step out of this vicious circle by elaborating a framework that can be used for comparative research into the party systems of at least seven Latin American countries: Argentina, Brazil, Chile, Colombia, Mexico, Uruguay, and Venezuela.

A second purpose of this chapter is to confront the larger issue of whether it is worthwhile to devote much attention to Latin American political parties. Douglas A. Chalmers raises this question directly in one of the few outstanding contributions to the "party" literature, and his answer articulates a position shared explicitly or implicitly by many other students of the area. He argues that the persistence of hierarchical, elitist, bureaucratic patterns of political control in Latin America, coupled with the corresponding absence of sustained class conflict and revolutionary change, limits the role that Latin American parties are likely to play in validating governmental authority, organizing political participation, and aggregating and articulating interests. Individual parties, so the argument seems to run, are likely to be relatively superficial aspects of the political process; and variations in party systems from one country to another are likely to count considerably less than economic dependency and the weight of the Iberian heritage in shaping political change.[3] Compared to the "class-based" parties of Western Europe, Chalmers suggests, Latin American parties of all sorts have little direct contact with the masses, play a limited role in representing interests, and have a highly restricted part in the decision-making process.[4]

Other writers, such as Philippe C. Schmitter, Guillermo O'Donnell, and Howard J. Wiarda have elaborated further on such themes.[5] Despite different emphases and explanations, all imply that the conventional political-science focus on parties and mass electoral behavior is misdirected and misleading in the Latin American context. The "stuff" of Latin American politics, they suggest, is found elsewhere—in government agencies and private corporations, in the interactions of bureaucratic officials and economic elites, and in the patterns of domination which persistently and successfully impeded more pluralistic forms of political activity.

In this chapter, I do not wish to challenge these comparative propositions about the relative importance of parties in Latin America and Europe, even though for the most part they have never been explored empirically.[6] And more important, I shall not dissent from what seems to be an emerging consensus about the hierarchical character of Latin American political development, a conception which underlies much of the theoretical downgrading of party activity in that area. On the contrary, the starting point of my analysis—a "given" which I will not seek to demonstrate extensively—is that two types of hierarchical principles, corporatism and clientelism, describe a considerable portion of the political structures and processes of the seven countries I have chosen to study. I will also suggest, however, that differences in national party systems can help to account for some important intra-regional variation in the workings of individual Latin American countries. The lines of national partisan conflict superimpose themselves in significantly different ways upon other social and political hierarchies so common in the area; and far from simply reflecting these structures, they interact with them in ways that may reinforce, alter, or even transform clientelist or corporatist patterns.

Corporatism and Clientelism

Let me be more explicit about spelling out the developmental "givens" that are to inform this analysis. Stated negatively, the assumption is that in Latin America the growth of national market economies, the expansion of communications, and relatively extensive industrialization have not produced strong tendencies toward the emergence of autonomous interest groups and class associations or toward dramatic increases in the scope of political participation. For good or ill, such societies have managed to avoid the great historical discontinuities and profound social cleavages associated with the modernization processes in Europe, the United States, and parts of Asia and Africa. In more positive analytical terms, I accept the increasingly widespread view that much of the Latin American political process—particularly that part having to do with the organization, representation, and control of political demands—can be characterized by two deeply entrenched operating principles which, for want of better terms, can be labeled corporatism and clientelism.[7]

The corporatist concept is best understood in contrast to the pattern of competition between spontaneously formed, fully autonomous voluntary associations that allegedly characterizes "liberal-pluralist" societies. The corporatist alternative envisions the monopolization of interest representation by noncompeting, officially sanctioned functional organizations, which are supervised by agents of the state bureaucracy. In ideal typical terms, corporatist systems are vertically segmented societies, encapsulating individuals within a network of legally defined guilds and corporations which derive their legitimacy from and are integrated by a single bureaucratic center.[8]

Although no concrete society can be fully described in these terms, the hierarchical legal matrix of colonial rule corresponded closely to the corporatist ideal. More important, corporatist assumptions continued, by most accounts, to govern the manner in which Latin American elites responded to the major challenges of the nineteenth and twentieth centuries; that is, to the diffusion of liberal aspirations for constitutional government and to the assorted "middle-sector" and working-class protests against established authority. On the whole, these challenges can be viewed as important, but still muted, counterthemes in the unfolding Latin American developmental process, a process characterized predominantly by attempts to expand the framework of corporate privilege in ways that would co-opt new social forces and defuse their revolutionary potential.[9]

By the mid-twentieth century, the structural expression of these corporate principles could be observed in a number of otherwise different national political settings. First, there were a few more or less full-blown corporatist systems, best exemplified by Mexico, in which entrenched elites explicitly justified their authority and purposively organized interests along the lines described above. At least since the time of Lázaro Cárdenas, organized labor and peasant groups have become institutionalized pillars of the Partido Revolucionario Institucional (PRI), while commercial and industrial interests have been grouped into compulsory "chambers" linked directly to the bureaucracy. Such groups, as Susan K. Purcell notes, "are best understood as adjuncts of the central authorities, more often the implementors of decisions of the latter then representatives and defenders of the interests of rank-and-file members."[10] Schmitter's detailed study of Brazilian groups amply documents the proposition that these patterns can also exist in countries that lack institutionalized formulas for selecting top governmental leaders. In spite of the uncertain tenure of Brazilian presidents between 1945 and 1964, the corporatist legislation and policies of the Estado Nôvo remained in force; and official employers' and workers' syndicates continued to occupy "political space," permitting bureaucratic officials to dominate associational activity.[11] These arrangements have aptly been termed corporatism without an apex.[12] Finally, there are a few Latin American systems in which corporatist principles predominate in linking organized groups to the policy process, even though presidents are regularly selected through more or less competitive elections. For example, this was probably the case in Chile, at least until recently. Organizations like the National Society for Agriculture, the Society for Industrial Development, and the Chilean Chamber of Commerce were tied directly into the decision-making process through formal representation on assorted governmental boards and agencies.[13] At the same time, successive Chilean governments attempted to use welfare measures and union codes to co-opt and control white- and blue-collar unions and, more recently, to organize and regulate peasant activity.[14] As an aspiration and assumption about the way group life should be organized, therefore, the corporatist notion seems to be alive and well throughout the continent.

Clientelism is the second major theme that seems to run through most current discussions of Latin American history and politics. The patron-client dyad, narrowly defined, is an informal, particularistic, exchange relationship between actors of unequal power and status.[15] As a somewhat broader operating principle, clientelism reflects an extensive distrust of impersonal authority; a tendency to rely on the activation of diffuse primary relationships in order to accomplish assorted social, economic, and political goals; and, most important, a posture of personal dependency on superiors within the status hierarchy.

Like corporatism, clientelism emphasizes relationships of domination and subordination. To some extent, however, the fluidity and personalism of clientelistic orientations contradict the legalistic, bureaucratic implications of corporatism, and a considerable proportion of Latin American history can be understood in terms of shifts in the balance between the two. The full flowering of Latin American clientelism—expressed concretely in landlord-peasant relationships, local elite autonomy, and caudillo movements—became possible only after the collapse of imperial bureaucratic authority in the nineteenth century. And clientelistic patterns seem at times to retard or subvert the trend toward formal centralism taking place in the twentieth century. Almost everywhere in Latin America, cliques and followings, *cabides*, *panelinhas*, and *camarillas* form major action units in the political process, cutting through the façade of centralized legal power. Public office is utilized as a resource for building personal machines; formal authority relationships are undercut; and the bureaucracy itself becomes a sprawling, decentralized, faction-ridden arena, impossible to control from a single point.

From another perspective, however, the relationship between corporatism and clientelism can be seen as highly functional. On the one hand, corporatist arrangements discourage autonomous group competition and perpetuate more particularistic forms of individual problem-solving activity. Clientelistic forms of problem-solving behavior, in turn, vastly increase the flexibility of what would otherwise be quite rigid corporatist legal structures. The symbiotic aspects of the relationship between the two principles is well illustrated by Eric Wolf's discussion of the colonial mestizos who—although excluded for the most part from the formal imperial network of power—acted as the smugglers, go-betweens, and influence peddlers who made this elaborate system work:

> As society abdicated to them its informal and unacknowledged business, they became the brokers and carriers of the multiple transactions that caused the blood to flow through the veins of the social organism. Beneath the formal veneer of Spanish colonial government and economic organization, their fingers wove the network of social relations and communications through which alone men could bridge the gaps between formal institutions.[16]

It can be argued that many of the clientelist interchanges which honeycomb modern Latin American societies perform similar functions. First, the informal bonds that connect the members of ostensibly separate corporate orders reduce the heavy integrative burden that is so often vested formally in the office and person of the chief executive. Second, in a context where corporate arrangements discourage autonomous associational "inputs" into the political process, clientelistic ties constitute mechanisms whereby a relatively large number of individuals can make demands upon the state, manipulate the political game, and acquire some degree of resources and security. Finally, through personal attachments to higher-status patrons and brokers, many unincorporated and otherwise atomized peasants and "urban marginals" are linked into the larger sociopolitical order in ways that preserve the essentially elitist character of that order. It would thus seem that in a great many countries, corporatism and clientelism form parts of a single developmental dimension. The symbiotic interconnection between the two, suggests Schmitter, "have endowed Latin American societies with a formidable capacity for co-opting potential opponents and absorbing dissident interests without destroying the basic structure of social and political domination."[17]

This brief synthesis of Latin American developmental patterns should make my earlier remarks about the theoretical "downgrading" of Latin American parties somewhat more comprehensible. The primary importance attached to parties by general development theorists rests essentially on the assumption that the process of "modernization" mobilizes and divides the mass of the population—that it creates a crisis of participation which makes the emergence of "strong" political parties essential to the organization of stable and effective political rule. There may be debate over whether parties will emerge in all cases, or over the form parties will take if they do emerge. The assumption is, however, that the resolution of these issues will be critical for understanding the overall direction of political development in a society.[18]

But the postulation of a persistent, adaptable corporatist-clientelist pattern of Latin American political development calls this assumption directly into question. For one thing, neither principle provides, in itself, a viable social basis for the emergence of mass-based political parties. Corporatist preferences for "administration" over "politics," the tendency to cope with social disorders through elite bargaining and bureaucratic co-optation, seem to relegate party activity to a minor role in the political process. From the other direction, clientelism nibbles away at large-scale organization of any sort, encouraging fragmented and personalized forms of electoral competition. Even more important, corporatist and clientelist principles can be considered as "functional substitutes" for political parties, adaptable in a variety of developmental settings to the task of regulating the interchange between the citizen and the state. Carried to its logical extreme, the implication of the preceding discussion is that neither the "weakness" of Latin American parties nor variation in party systems from one country to another seems to matter very much, at least not in terms of the general capacity of Latin American political systems to adapt to and manipulate the challenges of economic development.

Though it seems to flow logically from the corporatist-clientelist principles outlined above, however, this unqualified conclusion is untenable, in part because it ignores other aspects of a complex Latin American reality which the corporatist-clientelist models do *not* describe. From the perspective of party development, the most important of these aspects, mentioned in passing above, involves the diffusion of a relatively widespread, if only partial, commitment to the proposition that governmental leaders should be selected through competitive elections. In practice, of course, this norm operates only tentatively and intermittently in most countries, as might be expected in societies where hierarchical principles are so well entrenched. Yet despite widespread recourse to suffrage restrictions, fraud, and authoritarian interludes, competitive electoral norms have generally been used as weapons in the political game ever since the caudillo rebellions of the early nineteenth century. And as the expansion of national market and communications systems has made possible the emergence of a mass electorate, the capacity to win votes has become an important, if not decisive, political resource in most countries. As a consequence, one finds almost everywhere the appearance of a new type of actor, the *político*, who specializes in manipulating symbols, private benefits, and public patronage to win the support of a voting public.

These developments have provided the opening wedges for the entry of parties onto the Latin American political scene. Particularly in countries where the conflicts of the late nineteenth and early twentieth centuries were fomented and led by relatively polarized groups of *políticos*, psychological attachments to the symbols of competing parties were transmitted from one generation to the next and, by the 1950s and 1960s, had become fairly widely diffused throughout the politically active population.[19] In this context, political parties have become important vehicles for organizing electoral power resources and for mobilizing challenges to central bureaucratic authorities. In some instances, these parties grew out of the relatively feeble, but still visible, middle- and working-class protest against the political domination of upper-class elites. Here, partisan loyalties built upon and then reinforced the consciousness of competing group interests (another "countercurrent" in the Latin American experience), without fully replacing clientelist and corporatist orientations and patterns of behavior. In other cases, these identifications fused with decentralized clientelistic ties themselves, increasing the tension between otherwise complementary clientelist and corporatist principles.

Wherever competing partisan loyalties have become entrenched in the political culture of Latin American nations, however, they have added a new dimension to the political game. The party organizations rooted in these loyalties, though often fragmented and weak, have nevertheless shown a remarkable capacity to survive changes in electoral arrangements and to rebound from periods of dictatorship and repression. In so doing, they have managed to shape both elite and mass preferences about candidates for office; to structure the identification of political enemies; and to present both elected and imposed governmental officials with the nuclei of relatively strong, durable forms of opposition. It thus makes a great deal of theoretical sense to view these conflicting partisan formations not simply as the products of their environment, but also as independent variables in the political process which can react to and reshape the social forces out of which they were born.

Machine, Group-based, and Center-dominant Party Systems

The seven countries that will serve hereafter as the concrete referents for the discussion of Latin American party systems have been selected for two reasons. First, their socioeconomic development trends, painted in very crude brush strokes, appear to follow roughly the same lines. Despite important historical differences, all are offshoots of the imperial expansion of Iberian political and commercial institutions and in this general sense share a common colonial heritage. During the early nineteenth century, each experienced a period of agricultural involution, local elite autonomy, and caudillismo; and in the twentieth century, each experienced middle- and lower-class politicization which, with the partial exception of Mexico, resulted in nonrevolutionary adjustments of hierarchical orientations and structures.

There is, to be sure, substantial variation in the quantitative levels of wealth and industrialization which each country had achieved by mid-twentieth century. Yet by most aggregate measures of "modernization," these countries are among the most economically and socially "advanced" of the Latin American societies; and in qualitative terms, their existing socioeconomic structures do not look radically different. All seven countries were, by the 1960s, semiindustrialized, semiliterate, and highly urbanized. Each country was also heavily dependent on foreign trade and capital, but none had suffered the degree of American economic, political, and military penetration experienced during the twentieth century by Cuba, Panama, or other Caribbean and Central American countries. All seven countries were highly stratified socially, with sharp divisions between "incorporated" middle-class, upper-class, and blue-collar groups and a large, "marginalized" mass of urban and rural poor. On the other hand, none exhibits the sharp ethnic and linguistic polarities characteristic of, say, Peru, Guatemala, Bolivia, or Ecuador. For the speculative and exploratory purposes of this chapter, therefore, these countries can be treated as having roughly comparable socioeconomic systems.

Despite the similarities of social setting, on the other hand, these countries have displayed sharply contrasting configurations of partisan conflict in the years following World War II. They can thus be used as springboards for exploring in more detail the manner in which such conflicts interact with the corporatist and clientelist patterns outlined above. In Colombia and Uruguay, contemporary parties were generated largely by the caudillo struggles of the nineteenth century; and the strong loyalties on which these parties are now based continue to be activated largely through clientelist exchanges of patronage, protection, and material resources for political support. I have labeled these "machine" party systems.[20] In contrast, the party systems in Argentina, Chile, and (to a somewhat lesser extent) Venezuela developed relatively strong roots in the group identifications and functional associations which emerged in the process of commercialization and industrialization; hence, they are labeled "group-based" party systems. Though the Mexican and Brazilian party systems are structurally distinct, finally, each can be considered a variant of what I shall call "center-dominant" party systems. In the first country, relatively extensive partisan loyalties have been monopolized by a single "corporatist" party, the PRI, and the electoral process is thus employed as a device for consolidating, rather than challenging, the authority of governmental elites. In Brazil, partisan loyalties are neither durable nor extensive; and party organizations are, relatively speaking, too weak and ephemeral to counteract corporate authority. In both countries, the primary challenge to central government has been organized not by parties but by shifting cliques of individual *politicos* whose personal followings can be dispersed through the co-optation or repression of their leaders.

Machine Party Systems (Colombia and Uruguay)

As noted, the main parties in these countries are rooted in the local and personal patterns of authority that flourished during the nineteenth century, after the collapse of the Spanish monarchy and before the

emergence of a more complex social infrastructure.[21] The main characteristic of this nineteenth-century authority pattern was the predominance of the local patron or broker, whose connections and control of
private wealth permitted him to monopolize the political allegiance of
village communities and to control the interchange between the center
and periphery. The distinctive feature of both Colombia and Uruguay
in this regard was the prolonged attachment of local power brokers to
highly stable partisan factions operating at the national level of political
life, an attachment that was partly the cause and partly the effect of a
series of bloody civil wars racking each society. In this extended
crucible of domestic strife, the mass loyalties which had once flowed
exclusively to individual patrons were transformed into more permanent and generalized attachments to the party coloration of a
neighborhood, village, or region; and these in turn were aggregated into
a relatively stable two-party cleavage structure at the level of national
electoral politics.

This complex fusion of general partisan identification with particularistic, clientelist orientations carries with it a number of important
structural implications. On the one hand, party leaders continue to
mobilize supporters through narrow personal appeals and exchanges.
Each party, as a result, is a decentralized, socially heterogeneous amalgam of competing factions and cliques, organized around the personalities of individual national politicians and local *gamonales* (bosses). At
the same time, however, the diffusion of strong partisan loyalties
among the mass of the voters has made Colombian and Uruguayan
parties considerably more durable than the political structures which
form intermittently around "purer" patron-client transactions.[22] Although these loyalties have recently shown signs of erosion, they have
nevertheless insured that both intra- and interparty conflicts take place
within relatively fixed bipolar limits. This, on the one hand, has
inhibited the growth of separate parties tied more directly to working-
class interests.[23] On the other hand, as I shall subsequently argue, the
stability of the machine-type party system also militates strongly
against the development of more centralized and formal patterns of
corporate control.

Group-based Party Systems (Chile, Argentina, and Venezuela)

Partisan configurations in these countries are the products of two
different sets of nineteenth-century political arrangements.[24] In Chile
and Argentina, postindependence political disruptions were followed by
a prolonged period of direct political rule by relatively cohesive and
closed oligarchies. In Venezuela, extreme elite fragmentation and decentralization came to an end only at the turn of the century, when

that country finally achieved a modicum of political unification under the aegis of national caudillos. In both sets of circumstances, however, the decisive fact was that there was no stable pattern of upper-class polarization, and no diffusion of traditional party identifications that might have preempted the formation of new political allegiances. Although clientelist and corporatist principles remained important features of all three societies, partisan conflict tended to overlap roughly with the interest conflicts associated with the development of a relatively specialized and diversified social infrastructure. In Chile and Argentina, well-organized Radical parties became directly involved in the organization of public employees and white-collar associations, and Marxists and Peronists established strong bases of support within segments of the working class. Although partisan conflict was somewhat more diffuse in Venezuela, the Democratic Action party did attempt to unite labor and peasant movements in its attempt to wrest political power from landed and commercial elites.

I do not mean to imply by this that the Chilean, Venezuelan, and Argentine experience necessarily followed the "class-based" party systems which allegedly emerged in nineteenth-century Europe. Organizations like the Peronists, the Christian Democrats, and the Acción Democrática (AD) tend to define themselves ideologically in "populist" or "corporatist" terms, and neither they nor the Chilean Marxists have come close to gaining the support of all members of their respective working classes. Moreover, in all three countries (although less in Chile than in the others) a variety of important functional groups—employers' associations, sectoral organizations, and the military—did not become linked directly to any of the major parties. Thus, there is obviously no one-to-one correlation between class and parties in what I have called group-based systems.

The defining characteristics of these systems, rather, are that at least one (and usually more than one) of the major parties was directly involved with middle-class, labor, and peasant protest against elite domination of the political system; that these parties continue to draw the bulk of their support from one or a few status groups within the population; and that they continue to predominate in organizing and representing the interests of these social sectors vis-à-vis other higher-status groups and institutions. Even though in many instances these higher-status groups and institutions do not link themselves formally to parties of their own, they frequently define their collective interests in terms of their opposition to these perceived partisan challenges—they are anti-Peronist, anti-Marxist, and so forth. In this respect, the emergence of competing group-based parties colors political conflict within the system as a whole.

Center-dominant Party Systems (Brazil and Mexico)

In these societies, partisan loyalties are either too fragmented or too monolithic to facilitate significant partisan opposition to central authority.[25] As the rubric implies, center-dominant systems are characterized developmentally by a relatively weak nineteenth-century challenge to the preindustrial bureaucratic traditions. Instead, in both Brazil and Mexico, governmental elites were able to co-opt the leaders of private groups and to bind these groups to the state before they could develop autonomous organizations or independent political identities. Therefore, although the postwar party systems in these countries were structured quite differently, each in its own way can be considered a paradigmatic example of the relatively limited role played by parties within highly elaborated "corporatist" political orders.

In the case of Brazil, Getúlio Vargas's no-party Estado Nôvo was built upon a tradition of central imperial rule that, until the 1890s, was the unifying force in an otherwise segmented rural society. Like the syndical structures established during the dictatorship, post-1945 Brazilian parties were themselves initiated from above, the products of competition between different segments of the Vargas bureaucracy rather than the response to threats organized by opposing, nonbureaucratic elites. The role of these parties in structuring electoral competition and political recruitment was thus weak. National politicians (many of whom were unattached to any of the main parties) tended to mobilize support indirectly, through alliances with local bosses and intermediaries, who in turn commanded followings loyal primarily to them rather than to the national party groupings. At the national and state levels, power flowed from control of governorships or other bureaucratic resources rather than from attachments to particular party labels; consequently, parties like the Partido Trabalhista Brasileiro (PTB) or Partido Social Democrático (PSD) were loose and fluid affairs, shot through with factional alignments and tactical coalitions that cut across partisan lines. Under these circumstances, it is not difficult to understand why, when competition among *politicos* intensified in 1964, the military could reimpose more explicit forms of authoritarian rule with a minimum of disruption and why it could demobilize the society without large-scale partisan opposition.

Mexico's violent history, in so many ways strikingly different from Brazil's, is also noteworthy for the strength and durability of inherited colonial norms, even within the general Latin American context. In striking contrast to the other Spanish American countries, monarchism played a significant role in nineteenth-century Mexico, appearing shortly after the movement for independence and again during the 1860s. By the 1870s, the "liberal" revolt against this tradition had itself been diverted into a highly bureaucratic, positivist order; and this, in many ways, was the direct ancestor of the political system that followed the Mexican Revolution of 1911.

The Mexican PRI is, of course, in many respects distinct from the more fluid party system found in Brazil between 1945 and 1964. The PRI's claim to embody the ideals of the revolution has permitted it to dominate the electoral process and has thus contributed to the consolidation and institutionalization of central elite authority. Nevertheless, notwithstanding its extensive structural articulation, the Mexican "one-party" system shares a number of important features with its Brazilian "no-party" counterpart. Like the PSD and PTB, for example, the Mexican PRI was formed primarily through the preemptive initiative of governmental authorities and has remained, in essence, a creature of the central bureaucracy. Precisely because it embraces such a wide spectrum of the population, moreover, the PRI as a whole plays a relatively minor role in the organization of political cleavages. As in Brazil, rather, competition for offices is structured around clientelistic factions and cliques which do not attach themselves to opposing party labels. And, as Frank Brandenburg has argued persuasively, the levers of power are wielded primarily by presidential appointees, the heads of state corporations, and cabinet ministers, many of whom are only loosely tied to roles within the PRI itself.[26] Although the PRI is distinct from the Brazilian parties in its capacity to legitimate governmental decisions, therefore, its main role is that of ratifying decisions made in other, nonparty arenas. As in Brazil (although for opposite reasons), party labels are thus more or less irrelevant to many key aspects of the Mexican political process.

Since there is doubtless a great deal to find fault with in these ruthless oversimplifications, a few disclaimers are in order before I proceed further. First, it should be noted that the framework presented above does not consider many political factors which are often used to differentiate one party system from another. The systems clustered within the group and center-dominant categories are distinct in many ways. Party units within each category vary significantly in cohesion, centralization, and scope of support. In some cases the patterns of competition between these units are highly regularized, in others, more tentative and intermittent. Some of the larger political systems in each category are highly institutionalized; others, praetorian. Clearly, it is impossible to arrive at a full understanding of any one of these systems without taking these and many other differences into account. But the central purpose of any "framework" is precisely to highlight shared and contrasting characteristics that might be overlooked in more detailed, configurative analysis. Indeed, in so doing, it should make such detailed research more useful and informative. This is the criterion by which the present framework should ultimately be judged. In emphasizing the differences and similarities in the extent and structuring of partisan loyalties, I have made an informed bet that these factors will be more useful than others in explaining other differences among the seven countries.

The framework, ironically, can also be criticized from another perspective; namely, that it is too closely wedded to only seven countries and not sufficiently abstract to embrace other Latin American party systems. This criticism is at least partially justified. Some countries, such as Bolivia, Peru, Paraguay, and Costa Rica, fit only imperfectly into the categories I have devised, while others, particularly the less-developed ones, would probably require the introduction of still other analytical categories. The framework presented above, thus, should not be represented in its present form as a thoroughgoing, inclusive taxonomy of party systems.

At the same time, it should be noted that efforts to construct such general taxonomies usually flounder on one of two difficulties. Either they provide more categories than there are empirical cases, which makes it impossible to test propositions derived from them empirically; or they are so general that critical explanatory variables slip through their conceptual net.

This framework, I would argue, avoids many of these difficulties. On the one hand, it *is* sufficiently general to allow for comparison among the seven countries themselves, and it is at least potentially adaptable to the study of other cases as well.[27] At the same time, as I shall attempt to demonstrate, the framework has the advantage of suggesting some logical propositions about why party systems might make a difference at all—about how they might affect the shared hierarchical patterns so common in the area.[28]

These general propositions, already scattered throughout the preceding pages, can now be pulled together and summarized as follows: Machine systems, which freeze nineteenth-century clientelist orientations within a twentieth-century setting, both inhibit the tendency toward centralized, corporatist rule and reduce the opportunity for the organization of social cleavages around consciousness of class or group interests. The different party arrangements in center-dominant systems, on the other hand, are most conducive to the development of stable, reinforcing corporatist-clientelist patterns. Both no-party and one-party variants inhibit the formation of group cleavages without challenging corporate centralization. Governments in these systems should thus be most capable of shaping and controlling the modernization process in ways that adapt, rather than destroy, hierarchical principles. Group-based party systems, finally, reflect and reinforce orientations which promote the unraveling of corporatist arrangements and the emergence of more conflictual, if not class-based, political orders.

The remaining pages of this chapter will be devoted to refining these contentions by tentatively exploring the impact of partisan conflict on three more specific areas of political life. Focusing first on the "inputs" into the seven Latin American systems, I will look at two ways in which variations in partisan conflict can structure political demands: first, the way this variation affects the nexus between the government bureaucracy and organized labor and upper-class associations; and second, their impact on the mobilization of marginal sectors of the population. In the last section of the essay, I will suggest some propositions about the way variations in political demands are reflected in the outputs of political regimes in each of the seven systems.

My general arguments and the propositions derived from them are summarized in table 1.

Partisan Conflict and Corporate Controls:
Employers and Labor Associations

It should not be surprising that students of Mexico and Brazil were among the first to apply corporatist models of politics to group-state relations in Latin America as a whole.[29] By most available accounts, the structural and behavioral elaboration of corporatist principles has been extensive in both countries. Thanks to Schmitter's exhaustive analysis of Brazilian associational activity, the clearest empirical evidence for this proposition is found in that system. Administrative autonomy, Schmitter notes in his conclusion, is a predominant characteristic of the Brazilian policy-making process. Brazilian bureaucrats are neither subject to the control of an "ideological" party nor subordinated to organized private interests; rather, they use their roles within the administrative apparatus to play off competing elites and to pursue essentially self-interested policies.[30] Unhappily, we so far lack studies of comparable depth and sophistication to undergird these conclusions in the case of Mexico; but the writings of Brandenburg, Purcell, Kenneth F. Johnson, Vincent L. Padgett, and others point clearly to a similar pattern.[31] Within the weak one-party or no-party context of each society, there are no strong countervailing forces to counteract the corporate trend toward bureaucratic domination. Administrators are thus in a position to play a pivotal role in manipulating the organization and leadership of employers' and workers' associations alike, to seize from these groups the main initiatives in framing and choosing policy alternatives, and to reduce the role of representative associations to that of ratifying or protesting decisional *faits accomplis*.

Although one can certainly find examples of similar patterns em-

Table 1. Partisan Conflict, Associational Strength, Political Participation, and Government Policies

Timing of Emergence of Partisan Conflict	Type of Party System	Relative Strength of Associations and State	Political Participation (Voting; Unions)	Public Policy Patterns
Parties emerge during early agrarian-based caudillo period	Machine	Strong employers' association Weak workers' association	Low	Distributive
Parties emerge in period of economic modernization	Group-based	Strong employers' association Strong workers' association	High	Redistributive
Society modernizes without partisan conflict	Center-dominant	Weak employers' association Weak workers' association	Low	Growth-oriented

bedded in the legal structures and governmental policies of the other five countries, my preliminary survey of the still sparse secondary literature on group activity within these countries would suggest that the administrative domination of associational life is by no means as extensive as is the case in either Mexico or Brazil. I would tentatively suggest that the variations in group-state relations shown in table 2 are associated with the three categories of party systems I outlined earlier.

Table 2. Group-State Relations

Type of Association	Center-dominant	Machine	Group-based
Employers' associations	Administrative penetration and control	Group autonomy or penetration of bureaucracy	Group autonomy or penetration of bureaucracy
Workers' associations	Administrative penetration and control	Administrative penetration and control	Strong resistance to administrative penetration

A brief summary of contrasting descriptions of Brazilian, Chilean, and Colombian employers' associations should suffice to illustrate the proposition about employer-state relationships. In Brazil, Schmitter implies, the heads of individual firms may in fact be quite influential, but their influence is channeled through direct administrative contacts or through individual political brokers rather than through the formally organized syndicates. The syndicates themselves, argues Schmitter, are, like the "captive" trade unions, extremely susceptible to governmental manipulation. Their legal representation on numerous government boards gives these groups the appearance, but not the reality, of power. In fact, association leaders hold office at the pleasure of the bureaucrats. They are rarely consulted in the critical initiation and decision phases of the policy process. And the quality of information they can provide, their capacity to represent the interests of their constituency, and their effectiveness in taking policy initiatives are viewed somewhat contemptuously by the heads of Brazilian decision-making agencies.[32]

In Colombia and pre-Allende Chile, formal corporatist arrangements are similar to Brazil's, but the interchange between groups and government is much more symmetrical, with influence apparently flowing upward as well as downward. Constantine Menges's study of Chilean organizations, for example, asserts that the heads of the most important Chilean enterprises seek to dominate the main peak associations, rather than to by-pass them; and until the late 1960s, the officers of these associations regularly exercised veto power over—or actually dictated—

ministerial appointments. In contrast to their Brazilian counterparts, Chilean peak associations possessed technical staffs far superior to those of corresponding governmental agencies, and they regularly assumed the responsibility for gathering "official" data, drafting legislation, and even regulating new investment within their particular economic sectors.[33] Robert H. Dix's discussion of the Colombian Coffee Federation presents a similar picture. The minister of agriculture was regularly chosen from lists presented by federation leaders. These leaders not only initiated or vetoed important legislation but, like the Chilean peak associations, assumed a variety of quasi-governmental functions. In fact, federation officials have acted "as Colombia's representatives in the international negotiations seeking to stabilize the price of coffee on the world market."[34]

Space limitations and lack of information prevent me from exploring whether these patterns are also characteristic of other group-based and machine systems. But my impression is that employers' associations do display considerably greater strength in these countries than they do in either Brazil or Mexico. In some instances, this strength may take on a more "pluralistic" character than in Colombia and Chile, with a considerable proportion of the organizational life occurring outside the bureaucratic orbit. When employers' groups are brought into this orbit, however, a very different kind of "corporate" relationship tends to emerge: The groups are more likely to penetrate and colonize the state, rather than the other way around.

The degree to which these contrasting patterns are related to partisan antagonisms is somewhat less clear than the contrasts themselves. Compared to other social strata, after all, employers possess the education and resources to sustain a complex organizational structure without the protection of political parties; and many in fact are not directly linked to these parties. The relatively weakness of employers' associations in Brazil (and probably in Mexico as well), however, suggests that extensive bipolar or multipolar partisan conflict can contribute at least indirectly to the propensity of employers to form relatively strong interest organizations. The historical experience of partisan competition, for one thing, probably provides employers with a strong incentive to organize collectively, even when—as in Colombia and Uruguay—the parties in this conflict are not tied closely to class divisions. More important, partisan conflict tends to weaken the "patrimonial" authority of the center, from the president on down. However much the president may try to "rise above politics," he is invariably linked to one of several antagonistic subsets of the population. In turn, bureaucrats— both *técnicos* and patronage appointees—are vulnerable to political currents occurring outside the bureaucratic arena, which they can personally control only marginally and indirectly. In this context, the bargaining leverage of employers' groups, the importance of their organized support as counters in the political game, is likely to be increased considerably.

The relationship between partisanship and labor organization presents a different set of contrasts, since in all seven countries the scarcity of industrial employment, the instability of other lower-class occupational roles, high levels of unemployment and underemployment, and a general lack of educational and financial resources inhibit the organization of lower-class interests. Because of these factors, the impetus to form and maintain workers' and peasants' unions has generally come from higher-status actors, from middle-class *politicos* and governmental administrators who act as the protectors, tutors, and spokesmen for their lower-class constituents. In contrast to the employers' groups, which at least some of the time are structured and organized by status peers, hierarchical relationships are built into the fabric of union activity. Still, there do seem to be important variations in the way these internally stratified union structures articulate with the machinery of the state. This relationship will depend in part on how the union organizers themselves relate to the state—on their political commitments, their access to the resources of party organization, and the degree of partisan support that can be mobilized outside the bureaucratic power structure.

More specifically, I would argue that, in group-based systems, lower-class organizations exchange dependence on specific parties for a comparatively high degree of autonomy from bureaucratic control, at least when "their" party is out of power. In all three group-based systems, Marxists, Peronists, or Adecos dominate substantial proportions of the labor movement. But the resulting fusion between party and union leadership roles provides these movements with an identity and coherence that they probably would not otherwise have acquired. Thus, as James O. Morris argues, the otherwise tenuous unity of the Chilean Labor Confederation (CUT) "derives as much from a similarity of party allegiances among [Marxist] leaders at various levels of the confederated structure, and not from economic strength or statutory grants of authority as such."[35] This is probably also true of the Argentine Confederación General del Trabajo (CGT) and the Venezuelan Federación de Campesinos Venezolanos (FCV) as well.[36] Over time, moreover, as partisan identifications spread among rank-and-file union members, the overlap between party and union loyalties probably helps to reinforce the latter and to consolidate the internal structure of union authority. Jeane Kirkpatrick's survey of the Peronist movement is significant in this respect: Her findings indicate that Peronist identifiers

are more strongly pro-union than ordinary union members themselves.[37]

These sorts of party-union overlaps do not, of course, render the
unions in group-based systems invulnerable to co-optation or repression. In all three countries, as many writers have argued, workers'
organizations have shown tendencies to become part of the "establishment"—essentially concerned with protecting bread-and-butter interests
rather than in promoting large-scale structural change.[38]   And the
actions of the Chilean junta since 1973 have shown that military force
can subdue even the most militant unions, at least temporarily.

From the perspective of several decades, however, it is nonetheless
true that Chilean, Venezuelan, and Argentine unions have frequently
proved capable of strongly defending their immediate institutional
interests, at least when compared to the far more passive Brazilian and
Mexican syndicates. In the face of highly restrictive labor legislation
and frequently hostile governments, the Argentine unions have remained a strong, independent political force. This was clearly also true
of Chile until 1973, and the ruling junta of that country may well find
it difficult to demobilize and control Chilean labor over the long
haul.[39]   In Venezuela, finally, AD unions formed the nucleus of the
underground opposition to the repressive dictatorship of Marcos Pérez
Jiménez. And although these unions were vulnerable to manipulation
and purges during succeeding AD regimes, they did display a degree of
independence even then. During the early 1960s, the Federation of
Campesinos organized direct land seizures to push the agrarian reform
forward. And as the AD governments drifted slowly to the right, more
radical, union-based leaders precipitated a split in the party which
deprived the Adecos of the presidency in the elections of 1968.[40]
Apparently, then, partisan activity in these countries has provided at
least some resistance to the general trend toward governmental penetration and control of unions.

The position of unions in machine party systems is more complex
and requires some additional comment. At first glance, a system in
which competing partisan groups both attempt to mobilize lower-class
voters might seem to suggest the possibility of a more "pluralist" form
of labor activity, in which unions remain more or less independent from
both the parties and the government. Superficially, there are elements
of this pattern in both Uruguay and Colombia. Uruguayan labor legislation is far less restrictive than that of other countries, and union
organizations are not closely linked to either of the major parties. [41]
Colombian unions, though formed through the initiative of Liberal and
Conservative factions, are led by officials who rise through union ranks
and who generally do not hold top party offices. "Despite close links to

politics," comments Dix, "organized labor in Colombia today more nearly approaches autonomy than is the case in many other developing countries."[42]

But in societies where so many social, economic, and cultural factors militate heavily against collective working-class action, these forms of structural autonomy may weaken, rather than enhance, the capacity of unions to play an assertive role in the political process. This seems particularly true in the Colombian case, where the unions appear to have the worst of all worlds. On the one hand, the strength of territorially based partisan loyalties has inhibited the formation of workers' associations that cut across party lines. The union movement, rather, is bifurcated into two confederations—one, the Confederación de Trabajadores de Colombia (CTC) with a Liberal coloration, and the other, the Unión de Trabajadores Colombianos (UTC), connected to the Conservatives. On the other hand, the links between each union sector and its corresponding party are too loose to furnish it with sustained protection while that party is in opposition. Union officials, on the whole, have minimal direct representation in party conventions and decision-making bodies, but rather are linked indirectly to their partisan sector through the sponsorship of individual factional leaders. These leaders, in turn, must compete with many other party notables who rely on more traditional forms of clientage to mobilize support and who also have economic and status interests that are directly threatened by union activity.[43] Perhaps for these reasons, partisan oppositions are reluctant or unable to furnish support to "client unions" that are threatened by governmental harassment or repression. Thus, under the protection of the Alfonso López regime in the 1940s, the Liberal-oriented CTC flourished. But when the Conservatives came into office, that sector of the union movement went into a precipitate decline, while the church-sponsored UTC gained in membership. Both confederations, needless to say, were seriously weakened during Gustavo Rojas Pinilla's military regime.[44]

Uruguayan unions have had a considerably greater reputation for strength than their Colombian counterparts, and by the late 1960s they may in fact have evolved toward a more "pluralistic" pattern of independence. Even before the military crackdown of the 1970s, however, this reputation may well have been exaggerated. Some highly powerful blue-collar unions undoubtedly did exist; but impressions about the strength of the union movement as a whole may have been derived more from white-collar than blue-collar activities. By laying the basis for the extension of welfare benefits to urban workers, José Batlle's bipartisan *pactas*, formulated in the early 1900s, probably did much to defuse union protest. At least through the 1930s and 1940s, labor groups "were not able to organize with the intensity or ubiquity of certain other areas of the continent."[45] During subsequent decades, the Uruguayan labor movement, like Colombia's, became bifurcated into competing confederations of roughly equal size. Finally, while the membership of these confederations has been more stable than in Colombia (perhaps because of a less intense and exclusive set of partisan loyalties), the Uruguayan organizations have seemed considerably less aggressive than those of neighboring Argentina and Chile. From 1946 to 1966, labor confederations in these economically similar countries organized twenty-one and nine general strikes respectively. During the same period, and in spite of intense economic difficulties, only three such strikes occurred in Uruguay, and none took place in Colombia.[46]

Partisan Conflict and the Scope
of Direct Political Participation

Along with the relative passivity of interest associations, a low level of direct individual political participation is a frequently mentioned corollary of corporatist-clientelist patterns of development. Indirectly, to be sure, a large number of individuals may influence the political process through the manipulation of clientage ties. But corporate control of group structures tends to discourage rank-and-file activity within a formal associational context. And even where white- and blue-collar group competition is lively, the scope of such forms of political participation remains narrow. Suffrage restrictions and coercion, widespread poverty, illiteracy, and geographic isolation all converge to restrict the number of individuals who are capable of exerting direct, conscious influence on national politics. In almost every Latin American country, at least until recently, there has existed a large "marginal" mass of urban and rural poor who rarely engage in even minimal direct forms of political activitiy, such as voting; who are linked to the national political arena, if at all, only through their ties with patrons and brokers; who claim little and expect less from the national government.

The possibility of activating these masses and bringing them into the national political arena obviously depends on a host of social, political, economic, and psychological factors. Nevertheless, it seems plausible that one of these factors will be the variation in the distribution of partisan loyalties among existing political elites and their already activated followers. Where these groupings are already polarized around organized group interests—that is, in group-based party systems—I would expect there to be the greatest amount of pressure to attract the support of these uncommitted mass elements and to expand the scope of direct participation.

The impact of partisan conflict is less in center-dominant and machine systems for a number of reasons. In the Mexican one-party version of the center-dominant systems, a relatively cohesive bureaucratic elite lacks the competitive incentive to sponsor large-scale political mobilization. In the no-party variant, *políticos* are competitive but fragmented into a multitude of cliques and factions which are presumably inclined to generate support more through shifting alliances with one another than through an expansion of participation.[47] Actually, in the concrete Brazilian instance, increased elite polarization during João Goulart's presidency did produce serious pressures toward an extension of the voting franchise and the activation of mass groups. In the absence of a preexisting base of popular support for these elites, however, the polarization tendencies ended not with high degrees of mass mobilization but with military intervention, the abandonment of the principles of formal competition, and widespread, relatively successful military efforts to depoliticize the urban slums and the countryside.[48]

In machine systems, as the history of Colombia amply demonstrates, the fusion of intense partisan antagonisms with decentralized clientelist structures can at times produce highly combustible forms of mass activity. The famed *violencia* originated initially in the efforts of conflicting Liberal and Conservative elites to mobilize their mass followings against each other. But the elites lacked the organizational centralization needed to control this mobilization; and once activated, grassroots hatreds spilled over into a diffuse, uncontained communal conflict.[49] At the same time, however, machine systems do not on the whole seem any more likely than center-dominant ones to produce more structured forms of mass participation. The reliance of the party units on informal, hierarchical links between leaders and followers and the tendency of these units toward decentralization and factionalism make them unlikely vehicles for promoting mass organization; and as noted, such mass organization is likely to be perceived as a threat by the high-status elites at the apex of these parties. Moreover, the bipartite power-sharing arrangements devised in both systems to contain the destructive potential of partisan conflict seem to discourage even widespread electoral forms of participation. By substituting intraparty factional competition for interparty conflict, power-sharing arrangements reduce the salience of partisan identification in structuring electoral choice. Factional leaders are thus deprived of a "costless" symbolic resource in their quest for votes and must draw more exclusively instead on finite patronage and personal inducements, resources which are clearly of limited effectiveness in mobilizing a large electoral mass.

As in the machine systems, tacit or explicit power-sharing arrangements may be introduced in the group-based systems to restrict the entry of mass elements into politics. In Chile—the group-based system par excellence—tacit agreements among left, centrist, and rightist party leaders excluded the rural masses from access to the multiparty system for many decades. As a result, Chile had one of the lowest levels of political participation in Latin America. The equilibrium created by these arrangements, however, is likely to be much more precarious than in the other systems. As representatives of relatively differentiated group interests, party leaders are likely to be limited in their capacity to align with competing forces in order to increase their power within the system. Sooner or later, therefore, the balance between these forces is likely to be upset by the efforts of one or another to mobilize new sources of support at the expense of the others. Over time, the scope of participation is thus likely to be broader in the group-based systems than in the others.

Table 3, though it uses extremely crude indicators of participation, does provide some empirical support for this hypothesis. It is, of course, virtually impossible to determine how much of the differences shown in the table can be attributed to party system factors, and how much to different levels of industrialization, literacy, or to a host of other variables that are said to increase organization and participation. Nevertheless, it is noteworthy that the differences do hold up among subgroups of countries with more strictly comparable social and economic characteristics. Argentina and Uruguay parallel each other closely in economic development, literacy, cultural background, and racial composition; yet the former has a substantially higher voter turnout rate and organizational level than the latter. In spite of its unusually great oil wealth, Venezuela is socially similar to its Colombian neighbor and at approximately the same economic level as Mexico and Brazil. Union organization in Venezuela, however, far exceeds that of any other country, and its voter turnout rate exceeds that of Colombia, Mexico, and Brazil by at least 20 percent. It should be noted, finally, that Chile—which was once characterized by a strict exclusion of peasants and "urban marginals"—had undergone an expansion of participation in the past twenty years that before the 1973 coup brought it close to the level of Argentina. To a considerable extent, this expansion was the product of a competitive race between Marxists and Christian Democrats which caused both partisan groups to reach into the countryside and slums, to mobilize peasant syndicates, *centros de madres*, neighborhood associations, and other forms of lower-class participation.

Without much more extensive survey and anthropological data than is presently available, we are in no position to assess what these

Table 3. Voter Turnout and Unionization

System Type	Average Voter Turnout in Recent Presidential Elections as Percentage of Eligible Voters	Union Membership as Percentage of Active Labor Force
Group-based		
Argentina	88	34
Venezuela	90	68
Chile	79	30
Machine		
Uruguay	72	19
Colombia	53	24
Center-dominant		
Mexico	69	21
Brazil	72	11

Sources: For voter turnout figures, Brazil: *Brazil, Election Factbook* (Washington: Institute for the Comparative Study of Political Systems, September 1965); Colombia: *Colombia, Election Factbook* (Washington: Institute for the Comparative Study of Political Systems, March–May 1966); Uruguay: *Uruguay, Election Factbook* (Washington: Institute for the Comparative Study of Political Systems, November 27, 1966); Venezuela, Mexico: Ronald H. McDonald, *Party Systems and Elections in Latin America* (Chicago: Markham Publishing Company, 1971); Chile: computed by author with data from Direccion Electoral, Chile, and Chilean census.

Union membership figures were derived from U.S. Department of Labor, *Directory of Labor Organizations*; the size of economically active population, from International Labour Office, *Yearbook of Labour Statistics*. Data compiled by Phyllis M. Frakt, "A Cross-National Analysis of the Effects of Democratic Development of Governmental Responsiveness: The Case of International Labor Standards" (Ph.D. thesis, Rutgers University, 1975).

aggregate differences reflect in terms of psychological involvement, political cognition, demands, and expectations. Obviously a high proportion of union members and voters in all countries are only minimally involved in political affairs. And in Latin America, it is abundantly clear that the great issues articulated at the level of national politics trickle down slowly, if at all, to the grassroots level. As many writers are increasingly pointing out, even the most militant politicians often appeal for lower-class support in particularistic and paternalistic terms, sometimes exhibiting a style that is strikingly parallel to traditional forms of clientelism.[50]

Most of the scattered behavioral evidence I can find, however, does suggest at least some association between attachment to group-based parties and an expanded "political consciousness." In his study of Chilean *pobladores*, for example, Daniel Goldrich suggests that active party organizations were the most important factors in promoting politicization among these urban poor. More important, his findings indicate that it was the Marxist coalition of Communists and Socialists, rather than the more multiclass and corporatist Christian Democrats, that was most effective in "promoting an orientation toward group action and demands formulated in broad, rather than particularistic terms."[51] Kirkpatrick's study of Peronismo reaches similar conclusions. Peronist-oriented workers were more likely than non-Peronists of similar status to identify themselves as members of the working class.They were also more likely than other Argentinians to favor expropriation and redistribution of agricultural land, the elimination of private enterprise from key economic sectors, and greater independence from the United States.[52] Intracountry comparisons of those who do and do not identify with group-based parties thus suggest an important association with other attitudinal variations, although it is obviously not clear just what is the cause and what is the effect.

One of the few intercountry surveys bearing on the same subject, John R. Mathiason and John D. Powell's comparison of peasant attitudes in Venezuela and Colombia, points in similar directions. Although the authors note the parallels between traditional clientelism and new forms of party and union mobilization, their results suggest that the new agrarian syndicates organized by the Venezuelan AD and the Comité de Organización Política Electoral Independiente (Copei) do seem to produce important attitudinal changes. They conclude that

> although the old rural power structure in Colombia and the new union-based structure in Venezuela are superficially similar, it is evident that they are quite different in their effects. Participation in Colombia at best ties the individual to his traditional liege lord and at worst involves him in anomic, fratricidal violence. It certainly does not equip him to deal with the national government. Participation in Venezuela involves the peasant in a structure in which he can directly interact with government, change his local leaders if necessary, and which, up to now, has provided an alternative to violence in producing change. This experience of participation has been instrumental in fostering a feeling that the individual can influence government and thus channel the government's influence on him.[53]

When placed within the context of the preceding discussion, findings such as these underline the many different functions that clientelist interchanges can perform as they become linked to different configurations of partisan conflict. Clientelism is most likely to be supportive of the corporate order in center-dominant systems, where partisanship either does not interfere with or actually reinforces bureaucratic control. Detached from partisan antagonism, it keeps mass participation low and maintains groups in a subordinate position to the state. In Colombia and Uruguay, clientelism also keeps participation low, but in addition it weakens the center and, at times, produces pressures toward violent and destructive social behavior. As found within group-based systems, finally, clientelist interchanges may be devices for initiating citizens into broader, more organized, and more direct forms of political action, increasing the load on the system as a whole.

Partisan Conflict and Decision-Making: Demands and Outputs

The literature on the corporate-authoritarian models, to which the Latin American decision-making process has increasingly been linked, suggests that in Latin America the most direct inputs into policy formation flow primarily from within the narrow circles at the apex of the bureaucratic pyramid—either from development-oriented, technocratic administrators, or from old-style ministerial politicians who use the resources derived from their offices to build and maintain personal political machines. An examination of the preceding discussion of group activity and mass mobilization from a "whole-system" perspective, however, suggests that partisan conflicts can produce important deviations from this "modal" pattern—that they can produce different structures of both demands and outputs in the three sets of countries.

In the group-based systems, fairly extensive mass mobilization, linked through partisanship to group competition, would undoubtedly tend to place considerable strain on bureaucratic-centered policy-making arrangements. Even though many important decisions in Argentina, Chile, and Venezuela may be made behind the closed doors of the executive mansion, the major decision makers cannot escape links of one sort or another to socially differentiated partisan coalitions, if not as champions of one of these coalitions, then as their opponents. In a context of economic scarcity and underdevelopment, the leaders of these partisan coalitions are likely to perceive the group struggle over both governmental office and policy in more or less zero-sum terms: As one side gains, the others must necessarily lose. In group-based systems, in short, technocratic and clientelistic sources of policy inputs are likely to be supplemented by strong pressures for government policies which explicitly reallocate resources from one class or economic sector to another.

The parties in machine sytems reinforce the general tendency toward highly particularistic forms of problem-solving activity. "Machines," as James C. Scott argues, "by the nature of the rewards they offer and personal ties they build into their organization, may well impede the growth of class and occupational bonds implied by economic change and thus prolong the period during which family and/or ethnic ties are decisive."[54]   Given the extensiveness of support for these machine structures in Colombia and Uruguay and, consequently, their importance in shaping the struggle for power, it should not be surprising that the demand process in these countries should be characterized more than elsewhere by "corruption," favor-seeking, requests for special legislation, and other payoffs to small groups, families, and individuals.

Center-dominant systems, while also characterized by these types of inputs, recruit leaders through channels that are less closely linked to partisan conflict of any sort. Consequently, there is less incentive for leaders to attempt to purchase popular support through patronage, or to tie themselves to a particular coalition of organized groups. The decision-making bureaucracy is thus more susceptible to what Chalmers called a *técnico*-centered decision-making style, in which major policy initiatives flow from "nonpolitical" groups of development-oriented experts and specialists who have become entrenched in various administrative sectors and are relatively insulated from either group or clientelist pressures.[55]

There is not, of course, a perfect correlation between these different configurations of demands and the actual policy outputs emerging in the three sets of countries. The variations in demand produced by partisan conflict, for one thing, are superimposed upon, but do not fully replace, the more general patterns of demand formation suggested by the discussion of clientelism and corporatism. More important, as recent aggregate data studies clearly indicate, the conversion of "demands" into policy output will in any system be mediated by a host of environmental and governmental variables—the level of economic development, the nature of individual regimes, and of course the idiosyncrasies and preferences of particular governmental leaders.[56] Still, the logic of the three types of party system does present decision makers with a matrix of political costs and opportunities which should make the forms of policy output shown in table 4 more characteristic of some countries than of others.

Table 4. Policy Outputs

System Type	Policies
Group-based	Redistributive: land reform; labor-oriented wage policies; reallocations of resources among economic sectors
Center-dominant	Developmental: emphasis on expanding productive resources and gross national product; encouragement of private foreign capital; credits and subsidies to private enterprise; distribution of benefits toward upper-middle classes
Machine	Distributive: pork-barrel legislation; state-supported patronage, etc.

Although once again I am unable to test these propositions with "hard" comparative data, descriptions and analyses of policy performance drawn from available secondary literature lend credence to the general argument I have advanced and suggest the need for further comparative and case-study research.

Turning first to the concrete examples of group-based systems, it is striking that Venezuela and Chile are the first Latin American countries to undertake fairly extensive land reforms in a nonrevolutionary setting. In Venezuela, the process began under the auspices of the AD in the 1940s, when an estimated eighty thousand peasants received private parcels of land. Significantly, under the succeeding Pérez Jiménez regime, agrarian policies reversed direction, with most of the land being taken away from the beneficiaries of the earlier reform and redistributed to its former owners. The return of the AD to power in 1959, finally, produced a still more extensive process of land-tenure reform, in which land was again given to the peasantry.[57] In Chile during the 1960s and 1970s, intense competition between the Christian Democrats and Marxists produced even more radical agrarian measures, leading eventually to the expropriation of almost all of the large, privately owned haciendas.[58] Under Salvador Allende, moreover, the redistributive process went even further. Wage and price policies sharply penalized the middle sectors and at least temporarily increased the standard of living of the urban lower classes. Almost all of the foreign enterprises in Chile, and a good proportion of the domestically owned private sector, were nationalized.

Group-based systems are most likely to produce popularly oriented redistributive policies when, as was the case in Chile before 1973, party competition occurs within a constitutional framework. The behavior of authoritarian regimes that come to power in such systems is more complex. On the one hand, these regimes may well be inclined toward redistributive measures which favor the upper, rather than the lower strata, as was the case with both the Pérez Jiménez regime in Venezuela, and the post-Allende junta in Chile. The threat of a highly mobilized lower-class opposition, moreover, can produce harsher and more overtly repressive forms of authoritarian rule than elsewhere. On the other hand, however, authoritarian rulers may well behave differently in group-based systems where new, unattached lower-class sectors have not yet been mobilized by existing parties. In this situation, such rulers may be more inclined than their counterparts in other countries to undertake popularly oriented redistributive measures in order to outflank or undermine their partisan opponents.

The archetypal example of this latter phenomenon is the Peronist regime in Argentina. Like Vargas's Estado Nôvo, with which it has so often been compared, Perón's "justicialist" government attempted to bind all major groups to the bureaucracy in a corporatist fashion. But unlike Vargas, Perón came to power in a country already rent by partisan strife in which Radicals, Conservatives, and military factions vied for control. To consolidate his power, Perón was thus moved to engage in extensive mobilization and redistributionist activities which, according to Juan J. Linz, are unusual for authoritarian regimes.[59] The politically uncommitted *descamisados* were organized into a vastly expanded trade-union movement tied from that time on to Peronismo. The distance between lower- and middle-class incomes was sharply reduced as welfare and wage benefits flowed to newly activated lower-class constituents. And in an unsuccessful effort to pay for all of this, the government sought to extract resources from the traditional agrarian sector and to underwrite a large-scale expansion of the industrial sector. The ultimate result of the Peronist effort is well known: not corporatist centralism but increased polarization, with some segments of the Peronist coalition becoming linked to radicalism, some to the anti-Perón military interests, and a large, well-organized union structure remaining as the chief bulwark of the Peronist movement.

The present Peruvian military government provides a more contemporary example of "radical" authoritarian regimes. While I would not consider Peru a clear-cut case of a group-based party system, the dynamics of the historic conflict between the Peruvian Apristas and the military establishments does contain elements of that form of partisan antagonism; and these elements, in turn, help to explain in part the policy behavior of the current government. Committed on the one hand to remain in power, and faced, on the other, by a stubborn, independent union opposition dominated by the Alianza Popular Revolucionaria Americana (APRA), the Peruvian junta is presented with a strong incentive to organize the still uncommitted Indians of the Sierra and to attempt to consolidate their loyalties through a redistribution of land. If these measures and the other redistributive policies of the Peruvian government are extensive; if they are combined with a successful economic expansion; and if the Peruvian junta can retain the political unity necessary to coordinate these difficult tasks, we might see the emergence of a Peruvian political order that parallels Mexican corporatism. Synthesizing these conflicting goals within a coherent policy framework, however, is a formidable challenge. And, should the Peruvian government fail to deal effectively with this challenge, Peru could end up far more polarized than it was before 1968, looking much more like contemporary Argentina than like Mexico or Brazil.

The performance of the Mexican and Brazilian systems on the whole seems to correspond reasonably well to the proposition that center-dominant systems are likely to favor economic growth over redistribution. For the past thirty or forty years, each country has undergone an extensive process of industrial expansion that has transformed it from among the more "backward" Latin American countries to the more "advanced." In both cases, this economic expansion has occurred in a controlled, highly stratified political and social context.

It is, of course, impossible to ignore the fact that, prior to this period of economic growth, Mexican society had also undergone one of the most extensive property redistributions in world history—a fact that somewhat weakens the general propositions about policy outputs in center-dominant systems. But the reforms of the 1920s and 1930s were not the product of "politics as usual." They occurred during an explosive era in which mobilized agrarian and labor factions, private political armies, and entrenched local bosses still loomed large on the political scene; and I would tentatively suggest that the reforms of that period were much more a product of revolutionary upheaval than of the "normal" workings of the center-dominant systems that bracketed this upheaval. Perhaps because the revolutionary factions had not crystallized around stable partisan identifications, moreover, the effect of the redistribution was to depoliticize the lower classes and to co-opt their leaders, laying the groundwork for a strong policy shift toward intensive capital investment, forced savings, and close collaboration with the new entrepreneurial elite.

The postwar Brazilian pattern of development—in spite of the strains caused by electoral populism—seems remarkably similar to Mexico's. With the exception of the Goulart "interlude," the thrust of government policy has been toward encouraging economic expansion, a thrust which if anything has been accentuated by the post-1964 military governments. In sharp contrast to their Peronist and Peruvian counterparts, the Brazilian authoritarian regimes, like the Mexican political elite, have been profoundly oriented toward growth as an end in itself. They have encouraged the private entrepreneurial sector, held out incentives to foreign investment, imposed stern austerity measures, and systematically depoliticized the lower class. So far, the result has been an apparent resumption of the growth trends so evident in the 1940s and 1950s.

Continuing or even accentuated social inequalities, and a relative decline in the income of the marginal population, compromise the social underside of the "economic miracles" occurring within these two systems. This combination of growth and inequality suggests a potential for highly explosive forms of revolutionary behavior, with Brazil's relatively uninstitutionalized system being perhaps the most vulnerable to such outbursts. Up to this point, however, the relative autonomy of administrative authorities, the key role of *técnicos* in the decision-

making process, and the capacity of the center to manipulate demands
through co-optation and coercion have all permitted regimes in both
Mexico and Brazil to engineer economic change on their own terms.

The policy outputs of the two machine systems are characterized
neither by strong redistributive measures nor by an emphasis on economic expansion. In contrast to Chile, Venezuela, and Argentina, the
extensive support for machine-type parties inhibits the mobilization of
group pressures for reallocations of social resources. In contrast to
Brazil and Mexico, the persistence of strong, bifurcated partisan loyalties erodes the capacity of the central government to undertake developmental measures. In periods of open electoral competition
between partisan groups in Colombia and Uruguay, the executive is
inevitably challenged by an entrenched, hostile opposition. In periods
where partisan leaders opt for power-sharing arrangements—such as the
National Front in Colombia or the Uruguayan Executive Council—the
need for policy-making by consensus institutionalizes immobilism. It
should thus not be surprising that distributive, particularistic, pork-barrel measures are characteristic patterns of governmental output in both
countries, with the costs of these measures being borne diffusely by the
population as a whole rather than by a specific class or sector.

Uruguay's enormously bloated and overextended "welfare state,"
with its strong reliance on patronage, pensions, and sinecures, is a clear
illustration of this tendency. Almost 30 percent of Uruguay's economically active population is employed directly by the central government,
and 30 percent of the total population depends almost exclusively on
government pensions for its livelihood. These figures, according to
almost all observers, reflect the more general Uruguayan tendency to
use patronage, subsidies, and bureaucratic structures as forms of political payoffs and employment, rather than as instruments of either
development or redistribution. "What has occurred in Uruguay," argues
Phillip Taylor, is a type of "generalized 'corruption.' The State undertakes to pay something to everybody, although it may be only a little.
It maintains a bureaucracy intended to be inefficient, while producing a
maximum number of sub-sinecure jobs. It refuses to enact a law which
means what it says, since there is the attendant implicit promise to
review and revise it if it ever becomes inconvenient."[60]

Dix's study of Colombian politics suggests a similar pattern, although
one which has occurred within a context considerably less oriented
toward welfare. Although during the 1960s the National Front governments were rhetorically committed to the social changes outlined by
the Alliance for Progress and actually passed land and tax reform
measures, neither type of reform was implemented extensively. And
while the Colombian economy has by no means been as stagnant as

Uruguay's, its general pattern of growth has been neither as sustained nor as dramatic as those found in Mexico or Brazil. On the other hand, Dix gives the Colombian governments relatively high marks for measures that might be classified as distributive: constructing houses, building schools, and extending water supplies and sewer facilities. [61] Outputs such as these can easily be manipulated as political payoffs to loyal supporters, and they do not directly threaten any single group.

Ultimately, the use of such short-term benefits to purchase political support, coupled with an inability to confront the larger issues of redistribution and expansion, may have negative political consequences. There is a good deal of evidence in both Colombia and Uruguay of a high level of alienation and disaffection, and of an increasing sympathy toward authoritarian solutions to the problems of development. But the most extended example of overt authoritarian rule within these systems—Rojas Pinilla's seven-year dictatorship during the 1950s—suggests that the authoritarian solutions generated within machine systems share many vices with constitutional arrangements and contrast sharply with superficially similar regimes in the other countries. Although Rojas effectively subjugated the Colombian labor movement, working-class commitments to the traditional parties inhibited him from mobilizing one of his own. While the regime was vaguely populist and engaged in antioligarchical rhetoric, the relatively few concrete efforts to engage in radical reforms were effectively blocked by organized middle- and upper-class interests. "Lacking both ideological direction and mass support, the single attempt at a 'populist authoritarian' solution to Colombia's crisis of the traditional order thus proved abortive."[62]

Evidence of a recent decline in identifications with the traditional Colombia and Uruguayan parties, the activity of the Tupamaros and the Uruguayan military, and Rojas's own near victory in the Colombian elections of 1970 all indicate an erosion of the partisan constraints that inhibited the first Rojas dictatorship. There may, therefore, be forces at work which could ultimately permit Uruguay and Colombia to break free from the clientelist patterns that have characterized them for so long.

Still, the heritage of the past is likely to weigh heavily on future events. Partisan loyalties, after all, have eroded slowly and unevenly, with significant sectors of the population still retaining their inherited attachments. Moreover, the particularistic expectations, fostered for so long by the traditional parties, are likely to outlive these parties and to be reflected in ostensibly new forms of populist protest and/or authoritarian rule. This is quite clearly evident in Rojas's ANAPO movement (Alianza Nacional Popular) which, despite its posture of opposition to the National Front, espouses programs remarkably similar to those of past governments.[63] Extensive new opposition movements, in short, are likely to be far more vague and diffuse than those which have emerged in group-based systems. And while increased political conflict may ultimately lead to authoritarian rule which rejects the traditional forms of partisanship, this rule is likely to be less redistributionist than that of the Peronists and less developmental than that of Brazil.

Concluding Remarks

There is no doubt that the preceding framework and the propositions derived therefrom will require substantial modification as new empirical research uncovers new information and as the theoretical scope of comparative party studies is expanded into more rigorous and inclusive forms of classification. As both a guide and a rebuttable target for further research, however, this essay should prove useful to ensuing studies on at least three different levels.

First, although I have tried to build upon and add to "corporatist-clientelist" models of Latin American development, the result underscores the need to exercise considerable caution in applying these concepts to Latin America as a whole. The rash of military regimes in countries such as Brazil, Peru, Argentina, Chile, and Uruguay has led many to seize upon "corporatist-authoritarian" models of politics as useful tools for understanding the nature and direction of political change in that portion of the world. The preceding analysis of different forms of corporatism and different types of behavior on the part of authoritarian regimes, however, should make clear the need to avoid the teleological fallacy of assuming that "stable authoritarianism" is somehow predestined, either for a given Latin American country or for the area as a whole. In many parts of Latin America the principle of competitive elections, though often abused, is nonetheless likely to remain in uneasy conflict with corporate authoritarian principles, often in ways that preclude the emergence of stable regimes of any sort.

In the second place, I have tried to demonstrate that one important offshoot of competitive electoral principles—namely, the conflict among competing partisan groupings—may during the second half of the twentieth century play an important role in shaping the evolution of corporatist and clientelist patterns. Almost everywhere, to be sure, giving exclusive attention to parties would produce an extremely distorted picture of the way in which state and society are linked. But ignoring partisan formations a priori is just as likely to lead to distortions, especially in our understanding of the ways in which central governmental authority can be challenged and deposed. In a very general way, therefore, this chapter points to at least two broad avenues of comparative party studies that should be placed on (or given higher priority on) the agenda of research.

1. *How variations in partisan conflict get to be that way in the first place.* The comparative study of party development, which has received considerable attention in the European context, is still not very far along in Latin America.[64] Although I made some references to the development of party cleavages in the early part of the chapter, much more needs to be done in exploring the different ways that parties become articulated with the conflicts of the early twentieth century, how partisan leadership contributes to or defuses this conflict, how and whether party loyalties become "frozen," etc.

2. Where partisan loyalties have become more or less permanent parts of the political landscape, we need to know in more detail about *how they articulate with other social structures and processes.* The framework, in this respect, is only a starting point for asking several important questions: At the level of individual values and behavior, how do party loyalties relate to other psychological attachments to patrons, to members of the same status group, to nonpersonal administrative hierarchies, etc.? At the structural level, how do the partisan communications networks and transactions interact with bureaucratic, associational, and clientelistic ones?

Third, and most important, I have essayed, in a relatively systematic way, to propose why such comparisons should be expected to make a difference. Chalmers remarks in his article on Latin American parties that "contrasts between . . . party systems, once exposed, inevitably lead to the query, 'So what?' "[65] This framework has attempted to point to some nonobvious answers to that question for the seven countries treated above, and possibly for others as well. To this extent, it should serve as a starting point for advancing our understanding of the role of parties beyond the noncumulative configurative case studies and the arid general typologies that so dominate the literature.

NOTES

1. Russell H. Fitzgibbon, "The Party Potpourri in Latin America," *Western Political Quarterly*, 10 (March 1957):3–22.

2. Douglas A. Chalmers, "Parties and Society in Latin America," *Studies in Comparative International Development*, 7, no. 2 (1972):102–30; Peter Ranis, "A Two-Dimensional Typology of Latin American Political Parties," *Journal of Politics*, 30 (August 1968):798–832; Ronald H. McDonald, *Party Systems and Elections in Latin America* (Chicago: Markham Publishing Company, 1971); John D. Martz, "Dilemmas in the Study of Latin American Political Parties," *Journal of*

Politics, 26 (August 1964):509—31; Charles W. Anderson, "Central American Political Parties: A Functional Approach," *Western Political Quarterly*, 15 (March 1962):125—39; and Robert E. Scott, "Political Parties and Policy-Making in Latin America," in *Political Parties and Political Development*, ed. Joseph LaPalombara and Myron Weiner (Princeton: Princeton University Press, 1966), pp. 331—69.

3. Chalmers, "Parties and Society." This position seems to be shared at least implicitly by Anderson's discussion in "Central American Political Parties." After elaborating a detailed typology of such parties, Anderson contends that they all perform the same, more or less limited function: that of providing patronage and perquisites for the emerging middle sector.

4. Chalmers, "Parties and Society," pp. 19—26.

5. Philippe C. Schmitter, "Still the Century of Corporatism?", *Review of Politics*, 36 (January 1974):85—131; Guillermo O'Donnell, *Modernization and Bureaucratic-Authoritarianism* (Berkeley: University of California, Institute of International Studies, 1973); and Howard J. Wiarda, "Toward a Framework for the Study of Political Change in the Iberic-Latin Tradition: The Corporative Model," *World Politics*, 25 (January 1973):206—36.

6. For some interesting related comparative research, see Kenneth Paul Erickson and Patrick V. Peppe, "The Dynamics of Dependency: Industrial Modernization and Tightening Controls Over the Working Class in Brazil and Chile" (Paper delivered at the Fifth National Meeting of the Latin American Studies Association, San Francisco, November 1974); and Fernando Henrique Cardoso and José Luis Reyna, "Industrialization, Occupational Structure, and Social Structure in Latin America," in *Constructive Change in Latin America*, ed. Cole Blasier (Pittsburgh: University of Pittsburgh Press, 1968), pp. 19—55.

7. I am not implying, of course, that such patterns are at all unique to Latin America. "Corporatism" and "clientelism" have been used to describe a wide range of political phenomena in many different cultural settings. Also, I do not feel it necessary for my present purposes to become involved in explanations of and debates over why such patterns should be so prevelant in Latin America. Most explanations attribute the persistence of these patterns in the face of economic development to the weight of the Iberian tradition, to "late" economic development, and to economic dependency. (See Philippe C. Schmitter, "Paths to Political Development in Latin America," in *Changing Latin America*, ed. Douglas A. Chalmers [New York: The Academy of Political Science, Columbia University, 1972], pp. 83—109.) Suffice it to say that all three factors, as well as probably others, are at least somewhat operative.

8. For the relevant literature on the corporatist concept, see Juan J. Linz, "An Authoritarian Regime," in *Cleavages, Ideologies and Party Systems*, ed. Erik Allardt and Yrjo Littunen (Helsinki: The Westermarck Society, 1964), pp. 251—83; Susan Kaufman Purcell, "Authoritarianism," *Comparative Politics*, 5 (January 1973):301—12; Philippe C. Schmitter, *Interest Conflict and Political Change in Brazil* (Stanford: Stanford University Press, 1971); Wiarda, "Toward A Framework for the Study of Political Change"; and Frederick B. Pike, ed., "The New Corporatism: Social and Political Structures in the Iberian World," *Review of Politics*, 36 (Special edition, January 1974).

9. See especially Wiarda, "Toward a Framework for the Study of Political Change."

10. Purcell, "Authoritarianism," p. 302.

11. Schmitter, *Interest Conflict and Political Change*, pp. 108—33.

12. Chalmers, "Parties and Society," p. 111; and idem, "Political Groups and

Authority in Brazil: Some Continuities in a Decade of Confusion and Change," in *Brazil in the Sixties*, ed. Riordan Roett (Nashville: Vanderbilt University Press, 1972), pp. 51—77.

13. Constantine Menges, "Public Policy and Organized Business in Chile: A Preliminary Analysis," *Journal of International Affairs*, 20, no. 2 (1966):343—66.

14. James O. Morris, *Elites, Intellectuals, and Consensus: A Study of the Social Question and the Industrial Relations System in Chile* (Ithaca: New York State School of Industrial and Labor Relations, Cornell University, 1966), pp. 78—242.

15. For some general explications of clientelism, see John Duncan Powell, "Peasant Society and Clientelist Politics," *American Political Science Review*, 64 (June 1970):411—26; James C. Scott, "Patron-Client Politics and Political Change in Southeast Asia," *American Political Science Review*, 65 (March 1972):91—114; Rene Lemarchand, "Political Clientelism and Ethnicity in Tropical Africa: Competing Solidarities in Nation-Building," *American Political Science Review*, 65 (March 1972):68—91; and Rene Lemarchand and Keith Legg, "Political Clientelism and Development: Preliminary Analysis," *Comparative Politics*, 4 (January 1972):159—70.

16. Eric Wolf, "The Power Seekers," in *Conflict and Violence in Latin American Politics*, ed. Francisco José Moreno and Barbara Mitrani (New York: Thomas Y. Crowell Company, 1971), p. 23.

17. Schmitter, "Paths to Political Development," p. 97. For an excellent description of the reinforcing interaction of what I have called clientelist and corporatist patterns, see Anthony Leeds, "Brazilian Careers and Social Structure: A Case History and Model," in *Contemporary Cultures and Societies of Latin America*, ed. Dwight Heath and Richard Adams (New York: Random House, 1965), pp. 379—405.

18. See especially Samuel P. Huntington, *Political Order in Changing Societies* (New Haven: Yale University Press, 1968), pp. 397—463.

19. Conventional impressions, along with scattered secondary sources, provide much of the basis for contentions about the extent and distribution of partisan identifications. On the whole, more systematic survey evidence is lacking. However, some relatively hard comparative data for several of the seven countries are pulled together by Philip E. Converse, "Of Time and Partisan Stability," *Comparative Political Studies*, 2 (July 1969):139—72.

20. For an elaboration of the "machine" model, see James C. Scott, "Corruption, Machine Politics, and Political Change," *American Political Science Review*, 63 (December 1969):1142—59.

21. A large portion of the following discussion is based on Robert H. Dix, *Colombia: The Political Dimensions of Change* (New Haven: Yale University Press, 1967); James L. Payne, *Patterns of Conflict in Colombia* (New Haven: Yale University Press, 1968); Philip B. Taylor, Jr., *Government and Politics of Uruguay* (New Orleans: Tulane University Press, 1960); and idem, "Interests and Institutional Dysfunction in Uruguay," *American Political Science Review*, 43 (March 1963):62—74.

22. For a description of the more intermittent structures that emerge around relatively "pure" patron-client relations and are not grounded in generalized competing partisan identifications, see Carl H. Lande, "Networks and Groups in Southeast Asia, Some Observations on the Group Theory of Politics" (Paper delivered at the annual convention of the American Political Science Association, Chicago, 1971); F. G. Bailey, *Politics and Social Change, Orissa in 1959* (Berkeley and Los Angeles: University of California Press, 1963); and Eric R. Wolf and E. C.

Hansen, "Caudillo Politics: A Structural Analysis," *Comparative Studies of Society and History*, 9 (January 1967):168–79. In this chapter, as well, competing factional formations referred to in Brazil and Mexico would also fit into this category.

23. Although broadly speaking, the Uruguayan Colorados and the Colombian Liberals can be placed to the left of their main competitors, it is still fair to say that the major axis of partisan conflict continues to be organized along territorial lines which cut directly through class and functional interests.

24. Much of the ensuing discussion is based on Gino Germani, "The Transition Toward Mass Democracy in Argentina," in *Contemporary Cultures and Societies of Latin America*, ed. Dwight Heath and Richard Adams (New York: Random House, 1965), pp. 454–75; Arthur P. Whitaker, *Argentina* (Englewood Cliffs, N.J.: Prentice-Hall, Inc., 1964); Federico G. Gil, *Genesis and Modernization of Political Parties in Chile* (Gainesville: University of Florida Press, 1962); Robert R. Kaufman, *The Politics of Land Reform in Chile, 1950–1970* (Cambridge: Harvard University Press, 1972); James Petras, *Politics and Social Forces in Chilean Development* (Berkeley: University of California Press, 1969); John D. Powell, *Political Mobilization of the Venezuelan Peasant* (Cambridge: Harvard University Press, 1971); and John D. Martz, *Acción Democrática: Evolution of a Political Party in Venezuela* (Princeton: Princeton University Press, 1966).

25. See Frank Brandenburg, *The Making of Modern Mexico* (Englewood Cliffs, N.J.: Prentice-Hall, Inc., 1964); Vincent L. Padgett, *The Mexican Political System* (Boston: Houghton Mifflin, 1966); Roett, *Brazil in the Sixties*; Schmitter, *Interest Conflict and Political Change*; and Purcell, "Authoritarianism."

26. Brandenburg, *Making of Modern Mexico*, pp. 141–66.

27. Tentatively, for example, I would place Bolivia and Peru in the "group-based" category, Paraguay as a "center-dominant" system, and Costa Rica in the "machine" category. These countries have been excluded from the present analysis largely because divergent social and ethnic settings would require the introduction of other sorts of variables into the analysis. Various models of "pure" caudillo politics probably come close to explaining many of the other, less economically developed Latin American systems. Although these would bear some similarity to both center-dominant and machine systems, the lack of either partisan identification or a well-developed central bureaucracy implies that politics in these countries might obey a logic which is distinct from any of the categories in the current framework.

28. In many ways, this attempt to find a "middle ground" between a more general typology and "raw" empiricism is inspired by Sidney Verba's discussion of "disciplined configurative studies" in "Some Dilemmas in Comparative Research," *World Politics*, 20 (October 1967):111–28.

29. See, for example, Schmitter's "Paths to Political Development" and *Interest Conflict and Political Change*.

30. Schmitter, *Interest Conflict and Political Change*, pp. 317–66.

31. Brandenburg, *Making of Modern Mexico*; Padgett, *Mexican Political System*; Purcell, "Authoritarianism"; Kenneth F. Johnson, *Mexican Democracy: A Critical View* (Boston: Allyn and Bacon, Inc., 1971); and chapter 7 in this volume.

32. Schmitter, *Interest Conflict and Political Change*, pp. 317–65.

33. Menges, "Public Policy and Organized Business."

34. Dix, *Colombia: The Political Dimensions of Change*, p. 327.

35. Morris, *Elites, Intellectuals and Consensus*, p. 46.

36. See, for example, Powell's discussion of the symbiotic relationship between leadership roles in the AD and the Venezuelan Peasant Confederation in *Political Mobilization of the Venezuelan Peasant*, pp. 117–36.

37. Jeane Kirkpatrick, *Leader and Vanguard in Mass Society: A Study of Peronist Argentina* (Cambridge: MIT Press, 1971), pp. 145–54.

38. See especially, Henry A. Landsberger, "The Labor Elite: Is It Revolutionary?" in *Elites in Latin America*, ed. Seymour Lipset and Aldo Solari (New York: Oxford University Press, 1967), pp. 256–301.

39. See Robert R. Kaufman, "Transitions to Stable Authoritarian-Corporate Regimes: The Chilean Case?" Sage Professional Papers in Comparative Politics (Beverly Hills: Sage Publications, 1976).

40. Powell, *Political Mobilization of the Venezuelan Peasant*, pp. 182–212.

41. Moises Poblete Troncoso and Ben G. Burnett, *The Rise of the Latin American Labor Movement* (New Haven: College and University Press, 1960), p. 22.

42. Dix, *Colombia: Political Dimensions of Change*, p. 337.

43. John D. Martz, "Political Parties in Colombia and Venezuela: Contrasts in Substance and Style," *Western Political Quarterly*, 18 (June 1965):318–33.

44. Dix, *Colombia: Political Dimensions of Change*, pp. 330–41.

45. Poblete and Burnett, *Rise of the Latin American Labor Movement*, p. 92.

46. Arthur Banks, *Cross-Polity Time-Series Data* (Cambridge: MIT Press, 1971), pp. 283–97.

47. See Huntington, *Political Order in Changing Societies*, pp. 412–28.

48. Schmitter, *Interest Conflict and Political Change*, pp. 366–95.

49. Payne, *Patterns of Conflict in Colombia*, pp. 159–82.

50. See Powell, "Peasant Society and Clientelist Politics," and *Political Mobilization of the Venezuelan Peasant*; Kaufman, *Politics of Land Reform in Chile*; Petras, *Politics and Social Forces in Chilean Development*; and Sidney G. Tarrow, *Peasant Communism in Southern Italy* (New Haven: Yale University Press, 1966).

51. Daniel Goldrich, "Political Organization and the Politicization of the Poblador," *Comparative Political Studies*, 3 (July 1970):176–203. See also, Raymond Pratt, "Parties, Neighborhood Associations, and the Politicization of the Urban Poor in Latin America," *Midwest Journal of Political Science*, 15 (August 1971):495–524; and idem, "Community Political Organization and Lower Class Politicization in Two Latin American Cities," *Journal of Developing Areas*, 5 (July 1971):523–42.

52. Kirkpatrick, *Leader and Vanguard in Mass Society*, pp. 176–94.

53. John R. Mathiason and John D. Powell, "Political Participation and Political Attitudes: Attitude Change of Peasants Involved in Political Mobilization" (Paper presented at the annual meeting of the American Political Science Association, New York, September 1969), p. 23.

54. Scott, "Corruption, Machine Politics, and Political Change," p. 1156.

55. Chalmers, "Parties and Society."

56. See especially the "fifty-state" literature on policy outputs, for example, Richard I. Hofferbert, "The Relation Between Public Policy and Some Structural and Environmental Variables in the American States," *American Political Science Review*, 60 (March 1966):73–83.

57. Powell, *Political Mobilization of the Venezuelan Peasant*, pp. 65–117.

58. Kaufman, *Politics of Land Reform in Chile*, chaps. 3, 4, and 6.

59. Linz, "An Authoritarian Regime," p. 304.

60. Phillip B. Taylor, Jr., "Interests and Institutional Dysfunction in Uruguay," in *Latin American Politics*, ed. Robert D. Tomasek (Garden City, N.Y.: Doubleday & Company, Inc., 1966), p. 539.

61. Dix, *Colombia: Political Dimensions of Change*, pp. 147–58.

62. Ibid., p. 125; and V. L. Fluharty, *Dance of the Millions: Military Rule and the Social Revolution in Colombia, 1930–1956* (Pittsburgh: University of Pittsburgh Press, 1957).

63. Judith Talbot Campos and John F. McCamant, *Cleavage Shift in Colombia: Analysis of the 1970 Elections,* Sage Professional Papers, vol. 3, series 01-032 (Beverly Hills: Sage Publications, 1970).

64. Seymour M. Lipset and Stein Rokkan, eds., *Party Systems and Voter Alignments* (New York: The Free Press, 1967), chap. 1.

65. Chalmers, "Parties and Society," p. 102.

THOMAS E. SKIDMORE

6

The Politics of Economic Stabilization in Postwar Latin America

Inflation is one of the most intractable economic problems to have appeared in the capitalist world since the Second World War.[1] With industrial economies around the globe experiencing double-digit rates of price increase, it is understandable that economists and politicians should begin to study more closely those countries where inflation has long been a problem.[2] Latin America is such a region (see table 1).

If we go on to inquire about the relationship between inflation and political systems, the Latin American experience reveals a striking pattern. Since 1945 not a single major Latin American nation has been able to preserve a competitive political system and, at the same time, achieve sustained control of inflation once the latter has exceeded 10 percent per year for three years or more. Indeed, the social tensions exacerbated by inflation have contributed significantly to authoritarian coups in Brazil (1964), Argentina (1966), and Chile (1973). To state this fact is, of course, not to pronounce any "historical law." Rather, it is a conclusion that becomes unavoidable when one examines the Latin American record.

The pattern is startling enough to justify closer analysis. In this chapter I shall examine the experience of Latin America's three largest countries in an attempt to learn something about the relationship between regime type and economic policy. We may hope to understand better why, at least in the larger mixed (public-private) capitalist economies, stabilization has proved so difficult to achieve.

Our focus will be on the political consequences of applying anti-inflation measures. What effect have such programs had when attempted in relatively competitive political systems, such as in Argentina from 1958 to 1962, or in Brazil from 1961 to 1964? Have authoritarian regimes been better able to withstand the political opposition generated by the kind of stabilization programs attempted? In answering I shall be

149

analyzing one (among many) of the possible factors which have contributed to the breakdown of open systems.[3] I shall also be analyzing the advantages and disadvantages that stabilization managers find in countries where the advent of a noncompetitive regime has antedated rapid inflation.

Table 1. Rates of Inflation (annual percentage change in cost of living)

Year	Argentina	Brazil	Mexico
1945	20.7	—	7.2
1946	17.1	27.3	25.0
1947	12.2	5.8	12.6
1948	13.0	3.5	6.2
1949	32.7	6.0	5.4
1950	24.6	11.4	10.6
1951	37.2	10.8	12.6
1952	38.1	20.4	14.5
1953	4.3	17.6	−1.7
1954	3.5	25.6	25.9
1955	12.5	18.9	16.0
1956	13.1	21.8	4.9
1957	25.0	13.4	5.8
1958	31.4	17.3	11.5
1959	113.9	51.9	2.4
1960	27.3	23.8	4.9
1961	13.5	42.9	1.7
1962	28.1	55.8	1.2
1963	24.0	80.2	0.7
1964	22.1	86.6	2.2
1965	28.6	45.5	3.7
1966	31.9	41.2	4.2
1967	29.2	24.1	3.0
1968	16.2	24.5	2.3
1969	7.6	24.3	3.7
1970	13.6	20.9	5.2
1971	34.7	18.1	5.7
1972	58.5	14.0	5.0
1973	—	13.7	—

Sources: Argentina, cost of living, Buenos Aires, from *Boletín de Estadísticas Sociales*, no. 1 (April 1966), no. 16 (March 1973). Mexico, 1945–1967, "workers 'cost of living' " from B. Griffiths, *Mexican Monetary Policy and Economic Development* (New York: Praeger, 1972), table 4; 1967–1972, consumer prices calculated from IMF, *International Financial Statistics*. Brazil, *Conjuntura Econômica*, 28, no. 5 (May 1974).

Inflation as a Policy Problem

Economists are no longer as divided over the causes of inflation—at least, in the case of Latin America—as they were fifteen years ago. The once fierce controversy between "structuralists" and "monetarists" has been largely superseded. Most economists have found, on the basis of subsequent experience and more detailed analysis, that neither theory taken alone can satisfactorily explain the facts.[4] Although the explanation of any particular case is necessarily complex, we now have a solid body of evidence on which to analyze how and why stabilization managers have succeeded or failed (the definition of "success" is given in the note to table 2). It should be noted that I am leaving aside the question of whether the goal of relative price stability *deserved* the priority it was given and, therefore, whether its costs were justified.

As for the country sample, Argentina, Brazil, and Mexico have much in common. They are the three largest Latin American nations in area and population. All three have been able to attempt industrialization for a large home market. When faced with rapid inflation, however, they have adopted differing policies. These cases have been analyzed at varying lengths in the monographic literature, where emphasis is often placed on the unique features of each case. My purpose here is to explore the similarities in the political problems accompanying stabilization, in order to shed light on the nature of regime type.

First, a word about studying government responses to inflation. Inflation is an interesting policy problem because it directly affects the vital economic interests of every social group. Each group struggles to protect (or increase) its share of real income as its members shed the "money illusion." The battle is fought out not only over wages and salaries, but also over job definitions and pay differentials among job categories, all of which are fundamental determinants of income distribution. Tension is increased because social status, as well as income, is involved in the struggle.[5]

The response to inflation is also interesting for what it can tell us about Latin America's economic and political relationship with the centers of trade and finance abroad. Rapid inflation has usually been accompanied by deficits in the balance of payments (BOP), forcing governments to seek short-term international credits while also attempting to refinance long-term foreign debt. One obvious source is the International Monetary Fund (IMF), although it has not figured in all the cases to be discussed here. The IMF only enters the picture when a country seeks to draw from the fund to meet short-term debits on international accounts. The IMF charter requires borrowing nations to commit themselves to correcting the disequilibrium in the foreign sector. The applicant government must formulate a *plan* to carry out its commitment. In cases of "standby arrangements" (which are ongoing lines of credit), the plan must be spelled out in a "letter of intent" which becomes a virtual contract between the borrowing government and the IMF.[6] If the program is not followed, the fund can bar further currency drawings. This is a clear indication to other creditors that the IMF considers the debtor government to be abandoning or seriously compromising stabilization.

Although the IMF's potential credits are often relatively small in relation to the applicant country's needs, the fund's evaluations carry great weight with capitalist bankers and governments. Part of the reason lies in the fact that (especially since about 1960) the IMF staff studies (often carried out in cooperation with World Bank staff) have been so detailed and careful. Not beholden to any single government, these international bureaucrats believe they are uncommonly able to reach objective conclusions about any nation's "creditworthiness" or commitment to stabilization. Since the mid-1950s, the IMF often has been implicitly recognized by lenders in the United States and Western Europe as the "certifier" of creditworthiness.[7]

The criteria used by the IMF and the World Bank in approving hard currency loans to meet BOP crises (IMF) or for longer-term loans to finance public investment (World Bank) have aroused vehement debate in Latin America.[8] Critics have charged that the criteria are excessively "monetarist," rigidly conceived, and mechanically applied. These critics have gained support from "structuralist" economists, who aggressively championed a revisionist interpretation of the causes of (and therefore, the cures for) inflation in developing countries. Support came also from radical nationalists who mobilized political support by attacking the "exploitative" terms on which capitalist creditors (including multilateral agencies, as well as the United States and other wealthy nations) have dealt with dependent countries.

The political results are familiar. Governments seeking large foreign credits as part of a stabilization program are the very ones facing strong opposition at home. The economic ills that send them abroad in search of credit have also created loud dissatisfaction among workers, employers, exporters, importers, and bankers. Promises made abroad (typically including wage restraint, reduction in government employment, and devaluation) further threaten powerful economic interests at home. Although their interests diverge in the long run, these groups (for example, bankers and civil servants) forge an alliance in which each thinks it can best protect its fortunes if stabilization is scrapped. At a time when the government needs cooperation in getting the economy back on the road to real growth (within the prevailing mixed [public-private] capitalist model), it faces the charge that sacrifices will benefit only rich creditors abroad. Little wonder that experienced politicians dread the prospect of searching for the short-term financial help so essential for stabilization.

It would be wrong to offer a simple explanation to fit every attempt at stabilization. Any formulation of government policy—especially economic—is a complex process. Opponents often coalesce for widely differing reasons, not all of which can necessarily be traced to the opposition aroused by the stabilizers' painful measures. In response to opposition the government may abandon part of its stabilization program while attempting to maintain the rest—often a fatal compromise. In the necessarily brief discussion of individual stabilization efforts which follows, only the main features of each case can be sketched. Of course, the potential value of comparative analysis of stabilization can only be fully realized in a considerably more detailed investigation.

Background: The First Postwar Decade

Table 2 indicates the pattern of success and failure in major attempts to reduce and control inflation. Typically, great emphasis is given to wage restraint and an improvement in the foreign trade balance, as well as reducing the government deficit (and financing any deficit in a noninflationary manner). These stabilization attempts have usually been launched as part of a general government appeal for public support to overcome an economic crisis. Before turning to country case studies, we need to review briefly the economic history of Latin America in the first postwar decade as background for the stabilization struggles of the 1950s and 1960s.

When the Second World War ended, most Latin American nations had relatively large foreign exchange reserves. These gold and hard currency holdings had accumulated during the war when heavy exports to the Allies could not be balanced by Latin American purchases, because of a lack of shipping and the diversion of Allied production to war priorities. With the end of the hostilities, however, the release of suppressed demand resulted in heavy imports and soon led to trade deficits, which had to be covered by drawing on foreign exchange reserves. Within three years the reserves were exhausted.

Yet the Latin Americans had given little thought to diversifying and expanding exports, perhaps because they hoped that sales of their traditional products would carry them back toward the golden period of export-led growth, 1880–1914.[9] Furthermore, Latin American governments were not well prepared to intervene in their economies, even if they should have decided to act. Competently trained economists were in desperately short supply. Experience with large-scale planning (or even forecasting) was scant. An equally important liability was the policy-making climate. Neo-orthodox liberal doctrines (Manchester-type) still heavily influenced policy makers in Mexico and Brazil. In Argentina, Juan Perón was directing a strongly interventionist government role, but expertise and experience in implementing government plans were scarce, and Perón was to prove surprisingly orthodox when it came to fighting inflation.[10]

Table 2. Major Stabilization Programs

Country	Successful	Unsuccessful
Argentina	1949–1955	
		1958–1962
	1966–1970	
Brazil		1953–1954
		1955–1956
		1958–1959
		1961
		1962–1964
	1964–1968	
Mexico	1951–1956	

Note: "Major stabilization program" means a broad-based government effort to reduce the rate of price increase, usually including announced targets in fiscal and monetary policy. "Successful" is defined to mean reducing and holding inflation (for the life of the government) below 10 percent per year. "Success" is defined here *solely* in terms of price behavior and therefore leaves aside changes in other indicators such as GDP, the balance of payments, and employment. However, the Brazilian stabilization of 1964–1968 is classified as successful, although it does not satisfy these criteria. The reason is that the use of such devices as indexation and minidevaluations greatly neutralized the normally distortionary effects of the "residual" inflation.

The years between 1947 and 1949 brought a painful awakening. Governments could no longer ignore such harsh economic realities as rapid inflation (see table 1), insufficient foreign financing to cover BOP deficits (see figures 1–3), and the urgent need for rapid growth to offset rapid population increases in Brazil and Mexico. The population increase was smaller in Argentina, yet even there *any* increase in real Gross Domestic Product (GDP) was already proving difficult to sustain. Faced with these problems, Latin Americans looked abroad for advice.

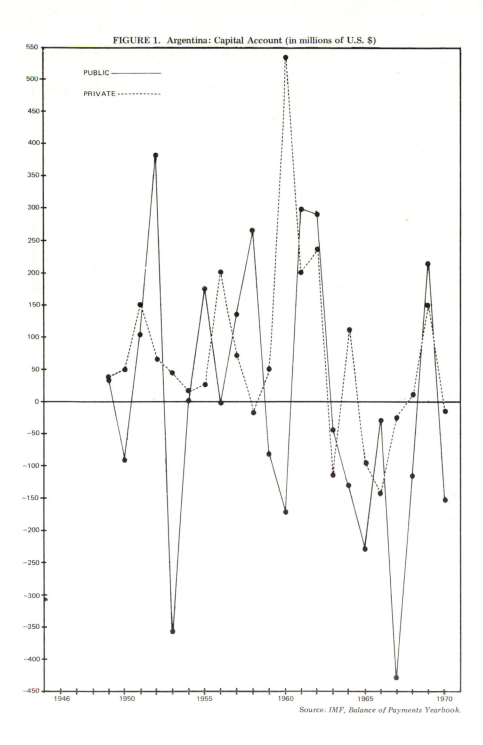

FIGURE 1. Argentina: Capital Account (in millions of U.S. $)

Source: *IMF, Balance of Payments Yearbook.*

FIGURE 2. Brazil: Capital Account (in millions of U.S. $)

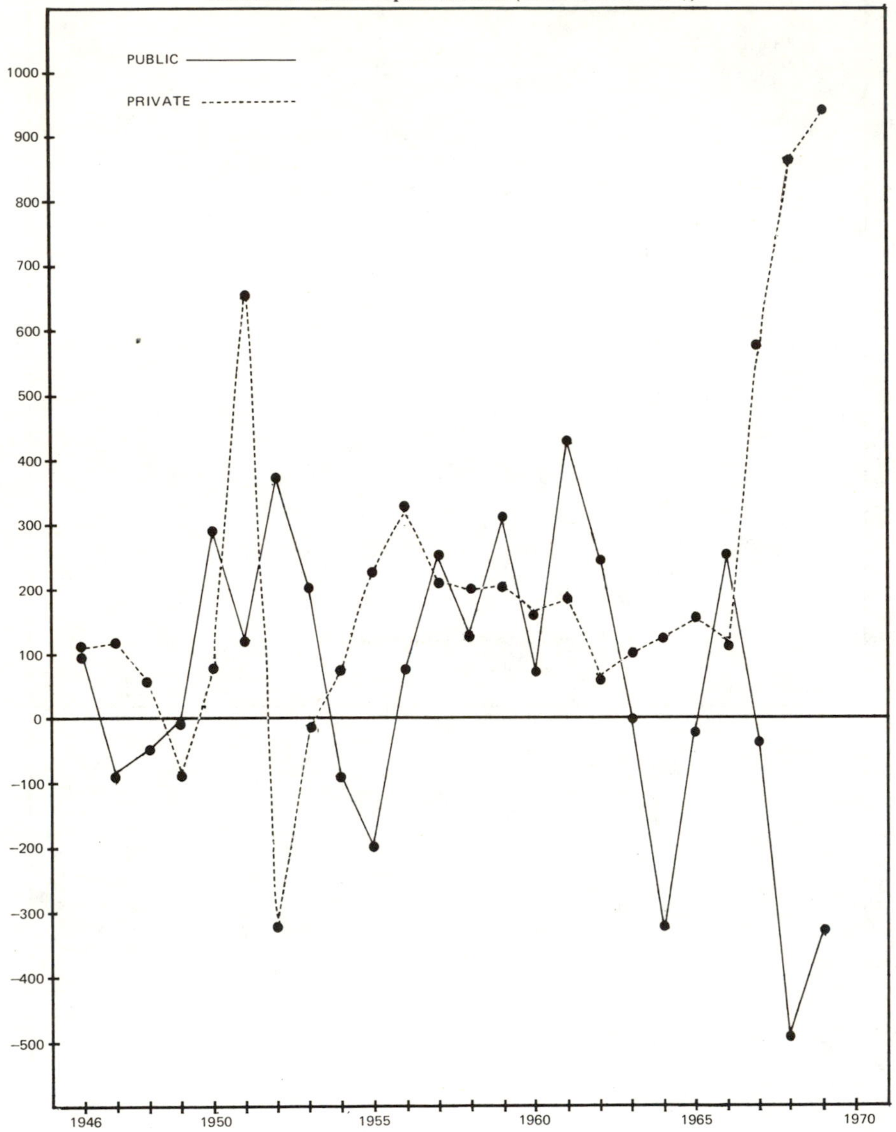

Source: *IMF, Balance of Payments Yearbook.*

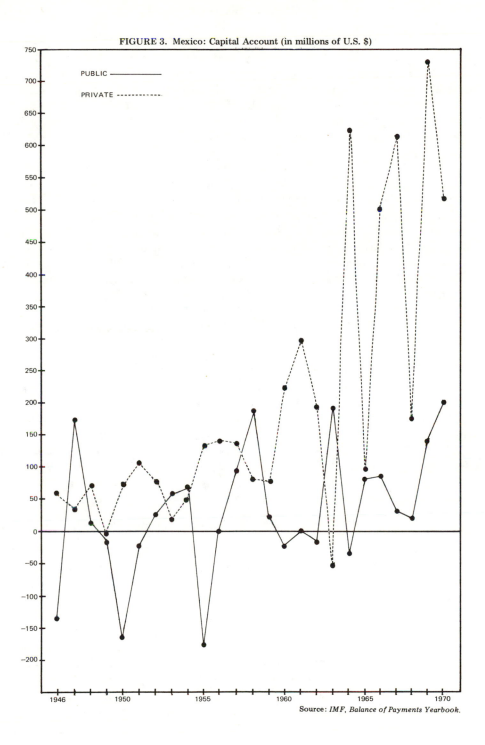

FIGURE 3. Mexico: Capital Account (in millions of U.S. $)

PUBLIC ————————

PRIVATE - - - - - - - - -

Source: *IMF, Balance of Payments Yearbook.*

They almost invariably heard voices counseling orthodox policies, that is, emphasizing price stability and urging the maintenance of a "favorable climate" for private foreign investment. They lacked theoretical models of their own which could help explain how to deal with persistent inflation and chronic BOP deficits and at the same time, continue to grow. Improvisation in policy-making was the usual response. The result was a varying combination of orthodoxy and innovation.

Between 1949 and 1955, Argentina, Brazil, and Mexico were all forced to attempt major stabilization efforts. The precipitating factor in each case was a sharp deterioration in the balance of payments. To reduce trade deficits on international account, they resorted to devaluation (see table 3), multiple exchange rates, and import quotas. The need for capital inflows, both private and public, became more obvious. Private foreign investment was more actively solicited. Such capital was needed to supplement domestic savings, cover debits on the current international account, and acquire badly needed technology.

During the early 1950s, the Mexican and Brazilian governments increased their direct role in their economies, a trend already underway in Perón's Argentina. In all three countries a new generation of technocrats was seeking to promote industrialization as a key element in growth. The theoretical rationale for such growth policies could often be traced to the work of the United Nations Economic Commission for Latin America (ECLA).[11] Economists identified with ECLA offered a systematic explanation for the persistent BOP deficits (the Prebisch-Singer terms-of-trade theory) and for inflation (the "structuralist" thesis).[12] Latin Americans were thus given a new theoretical basis for analyzing their economic problems. It was to be used often in the bitter arguments that arose over the causes of and cures for rapid inflation.

Argentina, 1949–1955: A Populist Tries Economic Orthodoxy

The Argentine stabilization experience under Perón was an example of an extraordinarily uncompromising application of orthodox monetarist strategy. This seems all the more surprising, since Perón was hardly known for orthodoxy in most of his economic policies.[13] The years between 1946 and 1949 have aptly been called the "euphoric" era for Perón because in that period his government seemed able to pursue freely its policies of economic nationalism and income redistribution. The overall increase in output was impressive in 1946 and 1947, when GDP grew 8.7 and 12.7 percent (see table 4). Even in 1948, when the increase dropped to 5.1 percent, it was a respectable figure by world standards. Increases in manufacturing output led the way, total-

Table 3. Exchange Rates

Year	Argentina (pesos per dollar)	Brazil (cruzeiros per dollar)	Mexico (pesos per dollar)
1945	—	—	4.85
1946	—	—	4.85
1947	—	—	4.85
1948	4.23	18.72[a]	5.76
1949	4.85	18.72	8.02
1950	6.56	18.72	8.65
1951	7.50	18.72	8.65
1952	7.50	18.72	8.65
1953	7.50	55.00[b]	8.65
1954	7.50	76.00	11.34
1955	10.12	66.75	12.50
1956	18.00	65.65	12.50
1957	18.00	90.50	12.50
1958	18.00	138.52	12.50
1959	80.63	203.77	12.50
1960	82.80	205.14	12.50
1961	83.13	318.51	12.50
1962	115.98	475.00	12.50
1963	138.61	620.00	12.50
1964	141.00	1,850.00	12.50
1965	171.62	2,220.00	12.50
1966	209.35	2,220.00	12.50
1967	333.50	2.715[c]	12.50
1968	350.00	3.830	12.50
1969	350.00	4.350	12.50
1970	379.17	4.950	12.50
1971	4.598[d]	5.635	12.50
1972	8.333	6.215	12.50
1973	9.998	6.220	12.50

Sources: Argentina, 1948–1970, from R. Mallon and J. Sourrouille, unpublished study of Argentine economic policy, table 1-4; 1971–1973 from IMF, *International Financial Statistics* (rate given as "trade conversion factor"). Mexico, 1945–1963, from Clark Reynolds, *The Mexican Economy* (New Haven: Yale University Press, 1970), table 2.14; 1963–1973 from IMF, *International Financial Statistics*. Brazil data are all from IMF, *International Financial Statistics* (rate given as "free rate").

a. From 1947 to 1953 Brazil used a licensing system to control imports.

b. A complex set of multiple exchange rates was used for 1953–1957.

c. A new Brazilian cruzeiro was introduced equal to 1,000 old cruzeiros.

d. A new Argentine peso was introduced equal to 100 old pesos.

ing 10.2 percent in 1946 and 13.2 percent in 1947, then falling to 4.9 percent in 1948. Less reassuring was the performance of agriculture. After a sharp decline of 20 percent in 1945, agricultural output rose 3.7 percent in 1946 and 8.7 percent in 1947 but leveled off in 1948, when it rose only 0.1 percent.[14]

The Perón government had come to power on a wave of militant labor support and in its first years rewarded organized labor with handsome increases in real income. Because of the industrial boom of 1946–1948, urban employment was high and increasing rapidly. Government pressure on employers (by manipulation of credit, selective allocation of foreign exchange for essential imports, etc.) helped unions win hourly money wage rate increases in industry averaging 35 percent annually for the three-year period 1946–1948. Since inflation

Table 4. Argentina: Annual Changes in Real Output (Percent)
(1960 = 100)

Year	Agriculture	Manufacturing	GDP	GDP + Merchandise Imports
1940	+ 5.3	− 3.4	+ 1.2	—
1941	+11.9	+ 5.1	+ 5.7	—
1942	− 2.6	+ 3.7	+ 0.7	—
1943	−13.2	+ 4.5	− 2.0	—
1944	+23.5	+11.1	+12.1	—
1945	−20.0	− 1.7	− 4.8	− 3.0
1946	+ 3.7	+10.2	+ 8.7	+12.1
1947	+ 8.7	+13.2	+12.7	+17.2
1948	+ 0.1	+ 4.9	+ 5.1	+ 5.0
1949	− 8.1	+ 0.7	− 1.5	− 4.5
1950	− 6.7	+ 2.8	+ 0.3	− 0.1
1951	+ 6.7	+ 0.9	+ 3.9	+ 5.4
1952	−14.9	− 2.6	− 5.9	− 7.7
1953	+30.0	0.0[a]	+ 6.1	+ 3.6
1954	− 0.3	+ 9.1	+ 5.0	+ 5.6
1955	+ 3.7	+12.1	+ 7.2	+ 8.0
1956	− 4.8	+ 5.6	+ 2.2	+ 1.7
1957	− 0.2	+ 7.7	+ 5.1	+ 6.2
1958	+ 4.3	+ 7.4	+ 0.5	+ 4.7
1959	− 0.8	− 7.5	− 0.5	− 5.2
1960	− 0.2	+ 6.4	+ 0.6	+ 7.6

Sources: First three columns calculated from Consejo Nacional de Desarrollo, *Distribución del Ingreso y Cuentas Nacionales en la Argentina*, vol. 3 (Buenos Aires: Presidencia de la Nación, 1965), pp. 64–65. GDP is the figure at market prices. Last column taken from Carlos Díaz-Alejandro, *Exchange-Rate Devaluation in a Semi-Industrialized Country* (Cambridge: MIT Press, 1965), p. 128, table S.3.

Note: Tables 4 and 8 represent two time series which do not always agree for the overlapping years. I have therefore given both series.

a. There is presumably an error in the original data which give the same figure for the value of industrial production in 1952 and 1953.

was far below this level, *real* hourly industrial wage rates increased dramatically over the three years: 5.6 percent in 1946, 25.3 percent in 1947, and 23.5 percent in 1948 (see table 5). Furthermore, because of productivity increases, high utilization of capacity, and very favorable foreign trade performance, profits also increased.[15]

In 1949 the euphoria ended. Two unmistakable signs of economic trouble appeared: a sharp increase in inflation and a severe foreign exchange bottleneck, to which the inconvertibility of sterling had contributed since 1947. Both problems required immediate action, and Perón reacted by firing his economic czar, Miguel Miranda, and replacing him with Alfredo Gomez Morales, who was to remain the principal economic policy maker until Perón's overthrow in 1955.

The cost-of-living index for Buenos Aires had been rising significantly since the end of the war, averaging an increase of 16 percent per year for the four-year period of 1945–1948. In 1949 the inflation rate jumped to 32.7 percent, almost double the previous yearly average. Inflation continued at that rate through the first half of 1949, when the cost of living increased 15.8 percent. The shortage of foreign exchange became even more critical, as reserves dwindled from $573 million at the end of 1948 to only $370 million at the end of 1949.

Faced with these problems, Perón opted for a notably orthodox approach to inflation. His new finance minister, Gomez Morales, believed strongly in exploiting the full potential of monetary policy.[16] A premium was placed on fighting inflation by tightening credit, contain-

Table 5. Argentina: Real Wage Rates

Year	Annual Change (%)	Year	Annual Change (%)
1946	5.6	1959	−20.5
1947	25.3	1960	3.2
1948	23.5	1961	9.7
1949	4.9	1962	−1.9
1950	−4.4	1963	0.7
1951	−7.0	1964	7.0
1952	−11.3	1965	5.1
1953	7.8	1966	2.0
1954	6.9	1967	−5.0
1955	−1.1	1968	−3.0
1956	0.5	1969	5.0
1957	7.2	1970	1.0
1958	4.7		

Sources: Figures for 1946–1965 from Carlos F. Díaz Alejandro, *Essays on the Economic History of the Argentine Republic* (New Haven: Yale University Press, 1970), statistical appendix, table 123. Figures for 1966–1970 from Felipe Pazos, *Chronic Inflation in Latin America* (New York: Praeger, 1972), table 18.

ing public expenditures, and holding down wage increases. Promoting exports—which would have been the most logical long-run step toward curing the foreign exchange bottleneck—proved far more difficult.

The initial years of stabilization began with an unpleasant finale to the postwar euphoria. In 1949 GDP declined by 1.5 percent. Subsequent GDP growth was only 0.3 percent in 1950 and 3.4 percent in 1951. A devastating drought in 1951–1952 contributed to the decline of 5.9 percent in 1952, which was sufficient to produce a negative annual average growth in GDP of 0.8 percent for the four-year period of 1949–1952.

Despite this stagnation, inflation continued. The rate of increase in the cost of living for Buenos Aires was 32.7 percent in 1949 and rose to an annual average of 33.3 percent for 1950–1952. The foreign exchange bottleneck also proved unresponsive to the new policies, at least in the short run. The negative trade balance of $138 million in 1949 was followed by a trade surplus of $113.6 million in 1950, but the gain was short-lived. Unprecedented trade deficits followed, totaling $211 million in 1951 and $392 million in 1952 (see table 6).

By 1952 neither inflation nor the exchange shortage had been cured, despite the sacrifice of years of potential domestic growth. Why this disappointing record? How did the Perón government manage to produce such a striking example of "stagflation"?

It should first be noted that the rate of total credit expansion was slowed down in 1949 and 1950, when the real average stock of money and quasi money rose only 1.7 and 1.4 percent, respectively. In 1951 that stock was actually *reduced* 11.8 percent, and it fell another 13.8 percent in 1952. In other words, for two years (1951–1952) the monetary authorities sought to choke off inflation by holding credit expansion down to a significantly lower rate in nominal terms than the rate of price increase.[17] Given the overall constraint on credit expansion, it was therefore very difficult to blame monetary policy for the continued inflation.

What about wages? Here the Perón government reacted with a far tougher policy than most contemporaries would have predicted. Real hourly wage rates, which had risen so dramatically between 1946 and 1949, *declined* 4.4 percent in 1950, 7 percent in 1951, and 11.3 percent in 1952 (see table 5). Although Perón had greatly consolidated his personal control over labor union leadership by 1949, the fall in real wages did provoke serious strikes. In October and November, 1949, the sugar workers in the province of Tucumán staged a bitter strike, which Perón denounced. Although the sugar workers managed to extract a 60 percent wage increase, the trend was not allowed to spread. Its only significant sequel was a railway strike between November 1950 and

Table 6. Argentina: Balance of Payments (in millions of U.S. dollars)

Year	Trade Balance	Capital Account	Errors and Omissions
1946	425.0	−399.1	−25.9
1947	−29.2	142.3	−113.1
1948	−81.2	−105.4	186.6
1949	−138.0	73.4	64.6
1950	113.6	−39.8	−73.8
1951	−211.2	346.7	−135.5
1952	−392.1	165.3	226.8
1953	356.0	−356.7	0.7
1954	86.2	12.3	−98.5
1955	−238.8	204.8	34.0
1956	−129.1	199.5	−70.4
1957	−300.5	197.8	102.7
1958	−256.1	254.1	2.0
1959	13.7	−30.9	17.2
1960	−197.9	374.4	−176.5
1961	−573.0	502.4	70.6
1962	−269.7	533.0	−263.3
1963	232.0	−160.2	−71.8
1964	34.2	−19.6	−14.6
1965	224.0	−318.0	94.0
1966	260.0	−172.0	−88.0
1967	184.0	−440.0	256.0
1968	−15.0	−104.0	119.0
1969	−219.0	364.0	−145.0
1970	−134.0	−168.0	302.0

Source: IMF, *Balance of Payments Yearbook.*

January 1951, which produced concessions that the government prevented from becoming a precedent for less militant workers. In general, the years from 1949 to 1952 demonstrated Perón's personal and institutional mastery of organized labor. It seemed that most workers were willing to separate dissatisfaction over erosion of their material gains from their political sentiments about the president and his stabilization policy. At least the dissatisfied workers, however large their number, were not able to influence union leadership, which Perón generally controlled. The populist caudillo was leading the faithful through an orthodox stabilization effort.

As for exports, they could have been increased by diverting agricultural goods from domestic consumption to foreign markets. Since Argentines enjoyed relatively high consumption standards, some cut in domestic intake of beef might have been attempted, at least as a short-term measure. Perón did the opposite. In 1951–1952, Argentina suffered a severe drought which greatly decreased production of meat, especially beef. It was the domestic market, not the export sector, which suffered least from this shortage (see table 7). The absolute level of beef exports in 1951 (255,983 tons) fell 40.3 percent from the 1950 level (429,499 tons).[18] The share of beef production going to the domestic market rose from 79 percent in 1950 to 86.4 percent in 1951. The balance between exports and domestic consumption continued at approximately that level until 1955. The Perón government had decided to keep beef on the Argentine worker's table to help offset the decline in real wage rates. Unfortunately, this concession also exacerbated the foreign exchange shortage.

The 1949 stabilization program had proved a bitter disappointment in its first two years. Both rapid price inflation and trade deficits continued. Argentine policy makers could not then have known that an orthodox stabilization strategy—such as the Perón policy—has often

Table 7. Argentina: Beef Production, Consumption, and Export

	Total Production (Metric Tons, 1000s)		Change from Previous Year (Percentage)		Amount Exported (Percentage)		Per Capita Consumption (Kgs. per person)	
Year	Meat	Beef	Meat	Beef	Meat	Beef	Meat	Beef
1940	2,010.7	1,690.1	—	—	35.2	34.3	93.3	77.2
1941	2,246.8	1,854.0	+11.7	+ 9.7	40.6	39.1	95.0	76.5
1942	2,233.8	1,724.9	− 5.8	− 7.0	41.9	41.4	89.4	68.5
1943	2,247.6	1,602.6	+ 6.2	− 7.1	39.4	40.9	89.2	65.3
1944	2,370.6	1,619.4	+ 5.5	+ 1.1	37.0	40.1	93.8	67.5
1945	2,113.2	1,455.7	−10.8	−10.1	25.7	31.2	94.5	70.3
1946	2,207.1	1,682.2	+ 4.4	+15.6	26.3	30.7	97.7	79.2
1947	2,458.8	2,023.8	+11.4	+20.3	31.8	34.4	101.2	86.6
1948	2,345.4	1,958.1	− 4.6	− 3.2	24.1	25.9	106.6	91.1
1949	2,386.9	2,003.2	+ 1.8	+ 2.3	23.3	24.4	107.7	91.7
1950	2,372.5	2,043.9	− 0.6	+ 2.0	21.0	21.3	108.7	93.0
1951	2,170.7	1,879.4	− 8.5	− 8.0	13.6	14.0	105.9	92.0
1952	2,117.1	1,788.2	− 2.5	− 4.9	15.4	17.0	97.4	83.8
1953	2,112.5	1,765.5	− 0.2	− 1.3	13.0	15.1	97.5	83.4
1954	2,176.5	1,814.9	+ 3.0	+ 2.8	12.8	15.1	98.5	84.4
1955	2,501.3	2,146.8	+14.9	+18.3	19.3	20.3	104.3	90.6
1956	2,856.1	2,475.6	+14.2	+15.3	24.3	24.6	110.5	96.1
1957	2,826.8	2,459.5	− 1.0	− 1.3	23.8	23.8	108.3	94.2
1958	2,893.4	2,540.9	+ 2.4	+ 8.1	25.5	24.5	107.8	93.5
1959	2,270.9	1,944.4	−21.5	−23.5	26.6	25.2	82.4	69.2
1960	2,241.8	1,833.3	− 1.3	− 8.4	20.4	19.9	85.7	71.5

Source: Calculated from Junta Nacional de Carnes, *Estadisticas Básicas: 1964.*

taken at least eighteen months to show significant results in reducing the rate of price increases, judging from the postwar Latin American experience.

In early 1952 the government became impatient. Perón announced a new stabilization plan with great fanfare. It coincided with the inauguration of the second Five Year Plan, which included much greater attention to the need for raising productivity, augmenting agricultural production, and increasing investment in neglected infrastructural areas such as transportation and energy.

The anti-inflation program, again drafted by Finance Minister Gomez Morales, called for a two-year wage freeze.[19] Perón's adoption of such a policy revealed once more the president's confidence in his ability to hold labor's loyalty in the face of their continued material losses. An intricate system of consultative procedures among representatives of labor, industry, and government was to decide on all wage and price hikes.

In fact, this new plan came just as the 1949 program was beginning to bear fruit. The inflation rate (cost of living for Buenos Aires) rose only 4.3 percent in 1953 and 3.5 percent in 1954, a dramatic drop from the annual average of 33.3 percent for the preceding three-year period. For 1955 (Perón was in office for only eight months of that year, since he was overthrown by a military coup in September 1955), the rate went up to 12.5 percent. GDP also resumed its growth, recording an increase of 5.4 percent in 1953, 4.1 percent in 1954, and 7.1 percent in 1955 (see table 8). In short, between 1952 and 1955, the Argentine economy enjoyed the "go" phase of the stop-and-go pattern evident throughout the postwar period.

The BOP also showed improvement. Goods and services produced a surplus of $356 million in 1953 and $86 million in 1954, although they slipped into a significant deficit ($239 million) in 1955. These variations occurred within a relatively static range. Surpluses were produced by constricting imports rather than as a result of any steady growth in export earnings. Furthermore, the latter were at the mercy of the weather, which brought devastating droughts in 1949 and 1951–1952. That meant that Argentina was failing to finance the minimum of imported inputs necessary to maintain and modernize its capital base. Domestic growth continued to be subordinated to the foreign exchange bottleneck.

Despite their rhetoric in the 1952 stabilization plan, the government's economic policy makers eased up on credit controls. In the "go" cycle it was necessary to provide liquidity for expansion. The average stock of money and quasi money rose by 15.3 percent in 1953, 8.1 percent in 1954, and 5.5 percent in 1955, the highest annual rates of increase since the war except for 1948 (5.7 percent).[20]

Table 8. Argentina: Real GDP
(at factor prices of 1960)

Year	Total GDP		Manufacturing		Agriculture		Per Capita GDP	
	Billions of Pesos	Annual Variation (%)	Billions of Pesos	Annual Variation (%)	Billions of Pesos	Annual Variation (%)	Thousands of Pesos	Annual Variation (%)
1950	689	—	192	—	124	—	412	—
1951	715	3.8	197	2.6	133	7.3	420	1.9
1952	679	-5.0	194	-1.5	114	-14.3	392	-6.7
1953	716	5.4	193	-0.5	149	30.7	407	3.8
1954	745	4.1	208	7.8	148	-0.7	414	1.7
1955	798	7.1	233	12.0	154	4.1	436	5.3
1956	820	2.8	249	6.9	147	-4.5	441	1.1
1957	862	5.1	269	8.0	146	-0.7	456	3.4
1958	916	6.3	292	8.6	153	4.8	477	4.6
1959	857	-6.4	261	-10.6	151	-1.3	437	-8.4
1960	925	7.9	288	10.3	154	2.0	465	6.4
1961	991	7.1	317	10.1	153	-0.6	490	5.4
1962	974	-1.7	299	-5.7	159	3.9	475	-3.1
1963	951	-2.4	287	-4.0	162	1.9	457	-3.8
1964	1050	10.4	341	18.8	173	6.8	495	8.3
1965	1146	9.1	388	13.8	184	6.4	533	7.7
1966	1154	0.7	392	1.0	177	-3.8	529	-0.8
1967	1183	2.5	397	1.3	184	4.0	533	0.8
1968	1238	4.6	424	6.8	177	-3.8	550	3.2
1969	1336	7.9	471	11.1	184	4.0	583	6.0
1970	1391	4.1		—	187	1.6	600	2.9

Sources: Calculated from Banco Central de la Republica Argentina, *Origen del producto y distribución del ingreso, 1950–69*, supp. to *Boletín Estadístico*, no. 1 (January 1971).
  Note: Tables 4 and 8 represent two time series which do not always agree for the overlapping years. I have therefore given both series.

Even though wage rates were supposedly frozen between 1952 and 1954, enough increases occurred so that the average real hourly wage rates rose 7.8 percent in 1953 and 6.9 percent in 1954. With the recrudescence of inflation in 1955, that index declined 1.1 percent. In fact, taking the period through 1954, real wages *per worker* never regained their 1949 level. Of equal interest, however, is the fact that between 1949 and 1955 the share of total net national income going to wages and salaries maintained the relatively high level of 57–61 percent. By contrast, in 1945 the level had been only 47 percent.[21]

In sum, the 1952–1955 period produced evidence of significant short-term success in fighting inflation. Prices increased at a lower rate for each of those three years than for any year since 1945. Perón had applied severe wage and credit constraints from 1949 to 1952 and thereafter reaped the "benefits" of his orthodox policy, although at the cost of low growth during stabilization. In retrospect, it seems unlikely that a government elected under a more open system could have survived the 1949–1952 phase of Perón's stabilization policy. Clearly the low growth and decline in real wage rates (partly regained by 1955) helped to disillusion some of Perón's supporters. It is thus noteworthy evidence of the political perils of stabilization.[22]

Brazil, 1953–1964: Stabilization Failures

Brazil also faced rapid inflation and continuous BOP deficits after 1948 (see tables 1 and 9).[23] By 1953 something had to be done. In that year President Getúlio Vargas (1951–1954) began Brazil's first serious postwar attempt at stabilization. It started with devaluation and the adoption of multiple exchange rates (see table 3). The latter were intended to give the government flexibility in earning the maximum foreign exchange value for Brazilian coffee exports, for which it was assumed that foreign demand was largely price inelastic. Wage policy became a bitterly debated issue, as the government pondered how much to increase the minimum wage, last raised in December 1951. In the interim, real wage rates had declined significantly (see table 10).

Less than a year after launching his stabilization program, Vargas allowed it to be sabotaged. He permitted his young labor minister, João Goulart, to increase the minimum wage 100 percent—which put the real minimum wage far above any year since 1945.[24] Vargas had jettisoned wage restraint in an attempt to mobilize labor support against the political enemies closing in around him. But it was too late. When Vargas chose suicide as his way out of the political crisis in August 1954, stabilization had long since been forgotten.

In the decade between the death of Vargas in 1954 and the coup of

1964 there were four more attempts at stabilization. None succeeded. The caretaker government that succeeded Vargas (President João Café Filho) lacked the time and political clout to carry out full-scale stabilization, although an attempt was made. The most important stabilization effort of this decade was launched in 1958 by President Juscelino Kubitschek (1956–1961), who had begun his presidency by giving first priority to an ambitious industrialization policy (the "Programa de Metas" which was to bring "fifty years' progress in five") and to extensive public works (especially the building of Brasília). Both goals were achieved, but only by exacerbating inflation and the BOP deficit. Like Vargas, Kubitschek agreed to a vigorous stabilization program, announced in October 1958. Within a year the costs of reducing inflation loomed large. The IMF was insisting on restraint in public

Table 9. Brazil: Balance of Payments
(in millions of U.S. dollars)

Year	Trade Balance	Capital Account	Errors and Omissions
1946	N.A.		
1947	−145.1	203.3	−58.2
1948	−37.3	23.5	13.8
1949	−117.8	7.4	110.4
1950	107.7	−91.6	−16.1
1951	−467.5	345.4	122.1
1952	−708.0	757.3	−49.3
1953	30.0	45.0	−75.0
1954	−230.0	212.0	18.0
1955	−27.0	−6.0	33.0
1956	20.0	34.0	−54.0
1957	−285.0	425.0	−140.0
1958	−264.0	475.0	−211.0
1959	−340.0	335.0	5.0
1960	−521.0	511.0	10.0
1961	−276.0	227.0	49.0
1962	−461.0	601.0	−140.0
1963	−186.0	306.0	−120.0
1964	39.0	81.0	−120.0
1965	209.0	−178.0	−31.0
1966	−110.0	135.0	−25.0
1967	−353.0	388.0	−35.0
1968	−548.0	549.0	−1.0
1969	−367.0	387.0	−20.0
1970	−502.0	613.0	−111.0

Source: IMF, *Balance of Payments Yearbook*.

spending as a condition for its help. Other creditors, in turn, waited for the signal of creditworthiness from the IMF.

Kubitschek gambled; he decided to denounce the IMF's conditions and press on with his economic program. By *ad hoc* financing abroad and loose fiscal and monetary policies at home, Brazil managed to maintain a high growth rate through the end of Kubitschek's presi-

Table 10. Brazil: Change in Minimum
Real Wage Rates Between Official
Adjustments for Guanabara
(Greater Rio de Janeiro)

Year	Change (%)
1947	−11.0
1948	6.7
1949	8.4
1950	−3.9
1951	−2.0
1952	−7.2
1953	−12.2
1954	48.1
1955	−10.3
1956	17.1
1957	2.4
1958	−7.9
1960 (Oct)	−6.5[a]
1961 (Oct)	8.9
1962 (Dec)	−9.5
1964 (Feb)	−14.3
1965 (Feb)	−1.2
1966 (Feb)	−3.3
1967 (Feb)	−9.3
1968 (Mar)	−3.4
1969 (Apr)	−0.7
1970 (Apr)	−2.5
1971 (Apr)	−1.9
1972 (Apr)	1.0
1973 (Apr)	3.8
1974 (Apr)	1.1

Sources: Figures for 1947–1958 from Raouf Kahil, *Inflation and Economic Development in Brazil* (Oxford: Oxford University Press, 1973), table II.13. Figures for 1958–1974 calculated from data in Kenneth Mericle, "Conflict Regulation in the Brazilian Industrial Relations System" (Ph.D. dissertation, University of Wisconsin, 1974).
a. Two-year period.

dency. His success in maintaining economic growth despite persistent inflation (see table 11) seemed to confirm the heterodox theories of inflation. Some economists even suggested that inflation was a serendipitously effective device to generate forced savings.

But when President Jânio Quadros assumed office in 1961 there could be no ignoring the endemic inflation and constant pressure from foreign creditors. Brazil's foreign exchange earnings and capital inflows were clearly inadequate to service the large short-term foreign debt accumulated in recent years. During his seven months in office, Quadros began a tough stabilization program, including a sizable devaluation of the cruzeiro (see table 3). His policy was beginning to provoke opposition when Quadros abruptly resigned in August 1961.

Table 11. Brazil, Real GDP (in 1949 prices)

| Year | Total GDP | | Industry, Annual Variation (%) | Agriculture, Annual Variation (%) | Per Capita GDP, Annual Variation (%) |
	Millions of Cruzeiros	Annual Variation (%)			
1948	215.6	7.4	11.3	6.9	4.7
1949	229.9	6.6	10.3	4.5	4.3
1950	244.8	6.5	11.3	1.5	4.0
1951	259.3	6.0	6.4	6.9	2.8
1952	281.9	8.7	5.0	9.1	5.6
1953	289.0	2.5	8.7	0.2	−0.5
1954	318.2	10.1	8.7	7.9	7.0
1955	340.0	6.9	10.6	7.7	3.7
1956	350.8	3.2	6.9	−0.2	0.2
1957	379.1	8.1	5.7	9.3	4.9
1958	408.3	7.7	16.2	2.0	4.6
1959	431.1	5.6	11.9	5.3	2.4
1960	472.9	9.7	9.6	4.9	6.6
1961	521.6	10.3	10.6	7.6	7.2
1962	549.0	5.3	7.8	5.5	2.3
1963	557.5	1.5	0.2	1.0	−1.3
1964	573.8	2.9	5.2	1.3	0.0
1965	589.5	2.7	−4.7	13.8	−0.1
1966	619.6	5.1	11.7	−3.1	2.2
1967	649.2	4.8	3.0	5.7	1.8
1968	709.7	9.3	15.5	1.4	6.3
1969	773.6	9.0	10.8	6.0	5.9
1970	847.2	9.5	11.1	5.6	6.4
1971	942.8	11.1	11.2	11.4	8.2
1972	1,040.8	10.4	13.8	4.5	7.3
1973	1,159.4	11.4	15.0	3.5	8.2

Source: Calculated from data in *Conjuntura Econômica* (May 1974).

His successor, Vice President João Goulart, was at first shackled by a parliamentary system which right-wing military leaders had forced the Congress to create in return for Goulart's succession to the presidency. After achieving full presidential powers in January 1963, Goulart endorsed a stabilization plan drawn up by the well-known economist Celso Furtado and Finance Minister Santiago Dantas. But their policies soon aroused the familiar protests against wage and credit restrictions. Both inflation and the BOP deficit worsened under Goulart, who gave up any serious anti-inflation effort after Dantas resigned as finance minister in the middle of 1963. The deepening economic crisis was a key factor in increasing military support for the conspirators who ousted the president in early 1964. No government since the end of Kubitschek's presidency had been able to find the will and the political strength to pursue a "successful" stabilization program. As we shall see below, Argentina exhibited a similar pattern of failure.

Argentina: 1955–1966: Stabilization Failures

For three years after Perón's ouster, military caretaker regimes governed Argentina.[25] When the first national elections were held in 1958 (with Peronist candidates barred), Arturo Frondizi won the presidency. His ambitions for industrialization were similar to Kubitschek's, although the Argentine economy offered less room to maneuver. Unlike Kubitschek, however, Frondizi quickly committed his country to an ambitious stabilization program. In line with IMF and World Bank thinking, Frondizi sharply devalued the peso. Since the step was long overdue, it had an enormous impact on domestic prices, which rose 113.9 percent in 1959, the second year of the Frondizi regime. The result was a decline of 20.5 percent in real wage rates (see table 5). Although the inflation rate was much lower thereafter (it dropped to 27.3 percent in 1960 and 13.5 percent in 1961), the policies cost heavily in terms of political support. Labor denounced the decline in real wages. Nationalists ridiculed the commitments (reduction of workers on the deficit-ridden state railways, etc.) extracted by the IMF and the World Bank in return for promising to help finance Frondizi's ambitious development plans.

Argentina once again experienced the "stop-and-go" pattern typical of postwar stabilization efforts. Frondizi's government had tried to pursue development and stabilization at the same time. In return it got continued (although declining) inflation (which apparently could be arrested only at the cost of stagnation) *and* BOP deficits (which threatened the financing of imports vital for industrialization). The president was caught in an impossible political position, between the

Peronists on the left and the military on the right. When the Peronists were given the right to run their own candidates in the 1962 elections (for the first time since 1955), they scored wide victories. That was too much for the anti-Peronist military. They deposed Frondizi and arranged for another civilian government to take office.

The politician who inherited the legacy of Frondizi's aborted stabilization attempt was Arturo Illia (1962–1966), a faithful if colorless Radical. During his four-year term, inflation averaged 25.7 percent, never dropping below 22 percent. This record was understandable, since the economic policy makers of the Illia government, realistically enough, expected only to stabilize the rate of inflation, not reduce it to zero. The BOP improved, but because of the stop-and-go tactics that continued to hinder Argentina's long-term growth. Once again the stabilization efforts aroused militant Peronist opposition. Like Frondizi before him, Illia was ousted in 1966 by military officers disturbed at the continuing Peronist electoral successes.

Brazilian experience up to April 1964 and Argentine experience up to June 1966 had made certain lessons very clear. The elected politicians seemed unable to find any formula that would cure rapid inflation and increase foreign exchange earnings while also achieving significant growth in the short run. As a result, any elected government which pursued a "successful" stabilization program could expect to undermine its own political position. Then how could inflation be controlled?

Mexico, 1951–1956:
Preparing for Price Stability and Growth

Mexico offers an interesting contrast to the Brazilian and Argentine experiences.[26] In the immediate postwar years Mexico appeared to be suffering the kind of endemic inflation that Argentina and Brazil were to experience after the mid-1950s (see table 1). The rate of price increase was high by the standards of the day—25 percent in 1946 and 12.6 percent in 1947. Successive deficits in the balance of trade led Mexican authorities to worry that the peso had become seriously overvalued (see table 12).

This disequilibrium in the foreign sector grew worse, prompting the Mexican government to devalue in 1949 (see table 3). One of the immediate results was an increase in the rate of internal inflation, which averaged 12.6 percent for 1950–1952. In 1952 real wage rates actually dropped 13.4 percent (see table 13). In 1954 the Mexican authorities once again grew concerned over the external sector, although effec-

Table 12. Mexico: Balance of Payments
(in millions of U.S. dollars)

Year	Trade Balance	Capital Account	Errors and Omissions
1946	−186.6	101.1	85.5
1947	−222.0	204.8	17.2
1948	−87.5	80.7	6.8
1949	30.9	−23.3	−7.6
1950	41.8	−92.8	51.0
1951	−110.9	83.5	27.4
1952	−48.9	103.8	−54.9
1953	−121.7	78.6	43.1
1954	−23.6	121.7	−98.1
1955	153.4	−47.0	−106.4
1956	−47.1	138.5	−91.4
1957	−200.2	235.9	−15.7
1958	−202.4	269.8	−67.4
1959	−44.7	103.3	−58.6
1960	−318.9	200.9	118.0
1961	−214.9	295.0	−80.1
1962	−156.1	175.6	−19.5
1963	−200.2	137.3	62.9
1964	−407.8	589.5	−181.7
1965	−398.0	180.0	218.0
1966	−391.0	584.0	−193.0
1967	−635.0	647.0	−12.0
1968	−757.0	201.0	556.0
1969	−609.0	868.0	−259.0
1970	−1057.0	721.0	336.0

Source: IMF, *Balance of Payments Yearbook.*

tively concealing their concern from the public. When Mexico again devalued in 1954, it hit the exchange markets as a shock. This time the peso was to remain significantly undervalued and thereby furnish a stimulus for Mexican exports. Competitive pricing of exports was more important for Mexico than for Argentina and Brazil, because Mexico's more diversified export list meant Mexicans could anticipate greater price elasticity of foreign demand for the goods and services they exported.[27] It should also be noted that Mexico's largest single foreign exchange earner was tourism, especially from the United States.

But this stimulus to the BOP was soon reflected in domestic price increases. The rate of inflation soared to a record level of 25.9 percent for 1954 and the following year was at 16 percent. Despite widespread popular protest, the government persevered. By 1956 the inflation rate was back down (4.9 percent), and the conservative money managers at the Bank of Mexico and the Finance Ministry consolidated their control over economic policy-making.

Mexico subsequently compiled an impressive record of price stability between 1956 and 1970, with inflation averaging 4 percent annually and exceeding 6 percent only once (1958). As a result, Mexico was able to pursue a growth policy (see table 14) in which price stability and a unified exchange rate made that country very attractive to foreign investors. Among the many factors which contributed to this record, decisive monetary policy was extremely important.[28] This policy was only possible because the politicians of the official government party (Partido Revolucionario Institucional or PRI) furnished an impregnable political base for conservative money managers, such as Antonio Ortíz Mena, minister of the treasury between 1958 and 1970. It seems reasonable to ask whether a freely elected government could have resisted the short-term interest-group pressures against such a policy. Another crucial factor was the government's control of the labor union movement, which was maintained by co-optation of cooperative labor leaders and by repression of the rebellious.[29] Finally, it is important to note that the benefits of this relatively inflation-free, conservative

Table 13. Mexico: Real Wage Rates

Year	Annual Change (%)
1951	−3.0
1952	−13.4
1953	7.1
1954	5.6
1955	−2.1
1956	5.4
1957	−2.0
1958	−2.1
1959	8.5
1960	3.9
1961	1.9
1962	8.3
1963	16.2
1964	8.0
1965	2.0
1966	0.0
1967	4.0
1968	2.6
1969	1.9
1970	1.2

Source: Calculated from volumes of IMF, *International Financial Statistics.*

macroeconomic management were distributed very unequally in Mexico, with business and commercial agriculture gaining far more than the rural poor.[30]

The inability of Brazil and Argentina to control inflation in the early 1960s added to the sense of desperation felt by politicians there. In both cases the military attempted to break the deadlock.

Brazil, 1964–1968: Triumph for the Gradualist Strategy?

In 1964 Goulart's ineffectual regime was swept aside by a conspiratorial movement in which the military held the upper hand.[31] Army General Humberto de Alencar Castelo Branco, a leading conspirator, was elected president by the Congress shortly after the coup. Direction of economic policy was delegated to Roberto Campos and Octávio Gouvéia de Bulhões, economists who had participated in the unsuccessful Brazilian stabilization efforts of 1955–1956 and 1958–1959. They were given broad powers, not only to fight inflation, but also to launch a major reorganization of institutions in the public sector. Campos proved to be the dominant figure. His economic team reduced inflation from 86.6 percent in 1964 to 45.5 percent in 1965, and 41.2 percent in 1966, a record which fell far short of its announced goals, although Brazil was soon to show it could combine growth with a stabilized rate of inflation. The figure for 1967, which saw the inauguration of a new government in April, was 24.1 percent. The short-run BOP situation also improved greatly, but this success came at the cost of virtual stagnation in per capita growth. Furthermore, real wage rates fell significantly over the three-year period (see table 10). The Castelo Branco government was able to sustain its unpopular program only by increasing its reliance on authoritarian methods.

Delfim Neto, the finance minister who replaced Campos as economic czar in 1967 when General Artur da Costa e Silva succeeded Castelo Branco in the presidency, decided to revise the strategy. He gambled on the assumption that excess demand was no longer a problem—indeed, that demand should be stimulated. He loosened credit, which led to a surge of growth. His assumption proved correct, and the new growth was not accompanied by any increase in inflation.

A crucial moment for the new government occurred in 1968. A wave of wildcat industrial strikes in the interior state of Minas Gerais spread to the industrial heartland of São Paulo.[32] Worker dissatisfaction was hardly surprising, given the fact that real wage rates had been driven down steadily over the last four years. The government reacted uncertainly to the strikes in Minas Gerais. By the time the unrest reached São

Table 14. Mexico: Real GDP (in 1950 pesos)

Year	Total GDP Millions of Pesos	Total GDP Annual Variation (%)	Manufacture Millions of Pesos	Manufacture Annual Variation (%)	Agriculture Millions of Pesos	Agriculture Annual Variation (%)	Per Capita GDP Pesos	Per Capita GDP Annual Variation (%)
1945	30,473	—	5,915	—	3,815	—	1,328	—
1946	32,477	6.6	6,469	9.4	3,857	1.1	1,378	3.8
1947	33,761	4.0	6,575	1.6	4,247	10.1	1,394	1.2
1948	35,278	4.5	6,989	6.3	4,709	10.9	1,417	1.7
1949	37,424	6.1	7,491	7.2	5,405	14.8	1,463	3.2
1950	41,060	9.7	8,437	12.6	5,999	11.0	1,562	6.8
1951	44,217	7.7	9,332	10.6	6,299	5.0	1,635	4.7
1952	45,933	3.9	9,744	4.4	6,017	-4.5	1,650	0.9
1953	46,029	0.2	9,632	-1.1	6,053	0.6	1,604	-2.8
1954	50,859	10.5	10,575	9.8	7,571	25.1	1,718	7.1
1955	55,312	8.8	11,605	9.7	8,417	11.2	1,810	5.4
1956	58,962	6.6	12,915	11.3	7,931	-5.8	1,868	3.2
1957	63,431	7.6	13,763	6.6	8,669	9.3	1,945	4.1
1958	66,918	5.5	14,500	5.4	9,430	8.8	1,985	2.1
1959	66,852	-0.1	15,800	9.0	8,711	-7.6	1,976	-.05
1960	74,317	11.2	17,116	8.3	9,178	5.4	2,062	4.4
1961	76,927	3.5	17,726	3.6	9,417	2.6	2,064	0.1
1962	81,742	6.3	18,862	6.4	10,013	6.3	2,095	1.5
1963	85,865	5.0	20,597	9.2	10,163	1.5	2,154	2.8
1964	94,601	10.2	23,523	14.2	10,986	8.1	2,293	6.5
1965	99,616	5.3	25,202	7.1	11,579	5.4	2,334	1.8
1966	107,238	7.7	27,999	11.1	11,764	1.6	2,429	4.1
1967	114,262	6.5	30,294	8.2	11,940	1.5	2,500	2.9

Source: Leopoldo Solís, *La realidad económica mexicana: Retrovisión y perspectivas* (Mexico: Siglo Veintiuno, 1970), tables III-1, III-2.

Paulo, however, there was no longer any hesitation. Strike leaders were arrested, protesters clubbed, and sympathetic Catholic clergy were interned, some even tortured. In short, four years after the advent of a tough stabilization policy, government leaders were still willing to use suppression against organizers of worker resistance. The 1968 strikes only made the military government *more* determined to impose its will. And they had confidence their strategy would work.

The Costa e Silva government soon felt itself justified by the resurgence of growth, which reached 9.3 percent for 1968. After 1968 Brazil's growth rate remained very high, averaging about 10 percent annually (see table 11). Brazil sharply increased exports and attracted a large flow of foreign capital, primarily in the form of loans. An ingenious policy of indexation of contractual obligations ("monetary correction") allowed Brazil to live with persistent inflation (between 21 and 24 percent through 1970), and the policy of frequent minidevaluations kept Brazilian exports competitive. All this was achieved by an authoritarian government which pursued its alleged enemies ruthlessly and gave no sign of an early return to an open political system.

Argentina, 1966–1970: Brilliance and Defeat

In 1966, two years after the Brazilian coup, the military also seized power in Argentina. This coup, led by General Juan Carlos Onganía, appeared to be more profound than any since Perón's overthrow in 1955. In deposing President Illia, the Argentine officers claimed for themselves a moral mission similar in rhetoric to that of the Brazilian military rebels two years earlier. The Argentine military, like their Brazilian counterparts, looked to the civilian sector for their chief economic policy maker.[33] The Argentine counterpart of Roberto Campos was Adalbert Krieger Vasena, an able economist who, like Campos, had served in several previous administrations but had remained critical of their inadequate stabilization efforts.[34] Now the military offered Krieger Vasena the umbrella of extraordinary powers. He quickly accepted the finance ministry and formulated a stringent stabilization plan which involved holding down wages and encouraging foreign investment.

Krieger Vasena's program *did* dramatically lower the rate of inflation, bringing it down from 31.9 percent in 1966 to 29.2 percent in 1967, then 16.2 percent in 1968 and only 7.6 percent in 1969. It appeared as if Argentina might be bettering the post-1964 Brazilian performance, while also maintaining growth that was extraordinarily high for a stabilization phase—2.5 percent in 1967, 4.6 percent in 1968, and 7.9 percent in 1969 (see table 8). Brazil, on the other hand, did not resume significant per capita growth until the fourth year of the military-backed stabilization program (1968). Indeed, the Onganía regime seemed to be well entrenched, partly because it had encountered less labor resistance than might have been expected and had even enjoyed the support of some important union leaders, such as Augusto Vandor. Thus, the sudden eruption of conflict in May 1969 in Córdoba, Argentina's second most important industrial center, came as a shock to the government. Confrontation with labor in Córdoba led to a full-scale political crisis after a bloody clash between the army and workers in what became known as the *Cordobazo*. The local army command lost control when trying to prevent protest marches. The troops fired, and the slaughter in the streets caused a revulsion among the public. It launched the kind of militant opposition that the military regime had previously escaped.[35]

The conflict bore many apparent similarities to the wildcat strikes of Brazilian workers in 1968. Whereas the Brazilian military saw popular protests in 1968 as a cause for more repressive measures, the Argentine officers (or at least enough of them to force a shift in policy) lost confidence in their mission. At least one wing of the Argentine military saw the violence as a sign that the government had lost its legitimacy. They were not prepared to continue supporting the Onganía regime's policies amidst such bloodshed. When Krieger's brilliantly conceived program had already seemed to be paying off, the government lost its political base.

The contrast with Brazil is all the more striking in view of the fact that real wages of Argentine workers had declined significantly less than those of Brazilian workers (compare tables 5 and 10).[36] But when it came to violent social conflict, the military in Argentina were much more seriously divided than the Brazilian military.[37] In part, this might be explained by the fact that Argentine urban workers had a far more independent union structure and a much greater tradition of militancy than their Brazilian counterparts. Krieger Vasena, embittered by the rapid decline in support, resigned soon after the *Cordobazo*. His successor, José Maria Dagnino Pastore, sought to push growth in a continuation of Krieger's policy.[38] But time had run out, and General Onganía himself fell victim to a coup at the hands of his fellow officers in 1970.[39]

Argentina was therefore unable to follow up stabilization with a new period of growth (assuming that a major reduction in inflation was the necessary prerequisite for sound growth). Looking back over the postwar era in Argentina, we see that both "successful" programs of stabilization—Perón's in 1952 and Onganía's in 1966—were dropped after three years. In neither instance did the stabilizing regime last long enough to gather the economic fruits of its unpopular measures. And the successor governments in both 1955 and 1970 were too divided to pursue *any* coherent long-term policy. It would appear from the Argentine experience that an authoritarian (such as the military government of Onganía) or a semiauthoritarian political base (the second presidential term of Perón) was a *necessary* condition for the control of inflation. Yet even these governments did not survive long enough to achieve sustained growth. Indeed, no postwar Argentine government has developed a politically viable strategy for sustained growth without rapid inflation.

After 1970, Argentina experienced a succession of weak military regimes. None offered hope of surviving long enough to allow economic policy makers to go beyond short-run policies. Inflation rates shot up again, while stagnation in exports left the country unable to finance vital imports. As a result, growth lagged, once again leaving Argentina with the worst of both worlds.

Conclusions

Why has stabilization proved so difficult to pursue, especially for elected governments (but also for military regimes in Argentina)? The reasons are several. First, stabilization programs have invariably led to a decline in real wage rates, at least in the short run. In theory, stabilization would not *have* to result in declining real wage rates. One can easily design (on paper) a strategy in which workers would maintain their real wage rate levels. In fact, however, real wage rates have declined in all four cases studied here, either through deliberate policy (Brazil, 1964–1968) or as a result of the manner in which stabilization was implemented. In none of the four successful stabilizations has the government avoided imposing this sacrifice on workers. Naturally, workers were unhappy. Their opposition, however, varied according to the structure of unions, the historical militancy of workers, and the degree of police repression. It seems fair to conclude that variation in the character of the labor movement (which may in turn be attributable to the level of economic development) is the most important single variable in explaining the success or failure of stabilization programs.[40]

The second common element in all four successful stabilization efforts was a sharp devaluation. Although the devaluation was designed primarily to adjust the exchange rate downward to compensate for past domestic inflation, the short-run consequence was a further increase in the domestic price of all goods and services with an import component (insofar as multiple exchange rates were not used to reduce this effect). It also resulted in higher earnings for exporters (insofar as the new prices paid by foreign customers were translated directly into domestic currency). Thus, a government could find itself forcing up domestic prices (affecting especially urban consumers) while at the same time rewarding a small social sector (exporters, especially in the case of agricultural exports). Resistance could therefore be expected from city dwellers, who include the political elements most likely to protest the higher prices earned by the rural exporters. It was in part to neutralize this effect that Perón turned to IAPI, the government's foreign trade monopoly, to channel the foreign exchange earnings from wheat and beef, and was thus able to control the earnings of the landowners. [41] Brazilian governments pursued a similar policy vis-à-vis coffee growers in the 1950s (although it was *not* a part of a successful stabilization), when the government expropriated a portion of coffee's foreign exchange earnings (*confisco cambial*) in order to finance imports necessary for industrialization.[42] This multiple exchange rate system, introduced in Brazil in 1953, was also used to subsidize the domestic price of wheat and oil, two imports which had an immediate impact on urban consumers, in the form of bread and bus fares.

We should also remember the international context of these devaluations. The IMF almost invariably required them as part of the stabilization program the fund had to approve before it would authorize any drawings from the fund. The IMF logic was clear: Overvalued exchange rates were an inevitable consequence of rapidly rising domestic prices and had rendered exports too expensive and imports too cheap. Chronic deficits in the BOP resulted. The cure lay in a more "realistic" exchange rate.

Stabilization has been accompanied by a third unpopular feature—painful credit restrictions for the private sector. In all four cases government credit policy alienated domestic businessmen (pinched for both long-term and short-term capital), who became yet another political sector opposed to paying what they saw as unfair costs in the cause of stabilization.

Taken together, these three policy consequences—declining real wage rates, higher prices for import components (along with increased earnings for exporters), and tightened credit—have constituted such a political liability as to erode more public support than any freely elected government could afford to lose. That result is apparent in the frequent scuttling of stabilization attempts, such as 1953–1954, 1955–1956, 1958–1959, 1961, and 1962–1963 in Brazil, and 1958–1962 in Argentina. Even the "successful" Argentine stabilizations of 1949–1955 and 1966–1969 ended with the fall of the chief economic planners (Gomez Morales and Krieger Vasena), along with the head of state, either at the same time (Perón) or shortly thereafter (Onganía).

From the postwar experiences of Argentina, Brazil, and Mexico we can draw some further conclusions about the relationships between economic policy-making and regime type: (1) governments in competitive political systems find it *extremely* difficult to reduce inflation, once it has exceeded 20 percent, and they have paid very high political costs for their efforts; (2) no such government has proved able to pursue a successful (as defined earlier) anti-inflation effort; (3) all the cases of successful stabilization have been carried out by authoritarian (or one-party) governments; and (4) even authoritarian governments must have a high degree of internal consensus to carry through a successful stabilization.

Let us summarize the political evidence which supports these conclusions. The coups against Goulart in Brazil in 1964 and Illia in Argentina in 1966 show how an economic crisis associated with inflation can push electoral systems toward authoritarianism. In both cases a government which had been chosen by direct popular election (although with Peronist candidates barred in Argentina) had been unable to reduce inflation rates which were then exceeding an annual rate of 20 percent. Both governments had maintained the official exchange rate at seriously overvalued levels because they feared the political consequences of devaluation and did not want to acknowledge the de facto depreciation of their currency. Both governments were swept aside by military conspirators who regarded stabilization as urgently necessary. The military were prepared to provide the political base for the stabilization efforts of civilian technocrats, since the officers favoring a coup thought an essential part of their mission was to create a regime strong enough to produce "order" in the economy.

In the other two cases, Argentina in 1949–1955 and Mexico in 1951–1959, semiauthoritarian (or noncompetitive) regimes already in power saw inflation rising above 20 percent. Stabilization was then carried out successfully (as defined earlier) by these governments, which had powers much greater than those of popularly elected regimes.

Finally, a word is in order about several economic aspects of the four cases of successful stabilization analyzed here. Two (Argentina, 1952–1955, and Mexico, 1951–1956) occurred in the first half of the 1950s, before inflation had become so endemic or so institutionalized in Latin America. Of the remaining two successful cases, both in the 1960s, one (Argentina, 1966–1970) did not create the base for a resumption of growth nor was the subsequent government able to maintain control over prices, which had shot up again by 1971. In the 1960s, only Brazil (1964–1968) proved able to combine stabilization with the resumption of sustained growth. But the anti-inflationary side of that policy consisted of stabilizing the rate of price increases at a relatively high level, approximately 20 percent per annum. In short, the Brazilians institutionalized a continuing rate of inflation which in the 1950s the IMF and most economists in the developed world would have thought intolerably high. And even bringing Brazil's inflation rate down to that "stabilized" level of 20 percent was accomplished only by a frankly authoritarian regime.

How valid are these conclusions? Is the sample adequate, since it consists of only three countries over only twenty-five years (1945–1970)?[43] It might further be objected that these conclusions are based on an oversimplified analysis, because the type of political regime (authoritarian versus competitive) has been correlated with only one variable, inflation. What about other causal factors which help explain the breakdown of democratic regimes? Have not sectoral conflicts over land reform or nationalization of foreign enterprises helped cause military leaders to believe that the elected government was heading for an irreversible change in social structure? Have not military officers intervened simply to protect the property and privileges of the middle and upper sectors, whose hegemony was threatened by the political mobilization of the lower sectors?

The conclusions in this chapter are obviously compatible with these and other explanations based on models including more variables. In countries with genuinely competitive electoral systems, for example, rapid inflation may be only one factor accelerating political polarization by frightening the middle sectors into supporting authoritarian measures which in the end also save the upper sector. In that case the danger to the government comes not simply from the social tension generated by inflation, but from the manner in which that tension is translated into new political alliances.

We cannot conclude without noting that this essay has raised several questions which deserve further research and analysis: At what point does a serious attempt at stabilization become unavoidable for a government? Is the precipitating factor rapid price increases or deficits in the balance of payments? If the latter, to what extent have governments attached a separate priority to reducing the rate of price increases, once the BOP deficit is significantly reduced and the outstanding foreign debt satisfactorily refinanced? Why should any powerful social sector strongly support an anti-inflation program per se? What advantage can such sectors expect to gain from stabilization in the short run (say, up to two years)? Finally, what is the relationship among stabilization, growth, and income distribution? The critics of stabilization—especially of the orthodox kind required by foreign creditors—have long argued that orthodox anti-inflation efforts would result in stagnation, sharply unequal social sacrifices, and growing foreign control of the economy. In this study Brazil and Mexico are the only countries which had "successful" stabilizations followed by high growth. Before making that transition, both suffered low growth rates (one year in Mexico but three years in Brazil). Both also appear to have experienced an increasing concentration of income and increased foreign control of key economic sectors.[44] A satisfactory explanation of the nature of the relationship among these phenomena obviously must await a more detailed comparative analysis. The enterprise deserves attention, since the issues in question could hardly be more fundamental for policy makers and populations in the developing world.

NOTES

Very helpful suggestions were made by participants in the Conference on Authoritarianism and Corporatism in Latin America held at the University of Pittsburgh in April 1974, and at the Cliometrics conference at the University of Wisconsin in April 1975, where earlier versions of this paper were presented. Especially valuable comments were also given by Roberto Cortés Conde, Peter Lindert, Joseph Love, Samuel Morley, Jorge Oclander, and Guillermo O'Donnell. I am indebted to Felicity Skidmore, Tom Holloway, Judy Mondello, Michael Kolstad, and Roseanne McKnew for research assistance. The American Philosophical Society and the Woodrow Wilson International Center for Scholars furnished financial support. Thanks are also due Roberto Cortés Conde, former director of the Instituto Torcuato Di Tella, for generously arranging access to the institute's facilities while I was in Buenos Aires.

1. Lord Balogh, an English economist with personal experience of the difficulties of economic policy-making, calls inflation "the most important of the economic ills now facing the Western World" (Thomas Balogh, "Inflation and the New Economy," *Challenge*, 16, no. 5 [November–December 1973]:6–13). By 1974 it was not unusual to hear commentators predicting the dire consequences of continued inflation. A columnist in *Business Week* warned that "if inflation worsens, a trend toward authoritarian governments could develop" (Gene Koretz, "Commentary: Economics," *Business Week*, March 16, 1974). The Cassandra calls of a World Bank bureaucrat are catalogued in Irving S. Friedman, *Inflation: A World-Wide Disaster* (London: Hamish Hamilton, 1973).

2. One feature of Brazilian stabilization policy which has aroused much interest in the United States is indexation (called "monetary correction" in Brazil). For examples of serious debate about indexation's possible value for the U.S. economy, see Walter E. Heller, "Has the Time Come for Indexing?", *Wall Street Journal*, June 20, 1974, and "The Deceptive Lure of Indexation," in *Business Week*, May 25, 1974. For a discussion of the application of indexation in Britain, see Milton Friedman, *Monetary Correction: A Proposal for Escalator Clauses to Reduce the Costs of Ending Inflation*, Institute of Economic Affairs Occasional Paper no. 41 (London, 1974). A very useful comparative study of inflation in Argentina, Brazil,

Chile, and Uruguay is Felipe Pazos, *Chronic Inflation in Latin America* (New York: Praeger, 1972).

3. My assumption is that a focus on the policy problem of stabilization will offer at least a partial insight into the relationship between political systems and public policy formulation. One of the most successful attempts to cast such analysis into a broad framework is the excellent study by Guillermo A. O'Donnell, *Modernization and Bureaucratic-Authoritarianism: Studies in South American Politics*, Politics of Modernization Series, no. 9 (Berkeley: Institute of International Studies, 1973). Much of O'Donnell's comparative analysis of stabilization politics in Argentina and Brazil is relevant to the questions being asked in this paper. Susan Kaufman Purcell's analysis of recent publications on authoritarianism includes studies of Mexico and Brazil ("Authoritarianism," *Comparative Politics*, 5, no. 2 [January 1973]:301–12). Extensive references to the burgeoning literature on corporatism, which is often linked to authoritarianism, may be found in the stimulating collection of essays edited by Fredrick B. Pike and Thomas Stritch, *The New Corporatism: Social-Political Structures in the Iberian World* (Notre Dame: University of Notre Dame Press, 1974).

4. A very useful analysis of differing interpretations of inflation in Latin America may be found in Rosemary Thorp, "Inflation and the Financing of Economic Development," in *Financing Development in Latin America*, ed. Keith Griffin (London: Macmillan, 1971), pp. 182–224. For an interesting analysis of inflation in which the price expectations of labor are stressed, see Samuel A. Morley, *The Economics of Inflation* (Hillsdale, Ill.: Dryden Press, 1971).

5. For a subtle analysis of the social struggles which accompany persistent inflation, see the chapter on Chilean inflation in Albert O. Hirschman, *Journeys Toward Progress: Studies of Economic Policy-Making in Latin America* (New York: Twentieth Century Fund, 1963). I should add that my analysis in this chapter makes no attempt to determine the extent to which government leaders *intended* to carry through their announced stabilization plans. This is obviously an important point, but (by the nature of the evidence) difficult to pursue. I have also not discussed the extent to which governments may favor stabilization as a way to increase their own revenues.

6. Details of this system are given in an IMF-sponsored study: Joseph Gold, *The Stand-By Arrangements of the International Monetary Fund* (Washington, D.C., 1970). The record of IMF operations through 1965 is analyzed in another official publication: Margaret G. de Vries and J. Keith Horsefield, eds., *The International Monetary Fund, 1945–1965: Twenty Years of International Monetary Cooperation* (Washington, D.C., 1969), vol. 2. A radical critique of the fund's operation may be found in Cheryl Payer, *The Debt Trap: The IMF and the Third World* (Harmondsworth, Eng.: Penguin Books, 1974).

7. The close cooperation among the multilateral agencies and other creditors is analyzed with remarkable frankness in Edward S. Mason and Robert E. Asher, *The World Bank Since Bretton Woods* (Washington, D.C.: Brookings Institution, 1973), pp. 538–58. For an excellent critical review of the record of the multilateral agencies, see Werner Baer, "The World Bank Group and the Process of Socio-Economic Development in the Third World," *World Development*, 2, no. 6 (June 1974):1–10. A very useful survey of the activities of the multilateral agencies in Latin America is given in Wolfgang König, "International Financial Institutions and Latin American Development," in *Latin America in the International Economy*, ed. Victor L. Urquidi and Rosemary Thorp (New York: John Wiley, 1973), pp. 116–63.

8. A critical analysis of the multilateral agencies (and USAID) from the radical viewpoint is given in Teresa Hayter, *Aid as Imperialism* (Harmondsworth, Eng.: Penguin Books, 1971). The author gives special emphasis to Latin America, including case studies of Colombia, Chile, Brazil, and Peru.

9. Even the Economic Commission for Latin America (ECLA), which was later to become the bastion of export pessimism, seemed to share the optimism about exports. In its 1948 *Economic Survey of Latin America* eleven countries were grouped under the category of "usual surplus" (including Argentina and Brazil), four as having "usual deficits," and five with a "variable balance" (including Mexico). Classification was based on the net trade data for 1937–1947 (United Nations, ECLA, *Economic Survey of Latin America: 1948* [Doc. E/CN 12], 1949, p. 226). The assumptions underlying export policies in the early postwar years clearly deserve further study.

10. Ironically enough, the Perón regime was building on the precedents—and even some of the governmental institutions—created by the Conservative governments of the 1930–1943 era. This was especially true of exchange rate policy and the marketing of agricultural exports. Further detail may be found in Carlos F. Díaz Alejandro, *Essays on the Economic History of the Argentine Republic* (New Haven: Yale University Press, 1970), pp. 94–106; and Roger Gravil, "State Intervention in Argentina's Export Trade Between the Wars," *Journal of Latin American Studies*, 2, pt. 2 (November 1970):147–73. The clarity and foresight with which these policy instruments were wielded, especially in the 1933–1936 period, is emphasized in a provocative (as yet unpublished) paper by Joseph Tulchin on Argentine foreign policy between 1930 and 1943, which Professor Tulchin kindly made available to me.

11. ECLA's theoretical positions can be found in a volume which attempts to synthesize a number of ECLA publications from the 1950s and 1960s: *Development Problems in Latin America: An Analysis by the United Nations Economic Commission for Latin America* (Austin: University of Texas Press, 1970). See also CEPAL, *El pensamiento de la CEPAL* (Santiago, 1969); and Werner Baer, "The Economics of Prebisch and ECLA," *Economic Development and Cultural Change*, 10, no. 2, pt. 1 (January 1962):169–82.

12. Interestingly enough, neither doctrine per se seemed influential in Argentina under Perón, where rapid inflation was successfully reduced during the president's second term.

13. Anti-inflation policies during the Perón era of 1943–1955 deserve more detailed study than they have yet received. Among the most important analyses are Javier Villanueva, *The Inflationary Process in Argentina, 1943–60*, 2d ed. (Buenos Aires: Instituto Torcuato di Tella, 1966); Eprime Eshag and Rosemary Thorp, "Economic and Social Consequences of Orthodox Economic Policies in Argentina in the Post-War Years," *Bulletin of the Oxford Institute of Economics and Statistics*, 27, no. 1 (February 1965):1–44. The starting point for any serious discussion of modern Argentine economic history is Díaz Alejandro, *Essays*. A stimulating reappraisal of Argentina's postwar economic history is given in Marcelo Diamand, *Doctrinas económicas, desarrollo e independencia* (Buenos Aires: Paidos, 1973). I am indebted to Professor Richard Mallon for allowing me to read several draft chapters of his important study, written with Juan Surrouille, *Economic Policy-making in a Conflict Society: The Argentine Case* (Cambridge: Harvard University Press, forthcoming).

14. It should be noted that a major portion of the foreign exchange reserves Argentina had accumulated by 1945 was in sterling. When England made sterling

inconvertible in 1947, Argentina found her BOP options greatly limited, especially since England had been her most important market. By contrast, the exchange reserves of Brazil and Mexico in 1945 included a much smaller share in sterling.

15. "The Situation in Argentina and the New Economic Policy," *Economic Bulletin for Latin America*, 1, no. 1 (January 1956):30.

16. Gomez Morales's ideas were spelled out in his "Plan de Acción en Materia Economica," presented to a cabinet meeting on June 1, 1959. I wish to thank Sr. Gomez Morales for making available to me the typescript copy of this and other documents in Buenos Aires in August 1972.

17. These data are from Díaz Alejandro, *Essays*, statistical appendix, table 123.

18. Junta Nacional de Carnes, *Estadisticas Básicas: 1964.*

19. Gomez Morales prepared for the Consejo Economico Nacional a detailed analysis of the economy in late 1951: "El Panorama economico del pais en el segundo semestre de 1951 y perspectivas para 1952." I consulted the typescript copy in the possession of Sr. Gomez Morales in Buenos Aires in August 1972.

20. These data are from Díaz Alejandro, *Essays*, statistical appendix, table 123.

21. "The Situation in Argentina," p. 44.

22. For an enlightening analysis of the political dimensions of economic policy-making, see Gilbert W. Merkx, "Sectoral Clashes and Political Change: The Argentine Experience," *Latin American Research Review*, 4, no. 3 (Fall 1969):89–114. A very interesting comparative study of the stabilization efforts of Perón, Frondizi, and Onganía may be found in Gary W. Wynia, "Economic Policy-Making Under Stress: Conflict and Exchange in Argentina," LADAC Occasional Papers, ser. 2, no. 11 (Austin: Institute of Latin American Studies, 1974). Further research will be necessary to determine how Perón's political support fluctuated. A recent study of elections during the Perón era suggests that, at least in Buenos Aires, there was a "growing popular disillusionment with the Peronist regime" after 1948–1949, which may have been a result of the government's economic troubles (Walter Little, "Electoral Aspects of Peronism, 1946–1954," *Journal of Inter-American Studies*, 15, no. 3 [August 1973] : 267–84).

23. Greater detail on Brazilian economic policy in the 1953–1964 period may be found in my *Politics in Brazil, 1930–1964: An Experiment in Democracy* (New York: Oxford University Press, 1967).

24. Raouf Kahil, *Inflation and Economic Development in Brazil, 1946–1963* (Oxford: Oxford University Press, 1973), p. 65. In this painstaking study of the causes of Brazil's inflation Kahil concludes that structural weaknesses did *not* play "a significant role in the evolution of the price level from 1945 to 1964 and that their aggravation towards the end of the period was more an effect than a cause of the acceleration of inflation" (p. 327).

25. Secondary sources on Argentine economic policy from 1955 to 1966 include five works cited earlier: Villanueva, *The Inflationary Process*; Eshag and Thorp, "Economic and Social Consequences"; Díaz Alejandro, *Essays;* Merkx, "Sectoral Clashes"; and Wynia, "Economic Policy-Making." A penetrating study of the relationship between stabilization and the external sector is Díaz Alejandro, *Exchange-Rate Devaluation in a Semi-Industrialized Country: The Experience of Argentina, 1955–1961* (Cambridge: MIT Press, 1965). Valuable also are the chapters by Aldo Ferrer and Mario S. Brodersohn in Aldo Ferrer et al., *Los planes de estabilización en la Argentina* (Buenos Aires: Paidos, 1969).

26. The secondary literature on economic policy-making in Mexico is less satisfactory than that for Argentina and Brazil. In part this can be explained by the

closed political system which Mexican politicians have taken great pains to preserve. One of Mexico's most distinguished historians recently observed that he lived in "a country whose public life is a true mystery" (Daniel Cosío Villegas, in Richard E. Greenleaf and Michael C. Meyer, eds., *Research in Mexican History* [Lincoln: University of Nebraska Press, 1973], p. 4). An ambitious study of Mexico's experience with inflation is B. Griffiths, *Mexican Monetary Policy and Economic Development* (New York: Praeger, 1972), although the author's credentials were sharply challenged in a review by Miguel Wionczek in *Journal of Latin American Studies*, 6, pt. 1 (May 1974):186–88. An indispensable guide to the secondary literature is Leopoldo Solís, "Mexican Economic Policy in the Post-War Period: The Views of Mexican Economists," *American Economic Review*, 61, no. 3, pt. 2, supp. (June 1971):1–67. Valuable surveys of postwar Mexican economic policy are given in Ariel Buira, "Development and Price Stability in Mexico," and Alfredo Navarrete R., "Mexico's Balance of Payments and External Financing," both in *Weltwirtschaftliches Archiv*, 101, no. 2 (1968):49–69, 70–85; Timothy King, *Mexico: Industrialization and Trade Policies Since 1940* (London: Oxford University Press, 1970); and Clark W. Reynolds, *The Mexican Economy: Twentieth-Century Structure and Growth* (New Haven: Yale University Press, 1970), esp. chap. 7. For a very convincing explanation of economic policy formulation in Mexico, see Susan Kaufman Purcell, "Decision-making in an Authoritarian Regime: Theoretical Implications from a Mexican Case Study," *World Politics*, 26, no. 1 (October 1973):28–54.

27. An analysis of the historical variations in the peso's valuation in relation to the U.S. dollar is given in Josué Sáenz, "Problemas Monetarios," *Comercio Exterior* (October 1957):535–38.

28. The ongoing debate over the proper economic policy for Mexico is illustrated in Barry N. Siegel, *Inflación y desarrollo: las experiencias de México* (Mexico: Centro de Estudios Monetarios Latinoamericanos, 1960), and Rodrigo Gómez, "Estabilidad y desarrollo: el caso de México " *Comercio Exterior* (November 1964):778–82, both of whom defended a relatively orthodox monetary approach. An early Mexican "structuralist" critic was Alberto Noriega Herrera, "Las devaluciones monetarias de México, 1938–1954," *Investigación Economica*, 15, no. 1 (1955):149–77.

29. The high degree of government control of the unions is stressed in Roger Hansen, *The Politics of Mexican Development* (Baltimore: Johns Hopkins Press, 1971), pp. 113–16; and José Luis Reyna, *Control político, estabilidad y desarrollo en México*, Cuadernos de CES, no. 3 (Mexico: Centro de Estudios Sociológicos, El Colegio de México, 1974), pp. 24–27.

30. For a systematic critique of the Mexican model, see Fernando Carmona et al., *El milagro mexicano* (Mexico: Ed. Nuestro Tiempo, 1970).

31. Greater detail on economic policy after 1964 in Brazil may be found in my "Politics and Economic Policy Making in Authoritarian Brazil, 1937–71," and Albert Fishlow, "Some Reflections on Post-1964 Brazilian Economic Policy," both in *Authoritarian Brazil: Origins, Politics, and Future*, ed. Alfred Stepan (New Haven: Yale University Press, 1973), pp. 69–118. A very original analysis of the relationship between economic policy makers and the political system both before and after 1964 is given in Celso Lafer, "El sistema político brasileño: algunas características e perspectivas," *Desarrollo Económico*, 14, no. 56 (January–March 1975):641–76. A systematic and sympathetic analysis of the post-1964 policies, along with many data, may be found in Donald E. Syvrud, *Foundations of Brazilian Economic Growth* (Stanford: Hoover Institution Press, 1974). Brazil's recent eco-

nomic history has generated heated debate among its analysts. For a detailed critique from the left, see José Serra, El "milagro" economico brasileño: ¿ realidad o mito? (Buenos Aires: Ed. Periferia, 1972). For the doubts of a much respected economist of the "structuralist" school, see Maria da Conceição Tavares, Da substituição de importações ao capitalismo financeiro: ensaios sôbre economia brasileria (Rio de Janeiro: Zahar, 1973), pp. 153–263. Celso Furtado's more recent criticisms have been spelled out in Analise do "modelo" brasileiro (Rio de Janeiro: Civilização Brasileira, 1972); A hegemonia dos Estados Unidos e o subdesenvolvimento da América Latina (Rio de Janeiro: Civilização Brasileira, 1973); and O mito do desenvolvimento economico (Rio de Janeiro: Paz e Terra, 1974). One of the most articulate defenders of Brazilian government policy has been Mário Henrique Simonsen, who became finance minister in 1974. His views can be found in Brasil 2001 (Rio de Janeiro: APEC, 1969); Brasil 2002 (Rio de Janeiro: Ed. Bloch, 1972); and in his two chapters in Ensaios economicos de Escola de Pos-Graduação em Economia da Fundação Getúlio Vargas (Rio de Janeiro: Ed. Expressão e Cultura, 1974).

32. For a detailed study of these strikes see Francisco C. Weffort, Participação e conflito industrial: Contagem e Osasco 1968, Cadernos CEBRAP, no. 5 (São Paulo: CEBRAP, 1972).

33. For studies of economic policy sympathetic to Finance Minister Krieger Vasena see Juan Carlos de Pablo, Politica Antiinflacionaria en la Argentina, 1967–1970 (Buenos Aires: Amorrortu, 1970); and John Thompson, "Argentine Economic Policy Under the Onganía Regime," Inter-American Economic Affairs, no. 24 (summer 1970):51–75. O'Donnell has given the most subtle and convincing explanation of the causes and characteristics of the 1966 coup in Modernization and Bureaucratic-Authoritarianism, pp. 115–65, although his correlation of economic and political indicators has been questioned (on the basis of newly available data) in Mario S. Brodersohn, "Sobre 'Modernizacion y Authoritarismo' y el estaneamiento inflacionario argentino," Desarrollo Economico, 13, no. 51 (October–December 1973):591–605; O'Donnell replied on pp. 606–12. For further background on the political context see Carlos S. Fayt, El Político armado: dinámica del proceso político argentino, 1960–1971 (Buenos Aires: Ed. Pannedile, 1971). For a stimulating analysis of the politico-economic rationale of the Onganía regime, see Tilman Tönnies Evers, Militärregierung in Argentinien: das politische system der "Argentinischen Revolution" (Hamburg: Alfred Metzner Verlag, 1972). A critical view of the Onganía era may be found in Oscar Braun, Desarrollo del capital monopolista en Argentina (Buenos Aires: Ed. Tiempo Contemporáneo, 1970). My analysis of the Krieger Vasena program makes no pretense at being comprehensive, especially since policies toward foreign investment have not been considered here.

34. For an enlightening comparison of Roberto Campos and Krieger Vasena, see O'Donnell, Modernization and Bureaucratic-Authoritarianism, pp. 96–106.

35. I am much indebted to Jorge I. Oclander for stimulating conversations about the Cordobazo, although he is not responsible for the manner in which I have used that information. For further detail, see Oclander, "Córdoba, May 1969: Modernization, Grass-Roots Demands, and Political Instability," in Alberto Ciria et al., New Perspectives on Modern Argentina (Bloomington: Indiana University, Latin American Studies Program, 1972), pp. 83–91. Further details on the background to labor discontent in Córdoba may be found in Francisco J. Delich, Crisis y protesta social: Córdoba, mayo 1969 (Buenos Aires: Ed. Signos, 1970); Beba Balve et al., Lucha de calles, lucha de classes; elementos para su análisis: Córdoba 1971–1969

(Buenos Aires: Ed. La Rosa Blindada, 1973); and Santiago Senen Gonzalez, *El Sindicalismo después de Perón* (Buenos Aires: Ed. Galerna, 1971).

36. As O'Donnell notes, often it is the *perception* of the economic position (relative to past positions and to past and present positions of others) which is most important for the historical actors. O'Donnell has chosen to stress the decline in real wages (using 1966 as the base year) which occurred during the Onganía government ("Comentario a la nota de M. Brodersohn," *Desarrollo Económico*, 13, no. 51 [October–December 1973]:610–11). Although there are no reliable unemployment data for Argentina, a recent study indicates that from 1965 to 1970 the rate of growth of industrial employment was much higher than in any of the preceding five-year periods since 1951 (Adolfo Canitrot, "Algunas características del comportamiento del empleo en la Argentina, 1950–70," *Desarrollo Económico*, 14, no. 53 [April–June 1974]:69–91).

37. A comparison of the Argentine and Brazilian cases is spelled out in a Marxian framework in Juan C. Portantiero, "Dominant Classes and Political Crisis in Argentina Today," *Latin American Perspectives*, 1, no. 3 (fall 1974):93–120. There is an excellent comparative analysis of stabilization in Argentina and Brazil in O'Donnell, *Modernization and Bureaucratic-Authoritarianism*, pp. 64–67. In comparing Brazil after 1964 and Argentina after 1966, O'Donnell suggests that "the significantly higher degree of coercion" which would have been required to deactivate popular opposition in Argentina would have created such social dislocation as to render "success," à la Brazil, unlikely (p. 101). The Chilean experience since the coup of 1973 has demonstrated a degree of repression far greater than that practiced by the post-1964 Brazilian regimes, thereby suggesting that we should not underestimate the government's potential for coercion in a country such as Argentina, which is relatively similar to Chile in its history of labor militancy. By a tragic irony, the Chileans do not even have any "success" at stabilization (as of July 1975) to show for their sacrifices.

38. For details, consult the collection of speeches by José Maria Dagnino Pastore, *Argentine Economic Policy, 1969–1970* (Buenos Aires: Ministry of Economy and Labor, 1970).

39. Little has been said here about exchange rate policy. Krieger Vasena carried out a major devaluation in 1967 and then invested much political capital in making credible his government's ability to maintain the announced exchange rate policy. It should be noted that signs of significant difficulty were evident in this area even before the *Cordobazo*.

40. As one economist specializing in inflation puts it, "stabilizing an economy after a period of inflation is probably the most delicate and difficult economic maneuver that a government can attempt. Stabilization at such a time means inevitably a cutting back in some direction—someone's spending and consumption must fall; someone must lose his job. It is the morning after an economic blast" (Morley, *Economics of Inflation*, p. 129). I owe to Peter Lindert the cautionary observation that the theoretical implications of this question deserve much more analysis. Can it be a mere accident that unemployment data for Latin American countries are virtually nonexistent? The lack of such data makes very difficult any attempt at analyzing the employment effects of stabilization attempts.

41. Curiously enough, IAPI has yet to receive any detailed analysis. Many leads for research may be found in Díaz Alejandro, *Essays*. The deleterious long-term effects on Argentine agricultural productivity of IAPI-type policies are spelled out in a *New York Times* article of January 23, 1975, and a *Wall Street Journal* article of July 16, 1975.

42. The interpretation in Nathaniel H. Leff, *Economic Policy-Making and Development in Brazil 1947–1964* (New York: John Wiley and Sons, 1968), pp. 9–34, overstates the disincentive which resulted from the *confisco cambial*. For details on how the coffee surplus purchase program operated, see Julian de Magalhães Chancel, "O café na formação do produto nacional," in Instituto Brasileiro do Café, Departamento Economico, Programa de Formação de Pessoal, *Curso de Economia Cafeeira* (Rio de Janeiro: Instituto Brasileiro do Café, 1962), vol. 2. Data on the response of Brazilian coffee growers to price fluctuations are given in Thomas Geer, *An Oligopoly: The World Coffee Economy and Stabilization Schemes* (New York: Dunellen, 1971), esp. chap. 4.

43. If we add Chile and Uruguay for the same period, our conclusions still hold, except for 1959–1961 in Chile, when inflation was reduced from 39 percent in 1959 to 12 percent in 1960 and 8 percent in 1961. But then the rate began to rise again, reaching 14 percent in 1962 and heading toward the hyperinflation of 1973 which helped erode support for the Allende government and led to the violent coup of September 1973 (Pazos, *Chronic Inflation*, p. 14).

44. A recent survey of income distribution classified both Brazil (data for 1970) and Mexico (data for 1969) as economies of "high inequality" (Hollis Chenery et al., *Redistribution with Growth* [London: Oxford University Press, 1974], table I.1). One of the most ambitious comparative analyses of the unequal distribution of the benefits of economic growth—where Brazil and Mexico are cited as important examples of high inequality—is Irma Adelman and Cynthia Taft Morris, *Economic Growth and Social Equity in Developing Countries* (Stanford: Stanford University Press, 1973), esp. chap. 6.

JOHN F. H. PURCELL and SUSAN KAUFMAN PURCELL

7

Mexican Business and Public Policy

The Mexican economy has been labeled "state capitalist," "semicapitalist," and "unclassifiable." Common to these terms is the recognition that the large role of the national government in the economy makes the economic system far from competitive, while the importance of the private sector makes "socialistic" a misleading designation.

The purpose of this chapter is to develop a model of the relationship between the public and private sectors in Mexico that highlights the major characteristics of Mexico's economy and suggests hypotheses to explain why it operates as it does. In particular, we are interested in the comparative implications of the model, especially the extent to which the Mexican system differs from the more obviously competitive economy of the United States. A major characteristic of the model is its focus on those characteristics of the Mexican economy determined by political factors. We contend that the relationship between government and business in Mexico is different from that in the United States mainly because of a difference between political systems, that is, between an authoritarian and a democratic-pluralist political pattern.

The principal questions dealt with include the following: What factors and/or interests influence the outcome of economic decisions and, particularly, what is the balance of influence between the public and private spheres? By what political process are decisions reached? Does this process result in coherent, conscious public decisions, or are decisions the residual or aggregate outcome of many uncoordinated private or public decisions?

In answering these questions, the observer is confronted with a range of variation sometimes seeming to suggest one kind of answer, sometimes another. In order to take these variations into account, a descriptive model must accommodate two dimensions: variation over time and variation according to the issue or policy area under consideration.

With regard to the first, it is apparent that relations between government and business in Mexico have undergone historical changes related to economic and political development, as well as cyclical changes related to presidential terms of office and internal and external crises. The descriptive model must therefore take account of the most important environmental factors that influence government policy and private-sector response.

Second, patterns of relations between government and the private sector vary, depending on the type of issue being decided. This concept of "arenas" of policy-making was originally developed in 1964 by Theodore Lowi in relation to business and government relations in the United States.[1] Lowi argued that there were at least three distinct patterns of decision-making, depending on the impact of government policy perceived by those involved. Not only were the patterns different in the different arenas, but so were patterns of influence and the locus of power.

It is neither possible nor desirable to apply Lowi's framework mechanically to Mexico. Nevertheless, some comparison with the Mexican case is useful because business-government relations in Mexico *also* appear to fall into relatively discrete arenas, although they are not the same ones that Lowi describes for the United States. Parts of the Lowi framework thus provide a systematic means of comparing two political-economic systems and, most important, for developing hypotheses about why they differ. Before discussing this concept of arenas further, however, it is necessary to describe the structural and ideological environment within which the Mexican issue process operates.

The Political, Economic, and Ideological Environment

The most obvious characteristic of public sector—private sector relations in Mexico is the overwhelming potential power of the government over the economy. As Raymond Vernon says: "The important point is that the private sector operates in a milieu in which the public sector is in a position to make or break any private firm."[2] The power of the government vis-à-vis the private sector has several ramifications which can be classified under four headings: (1) government involvement in the economy, (2) authoritarian political control, (3) unorganized constraints, and (4) the existence of a relatively well-defined ideology of "state interest."

Government Involvement in the Economy

The Mexican government has always played an important role in the economy as a result of a variety of factors, including the inheritance of concepts of commercial and mercantile law from Spain and a relatively late-starting industrialization process. The government owns or controls the most important industries in the country, such as the railroad, telegraph, telephone, electric power, steel, aviation, petroleum, natural gas, and petrochemical industries. In addition, there are an estimated four hundred public or mixed public–private sector enterprises in the country, most created since 1940. Needless to say, the government's pricing policies in these industries as well as its decisions regarding the purchase of goods and services for them can seriously constrict the options of the private sector. Furthermore, through its control of agencies such as CONASUPO (a government agency that distributes low-cost food to the poor), the government can engage in direct price competition with the private sector.

The government also plays a significant role in credit and finance through its involvement in approximately thirty public credit institutions including the Banco de México (the central bank) and Nacional Financiera (the government development bank). Its role is further magnified by the unwillingness of private and public foreign capital, particularly agencies such as the World Bank and the Export-Import Bank, to lend to private business in Mexico. The government can and has used its control of credit "to divert funds from construction, commerce, and real estate speculation toward industry."[3] It also can use the Banco de México to manipulate reserve requirements in order to influence the private sector's rate and direction of investment.

The private sector is also greatly affected by the government's policies toward industrialization. The government sets tariff rates, grants tariff exemptions, and allocates rights to import foreign-made light and heavy goods. Furthermore, despite a recent decrease in direct government investment, investments of government enterprises as a share of gross investment have increased since 1956.[4] Most of this investment is in irrigation, energy (especially petroleum and electric power), and transportation. Thus, the government's decisions regarding how and where to invest are of great significance to the private sector.

That the private sector is well aware of the government's influence is evidenced by the overwhelming desire and, often, necessity of locating firms in the Federal District where businessmen have easier access to strategic government officials. Firms that cannot or do not wish to locate in the Federal District compensate for their disadvantage by having their leaders make frequent trips to the Mexican capital. The directors of several large Monterrey firms, for example, fly weekly to the Federal District, where they often maintain a small office and staff. Less wealthy firms often band together and maintain an office and staff shared by several firms.[5]

Authoritarian Political Control

One of the coauthors has elsewhere characterized the Mexican political system as authoritarian and defined the basic elements of such a system as elite consensus, limited pluralism, low mobilization, and a patrimonial style of rulership.[6] The first of these will be discussed in the next section. The other three, with the addition of a fourth characteristic, centralization of power, provide a useful framework for documenting the extent to which the Mexican government's political control is translated into economic control.

1. *Centralization.* The Mexican government is characterized by the centralization of authority in the executive (the presidency and "cabinet"). Other branches of government, such as Congress and the courts, are virtually powerless. It is true that some bureaucratic agencies supposedly under executive control exercise considerable independence, as in the United States. This should not obscure the fact that the Mexican president has much more control over fiscal and monetary policy than does the American executive.

First, the Bank of Mexico (the equivalent of the Federal Reserve Board), as well as other government banks, is directly and closely controlled by the minister of finance, unlike its American equivalent. In fiscal policy, for example taxation, the president need not bargain with congressional committees such as the House Ways and Means Committee of the U.S. Congress.[7]

The courts are unable and usually unwilling to thwart the will of the Mexican executive. There are, for example, cases in which the Mexican Supreme Court has ruled against executive decisions only to have the executive declare that the court decision would simply be ignored.[8] In such cases the executive, not the court, prevails.

Finally, while Mexico is in theory a federal system, in fact the states and communities are firmly controlled by the federal government. The government's monopoly of financial resources is a major—but not the sole—mechanism of federal control which far exceeds anything in the United States.[9] All of this means that the government in Mexico is in a position to make fairly coordinated macroeconomic decisions without much input from the private sector or even a variety of government agencies.

2. *Limited pluralism.* Interest groups in Mexico are less numerous and varied than in the United States, and their autonomy is severely circumscribed by government power. Business groups are the *most* autonomous because they are the only segment of society with independent resources and organizational skills. Nevertheless, the government has various ways of controlling business groups.

First, all firms of any consequence *must* belong to either the

National Confederation of Chambers of Commerce (CONCANACO) or the Confederation of Mexican Chambers of Industry (CONCAMIN). A large part of the formal contact between government and business is carried out through these chambers, which allows the government to use them to implement its goals. Several observers have described the leadership of the chambers as unrepresentative of the membership and as to some extent co-opted by special benefits and close contact with government officials.[10] Disgruntled businessmen have little alternative to membership in the official chambers, since refusal to join can be prosecuted under tax evasion laws and the government usually discourages the formation of alternative groupings.[11] Furthermore, the government fosters its own captive groups within the chambers such as CNIT, a group of manufacturing firms relying heavily on government economic protection and support and willing to follow the government line on most policy issues.

Government control over the labor movement also is a tool for control of business. The government has encouraged strikes to exert pressure on recalcitrant businessmen.[12]

In general, government-business relations are characterized by government initiative and business reaction. Business groups seldom draft or propose legislation, although they may be asked to react to government drafts.

The lack of autonomous interest groups in Mexican politics has another implication which will become more apparent in a later section. There are very few, if any, nongovernment groups to provide a countervailing force to business interests. In the United States, while business groups may predominate, numerous regional, agricultural, labor, and even consumer groups are active and at times in conflict with business interests. In Mexico business has the nonpublic sector more or less to itself, suggesting the slightly paradoxical conclusion that while business in Mexico is weaker than in the United States vis-à-vis the government, it is stronger than in the United States vis-à-vis other nongovernment interests.

3. *Low mobilization.* The absence of political consciousness and activism among the mass of the Mexican citizenry is closely related to limited pluralism and helps to explain it. Low mobilization means the absence of a high level of interest-group activity and the tendency for the members of existing groups to be passive and allow the (usually co-opted) leadership great power and freedom of action. This pattern is evident even within business associations.[13] In addition, low mobilization helps to explain the reduced number of organized political demands upon the government and the corresponding tendency for government to take the initiative in political decision-making.

4. *Patrimonial rulership.* Patrimonial rulership includes the tendency for relationships to be personalistic and hierarchical (patron-client) rather than universalistic and egalitarian, and the tendency for political issues to become disaggregated and for government rules to be applied in a discretionary manner rather than equally to all. There are numerous examples of patrimonial rulership in the economic sphere, and the difference between U.S. and Mexican patterns in this regard was summarized by one Mexican businessman who commented, "You Americans have the know-how but we Mexicans have the know-who."[14]

One result of the patrimonial style of politics is the already noted and much deplored tendency for business firms to locate exclusively in Mexico City to increase their access to government officials. Another related pattern is the oft-noted "petitionary style" of business efforts to influence government, which contrasts with the bargaining or log-rolling style typical of American politics.

In the disaggregated milieu of Mexican politics, the technique of "divide and rule" is a prime weapon in the government arsenal. In order to prevent horizontal (for example, class or interest-group) linkages from forming in the private sector, the government encourages a variety of cleavages among business groups. The discretionary application of rules and regulations is one method of fragmentation, as is the formation of progovernment groups within business peak associations (for example, the formation of CNIT within CONCAMIN noted earlier).

The other side of the coin of the patrimonial, disaggregated style of decision-making is, of course, a certain lack of coordination in the implementation of government policy which will be discussed later.

Unorganized Constraints on Government Decision-Making

The power and cohesion of the Mexican government vis-à-vis the private sector sometimes are severely limited by what may be called unorganized constraints. These are to be distinguished from conscious organized attempts by business to exert political and economic influence. The latter are dealt with in a subsequent section.

First, there are constraints deriving from the nature and structure of the political system. The problem of lack of coordination among bureaucratic agencies which is likely to plague any government has already been noted. This is intensified in Mexico because of the discretionary and disaggregated style of decision-making, which may obscure basic policy goals. For reasons which will be discussed shortly, the Mexican bureaucracy sometimes lacks the capacity to implement policy decisions in areas where strict control of day-to-day decisions of lower-echelon officials is necessary. It is likely, for example, that the creation of the customs-free border zone in the north was partly determined by the realization that customs regulations could not be enforced along the border with the United States.[15]

Some authors have mentioned the executive's difficulty in controlling the bureaucratic momentum of the semiautonomous agencies such as those which administer the government-owned petroleum and electric power industries.[16] Still others have observed the more subtle influence of the *técnicos* in choosing the alternatives submitted to political leaders for choice. This is especially important in the economic sphere, where technical alternatives are complex, and in a country like Mexico, where most of the economic expertise is concentrated in government agencies such as the Central Bank.

A second kind of constraint is political. Most important, the authoritarian coalition, or what Frank Brandenburg calls the "Revolutionary Family,"[17] must be kept together, which means that certain accommodations and compromises must be built into the decision-making process at the highest level. A second political constraint appears only periodically, and its real influence is vague—this is public opinion. There appear to be issues and times when the authoritarian system must respond to unorganized but strong demands. Vernon's comment on the nationalization of the foreign-owned electric power industry is relevant here, though it may be somewhat overstated: "In the end the recapture of the quasi-public powers of the electric companies from the foreign hands which held them seems almost an inevitable step, ordained by some unwritten law of nationhood."[18]

The third constraint is the Mexican government's reliance on both foreign and domestic private capital to achieve the economic growth that is one of its major goals. "In spite of its declared policy of being 'socialist within the constitution' and despite its 'ethos of revolution' the Mexican government has relied more heavily on the private sector for growth than almost any major country in Latin America."[19] In addition to relying on the domestic private sector, Mexico depends heavily on foreign investment and loans to finance its development. As Roger Hansen shows, this reliance actually increased during the 1960s.[20] Despite its power, the government must take care not to frighten off foreign capital or overly discourage domestic capital. Such considerations have limited the extent to which policies feared by the business community could be single-mindedly pursued.[21]

Ideology and State Interest

While in the United States there is no clear, operationalizable definition of public interest that political leaders can use to legitimate policy intiatives, there *is* such a definition in Mexico. It is perhaps better called a "state interest" than a "public interest" for reasons which will be discussed shortly.

Writing on the capture of public authority structures by private interests in the United States, Grant McConnell notes that "a curious feature of American politics in the twentieth century is the absence of any articulated body of doctrine that may be taken as an orthodoxy on the central problem of private power."[22] In the absence of a definite ideology relevant to public-private relations, McConnell argues that most governmental bodies in the United States simply reflect, legalize, and enforce the decisions of private interests.

In Mexico, on the other hand, while many government decisions may favor the business community, the government (and particularly the executive branch) has its own separate concept of the public good. We call this "state interest" rather than "public interest" because it is essentially formulated by political elites and includes as a major component the maintenance of political control by the authoritarian coalition. Consequently, that which is in the interest of the state is not necessarily in the interest of the general public. By the same token, the fact that a policy is not in the interest of the general public does not imply that it is necessarily in the interest of some private group. Finally, a particular policy which is in the interest of the state may or may not be congruent with some private interest. If the latter is the case, this does not mean that the policy cannot primarily serve the interests of the state.

State interest has elsewhere been characterized as elite consensus and identified as one characteristic of authoritarian political systems. In Mexico, state interest consists of three major categories which are ranked in the following manner: (1) political control, (2) nationalistic economic development, and (3) social justice.

1. *Political control.* The Mexican system differs from that of the United States not only in terms of its political structure but also in terms of the determination with which elites work to prevent any decentralization or fragmentation of political power and to build political support for the dominant party, the Partido Revolucionario Institucional (PRI). When economic and political goals conflict, the political will dominate in Mexico. The most important priority, as noted, is the maintenance of the authoritarian coalition. A variety of policies in the economic sphere are determined with this goal in mind. Cycles of development-bank policy, as Charles Anderson shows, are a prime means of accommodating the conflict between conservatives and reformers within the elite coalition.[23]

2. *Nationalistic economic development.* The priority of political control does not mean that other priorities become vague, as in the

United States. Most important, the goal of nationalistic economic development has produced a relatively clear set of policies in the economic sphere and vis-à-vis private enterprise. The government's strategy of economic development is highly favorable to private enterprise since it emphasizes a high level of profits in order to promote savings and further investment. The government sees its role as encouraging private investment and business activity *as long as they lead to economic growth.* The government focuses on providing an infrastructure (especially the development and control of irrigation, transportation, and energy resources), breaking bottlenecks (as in the nationalization of electric power in 1960), and encouraging investment in needed areas or providing government investment when the risks or amount of initial capital needed are so great as to prevent private entrepreneurs from entering the field. An example of the latter situation is provided by the early growth of the Mexican steel industry. [24]

Clark Reynolds has called this close, cooperative relationship between government and private enterprise an "alliance for profits." [25] The alliance, however, is not dominated by the interests of the business community. The interest of the state and the state's conception of how economic growth shall be achieved are paramount. For example, when a basic industry (such as the electric power industry in the 1950s) is not expanding fast enough and is creating serious bottlenecks which slow growth, the government is never loath to assert state interest in economic growth over the private interest of any individual firm. The goals of integration of domestic industry and import substitution also supersede the interests of any private firm or sector.

The nationalistic component of the state interest in economic development clearly shows the limits of government–private-sector coincidence of interests. The most obvious element of this "protective, self-respecting nationalism" is to hold the foreigner in check. This means that foreign capital is not to control or even partially own any basic industries and that, whenever possible, domestic production should substitute for imports or foreign-owned production. In general, foreign investment is welcomed only where special, complex technology that cannot be provided domestically is needed. The interests of the state do not, therefore, preclude the possibility of nationalization of productive capacity in sensitive areas.

Another related element of nationalistic state interest in Mexico contrasts sharply with the United States. This is the notion of the primacy of the state over economic life and particularly the doctrine that nature's resources are part of the national patrimony and cannot be arbitrarily exploited by private interests. As Brandenburg says, "Economic freedom as that expression was known to the 'Robber

Barons' never entered Revolutionary vocabulary."[26] In contrast, in the United States,

> from the earliest days of the American nation, something approximating a natural right to the untrammeled occupation and exploitation of land and its resources for private benefit has been asserted by people living near the areas where publicly owned resources are located. . . . In a large sense, the persistent success of demands for private exploitation has become a tradition conferring a degree of legitimacy on a wide variety of actions that give control of land and land policy to limited groups within the general population.[27]

3. *Social justice.* The third priority in the triad which constitutes state interest in Mexico may be called social justice. The concern for maintaining this aim of the Mexican Revolution is sporadic and subordinate to the priorities of political control and economic growth, but it is nevertheless at times asserted over the interests of the private sector. A notable example is the use of CONASUPO (a government agency concerned with basic commodity distribution) to compete with and undercut private firms in the sale of basic foodstuffs in lower-class neighborhoods. It may be argued that the motivation here is as related to political control as it is to social justice, but the point is that such actions are legitimated by reference to social justice. A variety of price and rent controls, as well as the rather economically inefficient distribution of *ejido* land, are other examples of at least the overt maintenance of a state interest in social justice.

The existence of a state interest of the kind described above creates the potential for what Peter Bachrach and Morton Baratz have called the "mobilization of bias."[28] The generally accepted ideological perceptions in the political system can be utilized or "mobilized" to prevent certain issues from arising and to prevent challenges to the status quo. Whereas in the United States the mobilization of bias is mainly available for manipulation by private elites, often to prevent government action prejudicial to their interests, in Mexico it is mainly available to government elites to reinforce their decision-making authority. Business elites appear to accept many of the tenets of state interest outlined here, including a major government role in the economy.[29] They certainly favor various kinds of government protection, incentives, and provision of infrastructure. Indeed, the mobilization of bias often favors business over other groups in the society because it is so crucial for the attainment of economic growth. As David Shelton says, "A good revolution requires good business and good business requires a good revolution."[30]

In areas where business interests conflict with the state interest, however, the mobilization of bias is effectively used to prevent real opposition from arising. In the profit-sharing decision, for example, business was unable to criticize the concept of compulsory profit-sharing because it was written into the Mexican constitution.[31] Certain institutions also benefit from the mobilization of bias. While businessmen often express dismay at the degree of entrepreneurial activity by the state which competes with existing private enterprise, they are loath to criticize Nacional Financiera, the major government development bank, which is responsible for much of this deplored entrepreneurial activity.[32]

To summarize, an important difference between the pluralist system of the United States and the authoritarian one of Mexico is the existence of a concept of state interest in the latter which the state can manipulate to influence the relationship between the public and private sectors. While the interests of the sectors often *coincide* in Mexico, there is not the blurring of public and private interests found in the United States, which derives from a lack of any clear, politically useful doctrine of public interest.

Patterns of Government-Business Relations in Mexico

We move now to an examination of the major patterns of government-business interactions in Mexico. According to the information contained in the studies available to date, these patterns generally fall into three relatively discrete "arenas." Because the Mexican patterns of government-business interactions are derived from the structural and ideological characteristics of the Mexican political system outlined in the preceding section, they differ considerably from the patterns described by Lowi for the United States. Lowi called the three patterns of policy-making characteristic of government-business relations in the United States distribution, regulation, and redistribution. Each can be briefly summarized as follows:

1. *Distribution* policies are made without regard to limited resources and are essentially pork-barrel programs. They can be easily disaggregated and dispersed unit by unit. As a result, "winners" and "losers" need never confront one another. "In many instances the deprived cannot be identified as a class because the most influential among them can be accommodated by further disaggregation of the stakes (logrolling)."[33]

2. *Regulation* refers to policies which reduce or expand the alternatives of private individuals. They lay down general rules to guide the *use*

of private property. Thus, regulatory policies involve a choice as to who will be deprived and who will be indulged.

3. *Redistribution* refers, not to the dispersion of nonscarce resources or to the use of private property, but rather to the removal of property or wealth from one category of people in order to give it to another. This is a choice of who will be deprived and who indulged on a much more fundamental level than that of regulation, where the ownership of property is not involved.

Although Lowi does not state it explicitly, each of his arenas appears to be defined in terms of four main variables: (1) the formal or apparent outcome of a policy, (2) the expected outcome of a policy, (3) the scope of a policy, and (4) the extent of aggregation or disaggregation of a policy. The first two variables are self-explanatory. The third variable, the scope of a policy, refers to the number of units, individuals, or firms to which the policy applies. The fourth variable, the extent of aggregation or disaggregation of a policy, may be described as the scope of individual issues or decisions *within* a particular policy area. The distinction between scope and aggregation is that the former refers to the range of units and/or interests affected by a policy, while aggregation refers to the range of units and/or interests affected by *each individual decision* which forms that policy.

In Lowi's scheme, all four variables tend to change together. Distributive "policies," for example, have a distributive outcome and are so perceived by the protagonists. Distribution also has the smallest scope, since distributive "policy" is not really a policy at all but a series of individualized decisions which can be termed a policy only in the aggregate and after the fact. Distributive policy is also the most disaggregated (or the least aggregated). At the other extreme, redistributive policies have a redistributive outcome and are recognized by those involved as being redistributive. Redistributive policies have the broadest scope, since they apply to large categories or classes of individuals and to large numbers of people. Such policies are also highly aggregated, since they basically divide the relevant interests into two sides, winners and losers.

Although Lowi assumes that all four variables change together, there is no logical imperative that they do so. For example, a policy with a regulatory outcome theoretically can be fairly narrow or extremely broad in scope. An illustration of the latter would be the gas rationing policy which received serious consideration in the United States during the recent fuel crisis. In general, however, there does seem to be a tendency in the issues that Lowi examined in the United States for the four variables to shift together, which probably accounts for his assumption to that effect.

In Mexico, on the other hand, the four variables appear to be substantially independent of each other. For example, the formal outcome of a policy often differs greatly from the expected or anticipated outcome. Despite the greater independence of the four variables in the Mexican context, they nevertheless appear to cluster into three main policy arenas. The Mexican arenas, however, are both different from and substantially less distinct than those elaborated by Lowi for the United States.

We have called the three Mexican patterns of policy-making (1) regulatory distribution, (2) indirect, piecemeal regulation, and (3) regulatory redistribution. As will become evident, the first category corresponds vaguely to Lowi's distributive arena, the second, to his regulatory arena, and the third, to his redistributive arena. There are, however, significant differences between the Mexican arenas and those described by Lowi for the United States. In general, as can be deduced from the labels we have given to the three Mexican arenas, regulation is a much more salient aspect of all policy arenas in Mexico than it appears to be in the United States. Furthermore, regulation in Mexico is predominantly indirect, in part because the government lacks the ability to undertake direct regulation. Finally, all three policy arenas in Mexico are characterized by high degrees of policy disaggregation, in contrast to the United States, where disaggregation was principally a characteristic of Lowi's distributive arena.

Before discussing each of the Mexican arenas in detail, we wish to stress that they do not necessarily exhaust all patterns of policy-making present in Mexico. They are rather tentative categories based on data culled from an admittedly limited and unrepresentative number of available studies. Future research may therefore necessitate expansion or modification of the three Mexican policy arenas described in the following pages.

Regulatory Distribution

The vast majority of relationships between the public and private sectors in Mexico have a superficial resemblance to a model of distributive politics. This is because most rules and regulations affecting the interests of the private sector are applied in a highly discretionary and disaggregated manner. The general style of Mexican economic and other kinds of decision-making is informal, personalistic, and piecemeal. In fact, elsewhere we have described the Mexican political system as similar to the classic American model of the political machine.[34]

First, regulatory legislation in Mexico is purposely vague and to be applied needs the will and definition of the executive in the form of a decree or *reglamento*.[35] Most laws are applied case-by-case, and exemptions can be granted as benefits to individual firms or groups. The following list gives some idea of the vast area of government-business relations that can be applied in a highly disaggregated manner: import licenses for both the businessman *and* his competitor, qualitative controls, import quotas and exemptions, tariff rates, tax exemptions for "new" or "necessary" industries (with few guidelines on how to define these terms), exemptions to price ceilings, tax subsidies to individual firms, discretionary application of labor laws, rebates on import duties, delayed revenue collection, exemptions on maximum size restrictions for agricultural holdings, and exemptions from limits on foreign ownership.

In any situation the Mexican government chooses the method of regulation that allows the *most* disaggregation. It is possible, for example, to control the import of foreign goods in a number of ways—through currency devaluation, tariff protection, import quotas, and import licenses. Mexico has usually avoided the least disaggregated methods such as devaluation, and even tariffs are used less than quotas and licenses. Reynolds, for example, notes that while economists prefer tariffs because of their efficiency of application, the Mexican government prefers quotas coupled with licenses. "Since 1954 almost the entire burden of commercial policy for import substitution appears to have fallen on the licensing system."[36]

Another set of government-business relationships that exhibits a high level of disaggregation is that of the various benefits conferred on business by government. In terms of formal impact this group of decisions fits the literal definition of distribution, the doling out of material benefits. The government provides a number of financial benefits to business, including privileged access to loans, various guarantees against investment loss, ceilings on interest, and large-scale borrowing abroad by Nacional Financiera in order to relend to individual firms at favorable interest rates. Other benefits include tariff protection, price supports, subsidies (for example, lowering the price of agricultural equipment), provision of information on investment opportunities, and provision of infrastructure and services (for example, irrigation, roads, and river basin projects).

Some kinds of benefits are less disaggregable than those just listed. These include "bottleneck-breaking" through nationalization or government investment; a monetary policy by which labor involuntarily finances business profits through a conscious and controlled government policy of inflation;[37] a system of price-fixing and "accords" between government-owned and privately owned enterprises (for example, in the steel industry)[38] to make sure that private vested interests are not harmed by too much competition; government establishment of industries in areas that private enterprise cannot enter; and the subsequent turning over of shares in these enterprises to private capital.

This latter set of benefits can be seen to have a fairly clear policy objective behind it—economic growth and the Mexicanization of key areas of the economy, one of the major priorities discussed under "state interest." In fact, most benefits to business fall into this category, whether disaggregated or not. Given the commitment to rely partially on private enterprise for growth and the high priority placed on economic development, the government encourages business activities which help to develop the economy.

The goal of economic development lies not only behind most of the benefits distributed to business, but also behind the highly disaggregated system of exemptions from regulations discussed earlier. Although such discretionary exemptions may at first seem like "pure" corruption, or at best logrolling, such a perception is usually false. A number of observers have noted that behind the apparently arbitrary and disaggregated decision-making process in these areas lie definite policy objectives. Reynolds, for example, has argued that the broad flexibility of the import licensing system is used to reward firms that comply with the criteria for domestic industrialization.[39] They are assured that licenses will not be issued for similar imports. On the other hand, firms that do not produce at what the government considers reasonable prices are told that licenses may or will be granted for competing imports. Rafael Izquierdo also finds that the government withholds licenses from firms that do not follow through on their commitments for gradual industrial integration (substituting domestically produced intermediate products for imported ones).[40] Flavia Derossi summarizes the argument as follows: "The lack of a published economic plan, the uncertainty and variability of fiscal incentives and of tariff protection, the apparent inconsistency of certain government decisions . . . prevent the outsider from perceiving the constant logical thread and the rather unitarian trend of Government intervention which lie behind the apparently unstructured situation."[41]

Taking a slightly different tack, it is apparent that what in Mexico looks like a distributive arena in Lowi's terms does not quite fit his model. Distribution in the United States is lack of policy. The pattern described here is a disaggregated method or *tactic* used by the Mexican government to achieve policy ends. In the United States, the fragmentation of the political system leads to the prevalence of distributive politics in some areas. Regional elites, decentralized bureaucratic agencies, and powerful congressional committees and subcommittees encourage the logrolling "coalition of uncommon interests" that Lowi describes as typical of the distributive arena. In Mexico, the disaggregated decision-making process is carried out under a highly centralized and powerful executive-dominated system in which Congress is virtually irrelevant and regional elites are kept in check.

If, however, there are coherent policy objectives behind much apparently arbitrary decision-making in Mexico, why is this disaggregated style used rather than a more "efficient" one? A considerable price is probably paid in administrative costs and loss of bureaucratic efficiency and coordination as a result of the disaggregated style. The first answer is probably cultural and historical. The pattern described here for economic decision-making permeates the entire social and political system and comes partly from the Spanish colonial heritage. Security in the Mexican social system tends to derive from vertical, patron-client relationships rather than from horizontal ties of common interest or universally applied legal and individual "rights." It is perhaps not too speculative to say that in cultures which emphasize the zero-sum aspects of human relationships, as does Mexican culture,[42] a successful political system will emphasize the *non*-zero-sum aspects of political relationships as a means of mitigating and avoiding conflict. Conflict in such a system will be seen as much more destructive and potentially disastrous than in a culture where interpersonal relationships are seen as less threatening.

Another possible set of reasons for the prevalence of the disaggregated style of decision-making focuses on its political power functions. Such a style provides a number of benefits from the point of view of the government: horizontal alliances and potential opposition to executive policies are blocked through fragmentation of the private sector; centralization of authority is encouraged by vague laws whose interpretation can only be validated at the center; the possibilities for distributing patronage and co-opting potential opposition are enhanced; the private sector expends large amounts of time and energy running from government agency to government agency attempting to get around a variety of complex rules and regulations—activity which further integrates businessmen into the political system and tends to institutionalize the status quo; the government is provided with tremendous flexibility to adapt its policy to changing circumstances which, as Vernon says, enhances the "ability of the executive to avoid the clutch of the law's dead hand";[43] and broad control is extended over a wide variety of areas by allowing the executive to intervene in the details of administration.

The question may now be asked whether there exists in Mexican government-business relations a pattern of politics which could be called distributive in the U.S. sense—that is, disaggregated decisions without an orchestrating executive interest and will behind them. No doubt the pervasive discretionary style and the limits of the government's capacity to coordinate and control create cases of "loss of control" where corruption, personalism, and logrolling produce unintended "policies" through the aggregation of many small, individual decisions. It is not possible to say—given the underdeveloped status of research on business and politics in Mexico—exactly how common such patterns are. However, the generous distribution of political patronage (for example, party positions, government jobs) points to the existence of pure distributive politics in areas only peripherally involved with the economy.

Interestingly, a type of distributive, logrolling pattern appears to exist at the very highest level among the members of the "Revolutionary Family." The "benefits" distributed are not material goods but symbolic values. Since a certain amount of ideological disagreement exists within the elite over issues such as whether to emphasize social reform or economic rationality, whether to placate labor, agricultural, or business interests, a kind of high-level logrolling appears to take place which results in cyclical changes in policy emphasis, including the "reformist" or "conservative" image of succeeding presidents. Anderson notes a similar tendency regarding the policy of the development banks. At times economic rationality and "good banking" principles are given top priority; at other times reformist goals are emphasized.[44]

Whereas distributive politics in the United States occurs at the lowest levels of the federal system (among local elites, congressional committees, and decentralized agencies), in Mexico it appears at the highest level (within the "Revolutionary Family"). This illustrates an important difference between the two systems. In the United States, fragmentation of power and decentralization of the pluralistic system mean that the further from the center one gets, the less "coherent"is the policymaking process. In a highly centralized authoritarian system like Mexico's, the central elites cannot afford the disruptiveness of open bargaining and conflict. A more satisfactory method of resolving differences—given, of course, that ranges of ideological difference are not too broad—is a modified process of logrolling, giving everyone his turn. In fact, the notion of "taking turns" seems to be very prevalent in the Mexican system as a way of solving potential conflict among competing groups. In some ways this can be seen as an attempt to turn a situation calling for confrontation and/or bargaining into one in which all will have their way if they are patient.

The present pattern of government-business relations has been called the regulatory distributive arena. This is to indicate that while the formal impact of the policies in this arena is regulatory and their scope similar to those of the regulatory arena in the United States, the decision-making process is disaggregated and the expectations of most participants fit more closely a distributive than a regulatory pattern. Thus, this arena shares some characteristics of both the regulatory and the distributive arenas in the United States. Because of the prevalence of the disaggregated style of decision-making, this pattern probably blurs gradually into a more purely distributive pattern. In Mexico it appears to be considerably more difficult to identify discrete boundaries of decision-making patterns than it is in the United States.

Indirect, Piecemeal Regulation

The pattern described here is similar in some ways to regulatory distribution. In both cases government policy initiative is the moving force behind government-business relationships. This arena is called regulation rather than distribution, however, because decisions are less disaggregated. The *tendency* toward disaggregation is always present in the Mexican system, but the policies in the present arena deal with issues which, by their nature, are difficult to split into a series of smaller decisions. The scope of policy thus is not much different from that of the regulatory distribution arena, although the level of aggregation is considerably higher. The expectations of protagonists concerning policy impact correspond much more closely to the regulatory arena described by Lowi for the United States than was the case for the regulatory distribution arena. Both business and government participants appear to recognize that general restrictions and guidelines are being laid down that limit the use of private property. The formal impact of policies, however, differs considerably from anything described for the United States. While the *intent* of policies is to regulate, the *method* used is uniquely adapted to the Mexican political system. The formal impact may be described as *indirect* rather than direct regulation.

Mexican government-business relations are *not* characterized by a reliance on legislation or administrative rules. As noted in the previous section, legislation tends to be extremely vague and to allow numerous exemptions or even total disregard. Because the system operates as it does, legal action and law are virtually never used to regulate government-business relationships in Mexico.[45]

Instead of direct regulation, the Mexican government tends to use more indirect means to achieve policy objectives. This technique is more possible in Mexico than in the United States because of the major, direct role the Mexican government plays in the economy. Certain areas of economic activity do not need to be regulated in the way they are in the United States because they are government-owned. The response of the Mexican government to difficulties in regulating key areas of the economy in private hands has been either to nationalize, to threaten nationalization, or otherwise to limit the control of the private sector in order to bring private-sector activities into line with government priorities. In the 1920s, for example, when it proved difficult to regulate foreign-owned electric power companies, the strategy of the *técnicos* was to attempt to prevent private companies from gaining control of any further water resources, thus limiting their capacity for expansion.[46]

Financial devices are commonly used to regulate business and, as Anderson comments, they provide "a flexibility and adaptability not found in more conventional administrative techniques relying on political sanctions."[47] Credit is used as both "carrot" and "stick." Because credit is a scarce commodity in any developing country, the various government-controlled development banks can use credit, including differential interest rates, to channel further investment into priority areas and squeeze out "nonproductive" private enterprise (such as high-cost housing and commodity inventories).[48] This tool is useful in both the agricultural and the industrial sectors. Another technique is the use of the trust fund, whereby the government appropriates money to be administered by a development bank for a specific purpose— usually a neglected policy area.[49] Development banks are also used to carry out a variety of administrative tasks not directly related to financing. These include technical assistance, research, and supervision.

Another technique of indirect regulation is used in price controls. Through direct competition in the sale of basic food comodities, CONASUPO, as mentioned earlier, is able to regulate prices in some urban neighborhoods. CONASUPO and its predecessor CEIMSA also operated in agricultural purchasing, and in some regions of the country the combination of CEIMSA and the development banks eliminated the open market for agricultural commodities and was able to develop an effective distribution system as well as maintain price stabilization. [50] Calvin Blair notes that in Ciudad Sahagún ownership of Diesel Nacional allowed the federal government to regulate private producers through price and quality competition and to use its power as a buyer of component parts to generate integration of the national automotive industry.[51] In the same manner, the government is able to control prices and production of a variety of products through its ownership of AHMSA, the nation's largest steel company.[52]

Along with the tendency to regulate indirectly goes the failure of efforts to regulate directly. Although the Mexican government usually does not attempt direct regulation as a means of achieving policy objectives in high-priority areas, there are examples of such attempts which have failed miserably. One was the effort to achieve a consistent rate structure in the electric power industry in the 1950s. A report by a committee appointed by the government to study the problems of the electric industry in 1958 concluded that existing laws and regulations, "although similar to the regulatory systems in many other countries, simply did not work in Mexico."[53] Some idea of the extent of this failure is indicated by the fact that upon nationalization of the industry in 1960 it was found that 150 different rate structures existed in various parts of the country based on individual plants and that regional differences in rates for similar services varied by as much as 300 percent.[54]

The disaggregated style of the Mexican political system seems unable to sustain a concerted effort at direct regulation, and the result is the disaggregation of policy into a series of small decisions which begin to look like Lowi's distributive arena. In general, rules and regulations that are intended to be applied in a regulatory manner (as opposed to those that fit in the regulatory distribution arena of the previous section) tend to fall apart as a result of pervasive personalism and corruption. For example, the manager of a cement industry interviewed by Derossi, complaining that machinery which can be manufactured in Mexico is not allowed to be imported, commented, "The Secretaría de Industria y Comercio's famous Rule 14 is becoming increasingly tight and ever larger bribes must be given to customs inspectors."[55]

In addition to indirectness, a second characteristic of regulation of private enterprise in Mexico is its *piecemeal* nature. We are referring here to the relationship between the policy area and the decisions that are meant to implement policy goals. In Mexico there is an oft-noted lack of coordination between one regulatory decision and another, with the result that while particular, fairly narrow or short-term policies can be implemented, long-range or large-scale policies, including various kinds of economic planning, run into serious difficulties. As Leopoldo Solís puts it, "A sufficient level of coordination does not exist in the broad and dispersed public sector to conciliate . . . the decisions of the independent agencies and the governmental entities in a concerted action in the same direction."[56]

A good example of the ability to regulate (indirectly) on a small or piecemeal scale but not on a large scale is provided by the development banks. These are responsive to their relevant ministries and, as has been shown, wield considerable power over private enterprise. As Anderson notes, however, each individual development bank (there are eleven) resulted from a specific set of economic and political circumstances. The overall system does not correspond to any plan for economic development.[57] Another example that highlights the weakness of planning in the Mexican system was the Plan de Acción Immediata of 1962.

The strategy was to increase public investment and, through this and other measures, reactivate internal demand and create conditions more attractive to private investment. The estimates for the amount of private investment to be expected—an extremely crucial part of the plan—appear to have been entirely residual. They were calculated as the gap between total investment needs dictated by GNP growth goals and public investment possible. The private sector was not even consulted.[58]

A final and extreme example of the government's inability to plan is the "National Plan for Economic and Social Development, 1966–1970," commonly known as "The Secret Plan." Prepared by the Ministry of the Presidency, it remained a well-guarded secret. As one observer noted, "How can a plan succeed if the private sector and the other development forces of the country do not know about it and for that simple reason fail to give it their attention?"[59]

In general it may be said that indirect regulation in Mexico only works well when there is consistent attention by the executive. This means that the policy cannot be very long-term and probably cannot be broad in scope, at least with regard to that portion of the policy which depends upon action by lower-level government officials. During the change of presidential administrations every six years, for example, the executive often temporarily loses control of lower-level agencies, which frequently strike out on their own with policy initiatives.[60] In addition, different administrations have different priorities, so that the tendency toward *proyectismo*[61] is more apparent than in less executive-dominated systems. The need for constant executive attention has political advantages, as was pointed out in the previous section, but the weakness is the lack of coordination of public agencies and the related lack of capacity to regulate on other than an indirect and piecemeal basis.

Of course other countries, including the United States, share with Mexico the problems of coordinating government agencies. In the United States, however, much of the problem appears to be related to the "capture" of decentralized agencies by private interests in the form of "clientele" groups. While more research is needed on this topic in Mexico, it would seem that coordination problems in the public sector are not related to capture of public agencies. Two studies of public agencies which shed light on this subject are Anderson's analysis of development banks and Martin Greenberg's study of the Ministry of Hydraulic Resources. Neither one provides evidence of domination by clientele groups. On the contrary, Anderson, for example, shows that the banks play a "tutelary and directive role" vis-à-vis clientele groups.[62] Perhaps the capture of public agencies by private-interest groups is made more difficult in a system like that of Mexico, in which there is an operative state interest to be set against the private interest.[63]

In sum, there appear to be three main reasons for lack of coordination. The first is the tendency for bureaucratic agencies to develop their own particular interests. Attempts to coordinate tariff policy and quantitative controls since 1959, for example, have failed because tariff controls are under the Ministry of Finance while quantitative controls are with the Ministry of Industry and Commerce. The two have tended not to work together, probably because "the Finance Ministry was unwilling to relinquish its control over an important source of revenue."[64] Second, the lack of coordination is reinforced by the disaggregated style of decision-making and the personalistic authority structure of Mexico. For example, for all practical purposes, the Mexican president has no cabinet. Major issues are resolved between him and the minister or department head directly involved, with little coordination between agencies. This "makes it exceedingly difficult to achieve unity of action among all potential policy-makers, to say nothing of reaching agreement on what over-all policy should be."[65] Third, and related to the disaggregated style of decision-making, is the elite political culture which exhibits a tendency toward distributive politics. Distributive expectations are certainly more conducive to piecemeal than to broad-scale regulation. Furthermore, the related preference for reducing conflict by avoiding confrontation is exhibited in the preference for indirect rather than direct regulation. Indirect regulation acts on the economic system in order to control private activity and is thus less obvious in selecting out discrete sets of interests as subjects of government restriction. This presumably makes horizontal linkages or interest-group formation less likely and, as a result, reduces the opportunities for confrontation between the public and private sectors.

Regulatory Redistribution

Redistribution has been a major element in Mexican history. The Revolution was redistributive in a way never experienced by the United States. At a later stage Mexico witnessed some redistributive dramas featuring foreign capitalists who controlled Mexico's railroads and petroleum resources. The nationalization of the oil industry in 1938 can be regarded as redistribution "on the cheap," however. By defining a redistributive policy where the "losers" were foreigners, the Mexican government was able to polish its redistributive and nationalist image and unite the country at the same time.

As the authoritarian regime in Mexico has become more institutionalized, redistribution has become less redistributive. The nationalization of the mostly foreign-owned electric power companies in 1960 certainly cannot be seen in the same terms as the nationalization of oil. Expectations on both sides were concerned more with the regulatory than with the redistributive impact. The government, for example, was primarily interested in imposing a rational rate structure on the electric power industry. Although the government was willing to take political credit for nationalizing the power companies, its original motive was not redistributive. Similarly, the fact that the mostly foreign-owned electric companies were being paid handsomely for their installations took the redistributive edge off the nationalization decision and emphasized its regulatory aspects. Furthermore, the original suggestion for the take-over of the industry came from one of the foreign-owned companies rather than from the Mexican government and reflected a desire on the part of the former to combat overextension and to consolidate its investment patterns in Latin America.[66]

Today, there is little sign in Mexican government-business relationships of the redistributive policy arena as Lowi defines it. The definition includes policies at the broadest level of scope and aggregation which affect groups approaching classes—"haves" and "have-nots," "bigness" and "smallness." The impact is potentially extreme—property may be redistributed from one class or category to another. There are a clear winner and a clear loser. Categories confront one another, and the potential for conflict is high.

In fact, the issues described by Lowi as redistributive in the United States do not conform to his model either. This is a serious problem for Lowi's scheme as it applies to the United States, but it need not concern us unduly here. The interesting point is that, according to Lowi's description of the issues (if not the model), potentially redistributive policies in the United States inevitably get watered down and come to resemble the regulatory arena more than the model of the redistributive arena.

A similar process occurs in Mexico, at least in the case of the only recent redistributive policy which has been studied, the profit-sharing decision of 1961–1963.[67] We have called this arena regulatory redistribution to indicate that while the *formal* impact is redistributive (in this case, profit-sharing required all firms to distribute a share of profits among their workers), the *expectations* in great part were more appropriate to the regulatory arena. In other words, business peak associations, after a brief moment of panic, recognized (and were quietly told by government officials) that the actual impact of the decision would involve only mild redistribution and that the largest firms would be able to bargain with the government to reduce the impact of the profit-sharing decision. The business interests then shifted their attention to the regulatory aspects. Specifically, they were disturbed by the government's attempt to regulate via an obligatory profit-sharing system the private sector's use of its profits. Also at issue was the possibility that the government would use the labor unions to keep tabs on the accuracy of industry's profit-reporting procedures. The regulatory expectations produced by what was formally a redistributive decision account for our designation of this policy arena as regulatory redistribution and distinguish it from Lowi's redistributive arena.

The policy of profit-sharing differs from the two Mexican arenas discussed previously in that the scope of the issue was much broader and *did* affect large categories of individuals (in this case, employers and employees). In addition, while *some* disaggregation was possible, it was nowhere as extensive as under the regulatory distributive or the indirect piecemeal regulatory arenas. In the bargaining process that ensued between representatives of private-sector peak associations (mainly CONCAMIN and CONCANACO) and government *técnicos* (the captive labor movement was essentially a passive observer, at times manipulated by the government to provide leverage against business), the most modern and highly capitalized firms were separated from the less modern in the sense that the final profit-sharing formula required the former to distribute a much smaller share of their profits.

From what has been said of the Mexican system so far, it is not surprising to find that redistributive policies are lessened in impact and that potential confrontation is mitigated through very quiet bargaining between business and government. In fact, even the bargaining process characteristic of the regulatory arena is usually avoided in Mexico. In the case of profit-sharing, however, a variety of internal and external factors, including the Cuban Revolution, were putting pressure on President Adolfo López Mateos to make a gesture in the direction of social justice—to do something that would be considered redistributive. The response of the executive was essentially a decision that involved mild redistribution and regulatory politics.

Although redistribution in both pluralistic regimes like that of the United States and authoritarian regimes like that of Mexico is not particularly redistributive, compared with Lowi's description of the "welfare state" battle of the 1930s in the United States the Mexican profit-sharing decision appears to be *more* redistributive in its final impact than the American decision.

Profit-sharing legislation was developed by the government and was quickly passed by Congress without consulting either labor or business groups. Business peak associations reacted mainly by complaining about the high-handed procedure rather than about the principle of profit-sharing. In fact, the *principle* of compulsory profit-sharing was inviolable, since it was written into the constitution; the legislation that had been passed was simply enabling legislation. This focus on procedure immediately placed the issue in bargaining rather than ideological terms.

Business tried very hard, however, to water down the impact of the decision. Its main goal in negotiations with the government was to allow each firm to deduct a share (originally around 12 percent) of total capital investment from profits before distributing the remainder to workers. The result of this procedure would have been that any firm whose profit was less than 12 percent of its total capital investment would have been exempted from profit-sharing. This proposal seems analagous to the proposal during the social security debate in the United States to add the principle of individual contribution which, as Lowi says, "took away the redistributive sting."[68] The difference is that the proposal was accepted in the United States, whereas the deduction based on total capital investment was flatly refused by the Mexican government. Business organizations tried every means at their disposal to influence the government, including secret bargaining, lobbying in Congress, the bureaucracy, and the state governments, mounting a large-scale propaganda campaign in the press, and even proposing to labor leaders that workers accept an extra month's salary in lieu of profit-sharing. The latter ploy backfired, since labor immediately informed the government of the business offer. Government officials told labor not to accept, and labor mounted its own press campaign accusing business of trying to undermine the *principle* of profit-sharing—thus painting business as "unrevolutionary," a serious charge given the mobilization of bias on the issue.

Every attempt of business seriously to impair the original proposal failed. The government refused to accede to business requests on the grounds that such deductions would mean that profit-sharing would not apply to every firm. In this sense the government maintained the redistributiveness of the original proposal. Some bargaining was successful, however. Government officials finally allowed some deductions from profits before redistribution, but these were based on a percentage of the profits themselves rather than on a percentage of total capital investment. In addition, the firms with the highest ratio of capital to labor could deduct the highest percentage. This favored the large modern firms which, not coincidentally, were the most powerful in the business peak associations, CONCAMIN and CONCANACO. It was calculated that firms with the highest capital:labor ratio would have to share only around 2 percent of total profits, while those with the lowest ratios would distribute as much as 12 percent among their workers. Provisions such as these not only maintained the redistributive principle but also set up conflicts of interest within the business community.

In the American case, the deflation of redistributive impact appears in Lowi's account to have resulted from the influence of big business operating through the peak associations and through allies in the bureaucracy—in particular, the Treasury Department. In Mexico business did not have enough influence to remove the redistributive principle. This was *not* because labor was such a powerful antagonist, however. Labor, as noted, played an essentially passive role. It was the executive and government *técnicos* operating with a clear conception of state interest (which at this time demanded a credible redistributive gesture toward social justice) who dominated the policy arena. Furthermore, the bargaining process, while reminiscent of the U.S. regulatory arena in some ways, was unlike it in that bargaining was not between interest groups but between one set of private interests (business) and the government. In the United States, moreover, the original issue was initiated by "widespread support" for redistributive legislation. In Mexico the issue was initiated unilaterally by the executive based on its own conception of political necessity and state interest. Finally, business had no spokesman in the bureaucracy. The degree of accord finally reached on profit-sharing stemmed from the fact that the government *técnicos* were concerned not only with redistribution but also with economic growth. This meant that redistribution could not be too severe or it would endanger economic development.

In conclusion, the present arena shares certain characteristics of the model of the redistributive and the regulatory arenas. The ideological expectation of broad-scale confrontation between classlike categories is essentially absent from Mexico. Because of the mobilization of bias and state-interest priorities, business cannot challenge the redistributive policy on ideological grounds. Lowi argues that one of the major functions of peak associations in the United States is to mount an ideologically based challenge against redistributive threats (or imagined threats). In the United States, the absence of state interest and a mobilization of bias *favoring* private interest makes this a successful strategy. Ironically Mexico, the system where redistributive expectations on the part of business are kept most muted, fosters policies with the more redistributive impact.

Conclusions

What is the balance of power between the public and private sectors in Mexico? The question obviously implies that there are, in fact, two distinct sectors. The presence of organizations such as CONCAMIN and the Bankers' Association, which represent privat interests, is evidence of the existence of a Mexican private sector at least in some areas. This is not to deny that there are significant areas in which the boundaries between the public and private sectors in Mexico are somewhat blurred. The important question, however, concerns the direction of the balance of power. Theoretically, the scales can be tipped toward the public or toward the private sector. The former situation would seem to exist where the government's role in the economy is large, as in Mexico, with the result that the areas which remain the exclusive domain of the private sector are reduced. The latter situation often results from the capture of public agencies by private interests, a phenomenon frequently noted by students of business-government relations in the United States. Rather than assume that the balance of power in Mexico is tipped toward the government because of the significant role it plays in the economy, let us analyze the evidence for government power and the evidence for business power.

The Power of the Government

At least four kinds of evidence derived from the analysis in preceding sections suggest, although sometimes only indirectly, that the balance of power in most public-private relations is tipped toward the government.

1. If the three policy arenas described by Lowi are considered to represent three ascending levels of aggregation of decision-making and intensity of political conflict (distribution, regulation, and redistribution), then it is possible to compare the three arenas in the United States with their Mexican "equivalents" (regulatory distribution, indirect piecemeal regulation, and regulatory redistribution). Such a comparison shows that the Mexican arenas exhibit less confrontation and more disaggregation than their American counterparts. The first arena in Mexico (regulatory distribution) is based on the most personalistic and disaggregated expectations to an extent not found even in Lowi's distributive arena. Import policy in the United States, for example, is distributive but based on tariff levels for particular *products*. In Mexico it is based on import quotas or licenses for particular *products* in particular *instances* for particular *firms*. The indirect piecemeal regulatory arena is also more disaggregated (piecemeal) in Mexico than is its U.S. equivalent. In addition, the indirectness of the regulation helps to dampen conflict and business opposition to government policy. Finally, in the arena of redistribution, expectations in Mexico are muted and confrontation is more reminiscent (though not exactly similar) of the regulatory arena in the United States. In this arena, too, some disaggregation is possible in the sense of splitting

off some business interests from others (for example, allowing highly capitalized firms to distribute a relatively small share of their profits).

The result of this deflation of Mexican arenas relative to those of the United States is both evidence of and a further enhancement of the Mexican government's control over all policy arenas. It tends to fragment the opposition as well as dampen the potential for ideological conflict.

2. If aggregation and conflict are deflated in the Mexican as opposed to the U.S. arena, the *impact* of policy in Mexico is *inflated.* The distributive arena often accords with government policy goals in Mexico, but not in the United States. Regulation does not appear to be subject to "capture" by business interests in Mexico as it is in the United States. Finally, the principle of redistribution seems to be maintained in a way not evident in the United States.

In Mexico the differences among arenas (especially between distributive regulation and indirect piecemeal regulation) are based on differing government tactics which are connected to the objective nature of the matters being regulated. In the United States the differences among arenas are based on differing patterns and strategies of the private groups as they make demands on government and on each other. This suggests that the key to Mexican public-private relationships is government initiative, while in the United States it is private-interest initiative.

3. In the United States each arena is characterized by a different locus of decision-making authority (distribution: committees and subcommittees in Congress; regulation: Congress as a whole; redistribution: peak associations and the federal executive). In Mexico the locus of decision-making is the same for all arenas—the federal executive. Anderson, for example, notes that private groups attempting to influence development-bank policy most commonly take their case, not to the bank in question, but to the relevant minister or to the president himself.[69]

The pluralism of the U.S. system and the fragmentation of political authority provide multiple access points for private interests and the possibility of playing off one government agency against another. Such possibilities are highly restricted in Mexico, and this is evidence of the power of government vis-à-vis private interests.

4. The organization of private-interest groups in Mexico also indicates the greater power of the government vis-à-vis the private sector. In the pluralistic U.S. system, the form and organization of groups and coalitions are dictated by the interests at stake in a particular arena. Individual firms and pressure groups abound in the distributive arena, interest groups and shared-interest coalitions in the regulatory, and peak associations in the redistributive.

In Mexico, private group size and organization are *not* based on the comprehensiveness of the interests at stake, as in the United States. Rather, they can be seen as responses to the *style* of government decision-making on the one hand and the political interests of the state on the other.

There are two important kinds of private groupings in the Mexican private sector. The first is an informal association of different kinds of firms—usually based on a source of credit such as a bank and including a variety of economically complementary but dissimilar industrial and even commercial firms. Sometimes the various firms are owned by members of an extended family or allied families. There are approximately sixty such *grupos* in Mexico, and they tend to form cohesive economic units—for example, lending to each other at favorable interest rates.[70] In addition, there is some indication that they use political "connections" with government officials for mutual benefit. These *grupos* can be seen as a response to the somewhat arbitrary environment produced by the government's disaggregated style of decision-making. Their internal variety is particularly adapted to distributive politics. In this they are different from any of the common private groups found in the United States which are based on *shared* interests. As Grant McConnell points out, in the United States group homogeneity is a prime factor in political success.[71] In Mexico, a certain kind of heterogeneity is more important.

The other major type of grouping is the peak association represented especially by CONCAMIN and CONCANACO. In Mexico, however, these exist at the behest of the government, not as a response to redistributive challenges. The interest of the state in control and stability in government-business relations dictates compulsory membership in these two confederations. Through co-optation, divide-and-rule tactics, and direct control, the government keeps these organizations from becoming free representatives of private-sector interests. The government also, through its disaggregated style of dealing with most policy issues, makes sure that the confederations do not rally business opposition against the government. Because the government is successful in redefining redistributive issues, as was shown for the profit-sharing decision, it is mainly the interest of the state in controlling business which keeps the confederations together, not the common interest of business in the redistributive battle, as Lowi suggests for the United States.

What is missing in Mexico is the wide variety of influential coalitions of interests and interest groups characteristic of the regulatory arena in the United States. This is not because there are no shared interests among sectors of the Mexican business community, but because group formation responds to the initiatives and will of the executive branch more than to the scope of political decisions.

The Power of Business

The matters dealt with in this section are mainly speculations and pleas for further research, since basic empirical data are still unavailable.

1. *Areas where private decision-making predominates.* We do not claim that the three arenas described in this chapter are the only patterns present in Mexican public-private relationships. What has been done here is to synthesize available studies into common patterns. A useful function of the framework we have developed is to highlight possible gaps in our knowledge of economic policy-making. The basic question for further research that emerges from this study is, How much decision-making goes on outside the three arenas defined? With regard to the issue of business power there appear to be at least two possibilities.

Considerable decision-making may occur which fits the American distributive arena. This would include decisions based on bribery and other corruption or personalism and political connections *not* related to some government policy. In this regard it would be helpful to know more about the autonomous regulatory agencies such as PEMEX and particularly their relationship with various clientele groups.

If the distributive arena is very large—and there is little evidence other than numerous unsystematic references to corruption—then our conclusions regarding the power of the government would need revision. It must be kept in mind, however, that some apparently arbitrary (at least from an economic point of view) decisions have political co-optation and patronage functions. The disaggregated style of decision-making often makes business look more powerful than we believe it actually is. What appears on the surface is a variety of exemptions and special privileges for businessmen. The policy intent, when present, often lies below the surface.

A second possibility is that individual decisions of private entrepreneurs have a major impact—unregulated by government—on the society and economy as a whole. For example, the individual investment decisions of a large number of private firms might have a patterned impact on social and economic structure (for example, loans to the rich but not to the poor). This arena is beginning to be researched in the United States but has so far been ignored in Mexico. We suspect, however, that because of the large direct role of the government in the economic sphere, private decisions with major public impact in the aggregate are less important than in the United States. Nevertheless, it would be interesting to know, for example, what insurance companies do with their capital and what role their peak association, AMIS, plays.

One hint of a socially significant role for "purely" private decisions is offered by Brandenburg. He argues that in the consumer goods industry, freely competitive capitalism (in some cases monopolistic capitalism) operates in a way not allowed in the producer goods area. There are too many plants and too much productive capacity for the market. As a result, profits decrease, quality is low, and producers, having saturated the market, must "rely on their dealers to squeeze the impoverished masses into buying on long-term, virtually impossible terms." Probably as a result of this, more than 50 percent of the television sets and refrigerators sold in Mexico are repossessed by creditors.[72]

This state of affairs appears to be an example of business power, and to some extent it is. However, the producers are powerful relative to other groups in society, not relative to the government. This is *power in the absence of state interest* and is related to the limited pluralism and low mobilization of the Mexican political system.

2. *Consultation and advice.* Another way in which business might exercise power vis-à-vis the public sector is through membership of business leaders in government institutions. Representatives of the private sector sit on the boards of development banks, regulatory agencies and commissions, fiscal boards, and some government-owned enterprises such as the railroads. They thus have an opportunity to be consulted by the government on a variety of economic decisions. This kind of consultation has become broader over the years and now extends into agencies dealing with social as well as economic issues such as the social security commission (IMSS). Finally, high government positions are becoming increasingly available to business leaders. The most notable recent example is that of José Campillo Sainz, a former official of CONCAMIN who is at present minister of industry and commerce.

On the other side of the coin, however, are several factors that considerably limit the influence of business leaders in this consultation process. First, the process is consultation, *not* bargaining, and observers consistently note the "petitionary" style of business requests—probably a sign of lack of real influence. On all the boards and commissions with business membership, the private sector is always a distinct minority, and in the cases which have been studied—for example, the general tariff commission—business representatives have minimal influence and are usually shunted into areas of responsibility dealing with either very broad and vague policies or very small and detailed decisions.[73] In addition, the private sector is *not* represented on the boards of some important autonomous enterprises where it would very much like to be, for example, PEMEX and CONASUPO. The significance of most advice and consultation was perhaps best summed up by a high official of one of the peak associations in commenting on business consultation concerning proposed government economic legislation: "If we get shown controversial legislation beforehand, there is a good chance that the government is not very serious about implementing it."[74]

Our conclusion must be, therefore, that the balance of power in government-business relations is tipped considerably in the direction of the government and that unrestricted private decision-making is much less important in Mexico than it is in the United States. Furthermore, this situation appears to be a direct result of the authoritarian nature of the Mexican political system. Political patterns, structures, and ideologies in Mexico essentially dictate major features of the economic system rather than the reverse. Mexico is thus an example of a political system that molds its environment to a greater extent than occurs in more liberal-democratic systems.

As has been noted, however, our conclusion is based on information contained in the literature available to date. Future research may produce findings that will substantially alter the image of a dominant state interest which permeates the extant studies. Care must be taken, however, to formulate future research regarding the balance of power between the public and private sectors in such a way that the findings will be subject to confirmation or disconfirmation. There is a school of thought, for example, that argues that all government-business relations which are susceptible to study consitute "bargaining on the margins" and that the really important decisions are made behind closed doors and are therefore incapable of being studied. Such an assertion, which has much in common with the cruder "power elite" position in the pluralist–power-elite controversy regarding political power in the United States, can be neither proved nor disproved and thus is not scientifically valid or particularly useful.

The "mobilization of bias" aspect of power-elite theory, on the other hand, does hold some promise for future research. Despite the fact that the available studies indicate that the Mexican government manipulates the mobilization of bias to serve the state interest and limit the options of the private sector, additional research into business-government relations could conceivably produce evidence tending in the other direction.

Finally, there are those who may seek to challenge our conclusion regarding the direction of the balance of power between the Mexican public and private sectors on the grounds that the government's pursuit of its own interests also serves the interests of the private sector. Thus, the argument would go, as long as there is an "alliance for profits" between the government and the business interests, the latter obviously have substantial power over the government. Only when the interests of the state and the private sector are no longer congruent, and the government begins to pursue policies seriously detrimental to the private sector, would the proponents of this view conclude that the balance of power is clearly tipped toward the government.

The problem with this argument is that it seems to assume that there can be no such thing as a dominant state interest in an essentially capitalist economic system since, by definition, a capitalist economic system is one in which the private sector profits from the system. In this chapter, however, we have been concerned with the range of variation possible *within* two basically capitalist systems, those of Mexico and the United States. One can, for example, posit a continuum of capitalist systems. At one extreme the balance of power is tipped toward the government; at the other extreme, it is tipped toward the private sector. We have concluded that the former situation is more characteristic of Mexico. To argue, as some may, that such a situation is not logically possible would severely limit further analysis of authoritarian regimes, such as that of Mexico, which are characterized by essentially capitalist economic systems.

NOTES

We wish to thank Robert R. Kaufman for his detailed and incisive comments and suggestions. We are also grateful to our colleagues who participated in the Conference on Authoritarianism and Corporatism in Latin America for their many helpful remarks.

1. Theodore J. Lowi, "American Business, Public Policy, Case Studies, and Political Theory," *World Politics*, 16 (July 1964):677–715.

2. Raymond Vernon, *The Dilemma of Mexico's Development* (Cambridge: Harvard University Press, 1963), p. 26.

3. Clark W. Reynolds, *The Mexican Economy: Twentieth-Century Structure and Growth* (New Haven: Yale University Press, 1970), p. 255.

4. Ibid., pp. 284–89. In 1962, investment of government and government enterprise as a share of gross investment equaled 32.7 percent, a 10 percent increase over the percentage for 1956.

5. Flavia Derossi, *The Mexican Entrepreneur* (Paris: Development Centre of the Organization for Economic Co-operation and Development, 1970), p. 54; and David Barkin and Timothy King, *Regional Economic Development: The River Basin Approach in Mexico* (Cambridge: Cambridge University Press, 1970), p. 65.

6. Susan Kaufman Purcell, "Decision-making in an Authoritarian Regime: Theoretical Implications from a Mexican Case Study," *World Politics*, 26 (October 1973):28–54.

7. For a discussion of the situation in the United States, see Paul Halpern,

"Management of the Economy," in *American Government Today*, ed. Roger G. Emblen (Del Mar, Calif.: Ziff-Davis, 1974), pp. 83–106.

8. An example was the attempt to form a National Chemical Association (ANIQ) against government wishes in 1960. See Robert Jones Shafer, *Mexican Business Organizations: History and Analysis* (Syracuse: Syracuse University Press, 1973), p. 69.

9. Susan Kaufman Purcell and John F. H. Purcell, "Community Power and Benefits from the Nation: The Case of Mexico," in *Latin American Urban Research*, vol. 3, ed. Francine F. Rabinovitz and Felicity M. Trueblood (Beverly Hills: Sage Publications, 1973), pp. 49–76; and Charles W. Anderson, "Bankers as Revolutionaries: Politics and Development Banking in Mexico," in *The Political Economy of Mexico*, ed. William P. Glade, Jr., and Charles W. Anderson (Madison: University of Wisconsin Press, 1968), p. 175.

10. Competition for leadership is intense. Office in one of the confederations brings positions on government boards and commissions as well as business advantages.

11. As it did the formation of ANIQ as a breakaway from the progovernment chamber, CNIT. See Shafer, *Mexican Business Organizations*, pp. 69–70.

12. Pablo González Casanova, *La democracia en México* (Mexico: Ediciones Era, S.A., 1965), p. 24; and Guadalupe Rivera Marín, "Los conflictos de trabajo en México, 1937–1950," *El Trimestre Económico* 2 (April–June 1955):181–208.

13. Shafer, *Mexican Business Organizations*, pp. 57–58.

14. Derossi, *Mexican Entrepreneur*, p. 86.

15. Rafael Izquierdo, "Protectionism in Mexico," in *Public Policy and Private Enterprise in Mexico*, ed. Raymond Vernon (Cambridge: Harvard University Press, 1964), p. 247.

16. Vernon, *Dilemma*, p. 127.

17. Frank Brandenburg, *The Making of Modern Mexico* (Englewood Cliffs, N.J.: Prentice Hall, Inc., 1964), pp. 13–18 and passim.

18. Vernon, "Introduction," in his *Public Policy*, pp. 15–16.

19. Reynolds, *Mexican Economy*, p. 308.

20. Roger D. Hansen, *The Politics of Mexican Development* (Baltimore: Johns Hopkins Press, 1971), p. 46.

21. For example, the government made sure to pay a price that would satisfy the owners when they nationalized electric power in 1960 (Miguel S. Wionczek, "Electric Power: The Uneasy Partnership," in Vernon, *Public Policy*, p. 106).

22. Grant McConnell, *Private Power and American Democracy* (New York: Alfred A. Knopf, 1966), p. 51.

23. Anderson, "Bankers as Revolutionaries," p. 128.

24. William E. Cole, *Steel and Economic Growth in Mexico* (Austin: University of Texas Press, 1967), pp. 24–25.

25. Reynolds, *Mexican Economy*, p. 186.

26. Brandenburg, *Making of Modern Mexico*, pp. 209–10.

27. McConnell, *Private Power*, p. 196.

28. Peter Bachrach and Morton S. Baratz, *Power and Poverty: Theory and Practice* (New York: Oxford University Press, 1970), p. 43.

29. Derossi, *Mexican Entrepreneur*, pp. 62–63.

30. David H. Shelton, "The Banking System: Money and the Goal of Growth," in Vernon, *Public Policy*, p. 179.

31. Susan Beth Kaufman, *The Mexican Profit-Sharing Decision: Politics in an Authoritarian Regime* (Berkeley: University of California Press, 1975), p. 63.

32. Anderson, "Bankers as Revolutionaries," p. 157.

33. Lowi, "American Business," p. 690.

34. John F. H. Purcell and Susan Kaufman Purcell, "Machine Politics and Socioeconomic Change in Mexico," in *Contemporary Mexico: Papers of the Fourth International Congress of Mexican History*, ed. James W. Wilkie, Michael C. Meyer, and Edna Monzón de Wilkie (Berkeley, Mexico, London: University of California Press and El Colegio de México, 1975).

35. This is part of the Mexican legal system derived from the Spanish colonial legacy which has provided considerable background to the modern authoritarian system.

36. Reynolds, *Mexican Economy*, p. 236.

37. Hansen, *Politics of Mexican Development*, p. 49.

38. Calvin P. Blair, "Nacional Financiera: Entrepreneurship in a Mixed Economy," in Vernon, *Public Policy*, p. 234.

39. Reynolds, *Mexican Economy*, p. 222.

40. Izquierdo, "Protectionism," p. 275.

41. Derossi, *Mexican Entrepreneur*, p. 29.

42. For an excellent discussion of this aspect of Mexican culture, see George M. Foster, *Tzintzuntzan: Mexican Peasants in a Changing World* (Boston: Little, Brown and Co., 1967), esp. chap. 6, "The Image of the Limited Good."

43. Vernon, "Introduction," *Public Policy*, p. 12.

44. Anderson, "Bankers as Revolutionaries," p. 148.

45. Derossi, *Mexican Entrepreneur*, p. 41.

46. Wionczek, "Electric Power," p. 51.

47. Anderson, "Bankers as Revolutionaries," p. 143.

48. Vernon, *Dilemma*, p. 23.

49. Anderson, "Bankers as Revolutionaries," p. 152.

50. Ibid., p. 169.

51. Blair, "Nacional Financiera," p. 228.

52. Cole, *Steel and Economic Growth*, pp. 36–37.

53. Quoted in Wionczek, "Electric Power," p. 81.

54. Ibid., p. 104.

55. Derossi, *Mexican Entrepreneur*, p. 62.

56. Leopoldo Solís, *La realidad económica mexicana: retrovisión y perspectivas* (Mexico: Siglo Veintiuno Editores, S.A., 1970), p. 227.

57. Anderson, "Bankers as Revolutionaries," pp. 121–22.

58. Miguel S. Wionczek, "Incomplete Formal Planning: Mexico," in *Planning Economic Development*, ed. Everett E. Hagen (Homewood, Ill.: Richard D. Irwin, Inc., 1963), p. 175.

59. Cited in Guy Benveniste, *Bureaucracy and National Planning: A Sociological Case Study in Mexico* (New York: Praeger Publishers, 1970), p. 85.

60. See, for example, Vernon, *Dilemma*, p. 118; and Philippe C. Schmitter and Ernst B. Haas, *Mexico and Latin American Economic Integration* (Berkeley: Institute of International Studies, University of California, 1964).

61. Eyler Simpson's term quoted in Barkin and King, *Regional Economic Development*, p. 101. The term refers to a propensity for building specific projects as monuments to the current administration rather than implementing policies which span more than one term of office.

62. Anderson, "Bankers as Revolutionaries," pp. 167–68; and Martin Harry Greenberg, *Bureaucracy and Development: A Mexican Case Study* (Lexington, Mass.: D. C. Heath and Company, 1970).

63. See McConnell's discussion of the U.S. Forest Service in his *Private Power*, pp. 196—202.

64. Izquierdo, "Protectionism," p. 253. See also Solís, *La realidad económica*, p. 226.

65. Wionczek, "Incomplete Formal Planning," p. 179.

66. Wionczek, "Electric Power," p. 94.

67. This and all subsequent references to the profit-sharing issue are from Purcell, *Mexican Profit-Sharing Decision*.

68. This and all subsequent references to the social security issue are from Lowi, "American Business," pp. 703—05.

69. Anderson, "Bankers as Revolutionaries," p. 156.

70. For a discussion of the *grupos* and a list of the better-known ones, see Robert T. Aubey, *Nacional Financiera and Mexican Industry: A Study of the Financial Relationship Between the Government and the Private Sector of Mexico* (Los Angeles: U.C.L.A. Latin American Center, 1966), pp. 76—78. See also Brandenburg, *Making of Modern Mexico*, p. 22, and Vernon, *Dilemma*, pp. 20—21.

71. McConnell, *Private Power*, pp. 241—42.

72. Brandenburg, *Making of Modern Mexico*, p. 291.

73. Izquierdo, "Protectionism," pp. 256—258.

74. Interview by one of the coauthors with an official of a peak association, Mexico City, 1968, cited in Purcell, *Mexican Profit-Sharing Decision*.

EVELYN P. STEVENS

8

Mexico's PRI: The Institutionalization of Corporatism?

Mexico's political system is characterized by patrimonially controlled participation exercised by the political elite based on the underlying assumption of privilege rather than right. Decisions concerning distribution of social and economic goods are made according to pragmatic judgments about the need to balance economic growth and political stability. Changes in domestic or international political and economic conditions are reflected in decisions to expand or contract the benefits granted to participating groups. Not even the most privileged groups (that is, business, industry, and large-scale agriculture) are exempt from the effects of such contractions.

Historical events and cultural preconditions have reduced the influence of such social groups traditionally included in corporatist systems as the church, the military, and the universities. Conversely, the position of economic and political entrepreneurial groups has been enhanced.

The decision-making process is legitimated by massive support from precisely those sectors of society that participate least in the distribution of benefits: labor, peasants, and Indians. Continued manipulation of this support is made possible by the monopoly of the Partido Revolucionario Institutional (PRI) on the electoral process. For more than forty years the Party[1] has maintained this monopoly by preempting and institutionalizing the revolutionary myth and by creating for itself an image as the key component of an indissoluble trinity composed of Party, government, and political elite. Although the division of labor among these three components is apparent to the analyst, the distinction is blurred for the supporters by the concurrent occupation of roles by the same individuals.

Because a political party is only one element in the complex set of interrelationships that we call a political system, and because each nation's system is in some ways similar to and at the same time different from the systems of other nations, it will be necessary to examine the Mexican PRI in the context of the Mexican political system in order to understand the functions of one in relation to the other. Five elements will be the object of special attention in this examination:

1. The national decision-making elite (hereafter referred to simply as "the elite"), as a set of persons which at any given historical moment has the power to choose goals for the nation and to carry out programs for the achievement of those goals.

2. The government, as a set of persons utilizing formal-legal institutions as well as informal and extralegal processes to implement the decisions of the elite.

3. The Party, as the mobilizer of periodic expressions of consent by some sectors of the population.

4. "Other" groups whose concurrence or consent must be obtained if a program is to be successfully carried out. These groups may be designated as indispensable collaborators.

5. "Other" groups whose concurrence or consent cannot be obtained but who must be dealt with if the elite is to achieve its goals. These are the unavoidable dissenters and protesters.[2]

Establishment and Development of the Party

Since the Party was first organized in 1929, as the Partido Nacional Revolucionario (National Revolutionary party, PNR), it has undergone several metamorphoses. There is no evidence to suggest that its founding father, President Plutarco Elías Calles, anticipated some of the functions that it performs today.

One of the most significant aspects of the establishment of the PNR is that it signaled the end of the open and violent struggle for control of the presidency that had marked the years since the promulgation of the 1917 constitution. There had been other parties during the 1920s, most notably the Cooperatist party, the Agrarian party, and the Labor party, but they had served chiefly to promote the ambitions of individual contenders for power.[3] In the sense that their leaders had no synthesizing vision of Mexican politics, nor any apparent interest in fashioning one, it can be said that none of these parties had become truly national in scope.

There is a temptation to look for parallels in the conditions existing in Mexico prior to the organization of the Party and those conditions in Spain which led finally to Francisco Franco's choice of the Movimiento (the Movement) as the only legitimate channel for political activity. It is true, of course, that both of these efforts came about at least partly as an attempt to end the prolonged, bloody, and exhausting civil wars that had all but obliterated the political institutions of the past without establishing any viable substitutes for them. It is also true that the political leadership of both nations had to deal with populations whose national integration presented grave problems arising from economic underdevelopment (better understood as underindustrialization and undercapitalization), illiteracy, and (at least in the case of Spain) strong movements for regional autonomy or separatism.[4]

But the points of divergence are as important as the parallels. While the Franco government supplanted a republic that had enjoyed widespread popular support, the Mexican Party was organized to fill the vacuum created by miniwars among rival caudillos. In Spain, while much of the population was poor, illiterate, and intermittently apathetic, there was a tradition of interaction (much of it hostile, it is true) between the *comunidades* and the central government that reached back into the sixteenth century. In Mexico the consciousness of nationhood and the notion of political participation at that level are still alien to a large number of Mexicans, that is, the part of the population which is non-European or nonmestizo in culture.

Other important differences are evident. The Mexican Revolution drew much of its strength from anticlerical sentiment, and this sentiment was incorporated in the 1917 constitution as well as in the Party's early rhetoric; whereas the Franco revolution was supported by large numbers of Catholics who had been antagonized by the violent anticlericalism of the republicans. Finally, Plutarco Elías Calles and Lázaro Cárdenas, the chief architects of Mexico's Party, were pragmatists, lacking the education and political sophistication of Spain's Serrano Suñer. As a result, policy statements of the Mexican leaders lacked the intellectual tidiness that characterized peninsular formulations, although theory was never a major obstacle to the flexible development of either organization. While the Mexican Party was founded on the assumption that the electoral process is both necessary and desirable, the Spanish Movement rejects these premises.

Thus, while both the Mexican Party and the Spanish Movement arose against superficially similar backgrounds of political chaos, economic disorganization, and war-weariness, about the only real point of contact between them has been their origin in a historical period characterized by a multiplicity of efforts to provide a viable alternative to both communism and pluralist democracy, because both of these were considered inappropriate or had previously proved ineffective. In addition, it is likely that the flexibility noted above has been an important element in the long-term survival of both political systems.

Elsewhere I have argued that Mexico and Spain are two major

variants of an inherent authoritarian model.[5] The Spanish variant has been described as the result of the manifestly corporatist experiments of the 1920s and 1930s, involving "the establishment of functionally-representative legislative bodies and councils of state, the restructuring of worker-employee relations along corporatist lines, [and] the organization of corporations and organs of economic coordination to regulate social and economic relations."[6] The Mexican variant, which I have designated as "secular authoritarianism," relies far less on the formal-legal incorporation of functional groupings into the structure of government and much more on "an historic pattern of social and political culture and organization—elitist, hierarchical, corporatist, and patrimonialist—that is seemingly characteristic of virtually all the Iberic-Latin systems."[7]

To say, however, that one can discern the imprint of traditional patterns on present-day practices is not sufficient reason for applying the label of corporatism to the contemporary amalgam.

In Mexico, the convocation of the new Party's constituent assembly was a recognition that Mexico was entering a new stage of development that required a national approach to political problems. In providing an organization through which competing claims to national power could be processed in a relatively orderly way, the Party was to consolidate, regulate, and legitimate the government created by the constitution. For the first time since the departure of the dictator Porfirio Díaz, Mexican political activity was to be sufficiently structured to be described as a political system.

When issuing the call for an organizational meeting, Calles exercised decisive influence by making up the list of individuals who would be allowed to participate. Significantly, he excluded the Mexican Regional Labor Confederation (CROM), headed by the powerful Luis Morones, and the Partido Nacional Agrarista, at that time the largest aggregator of peasant interests in the nation.[8]

These omissions meant that the Party, in its first incarnation, was not conceived as a framework for functional interest groups. Instead, it grouped together into a national network those local or regional leaders who had shown most political (rather than military) ability. Although many of these politicians had risen to prominence by reason of their military victories during the Revolution, their political ability was the prime consideration. This makes it possible for historians to describe them as *líderes* (leaders) rather than caudillos. They brought with them into the new party their entire networks of followers, people whose personal loyalty was assured through one or another element of the sacred triad of personal relationships consisting of family, friendship, and *compadrazgo* (ritual coparenthood).[9]

At this early stage of the PNR's development, the image projected by its leaders was that of a party whose chief concerns were for the destitute, the exploited, and the proletariat. There were even scattered references to capitalist exploitation and the class struggle, but as a matter of fact these vaguely expressed notions were not translated into a coherent pattern of action.[10]

From the beginning, the Party has been a clearing-house for the personal ambitions of leaders whose ideological orientations—or lack of them—have often conflicted. Party followers who espoused a particular ideology could always find a statement by some leader that seemed to reflect their own political biases. There were few ideologues among either the leaders or the followers, however, and the ideological imprecision was combined with preemption of the revolutionary mystique (enshrined throughout the Party's name changes by inclusion of the word Revolution) to impart a protean flexibility to the new political organization.[11]

At the 1933 national convention of the PNR, two changes were introduced which eroded the incipient federalism and centralized decision-making power. First, the regional groupings were abolished, at a time when government institutions at the regional and local level were being weakened, with the result that local leaders became increasingly dependent on the national leadership for support and patronage. They were forced to find places for themselves in a vastly enlarged network of personal relationships by forging bonds of mutual obligation through one or another of the elements of the sacred triad at supralocal levels.

Even now, more than forty years after the change was introduced, the interlocking of local and national networks wtihin the party structure accounts for the otherwise unexplainable success or failure of many ambitious people. It has proved impossible for individuals to build outside the Party a power base broad enough to force acquiescence by the Party's national leadership. Men who have tried to do so usually find their political ambitions permanently blocked; they may even suffer sudden death.[12]

The second change that took place in 1933 was the substitution of party nominating conventions for the plebiscitary procedures that had been used until then. This removed the process of candidate selection from public visibility. From that time on, this important activity became increasingly arcane, culminating in the *tapadismo* that has been a distinctive feature of the Party for many years.[13]

It is almost impossible to overrate the importance of the changes made by Lázaro Cárdenas in the Party's structure in 1938, because those changes both defined the Party's place in the Mexican political system as a whole, and limited its power to affect the choice of national goals. Almost certainly, it was not Cárdenas's intention to bring about the latter result.

He wanted to provide a group basis of action for those elements of Mexican society whose support was indispensable for his exercise of governmental power. He accomplished this by creating four sectors: Peasant, Labor, Popular, and Military. His populist sympathies were manifest in the organization of the first three of these sectors; it is significant, for example, that he chose the denomination "Peasant" instead of the more inclusive "agriculture." The latter would have embraced medium and even large landholders, and he had worked ever since assuming the presidency to eliminate these elements from the agricultural economy of the nation, through his program of expropriation of large estates and redistribution of the land to peasants. The basis of the Peasant sector was the Confederación Nacional Campesina (CNC), an organization that drew its membership from the *ejidos* (communal farms) created and encouraged by Cárdenas.

The Confederación de Trabajadores Mexicanos (CTM) constituted the nucleus of the Labor sector. In 1936, Cárdenas had been instrumental in organizing the confederation, for the evident purpose of supplanting older corrupt labor groupings with a group headed by Vicente Lombardo Toledano, who could be counted on to mobilize support for Cárdenas's policies.

Now the Mexicans had a president who actively wooed the forces of labor and who bound their loyalty to him by conciliatory acts. But Cárdenas did not seek this rapprochement for the purpose of achieving a dictatorship of the proletariat; it was simply a prudent step to secure the mass support necessary for stabilizing the power of the central government. In turn, this implied the support of governmental institutions and processes for the consolidation of power into the hands of a few "trustworthy" labor leaders, with a consequent weakening of the influence that could be wielded by rank-and-file union members. [14] With the passage of time, this resulted in a marriage of convenience between the government and the labor leaders (the latter known as *charros*), with the workers themselves being regarded as wards in a perpetual state of tutelage whose duty is to obey their parents. Attempts by a few dissident leaders to break out of these restrictions have been met with severe sanctions. [15]

The Peasant and Labor sectors of the Party are the explicit acknowledgment of the Revolution's debt to these two main elements in the victory of the armed phase of the struggle. They are the embodiment of articles 27 (agrarian reform) and 123 (rights of labor) of the 1917 constitution; together, constitutional provisions and formal party structure can be seen as a way of paying off old debts with the symbolic coin of promised future benefits.

Cárdenas obviously regarded the workers and the peasants as the most important elements of society, as indeed they were, judged by numerical criteria. He also recognized that there might be other elements aggregating thousands or even millions of persons who did not fit into either of these categories; for them he created the Popular (or "people's") sector. Rather than designate a special sector for Mexico's Indians, he indicated that they should be included in the Popular sector. In doing so, he ignored the fact that they might have been more appropriately grouped with the peasants, as their mode of life was rural and predominantly agricultural.

Census figures for 1970 identify three million individuals as Indians, defined by language-usage criteria. Fewer than one hundred thousand of these are presently counted as PRI members. A small contingent of them is periodically rescued from obscurity and paraded in full traditional dress at the Party's national meetings. They are strange sector-fellows of the bureaucrats, professionals, urban women and youth, craftsmen, small businessmen, and small property owners who make up the other divisions of this sector.

With time, the Confederación Nacional de Organizaciones Populares (National Confederation of Popular Organizations, formed in 1943 and known as the CNOP) has come to occupy most of the political space in the Popular sector, crowding into impotence the members enrolled individually. The bureaucrats who compose a division of the CNOP have increased their influence to such an extent that they are now clearly the most powerful visible group in the PRI. Their strength vis-à-vis CTM and CNC, major supports of the other two sectors, can be gauged not only by the disproportionate material benefits they enjoy, but by their preponderant representation in the national executive committee of the Party and the number of members of the Chamber of Deputies who owe their seats to them.[16] In 1970, for example, eighty-nine of the nominations (with subsequent election guaranteed) came from the Popular sector, while thirty-eight and fifty-one corresponded respectively to the Labor and Peasant sectors.[17]

Cárdenas created a fourth sector for the military men. It was dissolved in 1940, with some of the displaced officers gravitating to the Popular sector, while others withdrew or were forced to withdraw permanently from politics. Cárdenas's purpose in creating a special sector for the military men as a group, but most particularly for officers, had been to bring them into the open and force them to channel their political activities through the Party, where they could be controlled by the checks and balances provided by the other sectors. After a number of officers bolted in 1940 to support the independent candidacy of General Juan Andreu Almazán, their political ineptitude was devastatingly demonstrated at the polls, and it was possible for

President Manuel Avila Camacho to consign them to organizational oblivion.

With the 1938 reorganization of the Party into sectors that were isolated from one another and related only to and through the central control apparatus, a superficial resemblance to the corporatist political model began to appear.[18] Even the most cursory of surveys, however, would reveal that not all of the important functional groups in Mexican society were represented in the Party.

Groups Beyond the Pale

Although military men had been included in the 1938 reorganization because of the possible danger of ignoring them, two other important components of Mexican society were excluded at every stage because the revolutionary tradition expressly repudiated them. The church was forbidden by article 130 of the 1917 constitution to participate in any political activities, and members of the clergy were deprived of the franchise. The hostility was mutual; if the *cristero* rebellion of the 1920s had not been sufficiently convincing, the continued activities of the *sinarquistas* during the 1930s would have tipped the balance against the church.[19]

During the 1940 campaign for the presidency it appeared for a brief time that this hostility might create problems for the Party, especially when General Almazán appealed to Catholics for support, hurling such epithets as "atheist" and "church desecrator" at the supporters of the Partido de la Revolución Mexicana (PRM). How fragile was this appeal and how eager were the voters to continue faithful to the Party can be seen when it is recalled that Avila Camacho, the presidential candidate, reassured them with the simple sentence, "I am a believer." Thus, with two words (*soy creyente* in Spanish) he was able to wrest the opposition's chief propaganda weapon from its grasp, and won the election easily.

The other excluded group was composed of the growing number of bankers, merchants, and industrialists whose influence on the economic goals of the nation and whose share of the economic benefits were to increase over the years, in spite of sporadic bursts of anticapitalist rhetoric required to preserve the Party's image as a friend of the people and an enemy of the moneyed class.

To a large extent, this group has become an important influence on the decision-making process, with a prominent advisory role in setting economic policy. However, it has no veto power over distasteful decisions on, for example, taxation. On the other hand, political decisions about the kind and amount of official response to protest activities are often affected by the insistence of businessmen on the need for a "climate of stability."

The six years (1934–1940) of Cárdenas's presidency were without doubt the high tide of populist policy in Mexico. The legend of Cárdenas as the friend of workers and peasants and defender of the poor and the weak is solidly based in contemporary accounts.[20] But Cárdenas was no ideologue; he was a visceral pragmatist whose policies responded to the exigencies of changing national and international circumstances.

In 1936, Cárdenas had already responded to allegations that he was encouraging communist activity in Mexico by stating that "the cause of social agitation does not center in the existence of Communist nuclei. These form minorities without particular influence in the country. . . . These small minorities exist in Europe, in the United States, and, in general, in all the countries of the earth. Their action neither compromises the stability of our institutions, nor alarms the government and it should not alarm the entrepreneur."[21]

At the same time that the nationalization of the petroleum industry was dramatizing Mexico's image as an independent nation, freed from domination by foreign investors, other steps were being taken to insure the continued viability of domestic private capital. In fact, in 1936 and 1937 the government moved to establish a confederation of national chambers of commerce (known by its Spanish acronym CONCANACO) and a confederation of industrial chambers (CONCAMIN).

Statutory provisions have made membership in these organizations compulsory for all but the smallest businesses and industries. Together, CONCANACO and CONCAMIN embrace all private enterprises of any economic importance in Mexico. Their financial solvency, based on a graduated dues schedule, makes it possible for them to sponsor special studies, formulate position papers, conduct propaganda campaigns, and communicate their attitudes openly to the bureaucratic structure. The government often (but not invariably) consults their leaders in matters perceived to touch on the interests of their members, thus giving them advance opportunity to influence the shape of legislation or executive action. "Virtually every business group of note possesses an intimate interrelation with government," observes one author, who goes on to conclude that "participation of trade associations and other business groups in decision-making processes has in fact become institutionalized."[22] Internally, these chambers are organized to reflect the interests of their largest and wealthiest constituents. This is made possible through rules that weight the voting strength of member firms according to the amount of dues paid.

Merle Kling has contributed valuable insights into the long-term strategy and day-to-day operations of a fairly typical group representing business interests.[23] The *instituto* he studied is an interesting example of how things are done in Mexico, even when the official political mythology tells us that they are never done that way.

The institute's membership was made up of financiers, industrialists, and heads of large commercial enterprises, some of them representing firms whose capital was derived wholly or in large part from foreign investors (for example, Sears Roebuck and Woolworth's). New members were constantly recruited from among the elite of Mexico's economy, with special care being taken to assure that the heads of the important *cámaras* (chambers) of commerce and industry were included. If through election or other circumstances a *cámara*'s leadership underwent change, the new leaders, if not already members of the institute, were immediately invited to join.

These men were constantly castigated in public statements by high government officials as "enemies of the Revolution," advocates of policies whose nefarious influence must be extirpated from Mexico's program of economic development. Yet in private, some of those same government officials were corresponding regularly with the institute's staff, recommending additional names of financiers and industrialists as prospective members, complimenting staff members on the quality of news releases, and in general sustaining a cordial relationship with men whose counterparts two generations previously had been the mainstay of Porfirio Díaz's regime.

During his term of office (1958–1964), President Adolfo López Mateos declared, in a speech in Guaymas, that his administration was the "extreme left, within the limits set by the Constitution." Such a statement should, if taken seriously, cause profound consternation in the ranks of conservative businessmen. Not withstanding the militancy of his words, the "reactionary forces" applauded the speech and praised López Mateos for his statesmanship.[24]

In López Mateos's administration, the government vigorously repressed the activities of rebellious labor unions that had tried to throw off the yoke of their corrupt leaders. The action of those leaders had made possible the emasculation of Mexico's labor movement and had made a mockery of the PRI Labor sector's claim to a share of influence in the policy-making process. Yet, in justifying its repressive actions, the government alleged that the leaders of the rebellion were "communist agents."[25] The incongruity of López Mateos's Guaymas speech and the government's actions is even more evident when it is recalled that the Communist party was a legal entity in Mexico, and by any definition its few avowed members were the "extreme left within the Constitution."[26] The government tried to resolve this apparent paradox by appealing in its propaganda to xenophobic sentiments: It was not communism per se that was antirevolutionary, but *foreign* communism. Charges—never substantiated—were made that the rebellious labor leaders had been "in daily contact with the Russian Embassy."[27]

Evidence of cordial relationships between business leaders and Party leaders has continued to accumulate. The social activities pages of Mexico's newspapers chronicle in news stories and pictures the delicate and complex process of cross-fertilizing loyalties through the ritual ties of *compadrazgo*, intermarriage, and secular festivities among Mexico's economic and political elites.[28] As might be anticipated, members of the economic elite are not expected to cool their heels in the public waiting rooms of government or PRI officials in order to press their claims for preferential treatment. According to an account by an important industrialist, whose multiple enterprises are heavily penetrated by foreign investment capital, the usual mode of approach is through informal unpublicized contacts.[29]

There is a danger that the foregoing remarks may leave the impression that the government is abjectly subservient to the bidding of private enterprise in Mexico. This is not true. Authors of a number of studies have concluded that government policy has vigorously and positively promoted a mixed economy by innovative manipulation of banking and credit facilities, investment in and management of a number of large-scale enterprises, and creation of new financial institutions—all without relinquishing control over the determination of economic ends and means.[30] Businessmen have not always been enthusiastic about the regime's choice of means; at least some of their public viewing-with-alarm that ritualistically accompanies every innovation is probably rooted in real apprehension about possible effects on profits.

Mexican government policies vis-à-vis Mexican business interests are also affected by the relative inability of the Mexican government to prevent penetration of the economic sphere by foreign (principally U.S.) capital, which derives its power from its ability to affect the international economic, political, and even military conditions within which dependent nations must operate. One might ask, for example, what would happen if the Mexican government were able really to implement its publicly proclaimed policy of "Mexicanization," that is, the limiting of foreign stockholders to a minority role in industrial and commercial enterprises. One is led to speculate that, given its relative powerlessness to enforce such policies, the Mexican government since 1940 has attempted to protect native business interests as much as possible. Although Mexicans point with pride to the 1938 expropriation and nationalization of petroleum holdings, it is unlikely that such vigorous action could be successfully initiated today.[31] The operation

of large private corporations has become much more sophisticated and
consequently better equipped to deal with such threats.

If Mexico enjoyed greater autonomy vis-à-vis the United States in
particular and transnational and multinational corporations in general,
it is entirely possible that the Mexican government would bring native
business interests under more direct control, much in the way that it
has done with the labor and peasant groups. Here again, however, we
must point out that large-scale agriculture has to a very great extent
escaped the effects of constitutional and statutory measures intended
for its control. It is not irrelevant to point out that large-scale agricultural production has already been heavily penetrated by U.S. investors.
The result has been a weakening of the Mexican government's ability to
implement land-tenure and land-use policies. Thus we have the spec-
tacle of a PRI sector that is labeled "peasant" that does not act in
behalf of any component of that sector; the "big" farmers negotiate
directly with the government, while the peasants enjoy mobilization
without representation.

Common to all the studies of Mexico's mixed economy is the
conclusion that government participation has made an important contribution to the country's impressive economic growth and that this
growth has clearly benefited the private sector of the economy. At the
same time, these writers and others point out that income distribution
has not improved since the end of World War II and that in fact income
inequality has increased in recent years.[32] With continuing inflation
outpacing wage increases, it is still appropriate to cite a comment made
nearly twenty years ago to the effect that "the true hero of the
Mexican investment boom is the ordinary Mexican worker, whose
acceptance of a declining real income has in effect [subsidized] much
of the nation's building."[33] Although the poorer half of the Mexican
population became progressively poorer, the growth rate of the economy maintained itself for over two decades at such a high rate that
some publicists dubbed the phenomenon "the Mexican miracle." This
development took place against a background of government and PRI
populist rhetoric accompanied by hostile allusions to the alleged malev-
olence of private enterprises, counterpointed by sporadic expressions of
alarm about government intervention in the economy voiced by groups
representing private enterprise.

Whatever the formula, it is clear that the relationship is now sufficiently stabilized to enable us to say that it has become institutionalized; not, to be sure, within the formal structure of the Party organization, but certainly in such a way that there is a high degree of
predictability about the interaction of government and business. In
establishing the sector basis of the Party, Cárdenas had undoubtedly

been influenced by the corporatist experimentation that was going on in Europe during the 1930s. However, he was wise enough not to try to lock all of the elements of society into the same mold.[34]

That the government is by no means a helpless captive of business interests has again been clearly demonstrated by its actions during the administration of President Luis Echeverría. Since 1970, there have been disquieting developments, resulting in part from the world economic situation and reflected especially in Mexico's external imbalance of payments and in rapidly mounting inflation. The resulting hardships for the masses of Mexico's poor have increased political tensions. The situation has also provided fresh incentives for a growing chorus of criticism from reformist dissenters. In response to these pressures, the government has hardened its attitude toward open demonstrations of protest and at the same time has applied corrective measures to the economy, including price controls, wage increases, and new taxes. While reformers have challenged the adequacy of these measures, businessmen have expressed alarm at what they see as government hostility toward them. The Mexican national political elite has shown that no one component of the political system enjoys unchallenged domination. While economic growth has been the main theme of Mexico's programmatic consensus since 1940, the timetable has clearly been altered in favor of a greater emphasis on political stability.

Bureaucratization of the Party and the Government

Throughout most of its history, the Party's effectiveness depended on an aggregation of local and regional leaders who exercised a monopoly of influence over the organization of electoral activity in their particular areas. The establishment of the Party in the late 1920s had marked the transition from reliance on armed combat to more disguised forms of attaining and retaining national power. The new paths to power required the exercise of new political skills, including the distribution of patronage, manipulation of organizational rules, informal alliances, and use of new communication methods made possible by technological advances. The bulk of these activities are carried out by the Party, but to reinforce the controls the government has frequently used formal-legal institutions as well as extralegal covert violent measures such as kidnaping of protesters, assassinations in the provinces, and armed intervention in constitutionally protected meetings. Effective control of the mass media has kept these events from becoming common knowledge.

A natural outcome of this division of labor has been the increasing rationalization of the Party's operations, involving the emergence of cadres skilled in the techniques of communication, parliamentary procedure, and conciliatory negotiation. The new technocrats are the product of expanding educational opportunities; they are less interested in ideology than in the opportunity to employ their skills and to earn a decorous salary.

Because both Party bureaucrats and government bureaucrats have a stake in the continued hegemony of established organizations, they find temselves sharing at least nominal interest in the Party's Popular sector, which aggregates the membership of middle-class elements such as professional, clerical, and technical workers, either as individuals or as members of formal groups. Even when organized as white-collar unions, such groups are distinct from the labor unions that constitute the Labor sector of the Party. The Popular sector unions refer to their members as *empleados* (employees), while Labor union members are known as *trabajadores* (workers).[35]

Government employees are indirectly affiliated with the sector through their membership in various employee unions which together form the Federation of Unions of Government Employees (FSTSE). Membership in these unions is not compulsory, but only the most impractical of nonconformists would reject such benefits incidental to membership as free or low-cost vacation resorts, discounts on the prices of consumer goods, and preference for occupancy of moderate-cost rental housing—all important contributions to the constant struggle for marginal differentiation between membership in the mobile lower-middle class and the working class.

The number of nonunion individual members of the Popular sector is cloaked by several ambiguities, not the least of which is a propensity for agglutination in several kinds of groups displaying various degrees of organizational complexity, ranging from informal blocs to unions that are duly certified by the appropriate section of the government arbitration board. Flexibility is the great advantage of this ambiguity: Within a matter of hours, and with a minimum of effort, a bloc can be formed, purporting to represent the interests of an occupational class of individuals; a day or two after such a development, the bloc can be officially recognized as a union, with preemptive powers to speak for and negotiate in behalf of that particular class. This device has proved useful in by-passing nascent groups of protesters. For example, in the 1964–1965 protest movement of government physicians, the members of the striking physicians' alliance found themselves outflanked and effectively disfranchised by a doctors' union that had sprung full-panoplied from the pen of the Popular sector leadership.[36]

Although the Party is the major conduit through which the government channels its communications to the masses, it does not provide an efficient mechanism for conducting a reverse flow of information, from the masses to the government. There is no indication that the Party's founders ever intended to establish such a mechanism. The practice initiated by Lázaro Cárdenas during his presidency of riding circuit throughout the country suggests that he did not expect to get the information he wanted from the Mexican people through any institutionalized means. In fact, the only formal link between the general party membership and the government is the national executive committee of the PRI, whose members are selected by the president of the republic and by manipulation of intrasectoral elections.

We spoke earlier of a division of labor between Party bureaucrats and government bureaucrats. Both kinds of bureaucrats implement the overarching decisions made by a third group: the elite. This is what we might reasonably expect to find in a modern political system. There is no reason to assume that the different activities required by this division of labor are performed by different sets of individuals. In fact, Mexican politicians may move back and forth freely in all three roles, often accomplishing the metamorphosis several times during a working day, and sometimes leaping back and forth between roles in a matter of minutes. This does not ordinarily disturb most Mexicans, nor does it even occasion expressions of surprise. Speaking before an American audience, though, a Mexican observer referred to the "PRI-government," and the "PRI-Establishment," concluding that all of Mexico is "PRI-infiltrated."[37]

In spite of the discrepancies between the picture of sectoral membership presented for public consumption and the actual practices revealed empirically, the Popular sector is the strongest of the three divisions of the Party. This is due in great part to its ability to produce leaders from within its own ranks of middle-class members who possess the requisite political skills of manipulation and conciliation. National and regional heads of the Labor and Peasant sectors, on the other hand, rarely come from the occupational strata that they purport to represent; instead, they are also middle-class, even though the rank and file of their membership is not. This similarity of class background at the leadership level has resulted in a situation on which the Popular sector capitalized to secure for itself a disproportionate influence, both in intraparty distribution of influence and in the *modus operandi* which the Party has evolved in its dealings with other elements of the political system. One writer has described the resulting style of political activity as "instrumental rationality." [38]

The remarkable nature of this achievement can be better appreciated if the basis of support for the Party is examined in greater detail. In 1958 the most optimistic claims of the Party leaders indicated an overall membership of nearly seven million persons, with the Peasant sector accounting for three million of the total and the other two sectors dividing the remaining four million equally. Payment of dues has never been a requirement for membership; Robert Scott reported that only 3 to 5 percent of the members made any financial contribution at all, and these were individuals who occupied leadership positions.[39] In 1968, a Party spokesman announced that membership had grown to a litte over eight million—an impressive gain for the ten-year period—but again there was no way of distinguishing between directly affiliated individuals and indirectly affiliated persons (by virtue of membership in an organization such as a labor union or peasants' syndicate) or between active and passive members.[40] It is hard to credit the claim of the PRI spokesman that only card-carrying members had been counted; my own experience at national Party headquarters in Mexico City indicates that only a small percentage of Party workers could produce any credentials attesting to membership. Figures for labor unions and peasant syndicates—the basis for indirect Party affiliation—are equally unreliable. Here again, payment of dues is not a requirement for affiliation, and there is no way of checking the organizations' claims. Official announcement of strike votes might provide an indication of membership in some unions, but again the figures would be partial and suspect, as experience shows that even when such votes are actually taken, it is by a show of hands. Many times the government arbitration board simply announces the total, with no attempt to substantiate it.

If we pass from this uncertain ground to an area more accessible to measurement techniques, it is possible to examine in greater detail the electoral basis of support for the Party. José Luis Reyna analyzes election data from 1952 to 1967 and shows that four socioeconomic variables are positively correlated with differentiated voting (that is, tendency to vote for a party other than the PRI). These variables are urbanization, industrialization, literacy, and income.[41] It is his conclusion that support for the Party is derived most heavily from the poorest, least educated, rural people living in the poorest areas of the country. These areas, consisting of the states of Chiapas, Guerrero, Hidalgo, Oaxaca, and Tlaxcala, gave almost no support to the opposition.[42]

Modernization and economic development can be shown in another way to be inversely related to electoral support for the Party: Compared with other groups and classes, Mexico's Indians, who are the poorest, least educated, and most traditional members of society, turn out better than anybody else to give their vote to the PRI.[43] Their docility at the polls is reminiscent of the mass baptisms through which tens of thousands of their ancestors became "Christianized" during the early period of the Conquest.

During the past decade, the agricultural sector of the economy, composed of Indians and peasants, accounted for only 25 percent of the total GNP of the nation.[44] These are the Mexicans described by Pablo González Casanova as "marginals," that is, those who are largely excluded from effective *participation* in the distribution of economic and political benefits emanating from the country's developmental process.[45]

Mexico thus provides a clear example of the distinction between *participation*, understood as action taken with the conscious intent of increasing the share of benefits from the system, and *mobilization*, seen as support of the existing distribution of benefits. Moreover, this mobilization occurs only at election time for the rural population. In the cities, union members are sometimes required to attend rallies or march in parades, or to take part in a mass demonstration of hostility to a protest group. In one case involving the latter kind of action, a truckload of union men being transported to a counterprotest rally chanted, "We're not *going*; we're being taken."[46]

Commenting on this situation, Reyna observes that "political control is exercised upon the more manipulable groups within the system. Furthermore, the degree of manipulation varies inversely with the bargaining power of the group. By the same token, the lower the degree of development of the group (or sector) the lower its bargaining power."[47]

If we look closely at the election data supplied by Mario Ezcurdia, another aspect of the Party's place in the system becomes clearer. In 1967, not a presidential year, the number of adult citizens was 18 million; of these, 15 million were registered to vote, and 10 million actually cast votes. The PRI received 8,335,244 votes, only 200,000 more than the number of members claimed by the Party.[48] Ezcurdia cited these figures to show that official claims of PRI membership totals were "independently" substantiated by election results. To accept this interpretation would require a suspension of disbelief on the part of the nonparticipant observer, especially when it is remembered that the electoral process itself is supervised by the Secretariat of Gobernación, the government department that has produced five consecutive victorious PRI candidates for the presidency. This pro-PRI bias will be further examined below; here, it is enough to consider the extent to which data analysis—a tool of bureaucratic instrumental rationality—is used to validate the Party's claim to legitimacy.

The PRI and "Other" Parties

In the foregoing discussion, we have examined some aspects of the internal dynamics of the PRI and some aspects of the Party's relationship to "other" groups not included in its sectoral format but whose concurrence or consent must be obtained if the program, which is formulated and implemented outside the Party, is to be successfully carried out. We have seen that internally, the middle-class elements housed in the Popular sector have triumphed over the other sectors with respect to the distribution of influence in the PRI and also in connection with their greater share of prestige and material benefits. The interests of this part of the PRI membership coincide with the economic goals of the regime, making its support of those goals a natural outcome. From an "objective" point of view, it is not so easy to understand the motivations of members of the other two sectors, the labor and peasant sectors, unless it is remembered that their leadership also comes from the middle-class element of society.

Thus, the Popular sector is seen as a *participating* group of citizens, while the other two sectors are masses *mobilized* for the purpose of conceding their acquiescence.

In its external relationships the PRI operates in such a way as to leave ample room for action by important groups not included in its format. By far the most important of such groups are those associated with large and medium capitalist enterprises. That there has been a clear realization of the necessity and desirability of including those elements in the design of the political system is evident by reference to the historical studies cited earlier.

So comprehensive is that design and so integral a part of it is the PRI that there seems to be little room for maneuver or, indeed, little reason for the existence of other political parties. Such parties do exist; the historical circumstances of their founding and their bases of electoral support (or lack thereof) are discussed in all of the standard reference works cited in notes 3, 10, and 13. Because only the Partido de Acción Nacional (PAN) has had any measurable impact on public opinion and on the electoral process, it will be discussed briefly.

The Partido de Acción Nacional was founded in 1939, in response to events whose implications for the future profoundly disturbed the "better element" of Mexican society: the property-owning classes, the devout Catholics, and politically conservative groups. Populist rhetoric, church-state conflict, agrarian reform with its accompanying redistribution of land to peasants, labor unrest, and nationalization of the petroleum industry were enough to spur even the most timorous of dissenters to some kind of reaction. It was to provide an alternative set of policies that the PAN, with encouragement from the Catholic hierarchy, began its existence: ironically, at a time when the high tide of populism and anticlericalism had already begun to recede.[49]

The PAN shares the same philosophical and ideological assumptions of Christian Democratic parties in other Latin American nations; indeed, if it were not for Mexico's constitutional strictures against the intrusion of religion into politics, there is little doubt that PAN's name would have included the word Christian. PAN leaders have often been in cordial correspondence with Christian Democratic leaders in other countries, expressing solidarity and exchanging information. In their most recent formulation, PAN's Principles of Doctrine show the continuing influence of Catholic social doctrine, including the new directions taken since Vatican II, and incorporating the principles enunciated in *Mater et Magistra* (1961), *Pacem in Terris* ((1963), and *Popularum Progressio* (1967).

Catholic influence is clearly visible in such concepts as the sacredness of the family as the basic unit of society, the organic nature of society, and the hierarchical ordering of society in the interest of the common good.[50] The Thomistic notion of the just wage, which has always been hostile to the development of capitalism, has resulted in much moral ambivalence for many Panistas who themselves are capitalists. Like Christian Democrats in other parts of Latin America, they have resolved the dilemma to their own satisfaction—if not to that of the growing number of radical priests—by accepting the necessity of capitalism as the most efficient way of promoting the economic growth of the nation, as long as that growth alleviates human misery. This latter point has been the basis of recent PAN criticisms of the government.

Since its founding, the party has grown slowly but steadily. At the present time, it probably has about 180,000 active, dues-paying members and is able to garner nearly two million votes for its presidential candidate.[51] The most recent amendments to the electoral law resulted in the concession of twenty-one "party deputy" seats in the national chamber of deputies, in addition to the four seats actually won at the polls in the congressional election of 1974.

In the congress, PAN deputies have been able to criticize the government's policies and to propose alternative approaches to the solution of social and economic problems. These proposals have invariably failed of adoption at the time of their presentation, but a surprising number of them have subsequently been resubmitted in virtually the same form by PRI deputies and have been adopted without opposition.

PAN's efforts to displace the PRI or, more modestly, to capture a share of power through electoral victories, have largely been unsuccessful over the years. The party leaders have consistently blamed these failures on massive frauds at the polls, carried out by collusion among the elite, the government, and the PRI. There is no doubt that fraud is widely practiced: A number of well-documented cases have been reported.[52] Localized victories have been won and nullified by governmental action in such widely separated areas as Yucatán and Baja California, but even if all disputed cases had been resolved in favor of the PAN, the results would not have constituted a serious challenge to the PRI's hegemony.

Paradoxically, PAN's continued existence has always depended on the fact that it does not present a threat to the PRI. Its arrested development is a result of its failure to present a clear-cut alternative to the electorate, as well as its inability to employ the techniques of mass mobilization. But these deficiencies have made it acceptable to the elite, whereas a party that would propose real structural changes would surely have been repressed within a short time after its founding. It tickles the political vanity of many citizens to be able to assure themselves and to tell foreign observers (*para inglés ver*) that Mexico is a multiparty state.

PAN's leaders are aware of their delicate position and are able to tolerate the ambivalence. However, they are uneasy about the future, especially as they find their middle-class support being drained away by desertions of individuals who now see no major ideological barrier to supporting the PRI and benefiting from being identified with the winner. In practice, the elite has co-opted PAN's policy preferences. By its use of rhetoric, the PRI has preempted many of the symbols of Christian Democracy while carefully avoiding doctrinally loaded language.

The deserters from PAN's ranks represent a class of individuals whose concurrence or consent is necessary for the achievement of the elite's broad economic policies. If the entire class of such persons had withheld their support from the PRI, the government could not have survived. As a matter of fact, the PAN businessmen numbered but a very small percentage of this category; they held out long after the conditions justifying their obstinacy had disappeared. Even before their capitulation, the PAN had become simply a luxury which the elite could well afford.

The other two parties that have participated in the national electoral process are the Partido Auténtico de la Revolución Mexicana (Authentic Party of the Mexican Revolution, known as PARM) and the Partido Popular Socialista (Popular Socialist Party, known as the PPS). Both of these parties owe their creation to personal relationships between their leaders and influential persons in the regime. The PARM was created in 1954 by President Adolfo Ruíz Cortines as an acknowledgment of his debt to General Jacinto B. Treviño, who headed a group of military veterans of the Revolution.[53] These men had been unable to obtain leadership positions in the PRI and found it beneath their dignity to become simple supporters. Cartoonists depict the PARM as an old people's home for retired veterans. The party consistently supports the PRI presidential candidate, and although it is virtually certain that the PARM does not fulfill the requirements for certification, it continues to exist on sufferance.

The Partido Popular Socialista had been allowed to exist because of sentimental regard for the early association between Vicente Lombardo Toledano and President Lázaro Cárdenas. Lombardo's exposition of an eclectic ideology combining Mexican nationalism with some elements of Marxism-Leninism rounded out the official image of the political system as a spectrum of left-center-right positions. With the death of Lombardo Toledano came a decline in the prestige of the PPS, as a result of which the PRI's gravitation toward the right became more apparent.

The Dangerous Groups

Unlike the "tame" political parties described in the preceding section, a number of movements have arisen during the past twenty years that have reflected a deep-seated dissatisfaction with the elite's choice of goals and a broad-based attempt to force the adoption of structural changes. Some of these protest movements and the measures used by the government to suppress them or to co-opt their leaders have been described in detail elsewhere.[54]

The "dangerous" activities have taken several forms. The most visible, involving the largest number of persons and evoking the most violent repression, have been the protest movements led by university students. Since 1956 there have been several such movements, but the only one that attracted international attention was the student strike of 1968 that culminated in the massacre of an estimated two hundred students and bystanders at Tlatelolco Plaza in Mexico City. That student resistance is tenacious is evidenced by the fact that smaller-scale incidents have continued to occur even up to the present, on or near the campuses of both the National University in Mexico City and the University of Nuevo León in Monterrey.

For two decades, labor unrest has been manifested in efforts by rank-and-file union members to free their organizations from the grip of corrupt leaders who are closely allied with the PRI. Demetrio Vallejo, an insurgent leader of restive railroad workers, led a series of massive strikes during 1958 and 1959 that were suppressed by the government

Jailed for eleven years on charges of subversive activities (under the now defunct Law of Social Dissolution), Vallejo was freed in 1970 but was prevented from participating in union activities. He then organized a "movement of railroad men" whose meetings have been forbidden by local government authorities. Vallejo himself is constantly harassed by the police, and as recently as May 1974 he was kidnaped by police in Ciudad Obregón and held incommunicado for a time.[55]

Mexico's hinterland has always been plagued by bandits whose motives are mercenary rather than political. Since 1968, however, there has been continued guerrilla activity, frequently marked by the kidnaping (and holding for ransom) of political figures or prominent industrialists. At least one such incident involved the abduction and disappearance of an American consular official in 1973. His body was discovered in July 1974. At first the mass media referred to these incidents as banditry, but more recently they have labeled them terrorism.

The only serious attempt to channel student and worker discontent under the leadership of prominent intellectuals had obscure beginnings in 1968 in statements by Carlos Madrazo, the deposed president of the PRI, who declared his intention of organizing a new political party of "genuine opposition." Madrazo was killed in 1969 in a rather mysterious plane accident. The initiative for the movement was then assumed by such personages as Carlos Fuentes and Octavio Paz, both internationally known literary figures, and Heberto Castillo and Tomás Cervantes Cabeza de Vaca.[56] They have not yet been able to attract a widespread following or to participate in the electoral process.

In its chosen role as a political party involved only in the electoral processes of the system, the PRI has remained aloof from these conflicts. Because of the Party's Siamese-twin involvement with the elite and their joint control of the government, it is no wonder that the Mexican public in general and some protesters in particular have been unable to distinguish between these different elements.[57]

The Party and the System

We have seen from the foregoing description that the apparent ubiquity of the PRI is an optical illusion, that Party and political system are far from synonymous; other elements not only exist, but act and are acted upon in ways that help to define the totality. Among these are the elite, consisting of the officeholders and unofficial but influential persons; the personnel and formal-legal institutions of government; the powerful economic groups; the consenters; the dissenters, and last (or first) the Catholic church. When this is said, however, we must be careful not to understate the centrality of the Party, for it is the PRI that processes the men who aspire to a place in the elite, eliminating many and choosing a few for greater influence. Even more important, however, is the PRI's role as mobilizer, manipulator, and controller of that "great beast," the people. If we try to picture the Mexican political system without the PRI, we are most likely to conjure up a vision of the unregulated and bloody competition of all the other elements of society; the chaos in search of a system that was called constitutional government during the 1920s.

Glen Dealy was right in calling the Mexican political system a *monistic* democracy, that is, "the centralization and control of potentially competing interests." But he was mistaken in attributing the beginning of true monistic nationhood in Latin America to the 1917 Mexican constitution.[58] The attempt to implement the prescriptions of that document gave rise to the bloodiest conflicts of the following decade between competing interest groups. It was not until Plutarco Elías Calles decided in effect to ignore the constitution and to establish the PNR that it was possible to institute the order that is so essential an ingredient of true monistic democracy. The *summum bonum* pictured by the 1917 constitution was one that denied the very existence of such functional groupings as the church and the property owners. In opening the back door to those elements of society while inviting the masses to enter the political system by the front door of the Party, Calles made it possible to begin to restore peace. As one Mexican lawyer expressed it in an interview, "We have the best constitution in the world, and some day it will be a reality." By postponing that reality indefinitely it has been possible to rebuild a community based on the traditional authoritarian values of the Iberic-Latin world.

Authoritarianism is defined by the nature of its processes; corporatism, by the structure of its institutions. Juan Linz has described the former as being characterized by limited, not responsible, pluralism; low popular mobilization (except when required for support of the regime); lack of articulated ideology but prevalence of a typical mentality ("programmatic consensus"); and the often arbitrary but usually predictable exercise of power by a leader or a small group.[59] The first application of this formulation to Mexico was made by Susan Purcell.[60] The preceding sections of this chapter have documented the development and interdependence of these processes. It thus becomes possible to state that limited pluralism is a function (in the mathematical sense) of low mobilization; programmatic consensus is made possible through the exercise of power by a small group (the elite) in arbitrarily defining the subject matter of consensus.

Our description of the stages through which the Mexican political system has evolved during the past forty-five years has emphasized the recognition and legitimation of certain preexisting functional interest groups (for example, business and industrial chambers), the creation of new forms through which to channel the activities of other groups (for example, functional sectors of the Party), and the largely successful effort to reduce the influence of other functional groups (for example, the church and the military) by denying them a place in the formal structure of power. Does that pattern fit the definition of corporatism as "a system of interest representation in which the constituent units are organized into a limited number of singular, compulsory, noncompetitive, hierarchically ordered and functionally differentiated categories, recognized or licensed (if not created) by the state and granted a deliberate representational monopoly within their respective categories in exchange for observing certain controls on their selection of leaders and articulation of demands and support"?[61]

Whatever the undeclared goals of policy makers may be, the public statements of most proponents of corporatism include references to the need for organizing the representation of functional interest groups and of protecting those groups from the harmful effects—to themselves and to the national interest—of unregulated competition. The implication is that the weaker groups—the landless, the unskilled and illiterate, and the small entrepreneurs—benefit at least as much from this arrangement as the stronger groups. Has this in fact been the case in Mexico? Based on the study of the operation of groups inside the PRI structure and outside it, the conclusion must be in the form of a qualified negative. We have seen that from the crude occupational categories composing the sectors there have emerged influential strata whose members have not only been able to protect their own particular interests but have also been able to manipulate sectoral activity to promote those interests. Meanwhile, outside the Party structure, other interest groups are able to choose from a much wider range of methods for enhancing their influence. Thus, while the formal-legal structure of the Party corresponds, albeit imperfectly, to the corporatist design, the function is one of control rather than representation. Given the pragmatic, piecemeal approach of Mexican leaders since the Revolution, the Party could hardly have evolved differently.

Mexico's experience provides an interesting contrast to that of the Spanish regime. Since its inception, the Franco-dominated government rejected class as a basis of functional representation, while at the same time integrating the church into the structure of formally recognized advisory groups whose opinions are supposed to have some influence on the policies adopted by the elite. Drawing on theological principles, the position of the church has traditionally been inimical to capitalism and industrialization. Without the concurrence of the church, it is doubtful whether the Franco government would have been able to survive during the first decade after the overthrow of the republic. In the initial phase of consolidation of power, Spain's post—civil war leaders were therefore constrained to abide by the economic consequences of their choice: the acceptance of limitations on the expansion of capitalism, which we may describe as characteristic of the slow-growth society.

Since World War II, however, we have seen the secularizing effect of pressures for rapid economic expansion, arising mainly from the development of a technocratic ideology that gradually won over an influential group of adherents within the powerful Opus Dei.[62] These pressures, with their accompanying demands for departure from the Christian concept of equity, have caused increasing tension between the economic elite and the ecclesiastical authorities.[63] The programmatic consensus of the authoritarian regime has retarded definition of issues which would lead to polarizing positions, but there are signs that the dialectical process cannot be indefinitely avoided. The result may be that the Spanish regime will ultimately be forced to dispense with the support of the church; already, in fact, there are numerous indications of estrangement.

Starting more than a decade earlier than the Opus Dei, Mexico's modernizing elite had to overcome similar obstacles before it could adopt policies favoring capitalist economic expansion. The populist and socialist principles embodied in Mexico's 1917 constitution, while deriving their moral premises from Marxism, were as inimical to capitalism and industrialization as was the Catholic tradition.[64]

In Iberic America, the moral confrontation has been evaded by a search for alternative principles of validating the decision to strive for rapid economic growth. In utilizing the revolutionary myth, and in choosing the PRI to control the potentially dangerous populist elements, the Mexican elite accomplished a new political synthesis. Other Latin American societies, lacking a myth of similar emotional appeal, have relied on military elites in attempts to bring about the same results.

The protest movements in Mexico during the past decade are portents that the revolutionary myth is losing its integrative power. The most telling attack has been mounted, not by Christian democrats, but by intellectuals who see themselves as essentially secular prophets of a new ethos. Whether they recognize it or not, they have drawn their most compelling arguments from the earlier Christian doctrines. In the face of this attack, the government has been obliged with increasing frequency to rely on military forces to maintain public order. Again, the army has proved an indispensable adjunct to the authoritarian exercise of power.

Although, as we have seen, the army was eliminated from the sectoral organization of the Party in 1940, this has not meant that it has been reduced to a negligible role in the political system. A recent paper ascribes to the army not one but a variety of roles, the most important of which, in my opinion, is that of "a significant force for authoritarian control and occasional political repression."[65] In all of the large-scale protest movements since 1956, the army has been the decisive element in eliminating opposition to the elite's preferred policies. In 1956, it was the army that invaded the campus of the Polytechnic Institute and closed it down for several months, dislodging recalcitrant students from the dormitories and handing over many of them to the police. The railroad strike of 1959 was broken when troops rounded up the strikers and forced many of them at gunpoint to operate the trains. In 1965, when striking doctors and nurses staged a sit-in at government hospitals, the army allowed riot police to dislodge the strikers and then moved in to take over the operation of the hospitals with military medical personnel. In August 1968 the army invaded the Mexican national university (UNAM) and expelled thousands of students who had been using the campus as strike headquarters; later that year (October), the bloodshed at the Plaza de Tlatelolco was a direct result of military intervention. The 1959 and 1968 events additionally involved rounding up thousands of participants in the protest movements. They were unconstitutionally detained in military camps, where interrogation by intelligence operatives was carried on as a preliminary to arraignment in police courts.[66]

Reporting of these events in the Mexican press left no doubt about the close coordination of the army, the police, and the powerful Secretariat of Gobernación. The latter agency is charged with a number of functions, such as controlling immigration and supervising elections, but its most important activities are in maintaining the internal security of the nation, especially through the operation of a nationwide intelligence network. Although it appears not to engage openly in repressive violence, there seems little doubt that this government agency exercises the preponderant influence in any decision to use force. There is no need to argue here whether it is the president or the secretary of Gobernación who actually makes the decision and issues the order. The incumbent president of Mexico, Luis Echeverría Alvarez, as well as four predecessors in an unbroken line (Miguel Alemán, 1946–1952; Adolfo Ruíz Cortines, 1952–1958; Adolfo López Mateos, 1958–1964; and Gustavo Díaz Ordaz, 1964–1970) all occupied the position of secretary of Gobernación immediately prior to being nominated for the presidency by the PRI. Such a long-term conjuncture of career patterns has no parallel in other nations. At the least, it would seem to indicate a continuity of policy with respect to internal security and control.

As long as the tools available to civilian governments are adequate to the task of controlling most of the population, there is little likelihood that the army will seek a larger role for itself. The Party's sectoral format, a creation of Lázaro Cárdenas, has given Mexico's authoritarian regime the tool that it needed. Lacking that tool and seemingly unable to forge a copy of it, other Latin American nations have been resorting to the only apparent alternative, military rule.

At the beginning of this exposition, we defined five elements of the Mexican political system: the elite, the government, the Party, the indispensable collaborators, and the dissenters and protesters. We have seen that the sectors of the population whose consent is mobilized by the Party compose the overwhelming numerical majority of the nation. While the Party appeals to the populace in the name of the government, the aura of legitimacy conferred by majority consent is extended by inference to cover all policies promoted by the elite. This extension of legitimacy is facilitated by the inextricable intertwining of the Party, government, and elite roles held by the same persons.[67] The Party has thus preempted a special and very privileged relationship with other important elements of the political system and has succeeded in preventing other parties from sharing in this privilege. In addition, the threefold interrelationship of roles has made it virtually impossible for dissenting and protesting groups to challenge either the operations carried out by the Party or the policies decided on by the elite.

The sectoral organization of the Party provides a rudimentary and incomplete kind of corporatism. But the PRI is only one component, albeit an important one, of the entire system. Other elements such as business and industry are accommodated within the framework of interaction, while still others such as the church and the military, that have traditionally been accorded prominent places in corporatist systems, have been successfully reduced to marginality in Mexico.

The special quality of the Mexican political system consists precisely in the successful marginalization of those institutions which have been the central—and centralizing—elements of the organic, corporative state in other parts of the world, and the substitution of an alternative set of institutions equally well adapted to the maintenance of authoritarianism, while at the same time providing the flexibility of decision-making required for rapid economic and social expansion. Mexico has been the first Latin American nation to accomplish this synthesis, perhaps because its Revolution was two-staged. The first stage atomized Mexican society, and the second stage recombined the elements, assigning them new and drastically altered measures of influence. The result is a new variant of authoritarianism, not a new kind of corporatism.

If we look backward in time beyond the 1910 Revolution, we can gain some historical perspective and see that the apparently corporatist structure of the PRI has provided a way of reconciling two recurring tendencies of Mexican politics: the strong populist surges evident sporadically since 1810, and the equally strong elitist tendency to restrain and manipulate the masses. Possibly the long life of the PRI can be accounted for by the acceptance of most Mexicans of the need for such a reconciliation. While the PRI of the latter half of the twentieth century owes little to the form and function of nineteenth-century parties, it resembles only faintly and superficially the fascist institutions of Italy and Spain of the earlier part of this century. There is no reason to believe that the Mexican political system as we see it today has exhausted the possibilities of innovation or ceased its development.

NOTES

I am grateful to Charles W. Anderson, Wayne Cornelius, and Howard J. Wiarda for their helpful comments on a draft of this paper.

1. When spelled with an upper-case *P*, the word *Party* refers to the present-day Partido Revolucionario Institucional (PRI) under any of its historical names (Partido Nacional Revolucionario, PNR, 1929—1938; Partido de la Revolución Mexicana, PRM, 1938—1946; PRI, 1946 to the present). In addition to other works cited below, much basic information on the organization and *modus operandi* of the Party can be found in Frank Brandenburg, "Mexico: An Experiment in One-Party Democracy" (Ph.D. dissertation, University of Pennsylvania, 1956); Patricia M. Richmond, "Mexico: A Case Study of One-Party Politics" (Ph.D. dissertation, University of California, 1965); and Lorenzo Meyer, "El Estado mexicano contemporáneo," *Historia Mexicana*, 23, no. 4 (April—June, 1974): 722—52.

2. Following Leonard Schapiro's usage, "dissent" is described as "a term which implies a claim to criticize and disagree with the policy of the government, but without any intention or plan of replacing that government by one composed of its critics" (Introduction to his *Political Opposition in One-Party States* [London and Basingstoke: Macmillan Press, Ltd., 1972], p. 3). The term "protest" as I use it is in some senses roughly equivalent to Schapiro's "pressure group," which he employs in the limited context of communist political systems. He distinguishes between "interest groups" (such as the military) that seek to enhance their own positions within the system, and "pressure groups" (such as the Soviet "democrats") that "seek to promote some policy or aim of a more general nature" (ibid., p. 7). In the more permissive context of the Mexican political system, such "pressure groups" are sometimes able to organize repeated large-scale demonstrations before they are eventually suppressed. It is this type of massive and open demonstration that characterizes the term "protest" as I use it here.

3. Robert Scott, *Mexican Government in Transition* (Urbana: University of Illinois Press, 1964), pp. 119—21; and idem, "Politics in Mexico," in *Introduction to Comparative Politics*, ed. Gabriel A. Almond (Boston: Little, Brown, 1974), chap. 12.

4. An excellent description and analysis of the elements involved in the Spanish situation is provided by Juan J. Linz, "From Falange to Movimiento-Organización: The Spanish Single Party and the Franco Regime, 1936–1968," in *Authoritarian Politics in Modern Society: The Dynamics of Established One-Party Systems*, ed. Samuel Huntington and Clement H. Moore (New York: Basic Books, 1970), pp. 128–204.

5. Evelyn P. Stevens, "Protest Movement in an Authoritarian Regime: The Mexican Case," *Comparative Politics*, 7, no. 3 (April 1975):361–82.

6. Howard J. Wiarda, "Corporatist Theory and Ideology: The Latin American Development Paradigm" (mimeograph, n.p., n.d.), p. 4. For the most complete formulation of corporatist theory as applied to the Iberic-Latin world, see also by the same author: "Toward a Framework for the Study of Political Change in the Iberic-Latin Tradition: The Corporative Model," *World Politics*, 25, no. 2 (January 1973):206–35; "Corporatism and Development in the Iberic-Latin World: Persistent Strains and Variations," *Review of Politics*, 36, no. 1 (January 1974):3–33; and the Introduction to his *Politics and Social Change in Latin America: The Distinct Tradition* (Amherst: University of Massachusetts Press, 1974), pp. 3–18.

7. Wiarda, "Corporatist Theory and Ideology," p. 4.

8. Scott, *Mexican Government in Transition*, p. 122.

9. For a description of the binding nature of these relationships, see Evelyn P. Stevens, *Protest and Response in Mexico* (Cambridge: MIT Press, 1974), chap. 3.

10. Bertha Lerner Sigal, "Partido Revolucionario Institucional," in *México: la realidad política de sus partidos*, ed. Antonio Delhumeau (Mexico: Instituto Mexicano de Estudios Políticos A.C., 1970), p. 67.

11. I have followed the Mexican custom of capitalizing the word *Revolution* whenever it refers to the conflict which began in 1910.

12. See Kenneth F. Johnson, *Mexican Democracy: A Critical View* (Boston: Allyn and Bacon, 1971), p. 82; and Evelyn P. Stevens, "Legality and Extra-legality in Mexico," *Journal of Interamerican Studies and World Affairs*, 12, no. 1 (January 1970):62–75.

13. *Tapadismo* is used to describe the secrecy surrounding the selection process until the final moment before official designation of the candidate. Frank Brandenburg, *The Making of Modern Mexico* (Englewood Cliffs, N.J.: Prentice-Hall, 1964), pp. 145–47. The September 1975 announcement of the candidacy of José López Portillo was a classic example of the arcane process of *tapadismo*.

14. Manuel Reyna, Laura Palomares, and Guadalupe Cortez, "El control del movimiento obrero como una necesidad del Estado en México (1917–1936)," *Revista Mexicana de Sociologia*, 34, nos. 3–4 (October–December, 1972): 785–814.

15. The most notable example of such an unsuccessful movement was that of the railroad men. For an account of their strike and its aftermath, see Evelyn P. Stevens, *Protest and Response in Mexico*, chap. 4.

16. José Luis Reyna, "An Empirical Analysis of Political Mobilization: The Case of Mexico" (Ph.D. dissertation, Cornell University, 1971), p. 106.

17. Sigal, "Partido Revolucionario," p. 80.

18. Arnaldo Córdova, "La transformación del PMR al PRM. El triunfo del corporativismo en México" (Paper presented at the Fourth International Congress of Mexican Studies, Santa Monica, California, October 1973).

19. Somewhat different aspects of the *cristero* rebellion and the church-state conflict in Mexico are described in David C. Bailey, *Viva Cristo Rey!* (Austin: University of Texas Press, 1973); Albert L. Michaels, "Fascism and Sinarquismo:

Popular Nationalism Against the Mexican Revolution," *A Journal of Church and State*, 8 (1966):234–50; and Jean Meyer, *La cristiada, I* (Mexico: Siglo XXI Editores, 1973).

20. Arnaldo Córdova, "La política de masas del Cardenismo" (mimeograph, n.p., n.d.) is typical of recent critical reexaminations of Cárdenas's policies. For a fresh defense of that president's place in Mexican history, see Wayne Cornelius, "Nation Building, Participation, and Distribution: The Politics of Social Reform Under Cárdenas," in *Crisis, Choice, and Change: Historical Studies of Political Development*, ed. Gabriel A. Almond et al. (Boston: Little, Brown, 1973), pp. 392–498.

21. Quoted in James Wilkie, *The Mexican Revolution: Federal Expenditure and Social Change* (Berkeley and Los Angeles: University of California Press, 1967), pp. 79–80.

22. Frank Brandenburg, "Organized Business in Mexico," *Inter-American Economic Affairs*, 12, no. 3 (Winter 1958):26–50. See also William P. Glade, Jr., and Charles W. Anderson, *The Political Economy of Mexico* (Madison: University of Wisconsin Press, 1963); and Raymond Vernon, *The Dilemma of Mexico's Development* (Cambridge: Harvard University Press, 1963).

23. Merle Kling, *A Mexican Interest Group in Action* (Englewood Cliffs, N.J.: Prentice-Hall, 1961).

24. Manuel López Gallo, *Economía y política en la historia de México* (Mexico: Ediciones Solidaridad, 1965), p. 581.

25. Stevens, *Protest and Response*, p. 106.

26. For the ineffectiveness of the Communists in Mexico, see Karl M. Schmitt, *Communism in Mexico* (Austin: University of Texas Press, 1965).

27. Stevens, *Protest and Response*, p. 125.

28. For an especially perceptive description of contemporary networks of mutually advantageous relationships involving a Latin American economic elite and its foreign counterpart, see Nancie Gonzalez, "Patron-Client Relationships at the International Level," in *Structure and Process in Latin America: Patronage, Clientage and Power Systems*, ed. Arnold Strickon and Sidney M. Greenfield (Albuquerque: University of New Mexico Press, 1972), pp. 179–209.

29. Stevens, *Protest and Response*, p. 37.

30. In addition to the works cited in note 16, see Raymond Vernon, ed., *Public Policy and Private Enterprise in Mexico* (Cambridge: Harvard University Press, 1964); Marjory Urquidi, trans., *Mexico's Recent Economic Growth* (Austin: University of Texas Press, 1967); Robert Jones Shafer, *Mexico: Mutual Adjustment Planning* (Syracuse: Syracuse University Press, 1966); and Clark W. Reynolds, *The Mexican Economy: Twentieth-Century Structure and Growth* (New Haven: Yale University Press, 1970).

31. For the delicate interbalance of factors that enabled Lázaro Cárdenas to "get away with" the petroleum expropriation, see Lorenzo Meyer, *México y Estados Unidos en el conflicto petrolero, 1917–1942* (Mexico: El Colegio de México, Centro de Estudios Internacionales, 1968), esp. chap. 9.

32. Manuel Gollás and Adalberto García R., "El crecimiento económico reciente de México" (Paper presented at the Fourth International Congress of Mexican Studies, Santa Monica, California, October 1973); Calixto Rangel Contla, "El desarrollo diferencial de Mexico, 1940–1960" (Thesis, Universidad Nacional Autonoma de México, 1965); Ifigenia de Navarrete, *La distribución del ingreso y el desarrollo económico de México* (Mexico: Universidad Nacional Autónoma de México, 1960); and Lucila Leal de Araujo, *Aspectos económicos del Instituto Mexicano del Seguro Social* (Mexico: Cuadernos Americanos, 1966).

33. Daniel Seligman in *Fortune*, January 1956, quoted by Charles W. Anderson in *Political Economy of Mexico*, ed. Glade and Anderson, p. 180. See also the comments in a similar vein with particular reference to railroad workers in Stevens, *Protest and Response*.

34. For a description of the largely successful struggle of Italian industrialists to retain their autonomy in spite of the loss of private status by business associations, see Roland Sarti, *Fascism and the Industrial Leadership in Italy, 1919–1940* (Berkeley: University of California Press, 1971), pp. 134–38. It is possible that Mexican industrialists would have had a like measure of success, but in fact their autonomy has never really been challenged.

35. This parallels the distinction between *impiegati* and *operai* reported in G. Lowell Field, *The Syndical and Corporative Institutions of Italian Fascism* (New York: AMS Press, 1968), p. 106.

36. Stevens, *Protest and Response*, pp. 154–59.

37. Manuel Moreno Sánchez, *México: 1968–1972; crisis y perspectiva* (Austin: University of Texas Institute of Latin American Studies, 1973), passim.

38. Reyna, "An Empirical Analysis," p. 107.

39. Scott, *Mexican Government in Transition*, pp. 166–67, 154 n.

40. Mario Ezcurdia, *Análisis teórico del Partido Revolucionario Institucional* (Mexico: B. Costa-Amic, Editores, 1968), p. 78.

41. Reyna, "An Empirical Analysis," pp. 119–20. My conclusions in the ensuing section of this chapter are drawn from Reyna's analysis.

42. Ibid., p. 122.

43. Ibid., pp. 134–35.

44. A. Labra, "La concentración del ingreso en México," *Comercio Exterior*, September 1967.

45. Pablo González Casanova, *Democracy in Mexico* (New York: Oxford University Press, 1970; originally published in Spanish in 1965).

46. Cited in Stevens, *Protest and Response*, p. 273.

47. Reyna, "An Empirical Analysis," p. 171.

48. Ezcurdia, *Análisis teórico*, p. 79. It should be noted that eighteen-year-olds did not vote until after this election.

49. Robert E. Quirk, *The Mexican Revolution and the Catholic Church, 1910–1929* (Bloomington: Indiana University Press, 1973). Quirk's book brings to light much new material on the role played by U.S. Ambassador Dwight Morrow in bringing about a settlement between the church and the Mexican government.

50. See Donald J. Mabry, *Mexico's Acción Nacional: A Catholic Alternative to Revolution* (Syracuse: Syracuse University Press, 1973), chap. 6, pp. 99–112; and Jaime González Graf and Alicia Ramirez Lugo, "Partido Acción Nacional," in Delhumeau, *México*, pp. 212–16.

51. Mabry, *Mexico's Acción Nacional*, p. 142.

52. Ibid., pp. 63–64, 77–80.

53. Luz María Silva Ortiz, "Partido Auténtico de la Revolución Mexicana," in Delhumeau, *México*, p. 312.

54. Stevens, "Legality and Extra-legality," *Protest and Response*, and "Protest Movement in an Authoritarian Regime"; and Bo Anderson and James D. Cockroft, "Control and Cooptation in Mexican Politics," *International Journal of Comparative Sociology*, 7 (March 1966):11–28.

55. Heberto Castillo, "Facilidades al fascismo," *Excelsior*, May 16, 1974.

56. Victor Manuel Durand Ponte, "Reformismo burgués y reformismo obrero: un análisis de la realidad mexicana," *Revista Mexicana de Sociología*, 44, nos. 3–4 (July–September, October–December, 1972):840.

57. A good example of the confusion that Mexicans as well as foreigners sometimes experience in trying to distinguish between the PRI, the government, and the elite can be seen in Salvador Hernández, *El PRI y el movimiento estudiantil de 1968* (Mexico: Ediciones "El Caballito," 1971). In spite of the title of this book, the author fails to establish any connection between the Party and the events of that period.

58. Glen Dealy, "The Tradition of Monistic Democracy in Latin America," in *Politics and Social Change in Latin America: The Distinct Tradition*, ed. Howard J. Wiarda (Amherst: University of Massachusetts Press, 1974), pp. 73, 83.

59. Juan Linz, "An Authoritarian Regime: Spain," in *Cleavages, Ideologies, and Party Systems*, ed. Erik Allardt and Yrjo Littunen (Helsinki: Westermarck Society, 1964), pp. 291–341. See also his "Opposition to and Under an Authoritarian Regime: The Case of Spain," in *Regimes and Oppositions*, ed. Robert Dahl (New Haven: Yale University Press, 1973), pp. 171–259.

60. Susan Kaufman Purcell, "Decision-making in an Authoritarian Regime: Theoretical Implications from a Mexican Case Study," *World Politics*, 26, no. 1 (1973):28–54.

61. Philippe Schmitter, "Still the Century of Corporatism?", *The Review of Politics*, 36, no. 1 (January 1974):93.

62. Leslie Mackenzie, "The Political Ideas of the Opus Dei in Spain," *Government and Opposition*, 8, no. 1 (Winter 1973):72–92.

63. Charles W. Anderson, *The Political Economy of Modern Spain: Policy-Making in an Authoritarian System* (Madison: University of Wisconsin Press, 1970), depicts the rise of the new development program and the policy choices that have resulted from it.

64. Arnaldo Córdova, *La ideología de la Revolución Mexicana: la formación del nuevo régimen* (Mexico: Instituto de Investigaciones Sociales de la Universidad Nacional Autónoma de México, 1973).

65. David F. Ronfeldt, "The Mexican Army and Political Order Since 1940" (Paper presented at the Fourth International Congress of Mexican Studies, Santa Monica, California, October 1973), p. 12.

66. Stevens, *Protest and Response*, pp. 122–23, 236, gives the most complete available account of these events.

67. With reference to the "organic" nature of the Spanish state, Charles Anderson describes a similar kind of role alternation as an "interlocking directorate" comprising representatives from the family, local government, and syndicates and from the main institutions of Spanish society, that is, the Cortes, the church, the military, the Movement, and the university (*Political Economy of Modern Spain*, pp. 60–64).

JOHN J BAILEY

9

Pluralist and Corporatist Dimensions of Interest Representation in Colombia

What are patterns of authority relationships between governments and interest associations? Which trends are universal and which seem more particular to a geocultural region? While this volume concentrates on Latin American cases, we should recognize certain secular patterns which establish a more general context for our inquiry. Almost universally, contemporary polities are characterized by (1) the proliferation of organizations of all types, (2) the expansion of the role of government in promotion and regulation, (3) the devolution of public policy-making to the bureaucracy, and (4) the preoccupation of governments with economics: growth, stability, and income distribution. Given the universality of these trends, the interesting questions concern how the Latin American polities have crafted institutions and practices to accommodate themselves to the modern setting, and it is from this perspective that I approach the analysis of government and interest associations in Colombia.

The purpose of this essay is to assess the utility of corporatism in understanding relationships between government and private associations in Colombia. Following a discussion of the images of corporatism in the recent literature, I shall attempt to examine the recent historical evolution of state administrative activity and interest representation in Colombia, and describe and analyze contemporary interest associations and their linkages to government agencies. Also, I shall speculate in preliminary fashion on implications of the system of interest representation for public policy-making. The purpose of the description is not to render an exhaustive account of Colombian interest associations, but rather to interpret the nature of government and interest representation in that country in relation to corporatism as an ideal construct.

To anticipate the conclusions, I shall argue that corporatist features

of Colombian interest politics do not reflect a reemergence of a sociopolitical logic of medieval and colonial Spanish institutions, as proponents of cultural determinism might suggest, but rather are associated
with the choices taken to expand the role of the central government in
promotion and regulation within a political regime of procedural
democracy and social pluralism. Also, I shall attempt to demonstrate
that while intellectual and institutional features of historicocultural
corporatism are to be found in the Colombian experience, the overall
pattern of interest representation may more accurately be described as
a variant of pluralism. This finding is of interest in that the historicocultural approach would imply that Colombia "should be" a country in
which Hispanic-Catholic corporatist practices are highly developed.
This, I believe, is not the case, and it may indicate that a reexamination
of the approach is needed. It is also of interest in that Colombia differs
significantly from the authoritarian patterns of Mexico, Brazil, Peru,
and Argentina. While it may be premature to designate Colombia as a
deviant case in Latin America, the findings from this study may offer
clues into the origins and maintenance of pluralism in a "developing"
polity.

For the most part, the methodology employed here is eclectic and
straightforward, with considerable reliance on secondary sources, even
though the literature dealing specifically with Colombian interest associations is scant.[1] Data are drawn principally from the public record:
publications by interest associations and government agencies, as well as
Colombian newspapers and periodicals. The latter part of the chapter
concentrates on the organizational features and interrelationships of the
interest associations and government agencies. While it would be useful
to examine interest politics at the departmental and municipal levels,
space constraints limit this discussion to an analysis of the central
government and national peak associations.[2] Because of present limitations, only marginal consideration is given to the Colombian military
forces and the Catholic church as actors in interest politics. The
strategies employed by the peak associations are only briefly sketched,
and assessments of their effectiveness lie beyond the present scope.
Furthermore, it is recognized at the outset that the formal associations
by no means monopolize interest articulation but rather complement
the pervasive webs of informal linkages between government authorities
and citizen claimants. An analysis of these linkages, their significance
notwithstanding, unfortunately also must be excluded.

Contrasting Images of Corporatism

Underlying the recent interest in corporatism as an approach to
understanding Latin American politics is a widely shared dissatisfaction

with the established theories of modernization and development. Theoretical assumptions and empirical findings from other areas of the world seem to have limited utility in the Latin American context.[3] Associated with the dissatisfaction is a recognition of the unique historicocultural heritage of Latin America. These are not "new" or "emerging" states as the general comparative texts are wont to describe them, but rather have existed as legally sovereign entities for more than one hundred and forty years. If the Latin American countries seem not to obey the logic of development theory in progressing toward liberal democracy or totalitarianism, the key to an explanation might reasonably be sought in the historical and cultural heritage of the region or in its relationship to the developed areas. Thus, recent thinking on the region has tended toward more particularistic explanations, which is an underlying common denominator in such diverse approaches as delayed development, dependency, and corporatism. The corporatist perspective is particularly useful, in my opinion, in analyzing the nature of authority relations between governments and interest associations. The assumptions here are that patterns of interest representation provide insights into the nature of public policy-making and political culture as well as a means of gauging the directions of government-societal influence relationships in the countries of the region.

Various conceptualizations of corporatism can be found in the recent literature, and an initial task is to assess which of these, if any, is useful in understanding the Colombian case. A manifest danger is that the usages of corporatism may become so broad and vague as to render the concept meaningless at the outset. In characterizing corporatism, a distinction might be drawn between a cultural emphasis, approaching in some cases a form of cultural determinism, and a structural one. While the conceptualizations to be found in both approaches share some traits, the assumptions and methodologies associated with them are significantly different.[4]

The position elaborated recently by Howard Wiarda is a representative example of the cultural argument.[5] To oversimplify somewhat, the argument suggests that certain institutions and practices were implanted in Latin America during the long colonial period. In turn, these institutional characteristics (hierarchy, authoritarianism, elitism, Catholicism, and corporatism) persisted throughout the national period largely uninfluenced by the liberal and socialist revolutions of the time. In this perspective, corporatist-authoritarian patterns to be found in Latin America at present are essentially the reemergence of the "traditional essence" of Hispanic culture. Thus, according to Wiarda, "corporate structures, reinforced by a political culture grounded on hierarchy, status, and patronage, enable the traditional socio-political forms to hang on so tenaciously."[6]

The structural-sequential image of corporatism, while admitting cultural elements in description and explanation, concentrates more on the timing of the expansion of the central government in relation to the formation of interest associations. In essence, the argument here is that in a polity in which the central government mobilizes resources and expands its jurisdiction prior to the spontaneous emergence of interest associations, there is a greater likelihood of a pattern of authority relations which resembles corporatist authoritarianism. The ideal type of this pattern, as elaborated by Philippe Schmitter, stresses the non-ideological nature of the regime, in which interest associations are dependent upon government authorities for the maintenance of group identity and access to public policy-making. On the other hand, in polities in which interest associations precede the expansion of state activity and are able to mediate and contain state power, a different pattern of authority relations emerges which more closely resembles pluralism.[7]

For the purpose of analyzing the Colombian case, the structural-sequential assumptions and approach seem more useful. While Colombia is my reference point in evaluating these images, and an argument might be made for the uniqueness of the case, the limitations of the cultural interpretation seem severe, especially in its stress on historical continuity and its vague depiction of contemporary interest politics.

In stressing the continuity of underlying institutions and practices over time, the cultural image deemphasizes a fundamental transformation in the nature of government which occurred in the mid-1930s in response to the worldwide depression and growing attention to the development and welfare functions of the state. Also, there is in this approach a rather casual assumption of equivalence of medieval structures and functions with contemporary institutions, which some proponents of modern corporatism reject.[8] In this sense, for example, one wonders whether the medieval or colonial system of guilds might validly be equated with contemporary interest associations, or whether royal charters are comparable to present-day juridical recognition. Apparent as well in the cultural position is the strain to account for structural differentiation and semipluralistic activity in the Latin American countries since the 1930s.[9] Finally, the cultural image implies determinism in the patterns of interest politics toward corporatist authoritarianism and fails to account adequately for voluntarism in the structuring of political institutions.

As applied to the structures and practices of contemporary governments, the cultural image is limited in that its key descriptive elements (state, hierarchy, authority, corporatist) remain vague as used in shifting contexts. While features such as hierarchy and authority may characterize macro features of Latin American societies and constitute themes in religious dogma, their presence in government institutions or in the relations of associations with governments should not be assumed but should be verified empirically. Further, it may be that the cultural image confuses the obvious and highly skewed distribution of wealth, social status, and presumed political influence with the notions of hierarchy and authority in corporatism. Finally, the historicocultural approach by its nature does not adequately account for patterns of interest representation in non-Hispanic countries which resemble in important respects those to be found in Latin America.[10]

The point of these criticisms is not to dismiss historicocultural interpretations as useless. Indeed, to ignore such influences on institutional development is simply wrong. Rather, the goal is to specify types of interest representation within and across countries of the region sufficiently precisely to forge a useful conceptualization of corporatism. For this purpose, the structural-sequential approach suffers fewer liabilities. Even within this approach, however, there remain several conceptualizations which define corporatism with varying degrees of precision. A rigorous definition has been proffered by Schmitter:

> Corporatism can be defined as a system of interest representation in which the constituent units are organized into a limited number of singular, compulsory, non-competitive, hierarchically ordered and functionally differentiated categories, recognized or licensed (if not created) by the state and granted a deliberate representational monopoly within their respective categories in exchange for observing certain controls on their selection of leaders and articulation of demands and supports.[11]

Moving from the generic type, Schmitter draws a distinction between two forms of corporatism, "state" and "societal." State corporatism is characterized by government penetration and control over interest associations, whereas societal corporatism is a system of relatively autonomous associations whose activity and support for government constitute a major source of political legitimacy. Viewed statically, these subtypes share structural features; yet they are the products of distinct socioeconomic and political settings.

> Societal corporatism is found imbedded in political systems with relatively autonomous, multilayered territorial units; open, competitive electoral processes and party systems; ideologically varied, coalitionally based executive authorities—even with highly "layered" or "pillared" political subcultures. State corporatism tends to be associated with political systems in which territorial subunits are tightly subordinate to central bureaucratic power;

elections are nonexistent or plebiscitary; party systems are dominated or monopolized by a weak single party; executive authorities are ideologically exclusive and more narrowly recruited and are such that political subcultures based on class, ethnicity, language, or regionalism are repressed. Societal corporatism appears to be the concomitant, if not ineluctable, component of the post-liberal, advanced capitalist, organized democratic welfare state; state corporatism seems to be a defining element of, if not structural necessity for, the antiliberal, delayed capitalist, authoritarian, neomercantilist state.[12]

The utility of this conceptualization is its explicitness and attempt to hypothesize on the origins of distinct forms of corporatism. Beyond the difficulty in operationalizing these concepts, however, there are at least three problems with this reasoning. First, structural characteristics (along with power relationships) and level of economic development tap two different dimensions, but here they are merged. Thus, societal corporatism presumably is correlated with postindustrial polities, while state corporatism is "delayed capitalist." Second, state corporatism, depicted as "authoritarian," denotes government penetration and control of interest associations. In this regard, however, Roland Ebel's discussion of small Latin American countries (essentially Central American states which would include a priori examples of authoritarian systems) conveys the impression of considerable associational autonomy vis-à-vis the state.

> Politics in the city-state is a struggle between elites for a particular allocation of goods and values. These elites tend to be organized corporatively. That is, the cotton growers, coffee planters, industrialists, the church, the military, and, to some extent, international business, seek to retain hegemony within their own domain and to ensure and control their "slice of the pie." Each major group has its own specialized point of access to the decision-making process: a specific ministry, an autonomous institute, or a specialized court.
>
> Latin American corporativists proceed under the assumption that decisions affecting their sector should be made by them free of outside interference. Once the decision has been made, it is the government's responsibility to see that it is carried out. Thus, the government has a twofold task: first, to shield the group from the claims of other groups by validating and legitimizing contracts negotiated between it and the corporate group; second, to extract sufficient resources from society (such as money, credits, and labor) to implement the previously negotiated policy. Corporativism, therefore, inevitably leads to statism and centralized administration.[13]

Yet, as Ebel goes on to point out, this form of corporatism also implies the decentralization of decision-making from the state to the corporate groups. Significant here is that policy-making activities may be compartmentalized in such a way that an "authoritarian" ruler and government may coexist with relatively autonomous interest associations. Group autonomy is also a characteristic of pluralist polities, which is simply to note that structures and processes of subsystems (in this case specialized arenas of policy-making) may be similar across analytically distinct regime types.

Third, while Schmitter's delineation of corporatism in structural-processual terms is useful, his hypothesized relationship between delayed capitalist development and state corporatism clearly is not supported in the Colombian case. The obvious point, however, is that a single case to the contrary does not disprove a hypothesis, and sufficient impressionistic evidence exists in the region to justify its retention and further investigation. Equally obvious is the danger of distortion in excluding by definition an alternative hypothesis linking forms of pluralism with delayed development. Schmitter's depiction by implication of delayed development linked with "nascent" or "incipient" pluralism leads the analyst to expect, rather fatalistically, the conversion of a developing polity at some point to a form of state corporatism, a fate not unlike that experienced by Chile after September 1973.

The argument of this essay is that neither the historicocultural nor the state image of corporatism is useful in understanding Colombian interest politics. Corporatist traits to be found represent a potential for, but not the reality of, state corporatism. A more accurate image to describe the Colombian case is elitist pluralism, in which middle-sector and upper-class producers' and professional associations are numerous, active, and closely interwoven with government agencies in fluid and complex linkages. At the same time, lower-class workers' and peasants' organizations are permitted to exist and influence policy-making, but under strict limitations imposed by elites. On the whole, the scope of organized interest activity is concentrated in urban areas and among the relatively affluent agriculturalists. While the logic of the system is elitist and somewhat co-optive, efforts have been made recently (for example, through Community Action programs and the Peasant Users Associations) to expand the scope of interest activity and possibly offset to a limited extent the monopoly on politics enjoyed by elite groups. Associations exist in varying degrees of independence from the government. Among elite groups, the agricultural associations seem most closely tied to government, while the remaining professional and producers' associations exist fairly independently and engage actively in bargaining over public policy. The government can and occasionally does impose policy on elite groups, but the more general pattern is one of compromise and negotiation.

Further, while corporatism has some utility in regard to certain aspects of Colombian interest politics, it must be carefully qualified. The most salient corporatist feature is the limited number of peak associations, which are functionally differentiated, licensed by the state, and granted something of a representational monopoly on government decision-making bodies. The structural linkages between government and private associations and the administration of public programs by private groups (FEDECAFE,* for example) carry corporatist connotations. On the other hand, important pluralistic dimensions should be noted: (1) There is unfettered spontaneity in the formation of associations, and state recognition is generally forthcoming; (2) the legitimacy of group autonomy from government is highly valued (yet there is little felt inconsistency in seeking, indeed demanding, government financial support); (3) there appears to be considerable intergroup policy dialogue at various levels, both within and apart from government structures. Finally, a significant factor to be considered throughout is the weakness of the central government *and its reliance on group support for political legitimacy.* In sum, it may be shown that Colombian interest politics is a hybrid of pluralist and corporatist features, but the overall logic and functioning of the system are more pluralist than corporatist.

Corporatism in the Colombian Historical Context

One finds in the Colombian experience ample incidence of authoritarianism in public institutions and political ideology; corporatism, however, is encountered much less. Present as well are traditions of procedural democracy, liberalism, and social pluralism. Indeed, it is typical in the literature to depict Colombia's history as a dialogue between these traditions.[14]

Corporatist-authoritarian characteristics, however, did not form the mold when the foundations of the modern Colombian state were established in the administration of Alfonso López Pumarejo (1934–1938). López drew upon Colombia's liberal, secular, and pluralist traditions as well as the interventionist and welfare-developmentalist currents which characterized the modern state of the 1930s. Essentially, the pluralistic institutional framework and interventionist policy orientations introduced by López have persisted to the present, despite both the massive rural violence of the two decades after 1948 and the quasi-falangist interlude of Laureano Gómez (1950–1953). Further, it is interesting that economic prosperity, the rapid proliferation of in-

*All abbreviations in this chapter are explained in the List of Abbreviations on pages 296–97.

terest associations, and the continued extension of government intervention coincide to a degree with the period of military rule under
Gustavo Rojas Pinilla (1953–1957).

Drawing on the sequential image, it may be argued that an important
factor in influencing associational autonomy in Colombia is the con-
fluence of political crisis and social modernization which accompanied
the rapid emergence of interest associations from 1946 to 1959. It is
under the leadership of the National Front (1958–1974) that the
principal interest associations have flourished and languished. To the
benefit of the associations, successive governments have promoted
group formation and have sought means of institutionalizing private-
sector participation in areas such as planning. To their detriment,
however, the central government bureaucracy has expanded markedly
in size, jurisdiction, and independence. The zenith of government
strength—and this will be qualified considerably—occurred during the
administration of Carlos Lleras (1966–1970), who labored mightily to
subject the maze of public agencies to a semblance of executive control.
The theoretical interest of the Colombian case is the preconditions one
finds at present for the maintenance of elitist pluralism, a trend toward
state corporatism, or stagnation and *immobilisme*.[15]

To support this interpretation, three areas will be briefly treated:
(1) the principal themes in the ideologies of the Liberal and Conservative parties; (2) state policy toward the formation of interest associations; and (3) the patterns of emergence of interest associations and the
expansion of central government administrative activity.

The purpose of examining the ideological themes in Colombian
political history is that political institutions are intentionally related to
ideational structures. De facto regimes may be legitimated in normative
terms, and political practices are structured in part by value prescriptions.[16] The nature of conservatism in Colombia merits particular
attention, since it is here that the historicocultural image suggests lie
the seeds of the "traditional essence" of Hispanic corporatism. Two
points may be suggested to account for the nonrealization of the
corporatist potential: First, Colombian conservatism became
"liberalized" in its acceptance of constitutional forms, republicanism,
and the minority representation of Liberals. Second, conservatism was
transformed early in the twentieth century (especially during the
Liberal administration of López) by the very materialism which it
opposed. To summarize this point schematically, the themes of "traditional" conservatism are sketched in table 1.

Notions of hierarchy, order, authority, and religiosity indeed perme-
ate the traditional variant of Colombian conservatism. The ideas of
"essence," "intrinsic," "transcendental truth," and "absolute values"

Table 1. Themes in Traditional and Transformed Conservatism in Colombia

Traditional	Transformed
Major Themes	
1. Essential ordering of universe and desirability of harmonizing secular with divine order 2. Central role of religion in secular affairs: established church and church control of education 3. Role of state to facilitate individual spiritual life 4. Protection of family: marriage, divorce, illegitimacy 5. Antimaterialism and anti-relativism 6. Order, authority, legality	1. Precedence of individual over state 2. Free enterprise and protection of private property 3. Economic development and income distribution 4. Anticommunism and antipopulism 5. Nationalism 6. Reinvigoration of spiritualism (antimaterialism) 7. Reinvigoration of intermediate institutions (parties, associations, local government) 8. Protection of family
Minor Themes	
1. Centralization in organization of state 2. Protection for national industry and artisan trades 3. Agrarian emphasis in development strategy 4. Corporate organization of representative structures (e.g., Senate) 5. Natural aristocracy 6. Private charity for social welfare	1. Agrarianism 2. Social welfare 3. Role of religion in society (education) 4. Interest group and party participation in state planning 5. Excessive burden of taxation on middle class

are stressed to underscore the contrasts to "relativism" and "materialism" presumed to characterize liberalism. The Thomistic influence is recognized and defended as well. As a leading Conservative writer put it, "The philosophy of Thomas Aquinas extends throughout as the master framework of our mental structure. That philosophy infiltrated our being during secondary education, and to the even greater horror and scandal of the freethinkers and anticlerics, we have the temerity to declare that it was none other than the hated Jesuit fathers who guided us onto this road."[17]

It is in the nineteenth century that one finds the duel of the traditional forms of liberalism and conservatism. The major questions concerned the role of the state and the place of religion in it, and the Colombian experience conformed sufficiently to the general Latin American pattern to obviate a detailed discussion here. To be stressed for present purposes is that values of constitutional democracy and representative institutions were retained in principle as the basis for the regime during the long period of Conservative ascendency, 1886–1930. These procedural values implied limited government regulation of interest associations, except in the sensitive areas of religion and labor unions.[18]

It is conventional to mark 1849 as the origin of the Liberal and Conservative parties in Colombia. While the parties have been plagued by internal fragmentation and dissension, it is possible to sketch the main lines of thought that characterized these movements. Liberalism was from an early period marked by two major tendencies, one which might be considered classical liberalism, and the other, socialism. Classical liberalism rested on the key assumption of the consent of the individual as the source of governmental legitimacy. Thus, its principal concerns were those of personal freedoms: religion, press, assembly, speech, and legal guarantees such as trial by jury. Associated concerns included private property, low tariffs, limited military expenditures, and regional autonomy (federalism). The socialist thread from the outset (1850s) was preoccupied with the role of the state in regulating the economy and effecting an equitable distribution of income. This thread was the minority influence in the liberal tradition.[19] These two main themes in liberalism interacted up to the period of transformation, 1934–1959, after which the interventionist position—although in a moderated form—gained ascendancy.

To reiterate, religion lay at the core of traditional conservatism. The Thomistic notions of hierarchy, organic society, natural aristocracy, and protection of the family as the basic unit of society predominated. Yet Colombian conservatism accepted for the most part the major contributions of the eighteenth-century liberal revolutions: popular sovereignty, civilian democracy, the rule of law.[20] This is not, however, to ignore the blatant authoritarianism of Conservative leaders, who—as often did their Liberal counterparts—simply ruled as military or civilian strongmen. To understand conservatism's acceptance of liberal forms, we might recall that both parties grew out of the independence movement and that the casuistry of Thomistic thought makes for considerable tactical flexibility on the part of its adherents. There is, for example, little basic incompatibility—at least in principle—between democracy and Thomistic tenets, even though monarchy might be preferable.[21] In fact, the Conservative Miguel Antonio Caro apparently acted in this vein in proposing corporate representation in the upper chamber of an essentially representative government in the constitution of 1886.[22] The basic point is that while nineteenth-century conservatism had the potential for corporatist authoritarianism, the tradition was committed to representative forms that were essentially liberal and republican. That century could offer no model of a corporatist state as the pattern for the reorganization of Colombian institutions; it would require the structural inventions of the Franco regime in Spain to elicit in 1953 the corporatist-authoritarian proposals of Conservative Laureano Gómez.[23]

The intense conflict between the traditional variants of liberalism and conservatism entered a pretransitional phase in the early 1900s. Materialism, or the commitment of the government to promote economic development, was the major influence at work. The ideological symbols of the traditional period became less salient in the growing attention to business and finance. The pragmatism of the age included the invitation for minority participation by the Liberals in the Conservative governments, and a shared probusiness orientation dominated both parties. Further, a working consensus was achieved between the parties on centralization in government organization, establishment of the church, and guarantees of individual liberties.[24] As might be expected, there arose a degree of overlap in party affiliation, which Gonzalo Restrepo Jaramillo has called the "nomadic tribe," moving its goods and quarters easily from one camp to the other.[25] This diminution of the traditional issues in conflict presaged the crisis of Colombian politics and the transformation of thought in that country.

The transformation of political debate in Colombia coincided in part with the government's response to economic crisis. It has been suggested that Colombia's expansion of government jurisdiction in reaction to the depression was more extensive than that of other nations of the Andean and Central American regions.[26] A consequence of this response was a rapidly increased role for government in regulating the economy and devising means for a more equitable distribution of wealth through direct intervention. This new orientation challenged the elitist bipartisan consensus on the more limited role of government in stimulating growth indirectly (as through infrastructure development) and supporting business interests on questions of union-employer conflicts.[27]

The more specific challenges to the traditional consensus issued by López included the government's determination of the social obligations of private property (especially in land tenure), government promotion and protection of organized labor, elimination of the church's monopoly in education, the renegotiation of Colombia's concordat with Rome, and tax reform to finance new programs.[28] These steps did not imply socialism from López's point of view; in fact, he believed public ownership of the means of production to be inappropriate at that point in Colombia's development (which created considerable tension in his supporting coalition). The reforms were perceived as drastic and socialistic by Conservative opponents, however, and they contributed to the political crisis of 1946–1959.

The chronology of political events leading to military dictatorship in 1953 and the subsequent creation of the National Front in 1958 has been discussed elsewhere.[29] Central to present concerns are the fragmentation of the Liberal party in 1946, the disciplined unification of the Conservative party under Laureano Gómez during 1946–1952, and Colombia's comparatively strong economic recovery in the postwar period up to the mid-1950s. In interpreting the political crisis, the Gómez presidency (1950–1953) might be best understood as the last attempt by members of his generation to settle the Liberal-Conservative conflict in traditional terms. The prominent Hispanic elements in his visions of Colombian government, with a strong president, established church, and weak, corporately organized legislature and provincial administration, clearly conform to the historicocultural image. These proposals, however, along with his harsh and arbitrary style of governance, provoked a split in the Conservative party and led ultimately to military intervention in June 1953. One might argue that the Gómez proposals illustrate the continuity of Hispanic values, but the more significant conclusion, it would seem, is that radical corporatist authoritarinism was a minority position even within the Conservative party.

"Transformed" conservatism was initially the product of the moderate wing of the Conservative party, the faction led by Mariano Ospina. Drawing upon the pragmatic and materialistic traditions in conservatism, Ospina—a product of business-oriented Antioquia—led a bloc opposing the radicalism of Gómez and seeking a reconciliation with Liberals to end rural violence and restore political civility. Major themes added to transformed conservatism were promotion of free enterprise, protection of private property, anticommunism, and reduction of the role of the state in the society and economy. The underlying premise here was the necessity for the Conservatives to address the public in terms established by the López era: How might wealth be generated most effectively? How might a just distribution of wealth be achieved? What should be the role of the state in these matters? The answers to these questions have basic implications for interest associations in Colombian society.

For transformed conservatism, the major problem that Colombia confronts is the omnipresent but inefficient and threatening state. To preserve individual liberties, it is necessary to structure into basic processes such as public planning a role for the traditional political parties. The enemy of transformed conservatism is the interventionist and apolitical bureaucracy; its allies are social and economic institutions which can combat populism and constrain the exercise of public powers. The implications for interest associations are clear: While such associations have social obligations, they should exist independently from the state and retain complete freedom of action in participating in political debate.[30]

The historicocultural interpretation of Latin American corporatism stresses the continuity from medieval and colonial times of corporatist and authoritarian values. This brief survey suggests that this view is of limited utility in the Colombian case. In short, very little in either traditional or transformed conservatism supports the corporatist-authoritarian image.

Ideology is only one factor in understanding the nature of Colombian interest politics. We should examine as well the legal policy of government vis-à-vis interest associations, and especially the use of licensing (*personería jurídica*) as a means of state control over associations. State licensing, the historicocultural approach suggests, is a central feature of Hispanic corporatism and is used as an instrument to control interest associations. It can be shown, I believe, that although this legal form has existed in Colombia, it has not been used as an instrument of coercion, again with the important exceptions of labor and religious associations.

Personería jurídica in Colombia is a legal construct which enables a corporation to exercise rights and contract civil obligations under the law and to be represented both legally and extralegally. Quite apart from the familiar North American idea of the limited liability corporation, there exist in Colombian practice as distinct categories "corporations and foundations of public utility" (*fundaciones de beneficiencia pública*) with juridical person. This means that private groups, religious and secular, must be licensed by the state if they are to exist legally. To gain recognition, the group must submit its charter and bylaws to the state for approval. Any subsequent change in its basic charter must be approved by the government if the group is to maintain its legality, and the state retains the right to dissolve the association under specified legal circumstances. As applied to interest associations, there is an interesting blurring between public and private entities. A leading legal scholar writes:

> Finally, public juridical persons are those created by the state to take care of a public service; for example, the National Petroleum Company, the Bank of the Republic, and the National Council of Railroads, the National University, etc. Also included here are the nonprofit entities which carry out activity for the community well-being, such as the foundations, corporations, institutions of common utility, the Catholic church, etc.[31]

Little wonder this legal tradition so intrigues students of corporatism, since it establishes the potential for state control of *all* interest associations. Historically, this potential indeed was partially realized in certain instances. The primary problem in the nineteenth century was establishing order.[32] Among the constraints on liberty imposed during the Regeneration, which itself was a reaction to previous years of anarchy and civil disobedience, we find the government's legal right to intervene in associations to maintain order. A law of 1888, for example, established that:

> The president of the Republic will exercise the right of inspection and vigilance over the scientific associations and institutions of learning; and he is authorized to suspend for the length of time which he deems necessary any society or establishment which under scientific or doctrinal pretext becomes a center of revolutionary propaganda or subversive teachings.[33]

It would seem, however, that regulation of interest associations did not reflect a hearkening back to the organic society of the Middle Ages, but rather was an attempt to fortify a central government with powers sufficient to maintain order. Thus, regulation was intended to prevent conspiracy and armed rebellion. Further, it should be recalled that the central government administration in the latter part of the nineteenth century was poor in money, personnel, and performance. The Justice Ministry in the 1890s is a case in point: "As far as judicial oversight is concerned, there simply did not exist uniformity, doctrine, workable priorities, or an effective system which would permit the Ministry of Justice to become an efficient administrative body."[34] Even so, the ministry's control over *personería jurídica* was administered almost as an afterthought, and the government's financial situation was so precarious that the Justice Ministry was abolished in 1895, not to be revived until 1947.[35]

More importantly, certain "nonfindings" would indicate that the administration of juridical person played a limited role in regulating interest associations. First, very few associations existed during the 1800s. Major advances in the economy were not registered until the early twentieth century, and interest associations did not become significant politically until the 1930s. Second, there is no prominent mention of the central government's withholding licenses as a means of regulating group activity or intervening in the internal policy-making of the very few associations which existed. The strongest emphasis was on simply preventing armed groups from overthrowing the established government for whatever reasons.

Generalizing on the evolution of interest associations in Colombia, Edwin Corr notes a progression in their emergence from agricultural through industrial and commercial groups to the most recent peasant and marginal urban organizations.[36] This is reflected in the sequence of the principal peak associations as shown in table 2. The majority of the Colombian peak associations were created just prior to or during the period of political crisis of 1946–1959.

Table 2. Date of Founding of
Principal Interest Associations

Date	Association
1871	SAC
1887	Society of Engineers
1927	FEDECAFE
1936	CTC
1944	ANDI
1945	FENALCO
1946	UTC
1951	ACOPI
1959	FANAL

This sequence is also reflected generally on a slightly larger scale. Although data on associations prior to 1936 are not readily available, it is evident from table 3 that in Bogota the pattern of interest-group formation resembles that of the peak associations in both rapid increase between 1949 and 1958 and the subsequent increase in lower-strata groups, in this case the cooperatives of workers and employees.

The other significant development to be considered in the historical perspective on interest associations is the extension and elaboration of the administrative apparatus of the central government and, to a lesser extent, the regional autonomous agencies, such as the CVC. Beginning with the creation of the Central Bank in 1923 and continuing to the present, the major administrative instrument for implementing the welfare-development agenda of the López era has been the public corporation and decentralized agency. "In general terms it may be said that approximately ten important decentralized organizations were created between 1930 and 1945. After 1945, however, the number increased so greatly that by 1963, some fifty were in operation."[37] The estimate of the number of such entities operating at present—and the lack of precise information is itself a datum—is approximately one hundred. To be emphasized is that the decentralized sector now spends more and is growing at a considerably faster rate than the central government line ministries.[38] Furthermore, Colombia is by no means unique in the importance of the decentralized sector; rather, it is very much in step with other Latin American countries.

Table 3. Proliferation of Interest Associations in Bogota

Type of Association	1936	1940	1944	1949	1952	1957	1961	1966	1970
Academia	1	1	2	2	2	3	3	4	4
Acción	1	2	1	1	1	1	1	1	1
Asistencia	—	—	—	—	—	—	—	—	—
Asociación	1	3	5	6	11	18	18	21	21
Cámara	2	2	2	1	2	2	2	2	2
Casa	1	—	—	—	—	—	—	—	—
Centro	1	1	3	3	4	4	5	5	5
Club	4	4	2	2	4	6	7	7	7
Comité	1	2	2	2	2	2	2	2	2
Cooperativa	2	4	6	11	28	44	48	75	81
Coordinación	—	—	—	—	1	1	1	1	1
Dirección	1	1	1	2	3	2	2	2	2
Directorio	—	—	—	—	3	2	3	3	3
Federación	6	3	5	8	7	6	7	6	6
Instituto[a]	1	1	3	4	14	17	17	18	18
Junta	—	—	2	2	2	6	6	9	27
Juventud	—	1	1	1	1	1	2	1	1
Sociedad	2	2	2	3	4	4	4	5	5
Unión	—	—	—	—	1	1	1	3	3
Total	24	28	37	48	90	120	129	165	189

Source: *Directorio Municipal de Bogota.*
a. Includes semipublic as well as private organizations.

A discussion of the rationale and efficacy of the decentralized sector lies beyond the scope of this chapter. To understand the nature of interest politics, however, it should be stressed that it is misleading to speak of "the state" or "the government" in relation to interest associations. To a significant degree, we find a multitude of complex organizations operating in varying degrees of freedom from the Congress, president, and line ministries and composing a labyrinth of policy linkages between public authorities and private groups. Interest associations have gained access to, and in many cases representation in, these agencies in part since the rationale of decentralization was to depoliticize administration, and the associations could claim to be nonpartisan, expert entities.

To oversimplify this interpretation even further, with the emergence of the decentralized sector, a basic bifurcation in Colombian politics has come about. Political parties and traditional conflict continue to the present, with a substantial part of the dynamics based upon patronage positions in the central government and departmental bureaucracies. At the same time, however, government intervention to promote development and welfare, the more substantive areas of policy, has gravitated to the decentralized sector. This trend was intensified during the period of crisis, 1946–1959. Interest associations responded to this orientation by seeking access to decentralized agencies, lending added support for the movement toward decentralized administration.

To summarize this historical overview, an important qualitative change in the nature of government may be seen in the 1934–1938 administration of Alfonso López, which greatly expanded the government's legal claims to promotion and regulation. While the concept of licensing (*personería jurídica*) exists in Colombia, there is little evidence that it has been used to coerce or control associations, with the notable exceptions of religious and labor organizations. There is little in traditional conservatism to support the notion of a corporatist-authoritarian regime, and the attempt in 1953 to move toward such forms was crushed forthwith. Transformed conservatism has taken as a principal theme the limitation of government power and the reinvigoration of political parties, interest associations, and free enterprise. The intensification of government intervention and subsequently the rapid postwar recovery were associated with the rapid proliferation of interest groups in Colombia. The logic of decentralization was to remove the cumbersome controls of the central government and minimize partisan conflict in administration, which had reached acute levels after 1946. These trends led to an extensive penetration of the decentralized sector by interest associations. The interface between government and the private sector in the decentralized agencies and the relative autonomy of associations vis-à-vis government constitute the subjects for analysis in contemporary interest politics in Colombia.

Interest Politics in Contemporary Colombia

Conventionally, the comparative analysis of interest politics stresses the structure of government institutions, the nature of elite and mass attitudes, and the characteristics of public policy as significant independent variables.[39] In Colombia, the general structural pattern is a centralized presidential system in which interest associations and administrative agencies are interwoven in complex patterns of overlapping representation. While elite attitudes toward the perceived influence of the peak associations appear somewhat negative, mass attitudes seem apathetic or hostile. State intervention is extensive, and the public agenda is heavily laden with promotional and regulatory activities which affect that portion of the population involved in the national market.

The truce which ended the nineteenth-century partisan wars included a centralized administrative system and a strengthened presidency. The most significant institutional trends in the present century have been the continual weakening of Congress to the point of virtual unimportance, the further strengthening of the presidency, and—as we have seen—the rapid expansion of the public sector, largely through the creation of public corporations and decentralized agencies. In the decline of Congress and rise of the executive, Colombia conforms to both regional and global patterns. Yet the stereotype of the omnipotent Latin American president is misleading. Constraints on presidential leadership to be found to a greater or lesser degree throughout the region include international economic and political pressures, domestic economic and social elites, and institutional actors such as the military forces and church hierarchy.

Additional constraints on the president specific to the Colombian setting are the cumbersome National Front agreements, and—by regional standards—an independent judiciary. Perhaps most important, and this will occupy considerable attention, the president encounters a complex public bureaucracy which has accumulated over the past forty years. Beyond formal-legal institutions, the independent interest associations, a generally unfettered press, constant regional pressures, and elite opinion further check his freedom. The comparatively highly developed and differentiated business and industrial sectors provide a general counterweight to government as a whole. While the traditional political parties have become weakened under the National Front, their leadership continues to exert influence on the president and ministers. Thus, while the president occupies perhaps the central position in the overall policy process, limitations on his influence are considerable.[40]

The political culture of Colombia, as manifested in attitudes expressed by elites and masses, further affects the activity of interest associations. While survey results are limited, if we accept the statements and behavior of interest association leaders, mass attitudes are perceived to be hostile. Apparent in their statements is a theme that the public misunderstands the groups' purposes, that their story simply is not being told.[41] To illustrate, an effort launched by industrialists and merchants to combat communism and create popular support for free enterprise soon became branded as the infamous "Black Hand" by a leading Liberal politician.[42] Further, and this is somewhat speculative, the principal peak associations have been identified with "the oligarchy," an odious symbol in the Colombian political lexicon.[43] Political violence and blatant opportunism, populism and not infrequent demagoguery have implanted a condition of potent mass hostility toward political and social elites. This has been reflected, I believe, in the electoral support for the antiestablishment positions taken by Gustavo Rojas and the ANAPO.

Elite attitudes are somewhat negative toward interest associations' perceived political influence. The findings from a 1966 survey of 1,003 intellectuals, congressmen, party leaders, and high bureaucratic officials indicate (1) the majority of those interviewed (59.3%) considered the actual influence of the groups to be "bad"; (2) the majority (69.3%) believed group influence had grown under the National Front; and (3) an even larger majority (70.6%) believed interest group influence would increase in the future.[44] Table 4 depicts elite perceptions of association influence by major categories. When one considers that the table depicts *elite* attitudes, the groups' plea for understanding is itself understandable.

Industrial associations follow only the press and "the oligarchy" (whose reification evidently seems reasonable to the respondents) in being perceived as exercising "excessive" influence. The clergy, agricultural associations, unions, and students also suffer a generally negative image among elites. Professional associations, however, are perceived as unduly weak. Opinion is nearly evenly divided on excessive versus adequate military influence, while the commercial associations (FENALCO and others) enjoy perhaps the strongest support among the business-industrial groups. Even though too much may easily be inferred from these limited data, a specific implication is that Colombian industrial and agricultural associations act in a hostile environment. Little wonder that the comparatively shielded and little-known arena of

Table 4. Colombian Elite Perceptions of Association Influence, 1966

	Labor	Industry	Commerce	Agriculture	Student	Professional	Clergy	Press	Military	Oligarchy
Excessive	47.1%	71.6%	36.0%	56.5%	46.5%	3.8%	69.5%	80.7%	40.5%	78.8%
Adequate	22.2	22.4	34.7	30.7	11.4	17.0	24.6	16.9	46.7	8.3
Insufficient	18.5	2.9	22.3	7.4	17.0	45.9	1.8	0.2	2.3	1.1
Nonexistent	8.9	1.0	5.0	3.4	23.2	31.6	3.0	0.2	8.1	6.3
No opinion	3.3	2.1	2.0	2.0	1.9	1.7	1.0	2.0	2.5	5.6
	(N=1003)		(N=1007)				(N=994)			

Source: Adapted from Fundación Tercer Mundo para el Desarrollo Humano, División de Estudios Sociales, "Estudio de las Estructuras Socio-Políticas de Colombia," 1966. Reported in Centro de Investigación y Acción Social, Estructuras políticas de Colombia, Colección Monografías y Documentos, no. 3 (Bogota: CIAS, 1969), p. 65.

the administrative agencies is the preferred turf of the peak associations.

The pattern of public policy in Colombia finds the state involved extensively in economic development and social welfare. Certain generalizations on interest-group politics apply: To the extent that the government's policy jurisdiction has expanded, we find both the creation of interest associations in response to intervention and the increased politicization of existing interest associations, which perceive a greater involvement of the state in what were formerly private activities. Also, interest groups tend to concentrate on the administrative organs of government and more on the implementation of policy than on its formulation.[45]

In order to demonstrate that patterns of contemporary interest representation in Colombia approach more nearly a variant of pluralism as opposed to state corporatism, two sets of relationships will be examined: (1) the types of controls which the government possesses and may exercise over the interest associations, and (2) the points of access which interest associations have to public policy-making, especially through the public decentralized agencies. In examining these relationships, I would stress the limitations inherent in a structural approach. The eventual goal of our collective research is to be able to associate types of governments and/or societies with patterns of public policy-making processes and outputs. Even with an ideal research design employing survey and elite interviewing, with access to agency documents and expertise in complex questions of public policy, it is hazardous to assess influences on policy-making. A more realistic goal in the present effort is to indicate some structural features and relationships which are obvious in the data and raise questions for further research. The instruments of government control over interest associations to be considered are licensing, subsidies, influence on leadership selection, and internal policy-making. Table 5 summarizes some information relevant to this analysis.

As noted above, licensing provides the potential for rigorous governmental control over the formation of interest associations as well as internal policy-making. Several factors, however, limit the realization of this potential. First, there is a pluralist norm in Colombian interest politics, particularly in regard to freedom of association. Juridical person is not essential to the existence of a group; rather, it facilitates group operations in owning property and conducting business. In fact, the purpose of juridical person is to assure an association of the safeguards and legal protection which exist under Colombian law. In this sense, it is a legal convenience. While the granting of juridical person implies the government's inspection of proposed constitutions and bylaws, the intent is to ensure that the association's goals are not contrary to existing law. In short, the norms supporting legality and free association inhibit the use of juridical person as an instrument of control. Second, juridical person may be obtained in at least two ways: formal recognition through a law or decree, or recognition through administrative action. One implication of the latter route is important: An association may receive recognition from any of thirteen national ministries or from a departmental administrative body.[46] Third, as will be shown, the tenure of office of government ministers is comparatively short. This suggests that an interest association can obtain juridical person fairly easily at some point from some agency. Once obtained, it is unlikely to be revoked, or even reviewed, unless complaints are made to the government.[47] In sum, while juridical person implies the potential for strict public regulation, cultural and legal norms, as well as structural factors, limit its use.

Money is certainly a key instrument in potential government control over private associations, and a brief review of comptroller reports, as shown in table 6, indicates the variety of groups and associations receiving money in various ways from the government. In considering the control potential of government spending, distinctions should be drawn among (1) annual and compulsory (that is, required by law) subsidies, (2) special grants, and (3) contracting for services.

Annual subsidies impose an obligation on the government (which it may choose to ignore in certain cases) to make payments which may produce little support or policy responsiveness from the associations. For example, evidence on the Chambers of Commerce, which receive a small annual subsidy, indicates little government control attendant on financing.[48] Also in regard to control, the form of payment may be significant. In the case of SAC, eighteen direct and equal payments are made to departmental associations, which would seem to weaken SAC's centralized control over its departmental affiliates without necessarily strengthening the government's influence over the local groups. I do not know whether the agricultural associations are exceptional in this respect.

Special grants are perhaps more capable of creating influence over association activities, since there is a degree of flexibility in their administration. Money, for example, to build a labor union's headquarters or to sponsor a labor congress, may buy policy responsiveness as well. But the very temporality of this type of spending, as well as an evident strain toward equity between the CTC and UTC suggest otherwise. Once transferred and spent, special grants become history in ongoing relationships between government and associations. Finally, payments for services contracted by the government seem limited as a

Table 5. Characteristics of Principal Colombian Interest Associations

	Gov't Control Over Leadership	Gov't Control Over Internal Policy	Gov't Control Through Finance	Membership
SAC	2 ministers on board which elects president	2 ministers on board	Subsidies from Agriculture Ministry	4,000 direct; 200,000 in allied groups
FEDECAFE	5 ministers on board which elects manager	5 ministers on 11-member board	Subsidies from Agriculture Ministry; contracts	185,000
CTC	Indirect, labor code	Indirect, labor code	Subsidies from Labor Ministry	150,000 (1963 est.) 446,000 (mid-1960s est.)
ANDI	None	None	None	540 firms (150,000 employees) (1963 est.) 600 firms (1967 est.)

FENALCO	None	None	None	5,000 firms (1967 est.)
ACOPI	None	None	None	13 regional associations
UTC	Indirect, labor code	Indirect, labor code	Subsidies from Labor Ministry	200,000 (1963 est.) 449,000 (mid-1960s est.)
FANAL	Indirect, labor code	Indirect, labor code	Subsidies from Labor Ministry	65,000 (1967 est.)

Sources: Corr, *Political Process in Colombia*, pp. 54–81; Dix, *Colombia*, chaps. 11–12; Koffman, "National Federation of Coffee-Growers," pp. 23, 42; Urrutia, *Development of the Colombian Labor Force*, pp. 170–73, 204–11; Asociacion Colombiana Popular de Industriales, "Que es ACOPI?" (Bogota: mimeo, 1970); Federación Nacional de Comerciantes, *Estatutos y resoluciones reglamentarias* (Bogota: ANTARES, Ltda, n.d.); Sociedad de Agricultores de Colombia, *Estatutos de la Sociedad de Agricultores de Colombia, SAC* (Bogota: n.p., 1970); Thomas E. Weil et al., *Area Handbook for Colombia* (Washington, D.C.: USGPO, 1970), p. 430.

Table 6. Colombian Central Government Payments to Interest Associations: Selected Examples

Amount (pesos)	Recipient (and Purpose)	Donor Ministry	Year
50,000	SAC	Agriculture	1962
70,000	SAC	Agriculture	1966, 1967, 1969
50,000	Agricultural Congresses (aid)	Agriculture	1969
157,115	Cattlemens' Associations (aid)	Agriculture	1969
7,000,000	(contract to improve cattle-raising)	Agriculture	1967
4,000,000	FEDEGAN (contract)	Agriculture	1969
1,483,070	FEDECAFE	Development	1966
300,000	CTC (building)	Labor	1966
150,000	CTC (Congress of Workers in Santa Maria)	Labor	1967
150,000	Peasant Congress	Labor	1967
100,000	FANAL and National Union Cooperative (aid)	Labor	1966
300,000	UTC (building)	Labor	1966
300,000	Union Congresses	Labor	1969
100,000	Shoemakers Cooperative, Barranquilla (subsidy)	Labor	1969
15,000	Bricklayers' Union of Sahagun	Labor	1969
100,000	Engineers' Society	Public Works	1967, 1969
80,000	Engineers' Society	Public Works	1966
10,000	Engineers' Society (annual prize)	Public Works	1969
50,000	ADEA (construction of headquarters)	Education	1966
10,000	Colombian Association of Physical Education Teachers (aid)	Education	1969
50,000	Colombian Association of Secondary Teachers	Education	1969
50,000	National Association of Teachers of Technical Training	Education	1969
10,000,000	39th Eucharistic Congress	Treasury	1967
20,000	St. Vincent de Paul Society, Pensilvania	Public Health	1966
2,000	Chamber of Commerce	Development	1962

Source: Contraloría General de la República, *Informe financiero*, 1962, 1966, 1967, and 1969.

means of controlling associations, since the purpose of contracting is to acquire some service presumed to be in the public good.

The obvious question to be raised concerning money as a control instrument is whether power and influence redound to the giver. Even this cursory glance at some aspects of the Colombian case would challenge an unqualified presumption of control accompanying government payments. Furthermore, this admittedly nonrigorous review of comptroller reports reveals no government subsidies to the principal industrial and commercial associations—ANDI, FENALCO, and ACOPI. While subsidies to labor unions may be explained in part by government preoccupation with controlling labor associations and the financial weakness inherent in the organized labor movement, an interesting pattern is the comparatively consistent and substantial support received by the various agricultural associations, which appear to have developed closer linkages with government than the commercial and industrial associations.

These findings suggest further questions on the origins and distribution of subsidies. Under what circumstances have groups sought and received subsidies? Was the intention of the subsidy to control the group or promote activities presumed to serve the public good (or some combination of these motives)? How have postdepression administrations manipulated subsidies to create political support? In regard to contemporary politics, how do the amounts of subsidies vary from one group to another? And, equally important, what groups are excluded from government aid and for what reasons?

Beyond licensing and subsidies, control over leadership selection by interest associations is a potential instrument of government influence. Again, unfortunately, there is virtually no published information on whatever informal consultation occurs between government and association actors in this area, and comments must be limited to the formal-legal evidence. In this respect, there appears to be a continuum of government controls with some formal influence over FEDECAFE and SAC, less control over the labor confederations, and apparently none over the industrial and commercial associations.[49]

Government control over internal association policy-making is not known. Certainly there is ample contact between public officials and associations in diverse arenas: private consultations, government representation in general meetings of the associations, airing of views in the press. Yet in this respect, as in the historical overview, the "nonfindings" seem more significant than the findings. Given the stress on legality and the associations' preoccupation with government regulation, it would seem that government intervention into the internal operation of the associations would soon be reflected in the public press or in association publications. This apparently has not occurred. Moreover, there is little need for government sorties into internal association policy-making, since a more effective and less controversial means of control is for government officials simply to ignore the associations altogether in cases of conflict over policy. This method *is* commented upon frequently and acridly, particularly by the industrial and commercial associations.[50]

In sum, it would seem that there is little evidence to support an interpretation of Colombian interest politics as state corporatism. While the potential for government control exists through legal instruments such as licensing and subsidies, and for direct intervention through extraordinary powers in cases of declared emergency, the pattern seems to indicate substantial association independence. A more effective method of political control over the associations is the manipulation of conditions of access of interest groups to public policy-making, especially at the implementation phase in the ministries and decentralized agencies.

A difficulty in analyzing the Colombian decentralized sector is the limited data available from or about the agencies themselves. This is complicated by their reluctance to define themselves as public entities. Until recently, government organization manuals did not include descriptions of them, comptroller reports routinely lament their refusal to cooperate, and the researcher is forced into the mines of public law to prospect for useful information. Rather than following the conventional distinctions between public and mixed corporations, national and regional decentralized agencies, and special districts (for example, industrial development zones), a more useful distinction for present purposes is between agencies in which the central government is dominant and those with significant private-sector participation. Some preliminary points on the agencies may be helpful.

Officially, decentralized agencies are presumed to meet certain criteria which justify a degree of autonomy from the central government. In the mid-1950s, these criteria were that (1) the agency be concerned with a function which falls within the domain of the state; (2) the function be highly technical; (3) the state legally endow the agency with sufficient financial and administrative power that it might effectively deal with its clienteles and other state agencies; and (4) the central government exercise sufficiently close control over the establishment to maintain administrative coherence.[51] As will become evident, not all of those conditions are fully realized in practice.

The rationale for the creation of the decentralized agencies has been discussed above. They provide asylum from partisan conflict in the central government; they have greater administrative flexibility, can pay high salaries, and thus can recruit able specialists. Yet what is most significant for the interpretation of Colombian interest politics is the logic of interest representation in the decentralized sector. The legitimacy of government intervention is conditioned in good part by guaranteeing interest associations structured access to policy-making. This pattern, it would seem, supports the notion of pluralism as opposed to state corporatism in the Colombian case. Further, there seems to be a process of flexible contracts negotiated by government officials and interest associations. In exchange for support of (or at least acquiescence to) government regulation, the associations receive a degree of power over public policy-making.[52] This process is not totally dissimilar from U.S. experience since the New Deal, but important distinctions should be drawn.

Corporatist structures are found in U.S. administration. At the federal level, the Pay Board, Price Commission, and Cost of Living Council are recent examples of structured coalitions of labor, government, and public members. Yet the more significant manifestation of corporatism is the enormous proliferation of advisory committees, some 1,439 by a recent count. Of these, 257 meet the corporatist criterion of official recognition (in this case statutory authorization).[53] In contrast, the Colombian variant of corporatism involves interest associations exercising voting power on the directive boards of the agencies.

Unfortunately, the data reported in tables 7 and 8 constitute a still photograph of a fluidly changing relationship. Whenever possible the most recent decree or law structuring the directive junta was consulted. This is important since Carlos Lleras strengthened considerably presidential control over the agencies in a series of administrative reorganizations in 1968. His principal instrument to achieve this was direct nomination of public members to agencies and indirect nomination by selecting representatives from lists submitted by interest associations. Lleras further fortified the central government and presidency by formally bringing the decentralized agencies under the policy control of the line ministers, themselves presidential appointees. For the most part, this was a reiteration of existing laws, but the reorganization had the effect of formalizing and enhancing the potential for central government control.[54]

No clear patterns of representation in relation to date of organization or type of activity emerge from these examples. This finding underscores the point that there is a complex diversity of interest representation within given countries, with considerable variation from one agency to another. Generalizations on interest representation, then, should be stated in terms of trends and patterns to describe a concrete polity as more nearly approximating a pluralist or corporatist system.

Three areas for priority in research seem obvious from these ex-

Table 7. Public-Private Sector Participation in Directive Boards of Decentralized Agencies: Private Sector Significant

Agency[a]	Representation	
	Public Sector	Private Sector
IDEMA (1968)	Min. Agriculture Dir., Bank of the Republic Dir., Agr. Bank Dir., INCORA Dir., ICA Dir., INDERENA Dir., INCOMEX	Dir., FEDECAFE Production guilds (1)[b] Peasant assocs. (1)[b] Agr. Co-ops (1)[b]
INCORA (1961)	Min. Agriculture Min. Public Works Armed Forces (1) Agr. Bank ICA Geographical Inst. Senate (2) Representatives (2)	SAC (1)[b] FEDEGAN (1)[b] Workers (CTC-UTC) (1)[b] Catholic Social Action (1)[b] Agr. Co-ops (1)[b]
INSFOPAL (1970)	Min. Public Health Pres. delegate (1) Planning (1) INPES (1)	Col. Assoc. of Municipalities (1)[b] Col. Soc. of Engineers (1)[b] FEDECAFE (1)[b] SAC (1)[b]

ICSS (1960)	Min. Labor
	Min. Health
		Nat. Acad. of Medicine—
		  Col. Medical Fed. (1)
		Employers (ANDI, FENALCO,
		  SAC) (1)
		Workers (CTC-UTC) (1)

ICT (1963)	Min. Development	Military Housing Fund (1)[b]
		Reps. of guilds & orgs. with
		  activities directly related
		  to national housing programs (4)[b]

SENA (1968)	Min. Labor Min. Education Nat. Planning	Episcopal Conf. (1) ANDI (1) FENALCO (1) ACOPI (1) SAC (1) UTC (1)
Financial Corp. for Transportation (1964)	Public member	Reps. of transporters (2)[b]

CVC (1960)	Min. Development
	Governors, Valle & Cauca
	Pres. delegates (2)
		SAC, Coffee Growers of Valle,
		  Col. Assoc. of Agr. Engineers (1)
		Bankers Assoc., ANDI, FENALCO,
		  Engineers' Assoc. (1)

INDERENA (1968)	Min. Agriculture Dir., Agr. Bank Dir., INCORA Dir., IDEMA Dir., ICA	Peasant assocs. (1)[b]

continued

Table 7, continued

| Agency[a] | Representation | |
	Public Sector	Private Sector
ICBF (1968)	Min. Justice Min. Education Min. Public Health Dir., Nat. Police Senate (1) Representatives (1)	Social science expert designated by Episcopal Conf. (1) Reps. designated by pres. from lists submitted by relevant orgs. (2)[b]
ICFES (1968)	Min. Education Pres. delegates (2) Dir., ICETEX	University rectors (4)
FFNN (1970)	Min. Public Works	Members from commerce, agr., & industry (4)[b]
Nat. Fund for Community Road (1970) (Nat.)	Min. Government Min. Public Works Min. Agriculture Public members (3)	Dir., FEDECAFE
(Departmental)	Sec. Public Works Rep. Min. Public Works Rep. Nat. Fund Commu- nity Action	Agr. & Cattlemens' Assocs. (1)[b] Guild representation FEDECAFE[b]

a. Date corresponds to year of decree consulted.
b. Government exercises some control over choice of representative, usually from lists submitted by associations.

amples: (1) What are the principal trends in government and interest association representation on the agencies? (Superficially, the pattern seems to be one of increased government control through nominations of public members and cross-representation among public agencies.) (2) What characterizes the politics of presidential appointments? De jure control over appointments need not translate into presidential power, however impressive the number and range of posts may be. A strong president, which was the Lleras image, might exercise considerable influence in the agencies. But a weak president would very likely engage in the kind of political *milimetría* (tediously balancing cabinet appointments among various partisan cliques and factions) which characterized the Guillermo León Valencia administration (1962–1966). Related to this, are interest associations interested and successful in influencing the appointments of public members? Rather than further empowering the president, the additional public posts might provide expanded access for interest associations and the enhancement of private control over public agencies. (3) What are the characteristics of the appointees themselves? Beyond the demographic variables of age, region, social class, etc., what additional factors (technical training, partisan activity) are relevant to appointments?[55] Particularly, to what

Table 8. Public-Private Sector Participation in Directive Boards of Decentralized Agencies: Public Sector Dominant

| Agency[a] | Representation | |
	Public Sector	Private Sector
TELECOM (1960)	Min. Communications Dir., Min. Communications Pres. delegates (2)	
COLPUERTOS (1959)	Min. Treasury Min. Public Works Pres. delegates (2)	
INRAVISION (1963)	Min. Communications Min. Education Pres. delegates (2)	
INTRA (1968)	Pres. delegate (1) Min. Public Works Min. Communications Dir., Nat. Railroads Pres., Financial Corp. for Transportation	
Nat. Corp. for the Dev. of Chocó (1968)	Min. Defense Min. Agriculture Pres. Delegates (4) Min. Mines & Petrol. Min. Communications Planning Governor, Chocó Dir., INCORA	Col. Soc. of Engineers (1)
ECOPETROL (1959)	Pres. delegates (4) Min. Mines & Petrol.	
IFI (1963)	Min. Treasury Min. Development Pres. delegate (1)	
Nat. Fund for Dev. Projects (1968)	Planning (2) Dir., Infrastructure Unit Dir., Urban & Regional Dev.	
Community Dev. Fund (1970)	Min. Government Dept. Governor Planning Community Action Pres. delegate (1)	
ICCE (1969)	Min. Education Min. Public Works Planning Pres. delegate (1)	

a. Date corresponds to year of decree consulted.

extent is there a circulation of elites between government agencies and leadership positions in the associations? Robert H. Dix suggests that the movement is strong:

> The overlap between the leadership of major interest associations and both legislative and high executive office is likewise of relatively great importance in Colombia. Men who are themselves past or present officers of such organizations as the Federation of Coffee Growers, the National Sugar Growers Association, the ANDI, or the professional associations are frequently to be found in high government posts, including the presidency. . . .
> The point is not that leadership in interest associations is a primary basis of recruitment to governmental office. Rather, the patterns of Colombian society tend to produce such an overlap and to this degree to fuse the interests of major organized groups with those of government.[56]

While the notion of movement and overlapping representation is clearly stated, the questions begged here are what interests are held in common by associations and government and whose interests prevail, under what circumstances, when and if differences arise.

The strength suggested by the central government's (and more specifically the president's) powers of appointment may be more apparent than real. In important respects, in fact, the central government is comparatively weak, and this weakness is magnified in its inability to control the decentralized agencies. Two areas will be sketched to illustrate the debility of the central government: ministerial tenure in office and budgetary controls.

Table 9 depicts the tenure in office of the line ministers over the period 1930 to 1970. Most obvious is the greater stability of tenure during the National Front in contrast to the preceding twenty-eight years. Nevertheless, it is reasonable to infer from this that whereas ministers are the principal coordinators of the decentralized agencies, in several cases they are in office for too short a time to exercise continuing policy direction, which creates a potential for pronounced agency autonomy and capture by interest associations. In this respect, it would be interesting to compare the relative tenure of public and private representatives on agency directorates. Once again, unfortunately, we must reason from an example rather than a representative sample.

SENA is an agency with significant private-sector representation on its national directorate. As table 10 indicates, the private-sector groups clearly have longer tenure in office than those in the public sector. Furthermore, these patterns are generally reflected at the department SENA directorates, where again the tendency is for much more rapid turnover of representatives from the public sector.[57] In reasoning from this example, two caveats must be noted: (1) SENA may be an excep-

Table 9. Average Tenure in Office of Colombian Central Government Line
Ministers (in months) 1930–1970

Ministry	1930–1957	1958–1970	1930–1970
Government	11.2	13.0	12.0
Education	8.4	13.0	9.5
Development	9.6	15.6	10.9
Foreign Relations	9.3	16.3	11.2
Defense	10.8	19.5	13.3
Agriculture (1937–70)	13.1	13.0	13.1
Communications	11.2	13.0	11.7
Treasury	12.0	19.5	14.1
Public Works	17.7	19.5	18.2
Justice (1946–70)	8.0	13.0	10.0
Labor (1938–70)	12.6	13.0	12.8
Public Health (1946–70)	11.1	16.3	13.1
Mines and Petroleum (1940–70)	8.7	15.6	11.6

Source: Richard Hartwig, "Cabinet Instability and the Colombian Political
System," (manuscript, University of Wisconsin, 1971), appendix.

tion among the decentralized agencies; and (2) one should not infer too
much about comparative influence on policy-making from tenure in
office. It may be plausible that expertise, interpersonal solidarity, and
facility in bargaining are associated with long tenure, but this need not
be the case.

The budgetary process, a principal instrument for administrative
control, has not effectively subordinated the decentralized agencies to
the central government. Despite efforts of Lleras and his predecessors
to exert influence over policy via planning and budgeting, complaints
by the comptroller of noncompliance by decentralized agencies persist.[58] Part of the weakness of budgetary controls stems from Colombia's economic dependence, which distorts and fragments the taxing
and allocative process. Also important is the preference of the government to employ spending rather than coercion as a means of dealing
with short-term pressures (strikes, bankruptcy).[59] In addition, the
decentralized agencies and public corporations in many instances enjoy
assured income through special taxes, earmarked appropriations, and
sales of goods and services. However, this does not imply that the
president or ministers lack any control through budgeting. Earmarked
appropriations can be ignored in certain circumstances (for example,
severe deficits or balance-of-payment problems), and transfers from the
ministries—which compose a substantial portion of certain agencies'
income—can be regulated to a degree. To the extent that money is
spent for investment, government control by the National Planning

Table 10. Interest Representation on SENA National Directorate, 1957–1972

	Number of Representatives	Years on Directorate	Longest Tenure (consecutive or broken)
Private associations			
ACOPI	2	9	7
ANDI	4	16	6
FENALCO	3	16	10
SAC	2	16	9
UTC	2	16	14
Church	6	16	10
Mean tenure: 4.86 years			
Public agencies			
Ministry of Education	14	16	4
Ministry of Labor	17	16	3
National Planning Agency	2	4	2
Mean tenure: 1.03 years			

Source: SENA National Directorate.

Department may be exercised. The point to be emphasized is that budgeting is embedded in a rigid yet fragmented body of legislation which legally commits a substantial portion of income and expenditures and provides agencies with legal claims in the actual bargaining over allocations. Legal rights, however, must be buttressed by political support, and here the influence of the private associations represented on agency directorates or benefiting from agency programs is significant.[60]

This discussion of representation and budgeting suggests an image of government weakness which should be qualified. The Colombian central government is not simply the passive instrument of associations; it can and does exercise coercion. But the targets, timing, and methods are carefully chosen. Riots or political kidnapings are often met immediately with declarations of state of siege and military suppression. General elections are conducted under heightened military preparedness. Labor unions and student groups are closely monitored by government officials, and there is a predisposition to intervene forcefully if strikes are declared disruptive or illegal.

Apart from physical coercion, the government may exercise significant direct influence. While the president has been described as subject to diverse pressures, his influence in selective instances is considerable.

In support of civilian supremacy, for example, President Valencia in 1964 removed Rúiz Novoa as minister of war, and President Lleras in 1969 forced the retirement of the commander of the army for airing political statements publicly.[61] More recently, President Misael Pastrana ignored the recommendations of the UTC leader and placed his own labor delegate on a study commission for labor reforms.[62] And a recent study of the ICT finds that "the president makes little use of his power to supervise the details of ICT operations through the Junta Directiva or the minister of development, but he does call upon his formal authority to initiate and approve major ICT policies."[63] Thus, a more accurate image of central government power would balance the institutional complexities of the ministries and decentralized agencies with the capacity to coerce to maintain order or to exercise presidential prerogatives.

The purpose of this overview has been to assess the utility of corporatism in interpreting Colombian interest politics. Unfortunately, the lack of data has necessitated reasoning from examples, which places the discussion rather awkwardly between case studies and a more comprehensive survey. I hope, however, that two goals have been met: (1) an interpretation of Colombian interest politics which conforms more closely to elitist pluralism than to state corporatism has been supported; and (2) specific questions and areas for further research have been targeted. If we accept the accuracy of this interpretation, some political implications of this pattern of interest representation might be noted.

Implications of Elitist Pluralism

I shall limit these concluding remarks to a brief, perhaps inelegant, and *ad hoc* balance sheet of some positive and negative consequences of elitist pluralism for economic development and social equality in the Colombian case.

The information functions of interest representation are important for effective government participation in promotion and regulation. Scarcity of expertise in Colombia is no longer the serious problem it once was, but the concentration of experts from the public and private sectors on the policy-making boards of the specialized agencies may be a more efficient use of resources than isolated and competing groups. Not only is the technical and policy-related expertise significant, but also the political information transmitted by group representatives provides a means for pretesting policy options and assessing the acceptability of programs to affected groups. Although I have no hard evidence on which to base this, I suspect the policy and political information exchange which characterizes the decentralized sector takes on added importance given the partisan and status preoccupations of Congress and parties, and the comparatively greater involvement of the ministers and ministries in status politics.[64] Thus, the comparatively shielded arena of the decentralized agencies may be the more significant locus of policy politics.

The central theme developed throughout the discussion of contemporary interest politics is that association autonomy and access to public policy-making constitute a major source of legitimacy for government activities. That this form of interest representation is in some way consistent with Hispanic corporatism, which is only partly true, seems to me more incidental than central to explaining its contemporary origins and functions. Participation by groups in the policy processes which affect them is not by any means limited to Hispanic countries. Indeed, public participation in administrative programs has become a major theme in the United States.[65] Of much greater import is that contemporary governments as a general rule adopt interventionist measures, not to approximate the sacred norms of order and hierarchy in secular affairs, but to pursue the rather conventional goals of economic growth and stability. The general logic is that groups possess resources (money, information, strategic services) which may be used to influence policy-making. These groups, themselves the products of economic and social differentiation, demand access to relevant decision-making arenas. By granting such access, government officials anticipate cooperation and support from the groups for public programs. This is a voluntary and secular process which, writ large, constitutes a basis of political legitimacy in which information, bargaining, and collaboration constitute more important currencies than persistent coercion or imposition.

Another positive characteristic of elitist pluralism is its relative flexibility. This is an arrangement which facilitates serial adjustments; successive governments can impose more or less regulation. Also, there is flexibility in the admission of new groups to policy coalitions, although there may be much greater rigidity in eliminating existing groups.

On the whole, then, information, participation, and flexibility may be viewed as functional for efficient policy-making. Some problems with this form of representation should be considered as well. Certain common criticisms of pluralism apply *mutatis mutandis* to the Colombian case.

First, not all relevant interests are represented in this system. The most obviously excluded interests are the marginally employed or unemployed in both the urban and rural areas, who constitute possibly the majority of the Colombian population. There is, overall, a strong middle- and upper-class bias to Colombian interest politics. Second, the assumption of sectoral representativeness of existing organizations may be misleading. In this regard, the groups are not comprehensive in membership, and their actual composition should be carefully studied. Moreover, given the near universality of oligarchy in organizations, the internal functioning of the peak associations should be examined to assess whose interests are being served by group involvement in policy-making. Finally, this form of interest representation is inherently conservative in the sense that the interests of group membership as presently constituted are undoubtedly a foremost consideration in policy debate. Thus, options which might result in short-term disadvantages, or whose consequences may be unclear for a group's membership, would likely be rejected in the absence of coercion. To the extent that the public administration is characterized by structured participation by elite groups, then, one might expect continuity and incremental decision-making.

These are offered as preliminary thoughts on some policy consequences of elitist pluralism. Certainly, much more research is needed on the relationships between government and interest associations in Colombia before generalizations may be stated with confidence. At a minimum, however, this case study demonstrates that the rather sweeping assertions on the cultural heritage of Latin America, involving as it does the political experience of three continents over two thousand years, should be carefully qualified in explanations of political behavior in specific national settings.

LIST OF ABBREVIATIONS

ACOPI	Colombian Association of Small Industrialists
ADEA	Association of Educators of Atlantico
ANAPO	National Popular Alliance
ANDI	National Association of Industrialists
COLPUERTOS	Colombian Port Authority
CSTC	Syndical Confederation of Colombian Workers
CTC	Confederation of Colombian Workers
CVC	Cauca Valley Corporation
ECOPETROL	Colombian Petroleum Enterprise
FANAL	National Agrarian Federation
FEDECAFE	Coffee Growers Federation
FEDEGAN	Cattlemens Federation
FENALCO	National Federation of Merchants
FFNN	National Railroads
ICA	Colombian Agricultural Institute

ICBF	Colombian Institute for Family Welfare
ICCE	Colombian Institute for School Construction
ICETEX	Colombian Institute for Educational Credit and Foreign Study
ICFES	Colombian Institute for Development of Higher Education
ICSS	Colombian Social Security Institute
ICT	Territorial Credit Institute
IDEMA	Agricultural Marketing Institute
IFI	Industrial Development Institute
INCOMEX	Foreign Commerce Institute
INCORA	Colombian Agrarian Reform Institute
INDERENA	National Resources Institute
INRAVISION	Radio and Television Institute
INSFOPAL	National Institute of Municipal Development
INTRA	National Institute of Transportation
SAC	Colombian Farmers Society
SENA	National Apprenticeship Service
TELECOM	Communications Enterprise
UTC	Colombian Workers Union

NOTES

In addition to the participants in the University of Pittsburgh Seminar, whose comments were most useful, I should like to thank the directors of the Centro Colombiano of Washington, D.C., and the Washington Chapter of the Sociedad Económica de Amigos del País for organizing a joint meeting in March 1974, at which an earlier draft of this chapter was presented. Ms. Maria Elena Aguero provided helpful research assistance in collecting data for this study.

1. Fernando Cepeda U. et al., *Los grupos de presión en Colombia: mesas redondas do "AEXANDES"* (Bogota: Tercer Mundo, 1962); Edwin G. Corr, *The Political Process in Colombia*, Monograph Series in World Affairs, no. 1–2 (Denver: The Social Science Foundation and Graduate School of the University of Denver, 1971–1972), chap. 3; Robert H. Dix, *Colombia: The Political Dimensions of Change* (New Haven: Yale University Press, 1967), chap. 12; Harvey F. Kline, "Interest Groups in the Colombian Congress: Group Behavior in a Centralized, Patrimonial Political System," *Journal of Inter-American Studies and World Affairs*, 16, no. 3 (August 1974):274–300; Bennett E. Koffman, "The National Federation of Coffee-Growers of Colombia" (Ph.D. dissertation, University of Virginia, 1969); John D. Martz, *Colombia: A Contemporary Political Survey* (Chapel Hill: University of North Carolina Press, 1962), pp. 20–30; and Fernando Sanclamente M., "Grupos de presión" (dissertation, Universidad Javeriana, Bogota, 1965).

2. John Walton's theoretically interesting and methodologically imaginative essay, "Political Development and Economic Development: A Regional Assessment of Contemporary Theories," *Studies in Comparative International Development*, 7, no. 1 (Spring 1972):39–63, quite properly investigates regional variations (Cali and Medellin in the Colombian case) in relation to generalizations on political development. See also David W. Dent, "Oligarchy and Power Structure in Urban Colombia: The Case of Cali," *Journal of Latin American Studies*, 6, no. 1 (May 1974):113–33; and Irene Fraser Rothenberg, "Centralization Patterns and Policy Outcomes in Colombia" (Ph.D. dissertation, University of Illinois, 1973).

3. Philippe C. Schmitter, "Paths to Political Development in Latin America," *Proceedings of the Academy of Political Science*, 30 (1972):83–105; and Alfred C. Stepan III, "Political Development Theory: The Latin American Experience," *Journal of International Affairs*, 20, no. 2 (1966):233–35, are useful critiques of development theory in the Latin American context.

4. On this point, see William P. Glade, "The State and Economic Development in Mediterranean Politics" (Paper delivered at the annual meeting of the American Political Science Association, New Orleans, September 4–8, 1973), pp. 13–22; and Philippe C. Schmitter, "Still the Century of Corporatism?" *Review of Politics*, 36, no. 1 (January 1974):86–92. In an earlier discussion, I characterized Colombian interest politics as "neocorporatist." This, however, tends to muddle further an already overburdened concept, and I now believe it is more useful to analyze Colombia as a variant of pluralism. See "La implementación política en un régmen neocorporative: algunos ejemplos de la educación Colombiana," *Estudios Andinos*, 4, no. 1 (1975):203–39.

5. Howard J. Wiarda, "Toward a Framework for the Study of Political Change in the Iberic-Latin Tradition: The Corporative Model," *World Politics*, 25, no. 2 (January 1973):206–35; and idem, "Corporatism and Development in the Iberic-Latin World: Persistent Strains and New Variations," *Review of Politics*, 36, no. 1 (January 1974):3–33. These themes are treated in the symposium "Colonial Institutions and Contemporary Latin America," in *Hispanic American Historical Review*, 43, no. 3 (August 1963):371–94. Ronald C. Newton, "On 'Functional Groups,' 'Fragmentation,' and 'Pluralism' in Spanish American Political Society," *Hispanic American Historical Review*, 50, no. 1 (February 1970):1–29, reaches a qualified conclusion in general support of the continuity theme. Newton's portrayal of U.S. pluralism in drawing contrasts with Latin America should be read critically. See also in this literature, Glen Dealy, "Prolegomena on the Spanish American Political Tradition," *Hispanic American Historical Review*, 48, no. 1 (February 1968):37–58, which questions the impact of liberalism on the Latin American nation-states in the early republican period. Donald E. Worcester, "The Spanish American Past—Enemy of Change," *Journal of Inter-American Studies*, 11, no. 1 (January 1969):66–75, carries the cultural determinism interpretation to its logical and perhaps least acceptable extreme.

6. Wiarda, "Toward a Framework," p. 225.

7. Schmitter, "Paths to Political Development," pp. 91–92, and "Still the Century of Corporatism?", pp. 102–07. See also Nathaniel H. Leff, *Economic Policy-Making and Development in Brazil, 1947–1964* (New York: John Wiley, 1968), pp. 109–31; and Roland H. Ebel, "Governing the City-State: Notes on the Politics of the Small Latin American Countries," *Journal of Inter-American Studies*, 14, no. 3 (August 1972):325–46.

8. In the Colombian context, see Alcibiades Riano R., *Actualidad del corporativismo: ensayo político-económico* (Bogota: Editorial y Litografía "CAHUR," 1950), p. 25.

9. Wiarda, "Toward a Framework," pp. 229–35.

10. Schmitter, "Still the Century of Corporatism?", pp. 89–90. A central difficulty in Professor Wiarda's approach is his insistence on merging a fairly precise structural definition of corporatism (derived from Schmitter) with his own elastic Weltanschauung: "The second sense in which we use the term corporatism is broader, encompassing a far longer cultural-historic tradition stretching back to the origins of Iberic-Latin systems and embodying a dominant form of sociopolitical

organization that is similarly hierarchical, elitist, authoritarian, bureaucratic, Catholic, patrimonialist, and corporatist to its core" ("Corporatism and Development in the Iberic-Latin World," p. 6).

11. Schmitter, "Still the Century of Corporatism?", pp. 93—94.

12. Ibid., p. 105.

13. Ebel, "Governing the City-State," pp. 336, 341—42.

14. J. Leon Helguera, "The Problem of Liberalism Versus Conservatism in Colombia: 1849—85," in *Latin American History: Select Problems*, ed. Frederick B. Pike (New York: Harcourt, Brace and World, 1969), pp. 224—59.

15. The ingredients of these preconditions include the transition from National Front government with the election in April 1974 (by a sizable majority) of the Liberal Alfonso Lopez Michelsen, the severe economic crisis of late 1974 and early 1975, and the "coming of age" of a significant stratum of the Colombian population during the seventeen-year "freeze" on partisan conflict. Again, the utility of Schmitter's approach lies in the attempt to specify the conditions associated with the emergence of state corporatism: "As for the abrupt demise of incipient pluralism and its dramatic and forceful replacement by state corporatism, this seems closely associated with the necessity to enforce 'social peace,' not by coopting and incorporating, but by repressing and excluding the autonomous articulation of subordinate class demands in a situation where the bourgeoisie is too weak, internally divided, externally dependent and/or short of resources to respond effectively and legitimately to these demands within the framework of the liberal democratic state" ("Still the Century of Corporatism?", p. 108).

16. In taking this position, I am aware that the significance of ideology is open to question. Harry Bernstein, for example, has argued that "the historians can show that political growth in Latin America was quite *ad hoc*, even pragmatic" ("The Concept of the Nation-State in the Caribbean," in *The Caribbean: Its Political Problems*, ed. A. C. Wilgus (Gainesville: University of Florida Press, 1956), p. 7.

17. Gonzalo Restrepo Jaramillo, *El pensamiento conservador: ensayos políticos* (Medellin: Tipografía Bedout, 1936), p. 211. Translations are my own unless otherwise noted.

18. See César Ferrero C., "Los sindicatos obreros colombianos," *Estudios sindicales y cooperativas*, 4, nos. 15—16 (July/December 1970):32—78, for a brief historical overview, and Miguel Urrutia, *The Development of the Colombian Labor Movement* (New Haven: Yale University Press, 1969), esp. chaps. 10 and 12, for a more detailed discussion. Masonic lodges, for example, were not granted official recognition until 1935, and the Communist labor confederation, CSTC, was still not licensed as of 1969.

19. Gerardo Molina, *Las ideas liberales en Colombia, 1849—1910* (Bogota: Universidad Nacional, 1969).

20. See the essays by Conservative activists of the period: José E. Caro, "Sobre los principios generales de organización que conviene adoptar en la nueva constitución" (1842), and Mariano Ospina Rodríguez, "Los partidos políticos en la Nueva Granada" (n.d.), in *Antología del pensamiento político colombiano*, ed. Jaime Jaramillo U. (Bogota: Banco de la República, 1970), vol. 1, pp. 87—148.

21. William A. Dunning, *A History of Political Theories from Luther to Montesquieu* (New York: Macmillan, 1923), pp. 144—45.

22. Miguel A. Caro, "Los fundamentos constitucionales y politicos del estado" (1885), in *Antología del pensamiento político colombiano*, ed. Jaime Jaramillo U., vol. 1, pp. 182—95.

23. Martz, *Colombia*, pp. 147–62.

24. Eduardo Santa, *Sociología política de Colombia* (Bogota: Ediciones Tercer Mundo, 1964), pp. 40–60, 85–86.

25. Restrepo, *El pensamiento conservador*, p. 11.

26. Charles W. Anderson, *Politics and Economic Change in Latin America* (Princeton: D. Van Nostrand, 1967), pp. 208–11.

27. Alfonso López stressed fiscal and monetary policy as key areas of conflict in the "new politics." See "El liberalismo y la transformación política de 1936," in *Antología del pensamiento político colombiano*, ed. Jaime Jaramillo U., vol. 2, pp. 215–58, esp. pp. 232–33.

28. For more detailed discussions of the *Revolución en marcha*, see Urrutia, *Development of the Colombian Labor Movement*, chap. 8; Dix, *Colombia*, chap. 4; and Albert O. Hirschman, *Journeys Toward Progress: Studies of Economic Policy-Making in Latin America* (New York: Doubleday Anchor, 1965), chap. 2.

29. Martz, *Colombia*, chaps. 3–10; Dix, *Colombia*, chap. 5; and Vernon L. Fluharty, *Dance of the Millions: Military Rule and the Social Revolution in Colombia, 1930–56* (Pittsburgh: University of Pittsburgh Press, 1957), chaps. 4–9.

30. Themes in transformed conservatism may be found in Centro de Estudios Colombianos, *Una política conservadora para Colombia: bases para la nueva plataforma social del partido* (Bogota: Centro de Estudios Colombianos, 1969); and Alvaro Gómez Hurtado, *Diálogos con Alvaro Gómez: política para un país en vía de desarrollo*, comp. Alberto Bermúdez (Bogota: Italgraf, 1973). Of significant comparative interest on this point is Samuel Beer's analysis of the evolution of British Conservatism (*The British Political System* [New York: Random House, 1974], chap. 9).

31. Jorge Ortega T., *Cógido civil: con notas, concordancias, jurisprudencia de la corte suprema y normas legales complementarias*, 6th ed., rev. (Bogota: Editorial TEMIS, 1969), p. 248.

32. From roughly 1830 to 1930, Colombia experienced ten large-scale revolts, some seventy smaller uprisings, and was governed under seven national constitutions (Jesus M. Henao and Gerardo Arrubla, *History of Colombia*, trans. J. Fred Rippy [1938; reprint ed., New York: Greenwood Press, 1969], p. 537).

33. Molina, *Las ideas liberales en Colombia*, p. 159.

34. Vasco A. Muñoz C., *El ministerio de justicia y la vigilancia judicial* (Bogota: Empresa Nacional de Publicaciones, 1957), p. 75.

35. Ibid., pp. 80, 83–110.

36. Corr, *Political Process in Colombia*, pp. 68–81. Interestingly, the Colombian associations lag some thirty to fifty years behind their counterparts in Chile (Constantine C. Menges, "Public Policy and Organized Business in Chile: A Preliminary Analysis," *Journal of International Affairs*, 20, no. 2 [1966]:343–65).

37. Organization of American States—Joint Tax Program, *Fiscal Survey of Colombia: A Report Prepared Under the Direction of the Joint Tax Program* (Baltimore: The Johns Hopkins Press, 1965), p. 231.

38. Contraloría General de la República, División de Control Interno y Análisis Financiero, *Cifras fiscales del gobierno nacional y las entidades descentralizadas nacionales* (Bogota, December 1972), "Introducción."

39. Harry Eckstein, *Pressure Group Politics: The Case of the British Medical Association* (Stanford, Calif.: Stanford University Press, 1960), chap. 1.

40. Dix, *Colombia*, chap. 7; Mauricio Solaun and Fernando Cepeda, "Political and Legal Challenges to Foreign Direct Private Investment in Colombia," *Journal of Inter-American Studies and World Affairs*, 15, no. 1 (February 1973):77–79,

89—93; and Rodrigo Losada Lora, *Los institutos descentralizados de carácter financiero: aspectos del caso colombiano* (Bogota: Fundación para la Educación Superior y el Desarrollo, November 1973), pp. 1—2.

41. Ignacio Betancur, "Qué es la ANDI?", *Revisita Trimestral*, 1, no. 2 (September 1966):6—11; ANDI, *Noticiero*, no. 290 (May 12, 1967), p. 6.

42. George F. Drake, "Elites and Voluntary Associations: A Study of Community Power in Manizales, Colombia" (Madison: University of Wisconsin, Land Tenure Center, Research Paper no. 52, June 1973), pp. 40—45.

43. See the comments of Mario Latorre in Fernando Cepeda U. et al, *Los grupos de presión en Colombia*, p. 42.

44. Centro de Investigación y Acción Social, *Estructuras políticas de Colombia*, Colección Monografías y Documentos, no. 3 (Bogota: CIAS, 1969), pp. 63—64.

45. Dix, *Colombia*, p. 328. Kline, "Interest Groups in the Colombian Congress," pp. 280—82, finds relatively little contact with the economic groups reported by Colombian congressmen. His association of the economic groups with the Independent bloc of the Conservative party (p. 287) is somewhat misleading.

46. The National Federation of Miners, for example, was established in and received juridical person from Antioquia (*El Tiempo* [Bogota], July 10, 1970, p. 10).

47. To cite an example, a minister of agriculture threatened to use decree 2420/1968 as a legal ground to intervene in the agrarian association to ensure that association money was being spent according to the group's statutes. The minister noted the problem was that the associations are not controlled by the Superintendency of Enterprises, the state, or their own members. This means that the government will intervene if association members call for such action. Decree 2420 gave the Ministry of Agriculture the power to grant juridical person and inspect the associations. If necessary, the ministry can thus visit, inspect, and impose sanctions, which may include retraction of juridical person or criminal prosecution (*El Tiempo* [Bogota], January 22, 1970, pp. 1, 26).

48. Antonio Abello R., *Cámaras de comercio* (dissertation, Universidad Javeriana, Bogota, 1961), pp. 27—28.

49. See Asociación Colombiana Popular de Industriales, Presidencia Nacional, "Qué es ACOPI?" (Bogota: mimeo., 1970); Federación Nacional de Comerciantes, *Estatutos y resoluciones reglamentarias* (Bogota: ANTARES, Ltda., n.d.), pp. 27—30; Sociedad de Agricultores de Colombia, *Estatutos de la Sociedad de Agricultores de Colombia, SAC* (Bogota, 1970), pp. 4, 10—11, 15; and Koffman, "National Federation of Coffee-Growers," pp. 92—96.

50. See, for example, Asociacion Nacional de Industriales (ANDI), *Informe del presidente* (place varies with city of conference), 1954, pp. 14—15; 1957, p. 5; 1958, p. 11; and 1966; ANDI, *Noticiero*, no. 352 (May 1, 1968), pp. 2—4; FENALCO, *Estatutos*, pp. 10—12; and *Boletin FENALCO*, no. 2352 (February 26, 1963).

51. Alberto Ruiz N., "El control de los establecimientos públicos," *Economia Colombiana*, 13 (1955):253—54. These criteria were reiterated and strengthened by the 1968 administrative reforms. For a useful brief discussion, see Jaime Castro, "Los organismos descentralizados," *Revista Cámara de Comercio de Bogota*, 2, no. 7 (June 1972):89—123. Significant recent research is reported in Fernando Guillén Martínez, *La nueva forma del estado* (Bogota: Universidad Nacional de Colombia, 1974).

52. A similar point is developed by Ebel, "Governing the City-State."

53. U.S. Senate, Committee on Government Operations, *Federal Advisory Com-*

mittees: First Annual Report of the President to the Congress, Including Data on Individual Committees (Washington, D.C.: U.S. Government Printing Office, May 1973), pp. 10, 12.

54. Roderick Groves, "The Colombian National Front and Administrative Reform," *Administration and Society*, 6, no. 3 (November 1974):324, suggests that there was some "slippage" of central control over the agencies following the Carlos Lleras administration. I have attempted to elaborate this point and assess the recent performance of the Lopez Michelsen administration in "Policy-making in Colombian Decentralized Agencies: Presidential Control Versus Agency Autonomy" (Paper delivered at the annual meeting of the American Political Science Association, San Francisco, September 1–4, 1975).

55. In regard to financial and development agencies, Rodrigo Losada suggests that the main factors in the recruitment of junta members is the representation of groups affected by the agencies' programs. The directors of the agencies are generally drawn from those with successful careers in the private sector. Party affiliation is not significant at this level (*Los institutos descentralizados de carácter financiero*, pp. 22–23).

56. Dix, *Colombia*, p. 328. The survey by the Fundación Tercer Mundo para el Desarrollo Humano (see n. 44) found that 56.4 percent of former ministers and high officials, 41.9 percent of congressmen, and 42.9 percent of high-level bureaucrats had held a position in an association.

57. Data on Medellin and Barranquilla SENA directorates were provided by regional directors for the years 1960–1970.

58. See *El Tiempo* (Bogota), August 9, 1970, p. 10. This situation was complicated recently by charges of corruption brought against the comptroller and several officials of the agency (*El Espectador* [Bogota], December 31, 1974, pp. 1, 8A).

59. John J Bailey, "Public Budgeting in Colombia: Disjoined Incrementalism in a Dependent Polity," *LADAC Occasional Papers*, ser. 2, no. 10 (Austin: University of Texas, 1974).

60. Gayle P. W. Jackson, "Making Policy in a Latin American Bureaucracy: The Cauca Valley Corporation of Colombia" (Ph.D. dissertation, Washington University, 1972), pp. 248–51 and passim, describes the interplay of interest groups and government agencies at the national and departmental level in regard to agrarian reform.

61. Alice S. Keller, "The Military as a Pressure Group Under the National Front" (M.A. thesis, Georgetown University, 1973), pp. 133–35, 138–42.

62. *El Tiempo* (Bogota), August 22, 1970, pp. 1, 15.

63. Rothenberg, "Centralization Patterns and Policy Outcomes in Colombia," p. 196.

64. James Payne, *Patterns of Conflict in Colombia* (New Haven: Yale University Press, 1968), chap. 1 and passim.

65. On this point, see Herbert Kaufman, "Administrative Decentralization and Political Power," *Public Administration Review*, 29 (January/February 1969):3–15; and Theodore Lowi, *The End of Liberalism: Ideology, Policy, and the Crisis of Public Authority* (New York: W. W. Norton, 1969).

KENNETH S. MERICLE

10

Corporatist Control
of the Working Class:
Authoritarian Brazil Since 1964

Since the military coup of April 1964, Brazilian governments have been
remarkably successful in pursuing two objectives: the demobilization of
peasant and working-class political movements, and the minimization of
overt class conflict. This study focuses on the system of corporatist labor controls which was used in 1964 and 1965 to dismantle
the urban working-class movement and has subsequently been used to
regulate and control labor protest.[1]

In this study the term "corporatism" is used to describe a system of
interest-group representation in which the state plays a major role in
structuring, supporting, and regulating interest groups with the object
of controlling their internal affairs and the relations among them. A
basic premise of the study is that state intervention and control are not
applied uniformly to all interest groups. Corporatist controls are aimed
primarily at lower-class organizations, and the extent of the state
control apparatus depends on the inherent organizational and disruptive
capacity of the lower-class group. Labor organizations score high on
both criteria. The organizational capacity of labor is high because large
numbers of individuals with common interests and grievances are in
daily contact with one another. Likewise, the potential disruptive
capacity of labor is enormous. Workers have the power to halt production and to impede the process of capital accumulation. Of all lower-
class groups, labor organizations are the easiest to organize and potentially the most powerful. For these reasons, the urban working class has
been the principal object of state corporatist control.

All governments regulate class conflict. The distinguishing features of
state conflict-regulation activities under corporatism are the extent and
nature of the role of the state. With respect to labor organizations, the
state specifies organizational structure, requires registration, accords

303

recognition, extends financial support, channels internal activities, controls leadership activities, intervenes directly in labor-employer conflict, etc. Most of this study consists of an analysis of the major features of Brazilian corporatist labor controls and the impact of these controls on class conflict since 1964.

The ability of the state to control labor protest depends primarily on two variables: the extent to which the corporatist control system has been imposed on labor organizations, and the will and capacity of the state to utilize the control apparatus. The main thesis of this study is that the low levels of class conflict which have characterized Brazil since 1964 can largely be attributed to a very complete and sophisticated system of corporatist labor controls. When employed by authoritarian governments, this control system has an amazing capacity to prevent the effective articulation of working-class demands and to suppress open conflict behavior.

The empirical data presented in the work that follows are based on a group of interviews with labor leaders from the Greater São Paulo metropolitan area which were conducted from May to July 1972.[2] During that period I visited thirty-five of the most influential *sindicatos* (union locals) in the region. These *sindicatos* account for only 2 percent of the Brazilian total, but collectively they represent 1,200,000 workers, or about one-sixth of the total number of wage and salaried workers in Brazil.[3] A group of the largest and strongest *sindicatos* in Brazil was deliberately chosen because these *sindicatos* were most influential in the pre-1964 working-class mobilization and were most likely to retain some degree of independence within the corporatist control system. In addition to the interviews, I have drawn heavily on secondary sources and Brazilian labor law.

Historical Background

Brazil's corporatist labor institutions were established under the Estado Nôvo dictatorship of Getúlio Vargas during the 1930s and early 1940s and were modeled on the labor system of fascist Italy.[4] This basic corporatist system was intact when the military seized power and has been subject to only minor modifications since 1964. Since the end of the Estado Nôvo in 1945, authoritarian and competitive governments have differed greatly in their use of the corporatist structure and control system. During the period of open political competition (1945–1964), many of the control measures of the system suffered from disuse. The government of João Goulart is particularly interesting because of its professed interest in radical reforms, its attempt to extend corporatist representation to rural workers, and its use of the corporatist labor structure to mobilize support for its reform program.

Goulart's ascendance to power and populist reforms had provoked serious divisions within the traditional ruling elites even before the mobilization of urban and rural workers began in earnest.[5] The mobilization had two major effects: First, it seriously frightened the middle and upper classes, greatly narrowing Goulart's base of support within these groups. Second, mobilization caused a rapid polarization among supporters and opponents of the regime. The alienation of middle- and upper-class support meant that Goulart was increasingly dependent on the mobilization of workers to carry out his reform program. As a result of Goulart's isolation and growing dependence on the working class, labor leaders were able to develop independent power vis-à-vis his administration even within the confines of the corporatist labor system. In fact, the control aspects of the system eroded very rapidly as militants and radicals displaced co-opted leaders in the official labor structure and created a parallel system of labor organizations outside the official structure, which they used to coordinate and lead strike movements.[6]

Goulart's ability to force his reform program on a hostile Congress depended on accelerating the mobilization, but each move in that direction helped solidify his opposition, particularly within the army. During 1963, Goulart vacillated between attempting to reassert control over the movement and encouraging further mobilization and militancy. In early 1964, he seemed finally to have opted for the mobilization strategy and militant pursuit of the reform program. The coup occurred before any serious threat to upper-class interests could develop.

Massive direct repression and a reactivation of all the control measures of the corporatist labor system played major roles in the original demobilization of the working class. Hundreds of militant and radical labor leaders were removed from office;[7] many others were incarcerated, tortured, and assassinated. Brazilian democracy was also a victim of the coup. In 1964 and 1965, the military regime eliminated most of its prominent political opposition by canceling mandates and political rights and abolishing all political parties. In 1968, another round of mass repression occurred as open defiance of the military government reached a peak. Working-class opposition took the form of two strike movements in Minas Gerais and São Paulo. In both cases the strikes were contained by a show of force before they could spread.[8] The student movement also reappeared and was repressed. Even congressmen succeeded in provoking the military regime enough to cause it to close Congress. These minor opposition movements can in no way be considered a serious threat to the regime. Nevertheless, hundreds of people lost their political rights as hard-liners within the military consolidated their power and pushed through new repressive measures.

The actions of the regime in 1968 clearly demonstrated that open, ideological opposition would no longer be tolerated. Since the minor upheavals of 1968, repression has been more selective and less frequent.

Working-class protest has been minimal in spite of the fact that the economy has been growing very rapidly since 1968 and few if any of the benefits of this growth have filtered down to the unskilled and semiskilled workers who make up the bulk of the urban labor force. One indication of the failure of the lower strata of Brazilian workers to participate in the economic boom is provided by changes in the official minimum wage. In 1970, about one-quarter of all wage and salaried workers in the Brazilian urban labor force earned wages which were less than or equal to the minimum. Another 16 percent earned between 1.0 and 1.3 multiples of the minimum wage.[9] The government's minimum-wage policy has a critical impact on the wages of all of these workers. Between 1964 and 1966, reduction of the real minimum wage was an important component of the stabilization program. In the eight-year period from March 1966 to April 1974 (during which real per capita GNP increased substantially), the real value of the minimum wage averaged only 68.2 percent of its average real value in the period from July 1954 to December 1962.[10]

The data on income distribution provide another clear indication of who is and who is not benefiting from Brazilian economic growth. A dramatic concentration of income occurred between 1960 and 1970. The top 5 percent of income earners increased their share of total income from 27.4 to 36.3 percent, while the share of the lower 80 percent fell from 45.5 to 36.8 percent.[11] Many urban workers are not participating at all in the economic boom; some have suffered absolute declines in real wages; and nearly all have seen their position in the income structure deteriorate relative to a privileged upper class. Under these circumstances, one might anticipate very high levels of violent class conflict. In the following section, the role of the corporatist labor control system in preventing open class conflict is explored.

The Corporatist Labor Control System

Structure

The current corporatist labor structure was specified in the labor law of 1939. At that time existing unions were forced to disband and reorganize in conformance with jurisdictions specified in the labor law. Thus, the existing structure is the artificial creation of the state: There is nothing organic or spontaneous about its evolution. Certain characteristics of this artificial structure have very important implications for the control of working-class protest.

The labor structure consists of three tiers at the local, state, and national level. At the bottom are the *sindicatos*, local unions which represent workers in small geographical areas, usually one *município* or unit of local government. The *sindicatos* are linked at the state level in federations which in turn are linked at the national level in seven nonagricultural confederations. No peak association similar to the Confederación General del Trabajo (CGT) in Argentina or the former Confederación Unica de Trabajadores (CUT) in Chile brings the confederations together.

The master plan (*enquadramento*) used to create the labor structure was based on three important principles:

1. *Exclusive representation.* Only one labor organization is officially recognized for each government-specified jurisdiction.

2. *Organization by craft and industry. Sindicato* jurisdictions cover all workers in "identical, similar, or connected trades."[12] Both craft and industrial organization are permitted, with the latter by far the more common.

3. *Geographical fragmentation.* Each *sindicato* is autonomous and independent within its geographical base. It has no formal direct horizontal links with *sindicatos* representing workers in other industries (or crafts) in the same area, and no direct links with *sindicatos* representing workers in the same industry in other areas. Within the formal structure, all linkage occurs vertically through the federations.[13]

Exclusive representation has meant that day-to-day competition between rival unions does not exist in Brazil. Once a *sindicato* has received government recognition, it becomes the official spokesman for all workers in the government-specified jurisdiction. Competition among rival political groups is effectively limited to leadership elections of recognized bodies. This means that radicals and militants cannot openly build independent bases in competing nonofficial organizations. They are forced either to attempt to gain control of the official bodies and do what they can within the official structure, or to operate underground and build informal groups capable of acting independently of the official bodies. Since the risks of the latter strategy are enormous, most opt for working within the official structure.

The three-tiered nature of the official corporatist system, when combined with the small jurisdictions of most *sindicatos*, results in a structure which lacks the capacity to produce a united labor response to unfavorable government policy. Even though industrial unionism is far more common than craft unionism in Brazil, much of the potential strength that this form represents is dissipated in excessive fractionalization because of narrow industrial definitions and restrictive geographical jurisdictions. For example, workers in the food industry in the *município* of São Paulo are represented by seven different *sindicatos* based on industrial subdivisions. There are three *sindicatos* in glass, three in clothing and shoes, and two in paper. But fragmentation owing to industrial grouping is far less serious than the geographical limitation.

According to the law, the geographic base of a *sindicato* can be part of a *município*, a single *município*, several *municípios*, a state, several states, and under exceptional circumstances the entire nation. In practice, most *sindicatos* are limited to a single *município* or a small group of *municípios*.[14] This means that most *sindicatos* represent workers in an industry (sometimes very narrowly defined) within a very small geographic area. In exceptional cases this structure can produce *sindicatos* which represent a substantial number of workers. In a *município* like São Paulo, the most populous and highly industrialized in the country, the jurisdictions of certain *sindicatos* are very large. The metalworkers' *sindicato*, which represents a very broad industrial base, has about 216,000 workers in its jurisdiction. The São Paulo commercial workers' *sindicato* represents 120,000 workers, the textile *sindicato* 78,000, and the chemical workers' *sindicato* 36,000.[15] But these *sindicatos* are clearly exceptions in a structure in which the norm is a small and weak organization representing about 5,700 workers of whom perhaps 1,000 are dues-paying members.[16]

Most national unions in North America or Western Europe would be very satisfied if each of their locals had a thousand members. The size of Brazilian *sindicatos* is a liability only because it is very difficult to use the official corporatist structure to coordinate militant activity by a group of *sindicatos*. In theory, the federations are supposed to perform this coordination function. The federations are composed of all *sindicatos* in a particular branch of industry, commerce, or the services in a given state.[17] Under authoritarian governments, the federations are very easily controlled and hence are rarely involved in the coordination of any militant activity.

The key to government control of the federations is a highly nonrepresentative election procedure for federation leaders. Each member *sindicato* has one vote, regardless of its size. This means that in the São Paulo Metalworkers' Federation, the São Paulo *sindicato*, which represents 216,000 workers, has the same voting power as the Guarulhos *sindicato*, which represents 18,000. Since the federations control considerable financial resources which they can use to provide technical and financial aid to member *sindicatos* (especially small ones in the interior cities), they have considerable power over how the *sindicatos* cast their votes in federation elections.[18] As a result, incumbent federation leadership of any sort is very difficult to displace.

When a hostile government replaces federation leadership with its own appointees, as happened in 1964, these appointees can use their influence over the small *sindicatos* to remain in office and perpetuate a progovernment line at the federation level.

This same election procedure exists at the confederation level. As a result, federation and confederation leadership tends to reflect the political persuasion of the regime in power. Under these circumstances, the possibility of federations or confederations leading coordinated militant activities in defiance of an authoritarian government is extremely remote. Since 1964 the role of the federations and confederations has consisted mainly of providing legal and other technical assistance to their members. In the *sindicatos*, where elections are fairly frequent and based on a one man–one vote principle, it is much easier for militants to regain leadership positions after government purges. However, the actions of militant leaders are constrained by the fact that they are forced either to act in isolation or to establish informal and illegal coordinating bodies outside the official system. In both situations, they are highly susceptible to government repression.

Thus, under an authoritarian government, the only labor organizations from which a protest response is likely are the *sindicatos*; however, the corporatist labor structure insures that the probability of effective united action by the *sindicatos* is minimal.

Leadership Controls

Intervention or threat of intervention is the government's most potent weapon in dealing with labor leaders. Intervention involves state seizure of union headquarters and union funds and the replacement of elected union officials with government appointees.[19] The mass intervention that followed the coup in 1964 was much more widespread than it had ever previously been. In a very short period, virtually all the radical and militant union leadership was replaced by passive progovernment appointees. Since this original wave, intervention has been used much more selectively to intimidate militants who have filtered back into leadership positions.

An event occurred while I was interviewing São Paulo labor leaders in early 1972 which illustrates the effectiveness of selective intervention as an intimidation device. The bank workers' *sindicato* in Rio de Janeiro had been especially outspoken in its criticism of the government's wage policy. Around the middle of April 1972, the *sindicato* was invaded by police carrying machine guns who arrested the four principal leaders. Later the *sindicato* was placed under intervention, and the entire leadership was removed from office.

A few days previous to these events a meeting had been scheduled in

São Paulo to assemble leaders from the major *sindicatos*. The purpose of the meeting seemed innocuous enough—its organizers wanted to make a public statement on the minimum-wage policy of the government. They intended to send a report to President Garrastazu Medici recommending that the real minimum wage be raised substantially on May 1, the normal date for annual adjustments. Between the scheduling of the meeting and its occurrence, the government intervened in the Rio bank workers' *sindicato*. The meeting collapsed, and only two labor leaders dared show up; fear of a general government offensive kept the others away. Prior to the intervention, most *sindicato* leaders would have attended the meeting with few misgivings; after it occurred, the new limits on behavior had to be slowly and carefully explored.

This incident clearly demonstrates how selective intervention intimidates and immobilizes union leadership. In periods of low working-class mobilization, intervention is effective precisely because it does not have to be used frequently. By intervening selectively, the government creates a high degree of uncertainty concerning the type of behavior it will tolerate; this uncertainty leads to self-censorship, perhaps the most efficient form of control.

Short of intervention, the government can apply other sanctions to union officeholders. Article 553 of the labor law, in addition to intervention, provides for fines ranging from one-fifth of the minimum salary to ten minimum salaries, plus temporary suspension from office.[20]

After an intervention, the government can use restrictive election eligibility requirements to prevent a return of the ex-leaders and to screen new candidates. Article 530 of the labor law reads as follows:

No one can be elected to administrative positions or positions of economic or professional representation, nor continue to exercise these duties:

1. who has not had his accounts approved while in administrative office.

2. who had injured the well being of any sindical entity.

3. who was neither a union officer nor a worker in the activity or profession within the territorial base represented by the union.

4. who had been convicted of fraud, during the period of punishment.

5. who had lost his political rights.

6. who, publicly and ostensively, through acts or words, defends the ideological principles of political parties whose registration has been canceled or of an association or entity of any type whose activities had been considered contrary to the national interest and whose registration had been canceled or whose functions had been suspended by competent authorities.

7. who was guilty of proven bad conduct.

8. who had been removed from administrative office or sindical representation.[21]

Items 2, 5, 6, and 8 can be used to prevent purged leaders and their sympathizers from gaining control of unions. Furthermore, the language of this article is sufficiently vague and comprehensive that almost any union leader out of favor with the ministry can be prevented from standing for election.

The repressive measures outlined above are complemented by a carefully controlled system of co-optation which is designed to reward "cooperative" labor leaders selectively. The co-optation system has two major features: (1) systematic restriction of channels of upward mobility within the labor structure, and (2) a lucrative system of upward mobility outside the labor structure, access to which is strictly controlled by the government.

The potential for upward mobility within the labor structure is strictly limited because of the small number of full-time paid positions available and strict limitations on the salaries for these positions. According to law, a union officer can receive a salary only if his position forces him to be absent from his regular job, and the union salary cannot exceed that which he received on the job. In practice, the former salary can be supplemented by food and transportation allowances and other emoluments such as use of the union car, but even with these extras, holding union office is not a lucrative business. [22] Still, most workers would find the prestige and working conditions of a full-time, paid union position preferable to their regular jobs. However, the possibility of using paid positions to recruit a cadre of loyal union militants is also restricted by the labor law, which limits the number of paid officers to seven, irrespective of the size of the union. [23] The law is clearly designed to prevent union leaders from using union revenues to create an independent power base within the union or to promote their own social and economic mobility.

In eliminating the labor structure as a channel of advance, the government has provided a series of substitute paths, which are very useful in enticing union officers to cooperate with government policy. The most important of these is the position of labor judge (*vogal*) in the lower-level labor courts. The labor court system consists of three levels: first-level conciliation courts (*juntas de conciliação e julgamento*) where individual grievances are resolved, the regional labor courts (*tribunais regionais do trabalho*) where wages are set and individual grievances are appealed, and the supreme labor court, a court of appeal for the regional labor courts. Labor is represented in the tripartite courts at all levels of the structure, but the positions in the lower-level courts are by far the most important because of their numbers. Every major population center has at least one *junta*, and each requires a labor judge and a substitute. In the *município* of São Paulo, thirty-two labor judges (and thirty-two substitutes) are chosen from eighty *sindicatos*. Each *sindicato* can nominate three people for any opening, but the final decision is made by the president of the Regional Labor Court that acts as the court of appeals for the *junta* in which the opening exists. This means that a government-appointed court official has nearly total discretion over who is appointed to the judgeship.

The labor court positions are very highly prized because of the minimal attention they require and the high salaries they command. Since the court positions are half-time—the judge must be in the labor court weekday afternoons—a full-time union position can be held simultaneously. In May 1972, the salary for labor judges in the São Paulo courts was 3600 NCr. per month, or almost thirteen times the then prevailing minimum wage. This salary level permits a life-style which would never be possible on a worker's wage or union officer's salary.

My experience in observing labor judges in several of São Paulo's labor courts is that they are usually very passive and play a minor role in court proceedings.[24] They seldom argue the cases of the parties or challenge the legalism of the government-appointed judge with equity arguments. In a large majority of cases, both the labor judge and the employers' judge vote to support the decision of the career judge. That labor judges do not take the role of militant articulator of class interests is not surprising. Since the government effectively controls access to the posts, passive individuals who support the government labor policy are most likely to be selected. Once they are in office, their high salaries contribute to the resocialization of any militants who filter through the selection process. Another factor which discourages militant behavior by labor judges relates to their lack of power. The government judge really has all of the power in the court; his decisions can be overturned only if both the workers' judge and the employers' judge vote against him. The likelihood of this happening is very low.[25] Since the government judge's criteria for making judgments must be legalistic, this sets the tone of the court. The labor judges tacitly accept this fact, and consequently their lack of legal training becomes a liability. Instead of being class spokesmen, they accept the role of neutral arbiter of justice—a role for which they are not particularly qualified.

In an interview in May 1972, the president of a large São Paulo *sindicato* who is also a labor judge was vehement in his criticism of the class judgeships. He charged that 90 percent of the labor judges care nothing about their constituents and are interested in the position only because of the money it provides. He recommended that the positions either be eliminated or be filled through direct elections by the workers in the court jurisdiction.[26]

Philippe Schmitter lists a number of public bodies which serve the same co-optive function as the labor court positions:

> In the Ministry of Labor, Industry, and Commerce [now the Ministry of Labor and Public Welfare], a vast number of permanent commissions, such as those governing *enquadramento*, the *impôsto sindical* [union tax], the *salário mínimo* [minimum salary] and social welfare, as well as ad hoc working groups, were established usually with equal representation of workers and employers. The Labor Court System, as we have seen, was organized on a similar principle, as were the Special Maritime Labor Delegations. The autarchic Retirement and Social Welfare Institutes for various categories of workers (IAPI, IAPM, IAPB, etc.) presently are governed by such tripartite councils [IAPI, IAPM, etc. have been combined into a single administrative agency, but the tripartite structure has been retained].[27]

He concludes that these tripartite bodies provide attractive and prestigious posts for interest-group leaders and that "the attraction for workers' leaders has been particularly strong, given their lower-status origins and the formal prohibition against direct remuneration for their syndical jobs [in excess of their salary as a worker]."[28]

Three facets of the Brazilian labor system are salient in the process of co-opting labor leaders: The law guarantees that leadership positions will be filled by workers, a group susceptible to the appeals of social mobility. It also severely restricts the possibility of mobility within the union by controlling salaries. A number of alternative routes of mobility are then provided, and access is closely controlled by the government.

In addition to the repressive and co-optive leadership controls, the government has recently taken an active interest in the training and socialization of labor leaders. Beginning in July 1972, the regional office of the Ministry of Labor in São Paulo initiated a full training program including practical courses in union bookkeeping, labor law, social welfare, the labor courts, and job indemnity rights. The program also includes a course with the title "Moral and Civil Education and the National Reality." Similar programs have been established in several other states, and the best graduates from the regional courses will be sent to Brasília for further training.[29]

Organizational Controls

Government controls aimed at labor organizations are based on the same system of repression and co-optation as the leadership control system. The most important form of organizational control results from the fact that the government is responsible for a major portion of the revenue of labor organizations, and access to this financing depends on using it in prescribed activities. The government guarantees a financially stable labor structure and in so doing channels union activity into nonmilitant endeavors.

The three levels of the labor structure are financed from two major sources: a government trade-union tax (*contribuição sindical*) and union membership dues. The trade-union tax is the primary source of government-guaranteed financing. It is collected from *all* workers in the local union's jurisdiction *whether they are union members or not* and is equal to the remuneration the workers received for one day of work during the month of March. The tax is divided as follows: 5 percent to the confederation, 15 percent to the federation, 6 percent to the Bank of Brazil for handling charges, 54 percent to the *sindicato*, and 20 percent to the Ministry of Labor.[30]

In addition to the tax, a worker must pay monthly dues to qualify as a union member. Although the dues are generally set at low levels, many workers are reluctant to pay both dues and the compulsory tax. However, incentive to pay is provided by the fact that most union benefits are tied to dues payment. In other words, union programs are financed by all workers through the tax, but most benefit programs require union membership (dues payment) as a prerequisite for participation.

A third source of finances which has emerged in the last few years is a special discount taken from the worker's paycheck during the first month of the annual wage increase. As with the tax, the unions are dependent on the government to gain the discount, and the discount is taken from all workers, not just union members. The discount is included as a clause in the labor court decisions. Because of its relative newness, not all unions have the discount, but among major unions in urban areas, it is very common. Of the unions studied in Greater São Paulo, twenty-seven of thirty-five had discounts in their 1971 court decisions or agreements. Unlike the tax, the discounts depend on the good will of the courts. The unions must justify the discount each year in their annual court appearance. Since the discount is an important revenue source for unions which have it, the ability of the court to grant or deny the discount is potentially a very powerful control device.

One other source of income which is important for some unions is money generated from building rents, service fees, investments, and other sources derived from union assets and internal activities. For most unions this money is of minor importance in total revenues.

The relative importance of the four main revenue sources for the *sindicatos* which I visited in Greater São Paulo is shown in table 1. These *sindicatos* were deliberately chosen from among the largest and most powerful in the country. In general, they represent some of the highest-paid workers in Brazil. They should be among the *sindicatos* most able to develop financial independence from the government. However, government-guaranteed finances, in the form of the tax and discount, account for 59 percent of the income even of this select group of *sindicatos*. It is important to note that it is very difficult to reduce this dependence by raising union dues. Higher dues discourage new members from joining the *sindicato*, and proposals to raise dues are also likely to meet resistance from the existing membership. In addition, the legal administrative procedure for raising dues is very complicated, and the increase must be approved by the regional office of the Ministry of Labor.

For a more representative national sample of *sindicatos*, the trade-union tax is by far the most important source of revenue for labor organizations. Schmitter presents data from a Brazilian government study which indicates that in 1965 the tax alone accounted for 99.2 percent of the income of labor confederations, 92.5 percent for the federations, and 70.0 percent of the *sindicatos'* income.[31] Since the discount did not exist in 1965, these data may overstate the current importance of the tax. However, since both the discount and tax depend on the government, this distinction is of little importance.

Guaranteed financing provides the government with a major lever for channeling union activities into nonmilitant endeavors. Article 592 of the labor law specifies the following approved uses of the union tax: job placement agencies; maternity assistance; medical, dental, and hospitalization assistance; legal assistance; professional and vocational training schools; credit and consumer cooperatives; vacation facilities; libraries; social and sporting activities; funeral aid; and expenses incurred in the administration of the above activities. In practice, legal, medical, and dental assistance are the most frequently provided servi-

Table 1. Sources of Revenue Among the Principal *Sindicatos* in Greater São Paulo, 1971

Sector	Number of *Sindicatos*	Percentage of revenue from:			
		Tax	Discount	Dues	Other
All *sindicatos*	33	38.4	20.6	33.7	7.3
Industrial	24	34.7	26.9	32.6	5.8
Nonindustrial	9	46.5	7.0	36.2	10.4

Source: Interviews conducted in May–July 1972.
Note: Two of the *sindicatos* interviewed would not provide these data. The nonindustrial category includes *sindicatos* in commerce, communications, transportation, and banking. The percentages are calculated from aggregate data.

ces.[32] The tax revenues cannot be used for strike benefits or in other militant activities.[33] Revenues derived from the union discount are also linked to specific activities, usually the construction of buildings or the expansion of social-service activities. *Sindicatos* must keep a very detailed record and file annual reports which demonstrate that the tax and discount have been used only to finance approved activities.

In Brazil the distinction is often drawn between union assistance and social assistance; both can be legally financed from the tax. Union assistance includes traditional union activities—legal assistance in the labor courts, placement agencies, cooperatives, and union education—and is associated with the trade unionism of Western Europe and North America. Social assistance includes the social welfare activities which Brazilian *sindicatos* provide. It is clear from the data presented in table 2 that the traditional union activities play a distinctly secondary role in Brazilian unionism. On the average, the unions in the sample spend about 2.4 times as much money on social assistance as on union assistance.

Presumably, the *sindicatos* are free to spend their nongovernment revenue as they please; however, for many *sindicatos* the influence of the tax in channeling activities extends far beyond its actual value. Over one-half of the *sindicatos* that provided me with financial data spent more money on the legally specified tax activities in 1971 than the tax revenues produced. This means that many *sindicatos* are using their dues and other revenues over which they presumably have complete control to support the government-specified activities. Thus, government financing determines that the main role of the *sindicatos* lies in the distribution of social-welfare services.[34]

The extent of the social-welfare program depends mostly on the size

Table 2. Expenditures by the Principal *Sindicatos* in Greater São Paulo, 1971

Sector	Number of *Sindicatos*	Percentage of expenditures for:	
		Union Assistance	Social Assistance
All *sindicatos*	27	29.1	70.9
Industrial	18	23.2	76.8
Nonindustrial	9	36.6	63.4

Source: Interviews conducted in May–July 1972.
Note: In eight of the *sindicatos*, the respondent would not or could not provide these data. "Nonindustrial" includes *sindicatos* in commerce, communications, transport, and banking. Percentages are calculated from aggregate data.

of the *sindicato*. The São Paulo metalworkers' *sindicato*, which represents about 216,000 workers, provides members with legal, medical, dental, hospital, placement, and maternity services as well as maintaining a pharmacy, a consumer's co-op, a vacation resort, and general and union education programs. Lawyers, doctors, dentists, nurses, pharmacists, and teachers all work in the union's headquarters. A special social-service building was under construction in 1972. On the other hand, the union which represents about 7,000 workers who produce toys and musical instruments provides only legal, medical, and dental services.

No union can ignore social assistance activities even in cases where the leadership is opposed, in principle, to this role. For many workers the union is the only practical source of these services. Private medical and dental care is far beyond the means of most workers, and the government medical service is notorious for its inadequacies.

The normal sanction for *sindicatos* that stray too far from the government-specified social-welfare role involves the removal of elected leaders through intervention. However, if this measure proves inadequate, the government has an even more powerful weapon: it can cancel the official registration of the disruptive labor organization, rendering it a legal nonentity. Official recognition is a prerequisite for use of the labor courts, dealings with government administrative bodies, negotiation of collective contracts, general representation of the workers, and access to government-guaranteed financing.[35] Given the legal monopoly that recognized labor organizations have on these activities, and the generally hostile attitude of authoritarian governments to nonofficial labor organizations, it is virtually impossible for a labor organization to remain outside the official recognition system. Loss of recognition means organizational demise.

There is an important constraint on canceling *sindicato* recognition. The large social-welfare programs of the *sindicatos* could not be eliminated without creating considerable hardship and discontent. Usually, replacement of the leadership with government officials is sufficient to defuse a maverick *sindicato*. In such cases social-welfare programs can be maintained as if nothing happened. Cancellation of recognition is only used under rare circumstances to restructure completely labor organizations in a given sector of the economy, as with the agricultural *sindicatos* in 1964, or to eliminate a *sindicato* in which the members have become highly politicized. However, it remains an important threat which is readily available for dealing with serious offenders.

The government also has a series of control mechanisms which limit the freedom of operation of labor organizations. Besides requiring detailed annual financial reports and budget proposals, the government

regulates voting procedures, the definition of quorums, affiliation to
and disaffiliation from federations, and many other activities. In addition, *sindicatos* must keep registration books with the name, age,
marital status, nationality, occupation, place of work, residence, and
worker identification and social security numbers of all members. These
books must be available for inspection by officials of the Ministry of
Labor at any time.

Control of Workers

In the post-1964 period, the government has modified the labor law
in two important ways which have significantly increased the risk of
spontaneous protest behavior by workers. First, the job-security provisions of the labor law have been significantly weakened, making protesting workers much more susceptible to employer retaliation.
Second, new restrictive strike regulations and a demonstrated willingness on the part of the government to enforce them have virtually
eliminated the strike, either planned or spontaneous, as a bargaining
tool or even as an expression of general discontent. These two measures
have greatly constrained both individual and group protest by workers.

Job security. Job security has never been particularly well protected
in Brazil. Rather than being based on the organization of workers at the
shop level and hence guaranteed by their power, job security is derived
from a variety of provisions in the labor law. This means that the
workers are dependent on the labor courts and ultimately on the
political system for this limited protection.

Prior to 1966, the law established two types of security against
layoff: Workers with up to ten years of service with an employer were
entitled to indemnity payments equal to one month's salary per year
of effective service in the event of layoff. Workers with ten or more
years' service were granted "stability" status which meant that they
could not be fired without a prior court appearance in which the
employer had to prove that the worker was guilty of a serious mis-
demeanor which justified the discharge. Any worker with one or more
years of service was also entitled to a thirty-day notice of layoff, or, in
its absence, the salary for the month.

Workers with less than ten years' experience could legally be fired
at any time without a prior court appearance. The employer's liability
in discharge cases was limited to the indemnity payment, the notice
payment, and a series of smaller payments. Even these payments did
not have to be made if the employer could prove that he had just cause
for dismissing the worker.[36] Workers had no right to reinstatement if
the employer failed to prove just cause. Thus, under the pre-1966
system, the only factor constraining an employer's ability to dismiss

permanently workers with less than ten years' seniority was the risk of having to make legal separation payments out of the day-to-day operating budget. For a worker with eight years' experience this cost could amount to eight to ten months' salary. If an employer was determined to get rid of a worker and was willing to pay the cost, this system provided the worker little protection. However, in the case of small and medium-sized firms which operated at low liquidity levels, each individual layoff was an important cost decision. Mass layoffs of experienced workers were difficult for firms of any size.

From the point of view of the worker, this system was far from ideal. In most layoff cases, workers were forced to go to the courts and invest a considerable amount of time and sometimes money to enforce their legal rights. The risk of an unfavorable court decision forced many workers to settle for a small portion of their rights in a compromise voluntary settlement.

In terms of providing effective job security, the pre-1966 law worked much better for the "stable" workers with more than ten years' seniority. If an employer attempted to discharge a stable worker but could not prove his charges in court, the employee was entitled to full back pay *and reinstatement*. In cases where personal animosities between the worker and employer made reinstatement inadvisable, the judge could allow the employer to discharge the worker, but only after the worker had been paid double the normal indemnity payments. [37] This alternative was available only to small employers who had frequent face-to-face contact with their workers; all other stable workers had reinstatement rights. Under the stability system, it was either very costly or impossible to fire a stable worker without proving in court that he had committed a serious offense.

In December 1966, the government issued comprehensive revisions to the job-security law which eliminated the special stability status of workers with ten years' seniority and eliminated the immediate out-of-pocket costs of discharging nonstable workers.

The elimination of stability means that employers can fire a ten-year worker without a special court hearing and without proving that the worker committed a serious offense. The new system draws no distinction between workers based on the length of service. A twenty-year veteran has no more job security than a one-year novice. Under the new system, employers are required to make monthly deposits of 8 percent of the wage in individual accounts in the worker's name. These deposits create a fund which replaces the indemnity obligations of the employer under the previous law. This vesting procedure has removed all major financial constraints on the employer in making layoffs.[38] As soon as the monthly deposits are made, the money is lost to the employer. The cash payments which previously made employers think twice before firing a worker no longer have to be raised at the time the worker is dismissed.

The new law is supposed to be optional—workers are given the choice of remaining under the indemnity-stability law or opting for the new vested procedure. However, for two important reasons nearly all workers opt for the new law. First, employers pressure new workers to choose the new law; it is a widely held belief among workers that they will not be hired unless they opt for the new system. Employers favor the new law because it gives them much greater freedom to adjust the size of their labor force to correspond to business conditions. Second, the law has certain attractive features from the workers' viewpoint. For example, opting workers must be paid in cash for any indemnity rights which they had accumulated while working under the old system. This means that a worker who was employed in a firm for eight years prior to the new law is eligible for a payment of eight months' salary if he opts for the new system. If the worker involved has stability, he collects two months' salary for each year of service. In other words, the worker is offered more money in one lump sum than he has probably had at any time in his life, in exchange for his signature on a piece of paper. Of course, the signature gives the employer the right to fire the worker whenever he chooses. But in spite of the risks involved, the financial incentives are so great that relatively few workers can resist them.[39]

The vesting procedure, which so seriously undermines job security, also has some advantages over the previous nonvested system. Because the funds are vested, workers can voluntarily quit a job without losing the cash rights they have accumulated. Under the former law the worker was entitled to indemnity payments only if fired without just cause. Now the accounts are simply transferred to the new employer, and he begins to make the deposits. Since the deposits are legally required and the worker has property rights over them regardless of the circumstances of his dismissal, he need no longer fear losing his termination payments in an unfair labor court decision or because his former employer could not pay. Highly skilled workers have been able to use this increased mobility and a favorable labor market (for skilled workers) to move to higher-paying jobs. Unskilled and semiskilled workers must compete with the unemployed and underemployed for a limited number of "good" jobs in the modern sector. They are much less likely to quit a job voluntarily.

Irrespective of its other advantages, the new law has been an unmitigated disaster for job security. Any worker who has opted for the new system can be fired at minimal cost to the employer, for any reason, at any time. No union can expect to confront employers at the shop level under these circumstances. Although Brazilian *sindicatos* have never had extensive representation on the shop floor, the union steward systems which did exist were highly dependent on the employment security provisions of the pre-1966 law. Shop stewards were almost always chosen from workers who had attained stability status. These same workers were most likely to act as spokesmen for general grievances in the labor courts. The effective elimination of stability under the new law has greatly reduced the likelihood of direct contact between union stewards and employers. In many cases the existing shop infrastructure of unions has been destroyed; in other cases, shop delegates still exist, but they have no direct contact with the employer and, in fact, keep their union affiliation a secret. Under the new law, no worker can take a personal grievance of an *offensive* nature to the labor courts without fear of employer reprisal, which in most cases involves immediate termination. The result is that the labor courts are used almost entirely to settle grievances of a *defensive* nature arising from disputes over termination rights.[40] Under these circumstances, an increase in the number of labor court cases can most accurately be interpreted as an increase in employer-initiated, involuntary layoffs, rather than an increase in worker or union militancy.

The most important impact of the weakened job-security provisions has been to magnify the risk of any kind of protest behavior, either organized or unorganized. Unskilled and semiskilled workers have neither legal nor market-derived job security. Any behavior which marks them as troublesome, whether it be initiation of a labor court case or something as harmless as a disagreement with a supervisor, could lead to their permanent dismissal. Under these circumstances, it is not surprising that most workers passively accept traditional paternalistic patterns of employment relations.

Strikes. Brazilian governments have always had extensive legal power to regulate strike activity. Article 723 of the labor law specifies that workers cannot strike under any circumstances, legal or not, without the previous authorization of the Regional Labor Court. Penalties for unauthorized strikes include suspension or firing of striking workers, removal of union leadership from office (they can also be barred from running for office for two to five years), fines for the union, and, if necessary, cancellation of the union's registration.[41] If the courts are willing to apply these sanctions, they have tremendous power to determine the situations in which strikes will be tolerated. The key to understanding the effective right to strike in Brazil thus lies in a knowledge of the administrative procedures of the courts.

On paper, the right to strike in Brazil is not very different from the right to strike as it is established in U.S. law and labor contracts. Both

countries bar strikes which are not directly linked to the employment
situation (political and solidarity strikes), both restrict the use of the
strike during the life of the contract, and both permit strikes to
establish new contracts. However, the chasm between legal principle
and practice is enormous in Brazil. Since 1964, labor courts have
authorized strikes in only two situations: (1) to force an employer to
make overdue salary payments and (2) to force an employer to pay a
court-established wage increase that he has been ignoring.[42] Both
situations involve enforcement of a legal wage contract (or court
decision). Even in these situations strikes are rare because of powerful
incentives for the employer to settle the dispute before a strike actually
occurs. If the strike is authorized by the labor court, and if the court
rules in favor of the workers when the dispute is decided, the employer
must pay all wages lost during the strike.[43] As a result most disputes
are settled before the authorized strike deadline.

When strikes are allowed, the behavior of strikers is highly regulated.
Violent acts such as sit-down strikes, sabotage, aggressive picketing, and
the blockage of entry of nonstriking coworkers are, of course, illegal.
The list of prohibited activities also includes "the use of picket signs
which are offensive to the authorities, the employer or others of equal
stature."[44] Insults are also banned, as are efforts "to incite disrespect
for the decision of the Labor Courts which ended a strike or to block
the execution of such a decision."[45] It is also illegal for anyone from
outside the union's jurisdiction to incite workers to strike. Workers
found guilty of any of the above can be fined or criminally prosecuted.

The main role of strikes in the United States—as a pressure device to
extract concessions in a new labor contract—has been completely
eliminated. Although the law appears to allow strikes in disputes over
wages and conditions of employment, the courts never authorize strikes
in this situation. Legally the *sindicato* must notify the regional representative of the Ministry of Labor of its intention to strike five days
before the strike deadline occurs. During this period the government
official has the power to submit the dispute to the labor court for a
decision which is binding on the parties. Strikes are prohibited while
the court is deciding the case. This sequence of events is always
employed to prevent strikes in union campaigns for new labor contracts.

The strike law is typical of other social control measures in the
Brazilian labor law. It defines a very narrow and highly regulated range
of behavior that will be tolerated. It then specifies a severe set of
sanctions which will be applied to violators. Finally, it provides a series
of positive incentives for remaining within the bounds of legitimate
behavior.

Effects of Corporatist Controls on Leadership and Participation

Government intervention, guaranteed financing, and control of union activities create a bureaucratic form of social-welfare unionism which breeds a bureaucratic form of union leadership. José A. Rodrigues describes this type of leader as follows:

> He must know the law and legal procedures for processing the grievances as well as a lawyer. He must know the problems of health and social assistance as well as a social worker. He must look after the functioning of the union, provide and administer resources, and manage budgets and accounts as well as an accountant. As one can see, it is not enough to be a leader of the masses but, at the same time, he must be a good organizer and administrator to be a good union leader. And many times the administrative activities are so complex and absorbing that they obscure or provoke the decay of the qualities of leadership for which he was elected. Thus, a metamorphosis occurs: The worker, leader of the masses, becomes the director of the bureaucratic-union—the designations reflect in this case a change in content.[46]

Regardless of their politics or their basic attitudes about unionism, it is very difficult for union leaders to resist this metamorphosis. The demands of running a social-welfare agency leave little time and energy for more militant activities.

There is considerable evidence that many leaders would prefer a more independent and less bureaucratic form of unionism. As indicated in table 3, 42.9 percent of the leaders interviewed were against the trade-union tax, and almost all of the 54.3 percent who favored the tax did so because they considered it a financial necessity for the survival of the *sindicato* in its current form. In 1963, J. V. Freitas Marcondes found that more than one-half of the union leaders he interviewed in the city of São Paulo favored abolition of the tax.[47]

Another indication of union leaders' dissatisfaction with the nature of Brazilian unionism is provided in table 4. Over one-half of the respondents (57.1 percent) felt that *sindicatos* should not be in the social-welfare business. Among those in favor of these activities, the major reasons cited related to the inadequacies of government services and the prohibitive cost of private services. In other words, they supported welfare activities primarily because union members do not have access to equivalent services elsewhere. Further evidence is provided by the fact that nearly three-quarters of the respondents felt the government should assume responsibility for all social-welfare services.

Many of the union leaders interviewed were highly critical of nearly all government social and labor policy. A large group favored total

Table 3. Responses of Presidents of Principal *Sindicatos* to the Question "Are You For or Against the Union Tax? Why?"

Response	Percentage	
Total for the tax	54.4	
It is a financial necessity		48.6
It obligates worker to take an interest in *sindicato*		2.9
Sindicato services are for all; all should pay		2.9
Total against the tax	42.9	
Destroys *sindicato* liberty and autonomy		25.7
Sindicatos are not responsive to members		8.6
Everybody pays but only members receive benefits		2.9
No reason given		5.7
No response	2.9	

N = 35.
Source: Interviews conducted in May–July 1972.
Note: Data do not add up to 100 percent because of rounding.

restructuring of the labor movement with the object of breaking its dependence on the state. Most of those interviewed favored a great expansion of the effective right to strike. The situations in which union leaders favored using the strike are presented in table 5. One-half of those responding went as far as to advocate using the strike as a pressure tactic to change the labor law, and one-third favored striking

Table 4. Attitudes of Presidents of Principal *Sindicatos* Toward Social-Service Activities

Question	Percentage	
"Should *sindicatos* provide social services? Why?"		
Total responding yes	42.9	
No adequate alternatives for members		25.7
Better quality and faster services in *sindicato*		8.6
Legitimate function—improves members' well-being		5.7
Required by law		2.9
Total responding no	57.2	
Not a proper *sindicato* function		48.6
Government taxes workers and employers for these services		8.6
"Would it be better if the government assumed the responsibility for these social service activities?"		
Yes	74.3	
No	25.7	

N = 35.
Source: Interviews conducted in May–July 1972.
Note: Data do not add up to 100 percent because of rounding.

for general political objectives. Clearly these respondents cannot be considered pawns of the Ministry of Labor.

Besides the "genuine" leadership, there are a substantial number of *pelegos* (self-interested careerists who support the current labor system and thrive on it) in leadership positions in the São Paulo unions.[48] José Rodrigues identifies the lucrative class judgeships of the labor court system as the favorite center of the *pelegos*. He differentiates between inefficient *pelegos* who depend on the union tax as an easy source of income but care little about applying the tax in social-assistance activities, and efficient *pelegos* who take great pride in the social-assistance system and treat it as though it were the only function of the union. [49] Both types were encountered in the interviewing. The *pelegos* are active supporters of the government and its labor system. They treat the union members as clients, with public condescension and private contempt. The attitude of *pelegos* toward the role of unions can best be summarized by a comment one of them made during the interviews. When asked his opinion of the government's wage policy, he responded, "The wage policy is very good. The government grants wage increases automatically. It saves me time—I don't have to fight for the increases."[50] He refused to answer a question on the effect of the wage policy on the workers' purchasing power.

Peleguismo is very common in Brazil, and the reasons for its perpetuation are not difficult to discern. Members relate to the union as they would to any welfare institution—they go there when they have a problem. The instrumentalist attitude of Brazilian workers toward their *sindicatos* has been well documented.[51] The *sindicato* is viewed primarily as a welfare agency because it *is* primarily a welfare agency. The fact that a government bureaucrat can run a welfare agency as well as if not better than a Communist party militant is not lost on the workers.

Table 5. Responses of Presidents of Principal *Sindicatos* to the Question: "In What Situations Should a *Sindicato* Be Able to Strike?"

Situation	Yes	No
To obtain late salary payments	83.3%	16.7%
To gain higher salaries	96.7	3.3
To gain a new collective contract or court decision	83.3	16.7
To change labor laws	50.0	50.0
For general political objectives	33.3	66.7

N = 30.
Source: Interviews conducted in May–July 1972.
Note: Five presidents refused to respond because of the sensitivity of the question.

Consequently, when the government intervenes in a *sindicato*, it means very little to the average member. Because the average member is unmoved, few leaders are willing to risk intervention by attempting to lead protest activity.

At present the likelihood of worker-initiated spontaneous conflict in the form of wildcat strikes or on-the-job protest also seems very remote. The government has substantially raised the cost of spontaneous protest behavior by weakening job security and strengthening strike prohibitions. In addition, press censorship means that workers remain unexposed to radical critiques of government policy. Some underground political propagandizing and organizing appear to be occurring, but so far there have been no visible indications of any worker response to this activity.[52] On the other hand, the Brazilian government is engaged in its own massive and highly sophisticated propaganda offensive. During 1972, workers everywhere encountered posters with the message "You are building Brazil." Radio and television announcements continually reminded workers that they too could get ahead if they acquired a little more education. Although the success of this campaign is impossible to assess with any accuracy, many workers probably believe that some day they or their children will benefit from Brazilian economic development.[53] In the absence of an economic downturn or a liberalization of censorship and prohibitions on political propagandizing, optimistic perceptions of future benefits are likely to persist, and spontaneous protest activity seems very unlikely.

Wage-Setting: Corporatist Controls in Action

Wage increases have traditionally been the most important focus of working-class protest in Brazil. Since hours, working conditions, and fringe benefits are regulated in great detail in the labor law, labor court decisions and voluntary collective contracts are limited almost exclusively to wage issues.[54] By far the most frequent demand of the strikes which occurred during the late 1950s and early 1960s was for higher wages.[55] A higher wage is probably the only issue which has any current potential for mobilizing Brazilian workers. Thus, government policy on wages and wage-setting constitutes an ideal example for illustrating the impact of the corporatist control system.

The government influences wages in two ways: First, it sets the minimum wage for all wage and salaried worders and second, the labor courts grant annual wage increases to the *sindicatos*. Prior to 1964, labor protest played an important role in both procedures. The minimum wage was adjusted at irregular periods, primarily in response to working-class pressure in the form of wage campaigns and strike movements. Between August 1956 and February 1964, adjustments were made five times at intervals ranging from twelve to twenty-eight months. Strikes and wage campaigns also played an important role in wage-setting in the labor courts. The strikes and demonstrations were aimed both at employers and at the labor court judges. A strike or an effective strike threat could lead to either a more favorable court decision on wages or a favorable voluntary agreement with the employers. Usually disputes were submitted to the Regional Labor Court before a strike was called; however, unauthorized strikes did occur, and late-night court sessions to end or avoid a strike were not uncommon.[56] The strike, in short, was an integral part of the wage-setting procedure in the late 1950s and early 1960s.

It is very difficult to get a clear picture of the exact patterns of strike activity during this period because of a lack of systematic research on the subject and the absence of official data.[57] The nature of workers' participation in the strikes is also unclear. Only two studies have examined the attitudes of Brazilian workers toward strikes prior to 1964, and each involved only one factory in the Greater São Paulo area.[58] Both of these studies suggest a very low level of class consciousness and identification with *sindicatos* and strike activity. Leôncio Rodrigues describes the task of the *sindicato* leadership in strike situations as follows:

> What predominates among workers is a remoteness from class problems, an absence of the tradition of collective action, of united and open opposition to the authority of those who occupy dominant positions in the social hierarchy. Thus, in order that the authority of management be challenged, the challenge must be made by another "authority," that of the *sindicato* leadership.[59]

Rodrigues views workers as passive participants in strikes who accede to the authority of the militant pickets from the *sindicato*. Militant leadership is thus the key element in the success or failure of strikes.

It is important to note that Rodrigues's research is very narrow, covering only the geographic area of Greater São Paulo and within this area only industrial workers. Several of the most militant sectors of the working class—the longshoremen, port workers, maritime workers, railroad workers, airport workers, and bank workers—were not included in his analysis. Furthermore, his study is based on interviews with employers who, given their paternalistic attitudes, are naturally inclined to view strikes as conspiracies led from outside. Nevertheless, this view of workers as passive participants, highly dependent on union militants, is supported by the other limited direct evidence available.[60]

The passive-worker image also has considerable intuitive appeal. Many workers were of recent rural origin;[61] they tended to retain traditional values and to be passive and individualistic. In general, they perceived themselves to be better off in urban industrial employment than in agricultural employment,[62] they perceived their industrial employment as a transitional step toward self-employment,[63] and their primary identification was with all the lower strata of the population, that is, unemployed, marginally employed, low-paid workers, etc., rather than specifically with the industrial working class.[64] The level of education of all industrial workers was low and the incidence of illiteracy high.[65] In addition, the rapid expansion of the economy throughout the 1950s had produced relatively high rates of intergenerational upward mobility.[66] Under these circumstances, Rodrigues's passive-worker hypothesis seems very plausible.

The mass mobilization which occurred in the early 1960s exposed hundreds of thousands of workers to direct participation in conflict situations. Many workers were undoubtedly radicalized by their exposure to political propaganda, their collective experiences, and the sense of power they gained from relatively frequent victories. The image of the *sindicato* as a welfare agency was probably beginning to change. However, it is likely that the general level of class consciousness was still very low and that the mobilization process was still highly dependent on the *sindicato* leadership when the coup occurred in April 1964.

Post-1964 governments have made several changes in wage-setting procedures which have significantly defused the wage issue. Most of the uncertainty formerly associated with setting the minimum wage has been eliminated. The minimum wage is now adjusted annually. The process is automatic. Workers know that on May 1 of each year a new minimum wage will be announced. Labor leaders can no longer use the uncertainty about the timing of the wage adjustment as an issue for mobilizing workers.

The control of inflation has also helped to defuse the minimum wage issue. The annual increases in the cost-of-living index in the period from 1958 to 1963 were 21.0, 46.8, 25.5, 47.8, 48.2, and 93.3 respectively. Since 1968, inflation has fluctuated between 13.5 and 23.8 percent.[67] The stabilization of inflation, even at these relatively high levels, means that workers can form a stable set of expectations about price behavior. The real value of wages is far easier to perceive, and the annual deterioration in the real value is much less disturbing. During 1963 a worker whose wage equaled one hundred cruzeiros at the beginning of the year had only fifty-two cruzeiros of purchasing power in December. In a study of major strike movements in the early 1960s, Kenneth

Erickson identifies the erosion of real purchasing power as a necessary condition for the success of the strike movement.[68] By standardizing the adjustment procedure and controlling inflation, the government has eliminated intraperiod erosion of the real purchasing power of the minimum wage as an important wage issue.

From the point of view of the *sindicatos*, wage-setting in the labor court is far more important. The *sindicatos* play a direct role in the court process, and the outcome of the procedure determines their members' wages. The courts are essentially compulsory arbitration bodies. The parties to a wage dispute can either negotiate an agreement and register it with the court, or submit the dispute directly to the court for a decision. Since 1964, two major changes have occurred which greatly limit the role of the *sindicato* in the wage-setting process. First, strikes have been eliminated in wage disputes. Second, neither the labor courts nor employers have any discretion over the size of the wage increase. Wages are now set according to a complicated government formula which bases the increase on the value of real wages in the twenty-four months previous to the increase, on the anticipated inflation for the upcoming twelve months, and on a national productivity figure. The most important feature of the new procedure is that the courts no longer have the power to influence the size of the increase. They must use the official formula to calculate the wage increase, and increases in excess of the formula figure are not allowed. The courts must also reduce any voluntarily negotiated agreements to the formula figure.[69] As a result collective bargaining is a sham, and the court decisions have been reduced to a ritualized formality. One prominent judge has suggested that the courts could be replaced by a computer.[70]

By eliminating the wage-setting power of the courts and employers, the government has eliminated the two main targets of the pre-1964 strike movements. Wage decisions are no longer made in the courts; they are made in the Ministry of Finance. A challenge to a court ruling is no longer a challenge to the court or an employer but a challenge to the entire wage policy. The government has shifted the center of gravity in wage disputes into the arena of national politics. Unfortunately for Brazilian workers, this has occurred at a time when government interventions and the nonrepresentative election procedures combine to produce national confederation leaders who are most accurately characterized as progovernment bureaucrats.

My interviews indicate that among the leadership of large *sindicatos*, discontent with the wage policy is widespread. In response to the question, "What is your opinion of the government's wage policy: Has it raised or lowered the purchasing power of workers?" only 9.4 percent of the respondents stated that purchasing power had risen as a result of the policy, 81.3 percent felt that it had fallen, and 9.4 percent felt that the policy had no effect.

In spite of opposition to the wage policy, the possibility of *sindicato* leaders challenging national policy is very slight. Since strikes are effectively banned in wage disputes, the government would intervene in any *sindicato* involved in a strike against the wage policy. Unless the movement spread very rapidly to other *sindicatos* it would be doomed to failure. Given the present lack of federation coordination, it is highly unlikely that such a general movement could develop. *Sindicato* leaders are well aware that labor organizations which "create obstacles to the execution of the political economy adopted by the government" can find themselves out of business. Union militants who incite workers to strike illegally can find themselves in jail. So the militant leadership waits. Selective interventions have taught them that militant behavior is a one-shot affair. The risks involved in militant endeavors are very great, the costs are very high, and the benefits are questionable. Few leaders are willing to perform acts which could have tremendously costly personal consequences and quite likely would have very little impact on the workers or the government. They are waiting for the costs to decrease or the benefits to rise before acting.

Most *sindicatos* continue to mount wage campaigns in spite of the fact that leaders are very pessimistic about the impact of the campaigns (see table 6). During the campaigns, union newspapers and pamphlets openly criticize the wage policy.[71] However, direct action in the form of marches, demonstrations, strikes, or other militant activities is carefully avoided.

Sindicato members also recognize the impotence of the campaigns.

Table 6. Attitudes of Leaders of the Principal
Sindicatos Toward Effects of Wage Campaigns

Question	Yes	No
Did the *sindicato* conduct a wage campaign in 1971?	91.2%	8.8%
Do wage campaigns influence the courts?	23.5	76.5
Do wage campaigns influence the employers?	20.6	79.4
Do wage campaigns influence the government in its wage policy?	14.7	85.3

N = 34.
Source: Interviews conducted in May–June 1972.
Note: One union leader refused to answer any of the above questions.

As the data in table 7 indicate, nearly one-half of the unions attracted less than 5 percent of their membership to the wage campaign meetings, and over 80 percent attracted less than 10 percent. These data vastly understate the extent of worker apathy, since they are based on active, dues-paying members. On the average, dues payers account for 25.1 percent of the workers in the *sindicatos*' jurisdiction.

Table 7. Attendance at Final Wage Campaign
Meeting of the Principal *Sindicatos*
of Greater São Paulo, 1971

Attendance (percentage of active members)	Percentage of *sindicatos*
Less than 1%	9.7
1–5	38.7
5–10	32.3
10–20	6.5
More than 20	12.9

N = 31.
Source: Interviews conducted in May–July 1972.
Note: "Active members" are dues-paying members of the *sindicato*.

The Brazilian government has changed the nature of the debate over wages. In the case of minimum-wage policy, the wage-setting *procedure* has been eliminated as an item of contention. Deterioration of real purchasing power and uncertainty about the timing of increases are issues which no longer have any mobilizing potential. In the labor courts the opposite situation prevails—the wage-setting procedure has become the key issue. *Sindicatos* no longer have the power to affect single wage decisions because single wage decisions are no longer made.

These changes do not mean that wages have been eliminated as an issue in Brazil. The decline in the real value of the minimum wage and the failure of most workers to participate significantly in the growth process are definitely potential sources of conflict. The main impact of the changes in wage-setting procedures has been to redefine the issues in a way that minimizes the potential for *sindicato*-articulated conflict.

Conclusion

The coexistence of an authoritarian government and a highly developed corporatist system of interest-group representation is primarily responsible for the low levels of class conflict in post-1964 Brazil. Under the corporatist labor system, labor leaders, labor organizations, and rank-and-file workers are highly susceptible to state control. Any government with the will and power to utilize fully the control apparatus has a tremendous capability to suppress, channel, and preempt labor protest. Under President Goulart, the government lacked both the will and the power to implement the controls fully. Goulart was dependent on working-class support and thus was forced to use the controls selectively and cautiously. Since 1964, authoritarian Brazilian governments have been virtually unrestrained in their application of the labor controls. The post-1964 suppression of civil liberties, freedom of the press, and political opposition is certainly a complementary if not necessary condition for full implementation of the control system. Political competition tends to undermine corporatist controls. There is a natural affinity between authoritarianism and corporatism.

The major aspects of the Brazilian labor control system have been described and analyzed in this study. Labor leaders are initimidated through repression and coaxed into conformity and passivity through co-optation. Labor organizations are structured in a manner which facilitates control. They are guaranteed financial and organizational stability by the state, but in the process they lose control of the main thrust of their activities. With the full control system in operation, it is very difficult for labor leaders to use the official labor organizations as a vehicle of protest.

The likelihood that collective conflict will be initiated directly by rank-and-file workers is also very low. The costs of conflict behavior are very high because of repressive strike prohibitions and the lack of job security. Furthermore, the level of class consciousness among workers is very low, and it is likely that many workers believe they are benefiting or will benefit from the continuing economic prosperity. Workers are highly dependent on leaders to articulate issues and initiate militant activity. There is considerable evidence that labor leaders are dissatisfied with the government wage policy, the lack of an effective right to strike, and the general social-welfare orientation of Brazilian unionism. They want to lead militant activities; however, they are constrained by the control system. They find themselves in a paradoxical situation: In order to mobilize the workers, they must escape the controls; but to escape the controls, they must have a mobilized base. The workers require leadership, but the government controls effectively stymie militant leadership activity.

Several factors could produce change in this apparently stable situation. First, continued success of the growth model could produce labor market conditions which are more conducive to spontaneous labor protest. A tight labor market would weaken one of the most important rank-and-file controls—insecurity over employment. Lack of effective job security is a major impediment to all protest activity. Given the vast reserves of unskilled labor in the rural areas of Brazil, it is highly unlikely that any *general* shortage of labor will arise in the immediate future. However, the labor reserves are unevenly distributed, and short-run regional shortages have already occurred.[72] It is possible that spontaneous conflict during a period of regional shortage could ignite more general labor protest.

A second condition which could produce higher levels of class conflict is an economic downturn. It is probably true that most workers expect to participate someday in the "Brazilian Miracle." Any down-turn in economic activity could result in a very rapid reversal of consumption expectations and rapid reassessment of the entire growth model. If a downturn occurs, higher levels of class conflict could develop in spite of the high risks involved.

A third possibility is that labor militants outside the official corpora-tist structure will successfully articulate the issues and initiate conflict activities. Illicit political activity of this sort is very dangerous. Brazil's secret police are both effective and ruthless. But the potential for success of clandestine organizing would be greatly enhanced by either the development of tight labor market conditions or an economic downturn.

One final factor which could result in higher levels of class conflict is a breakdown in the elite consensus on the basic growth strategy and a reintroduction of political competition. The benefits of rapid growth are certainly not distributed equally among the various segments of the upper classes. For example, the traditional home base of Brazilian domestic capital—industries which produce for mass consumption like textiles, clothing, food processing, beverages, etc.—has been growing at a much slower rate than the foreign-dominated consumer durables sector. The growth of mass consumption industries depends on increas-ing mass purchasing power, while the growth of the consumer durables sector depends on a concentration of purchasing power. As long as overall growth rates are very rapid, all sectors of the upper classes can benefit and all sectors are presented with opportunities to diversify their holdings. If growth slows, some of the inherent strains in the model will begin to show. It is possible that a segment of the upper classes allied with representatives of the military will seriously question the overall model. This raises the possibility of upper-class demands for a reintroduction of political competition and could even lead to the sort of upper-class-initiated mobilization of the labor movement that occurred under Goulart. Currently this possibility seems remote, but change could come rapidly if the economy falters.

One final question remains—Are corporatist controls viable in the long run if none of the above conditions prevail? It seems to me that time works in favor of the controls. The longer the labor leadership can be effectively controlled, the greater their susceptibility to the co-optive features of the system. Also, sustained economic growth provides the regime with the opportunity to expand its base of support further among the upper strata of the working class. Given favorable economic conditions, the continued "success" of the system seems very likely.

NOTES

1. As used in this paper, the term "working class" includes all nonsupervisory wage and salaried workers in the nonagricultural sectors of the economy. Nonpaid family workers, the self-employed, managers and supervisors, and all rural workers are excluded.

2. The interviews were conducted as part of the research for my Ph.D. dissertation, "Conflict Regulation in the Brazilian Industrial Relations System" (University of Wisconsin, 1974). Research support came in part from the David Dubinsky Foundation and in part from the Ibero-American Studies Department and the Center for the Study of International Business, both of the University of Wisconsin.

3. For a more complete description of the *sindicatos* studied, see Mericle, "Conflict Regulation," appendix A.

4. Evaristo de Moraes Filho, *O problema do sindicato único no Brasil* (Rio de Janeiro: Editôra a Noite, 1952), pp. 243–44.

5. Thomas E. Skidmore, *Politics in Brazil, 1930–1964: An Experiment in Democracy* (New York: Oxford University Press, 1967), pp. 207–52.

6. Kenneth P. Erickson, "Labor in the Political Process in Brazil: Corporatism in a Modernizing Nation" (Ph.D. dissertation, Columbia University, 1970).

7. According to the U.S. government, the Brazilian government intervened in at least 2,018 *sindicatos*. These data include 1,600 *sindicatos* in the agricultural confederation but exclude interventions of *sindicatos* in four of the smaller nonagricultural confederations. See U.S. Department of Labor, *Labor Law and Practice in Brazil*, BLS Report, no. 309 (Washington, D.C.: Government Printing Office, 1967), p. 40.

8. The best source available on the two strikes is Francisco C. Weffort, *Participação e conflito industrial: Contagem e Osasco 1968*, Caderno CEBRAP, no. 5 (São Paulo: Centro Brasileiro de Análise e Planejamento, 1972). See also "A greve de Osasco," *Unidade e Luta*, Serie Estudos, 2 (Santiago de Chile, November 1972); and "Contribuição a um balanço necessário das lutas de 1968 no Brasil," *Outubro: orgão Trotsquista Brasileiro*, no. 2 (Orsay, Fr., October 1972).

9. *Anuário estatístico do Brasil 1972* (Rio de Janeiro: Instituto Brasileiro de Geografia e Estística, 1972), pp. 525, 549.

10. The calculations are based on a monthly time series of the real value of the minimum wage. To perform the calculation, the nominal minimum wage was deflated by the cost-of-living index for each month included in the two time periods. The average monthly real value was then calculated for each period, and value for the latter period was expressed as a percentage of the former. The minimum wage and cost-of-living index are both for Guanabara. Sources of all data are *Conjuntura Econômica*, 27, no. 12 (December 1973), and 28, no. 5 (May 1974).

11. João Carlos Duarte, *Aspectos da distribuição da renda no Brasil em 1970* (Piricicaba, São Paulo: Escola Superior de Agricultura "Luiz de Queiros," University of São Paulo, 1971), pp. 40, 46.

12. Victor Valerius, *Consolidação das leis do trabalho* (Rio de Janiero: Editôra Aurora, 1971), p. 242, article 570. This is the basic consolidation of Brazilian labor law. The law is available in many different annotated editions. All of my references are to the Valerius edition, which will be referred to as *CLT* in subsequent citations. Translations are mine.

13. This does not mean that leaders of the official *sindicatos* do not meet and communicate with one another. Contact is frequent and open, but it is also limited to nonmilitant activities. An open meeting to plan a strike or demonstration or to discuss support of such actions would very likely lead to government repression.

14. See United States Embassy, "Labor Directory for Brazil: 1971 Revision" (Report, United States Embassy in Rio de Janeiro, 1971).

15. Interviews conducted in May–July 1972.

16. This profile is based on data from "Labor Directory for Brazil: 1971 Revision." The directory has data for 1,587 *sindicatos* in the six major nonagricultural confederations. These *sindicatos* represent an estimated 9,030,000 workers, for an average of 5,690 workers per *sindicato*. An estimate of the number of workers represented by the National Confederation of Education and Cultural Workers was not available, so it has been excluded from the preceding calculation. It is doubtful that the exclusion of this confederation would affect the averages significantly. The membership figure is based on a national estimate that only 18 percent of workers in *sindicato* jurisdictions pay dues. These data, based on averages, really overstate the size of a typical *sindicato*. The large *sindicatos*, like those included in the Greater São Paulo sample, tend to inflate the averages. The median *sindicato* would represent far fewer than 5,700 workers and have far fewer than 1,000 members.

17. If the number of *sindicatos* in a particular federation jurisdiction is insufficient to justify state-level representation, the geographic base of the federation is often extended. Of Brazil's 112 nonagricultural labor federations, 60.2 percent are confined to a single state, 22.2 percent include more than one state, and 17.6 percent are national in coverage ("Labor Directory for Brazil: 1971 Revision").

18. A president of one of the metalworkers' *sindicatos* reported that twenty-five of thirty-six *sindicatos* in the São Paulo Metalworkers Federation were housed in buildings provided by the federation (interview, July 7, 1972).

19. Legally, new elections are supposed to be held within ninety days of the intervention (article 554, *CLT*, p. 239).

20. Article 553, *CLT*, p. 238.

21. Ibid., pp. 226–27.

22. In a ruling in 1968, the Ministry of Labor granted that "the exercise of the *sindicato* mandate should not be the cause of impoverishment" and ruled that food and transportation allowances were legal. Reported in Adriano Campanhole and João Emílio de Bruin, *Pratica sindical* (São Paulo: Editôra Atlas, 1970), pp. 236–37.

23. Article 552, *CLT*, p. 222. This limitation is only important for the large *sindicatos;* most small *sindicatos* cannot even afford seven paid officers.

24. I spent approximately two weeks in April 1972 observing procedures in the first-level labor courts. During this time, I conducted several long interviews with the judges and court personnel.

25. Interview with Judge Wagner Giglio, April 1972. Giglio is the government-

appointed career judge in one of the São Paulo first-level labor courts. He estimates that both class judges have voted against his decisions ten times in fifteen years.

26. Interview, São Paulo, May 1972.

27. Philippe C. Schmitter, *Interest Conflict and Political Change in Brazil* (Stanford: Stanford University Press, 1971), p. 125.

28. Ibid., p. 126.

29. "MTPS promove curso," *O Estado de São Paulo*, June 21, 1972.

30. *CLT*, pp. 650–51.

31. The source of these data is Ministério do Trabalho e Previdência Social, "Relatório da Comissão Instituida pela Portaria," no. 439/65, August 24, 1965 (mimeographed), as cited by Philippe C. Schmitter, *Interest Conflict*, p. 21.

32. Ophelina Rabello, *A rêde sindical paulista* (São Paulo: Instituto Cultural do Trabalho, 1965), pp. 75–101.

33. Erickson, "Labor in the Political Process," pp. 66–67.

34. Mericle, "Conflict Regulation," pp. 115–19.

35. Article 513, *CLT*, pp. 217–18.

36. The concept of just cause (*justa causa*) is very important in Brazilian labor law. Article 482 specifies the reasons which constitute just cause for discharging a worker. They include: theft, fraud, habitual drunkenness, abandonment of employment, immoral or offensive behavior, etc. For a complete listing and short explanation of each reason, see Gualdo Amaury Formica, *Manual prático do chefe pessoal*, vol. 1 (São Paulo: Sugestões Literárias, 1971), pp. 123–27. To fire stable workers, the employer must prove just cause and *in addition* he must demonstrate that the reason for discharge, because of its *nature or repetition*, constitutes a "serious violation of the employee's duties and obligations" (article 493, *CLT*, p. 210).

37. Article 496, *CLT*, p. 211.

38. In cases of involuntary layoff without just cause, the employer still must make a deposit at the time of layoff equal to 10 percent of the total in the worker's account. For a worker with ten years of seniority, this deposit would equal about a month's salary, or approximately one-twentieth the amount due under the old system (Formica, *Manual pratico*, p. 153).

39. The law permits employers to buy out the worker's indemnity rights for a payment of 60 percent of the money actually due. These "friendly agreements" at the 60 percent figure are very common, and even at the reduced rate, few workers can resist.

40. Mericle, "Conflict Regulation," pp. 156–62.

41. Articles 723 and 724, *CLT*, pp. 307–08.

42. Mericle, "Conflict Regulation," pp. 127–32.

43. The strike law, no. 4330 of June 1, 1964, is reproduced in full in Companhole and Bruin, *Prática sindical*, pp. 145–51.

44. Ibid., p. 148.

45. Ibid., p. 150.

46. J. A. Rodrigues, *Sindicato e desenvolvimento no Brasil* (São Paulo: Difusão Européia do Livro, 1968), p. 146.

47. J. V. Freitas Marcondes, *Radiografia da liderança sindical paulista* (São Paulo: Instituto Cultural do Trabalho, 1964), pp. 64–65.

48. *Pelego* is a derogatory term used to describe union leaders who cooperate with the Ministry of Labor and further their own interests at the expense of those of the union's membership. The word means literally the sheepskin blanket placed between the saddle and the horse to ease the burden of the rider on the horse.

49. Rodrigues, *Sindicato e desenvolvimento*, pp. 151–52.

50. Interview, São Paulo, June 1972.

51. See Juarez Rubens Brandão Lopes, *Sociedade industrial no Brasil* (São Paulo: Difusão Européia do Livro, 1971), pp. 57–58; L. M. Rodrigues, *Industrialização e atitudes operárias* (São Paulo: Editôra Brasiliense, 1970), pp. 101–14; and Joseph F. Springer, *A Brazilian Factory Study 1966*, CIDOC Cuaderno, no. 33 (Cuernavaca, Mexico, 1969), pp. 2-21–2-25.

52. There are indications that leftist organizations are attempting to do base organizing. Since the Osasco strike, this organizing has not resulted in a single important strike. On the experience of one activist with base organization, see P. Torres, "Uma experiência junto ao proletariado" (Mimeograph, Santiago de Chile, 1972).

53. This statement is based on informal conversations with a number of São Paulo workers. Very little research on working-class attitudes with respect to Brazilian development in the period of rapid growth since 1968 has been done recently or is currently in progress. One important exception is a survey conducted in 1972 by Peter McDonnough and Amaury de Souza, both of the Survey Research Institute of the University of Michigan.

54. Mericle, "Conflict Regulation," pp. 225–31.

55. See Jorge Miglioli, *Como São Feitas as greves no Brasil* (Rio de Janeiro: Civilização Brasiliera, 1963), p. 95; Leôncio M. Rodrigues, *Conflito indústrial e sindicalismo no Brasil* (São Paulo: Difusão Européia do Livro, 1966), p. 53; and J. A. Rodrigues, *Sindicato e desenvolvimento*, pp. 155–56.

56. Wagner D. Giglio, *Direito processual do trabalho* (São Paulo: Sugestões Literárias, 1972), p. 253.

57. The Brazilian government does not publish comprehensive statistics on strikes. Professor Francisco Weffort of the University of São Paulo is currently working on the preparation of a series for the period from 1940 to 1964.

58. Lopes, *Sociedade industrial no Brasil*; and L. M. Rodrigues, *Industrialização e atitudes.*

59. L. M. Rodrigues, *Conflito industrial*, p. 164.

60. See Lopes, *Sociedade industrial no Brasil*; and L. M. Rodrigues, *Industrialização e Atitudes.*

61. In the factory Lopes studied in 1957, 64.3 percent of the workers were migrants from the northeast of Brazil, the states surrounding São Paulo, and the interior of the state of São Paulo. Most of these workers worked until adolescence or young adulthood in agriculture (*Sociedade industrial no Brasil*, pp. 32–33). In his 1964 study of an automobile factory, L. M. Rodrigues found that 53 percent of semi- and unskilled workers and 17 percent of skilled workers had previously worked in agriculture (*Industrialização e atitudes*, p. 11). Based on extensive open-ended interviews with workers, Luis Pereira concluded that the two principal sources from which the industrial workers are recruited are rural proletarian families and working-class families (*Trabalho e desenvolvimento no Brasil* [São Paulo: Difusão Européia do Livro, 1965], p. 160).

62. Pereira, *Trabalho e desenvolvimento*, pp. 147–48; L. M. Rodrigues, *Industrialização e atitudes*, pp. 43–83; Lopes, *Sociedade industrial no Brasil*, p. 46.

63. Lopes, *Sociedade industrial no Brasil*, pp. 46–48.

64. Ibid., p. 67; and L. M. Rodrigues, *Industrialização e atitudes* pp. 163–71.

65. L. M. Rodrigues, *Industrialização e atitudes*, pp. 10–14; and Ivan Gonçalves de Freitas, *Mão-de-Obra indústrial na Guanabara* (Rio de Janeiro: Instituto de Ciências Sociais, 1967). Rodrigues found that 36 percent of his sample had not completed primary education. Gonçalves de Freitas studied industrial workers in

eight major industrial sectors of Guanabara and found that 16.6 percent of the workers had never attended school. Of those who had some schooling, 43.6 percent had not completed their primary education.

66. Bertram Hutchinson, "Mobilidade de estructura e de intercambio na assimilação de immigrantes no Brasil," *Educação e Ciências Sociais*, 4, no. 10 (April 1959):36–49.

67. *Conjuntura Econômica*, 27, no. 12 (December 1973), Special Statistical Supplement, pp. 85–88; and 28, no. 4 (April 1974): 178.

68. Erickson, "Labor in the Political Process."

69. See Mericle, "Conflict Regulation," chap. 6.

70. Supreme Labor Court Judge Mozart Victor Russomano, quoted in *O Trabalhador Gráfico*, 51, no. 303 (March 1972):3 (monthly organ of the São Paulo printers' *sindicato*).

71. For example, see "A produtividade crese, mas nossos salários se reduzem," *O Trabalhador Textil*, 5, no. 13 (April 1973) (monthly newspaper of the São Paulo textile workers' *sindicato*); *O Trabalhador Gráfico*, 51, no. 303 (March 1972):3; "Política salarial; fator de envaziamento dos sindicatos," *O Trabalhador em Madeira*, 2, no. 5 (February 1972):3 (monthly newspaper of the São Paulo furniture workers' *sindicato*); and "As razões de nossa campanha salarial," *O Veículo*, 3, no. 8 (April 1972):7 (monthly newspaper of the land-transport workers' *sindicato*).

72. In late 1973 shortages of unskilled labor began to develop in the construction industry in the Greater São Paulo area. The shortages later began to appear in other industries. The shortages are primarily the result of an exceptional boom in construction and other industries which employ a large component of unskilled workers, and a temporary slowdown and partial reversal in in-migration from labor surplus areas. See "São Paulo precisa de reforço" *Visão*, September 24, 1973, pp. 65–68; "Dias de glória na construção imobiliária," *Visão*, October 15, 1973, p. 43; and "A grande feira da Mão-de-Obra," *Visão*, January 14, 1974, pp. 23–30.

KENNETH E. SHARPE

11

Corporate Strategies in the Dominican Republic: The Politics of Peasant Movements

> Thus we clearly see, by examples both ancient and modern, that no nation exists, no matter how rude, uncultured, barbarous, gross, or almost brutal its people might be, that can not be persuaded and brought to a good order and way of life and made domestic, mild, and tractable, provided the method that is proper and natural to men is used, that is, love, and gentleness, and kindness.[1]

The chill darkness of the mountain night is broken here and there by the light escaping through the rough-hewn plank walls of peasant dwellings scattered over the Dominican Cordillera Central. From inside the kitchens come the laughter and crying of children, the clanking of spoons on metal plates, merengues and news from battery-powered radios. One house is strangely quiet, but for a single voice. Twenty-odd adults and children from four neighboring families sit on rickety chairs and handmade benches placed in a circle on the dirt floor. A kerosene lantern atop the still warm hearth gives a yellow glow to the room and makes shadows stir on the walls. Men in their much-patched work pants, women with infants sleeping in their arms, boys and girls in their worn, hand-me-down shorts and frocks all listen attentively to their neighbor Teresa, a twenty-three-year-old *catequista* (catechism instructor). She explains the lessons that she and other peasant *catequistas* learned earlier in the month from instructors sent by the parish priest.

"The most important thing in our lives as human beings is love," she emphasizes, not simply love of God or some abstract love of man, but loving each other in daily life by helping each other, by struggling together to help the whole community. She reminds them of the newly formed marketing cooperative (itself actively encouraged and supported by the church) as a way they can live the love preached by Christ. When she finishes her remarks, she asks those around her to discuss "what is to be done."

What are we to do to eliminate envy from our life?

What are we to do here and now to give testimony to the presence of Christ in our life?

What are we to do so that others benefit from our talents?

Concretely, what will we do not to be slaves to possession and domination?

What will we do so that all feel themselves as true brothers of God and brothers of all the members of the community?

The class ends with songs Teresa learned in her week-long catechism course in the municipal capital. A favorite is "La Revolución," sung to the popular merengue tune "Palo":

> There is robbing and killing without reason,
> Because of this we need a revolution.
> Palo, palo, palo . . .
>
> Christ brought to the world an orientation,
> If man lived by it, there would be a revolution.
>
> Living the divine grace with faith and firmness
> Impels us toward the revolution.
>
> Looking at the future with faith and joy
> Is the new direction of my life.
>
> A communitarian life and a life without sin,
> This is a revolutionary idea.

Teresa's catechism class presents the peasants with a critique of Dominican society in the light of a new Christian community being urged as a replacement for the existing City of Man. This critique and this vision are fundamental elements in church-sponsored *acción social* (social action) programs which encourage peasants to form self-help programs, agrarian leagues, and cooperatives. Indeed, they are important parts of the post–Vatican II Catholic theology of Teresa's priest, the bishop of her diocese, and "activist" clergy throughout Latin America. In this chapter I will argue that in a non-Christian state like the Dominican Republic (one in which the ruling party does not even make pretensions to Christian or Christian-Democratic principles), social programs based on this theology have political results which are not only often contradictory to the visions of the theology, but difficult to account for within its conceptual framework. They challenge the forms of control experienced by "marginal" groups, such as peasants; yet they often result in the incorporation of such groups into a state or state-supported organization which places them under new forms of control unacceptable to many clerics. My major concern is not with the fact of incorporation but with the political question: Who gets incorporated, when, and how? I will argue that the theological framework fails to pose this question, and that this failure has serious consequences. I will first discuss some of the major elements in this new Catholic orientation, emphasizing some of its conceptual limitations. Then I will examine two important social programs which flow from this theological framework: land reform and cooperative organization. In each case I will explore how the church's new orientation encouraged the promotion of these programs; the nature of the challenge made to the existing forms of control; how such programs resulted in consequences antithetical to church goals; and, most important, how certain limitations in the very framework inhibited activist clergy both from understanding these consequences and from developing effective strategies for action. Although my explicit focus is on church-sponsored social reform, the problems discussed below have important implications for all who would encourage active participation in community development programs as a strategy for social change.

The "Activist" Theology and Its Limitations

Existing society, Teresa's teaching implies, is filled with envy and egoism, with human selfishness, with the desire to possess and to dominate. It is far from a truly Christian society where men, as children of God, would see that they are all brothers and thus members of a community where the bonds that linked them were those of love, not self-interest; where each sought to use his talents for the material, not simply spiritual, improvement of others; where all men were subjects of their destinies, not objects of the decisions of others.

Such a Christian society is antithetical to both liberal and Marxist models. These, Teresa's bishop emphasizes, make men into slaves and create relations of dependency. There is a need, he writes, to find a new humanism

> that will transcend the bourgeois ethos, with its individualism and egoism, and will put aside the values of personalism in order to discover a new relationship between man and man that does not make man into an instrument, and a new relationship between man and his work. We think that in this way there can be a humanism that moves towards socialization—a humanism that does not have to lie prostrate before the dictatorship of the proletariat or the com-

munist society, but that can nevertheless create a social solidarity that will prevail over all types of private property.[2]

The bishop's thoughts reflect the position paper on justice outlined by the Latin American bishops in their conference at Medellin, Colombia, in 1968:

The system of liberal capitalism and the temptation of the Marxist system would appear to exhaust the possibilities of transforming the economic structures of our continent. Both systems militate against the dignity of the human person. One takes for granted the primacy of capital, its power and its discriminatory utilization in the function of profit-making. The other, although it ideologically supports a kind of humanism, is more concerned with collective man, and in practice becomes a totalitarian concentration of state power. We must denounce the fact that Latin America sees itself caught between these two options and remains dependent on one or other of the centers of power which control its economy.[3]

Out of this position grows a critique of those social institutions which deny man's basic humanity by treating him as an "object" of change or economic development. The bishops of the Dominican Republic, for example, outlining their Christian conception of man in society, wrote:

"The principle, the subject and the end of all social institutions is and should be the individual" (Vatican Council II, *Constitution on the Church in the Actual World*, 25)

This means that in the social order man ought to find the opportunity to obtain with his own efforts the goods that he needs and the conditions of life that respect and foment his dignity and legitimate independence. For this reason, the social structure and social institutions should not enclose and condition man, denying him his power to choose and his responsibility. On the contrary, the organization of society in all its aspects should be the guaranty and the means for man to develop his life freely and responsibly.[4]

In the Dominican Republic, the practical implication of this position is the need for land reform and peasant organizations such as agrarian leagues and cooperatives. Land redistribution is considered important in order that peasants have "the opportunity to attain with their own efforts the goods that they need and the conditions of life that respect and encourage their dignity and legitimate independence." Peasant organizations are important because such "intermediary groups" stand between the individual and the state and allow men to be "active participants" in decisions—the subjects, not the objects of change. The declaration on justice at Medellin, for example, stated:

The Latin American Church encourages the formation of national communities that reflect a global organization, where all of the peoples but more especially the lower classes have, by means of territorial and functional structures, an active and receptive, creative and decisive participation in the construction of a new society. Those intermediary structures—between the person and the state—should be freely organized, without any unwarranted interference from authority or from dominant groups, in view of their development and concrete participation in the accomplishment of the total common good. They constitute the vital network of society. They are also the true expression of the citizens' liberty and unity.[5]

The critique of existing society and the call for new, more human institutions and organizations found in much of the activist Catholic theology are notably unconcerned with a number of concepts important in other social theories such as "power," "conflict," and "structures of domination." Perhaps it is not surprising that a "theology" would not deal with political knowledge, especially since such notions are antithetical to the Catholic image of an organic community in which the central bonds among the children of God are brotherhood and love, a community in which each person plays a specific role in the attainment of the common good. But the failure to give a firm, theoretical place to notions of power, conflict, and institutional structure presents practical difficulties when one turns to this progressive theology for action guidelines. The Latin American bishops' position on economic institutions, so different from the liberal-capitalist or Marxist view, highlights some of these difficulties:

> In economic enterprises it is persons who work together, that is, free and independent human beings created to the image of God. Therefore, the active participation of everyone in the running of an enterprise should be promoted. This participation should be exercised in appropriately determined ways. It should take into account each person's function, whether it be one of ownership, hiring, management, or labor. It should provide for the necessary unity of operations.
>
> However, decisions concerning economic and social conditions on which the future of workers and their children depends, are rather often made not within the enterprise itself but by institutions on a higher level. Hence, the workers themselves should have a share also in controlling these institutions, either in person or through freely-elected delegates.[6]

If, however, the "owners" and the "laborers" do not perceive themselves as serving specific "functions" (for the attainment of the *bien común* [Common Good]) but rather as unequal classes who either claim the right to rule or reject the need to obey, then the "necessary unity of operations" may be broken by conflict.

In a Christian state, such conflict is considered abnormal, since all should accept, and act on the basis of, the same Christian view of the *bien común*. It is only on those assumedly rare occasions that men do not so act that force or power takes on explicit importance. If, for example, there should be conflicts over the *bien común* among "freely-elected delegates" who share "in controlling . . . institutions," the state is responsible for resolving such conflicts. But a number of difficult questions are not asked: What does "active participation . . . exercised in appropriately determined ways" mean in practice? How are the limits of participation (according to "each person's function") to be decided? In cases of conflict, what criteria should be used to decide how force should be applied? Who should formulate these criteria? Indeed, the Christian state itself is not conceived of as an aggregate of power favoring certain interests but as the temporal head of an organic whole, and the possibility of misuse of force against the best interests of those involved in a conflict does not seem to be a possibility: A Christian state, which "knows" and rules in the light of the *bien común*, does not impose evil or sinful solutions against men's best interest.

But the limitations of this framework are even more serious in the Dominican Republic, where the state is not Christian and guidelines for Christian *acción social* are needed. Emphasis on change through "communitarian" efforts excludes the possibility that certain kinds of conflicts may be unresolvable within a "community" framework. Institutional structures which may pose serious obstacles to change are often not analyzed, nor are the difficulties of creating the power which may be needed to overcome these existing structures of domination. Such an analysis, I will argue, might reveal serious difficulties with the major guideline this framework does suggest: *concientización*, creating a Christian consciousness among men.

That this theology focuses on changing the minds and hearts of men and not on destroying existing structures of domination and creating power, makes sense given the central cause it sees behind social evils: the sinfulness, egoism, and selfishness of men. According to the Medellin conference:

> The Latin American Church has a message for all men on this continent who "hunger and thirst after justice." The very God who creates men in his image and likeness, creates the "earth and all that is in it for the use of all men and all nations, in such a way that created goods can reach all in a more just manner" (*Gaudium et Spes*, 69) and gives them power to transform and perfect the world in solidarity. (cf. Genesis 1, 25; *Gaudium et Spes*, 34). It is the same God who, in the fullness of time, sends his Son in the flesh, so that He might come to liberate all men from the slavery to which sin has subjected

them (cf. Genesis 8, 32–35): hunger, misery, oppression and ignorance, in a word, that injustice and hatred which have their origin in human selfishness.[7]

Social structures must also be changed, the bishops argue, but the primary emphasis is on creating new men who will form these structures:

> The uniqueness of the Christian message does not so much consist in the affirmation of the necessity for structural change, as it does in the insistence on the conversion of men which will in turn bring about this change. We will not have a new continent without new and reformed structures, but, above all, there will be no new continent without new men, who know how to be truly free and responsible according to the light of the Gospel.[8]

Socialization, not conflict, is the way to realize the *bien común*:

> Socialization understood as a socio-cultural process of personalization and communal growth, leads us to think that all of the sectors of society, but, in this case, principally the social-economic sphere, should, because of justice and brotherhood, transcend antagonisms in order to become agents of national and continental development.[9]

Thus, in the Dominican Republic, it is not surprising that the major focus of Teresa's bishop is on creating an *espiritu comunitario* (community spirit) among those in his diocese. In his words:

> The purpose of the weekly catechism classes is to make the people feel themselves active members of a community, the Church, which they themselves make up; to make them conscious that Christian life has an impact on everyday life, that this Christian life manifests itself in love; and for there to be love, the people have to open themselves up to others, creating a climate of brotherhood.[10]

He and others believe that when men come to understand Christ's teaching they will neither act out of self-interest nor accept injustice, but instead work together to realize the *bien común*. According to the bishops at Medellin, this "awakening" and "awareness" achieved by *concientización* will be the source of "revolution":

> Men are to be awakened to the meaning of their dignity, the redressing of their rights, giving them an awareness of their worth, encouraging them to demand of politicians, of technicians, of businessmen, of all those who hold key positions, the respect due the human person and his inalienable rights. This awareness could bring about a continental revolution and a genuine

living out of the Universal Declaration of the Rights of Man whose 20th anniversary we commemorate this year. This action is not to be inspired by passionate violence, but by the dynamic force of justice.[11]

Indeed, when people live this new orientation (the catechism merengue tells the peasants) this will *be* the revolution: "Christ brought to the world an orientation, / if men lived by it, there would be a revolution." It is the love of men who are naturally brothers, not the power of men originally isolated as individuals in the state of nature, which should provide the dynamism for the justice sought by the bishops at Medellin:

> Love, "the fundamental law of human perfection, and therefore of the transformation of the world" (*Gaudium et Spes*, 38), is not only the greatest commandment of the Lord; it is also the dynamism which ought to motivate Christians to realize justice in the world, having truth as a foundation and liberty as their sign.[12]

What happens when clerics act, or recommend action, based on this orientation? I will argue that their lack of attention to structural matters of power and conflict, and their conception of the state, have these results: They blind the clerics to the often anti-Christian consequences their programs will have within existing political and economic institutions; they hinder them from explaining these consequences; and they limit their ability to rethink their strategies of *acción social* and *concientización*. Land reform and cooperative organization, two programs some Dominican bishops and priests have actively encouraged, serve as useful examples of such limitations.

Land Reform

On July 30, 1967, the bishops of the Dominican Republic issued a declaration on the peasant situation. A better distribution of land was one of the central agrarian reforms it called for. Their position, similar to that taken in 1968 by the Latin American bishops' meeting in Medellin, Colombia, was based on papal encyclicals:

> a) God made the earth and all that it contains for the use of all men and not merely for a few, such that the goods of the earth are received by all according to a just norm (Paul VI: *Populorum Progressio*, 22; Pius XI: *Quadragésimo anno*, 45; Vatican Council II: *Gaudium et Spes*, 69).
>
> b) All other rights, no matter what they are, including that of private property and free trade, are subordinate to the fundamental right that all men be able to use the goods of the Creation in such a way that they can live with dignity (Paul VI: *Populorum Progressio*, 22) . . . .

d) When a conflict arises between the rights of private property and the needs of the community, it falls to those with public power to procure a solution with the active participation of the people and social groups involved (Paul VI: *Populorum Progressio*, 23: Vatican Council II: *Gaudium et Spes*, 71; Pius XI, *Quadragesimo anno*, 49).

e) "The *bien común* sometimes demands the expropriation of large rural properties" be it for their extensiveness, for the misery they bring to the population, or for the grave harm to the interests of the country (Paul VI: *Populorum Progressio*, 24; Vatican Council II: *Gaudium et Spes*, 71). "When the *bien común* demands an expropriation, the amount of indemnity should always be fair, and should take into consideration all of the circumstances (Vatican Council II: *Gaudium et Spes*, 71)."[13]

Importantly, it was to the state that the bishops turned their hopeful eyes. The state—"by means of new laws"—was to be the agency for bringing about agrarian reforms and, with the "active participation" of those involved, settling conflicts. As a Jesuit commentary on the bishops' declaration pointed out: "The state's duty extends . . . to the *redistribution of economic power.* . . . it is the state as tutelary of the *bien común* that has the responsibility to set norms such that the social functioning of individual rights complies with a foreseeable minimum of justice."[14] But how state power was actually structured or used in the Dominican Republic was not questioned. Nor was the existing relationship between the state and the large landowners ever examined.[15]

The bishops further argued that land reform itself was insufficient if the peasants, as subjects, were not given "an active part in the decisions that concerned them": "The peasant not only wants more land, more education, or more security in his work; he wants above all *ser mas* [to be more], in other words 'he wants to participate even more in the responsibilities [of running his life], free of all oppression and outside situations that offend his human dignity' " (Paul VI: *Populorum Progressio*, 9).[16] They insisted on the importance of the "freely organized . . . intermediary structures . . . between the person and the state" that were later called for at the Medellin conference:

Among the fundamental rights of a human being ought to be the right to form freely workers' associations that give authentic representation to the worker . . . as well as the right to participate freely in the activities of the associations, without risk of reprisals (Vatican Council II: *Gaudium et Spes*, 68; Pius XI: *Quadragesimo anno*, 29–37). These fundamental rights are explicitly applied by church doctrine to the cooperative associations and peasant syndicates (John XXIII, *Mater et Magistra*, 146).[17]

The Dominican bishops do not notice the serious problems facing the land reform they encourage precisely because of their failure to look at the institutional structure and public policy of the state, the power of landlords and lack of peasant power, and the kinds of conflicts that such a land reform program will generate. One problem is that land reform may never be achieved.[18] But I will focus on another problem. Even when land reform is achieved, the existing structures of political and economic power produce consequences antithetical to the bishops' goals; and the bishops' framework limits their ability to understand these consequences and to suggest guidelines for corrective action. Land reform in the rice-growing community of Los Canales provides an important case for examination.

The Community

Los Canales is a flat, irrigated, rice-growing community in the Cibao region of the Dominican Republic. Before government-built canals brought irrigation in the early 1960s, cattle grazed on the arid land and a few subsistence crops grew on the fertile strip bordering the river. The basis of economic power in the community was control over land. The peasants in Los Canales rarely owned more than the plots their houses stood on. They sharecropped the land along the river *a media* (paying the owners 50 percent of their gross profits) and worked for wages as day laborers on the extensive cattle ranches or on the plots of share-croppers. Cash for food, medicine, and ceremonial expenses was always scarce, and the peasants were forced to buy food on credit advanced by local dry-goods store owners (for prices slightly higher than cash prices) or to seek small personal loans at 5 to 10 percent monthly interest from the store owners or landowners. Under Rafael Trujillo, a powerful centralized state exercised complete political control over the peasants. The threat of violent action by the local military discouraged any opposition or autonomous organization. But although the order the state enforced usually supported the economic power of the land-owners, the state itself exercised little direct economic control over the peasantry. The assassination of Trujillo in 1961, the ensuing organization of popular elections, and the elimination of legal barriers to organization changed the political landscape of Los Canales. Urban politicians, activist clergy, and peasant leaders began to call for agrarian reforms and to mobilize the peasants for political support or direct local action.

It was in this context that state-organized land reform began in the mid-1960s. Forty-five peasants, many formerly sharecroppers and agricultural day laborers, received irrigated *parcelas* (parcels of land) or about fifty *tareas* (eight acres). The major land distribution came in the late 1960s. By 1970, there were about two hundred *parceleros* (parcel holders) in the project under the administration of a local office of the Instituto Agrario Dominicano (IAD), the government's land reform agency. The distribution of land, the administration of land and water, and the provision of capital needed for production now tie the peasant to new structures of political and economic control.

The Distribution of Land

The redistribution of land in Los Canales did not severely challenge the economic power of the large landholders. The only land "expropriated" by the state for land reform was 25 percent of the land opened by the new irrigation system. The 75 percent retained by the original owners was irrigated, cultivatable land much more valuable than the formerly arid cattle lands. A small additional amount of land was acquired for redistribution by buying plots of often poor-quality land at handsome prices, or by using public land.

The land thus acquired was distributed by officials from the national IAD office and the local administrator of the land reform project. When the peasants applied through the local IAD office, information was recorded about family size and economic situation so that relative need could be determined. But official criteria were often put aside by the government bureaucrats (usually political appointees chosen on the basis of their support for the ruling Partido Reformista). Some decisions were based on bribes. Indeed, not only is the price "paid" for a *parcela* often common knowledge, but a number of *parceleros* explained to me how they themselves received land by "giving something." Other decisions were based on political support. Active backers of the Partido Reformista are rewarded (often on the recommendation of regional or national political officials); those who have opposed the party or who are critical of the government or land reform program are usually left landless. The case of R., a small sharecropper, is revealing. An active proponent of land reform, R. publicly criticized the distribution process, denouncing the giving of land to people outside Los Canales who "had political pull or paid off the IAD officials." Soon afterward, R. discovered from a friend in the local IAD office that the administrator had placed his name on the blacklist, angrily swearing that "as long as I am administrator, R. can forget about getting land." R. could do little: He had no proof he was being blacklisted (the administrator would have denied it and R.'s friend would have lost his job for admitting it) and no recourse against those who controlled the distribution of land. Such incidents reinforce the already widespread belief that opposition to the government means no land. "One doesn't want to say anything against the government because, you know, when the division of land comes . . . you know what's going to happen!" One peasant explained: "We're all progovernment here because the president has made many promises here. And he's given out some parcels—although he hasn't given many to the local people here. But you always have the hope that someday he'll give you your parcel!"

Control Over Land and Water

To make his land yield rice, the *parcelero* needs equipment (tractors, plows, levelers) to prepare his land, rice seed for planting, fertilizer and insecticide to nurture and protect his crop, money to meet production costs and to sustain his family, and large amounts of water to irrigate his fields. Most of the goods to meet these needs are provided by two government agencies. The IAD office (staffed by the administrator, an assistant, a credit agent, and four inspectors) is responsible for obtaining and distributing seed and fertilizer, approving and distributing credit, and allocating the use of what common equipment the project has. Furthermore, through their control over seed and credit allocation, IAD officials often decide what type of rice will be planted when. The irrigation canals, all government-owned, are controlled by a local office of the Instituto Nacional de Recursos Hidraulicos (INDRHI), staffed by a chief inspector and three assistants. They control the allocation of water for both the small *parceleros* and the large rice growers: They grant permission for the use of water, open and lock the control gates, and fine those who use water without permission.

These administrative agencies thus have great potential power over the peasants, power which they often abuse for both personal and political ends; the peasants, excluded from any active participation in such administration, have little control over those who make crucial decisions affecting their production. Administrative power is commonly misused in the allocation of water. To insure access to water, the *parceleros* pay off the chief inspector, who then divides the money among his assistants. "He [the chief inspector] is a good boss," an assistant explained to me over rum one afternoon. "For every $5.00 he gets, he always gives us $2.00 or $3.00." Pedro, a *parcelero*, explained how he had obtained water the year before: "First, I greased the palms of the INDRHI inspector. I gave him $4.00. That was the first installment! And since I had no more money, I took the inspector to my plantain grove and gave him two bunches of plantains. And right away I had all the water I needed! The inspector said: 'Pedro's water, nobody is going to touch.' " Serious problems come when water is scarce (during dry spells or at times when everyone in the region is preparing his land and planting). Only the larger landowners (like the Rodríguez family) who are able to keep the inspectors well paid get the scarce water. "The Rodríguezes had the inspector bought. They would pass him $10.00 a week to make sure they would always have water. [How do you know this?] The inspector himself told me. And you know that the parcel holders in the agrarian reform project rarely have even $2.00 to give. So the parcel holders don't have water."

The power exercised by officials of the IAD is also frequently abused. Since 1967 fertilizer destined for the *parceleros* has "disappeared," sold by officials to warehouses and large landowners in the area; equipment (a tractor, a plow) "disappeared," sold to a tractor driver in a neighboring town by an IAD official who was finally "transferred" to another project after an investigation by a commission from IAD headquarters; sacks of harvested rice turned over to a credit agent to cover bank debts "disappeared" between the fields and the rice factories.

The administrative control of these government agencies presents even more serious problems for the *parceleros*. For example, the land granted to the *parceleros* is only granted "conditionally": Title can be canceled by the IAD at the recommendation of the project adminis-trator.[19] The provisional granting of titles was designed to prevent peasant misuse of land. Those who wanted land simply to sell to others or who did not farm their land could have their titles canceled; those tempted to sell land to meet ever present debts could not do so, for the land still belonged to the government. But this power to cancel land titles is often abused, and there are no procedural safeguards for the *parcelero* whose title is canceled. The IAD makes the final cancellation decision; the only way to appeal is to go directly to the capital to convince IAD officials to revoke the cancellation. One *parcelero* had his title canceled after he reported to the IAD office in the capital that the administrator of the project (a personal friend of the president-administrator of IAD) was selling small plots of agrarian reform land for housing sites. While I was there, a group of seven *parceleros* received cancellation notices. The administrator informed them that their debts to the Banco Agrícola (Agrarian Bank) were too great. Yet their debts were no greater than those of most other *parceleros*. More important, an employee of the local office admitted that they had received "word" from the capital that seven *parcelas* were "needed." One of them, it later turned out, was destined for the brother of a high official in the Corporación Estatal Azucarera (State Sugar Corporation).

But this administrative control over land has ramifications far beyond personal profit or patronage. In a region where an atmosphere of fear surrounds any "antigovernment" activity, the possibility of cancellation becomes an important tool for political control. Just as those without land are reluctant to support opposition parties for fear of never receiving land, those with land fear such activity will cost them the land they already have. A group of *parceleros* who tried to form an association to protect their rights were threatened with cancellation by the project administrator, a threat which proved a major factor in the dissolution of the group. Other *parceleros* who have opposed the government by supporting opposition parties have had their titles canceled, or been threatened with cancellation, for what one describes as *"razones políticas"* (political reasons). It is sometimes difficult to prove that political activity was the cause of cancellation, but even the belief that this is the reason reinforces hesitation to participate in such activity.[20] As we talked alone late one night, one *parcelero* explained that the government's land reform policy was a farce. Little land was actually being distributed ("just enough to keep people hoping"), and recipients were not given the money, equipment, fertilizer, or technical advice needed to make the land produce:

> The agrarian reform wasn't set up so that the peasant would be better off. It was set up to get votes. If they really wanted the peasant to get ahead, to better his life economically, they would give him land without waiting so long; they would give him enough credit so that he could use the land, and they would give it to him on time, when he needed it; and they would also give him the technical advice he needs.

But, he admitted, he and those who felt like him were hesitant to even vote for another party at election time:

> Here everyone knows who is against the government. And they could very easily take away the title to your parcel. They could invent some reason. And this parcel is the only hope that we have. For this reason, one is afraid to speak against him [the president] even though you're really hurting. You could go to him to criticize one of those shameless officials in the land reform office here—but only if you go as a united group. But here all the parcel holders are progovernment, even if in their hearts they're not.

Although the political uses of provisional titles and cancellations are not always explicit or public, attempts to discourage or eliminate autonomous peasant organizations which challenge government agency control are clear. Three attempts were made in Los Canales to form organizations publicly opposed to land reform policies and administration. The landless peasants who formed the first group in 1964 sought to organize community self-help projects and to inform the government of their land needs. When the first land was distributed in Los Canales, many of them were given titles by the president himself during a public ceremony. But when government officials came to assign *parcelas*, the few available were given to peasants from another community. Protesting that they had been given titles but no land, the peasants were publicly supported by the church-backed Federation of Peasant Agrarian Leagues (FEDELAC). FEDELAC transported them to the capital to protest to the newspapers and to officials at the IAD. In a paid advertisement in *Listín Diario*, a national daily, FEDELAC denounced the treatment of these peasants and went on to state "that the Dominican Agrarian Institute has served as a political instrument after 1963, ever since the antidemocratic *golpe* [coup] of September 25 put this institution into the hands of a political party that has been using it for its political campaign."[21] A few days later, three of the group's leaders were arrested and brought to the provincial capital for interrogation. They were told that it was dangerous to associate with FEDELAC, which was antigovernment and (thus) communist. Although soon released, neither they nor others in the group were anxious to continue their efforts.

In 1970, FEDELAC tried to organize an agrarian league in Los Canales to obtain land for the landless and to protect those who had already been given land against the injustices of government officials. Many were afraid to join. Despite FEDELAC's nonpartisan position, it was well known that agrarian leagues were still considered dangerous and antigovernment by the authorities. In some areas, their leaders had been arrested or murdered. The few local peasants who initially formed a provisional organizing group in Los Canales (in response to FEDELAC initiatives) disbanded soon after the local police began to make inquiries.

The third attempt is perhaps the most interesting. It was sponsored by an IAD promoter sent to the Los Canales project. But instead of organizing the *parceleros* into "self-help" projects as he had been trained to do, he began to organize a group that would, in the words of a member, "help us struggle for our rights." He told them that they had a right to administer the land reform project themselves, to have any official they did not approve removed, and to stop unjust cancellations. The administrator of the project began to pass the word that the promoter was a communist. "This administrator didn't want us to get together. He was raised under Trujillo and he did not want to know from nothing about meetings and associations and syndicates. And he was afraid of us. He threatened to cancel the titles on the parcels of all those who were involved with the association." Next, he requested an IAD commission to investigate the association the promoter was organizing. As a result, the promoter was "transferred." Those in the nascent group, uncertain of what to do without the promoter and fearful of losing their *parcelas*, ceased to meet. The organization, however, continued to exist on paper and a year later it began to meet again, now officially advised by a promoter from the government's Oficina del Desarollo Comunidad (Community Development Office, ODC). Its major focus was no longer on taking control of the administration of the local project, but on organizing road-building teams, getting a government loan for a tractor, and occasionally (without the support of the ODC promoter) protesting individual acts of injustice on the part of land reform officials.

The failures of the three attempts to organize autonomous peasant organizations and the co-optation of the last attempt are highlighted further by the two other groups that exist in Los Canales today: a mother's club and a youth club. Like the reformed parcel holders' association, they are officially advised by a promoter from the ODC; they are dependent on the government for technical assistance and financial support; and they are engaged in "self-help" projects which present no challenge to the structures of authority within the community. One peasant explained why only these kinds of organizations exist:

> The people are afraid they'll be called communists. For example, if I or anyone else tries to form a group through FEDELAC, it will fall apart. It's useless. You hear that there are FEDELAC leagues in such and such a place, but these don't function. People will join, but no one dares to take charge—so that they won't have trouble with the authorities, they just don't do it. The problem is that they'll accuse you falsely. They'll say that you're against the ideals of the government. And the ignorant peasants don't dare to get involved. Right now many people have an interest in organizations, but only through ODC, which is official. If it's not through ODC, it's almost impossible to organize. Here no group that is independent of the agrarian reform or the ODC is able to function. If you try to get together, you're sure to have some kind of problem. Because those in power are bound to spread some rumor. And for this reason, ODC controls all the groups here. Its the only organization that has any freedom!

The land reform of Los Canales did not seriously challenge the economic power of the large landowners, but it did change the situation of the few who received land. No longer did their lack of land force them to pay 50 percent of their gross earnings to the owner for whom they sharecropped, or to work for low wages in the fields of another. They had the chance to produce a cash crop whose potential yield held the promise of substantially improving their life chances. But the acquisition of land through land reform subjected the peasants to new forms of control. State administrative control over land, water, and materiel not only provided officials with private siphons for tapping peasant earnings but became a means for exercising low-cost political control over a peasantry which various leaders and groups tried to mobilize after the fall of Trujillo. Political opposition and autonomous peasant organization were easily discouraged, eliminated, or co-opted. Indeed, the new linking of everyday economic life directly to the state structured political action in important ways. The peasant who acquired land, or hoped to do so, was obligated to support the ruling party. Any economic problem involving actions of state officials might be given political meaning, and those who protested risked being branded as "antigovernment." The previous simple, face-to-face relations with landowners had been understood by the peasants, and those who wronged them were clearly identifiable; but the new system involved the peasant in a complex bureaucratic network in which he understood neither how decisions were made nor who was responsible for them. Political action was both diffused and defused. The peasants were continually involved in dealing with individual grievances against specific acts of state officials who claimed to be obeying the rules or following directives. There was little possibility for a political confrontation with the ruling party, and less that the political system as such would be challenged. For those without land, existing distribution was proof that someday they would get a plot if they were not labeled troublemakers; those with land were kept involved in continual battles over individual problems and no longer had a direct interest in any classwide action to broaden the distribution of land or challenge the government's land reform policies. But the new problems facing the *parcelero* are even more complex than these. Because his new form of production involves capital needs far greater than those he encountered as a sharecropper or day laborer, his dependence on those who control capital has increased dramatically.

Control Over Capital

The problems administrative control over land and water present the *parcelero* are compounded by his dependence on private and state sources for urgently needed capital. The expenses incurred in rice production (far greater than in coffee, tobacco, beans, or plantains) can be seen by examining the production needs of Mingo, a *parcelero* in the land reform project (table 1). In February, Mingo must prepare his seedbed (plowing a small area of land, buying and planting the seed, putting down insecticide and rat poison) and pay a tractor driver to plow his eight-acre *parcela*. Then in March, the plowed land must be carefully leveled and terraced, water obtained to cover the land, and the seedlings transplanted. In April, the land must be fertilized and treated with weed killers and insecticides. May brings expenses for weeding, water, rat poison, and fumigation against insects which attack the

Table 1. Monthly Income and Expenses for an Eight-Acre *Parcela*

	February		March		April
Major expenses			*Major expenses*		*Major expenses*
Production costs			Production costs		Production costs
Preparing seedbed			Leveling & terracing		Fertilizer $ 90.00
Paid labor	$ 3.00		Paid labor $104.00		Herbicide 20.00
Plowing	8.00		Water permit 27.00		Insecticide 17.00
Insecticide	2.00		"Gratuity" for inspector 5.00		Paid Labor 6.00
Rat poison	2.00		Transplanting seedlings 80.00		Food 42.00
Seeds	98.00		Food 42.00		Total expenses $175.00
Plowing *parcela*	175.00		Total expenses $258.00		
Food	42.00				
Total expenses	$330.00				
Major income			*Major income*		*Major income*
3 days hired labor	7.50		None		4 days hired labor 10.00
Total income	$ 7.50		Total income $ 0.00		Total income $ 10.00
Deficit	$322.50		Deficit $258.00		Deficit $165.00

	May		June		July	
Major expenses						
Production costs						
Paid labor	$ 48.00					
Rat poison	4.20					
Fumigation	10.00					
"Gratuity" for inspector	4.00					
None			$ 0.00			
Harvesting (cutting, threshing, transporting 148 sacks)					$234.00	
Food	42.00		42.00		42.00	
Total expenses	$108.20		$ 42.00		$276.00	
Major income						
None	0.00					
Sale of pig			35.00			
1 day hired labor			2.50			
Sale of rice					1,480.00	
Total income	$ 0.00		$ 37.50		$1,480.00	
Deficit / Surplus	Deficit $108.20		Deficit $ 4.50		Surplus $1,204.00	

maturing rice. In July (or sometimes August) the rice must be harvested. Production expenses for the first three months alone (beyond
Mingo's own labor) were $637. But in addition to these production
costs, Mingo must also care for his family. His expenses for food to feed
minimally his wife and five young children averaged about $42 a
month. (There were additional expenses for medicine, clothes, travel,
and ceremonial needs.) In the face of these expenses, Mingo's income
(from working as a day laborer and selling a pig) was woefully inadequate. For five of these six months he needed far more money than he
earned. Where did he get this needed capital?

One might suspect that a *parcelero* like Mingo, who has farmed for
three years, might have accumulated capital from past harvests. But like
over 80 percent of the *parceleros* in the Los Canales project, Mingo
started this harvest deeply in debt: he owed $913 from two previous
crop failures (one caused by drought; the other, by bad seed provided
by the IAD). To meet their capital needs, Mingo and the other *parceleros* can turn to two sources. One is the IAD in conjunction with the
government's Banco Agrícola. In principle, these agencies are committed to supply *parceleros* with seed, fertilizer, and money (at 8
percent interest), but in practice there are a number of serious problems
about which the peasants can do nothing. The distribution of needed
capital is entirely in the hands of government officials over whom they
have no power. One problem mentioned earlier is the abuse of such
administrative control: The private sale of fertilizer by officials means
that it is not available to the *parceleros* when they need it. Far more
serious, however, is the failure to give credit in sufficient amounts or at
the time needed to meet production expenses. Mingo's case is typical.
Not only was there insufficient fertilizer when he needed it in April,
but the first money he received from the bank ($460) came in late April.
By this time he had already needed $637 for production costs alone
and another $126 for food—a total of $763. The second bank loan
($290) arrived in late June. But on top of unmet earlier needs he
needed an additional $150.20 by this time ($66.20 for production
expenses and $84.00 for food).

Such difficulties arise year after year. To get needed capital, *parceleros* like Mingo must thus turn to private sources. Some food needs
can be met with credit from local stores. But the major sources of
production capital are either the small, local rice-processing factory or
the large rice *comprador* (buyer), a middleman who sells rice to the
major processing factories in the region. Mingo went to the *comprador*,
where he felt he could get cash more easily. In February he borrowed
$15 to help meet food expenses; in March, $70 to pay some of what he
owed to the laborers who helped him level and terrace; in April he

borrowed $10 more. Each loan was payable at harvest time with a 20 percent interest charge. (Thus the money borrowed in February and paid back six months later was effectively charged 40 percent annual interest; that borrowed in April, 60 percent.) The *comprador* dispatched a tractor to do Mingo's plowing, charging $.50 more per *tarea* than the cash price ($175 instead of $150). He also supplied Mingo with the needed insecticide, rat poison, herbicide, and fertilizer. The fertilizer cost Mingo $6.25 per sack, about $1.00 more than the price he would have paid if IAD had supplied it. Finally, it was the *comprador*, and not the bank, who paid the $234 harvesting costs.

The costs of the capital Mingo received from the *comprador* were, however, far greater than the interest charges and higher prices of plowing and fertilizer. The capital advanced obligated Mingo to sell his rice to this *comprador* at the latter's terms of sale. This control over marketing through control of capital often meant that Mingo suffered losses in at least three different ways. Commonly recognized by all the *parceleros*, these mechanisms for control were explained to me in detail by a former rice-factory buyer. First, the *parcelero* must accept a lower price for his rice as a cost for the credit and "help" given. Mingo had to sell his rice to the *comprador* for $14.25 per 120-kilo sack, while those rice growers who sold to the factory received $15.00. Second, the scales themselves are often fixed, with small pieces of lead inserted to plug holes bored out of the scale's weights. The final, and most serious, is the "fixing of the percentage." The price for rice is set per *fanega*, a *fanega* of rice normally being equivalent to 120 kilos of green rice containing 20 percent moisture. The rice, however, often contains more moisture, increasing its weight. Rice buyers adjust for this by determining the amount of moisture contained in the rice and then "increasing" the weight of a *fanega* accordingly: When rice has a moisture content greater than 20 percent, more than 120 kilos are needed to make a *fanega*. The profit comes in determining how much more. The buyers simply plunge their hands into the sacks, feel the rice, and declare the weight they will "give" to the *parcelero*. The *parceleros*' suspicion that they commonly lose a number of kilos in each *fanega* by an overestimation of the moisture content was confirmed by the former rice-factory buyer who explained why the factory does not use the accurate electronic measuring devices available for calculating moisture percentages:

These devices don't leave any profit for the factory. Analyzing the rice by hand always results in greater profits for the factory. When rice put in one of these devices registers 122 kilos, I could have put it at 125 or 130 kilos if I had just felt it in my hand. And its for this reason that the majority of the factories don't use these new devices, because the old way you can get five or six kilos more in each *fanega*. I often bought rice at 140 kilos a *fanega* that would have been only 125 kilos had I used one of these devices.

When Mingo finished his harvest, his net earnings on the sale of rice were $1,480. His debts for this harvest (to the bank, the *comprador*, the dry-goods store) totaled about $1,230. The $250 left would have been about enough to give his family food (but not clothes or medicine) for the six months until the February planting when he would begin to incur new debts, but he still owed the bank $913 plus interest from previous harvests. He hoped that next year's harvest would be better and that the bank would wait.

Although I have only briefly discussed the *parceleros*' problems in meeting their capital needs, it is clear that their lack of desperately needed capital subjects them to new forms of control and dependence beyond those involved simply with control over land. Land reform gave the *parceleros* some control over a plot of land, freeing them from the control often exercised by large landowners to whom they formerly had to pay rent or sell their labor. But these peasants still lack the capital needed to make that land produce. To get that capital, they frequently have to subject themselves to the control of a rapidly growing commercial elite with access to capital. A better alternative—a more efficient system of state-financed credits through the IAD and the Banco Agricola—might free the peasant from dependence on commercial elites, but it would tie him even more closely to the state, compounding the risks of corruption and political control already discussed.

The Church Response

The state-sponsored land reform program urged by the Dominican bishops yielded results in Los Canales not foreseen by these and other clerics. The creation of new forms of dependency on commercial elites and the incorporation of the peasants into the state bureaucratic apparatus made these peasants objects not simply of corruption but of new forms of economic and political control. The bishops themselves have recently begun to recognize such results and criticize their variance with Christian goals.

In 1972, five years after their initial statement on the peasant situation, they issued another entitled "Reflexiones y surgerencias pastorales sobre las leyes agrarias" ("Pastoral Reflections and Suggestions Regarding the Agrarian Laws"). This time they noted the "increase in state control over large peasant sectors" and criticized the politics and corruption in the administration of the agrarian laws:

It is evident that this greater control can be used to favor groups who support, and prejudice legitimate groups that oppose, the dominant political parties. It could also become a source of corruption. . . . The human being, created free and responsible, in the image of God, cannot be enslaved by other human beings or by institutions. This would be anti-Christian because it would be antihuman. . . . A system that in practice reduces to a minimum the participation of the peasant as an agent of his own destiny cannot be called anything but a technocratic dictatorship in the service of established political power.[22]

Further, the bishops criticized the failure of the state to encourage the autonomous "intermediary structures" between the state and individuals that they had called for in their first declaration. Within such groups, they argued, the peasant would realize "the fundamental rights that all men have . . . as subjects of their destiny and members of a community . . . to meet and to form themselves into associations with their fellow man." Peasants could help each other "in their efforts to improve themselves," could elect their own representatives, and could "exercise their rights."[23]

The bishops' recognition of certain "anti-Christian" results of the land reform program does not, however, probe the factors identified in the above analysis: the lack of resources needed by the peasants, the sources of power available to institutional structures such as IAD and INDRHI, and the military and bureaucratic sanctions available to discourage or destroy autonomous peasant organizations. Furthermore, no mention is even made of the new, post–land reform problems that are caused by peasant dependence on those who control capital.[24]

Instead, the bishops fall back on their own understanding of the world. They imply that the problems stem from the "mentality of men," the lack of consciousness in the ways men think about themselves and others. New structures fail because new men have not been created. It is when men fail to accept fundamental Christian principles (man as *"sujeto activo de su destino"* [active subject of his destiny] and *"miembro de una comunidad"* [member of a community]) that "quite probably even new laws and national plans adopted to promote the development of the country, might serve, *according to the mentality of those who direct them*, as instruments to maintain an oppressive order."[25] The bishops seem to be directing their declaration to the state in the hope that those who formulate and apply the agrarian laws will be guided in the future by more Christian principles. They suggest, for example, "a minimum of legal guarantees and above all recognition and support of autonomous peasant organizations." Peasants should be not only allowed, but encouraged, to form associations to take charge of each agrarian reform project. Agrarian laws should be administered with no "discrimination for political reasons," with no "party politics involved in their administration," and a clear understanding that the "so-called moral causes that can be used to separate a parcel holder from the project" will at no time affect "the free political choice of each person inside or outside the land reform projects."[26] If only the state would pass better laws, if only officials would recognize the Christian essence of men and work for the *bien común*, the difficulties would be solved.

It is difficult to question the bishops' position within their own framework: The failure of new or existing structures can always be explained by the lack of Christian consciousness among the men in them. Their approach, however, prevents them from raising the possibility that existing structures must be radically changed in order to change men, and from exploring the difficulties involved in creating the power to change such structures. Furthermore, the failure of any systematic conceptualization of the relations among power, conflict, structures of domination, and change does not encourage posing the questions needed to analyze the problems of land reform in Los Canales: What is the actual role of the state in the Dominican Republic? What kind of peasant organization is it likely to favor or oppose? What governmental bureaucracies direct land reform efforts? Who staffs these agencies? What criteria are used for the distribution of land? Who controls the administration of land, water, and capital, and how is this power used?

Beyond these fundamental political questions there is a crucial insight into the relation of the state to society that this framework misses but that the case of land reform makes painfully obvious. The state may actually be using social programs such as land reform as instruments to preempt the autonomous mobilization of peasants demanding basic structural reforms. Land reform may serve as a political tool for co-opting and controlling peasants by organizing them into isolated land reform projects and tying them directly to the state through control over land, water, and capital. Social scientists who have begun to perceive how corporatist structures are used by the state to control groups whose actual or potential demands might prove disruptive have encouraged the raising of important questions often missed by the church's conception of the state:[27] How does the state co-opt and control marginal groups (urban slum dwellers, rural peasants) and potential opponents "without destroying the basic structure of social and political domination?"[28] What is it about the economic class position of peasant groups which makes them dependent on the state both before and after land reform? Such questions indeed guided my analysis of the land reform in Los Canales, revealing a pattern that most of the activist clergy have been unable to understand within their own framework.

Such lack of understanding has two important consequences. The activist clergy can recommend few practical guidelines for corrective action even in the face of the problems they recognize. If their appeals to officials to act like Christians go unheeded, the very land reforms which they back will continue to incorporate the peasants into a state bureaucracy which fails to recognize their "Christian essence." But more important, the one major action guideline embedded in their framework—the formation of "intermediary groups" to allow "active participation" of peasants in decision-making and thus solve the problem of "the increase in state control"—ironically becomes another potential instrument for state "incorporation." Closer examination may help explain how this occurs.

Cooperatives

Within the activist theology, there is a simple if naive explanation for the peasants' failure to form these important "intermediary groups": a lack of Christian consciousness among the peasants themselves. Not surprisingly, then, church programs for *acción social*—actively encouraged by two Dominican bishops and a number of priests—have been directed toward promoting peasant *concientización*. The new catechism for adults and courses in "human promotion" have sought to make peasants aware that, as children of God, they are brothers bound by love to help each other. Such help is best given in community groups—cooperatives and agrarian leagues—in which each actively participates in improving his life by helping others do the same. Such groups prevent the *cosification* (the making into things) of the peasants as mere objects of change and prevent their exploitation by those who would deny them the life-giving material goods that God gave to all men. Men, made conscious of their Christian rights and duties, will organize the intermediary groups now lacking.

But here again there are certain problems with this position that are not immediately evident to activist clergymen exactly because their stress on consciousness and community rather than power and conflict puts blinders on them, and their conception of the state as guardian of the *bien común* does not raise the possibility of the state's use of corporatist structures to co-opt and control certain classes. One problem is that consciousness may not lead to action. Peasant fears (of loss of land or credit), rooted in existing structures of domination, may impede the formation of intermediary groups in spite of *concientización*. Another is that such action may be unsuccessful: The power of those opposing the peasants, and peasant lack of material resources and organizational skills, may destroy any organizational attempts.[29] But I wish to focus on yet another problem. Even when *concientización* is effective and intermediary groups of peasant "participants" are formed, the failure to consider either the power of existing institutional structures or the difficulties peasants have in creating power makes invisible this ironic consequence. The very groups which are seen as mediating between the individual and state are often forced to become dependent on the state—incorporating the peasants into a bureaucratic apparatus where they chance suffering the corruption and political control so deplored by the bishops—or fail. Here the example of the church-promoted cooperative in Jaida Arriba is instructive.

The coffee-growing peasants in the mountainous community of Jaida Arriba faced problems with middleman-merchants similar to those the Los Canales rice *parceleros* encountered with the rice factory and *comprador.* Needing money to sustain their families and meet coffee production costs, yet facing a near continual preharvest money shortage, these coffee growers were forced to turn to local *comerciantes* (merchants) for cash and credit (especially for food). But control over desperately needed capital gave the *comerciantes* a certain control over the coffee market. Peasants' urgent cash needs (to meet expenses of illness and death) a few months before the harvest enabled the merchants to buy coffee *a la flor* (before the harvest or, literally, at the flowering) for half its harvest value; peasants' needs for cash to pay harvesting costs allowed the *comerciantes* to make contracts at prices 10 percent below the market value; and obligations to sell harvested coffee to the merchant who had been advancing credit again forced peasants to accept prices below the market value. Further, the peasants' capital needs and credit obligations forced them to enter the coffee market through these local merchant-middlemen, preventing them from gaining access to significantly higher prices on the national coffee market.[30]

In late 1967, the bishop of the diocese and the parish priest began actively to encourage the peasants to form a marketing cooperative to gain better prices for their coffee and improve the economic condition of the community.[31]   Fidel, a Catholic layman from the municipal capital, agreed to help with the actual organization. Puro, a coffee-growing peasant in Jaida Arriba (and a former *comerciante*) was much taken by the bishop's promotion and, with the help of Fidel and a few peasants, began an intensive effort to organize a cooperative.

The cooperative strategy was to form an organization through which the peasants could save weekly to accumulate a capital fund with which they could protect their coffee from the losses of preharvest sale or obligation to the *comerciantes* and then sell it for the far higher national market prices. But there were many obstacles to such organization. The *comerciantes* expressed vociferous opposition to the cooperative—opposition that was influential, not only because of traditionally strong deference to the advice of these *sabios* (men who know), but because they exercised complete control over the credit needed for food and the cash needed for medical, ceremonial, and production expenses. There was also much distrust among the peasants (both toward outsiders like Fidel and toward themselves), and many were reticent to invest already scarce resources in the hands of men who might be out to deceive them. Further, the peasant leaders lacked basic organizational skills, knowing little of how to mobilize support, run meetings, or administer funds. Overcoming such obstacles was a long struggle. Organizational success depended heavily on good men: the administrative knowledge, patience, empathy, and pedagogical skills of Fidel; the deep trust most peasants had in Puro, and his innate intelligence and past experience as a *comerciante*. But it depended, too, on God's grace. The *comerciantes* never organized to use their potential economic power to withhold credit on food (an action that would have destroyed the cooperative at any time during its early months) but rather limited their initial opposition to moral suasion.

But organizational success in forming an "intermediary group" proved a limited victory. The peasants' economic class position did not give them the power to accumulate sufficient capital to break the control of the *comerciantes*. By harvest time, nine months after initial organization began, strenuous efforts by over thirty members to save money from their often scarce resources yielded a fund of only $2,000.00. This money (and the continued willingness of the *comerciantes* to advance credit for food) enabled them to protect their coffee against preharvest selling. But with these funds already circulating in small loans, there was no money to meet urgent harvest expenses (about $8,500 was needed simply to pay pickers) or to advance money desperately needed by members to pay the food debts which still obligated them to sell their harvested coffee to the *comerciantes*.[32] Meanwhile, the *comerciantes* were not only offering ready cash for coffee and reminding the peasants of their obligations to sell coffee to pay for food advanced on credit, but applying economic sanctions, too. They threatened to refuse future credit to anyone who sold coffee to the cooperative. Thus *concientización*, even when accompanied by successful organization, had not enabled the peasants to create the power they needed to break the control of the merchant-middlemen.

The cooperative had few places to turn for needed capital. Neither the large coffee-exporting houses (who financed the local *comerciantes*) nor the banks (which often financed the exporting houses) were willing to risk loaning money to a peasant organization. The only funds were those made available by the government's Instituto de Desarrollo y Crédito Cooperativo (Institute of Cooperative Development and Credit, Idecoop) and the Federación Nacional de Cooperativas Agropecuarias (National Federation of Agrarian Cooperatives, Fenacoop) funded by loans from Idecoop (which received its money from AID) and at that time directed by officials with close personal ties to the Idecoop directors. The cooperative had already received technical assistance from Idecoop and Fenacoop promoters for many months (for example, courses in cooperativism); and Fidel himself had been hired as an Idecoop promoter (a few months after he had begun working with the peasants) and officially been put in charge of the cooperative. To meet the cooperative's capital needs, Fenacoop offered a loan which the cooperative agreed to repay by marketing its coffee through Fenacoop. This coffee, Fenacoop promised, would be sold abroad, giving the peasants prices far higher than the exporting houses could offer on the national market. Fenacoop also specified that a 1 percent commission would be charged for the marketing, and 8 percent interest would be charged on the $40,000 loan.[33] But Fenacoop did not keep its oral promises.

Most seriously, the money did not arrive in the promised amounts (only $13,000 eventually came) or at the time agreed upon. Such limitations and delays, in the face of cash demands rigidly set by harvesting needs (ripe coffee needs immediate picking), threatened the cooperative's very existence. But there were other difficulties, too. When Puro went to Santiago to receive the first $4,000 payment, he discovered that the contract he was to sign set the marketing commission at 2 percent, made no mention of the interest to be charged on the loan, and, most seriously, set in advance the price Fenacoop would pay for cooperative coffee (despite Fenacoop's promises to pay prices received after marketing abroad). Puro called the president-administrator of Fenacoop in the capital, briefly discussed these problems, was told that the interest rate would be 11 percent, and received assurances not to worry. Anxious for the money, Puro signed the contract. The peasants, dissatisfied and suspicious, were nevertheless hesitant to act against the intelligent, well-placed, powerful city people who ran Fenacoop, the more so because they were dependent upon them for loans.

Fidel, however, encouraged them to protest, and he set up a meeting with Fenacoop officials in the capital. The peasants' criticism of the 11 percent interest rate brought a quick response from the Fenacoop auditor. The peasants must be mistaken; the interest was only 8 percent. He produced the account books as proof. Puro, turning to the president-administrator, then explained that this man had told him 11 percent on the phone, and that one of the Idecoop officials sitting at the meeting was present during the phone conversation and could confirm this. Puro described the embarrassing moments that followed for the administrator: "Perhaps the administrator wanted to take 3 percent for himself. I don't know. Even Fenacoop's administrative council didn't know. They were all sleeping. This was a very ugly thing—one thing on paper, and telling us something else." The administrator, insisting that there had been an error somewhere, agreed to write a new contract stating the interest rate at 8 percent and resolving the other difficulties.

But many other problems followed. The cooperative, for example, discovered that the higher prices Fenacoop had promised them they would receive by marketing abroad through Fenacoop were $1.50 to $2.00 less per quintal than the prices exporting houses were offering nationally; yet the cooperative was bound by contract to sell its coffee to Fenacoop to repay the loan. A potentially more serious difficulty was the pressure exerted on the cooperative by Idecoop and Fenacoop to formally affiliate with Fenacoop, to become part of the federation. Such affiliation not only meant that Fenacoop would handle the cooperative's marketing, but further required that 5 percent of the earnings be held by Fenacoop for use in making future loans. Idecoop was thus prodding a still somewhat autonomous peasant cooperative to become incorporated into a state-supported federation which would have complete control over its capital and marketing. Fidel, disobeying instructions from Idecoop, warned the cooperative leaders of the danger of giving capital to Fenacoop. He told them they should keep the 5 percent in their own fund to use when and how they chose. When the leaders refused to affiliate, Fidel openly defended them.

Throughout that year Fidel's criticism of Fenacoop's policies became ever more open, despite pressures from his employer, Idecoop, to lead "his" cooperative into the fold. Fidel came to believe that Fenacoop was a fiefdom, not a federation, that it was treating the peasants unfairly, and perhaps even intentionally trying to deceive them. He was joined in his criticisms by another promoter and the director of the local Idecoop office. The promoter was fired; the Idecoop official, transferred. An Idecoop functionary warned Fidel that he would lose his job if he did not bring the cooperative into the federation and stop attacking Fenacoop. Fidel was not quieted. That he did not lose his job was due to a special set of circumstances: a former friendship with the president-administrator of Idecoop (who had once worked with him in politics) and intercession on his behalf by the bishop.

The cooperative's success in maintaining some autonomy during its early years owed much to the actions of Fidel. His primary loyalty was to the peasants he was organizing and not to the state agency that employed him. But there is an important aspect of Fidel's behavior that should be noted. The ideological framework which oriented him was distinctively different from that of the bishop and priest who enlisted his support in organizing the cooperative. Although he fully embraced the Christian humanism of their activist theology and was himself a devout Catholic, he saw the new theology chiefly as a tool for mobilizing the peasants. It is important that he realized that simply motivating the peasants to act was a limited victory. A former buyer of peasant crops and once active in opposition politics, Fidel had a clear understanding of the structure of power exercised by local middlemen, banks, exporting houses, and government agencies. He viewed peasant problems, not as the products of evil men, but as the results of a profit-based economic system and a paternalistic, corruption-ridden political system. He always doubted the possibilities of cooperative success in such a system but hoped that even a failure would give the peasants organizational skills and a critical understanding of the system. Yet each time the cooperative faltered, he stepped in, explaining to the peasants what was happening and helping them work out a strategy. Such strategies involved far more than the *concientización* suggested by the church's position. We have seen that he helped them understand and protest actions of Fenacoop officials; he explained the dangers of incorporation into Fenacoop and actively defended the peasants' refusal to join. In other years, he used personal connections in exporting houses to help the cooperative get the capital needed to survive when loans from Idecoop failed to arrive on time. But perhaps most important, he used his personal contacts, political knowledge, and economic know-how to help the cooperative achieve more autonomy from national exporters and government agencies by gaining direct access to foreign markets. How the cooperative did this is instructive. It emphasizes that what little room there is for creating autonomous peasant organization depends on men oriented toward action beyond the mere formation of "intermediary groups," with skills much greater than those needed for *concientización*, and with access to sources of power far beyond the local community.

Fidel first began to explore the possibility of marketing coffee directly to Europe (avoiding both national exporting houses and Fenacoop) in late 1970. He was assisted by a personal friend, the head of a large, Dominican-based, European trading firm, who offered to make contact with coffee buyers in Europe. Samples of cooperative coffee were soon sent off to a prospective buyer.

That same year Idecoop offered to help the cooperative meet its capital needs with a $35,000 loan. At a grand ceremony in Santiago—replete with lunch, photographers, and smiling government officials—

the terms of the loan agreement were read to representatives of various cooperatives. Based on what they (and Fidel) heard, the leaders of the Jaida Arriba Cooperative signed the contract without reading it themselves. Officials from Idecoop and another cooperative federation (Federación de Cooperativas para el Mercadeo del Tabaco, Fetab) also encouraged the cooperatives to export their coffee abroad through Fetab. For a $3 per *quintal* (100 pounds) commission, Fetab offered to provide them with access to the international market. Direct export without Fetab would be difficult, the officials told the peasants, because it would take them at least three months to get an export license.

The $3 commission seemed strange to the cooperative leaders: It was twice as much as a commercial exporting house had just asked them for the same service. But things proved stranger still. A few weeks after receiving the Idecoop loan, the cooperative received a firm offer to sell coffee directly to Europe. A lawyer (a close friend of Fidel's who also worked for the European trading firm) began to make the necessary arrangements. He found that the export license could be obtained in one day by going to the capital and requesting it. But a serious obstacle did appear a few days later at an Idecoop gathering when Fidel informed other Idecoop officials of the cooperative's intention to export directly. He was informed that this was impossible, because the loan contract signed with Idecoop had committed the cooperative to pay back the loan by exporting exclusively through Fetab. Fidel denied this, for he himself had heard the contract read, but a copy was produced which indeed contained the restrictive clause. Fidel immediately contacted the lawyer of the trading house. The lawyer protested directly to the president-administrator of Idecoop in the capital. A few days later an editorial (written by the lawyer) appeared in the Santiago daily denouncing Idecoop (and indirectly Fetab) as new middlemen:

> In other words, no institutions of any kind, even those that exist to encourage cooperatives, can be permitted to substitute themselves for the role of the old middleman because the situation of the producer will simply continue to be the same. It is necessary that the producer at all times maintain his freedom to sell his harvest abroad directly, without any interference.[34]

After a complex series of events, such pressure proved successful and the restrictive clause was withdrawn.

These few examples of the many difficulties the cooperative had with agencies such as Idecoop, Fenacoop, and Fetab illustrate a central problem. Those upon whom the cooperative depended for urgently needed capital to break the control of local middlemen threatened to become middlemen themselves. The administrative control they had over capital did not simply allow the possibility that corruption would bring severe economic losses to the cooperative, but came to threaten the very survival of the cooperative itself. The success the cooperative had in maintaining some autonomy in the face of such control was largely the result of Fidel's active defense of the cooperative against these agencies and federations and his access to alternative sources of power. But such action is rarely successful in the Dominican Republic. The threats of dismissal that Fidel often faced have been carried out against other promoters. More seriously, cooperatives, dependent upon government promoters for administrative training and access to capital, are not likely to find many willing to risk their jobs by taking sides against their employer.

There are also important political implications here. The control exercised by state agencies such as Idecoop also gives them potentially great political power. All Idecoop promoters, for example, were expected to campaign actively among their cooperatives for the reelection of the ruling Partido Reformista and president (who, incidentally, personally signs the "incorporation" papers of each cooperative). They were further expected, according to an official memorandum, to hand over 2 percent of their salaries to the Reformist party for social services. The control over the promoters can be extended more directly to control over the peasants. One can imagine the potential for sanctions against a cooperative whose leaders actively support an opposition party. As hacienda owners once used indebtedness to incorporate individual Indians into the capitalist economic system, now the state can use the credit needs of "intermediary groups" to incorporate peasants into the political system.

Conclusion

The social reforms urged by the Dominican church face a serious dilemma: They fail whether they succeed or not. While the church puts its faith in the state to pass laws which will redistribute land and allow the formation of autonomous peasant groups, either the state does little, or the land it redistributes and the groups it encourages enable it to incorporate the peasants into a bureaucratic state system permitting widespread corruption and new forms of political-economic control, both antithetical to the goals of the church.

Activist clergy have begun to recognize such failures, but the framework that orients them hinders both an adequate understanding of the problems and the development of strategies for action. We saw earlier that the framework's failure either to conceive of the use of corporatist structures by the Dominican state or to deal with structural questions of power limited the bishops' ability to understand the often anti-Christian results of land reform. Now we have seen that the major *acción social* strategy this framework suggests for solving such problems encourages, ironically, further state control and corruption. The cooperative in Jaida Arriba, an intermediary group based on the active participation of peasants who had been *concientizadó (made conscious)* was itself unable to create the power needed to break the control of the local middlemen; to survive, it had to turn to state agencies and face the dangers of incorporation and control by these new, national "middlemen."

Conceiving of the state as a powerful bureaucratic apparatus which might seek to organize certain classes and groups into corporate structures in order to co-opt and control them would help make sense of consequences which seem like anomalies to activist clergy who see the world in terms of community and *concientización* and call on the state to serve the interests of the *bien común*. They might see, for example, that the state views the potential mobilization of peasants into autonomous organizations (such as those encouraged by the church) as a threat and is likely to respond by either preemptively organizing the peasants or co-opting autonomous organizational efforts. State agencies and state-supported federations (like ODC, Idecoop, Fenacoop, and Fetab) might then appear as instruments for organizing the peasants into groups before they organize themselves or are organized by others. It would thus seem to be no accident that parcel holders' associations and peasant cooperatives supported by the state were vertically tied to the state bureaucracy and subject to economic and political control. It would be clear that any attempt to organize independently of the state—such as the church-sponsored cooperative in Jaida Arriba—would continually face the dangers of co-optation. And if the state ever did give peasant associations "participation" in the local administration of land reform projects, the clergy who continually call for "active participation" would want to withhold their praise until they asked: Who organized these associations? Who finances them? What kind of power do they have to do what? If the state has set up and financed peasant associations which allow those in land reform projects to organize the distribution of water and fertilizer but give them little control over the distribution of land (how much, to whom?), the cancellation of titles, or the management of credit, then serious doubts must be raised about the adequacy of such "participation." If the activist clergy asked the question "Who does the state seek to incorporate, when, and how?" such problems and dangers would come more sharply into focus, and strategies for coping with them could at least be discussed.

Co-optation through incorporation into state-dependent organizations is normally a simple matter: not only do cooperatives (and other such peasant organizations) need legal state recognition (for example, a charter signed by the president on the recommendation of Idecoop), but they desperately need credit and technical assistance normally available only from the state, or from a state-supported cooperative "federation" which each cooperative is "encouraged" to join. That the Jaida Arriba Cooperative was able to maintain some limited autonomy (refusing federation into Fenacoop, bargaining over the terms of credit arrangements) was due to unusual but significant factors: The cooperative organizer was initially enlisted by the church, not the government; he had an understanding of the structural obstacles to organization and the dangers of the state very different from the activist Catholic theology; and he had personal friends with access to alternative sources of power (credit lines at banks, foreign marketing contacts, the media) which the cooperative could use to gain some independence.

Fidel's limited success does not provide the activist clergy with any certain strategy for future action. But the ways in which he acted outside the guidelines offered by their framework point to the dangers of ignoring structural questions of power and the corporatist structures of the state. Continuing simply to encourage *concientización* and active participation in community-based intermediary groups will not produce autonomous organizations which stand between the individual and the state and make peasants "subjects of their own destiny." Either such organizations will blindly crash against existing institutional structures or they will pay a high cost for salvation: incorporation and control by the state.

NOTES

1. Bartolome de las Casas, quoted in Eugene H. Korth, S. J., *Spanish Policy in Colonial Chile* (Stanford: Stanford University Press, 1968), p. 15.

2. Conferencia del Episcopado Dominicano, "Reflexiones y sugerencias pastorales sobre las leyes agrarias," *Estudios Sociales*, 6 (1973):62. This and subsequent translations are my own.

3. Second General Conference of Latin American Bishops (CELAM), *The Church in the Present-Day Transformation of Latin America in the Light of the Council*, vol. 2 (Bogota: General Secretariat of CELAM, 1970), p. 62.

4. Conferencia, "Reflexiones y sugerencias pastorales," p. 59.

5. CELAM, *The Church in the Present-Day Transformation*, vol. 2, p. 60.

6. Vatican Council II, *Gaudium et Spes*, p. 68, quoted in CELAM, *The Church in the Present-Day Transformation*, vol. 1, p. 140.

7. CELAM, *The Church in the Present-Day Transformation*, vol. 2, p. 58.

8. Ibid., p. 58.

9. Ibid., p. 63.

10. Kenneth E. Sharpe, "From Consciousness to Control: The Politics of a Dominican Peasant Movement" (Ph.D. dissertation, Yale University, 1974).

11. CELAM, *The Church in the Present-Day Transformation*, vol. 1, p. 42.

12. Ibid., vol. 2, p. 59.

13. "Declaración Conjunta del Episcopado Dominicano sobre la situación campesina," *Estudios Sociales*, 1 (1968):62.

14. Ibid., pp. 38, 36.

15. Indeed, the bishops actually exhorted the large landowners to act as Christians: "We remind the landlords of the grave responsibility they have not to block a fundamental agrarian reform and to show themselves willing to make available their lands for settlement of poor peasants" (ibid., p. 63).

16. Ibid., p. 61.

17. Ibid., p. 62.

18. This argument has actually been made by a Dominican Jesuit priest who recognizes the church's failure to consider the problem of power. José Luis Alemán criticizes the "path" suggested by the church for reforming land tenure: the introduction of appropriate legislation *by means of the state*. This solution "portrays a notable lack of practical realism":

> The modern state, especially in Latin American countries, is not some olympic state which is above all pressures of parties or special interests and attentive only to the common good.
> If it is true that the large landowning interests control or restrict the state's freedom of action, how can those who control public power bring about a legal reform which distributes land? The frequent pleas directed at the "rich" and the "powerful men of land" (*Gaudium et Spes*, p. 69; *Populorum Progressio*, p. 32; *The Speech of Paul VI to the Peasants*, Bogota, August 23, 1968) that they set aside their egoistic attitudes suggests, on the one hand, that the church is conscious of this problem, but, on the other hand, it suggests that the church has too much confidence in the "moral message" as the ultimate instrument of change.

He then argues that the "great instrument of change for introducing daring legislation on rural property" is the "peasant syndicates." (Note that his emphasis is on introducing legislation.) And he criticizes both "the formation of cooperatives" and "peasant cultural promotion" as being inadequate substitutes for "syndicate action" (José Luis Alemán, "La reforma agraria y la doctrina social de la Iglesia," *Estudios Sociales*, 1 [1968]:126–27).

19. The relevant articles are found in the Agrarian Reform Law no. 5879, April 27, 1962, as cited by Martin Clausner in *Rural Santo Domingo: Settled, Unsettled, and Resettled* (Philadelphia: Temple University Press, 1973), p. 381:

> Article 38. The distribution of parcels to the petitioners will be accomplished as indicated below by means of a conditional sales contract at the price, period of payment and under conditions which the Institute considers most reasonable, and in the manner provided by its regulations. . . .
> Article 43. The Institute will be empowered to revoke the rights conceded with respect to a parcel on the following grounds:
> a. Use of the parcel for purposes incompatible with the Agrarian Reform;
> b. Unjustified abandonment of the parcel or his family by the parcelero. In the latter case the Institute is empowered to award the farm to the wife or children, whichever in the opinion of the Institute has the greatest capacity and ability to comply with the requisites established by this law, and with the contract.
> c. Manifest negligence by the owner, demonstrated by his incapacity to work the farm, permitting the decline of its resources and the destruction of its improvements.

   d. Failure to comply, without justification, with the obligations contracted in
the conditional sales contract.

   20. It is erroneous to think of Los Canales as a community seething with
antigovernment sentiment kept just below the surface by clever manipulation of a
land reform program. On the contrary, many support the government exactly
because they see it as their only hope to gain needed land, or feel gratitude to the
president for having granted them a *parcela* (he personally signed and distributed
many of the provisional titles). But those who oppose land reform policy or would
support an opposition party are quite conscious of the dangers.
   21. *Listin Diario*, February 14, 1965.
   22. Conferencia, "Reflexiones y sugerencias pastorales," pp. 57–58.
   23. Ibid., pp. 58–59.
   24. At other times, at least some of the bishops and priests have recognized the
role cooperatives might play in overcoming the difficulties with *compradores*. But
here it is clear that the ways land reform might encourage new forms of domination
based on control of capital are not perceived.
   25. Conferencia, "Reflexiones y sugerencias pastorales," p. 60. Emphasis added.
   26. Ibid., pp. 58–61.
   27. See, for example, Bo Anderson and James D. Cockcroft, "Control and
Cooptation in Mexican Politics," in *Latin American Radicalism*, ed. Irving Louis
Horowitz, Josué de Castro, and John Gerassi (New York: Vintage Books, 1969),
pp. 366–89; Thomas E. Skidmore, "Politics and Economic Policy Making in
Authoritarian Brazil, 1937–71," in *Authoritarian Brazil*, ed. Alfred Stepan (New
Haven: Yale University Press, 1973), pp. 31–37; Philippe C. Schmitter, *Interest
Conflict and Political Change in Brazil* (Stanford: Stanford University Press, 1971),
chap. 5 and pp. 383–86; and chapters 3 and 10 in this volume. The literature is
often unclear on whether the state itself is to be conceived as corporatist (often
implying that all classes and groups are commonly tied to the state through
corporatist forms of organization) or whether corporatism is relevant only for some
classes and groups in society. The latter usage allows important empirical questions
to be raised such as: Which groups or classes are organized corporatively? Who
organized them? What are their particular relations to the state? In this essay I have
avoided referring to a "corporatist state" or a "corporatist regime" and instead
refer to the state's use of "corporatist structures."
   28. Philippe C. Schmitter, "Paths to Political Development in Latin America,"
in *Changing Latin America*, ed. Douglas Chalmers (New York: The Academy of
Political Science, 1972), p. 97.
   29. Such problems are discussed more thoroughly in Sharpe, "From Consciousness to Control," esp. chap. 9.
   30. A detailed analysis of peasant needs and the structure of middleman control
on the international, national, and local levels in the coffee market may be found in
Sharpe, "From Consciousness to Control," chaps. 2–4.
   31. The following year a position paper at the Medellin conference was to
argue: "Cooperatives, through the unification of many small resources, are able to
assume the strength found in the voice of the rich" (CELAM, *The Church in the
Present-Day Transformation*, vol. 1, p. 143).
   32. The peasants could not simply harvest their coffee and immediately sell it
for the cash to pay off the merchants because there was a one-to-three-month lag
before the cooperative processed (dried and hulled) a member's coffee and finally
sold it. It should also be noted that yet another $6,000 to $8,000 was needed for
processing and transportation costs.

33. This loan was to cover not only the more than thirty members of the Jaida Arriba Cooperative but approximately fifty more peasants in two other regional cooperatives (organized by the church and Fidel) which had affiliated with the Jaida Arriba Cooperative.

34. *La Información*, December 19, 1970.

DAVID SCOTT PALMER

12
The Politics of Authoritarianism in Spanish America

Students of Latin American politics have increasingly tried to come to grips with the phenomenon of persistent authoritarian modes of political activity there. Various explanations have been advanced. One is concerned with the Iberic heritage of a lengthy colonial experience.[1] Proponents of this explanation argue that authoritarian patterns of postindependence politics may be traced to the depth of penetration of authoritarian institutions of the *madre patrias* of Spain and Portugal during two hundred and fifty to four hundred years of colonial domination. The persistence of authoritarian politics in most countries thus reflects to an important degree the persistence of the colonial heritage. The "stability of instability" is a manifestation of the incongruity between underlying authoritarian social and cultural patterns imposed through the colonial experience and the liberal democratic ideology and political institutions which leaders of most newly independent nations tried to graft on the body politic. Therefore, it follows that the closer the new nation was to the core areas of Hispanic colonial penetration, the less likely such incongruent institutional innovations were to succeed.

A second explanation for authoritarian politics in Latin America emphasizes dependency.[2] Most governments of Latin America are severely constrained by international market forces over which they have little control. This is because they depend on tax revenues generated by exports of one or a very small number of primary products, and on external sources for loans and investments. These governments are further affected by the predominantly externally oriented asymmetrical growth generated by the processes of delayed dependent development.[3] The more dependent the nation has been, therefore, the more unstable and the more authoritarian its political structures and processes.

A third explanation of Latin American authoritarianism has to do with the multiple processes of social mobilization.[4] As change, largely induced from abroad, has reordered the lives of individuals, groups, and classes within each country, people's demands on their government increase. If governments are unable to meet, channel, or redirect these demands—or at least offer reasonable expectations of being able to do so in the near future—they are subject to severe strains. Authoritarian solutions, often brought about by military coups, are frequently sought to handle the destabilizing effects of social mobilization or political modernization. Thus, the higher the levels of social mobilization and the more rapid the rates of change, the more unstable and authoritarian the government is likely to be.

A principal objective of this chapter is to determine how strongly these three explanations of authoritarian politics in Latin America are in fact supported. It will also provide greater detail about the historical evolution of authoritarianism in one South American country, Peru, with particular emphasis on the military government there since 1968.

Authoritarianism

The most widely used definitions of authoritarianism include social and cultural as well as political elements. Juan Linz, for example, defines authoritarian regimes as "political systems with limited, not responsible political pluralism; without elaborate and guiding ideology (but with distinctive mentalities); without intensive nor extensive political mobilization (except at some points in their development); and in which a leader (or occasionally a small group) exercises power within formally ill-defined limits but actually quite predictable ones."[5] For our purposes, a more limited, more strictly political definition of authoritarianism is required. A number of possibilities suggest themselves. One is, quite simply, nonelected governments, or governments which are formally elected but without legal or effective opposition. Another is the degree to which coups d'état have imposed onto the political order de facto rather than de jure governments. A third encompasses the relative importance of the military establishment as a consumer of state resources. A fourth is a more specific type of nonelected government, military rule. Yet another indicator suggests the degree to which the executive branch of government has predominated over the legislative branch.

The historical data compilation efforts of Arthur Banks and others [6] make possible the construction of such a political definition of authoritarianism comprising the components just noted. Furthermore, it may be compiled for each Latin American country during the entire postindependence period. A first attempt is made in table 1 to combine these five indicators of authoritarianism and come up with an overall rank ordering of the Spanish American countries. This information may then be compared with similar rankings for our other hypothesized independent indicators: Hispanic colonial penetration, dependency, and social mobilization. A preliminary assessment may then be made regarding the degree to which these indicators relate to levels of authoritarianism in Spanish America.

Colonial Penetration

Any attempt to gather basic information reflecting the relative degree of colonial penetration in the various Latin American countries is hampered by a number of factors. Records are often incomplete and sometimes contradictory. The colonial administrative units do not always match the postindependence national boundaries. Some information may be obtained only by intensive examinations of primary sources in Seville, Mexico, or Lima. The present effort is a preliminary attempt to flesh out with concrete and comparative data the concept of colonial penetration.[7]

An underlying assumption in this effort is that Spain's colonization of the New World was anything but uniform. The variations in the depth of colonial penetration depended on such factors as the presence of precious metals, large concentrations of manageable native populations, proximity to principal navigation routes, and the like. Twelve indicators highlight these variations in the degree of Spanish colonial penetration.

1. Stages of effective occupation:[8] to suggest the varying lengths of Spanish rule of different parts of the New World.

2. Founding of capital cities:[9] a significant feature of Spanish occupation, given the importance the colonizers gave to the founding of capital cities "as outpost(s) of foreign politico-economic control . . . [to] dominate . . . its . . . regional hinterland."[10] The longer the city had been established, the longer it was in a position to dominate the surrounding countryside.

3. Type of administrative center established:[11] The importance which the Spanish attached to a region is reflected in the kind of center established—viceroyalties to the most important areas, followed by captaincies-general presidencies, and, finally, those frontier areas under the jurisdiction of a provincial governor.

4. Date of establishment of administrative centers:[12] suggesting the length and depth of control exercised over an area by the colonial administrative system.

Table 1. Authoritarianism

Country	Nonelective Rule[a] Rank	Ratio	Coups d'état[b] Rank	Ratio	Importance of Military[c] Rank	%	Military Ruled[d] Rank	Ratio	Executive Predominance[e] Rank	Ratio	Overall Rank[f]
Argentina	6	28.0	13	18.8	9.5	18.2	14	4.7	12	38.6	12
Bolivia	3	33.4	2	6.7	1	26.8	1	32.6	11	42.6	2
Chile	12	16.2	10	13.5	7	21.0	7	10.8	16	18.2	11
Colombia	15	11.6	9	13.4	11	18.1	8	8.2	14	29.9	13
Costa Rica	16	7.0	11.5	18.3	17	6.7	17.5	0	15	19.5	17
Cuba	4	32.3	16	21.8	14	13.3	13	6.2	2	83.1	9.5
Dominican Republic	1	50.0	8	11.0	3	22.5	10	6.8	3	72.8	4
Ecuador	9	19.9	6	8.1	6	21.2	15	3.7	6	61.8	8
El Salvador	10	18.8	7	10.7	9.5	18.2	2	32.0	9	47.7	7
Guatemala	13	14.4	14	19.1	13	14.1	16	2.6	10	44.4	15
Honduras	5	28.1	5	8.0	8	19.5	11.5	6.3	4	65.6	6
Mexico	11	17.8	4	7.0	4	21.4	3	29.5	8	53.4	5
Nicaragua	17	6.3	11.5	18.3	12	16.4	11.5	6.3	13	35.9	14
Panama	18	3.2	18	31.6	18	6.2	17.5	0	18	1.6	18
Paraguay	2	36.8	3	6.7	2	22.8	9	7.1	1	85.2	1
Peru	7	26.9	1	6.6	5	21.3	5	11.7	5	62.8	3
Uruguay	14	11.6	17	23.3	16	11.5	6	11.6	17	14.5	16
Venezuela	8	25.0	15	19.5	15	12.6	4	15.5	7	56.6	9.5

Note: In cases where countries with identical ratios have been assigned different ranks, the identity is due to rounding.
a. Number of years executive *not elected*/number of years since independence (to 1966), from Arthur Banks, *Cross-Polity Time-Series Data* (Cambridge: MIT Press, 1971), Segment 1, Field E.
b. Number of years since independence/number of coups, from Banks, *Cross-Polity Time-Series Data*, Segment 1, Field E.
c. Average military expenditures as a percentage of total budget of selected years, 1865–1963, from Banks, *Cross-Polity Time-Series Data*, Segment 3, Field E.
d. Banks categories of military or military-civilian governments, number of years since independence, from *Cross-Polity Time-Series Data*, Segment 1, Field D.
e. Banks categories of no legislature or ineffective legislature/number of years since independence, from *Cross-Polity Time-Series Data*, Segment 1, Field O.
f. Derived by combining the rank orders for each variable.

5. Date of establishment of *audiencias*:[13] suggesting the length and depth of control exercised over an area by the colonial judicial system.

6. *Audiencia* budgets and salaries:[14] to indicate the importance Spain attached to the various parts of the New World empire in terms of financial support for the judicial system.

7. Bullion production:[15] Those areas which produced the lifeblood of the empire would in all likelihood be more closely controlled and regulated than those which did not.

8. Church bishopric revenues:[16] an indication of the strength of the church establishment in different parts of the empire, hence of the degree to which this institution penetrated the fabric of colonial Latin American societies.

9. Major city populations:[17] The more importance attached to a particular area by Spain, the larger the population attracted to that region's urban centers.

10. Total population:[18] As vital to the crown and the church as natural resources were the human resources of an area. Therefore, a larger total population suggests greater administrative concern and control.

11. Population density: to suggest the degree of occupation of each specific area.

12. Total trade (exclusive of precious metals):[19] an indication of levels of commercial activity of different parts of the empire in addition to the obvious importance attached to precious metals.

Table 2 presents these various pieces of information for each subsequently independent nation in Spanish America and combines them for an overall rank order. This order may then be compared with the rank order derived for authoritarianism for a first approximation of the strength of the hypothesis that depth of colonial penetration and postindependence political institutions are directly related.

The Spearman rank order correlation between colonial penetration and authoritarianism is .35, which is significant at the .05 level.

Two cases deviate sharply in their comparative ranks: Guatemala (which ranks third in colonial penetration and fifteenth in authoritarianism) and Paraguay (which ranks seventeenth in colonial penetration and first in authoritarianism). Paraguay is most clearly a very exceptional case. There was a very strong Jesuit influence during most of the colonial period. The postindependence experience was marked by the devastating war with Brazil, Argentina, and Uruguay during which over half of the nation's population was killed, including almost 90 percent of the men.[20] As for Guatemala, it appears that the authoritarianism indicators used do not adequately reflect its prevalence, because the country has been ruled by dictatorships during

Table 2. Spanish Colonial Penetration

Country	Stages of Effective Occupation		Founding of Capital Cities		Type of Admin. Center		Date Admin. Center Established		Date Audiencias Established		Audiencia Budgets and Salaries	
	Rank	Stages[a]	Rank	Year	Rank	Type[b]	Rank	Date[c]	Rank	Date[d]	Rank	Amt.[e]
Argentina	18	3, 6	17	1580	12	4, 3, 1	13	1590	14	1661	5	42,726
Bolivia	12.5	2, 3	12	1538	14.5	3	10	1549	11	1559	3	53,470
Chile	16	2, 3, 6	14	1541	5.5	2	18	1778	13	1609	4	53,460
Colombia	7	1, 2, 3	12	1538	3	2, 1	11.5	1563	10	1549	9.5	36,300
Costa Rica	7	2	15	1560	11	2D	7	1527D	9	1543D	15	36,300
Cuba	2	1	12	1538	5.5	2	16	1764	18	1797	18	36,300D
Dominican Republic	2	1	1	1494	14.5	3	1	1500	1	1526	9.5	36,300
Ecuador	12.5	2, 3	8.5	1535	14.5	3	11.5	1563	12	1563	9.5	36,300
El Salvador	7	2	7	1528	8	2A	4	1527A	6	1543A	12	36,300A
Guatemala	7	2	5	1524	5.5	2	3	1527	5	1543	9.5	36,300
Honduras	7	2	5	1524	9	2B	5	1527B	7	1543B	13	36,300B
Mexico	12.5	2, 3	3	1522	1.5	1	8	1535	2	1527	2	94,000
Nicaragua	7	2	5	1524	10	2C	6	1527C	8	1543C	14	36,300C
Panama	2	1	2	1519	14.5	3	2	1510	3	1535	16.5	23,200
Paraguay	12.5	2, 3	10	1537	18	4	15	1700	16	1661B	7	42,726B
Peru	7	2	8.5	1535	1.5	1	9	1544	4	1542	1	105,000
Uruguay	17	4	18	1726	17	3A	14	1661	15	1661A	6	42,726A
Venezuela	15	2, 3, 4	16	1567	5.5	2	17	1773	17	1786	16.5	23,200

Country	Bullion Production		Church Bishopric Revenues		Major City Pop.		Total Pop.		Pop. Density		Total Trade		Total	
	Rank	Amt.[f]	Rank	Amt.[g]	Rank	No.[h]	Rank	No.[i]	Rank	Per km2[j]	Rank	Amt.[k]	Average	Rank
Argentina	6	1,046	8	10	8	38	10	330	18	0.3	4	5,790	11.08	13
Bolivia	3	4,600	2	73	5	49	4	1,100	12	2.6	6	2,807	7.92	4.5
Chile	7.5	1,000	13	5	9.5	30	9	440	16	1.5	11	1,700	10.58	12
Colombia	4	2,990	6	14	11	28	2	2,000	7	4.6	12	1,699	7.92	4.5
Costa Rica	15	0	16.5	3	14	20	17	59	9	3.0	14	895	12.38	16
Cuba	11	17	7	12	2.5	80	7	553	2	12.5	2	19,294	8.58	7
Dominican Republic	15	0	11.5	6	13	22	14	104	5	5.5	10	2,060	8.00	6
Ecuador	15	0	4.5	18	4	70	6	564	6	5.2	9	2,092	9.46	9
El Salvador	7.5	1,000	16.5	3	15.5	15	12	222	1	26.8	8	2,300	8.67	8
Guatemala	10	200	9.5	8	12	25	8	507	3	12.1	7	2,369	7.04	3
Honduras	5	2,000	16.5	3	7	40	15	94	14	2.2	13	1,350	9.67	11
Mexico	1	23,000	1	131	1	137	1	5,837	4	7.7	1	25,350	3.25	1
Nicaragua	15	0	16.5	3	18	?	13	159	8	3.2	15	635	11.21	14
Panama	9	500	11.5	6	9.5	30	16	80	11	2.7	17.5	?	9.50	10
Paraguay	15	0	4.5	18	17	10	11	300	15	1.9	16	551	13.04	17
Peru	2	6,240	3	30	2.5	80	3	1,400	10	2.8	3	9,288	4.54	2
Uruguay	15	0	14	4	15.5	15	18	40	17	0.5	17.5	?	15.25	18
Venezuela	15	0	9.5	8	6	42	5	898	13	2.5	5	4,162	11.67	15

a. 1=1492–1519; 2=1519–1543; 3=1543–1600; 4=1600–1763; 5=1763–1800; 6=after 1800.
b. 1=viceroy; 2=captain-general; 3=president; 4=governor; A, B, C, D=distance from seat.
c. A, B, C, D=distance from seat.
d. A, B, C, D=distance from seat.
e. In pesos, for 1788. A, B, C, D=distance from seat.
f. In thousands of pesos, for 1800.
g. In thousands of pesos, ca. 1800.
h. Thousands of people, ca. 1800.
i. Thousands of people, ca. 1800.
j. Ca. 1800.
k. In thousands of pesos, ca. 1800.

most of its independent life. The first freely elected civilian to complete his term of office was Juan José Arévalo, in 1951. If these cases are deleted, the Spearman rank correlation rises to .69, which is significant at the .01 level.

While more elaborate statistical techniques might be used to ferret out more subtle aspects of the colonial penetration–authoritarianism relationship, the basic hypothesis is supported in this preliminary examination.

Dependency

A salient feature of Latin American politics, societies, economies, and cultures has been the degree to which they have been shaped by external factors. The "dependency school" attributes most of the region's difficulties in achieving sustained economic growth, stable yet responsive political structures, and a truly autonomous society and culture to forces beyond national boundaries over which their governments have little control.

The historical record leaves little doubt that most Latin American countries have indeed been prisoners of external forces since their settlement by the colonizers in the fifteenth and sixteenth centuries. Spain's rigidly hierarchical administrative system and mercantilist economic apparatus left little room for autonomous local variation. The independence movements themselves were largely inspired by the dogma of French and English-American liberalism, as were the political structures which Latin American leaders attempted to graft onto their new nations once independence had been achieved. England soon took over Spain's former role as the dominant trading partner and the principal source of loans to and investments in the Latin American countries.[21]

The twin laws of comparative advantage and elite convenience combined to make all of Latin America a source of raw materials for Europe's factories and foodstuffs for her tables. Most of the capital came from Europe, and most of the risks were taken by European entrepreneurs; Latin American elites served as middlemen and reaped the benefits of commissions and fees for their services. Latin American governments derived most of their income from taxes on exports and imports. The periods of national consolidation experienced sooner or later by each country were facilitated by the new money made available from such taxes. As long as the scope of government remained small and the international markets stable, such revenues were more than sufficient to finance its needs. When markets were not stable and as government needs increased, bonds were floated in European capital markets and loans on easy terms were made to take up the slack. Economic growth certainly occurred in nineteenth-century Latin America, especially after 1850, but it was almost without exception dependent upon European and, later, American markets, investors, and entrepreneurs.[22]

Two central developments mark the evolution of Latin American dependency in the twentieth century. The first is the rapid increase in demands made on governments with the rise in consciousness of population sectors previously only nominally within their purview. As regimes strove to respond to these new requests, they required more resources than ever before to staff larger bureaucracies, provide welfare services, build roads and other infrastructure, and enlarge police and military establishments. Elites were generally unwilling to provide these resources even as they sought to maintain their hegemony and to find suitable positions for their sons and daughters within the enlarged service sector. The line of least resistance for most governments thus continued to be to seek loans and investments from abroad, to raise taxes on exports and imports, to apply certain general tax and welfare provisions selectively to the foreign investment sector, and to print more money.

The second major event was the collapse during the world depression of the market framework on which Latin America was so heavily dependent. Forced back upon their own resources, Latin American governments fared poorly on the whole. Budgets were reduced, demands went unheeded, and an intricate barricade of regulations was hastily thrown up to protect staggering domestic economies. Most governments were obliged by circumstances to expand their roles at the very moment their economic capacity for doing so was being drastically reduced. During this same period domestic industry was established or given incentives to expand, generally with small markets and always behind high tariff walls. Given in addition the absence of a strong national bourgeoisie capable of managing such enterprises, the results were all too often a combination of high cost, low production, inefficiency, and foreign control.[23]

The relative dependency of each Spanish American country is suggested by five basic indicators:

1. U. S. direct private investment:[24] the relative importance of foreign capital in national economic development.

2. Export dependence:[25] the degree of reliance on a single export product.

3. Market dependence:[26] the degree of reliance on a single foreign market for exports.

4. External debt:[27] the degree of reliance on foreign loans for domestic economic development.

5. Trade orientation:[28] the relative importance of all foreign trade for the national economy.

The presumable effect of high levels of dependency on the political systems of Latin America is one of increasing attempts by the executive to dominate, coups d'état, and military governments: in short, authoritarianism. Specific examples can be cited by any student of Latin American affairs to support this presumption. For Latin America as a whole over time, however, the hypothesis that there is a direct relationship between levels of dependency and authoritarianism is not borne out. The rank order correlation between overall levels of dependency (see table 3) and overall levels of authoritarianism in Spanish America is an insignificant .05. The close correspondence of dependency and authoritarianism ranks in Argentina, Bolivia, Chile, El Salvador, Nicaragua, Uruguay, and Venezuela is more than offset by the lack of correspondence in such countries as Costa Rica, the Dominican Republic, Guatemala, Panama, Paraguay, and Peru.

These are very gross and imperfect indicators, to be sure. More subtle relationships might be derived by looking at what occurs during shorter time periods, or by using more sophisticated statistical techniques, or by using more and/or different measurements of authoritarianism and dependency. These results do correspond, however, to the findings of Robert R. Kaufman et al. that there is a surprisingly low relationship between levels of dependency at two points in time and a series of internal economic, social, and political characteristics.[29] What these results suggest to me is not that there is no relationship between dependency and politics, but that it is much more subtle than dependency theorists would have us believe, and that dependency manifests itself politically in different Latin American countries in quite varied and even *sui generis* ways.

Social Mobilization

It is a truism to assert that political systems are affected by the social systems over which they exercise authoritative allocations of values. It is somewhat less obvious to assert the specific nature of the effects, or their sources, or their likely outcomes. Karl Deutsch and Samuel Huntington are among those who have attempted to flesh out some of these relationships between society and politics.[30] They hold that the increasing articulation of social forces, itself often government stimulated, serves to increase the kinds and levels of demands made on the political system. Governments which are more highly organized—better

Table 3. Dependency

Country	U.S. Direct Private Investment[a]		Export Dependence[b]		Market Dependence[c]		External Debt[d]		Trade Orientation[e]		Overall Rank
	Rank	Average	Rank	Average	Rank	Average	Rank	Average	Rank	Average	
Argentina	17	0.51	16	25.59	17	26.24	5	234.27	15	.25	16
Bolivia	15	1.43	5	65.48	8	53.93	1	794.54	2	.53	3
Chile	8	3.13	6	64.38	14	40.49	3	322.74	16	.24	11
Colombia	14	1.70	7	61.81	5	60.94	8	205.94	8	.32	8.5
Costa Rica	9	2.94	9	57.60	12	47.62	7	231.54	3	.50	7
Cuba	1	8.62	3	72.34	2	68.87	11	145.82	5	.41	2
Dominican Republic	6	3.90	12	52.28	11	50.56	17	85.86	17	.20	15
Ecuador	16	0.77	13	46.00	15	37.33	14	121.54	13	.27	17.5
El Salvador	12	2.03	2	73.90	13	44.84	15	110.14	9	.31	6
Guatemala	3	5.33	4	69.11	6	56.63	16	88.09	7	.33	4
Honduras	4	5.28	10	56.29	3	66.36	2	387.99	1	.56	1
Mexico	2	6.63	18	20.38	4	65.89	4	264.35	14	.26	8.5
Nicaragua	11	2.04	14	40.15	10	51.04	10	149.41	4	.44	12
Panama	5	5.05	8	61.64	1	76.86	12	137.67	12	.28	5
Paraguay	13	1.88	17	25.46	7	54.46	13	127.86	11	.29	14
Peru	10	2.33	15	26.05	16	31.83	9	160.36	6	.35	13
Uruguay	18	0.28	11	54.60	18	20.94	6	232.73	18	.13	17.5
Venezuela	7	3.65	1	81.29	9	51.64	18	44.69	10	.30	10

a. U.S. direct private investment as percentage of national government revenue, 1897–1970 (10 base years).
b. Leading export as percentage of total exports, 1887–1971 (8 base years).
c. Exports to leading country of destination as percentage of total exports, 1888–1971 (8 base years).
d. Total foreign debt as percentage of national government revenue, 1914–1969 (7 base years).
e. Total foreign trade as percentage of GNP, 1938–1965 (4 base years).

institutionalized—by the time social mobilization and political modernization occur are more capable of handling these new demands and of responding adequately to them. Governments with lower levels of institutionalization are less able to meet routinely or adaptively the effects of increased social mobilization. New or different demands often provoke governmental crisis in such situations, with inappropriate or inadequate responses, a loss of legitimacy in the eyes of the general population and elite sectors, and an attempt to avoid chaos or rebellion by such measures as suspension of constitutional guarantees or military intervention. In short, social mobilization and political modernization may produce authoritarian government.

Deutsch defines social mobilization as "the process by which major clusters of old social, economic, and psychological commitments are eroded or broken and people become available for new patterns of socialization and behavior."[31] The basic components of his operational definition include the following:

1. Population exposed to modernity
2. Mass media audience
3. Persons changing residence since birth
4. Urban population
5. Population in nonagricultural occupations
6. Literates
7. Per capita income
8. Voting participation

Deutsch maintains that the effect of social mobilization on political systems is related to both the overall level and the rate of change of these various indicators.

For Latin America it is somewhat difficult to get comparable basic information for each country in the several areas encompassed by the concept of social mobilization over a reasonable time span. It was necessary to make some adjustments to this end.[32] Urban population includes only the country's largest cities. The indicators of population exposed to modernity are taken to be the proportion of the total population speaking the national language and the miles of railroad per capita. Information on mass media audience, nonagricultural employment, and voting is readily available only for the years since 1940. Information on persons changing residence since birth is not available at all. An operational definition of literacy over time is the number in primary school in each base year. Educational levels are roughly measured over time by the proportion of the total population in all schools. Because gross national product or national income information was not available for most of Latin America until relatively recently, national government revenue per capita is used as a surrogate for per capita income. For this initial analysis, only changes in levels of social mobilization were used, not rates of change. Average results of these indicators of social mobilization levels and their rank ordering by country are provided in table 4.

The rank order correlation between average levels of social mobilization and average levels of authoritarianism in Spanish America over time is a startling −.31. The overall relationship is exactly the opposite of that hypothesized. Increased social mobilization is apparently related to decreased authoritarianism.

These findings may simply indicate that the social mobilization data on which they are based are not very good. They may suggest that the connections between social mobilization and authoritarianism are a good deal more complex than the simple hypothesis would have us believe. In short, there may be a number of intervening factors, such as government capacity or leadership quality, which muddy the relationship. Some of the elements of social mobilization, for example, are related both to increased awareness of the population and to increased capacity of government to provide services, such as education. This negative relationship may indicate that authoritarian governments on the whole are less likely to provide such services than nonauthoritarian governments. It is also possible that there may be idiosyncratic forces at work within particular Spanish American countries, such as economic crises, immigration, political movements, wars, regional variations, or individual caudillos. Finally, they may suggest just what they seem to: that the emergence and prevalence of authoritarian regimes is related on the whole and over long periods of time to factors other than those we commonly classify as composing social mobilization.[33]

Peru: The Continuing Authoritarian Tradition

Peru's present military government (1968−) comes as no great surprise to students of that country's history. Authoritarian politics of one form or another have dominated the national scene for most of the postindependence period. Peru ranks third in the authoritarian index (table 1). In the seventy years between 1824 and 1894 there were sixteen successful military coups d'état. The military budget during this period at times approached half of all government expenditures. With the exception of 1827−1829, nineteenth-century Peruvian politics until 1887 were marked by executive-branch predominance and a weak or nonexistent legislature.[34]

Peru was, after all, the heartland of the colonial empire along with Mexico, as the colonial penetration index suggests (table 2). The mines were numerous and productive; farming and pasture lands were exten-

Table 4. Social Mobilization

Country	Urban Population[a]		National Language[b]		Railroad Mileage[c]		Literacy[d]		Education[e]	
	Rank	Av.	Rank	Av.	Rank	Av.	Rank	Av.	Rank	Av.
Argentina	1	43.2	5.5	99.4	2	1.68	3	12.1	2	12.9
Bolivia	12	24.5	18	37.0	7	0.40	18	5.5	18	6.1
Chile	4	37.1	10	96.8	3	0.90	6	10.4	5	11.9
Colombia	14	21.5	8	98.4	18	0.12	15	7.1	14	7.8
Costa Rica	11	24.5	5.5	99.4	5	0.62	4	11.5	4	12.5
Cuba	9	30.2	2	100.0	1	3.27	1	23.2	1	14.4
Dominican Republic	15	21.2	2	100.0	13	0.24	11	8.8	12	9.4
Ecuador	17	19.7	15	69.6	14	0.23	9	9.2	11	9.7
El Salvador	13	22.7	4	99.6	15	0.16	13	7.3	15	7.8
Guatemala	16	19.9	17	46.4	11	0.27	17	5.8	13	8.3
Honduras	18	18.2	12	94.5	9	0.37	14	7.2	16	7.5
Mexico	10	28.6	14	91.2	6	0.47	7	9.7	9	10.4
Nicaragua	5	34.1	9	97.1	12	0.25	16	6.0	17	6.3
Panama	8	30.3	13	94.2	17	0.12	5	10.5	6	11.8
Paraguay	6	30.9	11	96.2	8	0.39	2	12.2	3	12.6
Peru	7	30.6	16	53.3	10	0.28	10	8.9	10	10.0
Uruguay	2	42.2	2	100.0	4	0.85	8	9.6	8	11.2
Venezuela	3	38.9	7	98.5	16	0.13	12	8.5	7	11.6

Country	National Revenue Per capita[f]		Mass Media[g]		Non-agricultural Employment[h]		Voting[i]		Overall Rank
	Rank	Av.	Rank	Av.	Rank	Av.	Rank	Av.	
Argentina	3	3373	2	190	1	76	3	38	1
Bolivia	18	599	17	23	15	37	11	23	17
Chile	2	4447	3	102	3	71	12	22	4
Colombia	14	1107	9	54	12	43	14	19	14
Costa Rica	6	2662	8	81	7	48	10	24	6
Cuba	5	3132	5	95	5	58	9	26	3
Dominican Republic	9	1849	16	25	14	38	4	38	11
Ecuador	16	1027	13	41	8	47	16	13	15
El Salvador	11	1346	12	46	13	43	8	27	13
Guatemala	13	1178	15	27	17	32	17	13	18
Honduras	15	1046	18	18	18	30	15	18	16
Mexico	10	1468	6	94	9	46	13	21	8
Nicaragua	12	1214	10	50	16	36	5	37	10
Panama	4	3291	4	95	6	51	7	28	9
Paraguay	17	912	14	30	10	45	6	29	7
Peru	8	1909	11	47	11	45	18	12	12
Uruguay	7	2649	1	243	2	76	2	38	2
Venezuela	1	7597	7	82	4	62	1	39	5

Note: In cases where countries with identical averages have been assigned different ranks, the identity is due to rounding.

a. 1857–1970 (7 base years).
b. 1960 figures.
c. 1880–1965 (6 base years).
d. 1880–1965 (6 base years).
e. 1880–1965 (6 base years).
f. 1880–1965 (6 base years).
g. 1947–1967 (4 base years).
h. 1937–1967 (5 base years).
i. 1940–1970 (up to 5 base years).

sive and fertile; and the Indian population available for labor and for conversion to the Catholic faith was large if not always submissive.[35] The numerous Spanish of the viceroyalty at Lima provided a bastion of conservatism; the independence movement which swept over Peru was stimulated largely from the outside rather than from within.[36] The small liberal movement in Peru was overwhelmed by conservative opposition. Therefore, when independence finally did come to Peru, in 1824, it represented no real break with the past and provided no basis for consolidation around democratic political ideals.

The continuance of authoritarianism into the postindependence period in Peru may be ascribed to the pervasiveness of the colonial experience, to the incompleteness of the independence movement, and to the attempts of various personalist movements to establish hegemony. Its maintenance and resurgence in the 1870s and 1880s was due more to the curious patterns of dependency which had evolved during the first period of national consolidation under Ramón Castilla (1845–1851, 1854–1862).[37] The War of the Pacific (1879–1883) itself broke out over the issue of Peru's (and Bolivia's) right to assert national sovereignty over its Atacama Desert nitrate deposits. They were almost entirely in the hands of Chilean and British entrepreneurs who resisted Peru's and Bolivia's attempts to increase taxes and regulations on nitrate exploitation and export.

The Chilean government took up the cause of its allegedly persecuted nationals and wrested control of the Atacama from Peru and Bolivia by force of arms. In the process they occupied almost half of Peru's national territory (including the capital, Lima), precipitated several coups, and completely disrupted the Peruvian economy as well as the government. National government revenues and expenditures declined more than tenfold between 1876 and 1896.[38] In order to pay off the large debts accumulated abroad, the Peruvian government was forced to grant extraordinary long-term concessions to British creditors in the country's first government monopoly, guano, as well as in the railroads, mines, and jungle territory. Any secular expansion of control over key economic sectors either by the central government or by a national bourgeoisie which might normally have occurred in Peru in the late nineteenth century was effectively cut off by the War of the Pacific debacle.

Peru in this postwar period may be characterized by sharply reduced central government capacity and control, and concomitant dependent—that is, foreign-controlled—capitalist economic development in the extractive and agricultural sectors. A war which Peru had neither sought nor desired thrust upon it a low-voltage government and a dependent economy. United States interests expanded rapidly, especially in mining. Ownership and exploitation of the fertile North Coast valleys were consolidated in the hands of U.S. and German interests, as well as a few immigrant and established Peruvian families. The products of these estates—mostly cotton and sugar—were sent to British, U.S., and European markets. The railroads remained in English hands under the Peruvian Corporation. The production for export of the government's guano "monopoly" was already attached at low prices for English creditors.[39]

The Civilian Democratic Interlude

Ironically, however, this period of sharply increased dependency and reduced governmental capacity brought to Peru its only sustained term of civilian democratic rule (1894–1914). Foreign military missions— predominantly French—were reorganizing and rebuilding the Peruvian military establishment at this time; a cornerstone of their training was noninterventionalist professionalism. Other power contenders, such as foreign business, banking, the oligarchy, and the small middle class, increasingly took advantage of the rapidly expanding opportunities in the private sector. Furthermore, world prices for Peru's primary products—especially sugar, cotton, minerals, and wool—were relatively high during most of this period. At the same time, neopositivist philosophy was gaining ascendancy in government, justifying limited expansion of the state's role in the economy in order to strengthen rather than restrict the private sector.[40] This neopositivist view and large debt repayments placed two major constraints on the expansion of national government.

During these twenty years, political participation expanded significantly. Direct election of national officials was instituted, and municipal elections were reestablished. For the first time major responsibilities rested with the Congress. Political parties, long weak and largely personalist vehicles for assuming executive power, became somewhat stronger and more institutionalized.[41]

Civilian democratic government could exist and be sustained in Peru during a period of increasing dependence, in part because the expanding private sector made the issue of who controlled government now relatively less important, and in part because the government left this private sector largely to its own devices. The War of the Pacific, for better or for worse, produced the break in Peru's historical evolution in the 1880s which the Wars of Independence in the 1820s had been unable to achieve.

The End of Civilian Democracy

This period of national political consolidation under civilian democratic governments was interrupted briefly in 1914 and definitively terminated five years later.

Why did the "civilian democratic interlude" come to an end? A major factor was certainly the insufficiently routinized political organization and procedures of the constitutional period. Individual leaders at times put their own welfare and advancement ahead of the system's. Some civilian sectors, most especially the more conservative elements, were willing to undermine civilian institutions by inducing the military to intervene, paradoxically enough, "to protect and uphold the constitution." They did not search for some compromise or solution within the civilian political arena, thus manifesting their felt or real organizational weakness. Regular elections were held, but there was rarely open and aboveboard competition in them. These difficulties may be traced in part to the insufficient precedent for constitutional civilian rule prior to 1894. The several formal contenders failed to develop the capacity to tolerate opposition if dominant, or to provide "loyal" opposition if not. Elections, still involving a very small percentage of the total population (less than 3 percent in 1915),[42] were not conducted in a spirit of fair play with the expectation that the outcome would be accepted, whatever it was. Intrigues, involuntary exiles, and abortive coups marked even this one relatively extended period of civilian constitutional government.

Peru's increasing dependency during this period had important but largely indirect effects on the capacity of the civilian regime to govern. The country's exports expanded fivefold between 1900 and 1919, but became much more diversified at the same time. Imports likewise increased during the period, though at a much less rapid rate, invariably giving Peru a favorable balance on current account. In 1900 about two-thirds of Peru's trade was with Great Britain; by 1919, about two-thirds was with the United States. While the large British interests in Peru increased very slowly between 1900 and 1919 (from about $100 million to about $136 million), U.S. investments increased rapidly (from about $10 million in 1900 to $111 million in 1919). Peru's substantial foreign debt, estimated at over $100 million in 1899 (£23 million), had been exchanged for the national railroad system and rights over guano, mines, and lands for sixty-six years under the British-held Peruvian Corporation. But nonfulfillment of some obligations under the 1890 agreement effectively kept Peru from receiving new loans abroad for years, until a new settlement was worked out in 1907. While the country's foreign debt increased rapidly thereafter, to upwards of $20 million, by 1919–1920 all but about $4 million had been paid off. On balance, then, Peru's external dependency increased through the period of civilian government but also became considerably more diversified in composition of exports and foreign investment.[43]

Because of the guarantees given foreign investors, however, the

Peruvian government was not consistently able to translate the rapid expansion of foreign trade into similar increases in national government revenues. Government income doubled between 1900 and 1909 but then fluctuated within a rather narrow range until 1919, when income doubled again in the space of two years. During several years, then, the government was not able to satisfy the increase in demands for services being placed upon it by newly articulate sectors within the country. While World War I did not adversely affect exports for more than a very short period, it did keep Peru's traditional supliers of imports from continuing their customary patterns. Imports dropped by more than half between 1914 and 1916 before adjustments could be made by turning to the United States. One effect was to increase inflationary pressures sharply. Wholesale prices more than doubled between 1914 and 1918, affecting most severely those elements of the population which were plugged into the national economic system but not into the export sector.[44]

Inflation was another adverse indirect effect of Peru's increasing export orientation during this period (1913 exports were about twice government revenues; by 1919 they were more than four times the government's income).[45] New foreign investment in the export sector bid up the price of land and mining concessions and brought numerous Peruvians who had previously been farmers and miners into the cities and into the economy's service sector. Scarce irrigated coastal land which had been used to grow foodstuffs was bought up by a few individuals and foreign interests and transferred to the production of sugar and cotton: Sugar cane land increased by more than a third between 1912 and 1918, while cotton land doubled between 1915 and 1920.[46] Thus food production declined at the very time that the urban population and nonagricultural working-class population were increasing in absolute numbers, if not as a percentage of the total population.

This pattern of absolute but not relative increases is reflected in other areas of social mobilization as well during the period of civilian dominance in Peru. Like urbanization between 1895 and 1919, industrial employment and railroad trackage increased markedly—all more than doubled—but not per capita. National government revenue did increase slightly more rapidly than population growth—about 5 percent a year on the average between 1900 and 1918—but only in 1919 did this revenue per capita exceed that of 1894. The proportion of the population in primary and secondary schools increased only slightly between 1903 and 1919, from 3.1 to 3.8 percent.[47] It seems reasonable to conclude, therefore, that a wave of rapid social mobilization was not sweeping the country during this period, even though the absolute increases in urbanization, industrial employment, education, and per capita income were contributing to new and greater demands on government.

The end of Peru's one extended period of civilian democratic government may be attributed, then, more to the perceptions and actions of the civilian political elite itself than to such forces as social mobilization or dependency. It is true that the nature of the development of Peru's dependency during the first two decades of the twentieth century contributed to the government's problems. The government's desire to encourage foreign investment and exports prevented it from increasing its own revenues or its own role in the economy as rapidly as it might have done otherwise. This attitude was also largely responsible for concentration of land ownership, a decline in food production, and many of the inflationary pressures of the 1913–1918 period. But the very diversity of Peru's dependency gave it a resiliency against the vicissitudes of external forces which encouraged the government to proceed on its "low-profile" course. Furthermore, the enclave nature of the development stimulated by foreign investment, especially in the mines of the central sierra and the cotton and sugar estates of the North Coast, actually insulated the central government from many of the pressures which a more generalized social mobilization would have produced.

Peru failed to take advantage of the sharp historical break produced by the War of the Pacific to institutionalize civilian democratic rule. After 1912 only one elected civilian president would complete his term of office without a coup. Responsibility for this failure, culminating between 1914 and 1919, lies fundamentally with the civilian political elite. Rates of change of social mobilization were still too low at this time to have played a decisive role in the collapse of civilian democratic government. Dependency's effects were multiple; some of them, such as inflation, certainly did contribute to the weakening of the government at this time. Others, such as the displacement of a growing native entrepreneurial middle class and the radicalization of an enclave working class, would have an important impact at later points in Peruvian political history. On balance, however, Peru's increasing dependency during this particular period was generally perceived as beneficial to the country and served as a model for development by subsequent governments, authoritarian and democratic alike, right up to 1968.

Populism and Entreguismo Under Civilian Dictatorship

Augusto B. Leguía (1919–1930) took power in 1919 with widespread support, even though he had no specific long-range program and followed no particular ideology. Furthermore, he came to power during a period of consolidation of foreign capital penetration of Latin America, and on the eve of its rapid expansion. For Peru at this time, the benefits accruing from such penetration were substantial, especially for the coastal elite. Hence Leguía's Oncenio (eleven-year rule) was heavily tinged with laissez-faire liberalism. The strategy of national development during this period in Peru was to generate new resources by continuing to expand foreign loans, investments, and the export economy.[48]

Politically, populism marked the Leguía Oncenio. Rather than build a strong political organization, Leguía tried to win and keep popular support by providing schools, roads, public buildings, and water supplies in personalistic and clientelistic ways. Political parties were actively discouraged, Congress was turned into a rubber stamp, and municipal officials were again presidential appointees rather than elected officials. In the international context of the Mexican and Russian revolutions, and in the domestic context of incipient labor organization and renewed student activism, the Peruvian coastal elite felt constrained to ensure the maintenance of their privileges. The evolving democratic procedures and organizations of the previous twenty-five years could no longer be relied upon to accomplish this. The populist solution of the Leguia Oncenio was essentially the elite's response to the potential rather than actual threat of mass social mobilization pressures. Furthermore, this solution, designed as it was to protect elite privileges largely based on Peru's foreign trade, investment, and loan structure, also protected and enhanced such external dependency relationships.

Given Peru's abundant and diverse primary product base and absence of industrial development, Leguía's populism could work only as long as international climate remained hospitable.[49] New taxes on exports and imports and massive foreign loans permitted the Leguía government to carry out many building projects. National government revenue per capita doubled. School enrollments almost doubled, railroad mileage was substantially increased, and the road network of coast and sierra alike expanded by more than eleven hundred miles. Urban migration was stimulated by this prosperity: The proportion of the population living in the country's largest cities increased from about 4 percent in 1920 to about 7 percent by 1930.[50]

With the onset of the world depression after 1929, Peru's domestic prosperity was soon over. Unlike the World War I period, which also provoked severe market and product dislocations, this period did not see prices of Peru's exports stay high, and an alternative market (the United States) was not available. Within two years exports had halved, and within four years, so had the national government's budget. In the suddenly turbulent domestic economic waters, Leguía possessed neither the resources nor the organizational base to weather the storm. He was swept away by a military coup in 1930. The fragility of thirty years of increasing external dependency was suddenly made manifest, as was the tenuousness of the civilian populist alternative of government.

Social Mobilization and Mass Political Organization

The eleven-year hiatus in Peru's political evolution had adverse political effects: Old political organizations atrophied and new organizations had no opportunity to be tested. As a result, one of the most significant political movements of twentieth-century Latin America burst upon the national scene full blown in 1930—1931. The Alianza Popular Revolucionaria Americana (APRA) had been forced to organize clandestinely in the 1920s but had done an extremely good job of it. APRA provided a radical alternative to the voices of moderate reform of the now all but defunct civilian parties and to the conservatism of the export-sector elite.[51]

The sudden appearance of the only well-organized party in Peru, which sported a radical rhetoric to boot, provided a source of grave concern to other political actors, especially the military and the coastal elite. They moved quickly to oppose and block APRA's entry into the circle of power contenders. Had other viable civilian political organizations survived the populism of the Oncenio, some form of democratic politics which incorporated APRA might well have returned to Peru in the 1930s. Open elections were in fact held in 1931: APRA lost to a military populist, Colonel Luis Sánchez Cerro. The victor was adamant against including APRA in the system on any basis. Increasing subversive politics resulted, including open warfare between APRA and the military and Sánchez Cerro's assassination in 1933. The political history of Peru in the 1930s and 1940s is thus the struggle between a well-organized party striving for the legitimacy on the national political scene it already enjoyed among its middle- and working-class followers; and the efforts by other political actors, especially the military, to deny APRA that legitimacy.[52]

APRA was too well organized and too ideological to be populist, however much one might dispute the coherency of its ideology. This stands in sharp contrast with the civilian populism of Leguía or the military populism of Manuel Odría (1948—1956), both of which strove to win the loyalty of the citizenry through government largesse on personalistic and clientelistic bases, without encouraging them to organize.

At this crucial entry period, APRA's real problem was that it had no equally well-organized civilian party alternative with which to do battle constitutionally in the political arena. The social mobilization threat which the elite had perceived between 1910 and 1919 had materialized by 1930, but in a much more fully developed form than they could possibly have imagined. In the 1930s the elite was too weak politically compared with APRA to fight a legitimate electoral battle because of the expansion of the electorate by virtue of the gradual increase in educational facilities and enrollments and owing to the absence of their parties in the political arena for eleven years. Therefore, the elite used the military to carry out via the coup and authoritarian rule what the civilian elite was unable to do by itself.

APRA served, somewhat perversely, to assist the elite in maintaining its dominant role by channeling and thereby controlling post-1920 increases in social mobilization. But the party was not permitted to play the role in national politics which would have institutionalized a democratic framework in Peru. The coastal elite remained in opposition to APRA, as did the military. Where APRA could control social mobilization by channeling social groups, the military could control it be repressing them. APRA, recognizing the strength of its adversaries and their commitment to keep APRA out of political power, pursued a dual strategy. With the military, APRA tried co-optation and subversion between 1930 and 1948 to achieve power extraconstitutionally. At the same time, a strategy of accommodation and compromise gradually emerged regarding the elite. APRA tried to trade its mass support and organizational strength with one or another civilian candidate in exchange for tacit or explicit recognition as a legitimate power contender. This dual strategy kept the military divided and off balance on the one hand, while on the other it permitted APRA finally to share constitutional government with a liberal independent president, José Luis Bustamente y Rivero, between 1945 and 1948. But APRA played the constitutional game badly, as it behaved irresponsibly in its important congressional role in order to maneuver for the presidency. At the same time APRA continued to play the military subversion theme. APRA thus undercut a reformist president and the constitutional process and was rewarded for its efforts with the Odría military coup of 1948 and proscription for eight years.[53]

APRA was thus unable to keep formal political power once it had achieved it. But the party had remarkable organizational strength and had attracted many of the new social forces which were emerging during the period. This was no mean feat. While overall social mobilization in Peru remained relatively low in the 1920s and 1930s compared with many Latin American countries, the rate of change increased markedly. Furthermore, the changes in social mobilization levels occurring within the country were asymmetrical, that is, concentrated disproportionately on the coast. Hence, changes in Peruvian society with potential effects on government were substantial through these important years.

For Peru, therefore, APRA played a vital role between 1924 and 1950. The party kept many of the newly articulated social forces bottled up and channeled while it tried to get into the political system, by and large on the system's terms (that is, via coup or elections). These newly mobilized individuals and groups might well have followed APRA on a more revolutionary course, had the leadership chosen that route. But the leaders did not, whatever their rhetoric. The hierarchy and strict organization of the party permitted the leadership to enforce its will on most of the rank and file. To the degree that social mobilization in Peru played a system-destabilizing role during this period, it did so *through* the country's one highly organized mass-based political party, not outside it.

While APRA was organizing many of the newly emerging social forces, the military was busily protecting the interests of the old, established social groups. It has been observed, in fact, that the Peruvian military in the twentieth century has been "the watchdog of the oligarchy," in spite of its predominantly middle-class origins. This assertion avoids consideration of the real corporate interests of the military itself; however, it is certainly true that the elite benefited from the military's regular intervention in the political system. This is because each intervention through 1962 (1914, 1919, 1931, 1933, 1936, and 1948) retained or restored the external dependency model of economic growth and/or kept APRA from obtaining or solidifying its control over the formal governmental apparatus. The military's own concern was to protect its perquisites and government budget share; after 1932, this was combined with a virulent anti-APRA strain.[54]

Backdrop to 1968: Military Populism and New Civilian Alternatives

The 1948 coup was followed by an eight-year period of military populism under General Manuel Odría. Odría's populism worked to restore government legitimacy by dispensing resources to citizens while proscribing popular organization save on a temporary basis for such manipulative purposes as a progovernment rally. APRA was banned, union activity virtually paralyzed, and the incipient cooperative movement held in abeyance. The objective of the Odría government and the military during this period was to undercut APRA support by means of "bread and circuses" rather than through alternative party and organizational apparatuses. These efforts were concentrated in Lima and on the coast rather than in the sierra, with the majority of the population and a far greater real need, in part because the coast was where the APRA organization was the strongest. Like Leguía, Odría obtained the resources for these populist initiatives primarily from external sources: foreign investment, loans, and taxes on foreign trade and established foreign enterprises. It was also a period of rapid internal industrial development, with important incentives to both domestic and foreign entrepreneurs. Political organizations languished while the economy became increasingly robust. Once again, the advantages to Peru's government of fundamental reliance on foreign markets and resources seemed amply demonstrated.

By the 1950s APRA, while still superbly organized, no longer served as the principal conduit within which new social forces could be channeled. When it became apparent that Odría would call for open elections in 1956 and that APRA would ally itself with a conservative candidate, former President Manuel Prado (1939–1945), a new reformist political group was established under the leadership of an ex-APRA congressman, Fernando Belaúnde Terry. This organization was the first to take advantage of the rapid social changes which had been occurring in the provinces since about 1940. The new party, soon to be called Acción Popular (AP), had remarkable success in attracting newly eligible elements of the population, especially outside Lima and the solid APRA North Coast, as their surprising 480,000 votes and second-place finish in the 1956 presidential election attest.[55] A new political organization had emerged to take up the banner of reform which APRA had dropped in exchange for the opportunity to return to the political arena. Furthermore, AP gave new social groups the opportunity to have a political voice, thereby channeling them into the system rather than forcing them to work outside it. Thus AP did for Peru in the 1950s and 1960s what APRA had done in the 1930s and 1940s.

There was at least one major difference between AP and APRA: Unlike APRA, AP did not incur the wrath of the military during its early years of organizational life. In part this was because the early rhetoric of AP emphasized nation rather than class struggle, and because AP tactics did not usually include recourse to actual (as distinct from threatened) violence.[56] And in part this was due to the increasing awareness among the military that national and internal security were best protected through centrally organized and directed social reform.[57] Whereas in 1936 the military had annulled elections which reformist APRA had won handily, in 1962 they staged a coup which permitted reformist AP to take over the presidency after its electoral victory a year later. It was the military's expectation, of course, that AP would be able to implement reform without threatening social, political, or economic stability.

Even at this juncture, though, there was no real questioning by political actors of the external dependency model of economic growth. True, there was an increased recognition of the need to provide better controls over foreign investments, especially with regard to the knotty problem of continued International Petroleum Company (IPC) control over the Brea and Pariñas oil fields on a shaky legal basis which many Peruvians felt was illegitimate. The intransigence of IPC and the U.S. government over Belaúnde's attempts to settle this question in a mutually satisfactory way not only helped undermine Belaúnde's democratic reformist regime but also brought into sharp relief to aware Peruvians, including many in the military, the inherent disadvantages of external dependence. Nevertheless, the Belaúnde government, like its predecessors, increasingly relied on external inputs to implement policies. In part this was because there was no real desire to change the model, in part because Belaúnde was unwilling to alienate those domestic sectors which profited from the status quo, and in part because APRA's dominance of Congress with its former archenemies, the Odría forces, kept AP from either legislating its reform package or funding legislation from internal sources.[58]

Although APRA and elite opposition effectively thwarted a number of social reforms, sometimes aided by AP's or Belaúnde's own ambivalence, a number of important measures were carried out:

1. Municipal elections were reestablished.

2. The cooperative movement was rapidly expanded.

3. Peru's first significant land-reform legislation was passed. Because it was partially emasculated by the exclusion of most coastal property, it forced the government to act in the previously neglected sierra.

4. Cooperación Popular, a program designed to strengthen rural economies and social organization, was established.

5. Important assistance for self-help and organization in the urban *barriadas* (squatter settlements) was provided.

6. A network of department development corporations was significantly expanded.

7. Urban and rural union activity was encouraged, and both organization and membership advanced markedly.[59]

These measures, because of their emphasis on organization and self-help, were neither populist nor personalist, in sharp contrast to the civilian populism of Leguía or the military populism of Odría. The challenge posed by increased social mobilization was finally being met by the significant expansion in organizational infrastructure for citizen participation. That this initiative persisted for so short a period (1963–1968) within a civilian democratic framework must be attributed to a number of factors: military impatience for more rapid results, especially after its experience with small guerrilla movements in 1965; continued APRA maneuvering for its own political advantage rather than the country's; increased divisions within the president's own party over the best way to proceed; and the insistence by some foreign actors, especially the United States and IPC, that certain of their prerogatives be retained whatever the cost to constitutional government in Peru.

Military Rule Since 1968: Corporativist Organization and Diversification of Dependence

When the military took over the government in 1968, they proposed to continue the reform objectives of the Belaúnde government, but in a context freed from the major constraints which had so severely hampered their full realization during the previous five years. These constraints included the civilian democratic political order, the APRA party in particular, and elite or foreign dominance of the principal levers of economic control. This was to be carried out primarily by the expansion and centralization of state influence and control under strict military supervision. To accomplish this the military felt that it must remain in power indefinitely. But this could be done only if its legitimacy as a reform government in the eyes of the populace was assured, and if its own corporate unity was maintained.[60]

Corporate unity was maintained by forced retirements of a number of officers who disagreed too significantly, increases in salary and perquisites, secrecy surrounding internal deliberations, regular rotation of subordinate officers between military and governmental posts, and the cumulative effects of its own early successes. Those civilians who disagreed too sharply and too publicly or who appeared to promote disunity within the military were unceremoniously deported. Legitimacy depended upon demonstrating the military's strength, effectiveness, and reform-mindedness. This was established almost immediately by the unilateral expropriation of all IPC facilities. It has been followed up in succeeding years by a series of dramatic decree-laws: a sweeping agrarian reform, nationalization of water rights, expropriation of the sugar estates, selective and highly publicized expropriations of a few highly visible foreign enterprises, reversion to the state of some mining concessions, industrial reform, the expropriation of the financially troubled fishing industry, the establishment of state marketing enterprises, partial state ownership of the communications media, a national all-inclusive organization of farmers, a social mobilization organization for stimulating and controlling citizen participation, and a social property law sharply curtailing private ownership. These measures are universally couched in an ideology of nationalism, a "fully participatory" society which is "neither capitalistic nor communistic," increased state influence within a pluralist social and economic order, rapid industrialization, and the end of dependence.[61]

The most impressive domestic accomplishment of the military regime in the years since 1968 has been the expansion of the scope and authority of government itself. As the above listing suggests, there are few areas which the Peruvian government has not significantly affected by legislative initiatives. A crucial area of their concern has been with the nature of the organizational relationship of the citizen to the state. Legislation has been decreed establishing, encouraging, or adjusting a number of citizen participation organizations. Industrial and mining communities have been created by which all members of an enterprise participate in profit-sharing and management. Neighborhood committees to deal with local concerns have been encouraged in the urban squatter settlements, now known as "Young Towns." The present government is also involved in the cooperative movement, already vitalized during the Belaúnde years. However, the military government has given much greater emphasis to production cooperatives; that is, enterprises which share the labor of the members rather than simply their money.[62]

The regime has also created numerous types of intermediary cooperative organizations, such as Agrarian Social Interest Societies (SAIS) or the Integral Agrarian Resettlement Projects (PIAR). Both involve all full-time farmers within a specific geographic area; however, the members come from different types of man-land relationships and have different economic and status relationships. Like the "industrial community" and production cooperative concept, some of the profits of the enterprises are distributed to the workers or to their agricultural unit (for example, peasant communities), and a management structure is created which provides for member and/or productive unit participation in some of the enterprises' decisions.[63]

Within the agricultural sector, these various local units are related to regional and national government entities through representation in the National Agrarian Confederation (CNA) by means of various all-inclusive, geographically arranged farmers' leagues. A similar organization exists in the industrial sector and includes industrial community representatives as well as private owners. At the same time, crosscutting these sectoral and vertically managed organizations are several union federations, two of long standing in Peru and two of recent creation. The Peruvian Workers Confederation (CTP, of the APRA party) and the General Peruvian Workers Confederation (CGTP, of Communist affiliation) now vie for members with the General Workers Confederation

(CGT, of Christian Democratic orientation) and the Workers Confederation of the Peruvian Revolution (CTRP, of the military government).

The responsibility for implementing, coordinating, and controlling the multiple legislative initiatives with regard to citizen participation rests with the National System of Support for Social Mobilization (SINAMOS). This organization combines under one roof older government bureaucracies such as the National Cooperative Development Office (ONDECOOP) and the Peasant Communities Agency (DCC). It has numerous responsibilities which are partially decentralized, in apparent contrast with most of the centralizing initiatives of the present government. Opportunities exist for joint citizen representative and government agent decision-making at the local and regional levels in matters relating to citizen participation. However, strict control over the agency is attempted by military officers, who compose the majority of national and regional directors.[64]

These various initiatives of the military government stand as important efforts to get Peru's citizens together to deal with problems of great significance to them—those of work place and residence. It is certainly true that the various enterprises are partially implemented at best, that they are generally closely controlled and regulated, and that legislation contains numerous safeguards against their utilization for partisan political purposes. The attempt to exert strong central organization and hierarchical control, the organization of participation units largely by functional sector, and the attempt to include disparate class elements within sectors all suggest the corporativist coloration of the government's initiatives to date with regard to the organization of citizen participation.

At the same time, there appears to be a conscious effort on the part of the government to undermine previously existing political organizations such as party, their affiliated unions, and peasant leagues. Political party member or union leader participation is limited in many of these new organizations; party labels are not permitted in internal elections; and with the new CNA, previously established federations lose their legal status as representatives of the peasants in dealings with the government. The government's more open policy with regard to unions seems to contradict this. But even here the government may well be pursuing a policy designed to undermine class organization which antedates the present regime. New organizations have been permitted, thereby increasing competition for members and the likelihood of intraclass conflict. Only the government's union receives strong official support and funding, however, making it likely that supporters of other unions will be drawn away. The CNA will eliminate alternative peasant federations when fully operational, and the industrial community is certainly viewed as an alternative to unions rather than as a complementary organization.

The present military government of Peru is thus meeting the challenge of social mobilization not with temporary populist expedients but by attempting to construct an organizational alternative to parties and by establishing interest groups with distinctly corporativist elements. The Peruvian military is violating Huntington's generalization that military governments tend to "shrink from a role as political organizers." [65] Rather, the present regime has apparently recognized the importance of the dictum that "in the modernizing world he controls the future who organizes its politics."[66]

The military government's position regarding dependency is a curious but perhaps realistic one. The rhetoric of the regime has hammered away at the need to eliminate dependency. In practice, however, the government has worked to diversify Peru's dependency. In some areas, in fact, the nation's dependency has even increased, but with much greater government supervision or direct control.[67] Socialist governments have been recognized. A truly independent Third World foreign policy has been pursued, leading to Peru's recognition as a major spokesman for this bloc. The two-hundred-mile limit for territorial waters has been vigorously advocated, in open defiance of the United States. The government has encouraged new loans and investments, public and private, outside their traditional American and British arrangements. The Andean Pact has been aggressively championed as a regional bloc potentially strong enough to neutralize big-power interests. And attempts have been made to find agreement among the big four copper producers for an export price formula which will be mutually advantageous. In addition to the IPC, a number of foreign enterprises have been expropriated, including some banking interests, the railroads, several fishmeal plants, the telephone company, sugar estates, and the large mining enterprises of Cerro de Pasco and Marcona Mining.

At the same time, however, major new investments have been actively sought and acquired in oil, copper, and iron, and the search continues for investors in heavy industry. Major new loans have been obtained from foreign and international sources, exceeding the total resources obtained during the Belaúnde government. These contradictions apparently flow from the realization that internal resources are insufficient and the frustrating experience of failing, in spite of generous incentives, to induce holders of private domestic resources to utilize them voluntarily for proposed investment projects.

This is the first government in Peru's history to question fundamentally the assumptions of the external dependency model and to insti-tute a new policy of sharply increased national government control over trade and investments. At the same time, however, the present regime is actively encouraging new investment and loans on the assumption that Peru's diverse resources and stable government will continue to provide sufficiently attractive incentives for responsible investors. Symbolic of their recognition of the continued importance of such external re-sources is their willingness to swallow some national pride to hammer out an agreement with the United States over all outstanding expropri-ated foreign investment, including IPC it appears, by providing a lump-sum payment to be distributed by the U.S. government.[68]

The Emerging Order: Participatory Corporativism

Over the past several years, the military government of Peru has amply demonstrated its capacity to govern. It has also defied all attempts by observers at definitive classification. The present govern-ment is most certainly authoritarian. While nominally adhering to constitutional principles, it rules in practice by the decree-laws which flow from the considerable talents of a military intelligentsia, with some important civilian input at the technical bureaucratic level. It keeps its ideology somewhat vague to keep options open, and decree-laws are often adjusted when confronted with realities different from those anticipated or when met by determined citizen opposition. It extends state control, thereby ending the laissez-faire liberalism which persisted in Peru up to 1968. It tolerates diversity within the military as long as a united front is presented to the public. It tolerates diversity outside the government only if opposition is muted and respectful. Deportation of leading spokesmen of particular causes, radical and conservative, has been a frequent occurrence; torture has not. A strong dose of pragmatism moderates considerably the radical rhetoric. The military's corporate interests and perquisites have been quietly ad-vanced; great personal sacrifices by many military men in government are also commonplace.

This is certainly not a populist government, although its general approach to the problems of Peruvian society during its first eighteen months in power might be viewed under the rubric of military populism.[69] Since that time, however, the regime has been pushing too forcefully the ideology of participation and working too diligently on organizational alternatives concerning the relation of the citizen to the political system. There is, to be sure, some continuing government largesse to co-opt and keep quiescent potentially troublesome elements of the population, especially in the squatter settlements. Yet the organizational thrust of this government remains. The old order with its parties and unions is not satisfactory to the present regime, but this government is doing much more than simply undermining that order. It is constructing a new order for citizen participation. Thus this military transcends the necessary and sufficient condition of populism.

True, this new order is not fully evident, and some of its manifestations are apparently contradictory, suggesting the continuing internal debate over the final shape of things. It is also a reason why the ideology is not more specific and why it takes an inordinate amount of time to legislate major alterations in social organization. But on the whole the new order may be characterized as having much more centralized government control, as anticlass and prosector, as recognizing the need for local units of citizen participation on the basis of work place as well as residence, and as providing for mechanisms which will eventually extend participation from the local to the national arenas.

The military is stung by criticism that it is trying to impose a corporate state in Peru. While such an arrangement is certainly compatible with Peru's Hispanic legacy and the *hispanismo* movement of the 1930s, the too obvious connections between corporativism and German or Italian fascism cause the Peruvian military to recoil from such attributions. Viewed with a cold analytical eye, however, in spite of the diversity and contradictions which are everywhere apparent, the overall model in process of construction in Peru is inescapably corporativist. It is also inescapably indigenous, and thus not likely to take on the virulent aspects of its German, Italian, or Spanish counterparts.

As long as the government is staffed by gradualists and as long as the country has its present revenue base and potential, the regime is probably going to be able to continue to construct this participatory corporativist model of political organization in Peru. The crucial problem here is the classical one—the relationship between central control and general citizen participation. But there appears to be in Peru the makings of a no-party alternative of political development whose progress should continue to be carefully watched by political analysts. This is not to say that the Peruvian example of a reformist military regime imposing a neocorporativist political framework on the body politic is likely to be widely imitated. The Peruvian case suggests that such a development is likely only where social mobilization is relatively low and has a history of organization within the system. The "modern" corporativist alternative also finds more fertile soil for cultivation where traditional corporativist roots of colonialism are deeply embedded in society. In addition, it will probably occur only in countries without a democratic past or where democracy has been repudiated by official excesses and leadership deficiencies. Finally, such a model is likely to be implemented only in countries with a diverse resource base which has the potential to satisfy the aware population's basic demands while the model is made reality.

NOTES

The research assistance of William T. Bayer III, David Ruccio, and Paul Wolff and the support of the Bowdoin College Faculty Research Fund in the preparation of this chapter is gratefully acknowledged. An earlier version was presented at the Latin American Studies Association meeting at San Francisco in 1974.

1. For example, Kalman Silvert, "National Values, Development, and Leaders and Followers," *International Social Science Journal*, 15 (1963):560–70; Ronald Newton, "On 'Functional Groups,' 'Fragmentation,' and 'Pluralism' in Spanish American Political Society," *Hispanic American Historical Review*, 50, no. 1 (February 1970):1–29; and Howard J. Wiarda, "Toward a Framework for the Study of Political Change in the Iberic-Latin Tradition: The Corporative Model," *World Politics*, 25 (January 1973):206–35.

2. For example, André Gunder Frank, *Capitalism and Underdevelopment in Latin America* (New York: Monthly Review Press, 1969); James D. Cockcroft, André Gunder Frank, and Dale L. Johnson, *Dependence and Underdevelopment* (Garden City, N.Y.: Doubleday-Anchor, 1972); and Oswaldo Sunkel, "National Development Policy and External Dependence in Latin America," in *Contemporary Inter-American Relations*, ed. Yale H. Ferguson (Englewood Cliffs, N.J.: Prentice-Hall, 1972), pp. 465–92.

3. For example, Guillermo A. O'Donnell, *Modernization and Bureaucratic-Authoritarianism*, Politics of Modernization Series, no. 9 (Berkeley: Institute of International Studies, University of California, 1973).

4. As elaborated in more general terms by Karl Deutsch, "Social Mobilization and Political Development," *American Political Science Review*, 55 (1961):493–514; and Samuel P. Huntington, "Political Development and Political Decay," *World Politics*, 17 (1965):386–430.

5. Juan Linz, "An Authoritarian Regime: Spain," in *Mass Politics*, ed. Erik Allardt and Stein Polekin (New York: Free Press, 1970), p. 255.

6. Arthur S. Banks, *Cross-Polity Time-Series Data* (Cambridge: MIT Press, 1971), from the Archives of the State University of New York, Binghamton, Center for Cooperative Political Research. In the interest of "band width," some "fidelity" was lost, but the data remain the best comprehensive historical information generally available.

7. One criticism of present "colonial" or "cultural" penetration literature has been its failure to distinguish the likely variation within the "Hispanic" culture, and hence its low utility as a tool of comparative analysis. The present effort attempts to overcome this admitted deficiency. The author gratefully acknowledges the important contribution to data collection and analysis of William T. Bayer III as part of his senior honors project at Bowdoin College, "The Spanish Colonial System and Subsequent Political Developments in Latin America," May 1974.

8. Hubert Herring, *A History of Latin America* (New York: Knopf, 1955), p. 151.

9. A. Curtis Wilgus, *The Development of Hispanic America* (New York: Farrar

and Rinehart, 1941); Edward G. Bourne, *Spain in America* (New York: Harper, 1904); and *The South American Handbook* (London: Trade and Travel Publications, 1964).

10. Richard M. Morse, *The Urban Development of Latin America* (Stanford: Stanford University Press, 1971), p. 9.

11. Wilgus, *Development of Hispanic America;* Bourne, *Spain in America.*

12. Ibid.

13. Ibid.; and Charles H. Cunningham, *The Audiencia in the Spanish Colonies* (New York: Gordian, 1971).

14. Cunningham, *Audiencia,* p. 21.

15. William Walton, *Present State of the Spanish Colonies,* 2 vols. (London: Paternoster-Row, 1810).

16. Alexander von Humboldt, *Travels to the Equinoctial Regions of America,* trans. Tomasina Ross, 3 vols. (London: Bohn, 1852); Sir Richard Henry Bonnycastle, *Spanish America* (London: Paternoster-Row, 1818); and E. G. Squier, *Notes on Central America* (New York: Harper, 1874).

17. Morse, *Urban Development;* C. H. Haring, *The Spanish Empire in America* (New York: Harcourt, Brace and World, 1947); Hubert Howe Bancroft, *History of Central America,* 3 vols. (New York: Bancroft, 1890); Humboldt, *Travels;* Donald E. Worcester and Wendell G. Schaeffer, *The Growth and Culture of Latin America,* vol. 1 (New York: Oxford, 1970); John Miers, *Travels in Chili and la Plata,* 2 vols. (London: Baldwin, 1826); Amy L. and William D. Marsland, *Venezuela Through Its History* (New York: Crowell, 1954); and Chester Lloyd Jones, *Guatemala: Past and Present* (Minneapolis: University of Minnesota Press, 1940).

18. Humboldt, *Travels;* Walton, *Present State of Spanish Colonies;* Jones, *Guatemala: Past and Present;* Bancroft, *History of Central America;* John Lynch, *Spanish Colonial Administration, 1782–1810* (New York: Greenwood, 1958); and E. G. Squier, *Notes.*

19. Bancroft, *History of Central America;* Humboldt, *Travels;* Lynch, *Spanish Colonial Administration;* Walton, *Present State of Spanish Colonies;* Bonnycastle, *Spanish America;* Richard Graham, *Independence in Latin America* (New York: Knopf, 1972); and Harris G. Warren, *Paraguay* (Norman: University of Oklahoma Press, 1949).

20. Warren, *Paraguay.*

21. Graham, *Independence in Latin America.*

22. William P. Glade, *The Latin American Economies* (New York: American Book, 1969).

23. O'Donnell, *Modernization and Bureaucratic-Authoritarianism.*

24. United Nations, Economic Commission for Latin America, *External Financing in Latin America* (1897, 1908, 1919, 1929, 1936, 1943, 1950 figures) (E/CN.12/649/Rev. 1), 1965; Organization of American States, *External Financing for Latin American Development* (1960 figures) (Baltimore: Johns Hopkins University Press, 1971); U.S. Department of Commerce, Bureau of Economic Analysis, Direct Investment Branch (1965–1970 figures).

25. *Statesman's Yearbook,* various years (London: Macmillan & Co.)

26. Ibid.

27. Banks, *Cross-Polity Time-Series Data.*

28. Ibid.

29. Robert R. Kaufman, Daniel S. Geller, and Harry I. Chernotsky, "A Preliminary Test of the Theory of Dependency," *Comparative Politics,* 7, no. 3 (April 1975):303–30.

30. Deutsch, "Social Mobilization and Political Development"; Huntington, "Political Development and Political Decay."

31. Deutsch, "Social Mobilization," p. 493.

32. Basic sources for all social mobilization indicators include *Statesman's Yearbook*, various years; and Banks, *Cross-Polity Time-Series Data*.

33. See Robert D. Putnam, "Toward Explaining Military Intervention in Latin American Politics," *World Politics*, 19 (October 1967):83–110, for comparable findings and discussion.

34. Frederick Pike, *The Modern History of Peru* (New York: Praeger, 1967).

35. See, for example, Lillian E. Fisher, *The Last Great Inca Revolt, 1780–1783* (Norman: University of Oklahoma Press, 1966).

36. Heraclio Bonilla et al., *La independencia en el Peru* (Lima: Instituto de Estudios Peruanos, Campodónico, 1972), esp. pp. 15–64.

37. For fuller elaboration of this dependency theme, see Ernesto Yepes del Castillo, *Peru, 1820–1920: un siglo de desarrollo capitalista* (Lima: Instituto de Estudios Peruanos, Campodónico, 1972).

38. Banks, *Cross-Polity Time-Series Data*, p. 124.

39. Yepes del Castillo, *Peru, 1820–1920*.

40. Pike, *Modern History of Peru*, pp. 159–68.

41. Carlos A. Astiz, *Pressure Groups and Power Elites in Peruvian Politics* (Ithaca: Cornell University Press, 1969); pp. 93–94.

42. Pike, *Modern History of Peru*, p. 203.

43. *Statesman's Yearbook*, various years, 1898–1922.

44. Ibid.

45. Yepes del Castillo, *Peru, 1820–1920*, tables 20 and 32, pp. 248 and 268.

46. Ibid., p. 264.

47. *Statesman's Yearbook*, various years, 1898–1922.

48. Howard L. Karno, "Augusto B. Leguia: The Oligrachy and the Modernization of Peru" (Ph.D. dissertation, University of California at Los Angeles, 1970).

49. The climate was indeed hospitable during most of the Oncenio. During the 1920s, foreign investments expanded, but U.S. sources exceeded British for the first time. Such investments remained largely in the extractive and primary product sectors. Exports increased annually between 1922 and 1929, almost regaining the historic high of 1920. Diversity of exports was retained while diversity of foreign markets was restored. Foreign loans, almost entirely from the United States, increased markedly, to something on the order of $100 million (*Statesman's Yearbook*, various years, 1920–1933; and Max Winkler, *Investments of United States Capital in Latin America* [Boston: World Peace Foundation, 1929], pp. 275–83).

50. Banks, *Cross-Polity Time-Series Data*, p. 85.

51. Harry Kantor, *The Ideology and Program of the Peruvian Aprista Movement* (Berkeley: University of California Press, 1953).

52. On APRA, see Peter Klarén, *Modernization, Dislocation, and Aprismo* (Austin: University of Texas Press, 1973); and Liisa North, "The Origins and Development of the Peruvian Aprista Party" (Ph.D. dissertation, University of California, Berkeley, 1973). On the military, see Victor Villanueva, *Ejército Peruano* (Lima: Mejía Baca, 1973).

53. Victor Villanueva, *La sublevación Aprista del 48: tragedia de un pueblo y un partido* (1954; reprint ed., Lima: Milla Batres, 1973).

54. Victor Villanueva, *El militarismo en el Perú* (Lima: Scheuch, 1962).

55. The vote in Peru was restricted to the adult literate population. In 1939, 4.9

percent of the population voted; in 1956, 14.8 percent (Kenneth Ruddle and Phillip Gillete, eds., *Latin American Political Statistics* [Los Angeles: U.C.L.A. Latin American Center, 1972]).

56. Jane S. Jaquette, *The Politics of Development in Peru* (Ithaca: Latin American Studies Program, dissertation series, Cornell University, 1971), pp. 84–92.

57. Liisa North, *Civil-Military Relations in Argentina, Chile, and Peru*, Institute of International Studies, Politics of Modernization Series, no. 2 (Berkeley: University of California Press, 1966); also Luigi Einaudi and Alfred Stepan, *Latin American Institutional Development: Changing Military Perspectives in Peru and Brazil* (Santa Monica: Rand Corporation, 1971).

58. Jaquette, *Politics of Development*, chaps. 3–5.

59. Details concerning these measures may be found in Susan C. Bourque and David Scott Palmer, "Transforming the Rural Sector: Government Policy and Peasant Response," in *The Peruvian Experiment: Continuity and Change Under Military Rule*, ed. Abraham F. Lowenthal (Princeton: Princeton University Press, 1975).

60. The early period of military rule in Peru after October 3, 1968, has been analyzed by Víctor Villanueva, *Nueva mentalidad militar en el Perú?* (Lima: Mejía Baca, 1969).

61. Major studies on Peru since 1968 include (besides Villanueva, *¿Nueva mentalidad militar?*, and Lowenthal, *Peruvian Experiment*) Julio Cotler, *El populismo militar como modele de desarrollo nacional: el caso Peruano* (Lima: Instituto de Estudios Peruanos, 1969); idem, "Bases del corporativismo en el Peru," *Sociedad y Politica*, 1, no. 2 (October 1972):3–11; Jose Z. García, "The 1968 Velasco Coup in Peru: Causes and Policy Consequences" (Ph.D. dissertation, University of New Mexico, 1974); David Scott Palmer, *"Revolution from Above": Military Government and Popular Participation in Peru, 1968–1972* (Ithaca: Latin American Studies Program, Cornell University, 1973); and David Chaplin, ed., *Peruvian Nationalism: A Corporatist Revolution?* (New Brunswick, N.J.: Transaction Books, 1976).

62. Palmer, *"Revolution from Above,"* pp. 126–43.

63. Cynthia McClintock, "SAIS Cahuide: Its Impact on Participation and Wealth in the Region" (Xerox, 1974); David Scott Palmer and Kevin J. Middlebrook, "Corporatist Participation Under Military Government in Peru," in *Peruvian Nationalism*, ed. David Chaplin (New Brunswick, N.J.: Transaction Books, 1976).

64. James M. Malloy, "Authoritarianism, Corporatism, and Mobilization in Peru," *Review of Politics*, 36, no. 1 (January 1974):52–84; also Palmer, *"Revolution from Above"*; Palmer and Middlebrook, "Corporatist Participation Under Military Government"; and Peter T. Knight, "New Forms of Economic Organization in Peru: Toward Workers' Self Management," in *The Peruvian Experiment*, ed. Abraham F. Lowenthal (Princeton: Princeton University Press, 1975).

65. Samuel P. Huntington, *Political Order in Changing Societies* (New Haven: Yale University Press, 1968), p. 243.

66. Ibid., p. 461.

67. David Scott Palmer, "Authoritarian Regimes and Reform: Military Government in Peru" (Paper delivered at the 1974 annual meeting of the American Political Science Association, Chicago, August 30, 1974).

68. From conversations by the author with some of the participants in the negotiations, April 1974.

69. The perspective of Julio Cotler in his early analysis of the military government of Peru, *El populismo militar.*

HENRY A. DIETZ

13

Bureaucratic Demand-Making and Clientelistic Participation in Peru

To view demand-making as one type of political participation is a large and ill-defined task. The term itself presents problems almost immediately: How are we to define a demand, and what sorts of acts constitute making or placing a demand? Demands can emanate from individuals, from small groups, or from widely flung political parties and pressure groups; they can be cast as pleas, petitions, claims, or ultimatums; and they can be presented peacefully, with threats of violence, or through openly violent techniques. Moreover, they can have as their aim the provision of a material good or service, the redress of a grievance, the enactment of a piece of legislation (or the prevention thereof), or—ultimately—the abolition of an entire political system.[1]

In many Latin American countries, much attention has been paid to both the potential and the actual predilections of the urban poor to opt for radical, nonconventional means of demand-making, or for their tendencies to support charismatic, strong-man caudillos. A good deal of energy has gone into the analysis of phenomena such as the *descamisado*'s support for Juan Perón in Argentina[2] and (most recently) the critical role of the inhabitants of Santiago's *campamentos*, or shantytowns, in supporting Salvador Allende.[3] Examinations of these and other urban mass movements and caudillismo have generally revolved around the questions of *why* the urban poor become involved in violent activities, and *how* society can best head off repetitions of such outbursts, either through repression or amelioration or some combination thereof.

Although these questions and occurrences doubtless merit attention, we may be guilty of assuming that the urban poor in Latin America are by definition passive until aroused by some caudillo-type figure, or until some psychological threshold is reached, after which an individual automatically becomes radicalized. In other words, we may permit the outbreak of violence or the emergence of some mass movement to obscure an equally important but less spectacular subject—namely, on what basis does *conventional, nondisruptive* political demand-making take place? While it may be clearly false to portray the urban poor throughout Latin America as in a constant state of unrest, it may not be as clear that these same people do in fact have demands, and that they have also established means of presenting them to relevant political authorities.[4]

The purpose of this chapter is to present a micro-level description and analysis of demand-making and participation by the urban poor in a particular national context and regime. Specifically, I shall concern myself with two ways through which the *poblador*, or inhabitant of the *pueblos jóvenes* (squatter settlements) of Lima, Peru, places demands and in general interacts with the Peruvian national political system—a system which is, at present, an authoritarian military regime.[5] The first of these ways is largely bureaucratic; it details the channels and strategies open to the *pobladores* for articulating their needs to a specific government agency. The second, however, deals with an attempt by the Peruvian government to create and institutionalize a multilevel organizational apparatus whose avowed aims are simultaneously (and paradoxically) the encouragement and the control of local, autonomous decision-making. My concentration upon these types of activities emerges from an assumption that of those members of the urban poor who do become politically active, the great majority spend their time and energy on conventional political activities designed to satisfy realistic, modest goals through incremental strategies. Furthermore, I assume that attempts to alter or restructure such strategies and behavior may prove disruptive and produce more turmoil than benefit.

Rapid Urbanization, Demand-Making, and Participation

Many theories of political development assume that rapid urban growth brought on in large part by massive cityward migration produces qualitative as well as quantitative change in demand-making focused at national governments. Karl Deutsch's classic formulation of social mobilization, which explicitly includes rural-urban transfer as a basic ingredient, posits a direct, causal linkage between mobilization and demand-making. Deutsch claims that as the numbers of city dwellers of every socioeconomic class increase,

> this growth . . . produces mounting pressures for the transformation of political practices and institutions. . . . As people are uprooted from their physical and intellectual isolation in their immediate localities, from their old habits

and traditions, and often from their old patterns of occupation and place of residence, they experience drastic changes in their needs.[6]

Deutsch then warns that it is highly probable that the increase in demands will outstrip the political system unless that system can demonstrate remarkable flexibility and adaptability.

Sometimes unstated, perhaps, but always implicit in such theorizing about sociopolitical change, is a chain of reasoning with a seeming logical inevitability:

1. Rural-urban migration contributes to rapid growth in the number of urban dwellers, especially in the lower sectors of society.

2. These new urbanites, uprooted as they are, undergo a dramatic shift in their needs.

3. Their exposure and proximity to governmental activities and agencies create an increasingly strong dependence upon the government for goods and services.

4. The political system of a developing nation, caught up in a seemingly exponential rise in demands upon it from all sectors, will not have the capacity to respond adequately.

5. Therefore, with basic needs and expectations unmet, the government will experience a drop in legitimacy as the urbanites become more and more disenchanted.

There are, however, a number of ways in which this sort of reasoning can be, and has been, challenged. For one thing, it is not at all inevitable that migrants (or the urban poor in general) will automatically approach the government when they perceive an objective need. Wayne Cornelius and I have argued that a definite series of steps must occur to translate needs into political demands.[7] Moreover, many recent descriptive and empirical studies have concluded that rural-origin migrants are not radicalized or alienated, thereby suggesting that the political systems of Latin America and the Third World frequently do manage to cope with demand-making, and that their coping is reasonably satisfactory *in the eyes of those making the demands.*[8]

The Revolutionary Government of Peru
and the Pueblos Jóvenes

Since October 1968, the government of Peru has been in the hands of its military forces. And despite the prevailing image of the military as a rightist, conservative, and repressive force, the Revolutionary Government of the Armed Forces has produced increasingly well-defined policies aimed at significant, far-reaching social and economic reforms.[9] It is not my purpose here to discuss the details of such policies nor to attempt to explain the origins of reformism in the Peruvian military. Rather, I shall concentrate upon identifying the military's perceptions of themselves and of the masses of Peruvian society, in particular the urban *poblador* or squatter.

On October 3, 1968, Fernando Belaúnde's constitutionally elected government was overthrown by the combined branches of the Peruvian military, acting in concert and as a unified, institutional force. It is essential to note these characteristics of the military's intervention; the *golpe de estado* (coup d'état) was not the work of a single general or colonel acting in the traditional caudillo or strong-man image. Rather, the military moved as an institution, led by institutional military leaders. General Juan Velasco Alvarado, who was named president (a post he held until August 1975), was at the time chairman of the Joint Chiefs of Staff; his cabinet officers were all high-ranking members of the army, navy, and air force officers' corps.

Since the overthrow, a good deal has been written—both in Peru and abroad—about the Revolutionary Government.[10] A number of observers have debated whether the military's rule can properly be labeled "revolutionary"; others have tried to account for the strongly nationalistic, reformist actions which the military has implemented, since much conventional wisdom posits an inherent contradiction between military rule and modernization.[11] Still other attempts have been made to classify the Peruvian military's model of development and to assess its possible impact on other Latin American and Third World countries. Numerous labels have been employed to characterize Peru's military: nationalist, reformist, Nasserist, modernizing, ruling in a Hispanic corporatist, authoritaritarian, divisive pluralist, or clientelistic fashion. I shall postpone the selection of labels. My more immediate goal is to investigate the military's relationships with the mass of Peruvian society, including such matters as the policies of the military in coping with the problems of mobilization in an authoritarian context and the mechanisms, strategies, and structures generated by the military to encourage participation as the military wishes it to be encouraged.

The Peruvian military possessed very little in the way of a coherent, complete ideology when it assumed power. Indeed, the motives used to rationalize its intervention were almost all based on issues such as the incapacity of civilian politicians and parties to govern and the presence of widespread corruption and scandal. Upon assumption of power, the military

based their legitimacy on their willingness to carry out reform, not on their willingness to include citizens as participants in the process. The military represented itself as acting on behalf of the marginal majorities, and appealed to them for support in their endeavors. Nowhere is this more clear than in the series of Sunday tours and speeches by ministers throughout the [*pueblos jóvenes*] ... of Lima, during which they continually explained that this government was working for them and needed their support.[12]

For the first eighteen months or so, therefore, the government made little actual effort to organize and mobilize the population, relying instead on "asking for support"—at best a vague way of handling the complex and pressing matter of involving the masses in a revolution being carried out in large part for their benefit. This is not to say, however, that the *pobladores* and other "marginal" groups were ignored by the Revolutionary Government.

Shortly after the 1968 *golpe*, a number of administrative decrees and reforms appeared, and the *pobladores* and their communities became the focus of a new national bureaucracy, one of several *organismos multisectoriales* (generally translated as "national offices") with the responsibility of dealing with several substantive areas: personal administration, community development, juridical matters, statistics and census, cooperatives, an advanced school of public administration, and the *pueblos jóvenes*. All of these offices were created under the immediate control of the prime minister, who in turn reports directly to the president; thus, these offices are (theoretically) supraministerial and serve as planning agencies as well as coordinating bodies for the ministries and for other governmental and nongovernmental organizations working in the areas mentioned.

The early enunciated policy stance of the Revolutionary Government of the Armed Forces toward the *pueblos jóvenes* represents a substantial shift in perceiving the "problem" of squatting and low-income housing generally. The initial reaction to these settlements on the part of power holders and elites generally has been one of fear, repulsion, or supposedly humanitarian concern, all of which frequently lead to policies of eradication of the "belts of misery" and "cancerous sores" preying upon the urban setting.

The literature counteracting such views is now both substantial and convincing; William Mangin and John Turner, along with many others, have presented persuasive cases that the squatters and their communities can fundamentally solve rather than cause the problem of low-cost housing.[13] Once considered radical or naive or both, this view has gained increasing acceptance in Peru since the beginning of the 1960s. Architects, engineers, and social scientists promulgated this perception; and the mass media, once rife with lurid tales of degeneration, promiscuity, and other social and physical ills, slowly changed and gradually gave wide coverage to the *pueblos jóvenes*, frequently playing up community projects in the settlements as examples for the rest of Peruvian society.[14]

More important, these views have been adopted by the Revolutionary Government. The Oficina Nacional de Desarrollo de los Pueblos Jóvenes (ONDEPJOV) was created less than three months after the *golpe* (December 13, 1968); it rests specifically upon the following definition:

> The *pueblos jóvenes* [are composed of] groups of people who with their own organization based upon a neighborhood system have directed themselves toward the solution of their problems in a progressive way, with the goal of attaining, by means of their participation based on common interests, integration into an urban way of life.
>
> These groups of people are located on the outskirts of, and in some cases within, major cities of the country which are undergoing rapid urban expansion, owing in large part to the phenomenon of nationwide migration; these communities by their own initiative are inhabiting the lands they occupy with the goal of constructing their houses; they require the installation or enlargement of running water, sewerage, electricity, and public transportation; they already contain incipient communal services such as schools, churches, markets, medical posts, police stations, and recreational facilities.[15]

This statement, which precedes the enunciation of the law establishing ONDEPJOV as an official agency, is remarkable in its positive tone: Nowhere is eradication mentioned, and nowhere are the settlements interpreted as something to be denigrated. Rather, much is made of the fact that the squatters have taken the initiative to solve their own problems, and that therefore the proper role of the government is to collaborate, assist, and coordinate these efforts, working within the structures and the conditions which the *pobladores* themselves have created. Under this definition, then, ONDEPJOV does not operate as an urban renewer, in the sense of the term in the United States; rather, ONDEPJOV must be sensitive to the conditions in the settlements and work within existing circumstances and situations. As the goal of ONDEPJOV states, the *pueblos jóvenes* and their *pobladores* are to be brought into the mainstream of urban life, and not be treated as or made to feel marginal. By 1970, a number of specific policies had begun to take shape and direction. These included administrative reorganizations, the beginnings of programs for basic physical infrastructure installation (electricity, roads, etc.), and others. Of all of these, the most important was the beginning of a massive distribution of land titles in 1971.[16]

In that year, instructions came from ONDEPJOV that titles were to be issued as quickly and as fully as possible throughout the administrative zones of Lima. A number of reasons for such emphasis are likely. For one thing, making land titles—*official* titles—available is clearly calculated to win support among the *pobladores*. The fact that prior to 1968 little effort had been made to distribute titles adds weight to this view. But at the same time, titles are not being forced upon the *pobladores*. An overwhelming majority classify obtaining a land title as highly important, and the reasons for such salience reveal the very urgent sense which many *pobladores* have concerning ownership. Legally, a *poblador* cannot sell his lot or will it to anyone in his family unless it is officially his (although de facto transfer of property in the *pueblos jóvenes* has been going on for years). Many *pobladores* prefer to perform such transfers in a binding and lawful fashion. Furthermore, for many *pobladores*, finally receiving an official title to land which they may have occupied for two decades or more represents the culmination of a process undertaken through individual *traspaso* (trespass) or group invasion and in effect vindicates their efforts and persistence. The rights and privileges of private property and of ownership constitute a major value for the *pobladores*, not only because of the desire to see their efforts succeed, but also because of the wish for security and permanence which a land title will give.[17]

ONDEPJOV is charged with the overall planning and coordination of a variety of activities. While its major focus and energies are directed toward the Lima situation, the office also carries on work in some twenty provincial cities. The national office in Lima has branches or departments with four basic aims: the coordination of sectoral work; the coordination of the local field offices (four in Lima and twenty in the provincial areas); the promotion of institutional resources; and the carrying out of national development plans for the squatter settlements. Thus the bulk of ONDEPJOV's work is administrative and coordinative. The actual field work—the execution of projects in one or more specific areas—is carried out by other agencies and ministries under the instructions of ONDEPJOV.

Most of the responsibility for executing ONDEPJOV policies falls to the Ministry of Housing and, within that body, to certain offices. The ministry was created shortly after the *golpe* of 1968 and took over the National Housing Board (JNV or Junta Nacional de la Vivienda), which in turn had been created from two previous agencies in the early years of Belaúnde's administration. Within the Ministry of Housing, of special concern is the office designated as the Dirección de Pueblos Jóvenes, best translated as Bureau or Agency for the *Pueblos Jóvenes*; we shall refer to it here simply as the DPJ. The DPJ is responsible for carrying out projects in the squatter settlements of Lima (in three of the geographic sectors; Callao has separate offices and agencies); most of the instructions to the DPJ come from the planning and other sections of ONDEPJOV. Within the DPJ exist several divisions, each responsible for particular types of work: programming, design, remodeling, property census and taxation, development, and legalization. It is the DPJ which implemented and carried out the land-title program mentioned above.

The major reasons for focusing upon the DPJ (admittedly out of proportion to its importance in the overall scheme of the Ministry of Housing) are (1) it is the executing and implementing body for directives from ONDEPJOV and therefore has the most intimate day-to-day contact with the settlements; (2) its personnel are the primary focus of demand-making activities and complaints (or both) on the part of the *pobladores* who wish to solicit assistance; since (3) the DPJ is *the* location to which any *poblador* from any settlement must come if he wishes to conduct any business with the Ministry of Housing or with ONDEPJOV.[18] Whether it be an individual matter—for instance, registering as an inhabitant of a specific settlement—or a communitywide project—for example, asking for assistance in surveying lots in a settlement or awarding land titles—a single *poblador* or an entire community must come to this specific office in order to make anything happen. This explains the reason for focusing upon the DPJ: Much of what the *pobladores* know of the government's work in the *pueblos jóvenes* derives from the actions of the DPJ. While the *pobladores* do, of course, develop opinions and attitudes regarding the performance and the effect of the government in many other ways, the personnel at the DPJ represent a factor common to all settlements.

The Office and the Pobladores

Having thus described the administrative roles which the Ministry of Housing and the DPJ play in terms of government-settlement relations, I can focus more closely upon some of the interactions which develop within the specific arena of the DPJ.[19] That is, I can probe into the established "rules of the game" or rituals of behavior for the *pobladores* in dealing with the DPJ and begin to analyze how (operating within these rules) a *poblador* can bring pressure to bear or at least attempt to make the personnel of the DPJ aware of his problems or desires. Bureaucratic rules and operations in the DPJ (and in most Peruvian governmental agencies) follow certain set, rigid, almost ritualistic patterns; and the success or failure of a bureaucratic undertaking will frequently depend upon an individual's being able to circumvent or break down these conventions. Of course, it can be argued that the Peruvian bureaucracy operates on just such a system of by-passing the written rules of the game, and that those people who cannot (for lack of connections) establish a particularistic tie with certain strategic members within a bureaucracy are doomed to interminable delays and minimally satisfactory results.

Perhaps the most fundamental rule of behavior in approaching the DPJ is simply not to break any rules—or at least not appear to be breaking any. Thus, coming to the DPJ either through one's own initiative or in response to a request by the DPJ, the individual presents himself as retiring (in the sense of not being pushy or impatient), eager to listen and to please, and thankful for the opportunity of coming to the DPJ. Such attitudes are especially apparent when the matter to be discussed is a new one. If the *poblador* appears because of ongoing discussions, he may display a businesslike attitude. But any display of belligerence or hostility would normally be considered not only bad form, but also prejudicial and harmful to the undertaking. The basic attitude, then, is compounded of respect for authority (probably real) and attentiveness and willingness to cooperate (perhaps less real).

This respect for authority stems from several sources and has several motives. In the first place, a *poblador* has a thoroughgoing respect for positions of authority and for the persons who hold them. Besides the fact that class and occupational differences create strongly felt and observed hierarchical perceptions, the presence (in some degree) of a patron-client relationship between the *poblador* and the DPJ personnel may be very real. Indeed, the DPJ itself may be perceived by the *poblador* as a patron, as an "individual" or source to which he can go for assistance or to plead his case.

Furthermore, in many ways, the *poblador* perceives himself (and correctly so) as in a weak position at best for demanding service. The inhabitants of any settlement—especially a recently founded invasion site—know full well that their situation is precarious and that a display of uncooperativeness will lead to delays of one sort or another. The remarks of a long-time leader are appropriate here. In discussing the level of conflict present within his community, he stated that:

> Here in —— there isn't much trouble, except when someone gets drunk and breaks up a bar or starts beating his wife—and then the neighbors try to calm things down if they can. Most people try to maintain tranquillity here because there are lots of kids. And besides, we don't want the authorities to think so, because then we won't get any help from them. When I go see someone at the mayor's office or at the *pueblos jóvenes* office, I always want to be able to tell them that our community doesn't cause trouble.

These remarks—although perhaps somewhat more cogently articulated than they might be by another person—illustrate a consistent desire on the part of a *poblador*: to present himself and his community as law-abiding and peaceful. Such an attitude is based in large part upon three beliefs: first, that such an attitude will convince the DPJ of the community's good intentions; second, that the *poblador* fully realizes his community's problems and the utility of the assistance the DPJ can offer; and third, that any attitude which might be interpreted as hostile could jeopardize the gains which the *pobladores* and their community have made. As many observers of the *pueblos jóvenes* have noted in the past, the *pobladores* operate in a high-risk position in that their occupancy and tenancy are normally illegal and de facto only. They may have risked a great deal to establish themselves, and they are in no way willing to gamble what they have gained. Therefore, attitudes which might in some way alienate the DPJ and its staff will normally be suppressed, and overt hostility will not be perceived as a positive strategy in demand-making.

The facts that the DPJ does exist, that it is charged with carrying out the policies of the Ministry of Housing and of ONDEPJOV, and that the *pobladores* are aware of this responsibility further reinforce the strict adherence to rules and to convention. In sharp contrast to their willingness to participate in a land invasion, most *pobladores* show great unwillingness to become involved in anything resembling an illegal act, and many of them admit that undertaking the invasion produced considerable fear of government retaliation through forced eviction or dislocation. For example, while less than half of a random sample (42%) report that their principal feeling during the invasion was one of fear, fully four out of five had expected resistance in one form or another.[20] The major motive for invasion participation—to become a landowner or homeowner—could not be met in any other way. However, since an institutional arrangement for satisfying the need for assistance and for other highly salient desires—for example, a land title—does indeed exist, the *pobladores* appear most willing to accommodate themselves to the patterns and rules of working within that framework. The desire for legality and, more broadly, for acceptance, along with a very low risk-taking potential, promote high levels of observance toward rules and procedures.

Interactions can be initiated either by the community or by the DPJ. But regardless of who first makes the contact, the interaction which takes place and the strategies employed by the *pobladores* in efforts to bring about a favorable (in their perceptions) resolution of a problem or an action remain largely the same. In exploring these strategies, I am in effect examining bureaucratic behavior of the bureaucrat himself. Moreover, I am concerned with an almost purely bureaucratic relationship. The personnel of the DPJ are public servants and are largely immune to electoral political pressures. In addition, indirect pressures—demonstrations against the administrator, for instance—are largely unattractive owing to the risk involved. Thus the question for the *poblador* is as follows: How can I act in such a way as to adhere to formal rules of behavior, and yet still generate responses in the DPJ favorable to my cause?

First, in dealing with personnel of the DPJ, most *pueblo joven* representatives are more than willing to demonstrate potential cooperation by offering their organizational efforts to contribute to whatever the project might be—ditch-digging for water or sewerage pipes, in the case of an undertaking requiring extensive physical labor, or simply promising to arrange within the community for facilities to be ready and the word passed if a DPJ representative or team plans to come to the community and speak at an *asamblea* (community meeting). Such offers may often be accompanied by references to past efforts (either real or exaggerated), during which the community—and its leaders—demonstrated all manner of collaboration and cooperation. Not only are such references meant to demonstrate the community's willingness to assist; they also present the community leaders as responsible, serious workers, able to mobilize their communities when called upon to do so.

A community representative will make every effort to develop and maintain his visibility in front of the DPJ personnel he encounters. One way of so doing has already been mentioned: references to previous contacts, exchanges, and undertakings. Another technique involves frequent, repeated visits, either to initiate a project (or express a need), or to push along one already in the works. The size of the DPJ (approximately one hundred and twenty employees) and the very large number of projects and responsibilities carried on by them at any given moment force community leaders to do anything they can to call attention to themselves and their needs. Repeated contacts and visits, then, are an attempt to fix the problems of a specific community in the mind of DPJ personnel and to prod along a project for the settlement. Along with this goes an unwritten rule for most community leaders: "Never leave the DPJ without making an appointment or setting a date for another visit." Not only does this commit the DPJ to see the community spokesman once again (whether or not any progress has been made); it also allows the leader to report back to his community that he has visited the DPJ, discussed the matter of present concern, and that he has obtained another meeting to continue the discussion.

Such visits may also permit a *poblador* to establish the most useful of contacts: a close relationship with a DPJ staff member which can develop to the point where a planner, architect, or social worker in the

DPJ will concentrate more fully on his problem and assign it priority in the DPJ's working schedule. This arrangement, of course, is highly valued and valuable, and something to be nurtured (but not overplayed or pushed too hard).

The techniques mentioned thus far concern the *poblador* spokesman and the DPJ in more or less general terms. That is, they are probable actions or maneuvers which might reasonably be employed by any individual. But it might still be asked: What possible means of creating pressure or for forcing the pace exist for the *poblador*, especially when he must adhere strictly to rules and decorum? Can he, in any modest or indirect way, place a demand in such a way as to threaten the DPJ? An answer to these questions calls for some discussion of what the DPJ would perceive as a threat or (at least) as a situation to be avoided.

Within the DPJ, perhaps the strongest desire for the personnel is that work flow roughly according to schedule, with the fewest possible interruptions or surprises. The workload and available time for completing work are mapped out in blocks of a month or several months; the upper levels of the Ministry of Housing expect projects to be carried out in the time allotted. Thus, when the massive push for the distribution of land titles began in 1971, the very substantial amounts of preparation which titles require placed a heavy burden upon the DPJ to keep up to date and to cope with unforeseen developments as quickly as possible. Occasionally, however, the DPJ is hit by totally unpredictable events.

In May 1971, one of the largest and most publicized land invasions of a decade occurred on land south of downtown Lima, near a settlement called Pamplona. At its height, an estimated twenty-five to thirty thousand people were squatting on public and private lands on both sides of the Pan American Highway. While the national political repercussions of the Pamplona invasion occupied most of the public's attention, the pressures which this event placed upon the DPJ strained its facilities and personnel severely. The policy reaction of the Ministry of Housing was to forbid the invasion to remain on the site, but to make available state lands further south in an area christened Villa El Salvador. Some fifty thousand lots were hurriedly surveyed and opened to the invaders, and the task of arranging for the distribution of these lots, and for checking each applicant for possession of land elsewhere in Lima, fell to the DPJ. Furthermore, because of the very high salience given the invasion by the press and other media, the government took great pains to insure that its policy was carried out promptly. A bureau head in the Ministry of Housing responsible for processing the applications for the official lots in Villa El Salvador incurred the personal wrath of President Juan Velasco who, upon visiting the agency and finding waiting lines of up to three city blocks, summarily fired the hapless bureaucrat for inefficiency.

While the Pamplona invasion represents an admittedly unusual or even unique event, it offered the *pobladores* of the *pueblos jóvenes* in Lima more than one way to apply some pressure to DPJ personnel. First, the total (and unexpected) dedication of all DPJ facilities to coping with the invasion brought about an abrupt halt to almost all other activity; plans and programs were put to one side while all ministry energies focused upon opening the new lands for the invaders. Quite naturally, people in areas in which work was underway or expected became bitter. As the same leader cited earlier stated:

> We've been after assistance from the DPJ for almost two years, and we've gone through all the red tape and the channels that we're supposed to—and now these invaders who've been there two weeks get everything that they ask for: land and titles and even street lights, while we've been waiting for twenty years for that. It's not right (*no es justo*).

Few community spokesmen felt any hesitation about stating such feelings to the DPJ personnel, who had little to say except that they had been following orders from above. The Pamplona invasion thus allowed the *pobladores* to criticize the DPJ with no fear of recrimination. The technique most commonly used involved four different stages: commiserating with DPJ personnel about the added work; complaining about the injustice (mentioned above); hurriedly reassuring the DPJ that the reasons for such injustice were understandable and that the blame actually lay elsewhere; and, finally, intimating that if the lost time and injustice were not made up, the community which they represented might become, in some way, unmanageable.

This last stage constitutes a veiled threat that is possible only under certain conditions at best; the large-scale Pamplona invasion was an ideal situation for its implementation. Normally all efforts are made to maintain the appearance of wanting to work only within the legal and customary structures of the DPJ. But if a *poblador* can make some sort of threat, he will in fact make it, thereby maximizing his chances for a favorable response. The Pamplona invasion allowed what both the *pobladores* and many of the DPJ personnel saw as a legitimate complaint—and beyond that, it put the *pobladores* on relatively firm footing for further demand-making.

Just how was the Pamplona invasion utilized? Perhaps the phrase which best sums it up would be "professed impotence" on the part of a *poblador* leader or spokesman in reference to his own position in the community. That is, he could claim (whether in fact the situation actually existed or not) that his community contained large numbers of people who were upset over the preferential treatment shown the recent invaders, and who might manifest their discontent through some sort of action—generally, by trying to circumvent the DPJ and going to the minister directly, to some other highly placed official, or (whether seriously or not) to the president. Such a move, if ever carried out, might reflect upon the DPJ staff and thus constitute a threat to their jobs. As mentioned above, the invasion very nicely permitted such a strategy; however, a *poblador* could use this technique at other times as well, when circumstances allowed a reasonable case for community dissatisfaction to be made.

Tied directly to the Pamplona invasion, of course, was the possibility of specifically informing the DPJ that some individual or group in the community was threatening to promote another land invasion elsewhere in the city. Revealing such conditions voluntarily (again, whether true or not) gave the spokesman a double advantage: First, by "revealing" such a possibility, he could demonstrate his good will, thus creating an image of himself and his community (except for a few renegade members) as willing to cooperate. While he could minimize the potential disruptive ability of these discontented *pobladores*, the leader would also admit that if his request were not acted upon soon, he might not be able to control this group, and thus—despite all his good intentions—another invasion might possibly take place, *and it would be the fault of the DPJ if it did.* The DPJ had been warned; community desires had been stated; and the community spokesman had done all he possibly could. If trouble occurred, the DPJ would have no one to blame but itself.

Such a strategy was employed more than once at the DPJ in the weeks immediately following the invasion; on each of these occasions, the community leader protested to the DPJ that the possible troublemakers in his community were not members of his association, that they had caused difficulties before, and that—insofar as he was concerned—"It's a pity that everyone in the community can't wait and be patient like me and the members of my association. But these other people have always caused trouble, and if there are any more delays, they may be able to get some more support, because everybody really is upset." Such reasoning thus removed the spokesman from a position of personally threatening the DPJ and yet placed the DPJ in the position of being threatened, either by disruption within a community or by the possibility of being circumvented. Pleading personal allegiance to and preference for operating in the "right" way, the *poblador* spokesman was nevertheless able to manufacture some small edge for manipulating the system at minimal risk to himself or his community.

While the desire to work within the rules of the game usually dominates most action choices among *poblador* spokesmen, occasionally the relationships between a community and the DPJ deteriorate or stagnate to such a point that the community may feel compelled to look elsewhere for a redress of wrongs. Just such a move was undertaken by the Association of Families in one community. After a protracted and (from their point of view) highly unsatisfactory relationship with a specific member of the DPJ staff, the community leaders drafted a petition addressed to the Ministry of Housing and spent several months and considerable money for lawyer's fees following it through the bureaucratic apparatus of the ministry. At the same time, however, the community leaders maintained contact with the DPJ, and although they carefully avoided the individual who, in their eyes, had caused much of their difficulty, they felt little hesitation in voicing their complaints about treatment received or in mentioning at convenient moments that their petition to the ministry was *en tramite* (being acted upon). DPJ personnel, for their part, expressed little overt interest in the petition, but the bureaucratic and procedural logjams which had tied up work in the community for many months did in fact finally break loose.

The option of going outside the normal boundaries or rules is, perhaps, always available; yet the difficulties involved prevent its becoming commonly employed. It is, for one thing, tedious, time-consuming, and expensive, generally involving repeated visits to the ministry and the advice of a lawyer, who must be paid. Furthermore, approaching the minister (or some other equivalent authority) involves, for the *poblador*, introducing a substantial element of chance into his calculations, in that the ministry and the minister constitute actors and an arena outside the usual and familiar. DPJ personnel are reasonably accessible, while the minister is a figure to whom a petition is submitted, after which it is beyond any sort of control or manipulation. All things considered, therefore, most community leaders would probably agree with one who said:

> It takes a long time to work things out at the DPJ; everywhere there's so much red tape (*papeleo*), and we have to keep going back over and over again, which takes a lot of time as well. But after a while they get to know you there; I know who is supposed to be working on the remodeling project, and I go right to him or to Engineer Fulano to see what's been done since I was there last. You've got to be patient, though, and keep on. Little by little things start to happen, but I have to keep on top of it all the time.

Poblador Evaluations of Government
Personnel and Performance

My approach to *poblador*-DPJ relationships has, up to this point, been highly descriptive; I have made little attempt to present data which touch upon overall perceptions of treatment by government authorities. Now that I have described the DPJ, its policies, and the nature of *poblador*-DPJ interactions, a discussion of *poblador* evaluations is more appropriate. That is, I can ask whether the activist—the individual who demands more from the DPJ, and who demands more consistently and frequently—develops a more critical attitude toward the government officials with whom he interacts.[21]

The data in table 1 indicate that differences between activists and the inactive are minimal. The two items dealing specifically with treatment at the DPJ vary but slightly, whether the contact with the DPJ originated for any reason or for the explicit purpose of making a demand. Predictions as to how courteous treatment might be during a hypothetical visit to a ministry again show no difference. Thus, neither the place of socialization, length of residence, specific community (with one exception), nor degree of activism appears to create a noticeable

Table 1. Treatment Received and Expected from National Political Authorities

Question	Activist	Inactive	X^2 Sig.
1. Are you acquainted with the ONDEPJOV office near Unidad Vecinal No. 3? Have you ever gone there? How do you think you were treated there? (Better, same as other people.)	83.2%	88.1%	>.05
		(N=149)	
2. Have you ever personally, alone, or with other residents of ——, gone to speak with some official of ONDEPJOV about some problem or need? What kind of treatment did you receive? (Officials paid much attention to request.)	86.8	78.4	>.05
		(N=128)	
3. If you were to go to the office of government—for example, the Ministry of Health—would you say that they would treat you better, the same, or worse than somebody else? (Better, same as other people.)	94.3	88.1	>.05
		(N=402)	

difference among the *pobladores* in terms of their reception at government offices.

But interpersonal relationships are one thing; evaluations of actual government performance may be quite another. Table 2 contains data which reveal that while place of socialization is almost completely irrelevant, length of residence varies directly with an increasingly favorable evaluation of government performance. In addition, evaluations of the government fluctuate very markedly across the five communities: Primer de Enero is much the harshest in its overall opinion, with Pampa de Arena next; Santiago and Zone A of 28 de Julio are almost equal; while Zone B is by far the most favorable. Finally, the activists appear to judge the government somewhat more unfavorably. However, analysis of activist-inactive differences demonstrates two further patterns: First, the number of activists decreases sharply as the community becomes more developed; and second, evaluation of government per-

Table 2. Evaluation of Governmental Performance,
by Selected Variables

	Favorable	Unfavorable
Migrant	48.0%	52.0%
Native	47.7	52.3
Activist	38.1	61.9
Inactive	53.9	46.1
Length of residence		
Short	28.8	71.2
Medium	53.0	47.0
Long	64.2	35.8
Community of residence		
Primer de Enero	21.6	78.4
Pampa de Arena	40.2	59.8
Santiago	55.9	44.1
28 de Julio, Zone A	59.3	40.7
28 de Julio, Zone B	78.2	21.8

N=411.
Notes: The evaluation of performance is an index derived from respondents' judgments of governmental success or failure in the following areas: providing water, electricity, sewerage, sidewalks, streets, police protection, land titles, educational facilities, and work for unemployed individuals.
X^2 significance level is less than .005, except for migrant-native differences.

formance becomes very much more positive for both the activist and the inactive as time passes.

These data, along with the accounts of *poblador* relationships with the DPJ, provide convincing evidence that as an agency and access point the DPJ functions successfully *according to the perceptions of the pobladores*. Their perceptions and evaluations are not those of a clientele which feels itself without knowledge of, or access to, the political system. Nor, as indicated by ways in which incremental strategies are at times employed with some success in dealing with the DPJ, do community spokesmen perceive the flow of influence as exclusively one-way. While many decisions come from the DPJ and are fed down to the *pobladores*, more than half of the activists have taken the initiative to contact the DPJ on more than a few occasions and (moreover) feel the DPJ to be receptive to such initiatives.

In addition, the *pobladores* do not expect the DPJ to respond immediately to their demands, a fact which helps to explain why the very modest strategies described satisfy the *pobladores*, and why the *pobladores* do not assume more aggressive or militant attitudes. A respect for authority figures, in turn embedded in a perception of rigid hierarchical stratification, acts to inhibit agressive or strident demand-making among a population which, it must be remembered, is in a position where such acts can be very risky. In addition, the *pobladores*—both the inactive and the activists—see their problems as solvable, either through their own efforts, through governmental assistance, or through a combination of both, and they remain firmly convinced that the government will eventually honor its responsibilities. An "informed cynicism" vis-à-vis interactions with the DPJ or with delays is certainly present among those *pobladores* with frequent contact. However, this cynicism is also clearly limited: Neither widespread alienation nor apathy nor frustration is noticeable among the *pobladores* in their relations with the DPJ or, for that matter, in their overall perceptions and interactions with the government in general. We have, therefore, a cluster of several factors: low risk-taking propensities; expectations for governmental assistance; a willingness to accept bureaucratic delays, procedures, and directives; and an overall belief or faith that the DPJ can (or will, in time) accomplish its responsibilities. This clustering maintains highly predictable patterns of behavior in dealing with the DPJ and keeps demand-making of an aggressive or (from the DPJ's point of view) unmanageable nature at a minimum. For the DPJ and its personnel, such a state of affairs is both desirable and vital; for the *pobladores*, little else appears to be available or realistic for coping with a situation in which the potential loss in delays and postponement of aid for erratic or strident behavior far outweigh any gain.

The Pobladores, Their Communities, and SINAMOS

This account of agency-*poblador* relationships describes one of the primary arenas available to the squatters for political action. Such petitioning and maneuvering are highly political, in that they clearly comprise activities which attempt to influence the distribution of governmental resources. But a question emerges: Is this political activity participation? Participation as generally defined includes voluntary involvement in one form or another. Lester Milbrath, for instance, claims that passive political behavior becomes active involvement only when an individual (for instrumental or expressive motives) *voluntarily* undertakes a political action.[22] Asking a bureaucracy (the DPJ) to satisfy a communal need through presentation of a demand might conceivably be considered a voluntary act, since (theoretically) a *pueblo joven* is not absolutely forced to request assistance from the government. But such bureaucratic petitioning is in no way equivalent to, for instance, demanding that new decrees be promulgated to broaden the scope of DPJ activity, or that new resources be made available to satisfy a need. Acts such as these are designed to create inputs to the system, while the *pobladores* aim only to request a share of predetermined policies and outputs. They do not attempt (or even think to attempt) to influence the choice of DPJ personnel, the formation of policy (except in the very narrowest community-specific sense), or resource-allocation processes. The *pobladores* are not a pressure group, because they concentrate on vying for those resources the government decides will be made available. In this sense, they must be classified, not as participants, but rather as clients.

Since the sorts of *poblador*-DPJ relationships I have described are more bureaucratic and clientelistic than anything else, we can reasonably ask whether the *pobladores* do in fact *participate* in politics, in the sense that they can become involved in those decisions which most clearly affect their lives. Such a question becomes especially important since political participation is often consciously or unconsciously thought to be associated with, and unique to, democratic systems.

The post-1968 military regime in Peru has concerned itself with the subject of participation, and at great length. Statements by various highly placed spokesmen reflect a considerable amount of thought behind the problems of mobilizing and involving large numbers of people in the programs of the Revolutionary Government. Purely bureaucratic relationships do not provide suitable scope for participation, in the judgment of the government. Thus the Revolutionary Government has, in the past few years, given increasing attention to strategies and mechanisms for creating new opportunities for greater and greater numbers of people—especially those groups previously on the margins of society—to develop a stake in its policies and programs.

The goal of mobilization is, of course, not unique to Peru. As Myron Weiner notes,

> Transformative elites . . . need public support to carry out their goals. Indeed, their object is typically to transform the attitudes and behavior of their citizens. Therefore most of the authoritarian elites governing the developing areas seek active rather than passive support and view some forms of political participation as desirable. Such governing elites often try to find new forms of political participation of the sort that will encourage or even mobilize citizens to support the regime and its goals.[23]

What concerns us here is the nature of the Peruvian attempt to mobilize support. By analyzing the characteristics, ideology, and structure of the program, the problems inherent in any such attempt, and the particular strategies through which the Revolutionary Government hopes to avoid them, I hope to develop a framework which can both incorporate these several elements and also be used in comparative analysis of similar regimes and attempts.

Early moves by the Revolutionary Government in this direction occurred in 1970 and 1971, when workers in industry and then in mining and fishing were granted a share of the profits and a voice in the management of their companies. But while these reforms and the "communities" they create within their respective economic sectors represent potentially significant innovations, two points should be made: First, workers in these sectors had been organized previously; and second, these reforms are sector-specific within the economic, and not the social, sphere of Peru. In other words, these reforms do not constitute a broad-range attempt at mobilizing those people who historically make up the masses of Peru—namely, the unorganized, the poor, and the marginal, whether rural or urban.

On June 22, 1971, the Revolutionary Government took the first large step to close this gap, through the promulgation of the Law of Social Mobilization. This law and its implementing agency, known as SINAMOS (Sistema Nacional del Apoyo a la Mobilizacion Social, National System of Support for Social Mobilization), appeared at least partially in response to the spontaneous emergence of Committees for the Defense of the Revolution, which developed largely in Lima/Callao and the coastal regions of Peru. The military government praised the idea of such progovernment support but soon took steps to co-opt these committees, ostensibly to prevent their use by partisan groups. However, a more fundamental reason lay in the very strong determination of the government to initiate, organize, and control any sort of grassroots organization. SINAMOS is the most far-reaching move yet by the government in this direction.

The goal of SINAMOS is to achieve the conscious and active participation of the population in the tasks of social and economic development. To this end, it

> stimulates and supports the organization of the people; it informs the basic social groupings about the meaning of the social transformations [of the government] and their relationships with revolutionary theory, with present-day society, and with the model for social organizations proposed by the revolution; it channels popular demands toward the government and also carries to the basic levels [of organization] the executive acts that stimulate and support free and democratic popular participation.[24]

According to Carlos Delgado, the process of social mobilization clearly includes participation and does not mean simply the organizing of people for public demonstrations or marches, but "more directly and ... with greater realism, undertaking *a historical process* ... to *change the structure of power of* [Peruvian] society."[25] To gain this end, Delgado posits two complementary and equally essential paths: *structural reforms*, to alter substantially the relations of power and property within the economy; and *popular participation*, to assist in the realization of economic and structural reforms and, in general, in the concrete tasks of the revolutionary construction of a new society in Peru.

For Delgado, the absence of meaningful mechanisms for participation among the lower levels of society explains in large part why formal democracy always maintained an elitist and discriminatory character in Peru, and why it always had something of a foreign character about it, since it failed to relate to the experiences and lives of the lower sectors of society. To rectify such a failure, Delgado calls for the creation of a web of participatory infrastructures which would integrate all organizations the population itself creates throughout all spheres of activity. These should become genuinely autonomous organizations, subject only to the decisions of their members. Experience gained in developing these institutions will thus point out the best routes for achieving a successful move from the local to the national level, and will allow policy decisions to be translated into coherent actions which will be authentically democratic and contain a high degree of genuine popular representation. Having stated these goals and methods, Delgado acknowledges that both are susceptible to being labeled utopian and abstract and therefore goes into a lengthy discussion of the philosophy, definition, operation, and organization of SINAMOS.

After its *golpe* in 1968, the Revolutionary Government had three alternatives: the creation of an official political party; the utilization of one or more traditional parties; or (and the route chosen) the rejection of all previous assumptions of the basis of political action and participation, and a redefinition of what constitutes political activity. This latter involved, for the government, a fundamental recasting of politics to include micro decision-making as well as the "great national issues" which had previously occupied center stage.

> Politics refers to the things that affect the real, concrete future of human beings on a smaller scale, but of very real (*indesdeñable*) significance. It [is] not a question, therefore, of reducing the meaningful universe of politics, but of enlarging it to guarantee that it [will] faithfully articulate the lives of those who make up society.[26]

Attaining this end calls for the development of an organizational structure which will simultaneously permit a massive broadening of participation *horizontally* throughout previously marginal sectors, while allowing needs, desires, and decisions to move *vertically* from micro, local levels up to the "superstructural levels of politics." Thus SINAMOS and a three-tiered organization emerged, which incorporate some eight state organizations, each of which in some way has access to large segments of Peru's population. These eight include:

1. National Fund for Economic Development, State Development Corporations, and Public Works Boards created by special legislation
2. National Office for the Development of the *Pueblos Jóvenes*
3. National Office for Community Development
4. National Office for Cooperative Development
5. General Agency for Community Development (previously called Cooperación Popular)
6. Agency for Peasant Organizations
7. Agency for Peasant Communities
8. Agency for Promotion and Diffusion of the Agrarian Reform

On the highest level, the National Office of Support for Social Mobilization (ONAMS) coordinates SINAMOS activities in six basic areas: cultural and professional organizations; economic organizations of "social interest" (cooperatives, etc.); labor; youth; rural areas; and the *pueblos jóvenes*, together with areas labeled "internal urban underdevelopment," or central slums. An intermediate level consists of eleven Regional Offices of Support for Social Mobilization (ORAMS), each of which has responsibility for one to five of Peru's *departamentos* (states).[27] Below this operate some thirty-five (of a projected seventy-five) zonal offices (OZAMS), which have the most direct contact with the local population. The most critical section in a zonal office is the Unit for Promotion of Base-Line Organizations, made up of teams of promoters who work directly with the people. It is the zonal offices, according to Delgado, which

> guarantee the direct presence of the population itself in the planning of local development actions. Here is made concrete the decisive focus of basic planning, through which the development of each locale and region will be the result of joint action by the state and the representative entities of the population. In this way, the actions of SINAMOS will be increasingly those decided by the participatory base-line organizations themselves.[28]

And of course it is at the zonal level that the most intimate and day-to-day contact occurs between SINAMOS workers—the field promoters, for the most part—and the *poblador*.

SINAMOS has, in effect, become a wholly new element in *poblador*-government relationships and has created new rules for mediating and governing *poblador* access to supracommunity resources. For instance, the program of land-title distribution has continued; however, for a community to receive land titles no longer depends only upon meeting the various bureaucratic criteria of recognition, remodeling, and so on. Rather, the basis and the internal structure of a community's local association must now be approved by SINAMOS.

Ostensibly, SINAMOS directives describe and encourage community reorganization on the grounds that a settlement must be well organized in order for community projects to succeed, and that all communities should have similar structures so that all can be treated equally and can respond equally to government decrees and policies. Based upon this assumption, SINAMOS' goal has become one of implanting a grassroots organization, based upon three representatives elected from each block or unit of the settlement in question. These three individuals—secretaries of coordination, organization, and economy—constitute neighborhood committees; all the secretaries of coordination elect from their members a General Committee of Promotion and Development. This committee then elects from its members a Central Governing Board (Junta Directiva Central), composed of six members: a secretary general, a subsecretary general, and secretaries of organization, economy, culture, and publicity. These six are the elected leaders of the community and link the settlement and the government for all negotiations; they also pass government directives on to the community.[29]

SINAMOS personnel have also directed numerous other activities in the *pueblos jóvenes*, including the promotion of electricity and water systems, self-help housing, and the like. Such projects, it should be

emphsized, are *promoted* by—but not actually accomplished through—
SINAMOS. SINAMOS is thus the arranger or broker who brings together the *pobladores* (who offer the manual labor and the guarantee to
repay a loan) and, say, a public utility which actually installs the
services. In Villa El Salvador (the government-sponsored settlement
organized after the Pamplona invasion), the secretary of economy
reported that with the assistance of SINAMOS, "we are grouping
together the shoemakers, carpenters, bricklayers, electricians, tailors,
cooks, bakers, and everyone else, in order to achieve a truly cooperative
undertaking. But not an undertaking which exploits us, but one where
all are members."[30]

The principal raison d'être for SINAMOS, shown in ideological
writings and pronouncements as well as in the actions of the field
promoters, emerges from the Revolutionary Government's determination to *organize* the whole of Peruvian society. "SINAMOS is a school
for participation," according to General Leonidas Rodriguez Figueroa,
its first director.[31] The individual citizen is thus the student, and
SINAMOS the instructor. Through its efforts, mechanisms of participation are designed and implemented (for example, the organization of
local associations in the *pueblos jóvenes*) so that a citizen can become
involved, *as long as he is willing to work within the approved structures.*
The Committees for the Defense of the Revolution, mentioned earlier,
were by all accounts a truly spontaneous grassroots phenomenon. Their
very spontaneity, however, caused their co-optation, eventual demise,
and replacement by SINAMOS.

Thus the goals, structures, and policies of SINAMOS and its hierarchical organization are fairly clear. I shall leave an analysis of
SINAMOS as a political entity, and the nature of *poblador*-SINAMOS
relationships, until later. But one further question must be addressed,
namely, how is the future of SINAMOS envisioned? Is it a permanent
or temporary fixture of the Revolutionary Government? While any
prediction as to what SINAMOS may do over the next few years is an
extremely hazardous business, can other nations' experiences with
mobilization campaigns of various kinds offer us any clue as to the
future course SINAMOS may follow, and the problems it may encounter?

In the essay from which I have quoted extensively, Delgado declares
repeatedly and emphatically that SINAMOS is *not* a political party,
that it does *not* inject itself into other organizations to direct or
manipulate them, that it is *not* meant to speak for a specific class or
sector of society, and that (most importantly)

it is not intended to be a permanent institution in [Peru]. Contrary to all
such assertions, SINAMOS can be defined as an institution for support, *and*

one of transitory life, that stimulates the growth of popular organizations so that, progressively, the decision-making power in all spheres of life . . . can be transferred to such organizations.[32]

Thus the organization of SINAMOS will, it is claimed, gradually disappear as the *instituciones del pueblo* (institutions of the people) become capable of assuming the functions and responsibilities now in the hands of state agencies. But as David Scott Palmer observers:

> [While SINAMOS] takes the important step of formalizing the commitment of the military government to the gradual turning over of responsibility for decision-making to organized citizens, . . . it is also apparent that the military government feels that the time has not yet come to relax its own final control over the participation stimulation process . . . the tension over freedom at the base and control from the center remains.[33]

I shall leave until the conclusion an analysis of the Revolutionary Government and the nature of the regime in general terms. Of more immediate concern here are questions which deal not so much with why SINAMOS has generated such acrimony,[34] but rather with some of the central problems the Revolutionary Government may face in attempting to impose SINAMOS on the *pueblos jóvenes* and with how best to characterize the nature of SINAMOS' relationship with the *pobladores*.[35]

Data of any nature about SINAMOS-*poblador* relationships, or on *poblador* evaluations of SINAMOS, are exceedingly scarce. Moreover, given the nature of SINAMOS, it is logical to expect that evaluations will vary from community to community. On the one hand, SINAMOS has, according to numerous reports, achieved considerable success in some newer settlements and invasion areas. In 1972, for example, promoters organized a group of families in a community and helped them form their own savings cooperative. By December 1973, this group then moved and took over a sizable portion of empty adjoining land and put up its collected savings as a down payment. SINAMOS then helped acquire the land through official expropriation and assisted in making land titles available.[36] We would expect that in such a community, which literally owes its existence to SINAMOS' collaboration and guidance, opinions of SINAMOS would be quite high.

On the other hand, a number of the *pobladores* in an area called 28 de Julio revealed a high degree of irritation over the wholesale restructuring of the local association. An ex-president of 28 de Julio, and a man of crucial importance in the successes of his community, claimed that his bitterness lay not in the fact that he and his colleagues were no longer in power, but rather in the fact that SINAMOS promoters had treated him (and by extension, the settlement as a whole) as someone who had never been able to do anything for himself until SINAMOS arrived on the scene. He resented this intimation very strongly.

SINAMOS does, in fact, display such an attitude:

> The *pueblos jóvenes* have, in the past, been a favorite spot for *"criollo"* politicians, for dealers who prey on want (*necesidad popular*), for the ternal promise makers. In the *pueblos jóvenes* literal "mafias" have grown up, intermediaries who prosper (as individuals or groups) by offering solutions to common problems in exchange for personal gain and influence over the *pobladores.*
>
> This situation of exploitation resulted in a great number of the *pobladores'* becoming accustomed to the idea that the central government or other authorities were going to resolve their problems, always in exchange for votes or other favors to the government. *This attitude, of waiting for everything from above* instead of attending a meeting or voting or creating public pressure, must give way to a new sense of individual responsibility, with the *pobladores* confronting problems themselves and increasing their capacity for decision-making by learning and practicing that capacity.[37]

This paternalistic attitude, which also finds expression in the constant theme of having to instruct and teach *el pueblo* how to participate in the programs of the Revolutionary Government, brings up the matter of whether—and how—SINAMOS may eventually withdraw from its position of stimulating and political organizing, and in fact devolve decision-making power to the *pobladores* and other previously marginal groups in Peruvian society. At present, it is far too early to predict; moreover, SINAMOS' future cannot be discussed *ceteris paribus*. SINAMOS and its goals have caused considerable and poorly hidden controversies within the military. A shuffling of power groups in the cabinet, or the demise of President Velasco, could bring an abrupt termination or reduction in SINAMOS activities. But aside from such "external" changes, the stated goal of turning power over to the population, set against a strong desire to retain control over the process of mobilization, provides a constant source of tension.[38]

An example with some striking similarities (and admittedly strong differences) that may offer some indication of problems is the United States' War on Poverty and the many attempts to encourage and force representatives from among the poor to participate on the local governing boards of community action agencies—attempts based on the "maximum feasible participation" clause of the Economic Opportunities Act which created the Office of Economic Opportunity (OEO). In a study of the War on Poverty in the Los Angeles area, Dale Marshall concludes that *participation* of the poor is not equal to their actually having *power;* rather, "while the poor are formally equal participants and in fact do participate actively in the discussions and work of . . . policy-making boards they have not gained power on [them]."[39] Instead, in Marshall's interpretation, this is an almost classic case of co-optation, in which the community representatives have been absorbed into the leadership or policy-making structure of the organization so as to avert any possible threat to the stability or existence of the organization itself.[40] In Peru, the actions of the government toward the original Committees for the Defense of the Revolution went well beyond mere co-optation, of course: The committees totally disappeared. But the moves by SINAMOS to make restructuring a prerequisite to such valued goods as land titles parallel the OEO's policies which—while providing access to resources for the poor—also discouraged and disarmed any competing autonomous groups, thereby maintaining OEO in a position of superiority. SINAMOS has commonly done away with existing local groups rather than utilize them. Whether these SINAMOS-backed organizations will be as effective as their predecessors remains to be seen. More important, the critical matter of whether SINAMOS can or will relinquish its penetration of the *pueblos jóvenes* remains totally open. Be that as it may, Richard Cloward's conclusion about the involvement of the U.S. poor on local action boards may possibly have relevance for Peru:

> Membership on policy-making bodies may confer a little prestige on the poor persons who participate, but . . . having been granted representation on . . . antipoverty councils, they now seem vaguely uneasy about their victory. They [may] begin to sense that they have been victorious on the wrong battlefield or a relatively non-strategic one.[41]

But the co-optive, controlled aspect of both the War on Poverty and SINAMOS constitutes only one facet of the participation question. Another side of the matter needs further exploration. For those individuals who become active in these innovations—the Community Action Agencies of the OEO, or the SINAMOS-inspired local community organizations—does such involvement have a basic politicizing effect beyond the fixed life of the institution itself? A study among Mexican-Americans who became involved as members of Community Action Agency boards in Los Angeles reveals that they developed a higher propensity to try to affect government, a greater capability in knowledge of the government and its workings, higher skills and techniques for creating pressure, and greater overall political participatory behavior. Experience as CAA members thus "took"; politicization among members remained significantly higher than among nonmembers, even after the War on Poverty itself, along with its structures and institutions, was dismantled.[42]

Comparable data among the *pobladores* are not available. But if the stated goals of SINAMOS do in the future become actualized, the result could be a rise in the numbers of *pobladores* who are familiar with the system, know how to operate within it, and may become increasingly difficult to satisfy. The initial problems facing SINAMOS of stimulating participation may fade over the long run and be replaced by the difficulties of coping with rising demand-making and expectations that these demands will be met. The burden may then be upon the government to fulfill its pledges of independent, autonomous decision-making, and to provide the resources needed for such fulfillment.

Another important test will come if the government has to decide whether to allow participation to take hold and flourish which starts to oppose SINAMOS or the government itself. SINAMOS was created because of the recognition that a means was needed to mobilize the citizenry to participate in the task of building a new society in Peru—an effort which is at present directed almost totally from the top. A possibility exists, however, that if SINAMOS succeeds in its task of mobilizing and politicizing the population, the Revolutionary Government may find that it will have created an organization as capable of opposing the government as of supporting it. If this point is reached, then the government will be faced with deciding whether it truly intends to abide by its pledges to permit full and active participation, even if this means opposition to its goals.

Finally, the most severe problem for SINAMOS may well be that of massive rejection by the *pobladores* (and by other affected segments of society as well). The tendencies of SINAMOS field workers and administrators to be dictatorial and highhanded as well as paternalistic, to intrude where they are not wanted, and above all to fail to carry through on promises may have caused more difficulty than either SINAMOS or the government has counted on. Indeed, by 1975 SINAMOS was in the midst of a thoroughgoing internal reorganization, and it was widely felt that much if not all of SINAMOS' responsibility in the *pueblos jóvenes* would revert to the Ministry of Housing, and that SINAMOS itself would be vastly reduced in its scope of activities, budget, and personnel.

SINAMOS as a Clientelist Participatory Mechanism

The identification of these potentially troublesome areas (paternalism, co-optation, and rejection) can now be brought together with another point from our discussion of the DPJ—namely, the clientelistic nature of the *pobladores'* demand-making. And what begins to emerge is a purposefully structured hierarchical system using carrot and stick to channel, control, and defuse potential demand-making among the *pobladores*. Prior to SINAMOS, ONDEPJOV had undertaken selective *pueblo joven* reorganization. Sara Michl noted that by "helping *pobladores* provide for their own physical development needs, and by creating and controlling organization within the settlements, the government may hope to confine demand-making to the institutional channels it has set up."[43] Despite the fact that SINAMOS has bureaucratically absorbed ONDEPJOV, Michl's conclusion is still convincing.

But the *nature* of the relationship between *poblador* and government remains less than fully explored, and the job of discussing these relationships in a more avowedly theoretical fashion is not yet done. To begin, we can recall our earlier argument that *pobladores* petitioning the DPJ are not participants, but clients. Delgado and other spokesmen claim that SINAMOS has injected a new element into this client-bureaucrat relationship, and that the eventual transfer of decision-making power to the *pobladores* will transform hat-in-hand petitioning into bargaining between equals—or, in more formal terms, from superficial petitioning over outputs into truly meaningful participation in input decision-making. Delgado thus argues that the *pobladores* will gain meaningful power, a term which Harry Scoble defines as "the probability that the claims of a group will be incorporated as the basis of *policy* by government decision-makers," thus permitting them to attain the "attentive interest" of relevant authorities when they (the *pobladores*) perceive their situation can be affected by an authoritative decision. In Scoble's terms, they will thus gain "access to politics." [44] Whether this transfer will ever occur, precisely when, to what degree, how rapidly—answers to these and to many related questions will be forthcoming only as time passes, and while speculation may be provocative, it is only speculation. Leaving the future to the future, I shall concentrate upon SINAMOS-*poblador* relations at the present time.

The descriptive data available suggest that what currently exists is a modification of the patron-client relationship so often encountered in peasant societies.[45] Here, we are concerned not with the highly traditional, dyadic relationship between individuals, but instead with a clientele system or clientelist state. While dependent upon the basic characteristics of the patron-client pattern—unequal status, reciprocity, and proximity—a clientele *system* also requires the presence of "mediators" or "brokers" who provide a linkage between the local and the larger social systems.[46] Moreover, in a clientelistic state, the loyalties which hold the ruled to the rulers do not require any belief in the ruler's unique personal qualifications, but are inextricably linked to material incentives and rewards.[47]

Rene Lemarchand and Keith Legg depart from the dyadic, micro patron-client pattern, as does John Powell; however, their main point lies in the expandable nature of this pattern within the framework of formal and apparently legal-rational institutions. The crucial element is provided through intermediary middlemen or brokers. But Lemarchand and Legg take the idea a step further:

> As the state structures become more and more differentiated and complex, as individual interests change and are transformed into collective interests, brokerage functions tend to be performed not only by nation-oriented influentials, but by national institutions, parties, and pressure groups .... Along with this change in the extensiveness of clientage networks, there occur substantial shifts in the type and source of resources available to these "middlemen" ... [who] are now in a position where they can use state resources (usually in the form of policy outputs) to exert new forms of control and manipulation over their clients. At this point the forms of control ... [become] a far more encompassing network of relationships, directly dependent upon the volume and allocation of resources from the center.[48]

I thus propose that SINAMOS-*poblador* interactions at present constitute an institutionalized clientelistic relationship, purposefully imposed on a systemic level.[49]

The success which SINAMOS has had (and will have) in invoking and maintaining this patterned relationship depends upon numerous factors, several of which are unique to the Peruvian situation.[50] In the first place, *poblador* demand-making as well as problem-solving most frequently revolves around communal interests. Such problems almost always concern the need for material resources or welfare benefits, many of which are available only through the government (for example, land titles). The desires for these goods, combined with the fact of state control, have created a situation where (as Powell observes) traditional patterns of behavior are consistent with, and adapted to, the requirements of modern organizational life.[51] I have already argued that the *pobladores* do not consider themselves as equals in their interactions with the government, owing in part to their high-risk position, the nature of the Peruvian political system across time, and the strictly hierarchical nature of the social system based on class distinctions. The *pobladores*, in other words, are not forced into a pattern of authority relationships unfamiliar or even undesirable to them.

This traditional willingness to behave as a client dovetails with the Revolutionary Government's perception of the "marginal" sectors of society. Despite repeated protestations by Delgado and others that SINAMOS is a temporary institution, at present SINAMOS acts precisely as a broker or middleman; its uniqueness lies in the fact that this broker has been created, sponsored, supported, and imposed by the national government. Two critical factors characterize nation-states in which the clientelist-broker system emerges. The first of these is relatively severe isolation of communities or regions; the second is centralized political power which only occasionally reaches into these communities or regions.[52] In Lima, no federation or association of *pueblos jóvenes* existed prior to 1968; furthermore, most regimes before that time paid attention to the *pobladores* only as potential threats to security or as a possible source of votes and support. In short, the *pobladores* and their communities were segmented from one another and were only partially integrated with the central government at best. According to Alex Weingrod, "It is within this context of relative segmentation that a category of 'mediators' arise who may act to bridge the different . . . levels."[53] SINAMOS, I would argue, has moved to fill the gaps within the system and to occupy the previously vacant political space. Not only does SINAMOS channel aid and recourses to the *pueblos jóvenes*, thus creating and maintaining a dependent relationship; it also, through its reorganization of the settlements, co-opts and/or replaces any grassroots, independent, or indigenous local association.

Peru presents a contradiction to Weiner's statement that authoritarian elites concerned with mobilization may seek support without allowing demands. SINAMOS has in fact facilitated the presentation of many *poblador* demands to government ministries and agencies. In addition, the Revolutionary Government does not seek to avoid these demands; indeed, the bureaucratic reshuffling, the creation of SINAMOS and ONDEPJOV, and the rather free reign given to SINAMOS all permit demands to be articulated. Moreover, the government makes resources available to answer them. But the stimulation of participation by SINAMOS encourages demand-making that (1) focuses on physical goods and community projects—that is, "approved" demands for "approved" goods and already available resources, and (2) uses "approved" and institutionalized channels for presenting these demands.[54] Demand-making and participation are therefore to a large extent controlled, predictable, and manipulable, just as the Revolutionary Government—or any government, for that matter—would prefer to have them. In sum, the *pobladores* occupy the position of participatory clients seeking patronage from a resource base—namely, the central government—while SINAMOS, in the role of broker, serves a variety of functions: It controls the content of these demands, while it also encourages and sometimes initiates their articulation; it co-opts and discourages other demand-making groups which might start to form; and through all of these roles, it continually seeks to stimulate support for the Revolutionary Government's policies and ideologies.

Clientelism, Participation, and Corporatist Authoritarianism

The original question which began this discussion has still not been directly confronted: Can this sort of clientelistic demand-making and petitioning, whether encouraged and controlled by SINAMOS or not, reasonably be labeled participation? The difficulty with this question is not so much in deciding whether or not participation is possible under authoritarian or corporatist rule; rather, the problem lies in attempting to define how systemic or structural features across different regime types can alter the *mode* of participation.

A good deal of recent analysis on the military in Peru has labeled both the government and its approaches to the organization of political life as corporatist in nature. More specifically, insofar as the attempts of the government to mobilize the urban poor are concerned, David Collier argues that while the military rule of General Manuel Odría proceeded on a clientelistic basis with the *pobladores*, the present government, by contrast, is relying on a system of control which is quite properly called corporatist.[55]

How can we define or describe a corporatist regime? One of the more recent and satisfactory attempts is that of Philippe Schmitter, who posits four features as distinctive:

> Corporatism can be defined as a system of interest representation in which the constituent units are organized into a limited number of singular, compulsory, non-competitive, hierarchically-ordered and functionally pre-determined categories, certified or licensed (if not created) by the State and granted a deliberate representational monopoly with the respective categories in exchange for observing certain governmentally imposed controls on their selection of leaders and articulation of demands and supports.[56]

Although Schmitter admits that his definition refers to an ideal-type regime, the structural components and roles of his definition parallel almost precisely the most important elements and functions of SINAMOS' relations to the national government and to the *pobladores*. All those features of SINAMOS which have been described—its sponsorship by the government, its hierarchical nature, and efforts toward monopolization—provide a very close empirical approximation to Schmitter's description.

Most analysts argue that pluralism is both distinctive and essential to corporatism. Schmitter argues that both pluralists and corporatists recognize the inevitability of structural differentiation and interest diversities in a modern state; the difference occurs when "the former suggest numerical proliferation, horizontal extension and competitive interaction" to meet such changes, while "the latter advocate quantitative contraction, vertical stratification and complementary interdependence."[57] As Juan Linz puts it, corporatism purposely *limits* pluralism by institutionalizing political participation in a limited number of groups and encouraging their emergence and growth. In addition, the co-optation of leaders, according to Linz, is a constant process through which individuals or groups become participants or are represented in the system.[58]

The very means by which SINAMOS was created—the fact that it took instant and full life by absorbing several ongoing national organizations—provides a clear example of the limited and controlled pluralism to which Linz and Schmitter refer. If the Revolutionary Government in fact operates through corporatist mechanisms, however, how can we reconcile this notion with the clientelist model presented above?

The answer lies in the realization that these two types are not necessarily opposites or mutually exclusive categories, but can be instead complementary and compatible. Susan Purcell makes the point clearly in her discussion of Mexico as an authoritarian regime; limited political pluralism (which she borrows from Linz) and systemic clientelism (which she refers to as patrimonial rulership) are both crucial ingredients in her definition.[59] In the Peruvian urban lower-class context, clientelism and corporatism can operate together with little trouble. Perhaps the most satisfactory way of keeping the distinction between them clear would be to characterize SINAMOS' interaction with the *pobladores* as dependent upon the essentially clientelistic nature of Peruvian politics, while the mechanics of the system created by the military are corporatist in structure. Clientelism thus refers to the underlying pattern or individual perception of political interaction; corporatism refers more precisely to the institutions and structures of the political system.

Nevertheless, both clientelism and corporatism allow participation, but in modes and under structural constraints and channels not usually encountered in electoral, democratic regimes. In an extension of their five-nation study, Sidney Verba et al. explored participation in Yugoslavia, a noncompetitive regime. Some obvious differences with democracies were found. For one, campaigning as a mode of participation disappeared. However, an alternative mode did emerge to fill this political "space," which Verba labeled "self-management." This mode, centering on involvement in self-management bodies in the specific areas of place of work and residential unit, represents a participatory innovation *not* found in the other countries. This innovation illustrates

> how significant structural differences within the political system (the absence of competitive elections and the presence of participatory opportunities in the workplace and the housing unit) modify ... [patterns of participation] .... the Yugoslavian case represents ... a most interesting example of the way in which the political structures in a nation can affect the general ways in which citizens take part in political life.[60]

Thus participation should not be defined without taking into consideration the type of regime or the expectations of a particular population subgroup. To argue that participation occurs only in electoral or democratic systems ignores the very real and successful efforts many regimes have made in involving their citizens in a variety of participatory structures. Co-optation, paternalism, manipulation, and participation itself cannot be identified solely by an outside observer; they exist in and through the individuals involved, and whether or not they feel that they control events and decisions that affect them. The evidence on SINAMOS and the *poblador* is still mixed and fragmentary, but clearly the Revolutionary Government has undertaken the implantation of a participatory mechanism whose potential is far-reaching.[61]

Conclusion

I have argued that *poblador* behavior patterns emerge as pragmatic adjustments to a wide range of systemic, structural conditions over which the *pobladores* have little or no control—or where control exists only as micro-level, individual responses to systemic, macro-level influences. For example, there is little doubt that while *poblador* achievements in creating the whole *pueblo joven* phenomenon constitute a remarkably successful, largely unaided, and independent (not to say illegal) effort, it is an effort which intentionally copes with a set of conditions rather than attempting to protest or to change them, and which demonstrates the lack of viable alternatives the Peruvian sociopolitical system provides the urban poor. Given the most salient goals of the *poblador*—acquisition of land and ownership of a house, education for his children, and overall general improvement of his living conditions—and given the system's incapacities and preferences, the alternatives available to living in a *pueblo joven* are simply unacceptable, consisting as they do of remaining in central-city rental housing, living with relatives or friends, returning to one's place of origin (if a migrant), or entering the commercial mortgage market. The squatter settlement doubtless is not an ideal situation for the *pobladores;* it is, however, probably the most realistic, and only therefore the "best," solution to a whole range of problems that confront inadequately prepared government institutions. Alejandro Portes reaches a similar conclusion:

> Problems of peripheral slums and their causation are of an essentially structural nature. . . . Ways of acting in the slum are structurally determined to the extent that individuals continuously look for the most efficient way of improving their positions within the limits and the barriers created by the existing social and economic organization.[62]

This finding in itself is not surprising. Almost without exception, studies of urbanization and political behavior in the Third World in general, and especially in Latin America, argue against any theory which pictures the rural-urban migrant as alienated, marginal, or radicalized.[63] My data agree completely with such findings; organized radical behavior—violent demand-making, demonstrations, and the like—has not been expected or encountered. But the question of why *poblador* demands and petitions to the government are as limited as they are does deserve attention. With the Revolutionary Government as anxious as it is to gain the support of the masses, the *pobladores* would appear to have an opportunity to press their demands and to ask for certain types of assistance and goods which they had not previously requested. Why is it that the *poblador* demands are as modest, conventional, and acceptable to the government as they are?

I have already mentioned a few of the reasons for the limited nature of government-focused demands. The *pobladores*, first and foremost, approach the government for assistance because they need help, not because they are obliged to do so. They want assistance and they are in general quite specific about the type of help they need. This being the case, the *pobladores* will not only behave in ways calculated to increase the probability of favorable response; they will also ask for those goods or services which are most likely actually to be delivered. The *pobladores* request only that assistance which they know a governmental office can in fact supply. They do not want to antagonize an agency with wild or unreasonable requests, thereby jeopardizing their chances of success; and they do not want to waste their own time and political resources in making unrealistic demands. The *pobladores* are very much aware that demands which the government considers *outré* will either be ignored (a considerable cost in itself) or will gain the community a reputation as a troublemaker.

Moreover, the *pobladores* recognize that the government operates under restrictions of its own, and that it is neither able nor willing to satisfy all needs of all groups in Peruvian society. The government also has a recognizable patience threshold which the *pobladores* approach but do not cross. Coupled with these realizations is another limitation which the *pobladores* themselves impose, and purposely—that some needs which are strongly felt are not politicized needs. Either by preference or distrust, the majority of the *pobladores*, for example, do not want government assistance—or what might be better labeled inter-ference—in house construction, since such aid would doubtless carry with it financial and other strictures which the *pobladores* want to avoid. Certain types of demands are not made, therefore, because the *pobladores* know that to make them would be foolish or risky, or both; others are not made because the *pobladores* do not want the assistance the government might offer.

Another mediating influence on the content of any demand has to do with the individual(s) who most frequently articulate that demand. Analysis elsewhere reveals that the activist *poblador*—the one who is most apt to participate in community affairs and most likely to con-front the government in the course of presenting a demand—is precisely that individual who feels the greatest stake in his investments in his community, and the most intense commitment to that community. [64] He also is disposed to give the established system of demand-making, including its formalisms and its incremental nature, credit for function-ing reasonably well. In other words, the *poblador* most probable to create and present demands is in many ways least likely to question the system and his place in it in any basic way; indeed, one might even suggest that the activists represent the sort of *pobladores* with whom the government would prefer to interact.

My conclusions as to why the *pobladores* articulate the types of demands they do, and why they present them as they do, should occasion little surprise. Throughout this analysis, nowhere has there emerged any sign that the *pobladores* are anything but willing to play by the rules; when and if pressure is exerted, it is done carefully and incrementally so as to maximize potential gains while guarding against any possible backlash.

The *pobladores* are poor; they operate at present under an authori-tarian military regime which gives them little space to maneuver. Other regimes at other times in Peru, whether electoral or not, have not given them a chance to experience any sense of decision-making power or independence. Basic needs, when politicized, become articulated by spokesmen from individual communities. When elections have been held, the *pobladores* have shown little tendency to support a single candidate or party.[65] Under the Revolutionary Government, which has attempted to impose a structured, hierarchical organization arrangement throughout the *pueblos jóvenes*, the *pobladores* show an equal reluctance to be cajoled or coerced in any mass-based fashion.

This lack of cohesion beyond the particular settlement might, to an outsider, appear to be detrimental to the *pobladores'* own best interests. After all, if a number of communities were to make demands on the authorities in concert, such an effort might produce more satisfactory results than if each one petitioned separately. The poor in any context seldom command much more than the sheer weight of numbers—a resource which can, of course, be extraordinarily persuasive if properly utilized. With probably a third of Lima now living in the *pueblos jóvenes*, two logical steps would thus seem to be in order: for the authorities (elected or otherwise) to try to co-opt or otherwise convince the *pobladores* to support them; and for the *pobladores* to unite in an areawide or even citywide organization of some sort. The Revolutionary Government has clearly taken the first step; the *pobladores* have just as clearly been unable or unwilling to take the second, and governmental efforts in this direction have been unsuccessful. What explains this inability or unwillingness (or both) of the *pobladores* to come together either voluntarily or forcibly?

Again, the conditions of poverty offer a partial explanation. The usual basis for creating and supporting indigenous positions of leadership—the ability to provide needed goods or services—does not lie within the local settlement, but rather outside it, with the national government.[66] Moreover, the goods and services the national government can supply are, from the *poblador*'s point of view, unique, highly desirable, and nonsubstitutable. Therefore, the *pobladores* turn to two loci of resources: themselves (and their immediate neighbors and surroundings) and the national government. Relevant resources for satisfying certain material, communal needs are nowhere else available, and the energy, costs, and time involved in attempting to create a unified *poblador* organization outweigh the potential gains. There are also at least two varieties of risk involved: possible negative sanctions from supralocal authorities who might see any independent organizing as a threat; and the possible risk each community would perceive itself taking by banding together and thereby losing flexibility and independence. The latter is especially important and deserves elaboration.

For the inhabitants of a special *pueblo joven*, the help which the government offers is seen as in scarce supply. This does not apply to material goods (few of which are actually offered) as much as it does to services, the scarcest and therefore most valuable of which is time. Obtaining the attention and time of office and agency personnel for

technical assistance, land titles, and the like is the major task of any
community and its spokesmen. Quite correctly, community leaders see
that demands upon government agencies are severe and conclude that if
officials direct their attention to one community, they cannot be
concerned about another. For example, the leaders of two separate but
contiguous communities both made it clear that each area had initiated
its own petition to the ONDEPJOV office. When ONDEPJOV announced that both would be treated equally and simultaneously, the
leaders were faced with conflict: While collaboration would advance
work as fast as possible, each feared that the other would somehow
extract more from the arrangement. The two zones are literally across a
street from each other and share many common problems; yet they
cooperated with much hesitation. Zone A, with manifestly poorer
conditions, felt it should receive priority, while Zone B claimed its
demonstrated competence in partially solving its own problems through
local efforts should be rewarded. The major source of concern came
from the realization that ONDEPJOV operated on a very tight schedule
and budget; neither zone wished to jeopardize its chances. This mutual
suspicion developed between two neighborhoods that are part of the
same general area. Magnify these feelings across the whole of Lima's
two hundred and fifty or so *pueblos jóvenes*, and intersettlement
collaboration becomes extremely difficult, basically because each community wishes to maintain a distinct identity and each wants to have its
problems treated separately.

These feelings offer another partial explanation as to why SINAMOS
has encountered such stubborn opposition from the *pobladores*. In the
first place, SINAMOS' insistence on organizing communities as it sees
best, along with its attempts to co-opt or close informal but highly
useful avenues of demand-making, deprive the *pueblos jóvenes* of their
separate identities as communities and quite possibly rob the communities of independent leadership. Bryan Roberts noted the same
phenomenon in Guatemala City:

> The more formally organized the neighborhood becomes the more likely are
> leaders to be perceived as unrepresentative and self-interested . . . the incapa-
> city of the poor to organize effectively is due to their overintegration into the
> city and not to their isolation from its political and social processes.[67]

While an outsider might see SINAMOS as a potentially positive contribution toward settlement improvement—representative local leaders,
defined channels for petitioning, etc.—the *pobladores* view it as a
threat, much as they view political party enticements or campaign
promises with high levels of skepticism. During periods of electoral

politics, *pobladores* often purposely avoid affiliation with one party, preferring the flexibility and superiority found in being able to play off one candidate against another, and not putting solid credence in any of them. A leader who overtly aligns himself with a party, or with SINAMOS, runs the risk both of losing legitimacy among his neighbors and of denying himself a sometimes extraordinarily useful source of political leverage. In effect, a government which compels acceptance of a formal organizational structure may destroy any genuine, indigenous sense of community present or nascent, thus denying to the settlement and to the government goals which both desire.

SINAMOS, for the *pobladores*, constitutes an intrusion. The bureaucratic, clientelistic relationships between a community and ONDEPJOV, while subject to unpredictability, inefficiency, and perhaps abuse, function in many ways vital to the *pobladores.* They produce, for the most part, the sorts of goods and services the *pobladores* want from, and for which they are dependent upon, the government, and produce them at costs measurable in time, money, and energy—but not in terms of daily interference and meddling with the community itself. Neither the *pobladores* nor the government would argue that the pre-SINAMOS arrangement was ideal; however, the government determination to improve the situation has resulted in its deterioration. The *pobladores,* prior to SINAMOS, were not dependent upon the government on any day-to-day basis; *poblador*-government relationships were confined to certain specified areas. SINAMOS threatens to increase the permeability and dependence of the *pobladores.* "In this respect, formalization of organization, however desirable from [an outsider's] view of participation and decision making, is inappropriate in environments where there is not the context of trust, public or private, to maintain it."[68]

As I have noted previously, a fully operational context of trust would have to extend both horizontally—within and across a single community as well as across various settlements—and vertically—from the community to the national government. At present, horizontal trust operates most fully within single communities; cross-settlement confidence is considerably less developed. Vertical trust, however, remains a major problem. A fundamental goal of the Revolutionary Government has been, and still is, the creation of support among those sectors of society either ignored or taken for granted by previous regimes. On the one hand, the government has given the *pueblos jóvenes* more attention, has expressed a clearly enlightened view of the squatter phenomenon, and has carried out some bureaucratic reshuffling.

On the other hand, the insistence upon externally imposed local organizational structures, the paternalistic attitudes assumed by

SINAMOS, and the overall intrusion of the government into daily life all constitute policies which, while understandable and perhaps even theoretically justifiable, in fact impede the support-gathering goals they are intended to promote. The possible repercussions of such policies can only be guessed at: The *pobladores* might start to take SINAMOS and the Revolutionary Government at its word and not be satisfied with demand-making for only those services which the government is ready and willing to make available; the legitimacy the *pobladores* accord the clientelistic participation mode of interaction might erode into apathy, cynicism, or outright alienation. Or—and not improbably— both of these scenarios might occur simultaneously; they are not mutually contradictory. A combination of rapidly broadening demand- making, coupled with a growing cynical dislike of the regime, would produce an exceedingly difficult situation for the Revolutionary Gov- ernment and for the *pobladores* as well.

Of course, such an outcome is by no means necessary or even likely. Existing broad opposition, not only among the *pobladores* but across society and within the military itself, may dampen SINAMOS and its most controversial aspects. Or widespread, passive nonacceptance of, or noncompliance with, SINAMOS directives may in time demonstrate to the government that the *pobladores* are, in some cases, much better left to their own devices.

With or without SINAMOS, the *pobladores* are in a number of crucial ways clearly dependent upon the national government. They realize this and accept it; the Revolutionary Government realizes it as well, and (despite disclaimers) is determined to encourage it. This may, in fact, be the most critical, basic source of friction between the *pobladores* and the present regime. Because of their low incomes, their occupational concentration in the service sector, the (until very re- cently) uncertain and fragile juridical nature of the communities, and their overall desire to be a part of urban, modern Peru, the *pobladores* present have little bargaining leverage which they can operate outside, or at least independent of, governmentally approved and controlled channels. Yet considering who and what they are, the *pobladores* survive and operate on a scale, and to a degree, which is quite remark- able. Their position as clients in an authoritarian state is one into which they have been forced by structural factors beyond their present individual or collective control. But they have, when necessary, de- veloped strategies which permit them to manipulate their objectively weak position and take as full advantage of it as realistically possible. Given the Revolutionary Government's emphasis upon local, partial participation and the very real limits imposed thereby, the *pobladores* in contemporary Peru can expect qualitatively little more in the future than they have at present in the way of autonomous, independent opportunity to make their own decisions.

NOTES

The material and data used in this chapter are part of a larger study which has been financed in part by the following institutions: the Social Science Research Council, the Center for Research in International Studies at Stanford University, the Institute of Latin American Studies at the University of Texas (Austin), and the American Philosophical Society (Philadelphia). I have also benefited from assistance by Sam Popkin, Norm Frolich, and Rick Moore, all of the University of Texas; Wayne Cornelius, of MIT; and Richard Fagen, of Stanford University.

1. See James Davis, "Citizen Participation in a Bureaucratic Society: Some Questions and Skeptical Notes," in *Neighborhood Control in the 1970's: Politics, Administration, and Citizen Participation*, ed. George Frederickson (New York: Chandler, 1973), pp. 59–72.

2. See two works by Peter Smith, *Politics and Beef in Argentina* (New York: Columbia University Press, 1969); and "Social Mobilization, Political Participation, and the Rise of Juan Perón," *Political Science Quarterly*, 84, no. 3 (March 1969):30–49.

3. James Petras, "Chile: Nationalization, Socioeconomic Change, and Popular Participation" (Paper presented at the 1972 meetings of the American Political Science Association, Washington, D.C.); and Franz Vanderschueren, "Political Significance of Neighborhood Committees in the Settlements of Santiago," in *The Chilean Road to Socialism*, ed. Dale Johnson (Garden City, N.Y.: Doubleday-Anchor, 1973), pp. 256–83.

4. Along this line see Wayne Cornelius and Henry Dietz, "Urbanization, Demand-Making, and Political System Overload: Political Participation Among the Migrant Poor in Latin American Cities," in *Frontiers of Urban Research*, ed. Rodney Stiefbold (Coral Gables: University of Miami Press, forthcoming).

5. Throughout I shall use *poblador* as a generic term rather than translate it. Likewise, I shall use *pueblo joven* (plural, *pueblos jóvenes*) instead of attempting some clumsy English translation such as "young towns."

6. Karl Deutsch, "Social Mobilization and Political Development," in *Political Development and Social Change*, ed. Jason Finkle and Richard Gable (New York: John Wiley, 1971), pp. 386–87, 390–91.

7. See Cornelius and Dietz, "Urbanization," passim.

8. For summaries of this point of view, see Wayne Cornelius, "The Political Sociology of Cityward Migration: Toward Empirical Theory," in *Latin American Urban Research*, vol. 1, ed. Francine Rabinowitz and Felicity Trueblood (Beverly Hills, Calif.: Sage Publications, 1971), pp. 95–150; and Joan Nelson, *Migrants, Urban Poverty, and Instability in Developing Nations* (Cambridge: Harvard University, Center for International Affairs, 1969).

9. The military in Peru refers to itself as the Revolutionary Government of the Armed Forces, and so shall I.

10. See, *inter alia*, Carlos Astiz, "The Military Establishment as a Political Elite: The Peruvian Case," in *Latin American Prospects for the 1970's: What Kinds of Revolutions?*, ed. David H. Pollock and Arch R. M. Ritter (New York: Praeger,

1973), pp. 203—29; Francois Bourricaud, "Los militares: por qué y para qué?"
Aportes, 16 (April 1970):13—55; idem, "Voluntarismo y experimentación: los
militares peruanos mano a la obra," *Aportes*, 18 (October 1970); Luigi Einaudi,
"The Military and Government in Peru," in *Development Administration in Latin
America*, ed. Clarence Thurber and Lawrence Graham (Durham, N.C.: Duke University Press, 1973), pp. 294—313; George Grayson, "Peru's Revolutionary Government," *Current History*, 64 (February 1973):661—66; Jane Jaquette, "Revolution
by Fiat: The Context of Policy-Making in Peru," *Western Political Quarterly*, 25,
no. 4 (December 1972):648—66; Charles W. Johnson, "Peru: los militares como un
agente de cambio económico," *Revista Mexicana de Sociología*, 34, no. 2 (April—
June 1972):293—316; James Malloy, "Dissecting The Peruvian Military: A Review
Essay," *Journal of Inter-American and World Affairs*, 15, no. 3 (August
1973):375—82; idem, "Authoritarianism, Corporatism, and Mobilization in Peru,"
Review of Politics, 36, no. 1 (January 1974):52—84; David Scott Palmer, *"Revolu-
tion from Above": Military Government and Popular Participation in Peru, 1968—
1972* (Ithaca: Cornell University Latin American Dissertation Series, No. 47,
January 1973); Victor Villanueva, *¿Nueva mentalidad militar en el Peru?* (Lima:
Mejía Baca, 1969); and idem, *El CAEM y la revolucion de la fuerza armada* (Lima:
Instituto de Estudios Peruanos, 1972).

11. For such a statement see Samuel Huntington, *Political Order in Changing
Societies* (New Haven: Yale University Press, 1968), p. 243; see also Eric Nord-
linger, "Soldiers in Mufti: The Impact of Military Rule Upon Economic and Social
Change in the Non-Western States," *American Political Science Review*, 64, no. 4
(December 1970):1131—48.

12. Palmer, *Revolution from Above*, pp. 43—44.

13. Both Mangin and Turner have written widely; see William Mangin, ed.,
Peasants in Cities (Boston: Houghton-Mifflin, 1970), which contains chapters by
both Mangin and Turner; John Turner, *Urban Dwelling Environments* (Cambridge:
MIT Press, 1969); and Mangin, "Latin American Squatter Settlements: A Problem
and a Solution," *Latin American Research Review*, 2, no. 3 (Summer 1967):65—97.

14. Editorials in such newspapers as *La Prensa* and magazines such as *Oiga*
during the early 1970s frequently carried such a point of view.

15. ONDEPJOV, *Guia para la organizacion de los pueblos jóvenes* (Lima: 1970),
pp. 2—3. This and translations throughout the chapter are mine. ONDEPJOV was
subsequently absorbed into the bureaucratic structure of SINAMOS in 1972; see
pp. 432—44.

16. By 1975, the land distribution campaign had diminished considerably, even
though some settlements lacked titles and others had been given only provisional
instead of definitive titles, thereby causing some significant discontent in a number
of settlements.

17. See Cornelius and Dietz, "Urbanization," pp. 9—10.

18. This office was, as noted, the only one in 1970—1971. In the next few years,
four branch offices in the four administrative districts of Lima were opened.
However, the manner in which demands and petitions were to be presented to these
branches remained very much the same, whether they were made to one or several
offices, and whether made to ONDEPJOV or to SINAMOS. Indeed, a long-time
active member of a community said in 1975 that SINAMOS had done little except
to create an additional bureaucratic layer which, more often than not, did little
except impede the whole process.

19. The materials described in this case study were collected during various trips
to Lima during 1964—1966, 1967, 1970—1971, and 1975, through interviewing,
participant observation, attendance at meetings, and other ethnographic techniques.

20. These figures refer to data collected through survey techniques in 1970–1971. For a complete description of this study, see Henry Dietz, "Becoming a Poblador: Political Adjustment to the Urban Environment in Lima, Peru" (Ph.D. dissertation, Stanford, 1974). Briefly, the data come from approximately four hundred and twenty-five interviews conducted with male heads of household in five squatter communities of Lima.

21. For a complete description of the activist poblador, see Henry Dietz, "Some Modes of Participation in an Authoritarian Regime" (Paper delivered at the 1975 meetings of the American Political Science Association, San Francisco).

22. Lester Milbrath, *Political Participation* (Chicago: Rand-McNally, 1965), p. 18.

23. Myron Weiner, "Political Participation: Crisis of the Political Process," in Leonard Binder et al., *Crises and Sequences in Political Development* (Princeton: Princeton University Press, 1971), p. 197.

24. Carlos Delgado, "SINAMOS: la participacion popular en la Revolucion Peruana," *Participacion*, 2, no. 2 (Lima, February 1973):6–22. The following information is derived from this article. Delgado was named in April 1972, upon the formation of SINAMOS, as general director of the national office (ONAMS), the second highest post in the organization, and the highest-ranking civilian position. Delgado is a U.S.-trained sociologist and anthropologist, head of the expropriated Lima newspaper *Expreso*, former member of the splinter left-wing APRA movement, ex-director of the National Institute of Planning, and a forceful and prolific spokesman for the Revolutionary Government. He is cited at length here because his is a viewpoint from within the government, and because his article constitutes a coherent, integrated treatment of the subject.

25. Ibid., p. 14.

26. Ibid., p. 17.

27. Strictly speaking, nine of the regional offices take in all of Peru except for Lima-Callao, which is covered by the tenth. The eleventh is concerned exclusively with the *pueblos jóvenes* of Lima, an indication of the importance of the settlements as perceived by SINAMOS and by the government.

28. Delgado, "SINAMOS," p. 23.

29. See Sara Michl, "Urban Squatter Organization as a National Government Tool: The Case of Lima, Peru," in *Latin American Urban Research*, vol. 3, ed. Francine Rabinovitz and Felicity Trueblood (Beverly Hills: Sage Publications, 1973), p. 167; see also ONDEPJOV, *Guia.*

30. *SINAMOS Informa*, 2, no. 3 (Lima, 1971):30.

31. Interview in *La Nueva Crónica* (Lima), April 8, 1972, p. 6.

32. Delgado, "SINAMOS," p. 18 (emphasis added).

33. Palmer, *Revolution from Above*, pp. 99–100.

34. As might be inferred from its goals, policies, and methods, SINAMOS has been the focus of extremely heated debates. A pamphlet issued in 1973 by SINAMOS itself has as its title *Why Is SINAMOS Attacked?* and states that "few times in the recent history of Peru has an organization been more violently attacked by traditional groups of all descriptions than the National System for Support of Social Mobilization." Capitalists, the old oligarchs, ultraleftists, political parties and their leaders, administrators, and bureaucrats—all, the pamphlet acknowledges, have bitterly assailed SINAMOS, and for a variety of reasons. Nine main motives are then listed and replied to: that SINAMOS is, or will become, an official party; that it is an octopuslike structure involved everywhere throughout Peruvian society; that it is a hotbed of radicals of various types; that it manipulates grassroots organizations; that it wishes to take over labor unions; that it intends to become a new labor

confederation; that it wants to control peasant organizations; that it is a corporatist and/or fascist entity; and that it retards the "true" workers' revolution. Opposition has come from a variety of sources, both verbal and written; responses from SINAMOS and the government range from written replies to occasional deportation. One of the severest, and yet most reasoned, criticisms of SINAMOS and of the military in general appeared in the magazine *Sociedad y Politica (Society and Politics)*; after four issues, the journal was confiscated and its editors, Anibal Quijano and Julio Cotler, deported.

35. My survey work concluded in Lima in August 1971, well before SINAMOS and its organizational structure came into existence. Thus I have little empirical or quantifiable data. What is available, and what is presented here, comes from a six-week field trip to Lima during the summer of 1975, and from conversations with *pobladores*, government officials, SINAMOS employees, and from the few scattered written accounts.

36. Austin Ligon, "The Peruvian Revolution: An Analysis" (Ms., Austin: Department of Government, University of Texas, 1973), pp. 28–29.

37. This rather extraordinary and insensitive statement appeared in the magazine which SINAMOS publishes, called *SINAMOS Informa* (1972):14–15, emphasis added. For more than twenty years, observers have been making the point that the most unique and remarkable aspect of the *pueblos jóvenes* lies in their ability to provide for themselves despite the lack of governmental assistance (or, at times, in spite of it). Indeed, "individual responsibility" could well be said to be the most outstanding characteristic of the settlements.

38. See Palmer, *Revolution from Above*, p. 104. As I noted above (see notes 16 and 18), the most likely reason for the decline and reorganization that took place in 1975 had to do with the very wide rejection of SINAMOS by those segments of the population it was designed to serve. On several occasions, SINAMOS branch offices were the target of violent mass activities, especially in Chimbote, Cuzco, and Puno, where the offices were burned by mobs. While no such violence has been specifically directed at a SINAMOS office in the *pueblos jóvenes* in Lima, the popularity and acceptance of SINAMOS by the *pobladores* has been (at least in the communities studied) minimal, and numerous acquaintances and informants spoke both openly and heatedly against it in 1975.

39. Dale Rogers Marshall, *The Politics of Participation in Poverty* (Berkeley: University of California Press, 1970), p. 144.

40. Ibid.

41. Richard Cloward, "The War on Poverty: Are the Poor Left Out?", *The Nation*, 21 (August 1965):56.

42. Biliana Ambrecht, *Politicization as a Legacy of the War on Poverty: A Study of Advisory Council Members in a Mexican-American Community* (Los Angeles: University of California at Los Angeles, Dept. of Political Science, 1973).

43. Michl, "Urban Squatter Organization," p. 172.

44. Harry M. Scoble, "Access to Politics," *International Encyclopedia of the Social Sciences*, vol. 1 (New York: Free Press, 1968), p. 10.

45. The anthropological literature on the patron-client relationship is, of course, very large. Major sources include George Foster, "Peasant Society and the Image of the Limited Good," in Jack Potter et al., *Peasant Society: A Reader* (Boston: Little Brown, 1967); Rene Lemarchand and Keith Legg, "Political Clientelism and Development: A Preliminary Analysis," *Comparative Politics*, 4, no. 2 (January 1972):148–65; John D. Powell, "Peasant Society and Clientelist Politics," *American Political Science Review*, 62, no. 2 (June 1970):411–25; and Eric Wolf, "Kinship, Friendship, and Patron-Client Relations in Complex Societies," in *The*

Social Anthropology of Complex Societies, ed. Michael Banton (New York: Barnes and Noble, 1966), pp. 1–21.

46. Powell, "Peasant Society," passim.

47. Guenther Roth, "Personal Rulership, Patrimonialism, and Empire-Building in the New States," *World Politics*, 20, no. 2 (October 1968):196.

48. Lemarchand and Legg, "Political Clientelism," pp. 154, 158–59.

49. Peter Berger and Thomas Luckman make a relevant observation when they argue that "the more conduct is institutionalized, the more predictable and thus the more controlled it becomes. . . . The more . . . conduct is taken for granted, the more possible alternatives to the institutional programs will recede, and the more predictable and controlled conduct will be" (*The Social Construction of Reality* [Garden City, N.Y.: Anchor, 1967], p. 140).

50. Lemarchand and Legg note that "clientelism cannot meaningfully be considered apart from the setting in which it exists. The forms which it takes depends to a considerable extent on the structure of the society and on the political system in which it operates" ("Political Clientelism," p. 158).

51. Powell, "Peasant Society," p. 424.

52. Alex Weingrod, "Patrons, Patronage, and Political Parties," *Comparative Studies in Society and History*, 10 (1968):382.

53. Ibid.

54. This second condition caused occasional difficulty, since channels are not always well defined. SINAMOS field promoters often take their assignments and mandate enthusiastically, resulting in clashes between SINAMOS-inspired actions and programs carried on by other agencies and ministries. The problem, however, is not one of the *pobladores* themselves going outside the rules of the game; instead, the difficulty is in the ill-defined boundaries under which SINAMOS operates. Given its very broad range of responsibilities and operation, it is inevitable that SINAMOS and other agencies would overlap and at times find themselves with contradictory jurisdictional mandates.

55. David Collier, *Squatters and Oligarchs: Urbanization and Public Policy in Peru* (Baltimore: Johns Hopkins University Press, 1976).

56. Philippe Schmitter, "Still the Century of Corporatism?", *Review of Politics*, 36, no. 1 (January 1974):94.

57. Ibid., p. 97.

58. Juan Linz, "An Authoritarian Regime: Spain," in *Mass Politics*, ed. Stein Rokkan (New York: Free Press, 1970), pp. 255–56.

59. Susan Kaufman Purcell, "Decision-making in an Authoritarian Regime: Theoretical Implications from a Mexican Case Study," *World Politics*, 26, no. 1 (October 1973):30–31. Purcell does not use the term "corporatism" specifically, but instead refers to "authoritarianism" as does Linz. Just where and how these two authors might differ from Schmitter and his "corporatism" is not clear. In any case, I prefer to view these terms as approximately equal, although I choose to speak of corporatism.

60. Sidney Verba et al., "The Modes of Participation: Continuities in Research," *Comparative Political Studies*, 6, no. 2 (July 1973): 247, 248.

61. As I noted on p. 440, it now appears clear that SINAMOS *as constituted at present* has probably been judged a failure by both the *pobladores* and the Revolutionary Government. The reorganization and expected return of all matters dealing with the *pueblos jóvenes* to the Ministry of Housing indicate that SINAMOS will not be maintained, although some of its programs and techniques doubtless will. And despite any reorganization, the possible impact SINAMOS may have had on the *pobladores* in terms of politicization still remains to be seen, as I suggested.

62. Alejandro Portes, "Rationality in the Slum: An Essay on Interpretive Sociology," *Comparative Studies in Society and History*, 14, no. 3 (June 1970):286.

63. For summaries of this view, see Cornelius, "Political Sociology of Cityward Migration," and Nelson, *Migrants*.

64. See Henry Dietz, "Some Modes of Participation."

65. Sandra Powell, "Political Participation in the Barriadas: A Case Study," *Comparative Political Studies*, 2, no. 2 (July 1969):195–215.

66. Bryan Roberts, *Organizing Strangers* (Austin: University of Texas Press, 1973), pp. 307–08.

67. Ibid., p. 311.

68. Ibid., p. 337.

JAMES M. MALLOY

14

Authoritarianism and Corporatism: The Case of Bolivia

Bolivia is one of the most extreme cases of delayed dependent development in all of Latin America. Rapid development came late, in the penultimate decade of the nineteenth century, and was based exclusively on the exploitation of minerals for export, with tin by far the most important export product. Bolivia is literally a case of mono-product export economy and therefore is in many respects (despite its geographic size) more comparable to the smaller Central American republics than its larger neighbors. If Guatemala was a banana republic, Bolivia was a tin republic.[1]

The overwhelming reliance on tin had numerous secondary effects. In the first instance, Bolivia has been much more dependent than most Latin American countries on the vagaries of the external market. Internally, the economic structure was skewed more exaggeratedly than in most nations, with the resulting structural dualism and internal colonialism being particularly pronounced. Moreover, by the early 1920s over 80 percent of tin production was controlled by three giant corporations, Patiño, Aramayo, and Hochschild. Their monopolistic control over the tin industry made "the big three" the most powerful interest combination in the country, dwarfing all potential competitors including the state.[2]

As Laurence Whitehead has pointed out, Bolivia has been characterized throughout the twentieth century by a particularly weak formal state.[3] Given the extremity of the Bolivian case, we can see somewhat more clearly how external economic dependence reverberates into the peripheral country, distorting the political process and undermining the local state's capacity for autonomous action.

The Effects of Economic Dependence

In the first instance, external stimuli from the industralized nations called forth the development of the tin industry, which was quickly

459

organized around monopolistically controlled enclaves rooted in isolated mining camps. The growth of the tin industry in turn stimulated
the parallel development of a service sector organized to facilitate the
flow of tin out of Bolivia and the return flow of manufactured goods
into Bolivia. The city of La Paz became the hub of the system and
thereby a center of social, economic, and political power that dwarfed
all other urban centers. As Roland Ebel has pointed out, this type of
situation is tantamount to that of a "city state" in which the national
capital becomes a self-contained metropolis living off the rest of a
nation which is largely rural.[4]

In this type of structural situation, the middle and lower-middle
classes are concentrated in the capital, where they fill positions in the
service sector (that is, as suppliers, providers of commercial services,
professionals, and public or private bureaucrats). As products of the
service sector, the urban middle classes are economically dependent.
Their security is tied to the fortunes of the export sector, which
fluctuates with the ebb and flow of external stimuli. Thus, their
position is marked by insecurity and uncertainty. In Bolivia, as elsewhere, concentrated economic power in the export sector spread by
means of investment into the control of the most important activities in
the service sector.[5] Hence, control of the two most vital sectors of the
economy came under either the direct or indirect control of relatively
few powerful individuals. As a result, the bulk of the urban middle class
found its fortunes directly dependent on the good will of such powerful
individuals and the upper-middle class of managers who oversaw their
enterprises.

Economic insecurity and dependency among the urban middle class
spawns a particularistic patron-client orientation because individuals
must advance their careers by forging personal links with the relatively
few powerful individuals who control the vital jobs, contracts, and
capacity to pay for services that determine mobility possibilities. In the
Bolivian "city state," as elsewhere, the fact that an increasingly large
part of the middle class came to rely on public employment infected
the political process with the same particularistic and clientelistic style.
Relevant political life in the "city state" is overwhelmingly concentrated in the capital city and, owing to voting and other restrictions, is
monopolized by the middle and upper-middle classes. As dependent
appendages of the dominant entrepreneurial class, the bulk of the
"political class" is motivated primarily by the control of jobs. Hence in
Bolivia political parties degenerated into personalistic factions involved
in a job-oriented interplay between "ins" and "outs." These factions
cut vertically across class lines, penetrating down into the lower social
echelons. Factionalism in the "political class" undermined govern-

mental stability and hampered administrative efficiency because of the high rate of turnover among elected and appointed personnel.[6] Aside from undermining stability and efficiency, the economic dependence of the members of the "political class" and the tenuousness of any faction's hold on office rendered government officials and politicians highly vulnerable to pressure from the few private interests that controlled real economic power. In a real sense, then, the dependence of the urban upper-middle and middle classes was carried over by the "political class" into the state, undermining its ability to function as an autonomous national actor.

Another source of weakness which undercut the autonomy of the Bolivian state was financial dependence. Again Bolivia manifests an extreme case of the modal pattern described in chapter 1. During the first three decades of this century, the Bolivian government expanded in size and assumed the responsibility of financing numerous infrastructure projects to support the export sector. And, like other Latin American states, Bolivia supported an outsized military establishment. The need for public revenue grew apace. Given the internal structure of the country, however, the national tax base was small and unequal to the large financial task. From 1900 to 1930 Bolivian governments relied mainly on limited export taxes and loans from foreign banks. By the late 1920s the country was burdened by an enormous public debt; during those years the two largest budget items were debt-service payments and defense. In 1930 Bolivia defaulted on its external debt, and from then until 1952 the state relied overwhelmingly on export taxes and loans from banks controlled by the tin magnates.[7] By all odds Bolivia was saddled with one of the weakest, least autonomous, and most dependent state structures in the entire region.

Bolivia also manifested an extreme form of the structural dualism characteristic of the region as a whole. By 1952, well over 65 percent of the population were Indian-speaking peasants who were racially and culturally distinct. Well over 70 percent of the population functioned in the backward rural sector, while only 20 percent lived in urban areas of over twenty thousand, the bulk of them in La Paz. Urban groups were in turn divided culturally among cholos, mestizos, a small Creole elite, and influential foreigners. The modern working class was very small. The most significant worker groupings were exurban miners and railway workers who lived in isolated mining camps or dispersed along the rail lines, and manufacturing employed less than 3 percent of the population, so the urban working class proper was minuscule. In the primary city the bulk of the lower orders was made up of the marginally employed, artisans, taxi and bus drivers, and low-level white-collar workers. Racial, cultural, occupational, and residential distinctions divided the low orders and minimized horizontal communication. Again, dependency born of land-tenure problems and occupational insecurity, as well as poverty and cultural backwardness, fostered particularistic and clientelistic orientations among all the lower-order groups, undercutting the possibilities of horizontally organized class action.[8] In Bolivia we have an extreme case of a polarized social structure held together by vertically organized patron-client nets that reverberated through an interlocking hierarchy of dependency relations pervading the entire system.

Another factor contributed to the extremity of the pattern of delayed dependent development in Bolivia. Tin was the backbone of the economy; but by the late 1920s the amount and quality of tin mined began a steady downward spiral which has continued to this day—a situation further exacerbated by the fact that Bolivia is a high-cost producer which has found it increasingly difficult to compete with other tin producers such as Malaya. Thus, not only was the nation's economic base initially narrow, but it has in a real sense been stagnant and/or contracting for some four decades. On top of everything else, then, Bolivia has been plagued by an extremely limited base of disposable resources to cope with accumulated social problems.[9]

During the 1930s and 1940s, Bolivia was a microcosm of the region. The effects of the depression and the exhaustion of the export-oriented growth model were heightened by the humiliating defeat Bolivia suffered in the Chaco War. Thus, Bolivia's hegemonic crisis was particularly intense; indeed so intense that the pressures generated in this period were never effectively contained, and in 1952 the system collapsed in violent revolution.

Hegemonic Crisis and the Rise of Populism

As in the rest of the region, the response to the hegemonic crisis in Bolivia was the emergence of a middle-class-based populist movement that sought to mobilize cross-class support to seize the state and assert its role as an autonomous regulator of the national political economy. Between 1936 and 1946, three civil-military populist governments sought to impose structural reforms from above. All three were unseated because of intense factional divisions in the military and the weakness of formal governmental authorities in the face of pressure marshaled by the tin companies.[10]

These early populist experiments in Bolivia were similar to experiments in neighboring states. Based on an alliance of civil and military elites, they seized power by means of a coup and sought to mobilize a mass base from above within an authoritarian and decidedly corporatist framework. Although short-lived, they did succeed in restructuring the terms of political debate, implanting new concepts of legitimacy, establishing the outlines of a welfare state, and launching policies designed to favor import substitution. During this period, the formal state apparatus expanded significantly, and political mobilization became broader and more intense.

Unlike the situation in other states, however, the Bolivian system was too weak internally to use a strategy of co-optation and segmental incorporation to contain the pressures generated in this period. The extremity and multiple effects of dependency foreclosed this "time-buying" approach in Bolivia. In the first place, as I pointed out earlier, the effective resource base was too narrow to underwrite such an approach. Secondly, structural dualism was so deep in Bolivia that the capacity for horizontal growth based on import substitution was very limited; Bolivia had neither the entrepreneurial leadership nor a sufficient internal market to support import substitution growth. Unlike the larger and more economically diverse states around it, Bolivia has yet to go through a significant import substitution phase and thus in this respect diverges sharply from the modal pattern of the region.

A critical factor during this period was the deep and permanent split of the military along ideological and generational lines. Younger middle-class officers tended to support the populists, while older, more established officers aligned with the status quo. Rebel officers could help the civilian populists seize power but were unable to underwrite a populist regime for any length of time. By the same token, the forces of the status quo were able to block systematic reform but were incapable either of buying time through segmental incorporation and co-optation or of excluding, by means of force, groups mobilized by the populists. The upshot was an extreme praetorianization of political life and a further debilitation of central governmental authority. Intense mobilization within the narrow confines of the reality of delayed dependent development transcended the system's adaptational capacities, creating a situation where formal governmental authority began to collapse.

In 1941 the populist forces were organized into a political movement called the Movimiento Nacionalista Revolucionario (MNR). Prior to 1946 the leadership of the MNR preferred to come to power directly by means of a coup and then structure relationships with its popular bases from above. After 1946 the party shifted tactics and sought to mobilize a mass base from below. In this effort, the MNR was largely successful. It drew the bulk of its support during this period from the urban middle class, organized labor, artisans, and "urban marginals." However, all of these groupings themselves were highly fragmented. Labor, for example (numbering at most one hundred thousand people), was not organized nationally and remained split into a series of independent federations and local unions. Other groups were split along factional, regional, and cultural lines. Hence, while the MNR had become a broad-based, cross-class alliance, it was not an internally integrated or centrally organized movement. The party did not directly incorporate its new supporters but rather formed alliances with leaders of discrete professional associations, artisan *gremios* (guilds), locality groups, unions, etc. Labor did not enter the MNR as a piece but joined on a functional, sector-by-sector basis through alliances between specific union leaders with specific MNR leadership factions; the core MNR leadership was itself split into a number of factions.

One close student of Bolivia, Christopher Mitchell, has aptly termed the MNR a sectorist party, that is, a party based on social groupings or sectors which are "taken to be a social organization, expressing material or status interests, whose membership is direct, exclusive and unique. Examples are professional associations, labor unions, neighborhood associations, or peasant *sindicatos*. A sectorist party is an alliance of such organizations into a national political force."[11] As an example of a relatively organized populist movement, the MNR points up the sectorist nature of all populist movements in the region. One reason populism became such a dominant force in the area after the 1940s was that it reflected rather accurately the essential sectoral, as opposed to class, organization of most Latin American societies.

In general, one might make the following argument regarding the linkages among delayed dependent development, populism, corporatism, and authoritarianism.[12] Many have pointed out that the colonial period left a legacy of corporatist social values and corporatist modes of essentially sectoral organization which persisted in the region despite the liberal democratic concepts and modes of organization enshrined in the new constitutions. The process of delayed dependent development did not supersede this de facto mode of social organization but rather grafted onto it new elements which actually reinforced the inherent structural tendency to sectorist and particularistic modes of social organization. Neither liberal democratic nor Marxist theories perceived the full extent of this structural reality. When the first crisis of delayed, dependent capitalist development occurred, populism came to the fore mainly because it recognized at least implicitly the de facto sectorist structures in Latin American society. Populist movements, whether organized (such as the MNR and the Alianza Popular Revolucionaria Americana [APRA]) or *ad hoc* (such as those led by Juan Perón and Getúlio Vargas), mobilized a range of sectorist base support groups and thus recapitulated within themselves the inherent sectorist structure of Latin American society. Hence, when populist elites sought to organize and control their constituent parts so as to underwrite an autonomous power capability, they naturally moved toward a formalization of a corporatist party and state structure. Although they were formally committed to a democratic style of corporatism, the elitist orientation of the populist leadership and situational constraints created, even in the early stages, a tendency toward authoritarian modes of behavior. As we have seen (chapter 1), most of the civil populist movements of the first stage (1930s–1950s) failed but left behind an ideological legacy as well as expanded governmental structures and increased levels of political mobilization. Most nations of the region lapsed into a de facto sectorist politics of segmental incorporation in which the formally powerful state structures were disarticulated and "parceled out" in a mode of informal corporatist decision-making. [13] The results were weakened states, inflation, and increased praetorianization of politics; these were reinforced when import substitution reached its limits and opened a new hegemonic crisis. In many cases, the response to the crisis engendered by the failure of civil populists cum corporatists was the emergence of institutionalized military regimes (1960s) which in alliance with civil technocrats sought to resolve the crisis by enforcing demobilization (political exclusion of some groups) and establishing the autonomous regulatory power of the state by reformalizing corporatist organizations within an authoritarian framework.

In the specific case of Bolivia, an interim crisis came early because of the inability to "buy time" through segmental incorporation as a result of the limited resource base and the lack of capacity to generate import substitution growth. In addition, the internal disintegration of the military foreclosed the possibility of an institutionalized authoritarian regime of the armed forces. Rather, after 1946, the tremendously weakened state began to collapse, and Bolivia degenerated almost literally into an invertebrate sociopolitical society. In that situation the MNR incorporated sectorally an ever widening spectrum of social groupings. In so doing, it recapitulated within itself the extremely fragmented sectorist organization of Bolivian society. In a real sense the task of the MNR (like the Partido Revolucionario Institucional [PRI] in Mexico, see chapters 7 and 8) was to seize power and to organize its component parts so that the party would become the political vertebrae that could bind the segments of the society to a skeletal framework to underpin a more autonomous central governmental authority. In its attempts to achieve this end, the MNR tried to elaborate a corporatist infrastructure within the party consciously modeled on that of Mexico.

Bolivia After 1952

The insurrection of April 9–11, 1952, toppled the old regime and brought the MNR to formal power, but it also stimulated a tremendous expansion of political mobilization. Most significant was the emergence of organized political activity among a large portion of the rural Indian peasantry. By mid-1953 Bolivia was an almost completely mobilized society. Moreover, during this period weapons were dispersed widely among the civilian populace and provided the base for spontaneous organization throughout the nation of paramilitary militia groups. From the outset, then, the MNR national leadership was confronted with the task of controlling and organizing a highly mobilized and well-armed populace.[14]

In the first stages of its postinsurrectionary organizational efforts, the MNR took what might be called a radical inclusionary approach. The party sought to include in its structure all social sectors except the so-called oligarchy, and in terms of individual membership (which applied mainly to the urban middle class) the party demanded little more than an oath of loyalty in exchange for a party card. Other members of the populace (workers and peasants) were nominal MNR members by dint of prior membership in organizations formally incorporated into the party; hence, the vast bulk of the populace belonged at least nominally to the party. The leadership sought to fashion a centrally coordinated organization radiating from the party chief and central political committee down to base organizations organized along both territorial and functional lines. Following MNR ideology (populist ideology is discussed in chapter 1), the party structure was fashioned to relate to three broad social classes: the middle class, workers, and peasants. The middle class was organized in the main along territorial lines in terms of departmental and zonal organizations; however, parts of the middle class related through functional organizations as well (that is, cells of professionals, shopkeepers, women, military officers, etc.). Labor related through functional organizations (*comandos funcionales*) on a union-by-union basis. The peasantry, in turn, related throught the quasi-functional but territorially rooted multiplicity of rural *sindicatos* (unions).

Following the Mexican example, the MNR sought to establish itself as a dominant inclusionary political organization that would control the state but within a formal democratic framework that allowed opposition so long as it did not pose a serious threat to MNR hegemony. The party's structure was clearly corporatist in that it attempted to organize the bulk of the populace into a limited number of discrete, officially sanctioned organizations coordinated from the top by the central political committee. The operative principles were that one representational organization per territorial or functional unit was allotted and that effective representation depended upon official recognition.

In a real sense, however, the party did not so much centrally organize its base as adapt to and ratify previously existing organizations with their own leadership cadres. This was particularly true of labor but held also to some degree for middle-class and peasant organizations. Also, while party myth held that the MNR was a multiclass party based on three primary classes, the reality remained that the MNR was a sectorist party that recapitulated within itself the now even more vertically fragmented sectoralized structure of Bolivian society. Christopher Mitchell has given us an excellent description of the real organizational nature of the MNR:

> But in organizational terms, the party was poly-sector: its members were grouped into well-defined functional and geographic hierarchies, each specialized or localized and relating to the party (if at all) directly to the central organs: the CNP and the *Jefe*. Thus there were no *commandos* uniting workers in many trades, but instead specialized ones for taxi-drivers, truckdrivers, construction workers, miners, and so on. One did not relate to the party as a *peasant*, pure and simple, but as a member of such-and-such a *sindicato* on a particular *ex-hacienda*. The party organization did not cut across, but was conditioned by these sectoral divisions in society, and if sectors in a given social class tended to act together . . . that was a result more of converging interests than of party structures able to coordinate them.[15]

Whatever the party leadership's aspirations regarding the formation of a party structure to underpin governmental authority and autonomy, the fact remained that the MNR's control over certain sectors was extremely tenuous. This was particularly true of labor, which, under the leadership of Juan Lechín Oquendo, was for the first time welded into a national confederation (Central Obrera Boliviana, COB) established parallel to and outside the party structure. Labor demanded and received recognition of its *"fuero sindical"* (autonomous jurisdiction), which the COB assumed the authority to implement. In addition the COB demanded and received a system of cogovernment (*cogobierno*) in which, in theory at least, governmental authority in specific functional areas was delegated to the COB. Under the new concept, the COB was granted the right to name four ministers (mines, labor, public works, and peasants) who in principle were mandated representatives of labor in the government. The concept of a cogovernment was also carried over to the new national mining corporation (COMIBOL), where at every administrative level the mine workers' federation (FSTMB) had the right to name members to administrative bodies and to veto policies with which it did not agree.

The COB itself, however, was far from a monolith in firm control of its constituent parts. On the contrary, sectoralism prevailed there as well, with each federation oriented to its own interests and the prerogatives of its leadership groups. Indeed, within the COB authority was parceled out to functional elites formally empowered autonomously to represent and regulate their members' interests. Sectoralization and division of authority were demonstrated by the fact that each of the three major federations named a specific labor representative to the ministry of most concern to it: the mine federation named one for the ministry of mines, the factory workers for the ministry of labor, and the railway workers for the ministry of public works.

Although the peasants were theoretically a part of the COB, a separate national confederation of peasants was formed to represent the global peasant interests both before the government and within the COB. The peasant confederation was, however, even weaker than the COB, and effective peasants' organizations remained only at the regional and local levels.

The MNR initiated a number of well-known revolutionary reforms such as nationalization of the mines, agrarian reform, and universal adult suffrage. In addition, the party implemented numerous policies designed to make the state the regulative pivot of national economic life. Not surprisingly, the public sector of the economy expanded rapidly until, in formal terms, it was preponderant. A large part of the public sector was in turn organized around autonomous public corporations charged with regulating specific functional areas: the mining corporation, the state petroleum enterprise, national railways, national airlines corporation, the mining bank, a development corporation, and many others. Hence, a significant amount of public authority was parceled out to these autonomous public units, which quickly became particularized fiefdoms controlled by interest sectors and party factions.[16]

It seems evident that postrevolutionary Bolivia was explicitly organized along corporatist lines. At its base the bulk of the society was divided into a series of functionally and territorially discrete sectors, each with a single officially recognized representational organization. A large number of these sectoral units (those of the middle classes) were represented mainly through the party, which in turn was theoretically the primary intermediary link between the sectors and the state. However, in the case of labor and the peasants, functionally specific intermediary associations were formed parallel to the party and granted corporate status. In principle, then, labor and the peasants had two lines of representation into the government: the party and the separate functional confederations. In practice, however, the peasant confederation was a paper organization; the COB did establish an autonomous mode of corporate representation for labor but was itself sectorally divided.

Atop the primary and intermediary layers stood the much expanded formal state apparatus. Organizationally, however, state authority was decentralized and parceled out among a number of autonomous public corporations and through the practice of *cogobierno* into the peak labor sectoral organization, the COB. Indeed, division within at least one specific public sphere, COMIBOL, went even further in the form of workers' control (FSTMB) with the right of veto.

But from the beginning, the peak of organizational control at either the intermediary or the state level was, to say the least, problematic. Structural organizational principles and particularistic orientations generated de facto sectoral fragmentation and decentralization. This tendency was reinforced by uncontrolled mobilization, especially in the rural sector, and by the fact that the ability to deploy armed forces was dispersed to primary territorial and functional sectoral organizations. Instead of a centrally coordinated corporate state structure, Bolivia was characterized by an extreme form of decentralized corporate structure which, when subjected to pressure, tended to degenerate into unrestrained anomic sectoralism.[17]

Although the revolution was made in the name of anti-imperialism and the assertion of national autonomy, the revolution in fact did not reduce external dependence and in some sense actually increased it. Bolivia remained primarily a mineral export economy with the United States the single most important consumer of Bolivian minerals. Nationalization eliminated the private mine companies as a primary source of public revenue. Public spending and hence the need for revenue expanded dramatically, but the available resource base did not. In addition, the MNR's tenuous control of its support groups reduced the state's ability to generate resources by internal extractive means. The upshot was that the U.S. government stepped into the breach, and the fledgling revolutionary government became extremely dependent on financial aid from the United States and United States-controlled international financial agencies such as the International Monetary Fund (IMF). Post-1952 Bolivia was thus doubly dependent on the United States, both as a primary consumer of Bolivian exports and as a major source of economic aid. This new reality projected the United States as a major actor in the unfolding revolution, and some have argued that

specific programs such as Food for Peace actually retarded local economic growth by undercutting incentives to develop local wheat production and processing. In the external dimension the state remained
extremely weak.[18]

Internally the situation was similar. Instead of providing a stable
national political structure to underpin an autonomous state, the MNR
degenerated into a disaggregated penumbra dependent on the multiplicity of particularistic sectoral organizations and factions it had mobilized. As time went on, the party was converted into little more than
a mechanism through which particularistic interest combinations as-
saulted the state's meager resources. In effect, the internal dependence
of the party was transferred into the state, which vis-à-vis internal
actors remained weak and dependent. The internal weakness of both
the party and the state was manifested in a steady increase of public
spending to support generalized popular consumption. Unable to control its mobilized support groups, the MNR fashioned public policies
designed to win support by buying it. Again, however, the nation's
resource base was too small to underwrite such consumptionist policies,
and Bolivia was subjected to a particularly vicious inflationary process.
Rampant inflation contributed to a generalized perception of a zero-
sum political game which in turn reinforced internal fragmentation,
particularism, and institutional atrophy.[19]

Unable to control its support groups within a stable set of institutions, the party's core leadership sought to cling to the formal symbols
of power by playing upon internal fragmentation and sectoralism. As
institutional constraints diminished, leaders such as Víctor Paz Estenssoro attempted to achieve some semblance of stability by fostering
linkages among state, party, and sectors within a system of clientelistic
politics. Behind the formal institutional façade, the de facto structural
reality was a proliferation of patron-client networks that radiated
outward from party leadership factions into sectoral and regional
groupings. Central party leaders such as Paz survived by balancing the
factions through compromises and logrolling. As in pre-1952 Bolivia,
clientelism was a system based on interconnecting points of dependence
and weakness. The party was weak and factionalized, creating the need
to generate support by parceling out sections of the government which
became the basis of patronage to be doled out within specific patron-
client nets. Sectoral organizations in turn were also weak owing to
fragmentation and a general lack of resources at lower levels; clientelistic politics provided a system in which sectoral leaders linked with
party leadership factions could get at least a piece of the national
government resources. It was, in effect, a system in which the weak and
dependent reinforced the weak and dependent.

This new, MNR-created, clientelistic system enforced the formal hegemony of the MNR and created a certain stability as most sectors and factions developed a vested interest in keeping the game going; but it also had a number of pernicious results. In the first place it contributed to a further weakening of the state manifested in the inability of the government to mount and sustain a coherent policy thrust. Just as important, clientelism weakened the ability of groups to form on a horizontal, class-type basis and sustain a coherent ideological position upon which an alternative definition of the revolution could be based. Left-wing ideology, for example, projected the notion of a socialist revolution to be based on an alliance of workers and peasants. Early on, however, the MNR core leadership was able to drive a wedge between workers and peasants and in the late 1950s actually mobilized peasant militias against workers' groups such as the miners. Within the working class itself, the middle-class MNR core leadership was able to provoke fragmentation and division by playing various working-class leadership cadres off against one another. Clientelism not only weakened the state but also debilitated the COB's ability to act as a unified revolutionary force. Another pernicious and long-term effect arose from the co-optation of lower-level leadership groups. This was particularly true in the case of both worker and peasant organizations. Co-opted leaders often developed a vested clientelistic interest that ran counter to those of their immediate followers; and, as might be expected, corruption became a way of life for many leaders. The upshot was a separation of leaders from followers accompanied by a crisis of authority as the mass of workers and peasants lost faith in anyone who held a leadership position.[20] The bulk of Bolivia's political leaders from the top to the bottom developed a tainted image in the minds of an increasingly cynical populace. This fact helped to weaken further the ability of broad horizontal aggregates such as workers and peasants to participate in coherent organized actions either to defend their "class" interests or to back attempts to transform the system. Political weakness at the center had been counterbalanced by weakness at the base.

From Populism to the Politics of Exclusion

Between 1952 and 1956 the MNR regime followed a policy of maximum inclusion of the populace within its ranks along with a policy of garnering support by increasing popular levels of consumption. The nation's resource base, however, could not sustain that approach, as was made manifest by chronic inflation and the degeneration of politics into an increasingly bitter zero-sum reality which began to undermine the de facto clientelistic system that had evolved. Inflation fell particularly hard on the urban middle sectors, who began to turn against the revolution in increasing numbers. But the inflation also hit some sectors of the urban working class who did not have the capacity to defend themselves on a sectoral basis as the mine workers did. Finally the rampant inflation called into question Bolivia's financial credibility in the eyes of the U.S. government and the lending agencies it influenced.

Between 1956 and 1960 the single most important issue facing the new MNR government of Hernán Siles was inflation and ways to control it. Behind that issue, however, was the more profound reality that a politics of mobilization and inclusion could no longer be sustained. The regime had to confront the choice of which of its multiplicity of support groups would gain and which would lose; in short, the early phase of inclusion gave way to the perceived need to shift to a politics of exclusion. In this shift the overwhelming financial dependence of Bolivia on the United States played an important role. For in order to get the further assistance it needed, the Bolivian government had to adopt an IMF-formulated stabilization program,[21] a plan which in that context amounted to an implied set of rules as to who would benefit or lose, who would be included or excluded. The brunt of the plan was to fall on sectors of the working class and, in particular, on the powerful mine workers. This put Siles onto a collision course with the miners and other segments of the COB.[22]

During his term, Siles made a concerted attempt to impose the plan by attempting to render the office of the presidency an independent source of regulatory power, standing above both the party and sectoral organizations like the COB. As one observer has perceptively put it:

> The CPN, no longer the forum where basic decisions were hammered out, served (with the cabinet) merely to ratify lines of policy adopted by the stabilization council. Inter-sectoral bargaining and trade-offs were now replaced by centralized presidential decision-making. The rules of the game were changing abruptly, and players at the old table felt (with justification) excluded from the new pattern of power and authority.[23]

Siles' four-year tenure was a turbulent time marked by incessant strikes, confrontation, and violence. However, Siles hung on and made the stabilization plan stick.

In his confrontation with the COB and particularly with the miners, Siles used a three-pronged strategy. First he played skillfully upon the sectoral divisions in the COB and the fact that the stabilization plan did not fall as heavily on some working sectors as others. His divide-and-conquer strategy was successful: By the end of his term the COB was a shattered organization which to this day has not been able to find even the tenuous unity of 1952 to 1956. Secondly, he used a combination of anticommunism and judicious patronage to mobilize some armed sectors of the peasantry (especially in Cochabamba) against the workers. Finally and perhaps most significantly, Siles used renewed U.S. military aid to rebuild and modernize the Bolivian military.[24] Even as he used the armed power of one sector, peasants, against that of another sector, miners, Siles moved to re-create an independent armed capacity for the state. Despite the turbulence of the 1956 to 1960 period, the MNR did not fall completely apart—partly because Siles did not try to crush his opponents completely, partly because the MNR remained the only political game, and partly because the alienated sectors of labor anticipated that the return of Paz in 1960 would mean a return to the old rules of the game.

If stabilization of hyperinflation was the central issue from 1956 to 1960, the prime issue of the new Paz Estenssoro administration inaugurated in 1960 was a concerted attempt to stimulate economic development. In confronting this problem, Bolivia's external weakness and fundamental dependency on the United States were again critical factors. In 1960 the Bolivian government sought briefly to diversify its external sources of support by negotiating with the Soviet bloc for credits and aid in building a tin smelter. However, the United States protested these moves, and in the face of U.S. pressure the Paz government capitulated. In return for increases in U.S. economic assistance, Paz accepted completely the development strategy embodied in the much heralded Alliance for Progress.[25]

In the Bolivian context, the alliance strategy was based on a modified system of state capitalism in which the state was to limit its further expansion into the economy, existing public-sector organizations would be rationalized and modernized, and the state apparatus would be used to stimulate activities in the private sector. Specifically the Paz government sought to stimulate growth by means of economic diversification, especially around agricultural products in the eastern region of the interior. Central to this thrust, however, was the conviction on the part of Paz and his U.S. advisors that the state mining corporation, COMIBOL, had to be converted from a position of heavy losses to at least a break-even operation. This aim was to be achieved through the United States-designed Triangular Plan for the tin industry, which aimed for administrative reorganization, a reduced labor force, imposition of labor discipline, and a reduction of subsidized foodstuffs in the camps.[26]

Again the issue of who would bear the costs of development became critical, and again a United States-designed economic program in effect defined the winners and losers. In that context the major direct loser was to be organized labor. Hence Paz, like Siles, confronted the need to enforce the exclusion of one of the major components of the original populist coalition. Paz's confrontation with labor was much more general and profound than that of Siles, and the level of conflict escalated accordingly.

While Paz sought to maintain control over the party apparatus, he did not use it as an instrument of government but sought even more than Siles to turn the formal governmental apparatus in general and the presidency in particular into an independent source of authority and decision. Originally MNR leaders saw the party as an institutional infrastructure which by organizing the major sectors of the society would provide popular support which would, in turn, confer authority on the government. But as we saw above, zero-sum politics stimulated sectoral factionalism which engulfed the party and through it systematically reduced the government's ability to act. By the 1960s, Paz and other leaders no longer saw the party as the backbone of the state or as a source of authority; they viewed it as an instrument to be tamed and controlled by an independent governmental authority. Hence from the political point of view Paz's task was to enforce the exclusion of the labor sector from governmental participation; depoliticize the party and turn it into an instrument of manipulation; and find alternative means to buttress the independent power and authority of the state.

Even more than Siles, Paz sought to buttress independent governmental power by rebuilding (with expanded U.S. aid) the military and making it a pivotal national institution. This was done in part to counter labor's armed power and to give the government the power to force labor's exclusion through coercion. But the military was also charged with an important role in the development effort. Through the United States-funded civic action program, the military built roads and schools, opened up new areas, and provided a pool of technical expertise—at least that was the theory.[27]

Simultaneously Paz sought to depoliticize major governmental posts and adopt a general technocratic style of government. He brought to the fore a new generation of young party people who were not identified with any of the traditional party sectors and therefore did not have their own power bases. In effect, they were his creatures and directly dependent on the president for their power and prestige. Their task in theory was to execute rationally determined technocratic policies without fear or favor to party or sector. Thus at one level the attempt was made to project the image of an independent, nonpolitical, technocratic government based on an alliance among U.S. technical experts (the AID mission), the military, and a civilian clique of apolitical governmental experts backed by U.S. economic and military aid.

Toward the party, Paz assumed a high-handed and autocratic posture and sought to impose discipline from above through a hand-picked executive secretary, Federico Fortún Sanjines, who was known for his personal loyalty to the president. Under Fortún the national party office gained apparent ascendancy by rigging party elections, disciplining dissidents, and manipulating intraparty factions by means of the well-honed patron-client techniques. Here too, the major thrust was to depoliticize the party and impose a system of government as central management. The effect, however, was to divorce the party even more from its original popular bases, thereby widening the organizational distance between the state and the fragmented populace.[28]

Between 1960 and 1964 Bolivia did experience some economic development but it did not diminish social conflict, which was the theory behind the Alliance for Progress. In the Bolivian context the resource base remained small, and its unequal distribution—not to mention the heavy costs imposed on labor—only heightened social conflict. In dealing with rising levels of social conflict the president employed a combination of coercive and manipulative techniques. Paz used force to impose his decision on labor as well as effectively to wipe out labor's influence in the party and the government. But he did not destroy the union organizations, which, although weakened, remained capable of harassing the government through strikes and demonstrations. In dealing with other social sectors, such as the peasants and urban middle classes, Paz came to rely more and more on personal manipulation of patron-client nets which now ran not through the party into the sectors but from the presidential office into the sectors.

Hence Paz succeeded in eliminating the significance of previous intermediary structures such as the party, the COB, and the peasants' confederation. But he was never able to create an independent governmental authority capable of acting as the organizational principle of national life. Rather, he cut the government off from the few organizational anchors that previously connected it (even if negatively) to the major social sectors so that it in effect floated above society in an illusion of apolitical technocratic authority. Coercion and clientelistic manipulation were the major ways the government articulated its relationship to society. Such means of interaction were hardly likely to breed either stability, public confidence, or a sense of governmental legitimacy.

In some senses it could be argued that Paz attempted to deal with the outstanding problems of the revolution by resorting to a system of bureaucratic authoritarianism.[29] But he was incapable of converting the illusion of independent governmental authority legitimated by technocratic norms into reality. The reasons are many but are all traceable to the extremity of Bolivia's delayed dependent development pattern. Bolivia had neither the resources, nor the infrastructure, nor the social cadres to back up Paz's model. The same structural factors born of extreme dependency which undercut Paz's attempt have continued to hinder subsequent attempts to impose a modernizing authoritarian solution in Bolivia.

It should be kept in mind that Bolivia has yet to experience any significant secondary development based on import substitution. Hence there is no significant national bourgeoisie of entrepreneurs able to support and provide the drive for a state-capitalist economic model. Of more importance is the fact that the "modern" component of Bolivian society is comparatively backward and hence has not provided a base to generate a cadre of middle-class technocrats. Paz tried to impose a technocratic model, but he had precious few technocrats to articulate the necessary values and perform technocratic roles. The group of young civilians with which Paz surrounded himself were often referred to as *técnicos*, but in reality they were middle-class professionals of a rather traditional sort.[30]

The Bolivian urban middle class was and remains largely a traditional dependent middle class of professionals and bureaucrats. Given the paucity of private employment, the state still remains its major source of employment. If anything, the revolution of 1952 exacerbated the problem by expanding public employment tremendously and making political criteria and clientelism the major means of securing a public post. Thus the middle class does not provide either significant entrepreneurship or a technocratic cadre to stimulate production and rationalize administration. It is, however, a class with high consumption aspirations which, in effect, drains national resources to support a swollen and inefficient bureaucracy. Furthermore, the nature of the game involved in securing public employment supports a set of values that directly contradicts those necessary to implant technocratic efficiency and to maintain a commitment to national over particularistic goals.

This reality was particularly evident in the MNR party during the 1960s. Under Paz the party was reduced to little more than an aggregation of office seekers. Paz reduced the significance of the party as a mechanism to articulate sectoral interests and formulate authoritative decisions, but one of the ways he did this was by manipulating the traditional clientelistic system of job apportionment. One result was that beneath the apparent central control of the secretariat, the party was in reality a fragmented collection of office-hungry factions that played its own divisive game of ins and outs. A significant problem was that despite the size of the public sector there were not enough positions to reward all of those who felt that their possession of a party card entitled them to hold a public post. Hence the buying off of some factions only alienated others, and the attempt to manipulate the party through patronage undermined Paz's attempt to depoliticize and "technify" the government structure. In short, the party continued to undermine the state.

One upshot was that Paz and his coterie of so-called technocrats, as well as his hand-picked party leaders such as Fortún, appeared in the eyes of the party and society at large to be little more than another faction whose claims on governmental posts were no more legitimate than those of any other faction. In fact, what started out as government by an inclusive single party in 1952 had by the 1960s degenerated, in the public mind at least, into government by a personalistic faction. [31] This reality, notwithstanding Paz's attempt to project an image of government by disinterested technicians, undermined the legitimacy of his government in the party and in society at large. In fact, large sections of the party began to conspire against the president and ultimately played an important part in his overthrow in 1964.

Military Authoritarianism

In the general disintegration after 1960, the military steadily emerged as a critical political factor. Beginning with Siles, the core MNR leadership came to rely more and more on the military rather than the party to enforce the exclusion of labor and uphold independent governmental authority. As in other Latin American states, the inability of civil elites to control a highly mobilized society created a situation where the military felt constrained to eliminate civilian leaders and impose a direct authoritarian solution through a military government. In the wake of widespread civil disorder, the military in November 1964 deposed Paz and pushed the entire MNR apparatus out of the government.

The fact that the military overthrew Paz is not surprising; the important factor from the point of view of this chapter is the way it was done. The Bolivian military did not act as a singular institution with a more or less coherent notion of its purpose in seizing power. Rather, the coup was an "old-fashioned" action in which factions of the military allied with certain civilian factions to depose a set of civilians in power. This factor is important in that it attests to the reality that in comparison to neighboring states the Bolivian military was (and remains) a rather backward and traditional institution.

The Bolivian military never was and is not now a modern professionalized institution. Despite attempts by Paz and the United States to modernize the Bolivian military and develop within it a sense of professional and institutional coherence, it continues to be a fragmented institution dominated by personalities who attempt to use it to further their own ambitions. Compared to the Peruvian and Brazilian militaries, for example, the Bolivians never developed an institutional doctrine regarding national reality and the role of the military within it. Nor has the Bolivian military developed a minimal notion of corporate identity or internal authority expressed in an effective chain of command. Rather, the operative reality has been that in moments of political crisis the chain of command collapses and the relevant actors are personalistic factions dominated by individuals of varying rank.

Backed by the United States, Paz attempted to constitute an independent governmental authority capable of imposing a developmental solution. His ability to do so was weakened because the deformed and backward structures of Bolivia could not produce the social cadres essential to that approach, and the military found it easy to overthrow him. But, in attempting to govern since 1964, military leaders have had to confront the fact that the military is itself underdeveloped and dependent and thus part of the general problem.

Since 1964 Bolivia has been governed by a succession of authoritarian regimes headed by individual strong men drawn from the armed forces. Throughout, Bolivia has constituted an extreme case of what Samuel Huntington has called a praetorian society, a situation in which levels of political mobilization have gone beyond the capacity of existing political institutions to control mobilized social forces.[32] One might add that in Bolivia, praetorianism has been exacerbated by a limited resource base and the fact that all relevant political actors perceive themselves to be involved in a zero-sum political game. In Bolivia as elsewhere the military seized power in response to a praetorian situation that civilians could not control. However, Bolivia also demonstrates that unless the military has achieved a high level of institutional autonomy and professional identity, and unless a cadre of civilian technocrats willing to ally with the military exists, the possibility of establishing a stable modern authoritarian regime within a corporatist infrastructure is highly unlikely. Lacking these factors because of severe underdevelopment and dependency, the Bolivian military has itself been praetorianized; as the MNR before it recapitulated within itself the fragmented structure of Bolivian society, so has the Bolivian military.

Between 1964 and 1969 Bolivia was dominated by the personality of Air Force General René Barrientos Ortuño. Under Barrientos, economic growth continued at respectable rates primarily because labor was effectively excluded from the political equation and forced to bear the costs of development. Following essentially the same state-capitalist strategy as Paz, Barrientos spurred development by supporting private mine and oil companies (both local and foreign) in the export sector; supporting private business and agricultural interests in the east; and pushing investment into existing public corporations; in short, by forming an alliance between public and private large-scale economic enterprises.[33] Barrientos did not and could not forge an institutional structure to solidify the alliance and back the state as the prime regulator of the state-capitalist thrust. In fact, during his tenure most intermediate political structures were effectively destroyed. He ruled primarily through brutal repression, directed mainly at labor, and skillful manipulation of patron-client networks.[34] The latter were used particularly to control segments of the dependent urban middle class, including the military, and the more articulate sectors of the peasantry. While the bulk of the economic costs fell on labor, the peasantry was also probably a net loser during the period.[35] Barrientos maintained his control over the peasantry, however, through demagogic manipulation and buying off of peasant leaders, as well as the fact that the development thrust was in areas other than where the bulk of the peasantry lived and therefore not perceived as having a direct impact upon them.

While a modicum of control was established over workers and peasants, Barrientos, as well as successive military leaders, could not assert control at the elite level. There was simply not enough largesse to go around among the dependent urban middle class. Hence, fragmentation among ins and outs became and remains the rule, and factionalization has carried over into the military. Before his death in 1969, it was evident that a significant coalition of civil and military factions was conspiring against Barrientos and that his days were numbered.

Between 1969 and 1971, Bolivia appeared to move in a leftist nationalist direction; first under General Alfredo Ovando and then under General Juan José Torres. Both attempted to forge coalitions among factions of the military, civilian elite factions, university students, and a revived labor movement. Both reversed the thrust away from exclusion and demobilization to a renewed attempt at mobilization and inclusion of mass sectoral support. Neither came close to achieving the minimal structural links established by the MNR in its early years, and hence both leaders ended by floating above an intensely renewed game of intersectoral and interfactional zero-sum politics. With every major group and institution fragmented, the state has become even weaker than it previously was and government almost an epiphenomenon. This was particularly apparent during the Torres regime when labor forced the hapless leader to acquiesce in the convening of a popular assembly which would ultimately form a government. However, the popular assembly, like everything else, was characterized by disarray, factionalism, and intersectoral struggle. Shortly thereafter a countercoalition of military factions, civilian outs, and private economic interests moved against Torres and toppled him with ease.

Since August 1971 Bolivia has been governed by a mixed civil-military regime headed by Colonel Hugo Banzer. Under Banzer the government has attempted to return to the state-capitalist model of the 1960s. Again the primary political thrust has been toward exclusion and demobilization, with labor (and left-wing political groups) the main target. Again severe repression and clientelistic manipulation have been the main instruments of rule. Banzer sought to underpin his regime by forging an alliance among the MNR, its old rival the Falange Socialista Boliviana (FSB), private business interests, and sections of the military; a formula was worked out within which the formal government was divided proportionately among these groups. Rather than providing structural stability, however, the alliance brought an increased number of factions into the government and has reinforced intraelite fragmentation and debilitated even further the state structure. Thus Bolivia remains a society that at its base is characterized by deep sectoral fragmentation and repressed mobilization, while at the top it is characterized by elite fragmentation and an intense struggle among in and out factions to control pieces of the state. Between the two levels there are no effective intermediary structures, and political life has degenerated into unstable caudillistic authoritarianism with the fragmented military producing the caudillos as elite factional alliances form and re-form. So it is apt to remain for some time to come.

Conclusions

A corporate political structure is a specific way of organizing the relationship between the state and the major interests in the society that it rules. In liberal democratic theory the state is a reflexive phenomenon that processes the inputs of independent, voluntarily formed societal interests into policies. In a corporate state, however, the state plays a more active positive role in defining legitimate interests, authoritatively recognizing which associations can express interests, and defining formal rules of access. In the liberal democratic model, group formation is spontaneous and unlimited, and social stability is maintained by an intermediary group structure that generates horizontal communication at the base by fostering multiple overlapping group memberships.[36] Corporate structures conversely are based on a limited number of compulsory groups formed along vertical functional lines, creating a columnar structure which minimizes horizontal communication at the base while fostering cross-sectoral communication at the elite level. Thus a corporate structure does not rest on an integrated base but radiates in vertical compartmentalized lines from a horizontally integrated "cartel of elites."[37] In this structure the core of the polity is transsectoral and thereby renders the state to some degree capable of asserting a constitutive rather than reflexive role. Contrary to the liberal democratic model which stresses behavioral over institutional criteria, the corporate model stresses the causal significance of formal governmental structures in regulating behavior. Corporate states may be democratic in the sense that the Netherlands, Sweden, and Norway are democratic. As we have seen, however, with few exceptions (Venezuela and Colombia) the trend in Latin America is toward authoritarian corporate structures.

Authoritarian corporatism in Latin America is to some degree linked to the region's Hispanic patrimonial past and the principles and modes of organization derived from it. However, this cannot be advanced as the major explanation of the contemporary trend. Contemporary corporate systems in Latin America and elsewhere are also systems of political economy linked to various developmental stages of capitalism.[38] In Latin America the linkage is to delayed, dependent capitalist development which introduced modern elements into the region as overlaps on previous patterns, creating the "living museum" effect. [39] One result was a fragmented, sectoralized social structure articulated in de facto vertical hierarchies which despite formal institutions constituted a system of what Ronald Newton has called "natural corporatism."[40] In one sense, contemporary corporatist systems can be seen as an attempt to formalize, institutionalize, and thereby control a de facto "natural corporatist" social structure.

The present situation in most nations of the region can be seen as an outgrowth of the crisis of export-oriented dependent capitalism which emerged in the 1930s. The critical link between the present and the 1930s was the phenomenon of populism, which was the characteristic regional political response to the crisis. Populism was implicitly (sometimes explicitly) corporatist and sought to mobilize a broad popular base to support a state-capitalist import substitution development model. But there was an inherent tension in most cases between populist inclusive mobilization and formal control that was to one degree or another aggravated by environmental conditions of scarcity. Populism in a sense bred a tendency to praetorianism, the manifestation of which varied from country to country in terms of degree of mobilization and the ability to buy time by segmental incorporation, which in turn was linked to the capacity to sustain import substitution growth. In many cases, however, a limit was reached, creating zero-sum political games that could be resolved only by excluding certain actors. But often under the extant constitutional rules civilian elites were incapable of enforcing exclusion, thereby reinforcing praetorian tendencies which created political immobilism and erratic economic performance. The upshot was a trend in many states toward the emergence of military-backed authoritarian regimes that seek to force exclusion, assert control, and stimulate development within a corporatist framework.

Bolivia can be seen as a case that followed most of the stages in this pattern but owing to the extremity of its delayed dependent growth experience veered from the modal path at critical junctions. Critical to the Bolivian situation was the extreme weakness of the state and the inability to stimulate import substitution growth. Previously high levels of mobilization were pushed to an extreme by the revolution of 1952 and soon went far beyond the limited resource capacity of the nation. The MNR sought to control the situation through a corporatist structure based on inclusion of all relevant social sectors. Limited resources, however, fed an inflationary zero-sum political situation in which central control gave way to sectoral bargaining, weakening the state and excerbating the inflationary spiral.

Attempts to control the inflation gave rise to a strategy of exclusion that was in part externally defined, an approach that was reinforced further after 1960 when the government sought to impose a United States-backed, state-capitalist development model. The inability of the MNR (or factions of it) to enforce exclusion and control praetorianism stimulated a military coup and an attempt at an authoritarian state-capitalist solution. However, because of the extremity of Bolivia's backward dependent situation, neither the technocratic cadres nor the military was sufficiently developed and institutionally self-conscious to back the thrust.

Bolivia demonstrates negatively and other states confirm positively that in modernizing authoritarian corporate regimes there are certain prerequisites to the achievement of more or less stable control.

The first is that the level of mobilization relative to economic and political resources must not have gone too far. In Brazil in 1964 mobilization was intermediate, while in Peru in 1968 it was relatively low; in Argentina it was and is very high; in Bolivia it is almost astronomic.[41] In addition, development must have achieved a level sufficient to have produced a modern professionalized military with an institutional identity and a relatively coherent image of its society and the military's role in it; a cadre of technocrats alienated from society and willing to ally with the military to force a restructuring of society to meet the technocrats' image; and groups (such as native and foreign entrepreneurs) willing and able to respond to incentives provided by the military-technocrat controlled state. One should probably also mention the existence of a resource base sufficient to underwrite the incorporation of the bulk of the dependent middle class into public and private bureaucratic employment so as to forestall fragmentation into an intra-elite game of ins and outs.

Argentina meets most of the criteria, but the level of mobilization and the sophistication of sectoral organizations appear to be the major destabilizing factors. In Bolivia, the level of previous development is too low to provide the essential prerequisites to fashioning a modernizing authoritarian corporate regime; a certain level of modernization and development is a basic prerequisite. But the level of mobilization in Bolivia has gone so far that the possibility of a stable traditional authoritarian regime has been precluded. Bolivia is literally caught in the middle, and as a result anomic praetorian authoritarianism has become that nation's dominant mode of politics.

NOTES

1. Prior to 1952 mineral exports accounted for over 95 percent of foreign exchange.

2. For an analysis of the early phase, see Herbert S. Klein, *Parties and Political Change in Bolivia, 1880–1952* (Cambridge: Cambridge University Press, 1969).

3. Laurence Whitehead, "The State and Sectoral Interests" (mimeograph, Oxford, 1974).

4. Roland H. Ebel, "Governing the City-State: Notes on the Politics of the Small Latin American Countries," *Journal of Inter-American Studies and World Affairs*, 14 (August 1972):325–46.

5. As early as 1922, Patiño was clearly the largest single financial power in the country. The following paragraph gives some idea of the breadth of his holdings as of that year:

Señor Patiño's activities are not confined to the field of mining; he is also the sole owner of the Mercantile Bank of Bolivia, which has a capital of four million dollars. In addition to his banking and mining activities he is connected with the company administering the monopoly of alcohol and spirits, the importance of which is indicated by the fact that over 400,000 pesos have to be paid annually to the Government for the privilege. He has a large interest in the Colonizing Company of Isoboro, the Machacamarca-Uncia, Llallagua and Amayapampa. He has, moreover, secured a concession for constructing a railroad from Cochabamba to the Mamore River, which, when finished, will give the products of Bolivia an outlet to the Atlantic. (William Parker Belmont, ed., *Bolivians of Today*, 2d ed., rev. [New York: Hispanic Society of America, 1922], p. 214)

6. I use the term "political class" here to denote those members of the middle and upper-middle class who lived primarily off politics. For an expansion of the analysis presented here, see James M. Malloy, *Bolivia: The Uncompleted Revolution* (Pittsburgh: University of Pittsburgh Press, 1970), chap. 2.

7. See Klein, *Parties and Political Change*, and Whitehead, "State and Sectoral Interests."

8. The role of personal dependency in undercutting class-oriented action is analyzed in June Nash, "Industrial Conflict in the Andes: The Bolivian Tin Miners" (mimeograph, City College of New York, 1972).

9. For a fuller analysis, see James M. Malloy and Richard Thorn, eds., *Beyond the Revolution: Bolivia Since 1952* (Pittsburgh: University of Pittsburgh Press, 1971).

10. For a detailed analysis of the period, see Klein, *Parties and Political Change*, chaps. 6–9; and Malloy, *Bolivia*, chaps. 5–6.

11. Christopher Mitchell, "Reformers as Revolutionaries: The Tragedy of Bolivia's Movimiento Revolucionario 1952–1964" (Ph.D. dissertation, Harvard University, 1971), p. 34.

12. See chap. 1 of this book for a general discussion of concepts.

13. This informal mode of corporatist decision-making has been referred to as "natural corporatism." See Ronald C. Newton, "Natural Corporatism and the Passing of Populism in Spanish America," *Review of Politics*, 36 (January 1974): 34–52.

14. For an expansion of the analysis, see Malloy, *Bolivia*, chaps. 9–10.

15. Mitchell, "Reformers as Revolutionaries," pp. 101–02.

16. Ibid., p. 114. Also see Richard Thorn, "The Economic Transformation," in Malloy and Thorn, *Beyond the Revolution*; and Melvin Burke and James Malloy, "From National Populism to National Corporatism: Bolivia 1952–1970," *Studies in Comparative International Development*, 9 (1974):49–73.

17. Malloy, *Bolivia*, chap. 12.

18. Melvin Burke, "Does Food for Peace Damage the Bolivian Economy?", *Interamerican Economic Affairs*, 25 (1971):3–26. For data on economic and military assistance, see Cole Blasier, "The United States and the Revolution," in Malloy and Thorn, *Beyond the Revolution*, pp. 111–56.

19. The postrevolutionary inflation in Bolivia was one of the most severe in the history of any Latin American nation. Taking 1950 as 100, the cost-of-living index shot to 9,980 in 1959. See Appendix, table 4, in Malloy and Thorn, *Beyond the Revolution*, p. 376.

20. This problem is analyzed in Nash, "Industrial Conflict in the Andes."

21. For a sympathetic analysis of the stabilization program which also demonstrates clearly the U.S. role in its implementation, see George Eder, *Inflation and Development in Latin America: A Case Study of Inflation and Stabilization in Bolivia* (Ann Arbor: University of Michigan, School of Business, 1968).

22. Malloy, *Bolivia*, chaps. 12–13.

23. Mitchell, "Reformers as Revolutionaries," p. 139.

24. For data see Blasier, "United States and the Revolution," p. 93.

25. Thorn, "Economic Transformation," pp. 194 ff.

26. Malloy, *Bolivia*, chap. 13.

27. For a study of military civic action, see William Brill, "Military Civic Action in Bolivia" (Ph.D. dissertation, University of Pennsylvania, 1965).

28. Mitchell, "Reformers as Revolutionaries," chap. 5.

29. For a development of this concept, see Guillermo O'Donnell, *Modernization and Bureaucratic-Authoritarianism: Studies in South American Politics* (Berkeley: Institute of International Studies, 1973).

30. In his last term Paz was obsessed with creating a cadre of technocrats. To this end he established, with U.S. assistance, a technical school outside the university framework. This provoked widespread opposition and contributed to his fall.

31. For a discussion of factions, see Mariò Pando Monje, *Las movimientistas en el Poder* (La Paz: Editorial Juventud, 1968), pp. 236–39.

32. Samuel P. Huntington, *Political Order in Changing Societies* (New Haven: Yale University Press, 1968).

33. For a detailed analysis see Burke and Malloy, "From National Populism to National Corporatism."

34. Barrientos's repression of labor was notorious. Troops were sent into the mines in September and May, 1965. And after a particularly bloody invasion in June 1967 the mines were permanently occupied.

35. For an analysis see Burke and Malloy, "From National Populism to National Corporatism."

36. The best-known formulation is William Kornhauser, *The Politics of Mass Society* (Glencoe, Ill.: Free Press, 1960).

37. For an analysis of this type of structure in a different setting, see Martin O. Heisler and Robert B. Kuavik, "Patterns of European Politics: The 'European Polity' Model," in *Politics in Europe*, ed. Martin O. Heisler (New York: David McKay Co., 1974), chap. 2.

38. This argument is effectively made in Philippe C. Schmitter, "Still the Century of Corporatism?", *Review of Politics*, 36 (January 1974):85–131.

39. Charles W. Anderson, *Politics and Economic Change in Latin America* (Princeton: D. Van Nostrand Co., 1967).

40. Ronald Newton, "Natural Corporatism," pp. 34–51.

41. In looking into this matter researchers should consider not only the quantity of mobilization but also its quality, that is, organization, leadership, etc. In Argentina mobilization is not only high but also very sophisticated.

IV

Conclusions and Implications

DAVID COLLIER and RUTH BERINS COLLIER

15

Who Does What, to Whom, and How: Toward a Comparative Analysis of Latin American Corporatism

Recent research on Latin American politics has placed substantial emphasis on the authoritarian relationships between national states and interest groups characteristic of the region. Particular attention has been paid to the limitation of pluralism and to "corporative" patterns of interest representation as distinctive features of the systems of state-group relations that have emerged. However, though many theoretical statements and descriptive case studies have examined these themes, little cross-national research has systematically compared state-group relations across a number of cases. Yet systematic comparison can yield important benefits, both as a means of sharpening conceptualizations and ultimately as an approach to testing propositions about the emergence of different types of state-group relations.

This chapter explores opportunities for the comparative analysis of state-group relations in Latin America. It first evaluates the contribution that quantitative cross-national research on national political regimes has made to the analysis of interest representation. Building on available conceptual discussions of corporatism, it proposes an approach to comparing corporative structures cross-nationally. It then argues that though the examination of corporative structures is an important starting point, it is essential to consider as well the differing relationships of economic and political power that are ratified or consolidated by means of these structures. The answers to the question, "Who does what, to whom, and how?" may be used for identifying a series of dimensions in terms of which these relationships can be compared. An examination of the answers to these questions with reference to one major aspect of state-group relations—the relationship between the state and organized labor in the modern sector—is presented to illustrate the wide variety of uses to which corporative

489

structures have been put in Latin America. It is argued that the answers to these questions have appeared in certain recurring patterns and that an essential task of future research is to identify the variety of different patterns that have emerged in Latin America. Finally, it is suggested that if the comparative analysis of state-group relations is to be meaningful substantively, a research strategy based on the analysis of relatively small numbers of cases and relatively simple cross-tabulations of nominal and ordinal scales derived from careful scoring of historical data must be employed.

Cross-National Analyses of National Political Regimes

Cross-national research that has included Latin American countries has given extensive attention to the analysis of national political regimes but has made only a limited contribution to the comparative analysis of authoritarian patterns of interest representation and state-group relations.[1] One reason for this limitation has been the fact that the substantive concerns of much of this literature have been embedded in a tradition of research on political change oriented around the analysis of democracy and the evolution of territorially based systems of representation. These themes were emphasized in part because of a desire to deal with aspects of political life that lend themselves readily to counting and quantification, and in part because of the widespread belief in the 1960s that formal democracy and democratization were central issues of political development. These studies focused on such things as extent of suffrage; degree of competitiveness of the party system (which involves the results of territorial elections and the distribution of seats in a territorially based legislature); and the regularity of elections and of constitutional succession.[2] The most important cross-national data banks that have included Latin America emphasize these same kinds of variables.[3]

In contrast to the heavy emphasis on territorial representation, relatively little attention has been given to the system of interest representation. The greatest problem with efforts to analyze interest politics cross-nationally is the limited investment that has been made in developing relevant measures. As a result, most studies that have employed indices measuring characteristics of interest representation have used the same indicators, those developed by Arthur Banks and Robert Textor.[4] Banks and Textor constructed two indices that dealt with interest-group representation. The first is a measure of freedom of group opposition that distinguished countries where groups were free to organize and able to oppose, free to organize but limited in ability to oppose, tolerated informally but effectively outside the established political system, and not tolerated. They also classified interest articulation by associational groups as either significant, moderate, limited, or negligible.

Three observations may be made about the Banks and Textor indicators. First, from the perspective of political science, their efforts were particularly interesting because of the extent to which their data bank, unlike many, was made up predominantly of *political* variables. Their work clearly represented a bold attempt to get at some of the more complex aspects of political life. Second, however, in any attempt to score all the nations of the world on a large number of complex variables, there are likely to be major problems of reliability. Reliability is indeed a problem for the Banks and Textor assessment of interest politics in Latin America. For a number of countries the scores have only a weak correspondence with the conventional wisdom among Latin American specialists concerning interest politics in the region.[5] Finally, their categories represent highly aggregated descriptions which fail to deal conceptually with the different mechanisms through which state control and regulation are exercised and which do not take into account the fact that in any particular country there are likely to be a number of distinct "subsystems" of interest representation that may differ greatly across sectoral or class lines.[6]

A limited number of additional studies have appeared that make some contribution to the comparative analysis of interest representation. Deane Neubauer developed two ordinal variables on which he scored the extent of organization of voluntary associations as high or low and the degree of group autonomy as high, medium, or low.[7] However, he unfortunately included only two Latin American countries among the ten that he considered. Other studies have overcome the problem of the high degree of aggregation involved in characterizing the entire system of interest representation by focusing on only one aspect: the labor movement. Irma Adelman and Cynthia Morris scored eighteen Latin American countries on an ordinal measure of the strength and autonomy of the labor movement.[8] Other authors have analyzed the extent of union membership and strike activity.[9] Though one of these studies includes only one Latin American country and another analyzes all of the data in dichotomous form, thereby losing a great deal of information, they do have the advantage of including more concrete comparative data on what are clearly important aspects of interest representation. However, though they include variables that would be very useful in the comparative analysis of authoritarian systems of interest representation, they do not directly measure the authoritarian characteristics of these systems.

On balance, then, little in the cross-national literature can be of use in analyzing interest groups and state-group relations in Latin America. Cross-national studies have made a heavy investment in measuring and analyzing features of national political regimes related to democracy and territorial representation and have devoted only limited attention to interest representation.

Ironically, one of the most important critiques of this neglect might be made not from the point of view of the scholar interested in authoritarianism and corporatism, but from the point of view of democratic theory: While cross-national analysts have been measuring democracy in terms of elections and parties, the pluralist school of democratic theory has emphasized interest-group politics as a principal basis for democratic representation.[10] The "antipluralist" tradition within the literature on American politics places a similar emphasis on the role of interest politics, though with less optimistic conclusions regarding the implications of existing patterns of group interaction for American democracy.[11] The conspicuous neglect of interest politics in most cross-national studies obviously represents a serious limitation from both of these perspectives.

From the point of view of scholars interested in authoritarianism and corporatism, this neglect of interest politics is equally serious. Some of the most important aspects of political life emphasized in analyses of authoritarian politics are the ways in which pluralism is limited and the ways in which elites control interest aggregation and articulation through a variety of means, in considerable measure through establishing corporative structures. Yet no effort has been made to construct indices dealing with these mechanisms. Cross-national studies have thus to a substantial degree become divorced from the central analytic concerns of a growing body of research on Latin American politics. Because of the heavy emphasis in cross-national studies on indicators of democracy and territorial representation, regimes have too often been conceptualized in terms of a continuum with democracy at one end and an unspecified nondemocratic, authoritarian, or undeveloped political system at the other. Relatively little attention has been devoted to the numerous dimensions of variation among the nondemocratic systems, or to the extent to which certain features usually associated with authoritarianism, such as corporatism, cut across a democratic-nondemocratic dimension. It is therefore time to go beyond the early scoring of regimes to construct indicators of the various techniques for channeling and controlling interest representation as a fundamental dimension in terms of which regimes may be compared.

Comparing Corporative Structures

Given this neglect of interest representation in cross-national research, what direction can cross-national studies of this aspect of political life most usefully take? One promising focus is suggested by recent writing on interest representation in Latin America that emphasizes the concept of "corporatism." Though this term has been applied to a wide variety of different phenomena—including ideology, broad cultural traditions, modes of political action, and types of political participation[12] —there appears to be a growing consensus regarding its meaning when it is used to describe systems of interest representation. Philippe Schmitter, Howard Wiarda, Kenneth Mericle, Guillermo O'Donnell, Robert Kaufman, James Malloy, and Alfred Stepan have all presented essentially structural definitions that treat corporatism as an approach to *organizing* state-society relations.[13] While using different vocabulary and phrasing, they all treat corporatism as a type of interest representation based on noncompeting, officially sanctioned, state-supervised groups. In contrast to the pattern of interest politics based on autonomous groups that is posited by the pluralist model and approximated to a substantial degree in some empirical cases, in the case of corporatism the state encourages the formation of a limited number of officially recognized groups that interact with the state in clearly defined and regularized ways.

Though these definitions have not been applied to the systematic comparative analysis of corporatism, their empirical referents are sufficiently clear that they are useful for developing such a comparison. They point to three specific types of mechanisms used in regulating state-group relations: *structuring*, *subsidy*, and *control*. The following working definition may be employed as a synthesis of available definitions:

> A system of interest representation is defined as corporative to the extent that it is characterized by a pattern of state *structuring* of representation that produces a system of officially sanctioned, noncompetitive interest associations which are organized into legally prescribed functional groupings; to the extent that these associations are *subsidized* by the state; and to the extent that there is explicit state *control* over the leadership, demand-making, and internal governance of these associations.

This definition lends itself relatively easily to comparative analysis because it is explicitly criterial.[14] That is, it identifies a series of traits that may be present or absent to varying degrees. It thus avoids an excessively narrow conception of corporatism as a phenomenon that is either present or absent and views it instead as a dimension (or, potentially a set of dimensions—see the next section) along which cases may be arrayed.

What types of data can most usefully be employed in the compara-

tive analysis of these corporative traits? Various authors have emphasized that the relationship between the state and interest associations in
Latin America is, to a substantial degree, formalized in the legal
system.[15] One useful point of entry is therefore to examine the formal
legislation that regulates state-group relations. The analysis of law also
has two important practical advantages. First, many of the relevant laws
are readily available, providing a convenient source of comparative data.
Second, the analysis of laws from different historical periods makes it
possible to develop data involving relatively long time series, permitting
not only comparative analysis among countries but also extended
longitudinal analysis within countries.

As part of an ongoing study of state-labor relations in Latin America,
we have attempted to take advantage of this opportunity for com-
parative-longitudinal analysis by using labor law as a principal source of
data on one important aspect of state-group relations. A code for
scoring labor law has been developed that identifies thirty-six different
provisions for state structuring, subsidy, and control of organized labor.
The relevant provisions concerning state structuring can be classified
under the following subheadings: registration and recognition of
unions; compulsory membership and the representation of nonmembers; definition of the sectors into which unions are to organize;
hierarchical and horizontal structuring of unions; monopoly of representation; and creation of multiclass representative bodies in which
workers' representatives participate. Two types of subsidy of unions
have been identified: state financing and direct state involvement in
sponsorship. Three types of control have been identified: control of
demand-making, control of leadership, and direct state monitoring and
intervention in union affairs. On the basis of this code, the labor laws of
ten Latin American countries have been scored annually for the period
1905 to 1974.[16]

Data collected on the basis of a code of this type can be aggregated
and analyzed in a variety of ways. One approach is to construct an
overall index of the extent to which corporative provisions are present
in the laws of each country. Such an index permits a detailed analysis
of the timing and degree of changes in the legal framework of state-
labor relations. The order and patterns in which different corporative
provisions appear in different countries may also be tested to see
whether they fit any recognized scaling patterns. The three different
approaches to shaping state-labor relations—structuring, subsidy, and
control—may be analyzed to discover whether, to some degree, they
represent distinct dimensions that appear in different combinations in
different settings. Data on labor law can also be analyzed in connection
with other variables in an attempt to explain variations in the extent to

which these corporative legal provisions have appeared in each country and in the timing of their appearance.

The analysis of the legal framework of state-group relations obviously represents only a starting point in the analysis of corporative structures. One must also consider the application of law and certain aspects of corporative practice that may never be ratified in law. Such an extension of the analysis would have to rely on available monographic literature on state-group relations or on new field research, and hence would not lend itself as readily to the comparison of large numbers of cases. It would be more appropriate to use this supplementary type of data in more focused comparisons of small numbers of cases or in the analysis of change over time within a single country. Even with these limitations in the scope of comparison, however, it appears that an analysis of this type focusing on both law and informal practice would provide a valuable approach to comparing corporative structures.

On the basis of available conceptual discussions of corporatism, it is thus possible to derive a set of criteria for evaluating the degree to which any particular case is characterized by corporative structures of state-group relations. However, conceptualizing corporatism only in terms of structure, whether formal or informal, cannot by itself form the basis of an adequate analysis. Similar *structures* may have very different *functions* in different settings.[17] They may be used to ratify or consolidate very different distributions of political and economic power. To the extent that this is the case, an understanding of structure provides insights into the *means* through which certain ends are accomplished, but not into what those ends are or who seeks to accomplish them. Yet it is precisely this context of power relationships that makes the analysis of structure interesting.

Who Does What, to Whom, and How?

If one is to move beyond a concern with structure and study the relationships of economic and political power that are ratified or consolidated by means of corporative structures, it is essential to identify dimensions in terms of which these relationships can most usefully be compared. With Lasswellian brevity one may ask, "Who does what, to whom, and how?" The answers to this question may be used as a starting point for identifying the different types of corporative state-group relations that have emerged in Latin America.

In the analysis that follows, as in the discussion of labor law presented earlier, the focus will be restricted to the relationship between the state and organized labor. This may be justified not only because it makes the task at hand more manageable, but also because, as O'Donnell has emphasized, state-labor relations are a particularly crucial aspect of the reality of Latin American corporatism.[18] If one were to consider the relations between the state and other interest associations, a set of parallel, yet distinct, answers to these questions would emerge.

Who?

When one says that corporatism ratifies or consolidates relationships of economic and political power, it is essential to ask, Whose power? Who creates or uses corporative structures? Whose interests are being served?

Since the focus of this portion of the analysis is on state-labor relations, it is convenient to begin by considering these two "actors"— the state and organized labor. Corporatism may enhance either the power of the state or the power of the labor movement—or, in many cases, of particular sectors or factions within the state or the labor movement. In some cases, corporative structures of state-labor relations are introduced or actively retained in settings in which a strong state is consolidating its domination over the labor movement. At the other extreme, a weak state may enter into a coalition with a powerful, often highly mobilized, labor movement, introducing corporative provisions desired by labor organizations or labor leaders in exchange for political support. A wide range of empirical cases, involving a variety of different power relationships and alliance patterns, are found between these extremes.

The way in which these apparently opposite outcomes can be achieved may be understood by considering separately the three component elements of corporatism discussed above: structuring, subsidy, and control. Whereas structuring can be used to reduce the ability of organized labor to engage in active and effective demand-making, it may also be used to ratify or reinforce the dominance of a favored sector of organized labor which is an ally of the government over other sectors of the labor movement. Though subsidy can reduce the autonomy and militancy of organized labor by making labor leaders dependent on the state and reducing their concern with defending and winning support of their own rank and file, it may also be used selectively to reinforce the power of a favored sector of the labor movement in relation to other sectors. Finally, though mechanisms of direct control may be used against the entire labor movement, they may also be used selectively against certain sectors of organized labor in a way that strengthens the position of the sector that is allied with the government.[19]

The difference between these two patterns corresponds to a distinction that Schmitter, drawing on the literature on European corporatism, has identified as the contrast between state and societal corporatism. Following Mihaïl Manoïlesco, he characterizes state corporatism as that in which "singular, noncompetitive, hierarchically ordered representative 'corporations'* are created by and kept as auxiliary and dependent organs of the state which found[s] its legitimacy and effective functioning on other bases." In the case of societal corporatism, "the legitimacy and functioning of the state [are] primarily or exclusively dependent on the activity of 'corporations.' " In the first case, interest associations are thus "dependent and penetrated"; in the second case, they are "autonomous and penetrative."[20] Schmitter identifies societal corporatism primarily with the "postliberal, advanced capitalist, organized democratic welfare state" that has emerged in the most advanced North Atlantic societies and state corporatism with the "antiliberal, delayed capitalist authoritarian, neomercantilist" state that is more characteristic of Latin America.[21]

It is certainly correct that societal corporatism is more prevalent in North Atlantic societies and state corporatism more prevalent in Latin America. However, it is evident that there are significant variations along this dimension *within* Latin America as well. The instances of state corporatism are numerous, with the contemporary authoritarian regimes in Brazil, Uruguay, and Chile obvious examples. A striking example of societal corporatism is Cuba in 1933, when a powerful labor movement won important concessions from a relatively weak government.[22] In many other cases, there is a complex mix of control from above and mobilization from below—including Venezuela in the period after 1945, Argentina after 1943, Mexico under Lázaro Cárdenas, and Colombia during the Liberal era.[23]

Though the state-societal distinction provides a useful starting point for answering the question of "who," it is important that it not lead one to treat society and the state as unified entities. The present discussion has already employed a relatively disaggregated conception of the societal side of the distinction, both because the analysis has been restricted to the labor movement and because the implications of corporatism for organized labor were explained in terms of its consequences for the relations among different sectors of the labor movement. In dealing with the state, one must likewise be careful not to treat it as a "black box," thereby neglecting to consider the question of "who" the state is, or which economic or political groups are acting through it.

---

*That is, multiclass interest associations that appear in the most extreme cases of "corporatism" as defined earlier in this chapter.

In the case of societal corporatism, it is primarily the labor movement, or a sector of it, that is acting through the state—or, more specifically, extracting concessions from the state or winning concessions by allying with other actors in the state or associated with it. In the case of state corporatism, and in those cases which involve a complex mix of initiative from above and mobilization from below, a variety of economic and political interests may come into play. These may again include the interests of the favored sectors of the labor movement, but in a context of more initiative from above and less autonomous initiative on the part of labor. Other interests served have included those of elements of the urban middle class, national industrialists, foreign capital, and civilian technocrats inside and outside the state. Military elites have often played a central role, including both national political leaders who have risen from the military and in some cases the military acting as an institution. Finally, political parties have played a crucial role in the development of corporatism in a number of countries.[24]

What and to Whom?

In emphasizing that corporatism ratifies or consolidates relationships of economic and political power, it is important to ask, "Power to do what, and to whom?" The exercise of political power is of interest, not in itself, but rather in terms of how it is used for pursuing certain objectives or policies. The question is "what" policies and objectives, and at "whom" are they directed?

An important part of the answer to this question involves the impact of corporative provisions on labor-management relations. These provisions may greatly strengthen the position of labor vis-à-vis management, as when corporative structures are used to protect major sectors of the working class that have not previously been organized in unions or have not participated in collective bargaining.[25] Alternatively, corporative provisions can be used to weaken the labor movement in its relations with management. In some cases this is done through a general tightening of control over the entire labor movement.[26] In other instances, it may be done by deliberately supporting a portion of the labor movement that is clearly more moderate and less militant in its demands.[27] In these different contexts, the answer to the question "to whom" thus varies. In some instances, corporative structures aid organized labor and to some degree are directed against employers. In other instances, they favor employers and are directed against organized labor.

Apart from the immediate consequences for the labor movement, answering the question "what and to whom" requires a consideration of the broader policy objectives being pursued by the state. These are relevant because corporative structures may be used either to win the support of the labor movement in a way that enhances the ability of the state to pursue certain broad objectives or to facilitate the control of the labor movement in a way that reduces its ability to oppose the state as the state pursues objectives that may conflict with the interests of an important portion of organized labor.

A striking variety of policy orientations—in terms of a right-to-left spectrum—has been associated with corporatism.[28] A convenient means of summarizing this spectrum is in terms of the overall development strategy pursued by the state. Drawing on the classification proposed by Charles W. Anderson, three types of development strategies may be identified: conventional, based on the elaboration and subsidy of the established modern sector; populist, based on the subsidy of the established modern sector and the active attempt to extend benefits to less privileged groups within society; and revolutionary, which views the established modern sector as an obstacle to development.[29] The relationship among these three categories may be conceptualized in terms of the degree to which they are oriented around the redistribution of wealth to the lower classes.

In terms of these categories, there is great diversity among the regimes under which corporative structures of state-labor relations have played an important role in Latin America. The post-1964 regime in Brazil and the Juan Carlos Onganía period in Argentina clearly fall at the conventional end of the spectrum. In the populist category at the middle of the spectrum, Juan Perón's first government in Argentina, Getúlio Vargas's first government in Brazil, and the Cárdenas period in Mexico are obvious examples. Other regimes that fall in the populist category include Venezuela from 1945 to 1948, Cuba in 1933, and the experiment in "military socialism" in Bolivia in 1936.[30]

Finally, one case in which a number of new corporative structures of state-labor relations were introduced fits in the revolutionary category— contemporary Cuba. Because of the degree to which the content of public policy in Cuba diverges from that which is traditionally associated with corporatism, this case underlines the importance of analyzing the *functions* performed by particular corporative *structures*.

The labor movement in pre-Castro Cuba had to a substantial degree been dominated by relatively conservative, and often corrupt, leaders who did not play a significant role in the overthrow of Batista. Important sectors of organized labor did not initially support the revolution, even though the overall thrust of the revolution involved a major redistribution of resources to the lower classes. In the context of massive foreign opposition to the revolution, the Cuban government was inevitably concerned about ensuring the loyalty of domestic groups

and introduced a series of new corporative provisions in labor legislation as a means of building a labor movement that would support the
revolution. This sharp increase in corporative provisions produced some
of the highest scores on the aggregate "corporatism" variable that have
appeared among the countries considered in our analysis of labor
law.[31]

Corporative structures of state-labor relations have thus played an
important role under regimes that span the full spectrum from right to
left. The introduction or consolidation of corporative structures has
made it easier for these regimes to promote very different patterns of
distribution of resources in society. The answer to the question "to
whom" has thus varied greatly, since these policies have benefited, and
have been directed against, very different combinations of groups within society.

The contexts in which corporative structures emerge may be analyzed in terms of more immediate political goals, as well as in terms of
broad development strategies. Specifically, political elites have used the
introduction of corporative structures as a means of winning and
consolidating political power. In Bolivia in 1936 and in Argentina after
1943, corporative structures were used to win labor support for political leaders who rose to power from the military.[32] Corporative structures have also played an important role in the winning and consolidation of power by political parties. In some cases parties have sought to
expand their electoral base by encouraging the formation of a new
labor movement; in some cases a new party and a new labor movement
have emerged together; and in still others, a new party has been built
onto a labor movement that already had substantial power.[33] Finally,
corporative structures may be used to facilitate the consolidation of
power by political coalitions that wish to pursue policies opposed by
organized labor. In these cases, corporative mechanisms are used to
reduce the political power of organized labor.

How?

The final step in addressing the question, "Who does what, to whom,
and how?" involves an analysis of the ways in which the corporative
ordering of state-labor relations is achieved. This brings the discussion
back to the issues of structure considered in an earlier section of this
chapter. However, structure is now treated as only one of several
dimensions in terms of which specific cases of corporatism can be
compared.

In addressing the question of "how," one must consider the different
patterns of corporative provisions present in each country.[34] In what
combinations and variations do they occur? Do different combinations

of provisions for structuring, subsidy, and control appear in different settings?

Important variations *within* each of these broad categories of structuring, subsidy, and control are also present. Some of the most striking differences are found in the approaches to structuring labor representation. These include variations in terms of the presence or absence of particular provisions. In addition, highly varied partial approximations of certain important corporative "traits" have appeared. Conceptual discussions of corporatism emphasize such features as the replacement of "horizontal" class organizations with "vertical" organizations that correspond to functional sectors of the economy; the granting of monopoly of representation; and compulsory membership. Yet these features of corporatism rarely appear in their most elaborated form. Instead, they are often achieved indirectly through various combinations of legal provisions and informal practices.

With regard to the vertical organization of representation along functional lines—as opposed to horizontal organization along class lines—perhaps the closest approximation in contemporary Latin America is the attempt to supersede horizontal organization by establishing self-managing enterprises such as those which have appeared in Peru. In general, however, the fundamental basis for organizing interest representation in Latin America remains horizontal, along class lines. Within this framework, many attempts have been made to achieve some degree of vertical integration among different class groups through the formation of public or semipublic representative bodies that bring together representatives of business and labor. These include various kinds of social and economic councils and a variety of agencies concerned with specific policy areas such as social security.

Another, very different, approach to fragmenting worker representation and substituting vertical for horizontal integration has appeared in several countries. Laws have emerged that appear to do this by orienting worker representation around local "enterprise" unions (also referred to as "plant" unions, "works" unions, and "industrial" unions).[35] Particularly in countries at lower levels of industrialization, where factories are small, such a unit of organization appears to lend itself readily to the formation of labor organizations which resemble "company unions" and which help perpetuate a paternalistic relationship between workers and managers. In one case, the requirement that a portion of the profits of the enterprise go directly to the union appeared to strengthen this relationship.[36]

In some cases, an exclusive monopoly of representation has been granted outright to particular unions, but with this feature of corporatism as well, perhaps the most striking thing is the variety of partial approximations that have appeared. These may be ordered in terms of a broad spectrum of degrees of monopoly, including the extension of certain privileges associated with monopoly of representation to more than one union, but not to all unions, in particular occupational groupings; granting of monopoly of representation to an interassociational committee that represents all unions in the particular occupational grouping; granting many privileges associated with monopoly of representation to one union, but permitting other unions to exist; and granting a monopoly of representation to one union and completely prohibiting competing unions.

Provisions for compulsory membership are in fact relatively rare. Once again, what one finds is a variety of provisions that indirectly perform the same functions as compulsory membership. These include laws that give unions the right to represent nonmembers (such as provisions that make collective bargaining agreements entered into by the union applicable to nonmembers); provisions concerning open, closed, and union shops; and syndical taxes that apply to nonmembers as well as members.

The state may subsidize organized labor in many different ways as well. Along with the great variety of funds available through ministries of labor and public welfare programs that directly or indirectly subsidize union leaders or union activities, the most crucial form of subsidy involves state assistance in the collection of union dues. The most comprehensive means of doing this is the syndical tax, which is paid by all workers under the union's jurisdiction—whether or not they are union members—and is distributed among the various levels of union hierarchy. Such taxes have rarely appeared, however, and provisions that facilitate the collection of union dues generally involve such things as dues checkoffs, requirements regarding open, closed, and union shops, and laws concerning compulsory membership.

One also finds a variety of mechanisms of direct control of labor representation. A number of different provisions limit the right to strike and specify when strikes may occur in relation to conciliation and arbitration procedures. Many different requirements have appeared concerning who may be a union leader. Finally, a variety of provisions give legal sanction to direct state involvement in the internal governance of unions, including provisions that allow a state official to attend a union meeting; permit a state official to preside over a union meeting; authorize the state to assume direct control of unions; and give formal legal sanction for the state to disband unions. The various forms that these and other mechanisms of control have taken merit central attention in any attempt to answer the question of "how?"

Varieties of Corporatism

In considering the various answers to the question " Who does what, to whom, and how?" it is evident that different answers cluster to some degree in recurring patterns. Two of the most widely discussed patterns are associated with regimes based on the "populist coalitions" that have emerged in the phase of import-substituting industrialization in some Latin American countries and with the "bureaucratic-authoritarian" regimes that have emerged in some countries in the context of economic crises associated with the apparent "exhaustion" of the initial "easy" phases of import substitution. The most conspicuous examples of these populist regimes are the first Vargas government in Brazil and the first Perón government in Argentina, with the Cárdenas period in Mexico exhibiting many similar features. The "bureaucratic-authoritarian" pattern is best exemplified by the post-1964 regime in Brazil and the Onganía period in Argentina. It has also been followed to some degree by the post-1973 regimes in Chile and Uruguay.[37] Though much remains to be done in terms of elaborating and systematically testing arguments about the emergence and characteristics of these regimes, a brief summary of available arguments provides a useful illustration of what two important varieties of corporatism may look like.

In the case of regimes based on populist coalitions, the answer to the question "who" is often intermediate with regard to the distinction between state and societal corporatism. Organized labor, or a sector of it, is in alliance with the government, which derives its legitimacy in part from the support of labor. Other actors in the dominant political coalition include a newly emerging class of national industrialists, important sectors of the newly emerging labor movement, and the political elites that lead these coalitions. These may involve leaders who have risen from the military, as in the case of Perón; the elite of a political party, as in the Cárdenas era in Mexico; or other civilian political leaders, as in the case of Vargas in Brazil.

These regimes tend to strengthen the bargaining position of organized labor. Their emergence frequently either coincides with or shortly follows the first major elaboration of corporative provisions in labor law.[38] These provisions often mark the end of long periods in which governments attempted to deny or at least limit the right of unions to exist and a shift to active government protection of unions, generally focused on one sector or confederation with which the government seeks to form an alliance. This protection is accompanied by active support for the formation of new unions and for broadening worker benefits through expanded social security programs and wage increases. The immediate answer to "what," in terms of the working class, is the protection, and sometimes the creation, of an organized labor movement and an extension of benefits to the working class.

In terms of broader economic policy, these regimes pursue the "populist" development strategies that are intended to promote import-substituting industrialization: the termination of free-trade policies, the development of domestic industry, and the expansion of the domestic market for consumer goods. The protection of organized labor and the extension of benefits to the working class appear to complement the goal of promoting industrialization in two ways. First, they win the allegiance of organized labor to the political coalition which supports the public policies that directly encourage industrialization. In addition, they increase labor income and thereby expand the domestic market for nationally produced consumer goods.

Politically, a common feature of the way in which corporative structures are employed under these regimes is in building a strong political party. The "incorporating," "inclusionary" thrust of the use of corporatism under these regimes serves to win the support of labor and often gives these parties a powerful base in the labor movement.[39]

In the case of bureaucratic-authoritarian regimes, the answer to the question "who" emphatically involves state corporatism rather than an intermediate case between state and societal corporatism. In these regimes the state does not depend on labor for legitimacy and support. The ruling coalition includes technocratic elites within—as well as outside—the state bureaucracy; the military, often acting to a substantial degree as an institution; and, directly or indirectly, foreign capital.

These regimes tend to weaken the bargaining position, as well as the overall political power, of organized labor. They exclude the labor movement from political power and adopt a policy of holding down wages or at least producing a shift in labor income unfavorable to large sectors of the working class.[40] Corporative structures play a central role in implementing these policies. This control of organized labor and labor income—as well as the broader "conventional" development strategies of these regimes—is part of the effort to overcome the crises of inflation and balance-of-payments deficits associated with the apparent "exhaustion" of import substitution, to facilitate capital accumulation, and to attract new foreign investment.

Politically, corporative structures are employed to protect the position of the military as it tries to rule as an institution. In contrast to the earlier period, the primary thrust of corporatism is "exclusionary," and the purpose is to control the political demands of organized labor.[41]

This schematic summary of these two patterns shows how particular combinations of answers regarding "what and to whom" as well as "who" have been grouped together in the context of two phases of industrial growth in certain countries in Latin America. In each phase, a certain economic and political "logic" appears to have produced these particular recurring patterns. Much remains to be done in terms of exploring the way these different features are linked even in the most often discussed examples of these regimes, and assessing the way they appear in modified form in other countries during different phases of economic growth.[42]   Nonetheless, these do appear to be two of the most important patterns that have emerged in Latin America.

These two phases of industrial growth are by no means the only contexts in which it is relevant to look for patterns. An important direction that studies of corporatism must take involves the analysis of other modal, as well as deviant, patterns. For instance, attention needs to be given to cases in which a substantial elaboration of corporative structures of state-labor relations has occurred in preindustrial settings. In these contexts, rather different combinations of interests of other urban middle-class and rural elite groups appear to come into play, along with a variety of military, party, and other political interests.[43]

Conclusion

A remarkable variety of answers to the question, " Who does what, to whom, and how?" thus emerges, even when one considers only one aspect of the system of interest representation—state-labor relations. This finding may suggest that the concept of corporatism casts too broad a net and perhaps obscures a variety of interesting distinctions that ought to be made within the Latin American context. In a period in which the study of corporatism is increasingly popular in research on Latin America, it may be too easy to achieve a sense of intellectual closure by simply applying the label "corporative" to a given political situation. Because corporative structures appear in such a wide variety of contexts, this sense of closure may be illusory.

The concept of corporatism does usefully highlight certain features of systems of interest representation that distinguish them both from pluralism and from situations in which there is a denial of the right of groups—most commonly labor unions—to exist.[44]   Corporatism is a system of nonpluralist group representation both because it is nonpluralist and because it *is* a system of group representation. The approach to the comparative analysis of corporative structures proposed earlier provides a basis for determining the degree to which corporatism, in this sense, is present in any particular case.

Once one has considered these important issues of corporative structure, however, it is essential to analyze the relationships of economic and political power that are ratified or consolidated through these structures and to use differences in these relationships as a basis for identifying different varieties of corporatism. In this chapter, we have tried to take a first step in this direction by identifying dimensions in terms of which one might distinguish different varieties of corporatism. We then presented a preliminary discussion of the combinations of answers that go together in recurring patterns.

If the next task for comparative analysts is the further exploration of different varieties of corporatism, what implications does this have for the types of cross-national comparisons that are most appropriate? It was suggested that certain aspects of the legal structure of corporatism—and hence an important part of the answer to the question "how?"—lend themselves to fairly elaborate measurement and scaling across large numbers of cases and over long periods of time. On the other hand, the informal aspects of structure and the answers to the questions "who, what, and to whom" require a very different kind of analysis.

What is called for is a type of "event scoring" of historical data that involves the classification of cases in terms of nominal or ordinal scales on the basis of available historical evidence. Because of the difficulty of collecting this type of data, it may not be possible to analyze large numbers of cases. The kinds of comparison that can be made on the basis of these data will often not involve elaborate, multivariate tests of hypotheses, but rather a type of "small-N" analysis based on selected cross-tabulations of categorical variables.[45] This may not allow for sophisticated statistical analysis, but it will permit *systematic* cross-national comparison. This approach obviously loses a great deal in terms of the number of cases that can be considered and the kinds of data manipulation that can be performed, but these losses appear to be a small price to pay for greater substantive relevance.

NOTES

We would like to acknowledge helpful suggestions made by Guillermo A. O'Donnell, Kenneth Mericle, Juan Carlos Torre, Robert R. Kaufman, Abraham F. Lowenthal, Louis Wolf Goodman, and Benjamin A. Most, as well as the hospitality of the Center of International Studies at Princeton University, where much of the research reported in this chapter was carried out. This chapter is part of a larger project on state-labor relations in Latin America, portions of which have been supported by National Science Foundation Grant no. SOC75-19990, the Social Science Research Council, and Indiana University. Leslie Spencer, Cherri Waters, and Lila Milutin have provided energetic research assistance in several phases of the project.

1. Following Linz, we are using the expression "regime" broadly to refer not only to the state itself, but also to the patterns of interaction between the state and

society. See Juan J. Linz, "Totalitarian and Authoritarian Regimes," in *Handbook of Political Science*, ed. Fred I. Greenstein and Nelson W. Polsby (Reading, Mass.: Addison-Wesley Publishing Company, 1975), vol. 3, p. 265.

2. See, for instance, Phillips Cutright, "National Political Development: Measurement and Analysis," *American Sociological Review*, 88 (April 1963):253–64; Fred R. Von der Mehden, *Politics of the Developing Nations* (Englewood Cliffs, N.J.: Prentice-Hall, 1964); Dick Simpson, "The Congruence of Political, Social and Economic Aspects of Development," *International Development Review* (June 1964):21–25; Ted Robert Gurr, "A Causal Model of Civil Strife: A Comparative Analysis Using New Indices," *American Political Science Review*, 62 (1966):1104–24; Deane E. Neubauer, "On the Theory of Polyarchy: An Empirical Study of Democracy in Ten Countries" (doctoral dissertation, Yale University, 1966); Irma Adelman and Cynthia Taft Morris, *Society, Politics, and Economic Development: A Quantitative Approach* (Baltimore: Johns Hopkins Press, 1967); Phillips Cutright, "Political Structure, Economic Development, and National Social Security Programs," *American Journal of Sociology*, 70 (1967):537–48; Russell Fitzgibbon, "Measuring Democratic Change in Latin America," *Journal of Politics*, 29 (February 1967):129–66; Donald J. McCrone and Charles F. Cnudde, "Toward a Communications Theory of Democratic Political Development: A Causal Model," *American Political Science Review*, 41 (1967):72–80; Deane E. Neubauer, "Some Conditions of Democracy," *American Political Science Review*, 61, no. 4 (December 1967):1002–09; Douglas P. Bwy, "Political Instability in Latin America: The Cross-Cultural Test of a Causal Model," *Latin American Research Review*, 3, no. 2 (Spring 1968):17–66; Martin C. Needler, "Political Development and Socioeconomic Development: The Case of Latin America," *American Political Science Review*, 62, no. 3 (September 1968):889–97; Marvin E. Olsen, "Multivariate Analysis of National Political Development," *American Sociological Review*, 33 (1968):699–712; Phillips Cutright and James A. Wiley, "Modernization and Political Representation: 1927–1966," *Studies in Comparative International Development*, 5, no. 2 (1969):23–44; Betty A. Nesvold, "Scalogram Analysis of Political Violence," *Comparative Political Studies*, 2, no. 2 (July 1969):172–94; Arthur S. Banks, "Modernization and Political Change: The Latin American and Amer-European Nations," *Comparative Political Studies*, 2, no. 4 (January 1970):405–18; Richard A. Pride, *Origins of Democracy: A Cross-National Study of Mobilization, Party Systems, and Democratic Stability*, Sage Professional Papers in Comparative Politics (Beverly Hills: Sage Publications, 1970); Harold D. Clarke and Allan Kornberg, "A Note on Social Cleavages and Democratic Performance," *Comparative Political Studies*, 4, no. 3 (October 1971):349–60; Robert A Dahl, *Polyarchy: Participation and Opposition* (New Haven: Yale University Press, 1971); William Flanigan and Edwin Fogelman, "Patterns of Democratic Development: An Historical Comparative Analysis," in *Macro-Quantitative Analysis*, ed. John V. Gillespie and Betty A. Nesvold (Beverly Hills: Sage Publications, 1971), pp. 475–98, and "Patterns of Political Development and Democratization: A Quantitative Analysis," ibid., pp. 441–74; Ronald H. McDonald, *Party Systems and Elections in Latin America* (Chicago: Markham Publishing Company, 1971); Philippe C. Schmitter, "Desarrollo retrasado, dependencia externa y cambio político en América Latina," *Foro Internacional*, 12 (October–December 1971):135–74, and "Military Intervention, Political Competitiveness and Public Policy in Latin America: 1950–1967," in *On Military Intervention*, ed. Morris Janowitz and Jacques van Doorn (Rotterdam: Rotterdam University Press, 1971), pp. 426–506; Robert W. Jackman, "Political Democracy and Social Equality: A Comparative Analysis"

(paper presented at the annual meeting of the Midwest Political Science Association, Chicago, 1973); and David Collier, "Timing of Economic Growth and Regime Characteristics in Latin America," *Comparative Politics*, 7, no. 3 (April 1975):331–59.

3. Bruce Russett et al., *World Handbook of Political and Social Indicators* (New Haven: Yale University Press, 1964); Charles L. Taylor and Michael C. Hudson, *World Handbook of Political and Social Indicators*, 2d ed. (New Haven: Yale University Press, 1972); Arthur S. Banks, *Cross-Polity Time-Series Data* (Cambridge: MIT Press, 1971); R. J. Rummel, "The Dimensions of Nations Project Data Bank" (unpublished); Kenneth Ruddle and Philip Gillette, eds., *Latin American Political Statistics* (Los Angeles: Latin American Center, University of California, 1972); and Kenneth Ruddle and Donald Odermann, *Statistical Abstract of Latin America 1971* (Los Angeles: Latin America Center, University of California, 1972). Arthur S. Banks and Robert B. Textor, *A Cross-Polity Survey* (Cambridge: MIT Press, 1963), is unique in terms of the wide variety of political variables it contains.

4. Banks and Textor, *Cross-Polity Survey*. Studies using the Banks and Textor indices are Simpson, "Congruence of Political, Social and Economic Aspects"; Olsen, "Multivariate Analysis"; Dahl, *Polyarchy*; and John M. Orbell and Brent M. Rutherford, "Can Leviathan Make the Life of Man Less Solitary, Poore, Nasty, Brutish and Short?" (paper presented at the annual meeting of the Midwest Political Science Association, Chicago, 1973).

5. Philippe C. Schmitter, "New Approaches to the Comparative Study of Latin America," *Latin American Research Review*, 4, no. 2 (Summer 1969):83–110.

6. See O'Donnell's analysis of these variations in chapter 3 of this volume.

7. Neubauer, "On the Theory of Polyarchy."

8. Adelman and Morris, *Society, Politics, and Economic Development*.

9. Ted Robert Gurr, *New Error-Compensated Measures for Comparing Nations: Some Correlates of Civil Violence* (Princeton: Center of International Studies, Princeton University, Research Monograph no. 25, 1966), and idem, "Causal Model of Civil Strife"; Nilda Sito, "Estructura ocupacional, desarrollo y sindicalismo en los paises latinoamericanos," *Revista Latinoamericana de Sociología*, 7, no. 1 (1971):6–36; Schmitter, "Desarrollo retrasado"; and Kenneth Erickson and Bernard Grofman, "A Comparative Longitudinal Analysis of Strike Activity: Applications to Industrialized and Industrializing Economies" (paper presented at the meeting of the International Political Science Association, Montreal, August 1973).

10. This has been the orientation of a substantial body of research on interest politics that grew out of the work of Arthur Bentley and David Truman.

11. See, for instance, Grant McConnell, *Private Power and American Democracy* (New York: Alfred A. Knopf, 1966); and Theodore J. Lowi, *The End of Liberalism* (New York: W. W. Norton and Co., 1969).

12. Howard J. Wiarda, "Corporatism and Development in the Iberic-Latin World: Persistent Strains and New Variations," *Review of Politics*, 36, no. 1 (January 1974):3–33; Ronald Rogowski and Lois Wasserspring, *Does Political Development Exist? Corporatism in Old and New Societies*, Sage Professional Papers in Comparative Politics, no. 24 (Beverly Hills: Sage Publications, 1971); and David Scott Palmer and Kevin Jay Middlebrook, "Corporativist Participation Under Military Rule in Peru" (manuscript, 1974).

13. Philippe C. Schmitter, "Still the Century of Corporatism?", *Review of Politics*, 36, no. 1 (January 1974):93–94; Wiarda, "Corporatism and Development," p. 6; Kenneth Mericle, chap. 10 in this volume; Guillermo O'Donnell, chap.

3 in this volume; Robert R. Kaufman, chap. 5 in this volume; James J. Malloy, chap. 1 in this volume; and Alfred Stepan, *State and Society: Peru in Comparative Perspective* (Princeton: Princeton University Press, forthcoming), chap. 2. The structural emphasis in available analyses of corporatism is also discussed in Stepan, *State and Society*, chap. 2.

14. James A. Gregor, *An Introduction to Metapolitics* (New York: The Free Press, 1971), p. 131.

15. See Ronald C. Newton, "On 'Functional Groups,' 'Fragmentation,' and 'Pluralism' in Spanish American Political Society," *Hispanic American Historical Review*, 50 (February 1970):1–29; Philippe C. Schmitter, "Paths to Political Development in Latin America," in *Changing Latin America: New Interpretations of Its Politics and Society*, ed. Douglas A. Chalmers (New York: The Academy of Political Science, Columbia University, 1972), p. 96; Alfred Stepan, *State and Society*, chap. 1; and Robert R. Kaufman, chap. 5 in this volume.

16. The principal source of data on labor legislation was the annual *Legislative Series* published by the International Labor Office. In addition, the standard editions of labor laws published in each country were used both to examine the laws in the original language and to fill in gaps in the *Legislative Series*. For a preliminary presentation of the data derived from this code, see David Collier, Leslie Spencer, and Cherri Waters, "Varieties of Latin American Corporatism" (paper presented at the 1975 annual meeting of the American Political Science Association).

17. In his *State and Society*, chap. 2, Stepan has likewise emphasized the limitation of structural definitions. Rather than focusing primarily on the functions performed by corporative structures, however, his concern leads to a different, but very important, question: What conditions affect the success of the installation of these structures and their legitimacy?

18. See chap. 3 of this volume.

19. These alternative functions of the structures linking the state with labor have been analyzed by Erickson in terms of the idea that skillful labor leaders may turn "sources of uncertainty" in labor regulations into sources of political power. See Kenneth Paul Erickson, "Corporatism and Labor in Development," in *Contemporary Brazil: Issues in Economic and Political Development*, ed. H. Jon Rosenbaum and William G. Tyler (New York: Praeger, 1972), p. 146.

20. Schmitter, "Still the Century of Corporatism?", pp. 102–03.

21. Ibid., p. 105.

22. See Favio Grobart, "The Cuban Working Class Movement from 1925 to 1933," *Science and Society*, 39, no. 1 (Spring 1975):73–103; and Cherri Waters, "State-Labor Relations in Pre-Castro and Castro Cuba" (honors essay, Department of Political Science, Indiana University, 1975).

23. These cases are discussed in a number of standard labor histories. See note 30.

24. Examples of the specific combinations of groups involved in particular historical periods will be presented shortly. For an important statement regarding the role of political parties as an intervening actor in state-labor relations, see Kaufman's analysis in chapter 5 of this volume.

25. With reference to Colombia and Argentina, see Miguel Urrutia, *The Development of the Colombian Labor Movement* (New Haven: Yale University Press, 1969), chap. 8; and Robert J. Alexander, *Labor Relations in Argentina, Brazil, and Chile* (New York: McGraw-Hill, Inc., 1962), pp. 167 ff.

26. See, for instance, Mericle, chap. 10 in this volume.

27. For a discussion of the way this was done in Brazil in the 1930s, see Howard J. Wiarda, *The Brazilian Catholic Labor Movement: The Dilemmas of National Development* (University of Massachusetts, Labor Relations and Research Center, 1969), pp. 15–16.

28. Schmitter, "Still the Century of Corporatism?", p. 87; and Wiarda, "Corporatism and Development," p. 4.

29. Charles Anderson, *Politics and Economic Change in Latin America* (Princeton: D. Van Nostrand Company, Inc., 1967), chap. 7. The first and third categories employed here involve the same labels and roughly the same content. The middle category differs both in its label and to some degree in its content. It is referred to here as "populist" rather than "democratic reform" since this approach is frequently adopted by regimes that are clearly nondemocratic. The middle category in the present analysis, like that in Anderson's analysis, includes development strategies based on "a belief in the centrality of the public role in the developmental effort" (p. 176) and on the conviction that public policy should "incorporate" social groups that had previously been marginal to the national society (p. 175). However, given the focus of the present analysis on organized labor in the modern sector, the concern here is particularly with populist policies toward groups in the modern sector, and not with the incorporation of the traditional sector, as in Anderson's analysis (see p. 174). I would like to thank Elizabeth Jelin and Oscar Oszlak for helpful comments regarding the issues involved in classifying development strategies.

30. Guillermo A. O'Donnell, *Modernization and Bureaucratic-Authoritarianism* (Berkeley: Institute of International Studies, University of California, 1973); Alexander, *Labor Relations;* Joe C. Ashby, *Organized Labor and the Mexican Revolution under Lázaro Cárdenas* (Chapel Hill: University of North Carolina Press, 1967); Anderson, *Politics and Economic Change*, pp. 284–86; Luis E. Aguilar, *Cuba 1933: Prologue to Revolution* (Ithaca: Cornell University Press, 1972); R. L. Woodward, "Urban Labor and Communism," *Caribbean Studies*, 3, no. 3 (October 1963): 17–50; and Herbert S. Klein, *Parties and Political Change in Bolivia 1880–1952* (Cambridge: Cambridge University Press, 1969).

31. For a discussion of this period, see Roberto E. Hernández and Carmelo Mesa-Lago, "Labor Organization and Wages," in *Revolutionary Change in Cuba*, ed. Carmelo Mesa-Lago (Pittsburgh: University of Pittsburgh Press, 1971), pp. 209–49. The relevant labor legislation is reported in the International Labor Office *Legislative Series* and in Grupo Cubano de Investigaciones Economicas, *Un estudio sobre Cuba* (Miami: University of Miami Press, 1963). Since complaints about the "authoritarian" control of the Cuban working class under Castro have been used as the basis for counterrevolutionary attacks on the Castro regime, it is noteworthy that writers sympathetic to the Cuban Revolution, such as Maurice Zeitlin, have reported the total replacement of the traditional, often corrupt, labor leadership and a "withering away" of the labor movement during the revolutionary period (Maurice Zeitlin, *Revolutionary Politics and the Cuban Working Class* [New York: Harper Torchbooks, 1970], pp. xxv–xxvii). For an interesting discussion of the emergence of conservative "labor bureaucrats" as an obstacle to revolutionary change, see Leon Trotsky, *Marxism and the Trade Unions* (London: Plough Press, 1968), pp. 5 ff.

32. See James M. Malloy, *Bolivia: The Uncompleted Revolution* (Pittsburgh: University of Pittsburgh Press, 1970), chap. 5; Klein, *Parties and Political Change*, chap. 8; and Samuel L. Baily, *Labor, Nationalism, and Politics in Argentina* (New Brunswick, N. J.: Rutgers University Press, 1967), chap. 4.

33. Colombia is an example of this first pattern (see Urrutia, *Development of the Colombian Labor Movement*, chap. 8); Venezuela is an example of the second (see John D. Martz, *Acción Democrática* (Princeton: Princeton University Press, 1966):256–73; and Robert Alexander, *The Venezuelan Democratic Revolution* (New Brunswick, N.J.: Rutgers University Press, 1964), chap. 18; and Argentina is an example of the third (see Alexander, *Labor Relations*). The first pattern corresponds to Kaufman's machine systems, and the second and third to his group-based systems (see Kaufman, chap. 5 in this volume).

34. The following discussion is drawn primarily from the preliminary analysis carried out in connection with the scoring of labor law discussed earlier.

35. Examples include the 1907 law in Brazil, the 1924 law in Chile, and the 1944 law in Colombia. See Arnaldo Susskind, *Direito brasileiro do trabalho*, vol. 1 (Rio de Janeiro: Empresa "A Noite," 1943), p. 100; Philippe C. Schmitter, *Interest Conflict and Political Change in Brazil* (Stanford: Stanford University Press, 1971), p. 111; Moises Poblete Troncoso, *Labor Organizations in Chile* (Washington, D.C.: United States Government Printing Office, 1928), p. 3; James O. Morris, *Elites, Intellectuals, and Consensus* (Ithaca: New York State School of Industrial and Labor Relations, Cornell University, 1966), p. 130; and Urrutia, *Development of the Colombian Labor Movement*, p. 155.

36. See Alan Angell, *Politics and the Labour Movement in Chile* (London: Oxford University Press, 1972), p. 63.

37. For an interesting early statement regarding the basic coalitional alternatives involved in these two patterns, see Trotsky, *Marxism and the Trade Unions*, pp. 10–11. James Malloy provides a valuable introduction to these patterns in chap. 1 of this volume. Standard general works on these patterns include Fernando Henrique Cardoso and Enzo Faletto, *Dependencia y desarrollo en América Latina* (Mexico: Siglo Veintiuno, Editores, 1969); Fernando Henrique Cardoso, "Associated Dependent Development: Theoretical and Practical Implications," in *Authoritarian Brazil: Origins, Policies, and Future*, ed. Alfred Stepan (New Haven: Yale University Press, 1973), pp. 142–76; and O'Donnell, *Modernization and Bureaucratic-Authoritarianism*.

38. These shifts emerge clearly in the preliminary analysis of labor law that we have carried out.

39. For a discussion of the concepts of incorporation and inclusion, see O'Donnell, *Modernization and Bureaucratic-Authoritarianism*, pp. 53 ff.; and Stepan, *State and Society*, chap. 3.

40. For a discussion of issues of income distribution under one of these regimes, see Kenneth S. Mericle, "Conflict Regulation in the Brazilian Industrial Relations System" (doctoral dissertation, University of Wisconsin, 1974).

41. For discussions of the concept of exclusion, see O'Donnell, *Modernization and Bureaucratic-Authoritarianism*, pp. 53 ff.; and Stepan, *State and Society*, chap. 3.

42. For a discussion of the differing patterns of development followed by bureaucratic-authoritarian regimes—and of the differing patterns of economic and political "logic" through which these regimes select policies—see Guillermo A. O'Donnell, "Reflexiones sobre las tendencias generales de cambio en el Estado burocrático-autoritario" (Buenos Aires: Centro de Estudios de Estado y Sociedad, 1975).

43. For an extended discussion of the configuration of interests that surrounded an important, early law in Chile, see Morris, *Elites, Intellectuals, and Consensus*.

44. For a general discussion of these issues involving the denial of the right of

association and the right of combination, see Reinhard Bendix, *Nation-Building and Citizenship* (New York: John Wiley and Sons, Inc., 1964), pp. 80–87.

45. Two recent studies of Latin America which make interesting causal inferences on the basis of relatively small case bases and the careful use of cross-tabulation of categorical variables are Kaufman, chap. 5 in this volume, and Stepan, *State and Society*, chap. 3. Other examples of this approach include Ted Robert Gurr and Muriel McClelland, *Political Performance: A Twelve-Nation Study*, Sage Professional Papers in Comparative Politics (Beverly Hills: Sage Publications, 1971); Pride, *Origins of Democracy*; Clarke and Kornberg, "A Note on Social Cleavages;" and Ruth Berins Collier, "Electoral Politics and Authoritarian Rule: Institutional Transfer and Political Change in Tropical Africa (doctoral dissertation, University of Chicago, 1974), chap. 6.

SILVIO DUNCAN BARETTA and HELEN E. DOUGLASS

16

Authoritarianism and Corporatism in Latin America: A Review Essay

In general, the authors in this volume treat corporatism and authoritarianism in terms of their implications for the study of political change. At the onset of any discussion on political change, a preliminary word seems imperative. As Simon Schwartzman points out in his chapter, such discussions are very easily influenced by the climate prevalent in any given epoch. In the fifties and sixties, representative democracy was assumed to be the most desirable end state of any developing nation. Analyses of political change were, therefore, organized around the factors facilitating or impeding the attainment of such an end state. In the seventies, following the dismissal of most civilian regimes in Latin America, a new mood seems to pervade the works of social scientists. We now talk about corporatism or corporate authoritarianism and treat liberal democratic institutions as a façade; the "true" Latin America, we say, has finally surfaced in the seventies.

If nothing else, the destiny of our early theories should warn us against repetition of the same errors. In our view, three related fallacies endanger the emerging literature on corporatism. First, we have the tendency—just mentioned—to counterpose corporatism, as the "true," "deep" normative pattern which organizes the relationship between state and society in Latin America, to democratic pluralism, as a "grafted," superficial pattern of organizing these relationships. Such a way of thinking is not necessarily warranted: There is no reason to assume that the seventies are a better expression of Latin American reality than the fifties or sixties, or vice versa. The oscillation between times of greater and lesser control of the state over society has characterized politics in the region since the nineteenth century. If there is a fundamental normative pattern, and if it is really continuous throughout Latin American political history, it must be general enough to encompass these historical variations or, minimally, to render them understandable contradictions. That is, it must be compatible with both democratic and authoritarian moments of the history of political institutions. This is a minimum requisite which the concept of corporatism has to fulfill, whatever its content. It is important to note that corporatism, treated as a constant normative pattern, cannot account for regime changes. As James Malloy points out, the emergence of overt authoritarianism has to be explained through the use of a "developmental focus" (that is, by tracing the evolution of dependence of the region relative to the developed capitalist world). In this case, the stabilization of one normative pattern in the form of an institutionalized system of political authority can only be understood and evaluated in conjunction with changes in the economy and the system of stratification.

Second, we have what might be called the "fallacy of uniqueness." Schwartzman observes that the use of the concept of corporatism is an attempt to answer the old questions of how and in what sense Latin America may be different from Europe and the United States. This is certainly a correct assessment of the use of corporatism; but, as he points out, it might too easily lead us to the extreme of assuming that there is something absolutely singular in the political development of Latin America. However, if we take as our characterization of corporatism the presence of a strong governmental structure which imposes upon society an enforced, limited pluralism, as more than one author proposes, such uniqueness is far from evident. A clear way to make this difficulty manifest is to quote from the work of an expert on Africa :

> If manipulation of the electoral laws is insufficient to assure the one-party state, other mechanisms are available. African governments have outlawed parties, or refused recognition to parties newly created, for example in Morocco, Sudan, the UAR, Senegal, Mauritania, Upper Volta, Niger, Mali, Cameroon, the Central African Republic. . . .
>
> Another form of restriction in the one-party state is that related to voluntary associations. There has been considerable pressure to keep them in line with the position of the party. When these groups have deviated sharply, they have been pressured, either by purges inspired by the party, or by withdrawal of financial and other aid by the government. Instances include the trade unions in Tunisia and Senegal, the women's organization in Ghana.[1]

Allowing for differences in language, Immanuel Wallerstein is pointing out that African governments are strong and impose upon society an "enforced limited pluralism." Since any fundamental cultural identity between Africa and Latin America is out of the question, two observations seem in order. First, corporatism, as characterized above, might be less a unique way of organizing the relationship between state and society than a consequence of the similar positions of dependence of Africa and Latin America in relation to the developed world. A serious confrontation with this alternative hypothesis is necessary if this version of the corporatist thesis is to be maintained.

Second, the possibility exists that thus far the "uniqueness" of corporatism (as a normative system regulating the relations of state and society) has not been clearly specified. There is a whole body of literature which shows (or tries to show) how cultural elements (specifically the world-oriented asceticism associated with the Protestant Reformation) facilitated the extension of entrepreneurial capitalism in the West. In a parallel fashion it is perhaps feasible to elaborate the notion of corporatism as a culturally specific view of state-society relations, and then show its particular consequences for the constitution of nation-states in Latin America. In crude terms, this suggests one direction in which an elaboration of the concept of corporatism could be proved useful.

Third, and finally, we have the "fallacy of the immutability of cultural patterns." When corporatism is understood at this level, there is a tendency to think about it as a constant pattern, as Schwartzman remarks. Two dangers are implied in such a tendency, one theoretical, one political. Theoretically, it is easy to overlook the complexity of the issue and attribute to cultural dispositions a sort of "immunity" to change. This constancy—if indeed it exists empirically—is not of a simple nature. A theory of symbolic systems has yet to be developed which would explain how these systems successfully isolate themselves from change in the social and political spheres, and how they may accomplish successful adaptation to modified environments. In the absence of systematic knowledge of this nature, the idea of the existence of constant cultural patterns easily lends itself to political uses, especially given the fashionable claim that democratic institutions have been "grafted" onto Latin American political realities. Under these circumstances, notions of corporatism can be used to legitimate authoritarian regimes, irrespective of the intentions of authors in this volume. Awareness of these questions is important if a successful distinction is to be made between the true theoretical and ideological implications of a position, and illegitimate derivations which might serve specific interests.

The criticisms contained in each of the three "fallacies" are largely directed against the use of the term *corporatism*. Labels tend to focus attention on themselves and away from the realities for which they stand. Also, as they become independent of their referents, labels are much more easily charged with ideological connotations. For these reasons, we think it necessary to make a conscious effort to ignore temporarily the word *corporatism* and look at the substantive realities analyzed by the several chapters under review.

When this is done, it becomes evident that most authors have addressed themselves to the classical question of how political institutions adapt to the growth in numbers and types of demands which arise with modernization. This problem is especially crucial for late developers, whose states confront simultaneously requests for social justice, political participation, and maintenance of a high rate of economic growth. One important way in which states have tried to manage this multiplicity of contradictory pressures is by penetrating private organizations, imposing limits on associational activity, and thereby limiting the number and kinds of legitimate demands. The main subject of this volume can be respecified, then, in the form of three questions: First, is corporatism the most convincing way of describing the efforts of Latin American states to control mobilization in their societies? This leads immediately into the second question: What means have states used to keep their control over different social forces through time? And third, does state control over society imply the implantation of authoritarian regimes in the area? In other words, does corporatism necessarily presuppose authoritarianism? Our previous comments have already indicated some of the problems surrounding answers to these three questions. The remainder of this review will be dedicated to a more systematic exploration of these issues.

Latin American politics has been analyzed under very different perspectives. Two different approaches can be distinguished among the authors in this volume. The first, represented by Douglas Chalmers, emphasizes the fluid character of politics in the region, while the second—of which Guillermo O'Donnell is perhaps the most extreme representative—pays closer attention to the impact of structural, extra-political factors upon politics. The first approach regards corporatism as a set of formal ties between government and social groups. These ties are instruments of political struggle and consequently subject to continuous reformulation. The second, the structuralist approach, posits the emergence of corporatism as a response to—or an anticipation of—the rapid mobilization of social groups, as Latin American societies become industrialized and integrated (in a dependent fashion) into the world economic system. By concentrating on the two authors just mentioned, we can discern a fundamental difference between the two perspectives, a difference that is often obscured by unsuccessful attempts to combine them.

Central to Chalmers's view is his notion of the "politicized state."

Such a state is characterized primarily by the lack of a permanent framework of legal norms and institutions for politics. In other words, norms and institutions are viewed instrumentally, and their particular forms are the object of conflict among political actors. This applies equally well to electoral rules and constitutional and administrative procedures. The central role of the state in Latin American societies reinforces politicization. Chalmers points out that the origin of this centrality is the participation of the state in a great number of decisions concerning social and economic affairs, a feature which gives political incumbents extensive patronage powers. These can be used both to benefit supporters and to attract new ones. Because control of the state is the major prize of political struggle and institutionalized rules are nonexistent, the chief executive is under constant threat of being overthrown. To meet this threat he must permanently rebuild his political base and widen it as much as possible. Supporters, on the other hand, tend "to jump on the bandwagon of an apparently successful opponent." Support is sought indistinctly among partisan electoral and administrative entities, the church, or powerful individuals like local chiefs. Interest groups are undermined and rarely achieve political expression. The reason lies precisely in the active efforts of incumbents to extend their political bases: Factions within groups compete for the privilege of supporting the government, thereby guaranteeing its favors. In short, major divisions are not among classes and interest groups, but among supporters and opponents of a political situation.

Chalmers proceeds to observe that "establishment of controls from the top over the requisite political resources, and the anxiety from below to find a place in the complex vertical links of political power, yield a variety of structures." Clientelism, one of these structures, is "a pattern of relationships in which goods and services are exchanged between people of unequal status." Corporatism stands for the formal links between government and social groups. Government manipulates these links to ensure political support, while social groups demand (and obtain) services and privileges in exchange. Finally, Chalmers draws the implications of his approach for the analysis of Latin American politics. First, he notes, authoritarianism is as experimental as democracy in Latin America, both kinds of regime being incapable of institutionalizing themselves. Oscillation between regime types is precisely the major characteristic of the politicized state in the area. Second, on the basis of his previous analysis, he criticizes theories that postulate high correlations between kinds of regimes and modernization of state and society. Third, and most interesting, he suggests that the politicized state might be as enduring as any institutionalized regime. He adds that the "politicized state may be a realistic response to changing conditions, in which political action continually focuses on questions of the shape and consequences of basic political institutions. Every arrangement is open to question since their appropriateness for achieving political goals is constantly being reevaluated, and the goals themselves are changing as the society changes."

There are reasons for feeling discomfort about Chalmers's analysis, though it is without doubt very insightful. In the final pages of his chapter one catches glimpses of the same temptation that afflicts other theoreticians of Latin American politics: the temptation to predict the political fate of the region. The suggestion that the politicized state might endure indefinitely is challenging and deserves close attention. However, one should not overlook the fact that Chalmers offers no explanation of *why* politicization occurs, limiting himself to a description of its characteristics. The central position of the state reinforces but does not determine politicization, as totalitarian systems well demonstrate. The question to be debated is, then, What factors account for the recurrent lack of institutionalization of any regime type in Latin America? We have no general answer to this problem; as long as there is none, attempts at prediction will be futile and will simply state that the future of the area will repeat some moment of its past.

It should also be noted that a few Latin American political systems already cast doubts on the general applicability of the politicization thesis: Mexico, as interpreted by Evelyn Stevens, seems to have reached at least a degree of political institutionalization. Legitimate authority in Mexico is the product of the double nexus of revolution-party, on the one hand, and party-executive on the other. The role of the party, as the institutionalized articulation of the body politic (composed of a hierarchical ordering of included groups), mediates the relation between those who participated in the birth of independent Mexico and the state which carries on the intentions of the revolutionary leaders. This double nexus provides the state with an authority base by ensuring continuity between those who organized the revolution and those who now participate in its realization. The capacity of the Partido Revolucionario Institutional (PRI) to provide this mediation, of course, is due in large part to the manipulation of personal ties between leaders and followers of sectional groups. But the latter is of a *different dimension* than the mediating role that the PRI plays between the past and the present. It is this mediating role which is the essence of legitimate authority.

A few more comments should be added on Chalmers's thesis. A central tenet of his argument is that classes and interest groups are undermined by politicization coupled with the central role of the state in social and economic life. This is true as long as it means that classes and interest groups have no political expression as *organized* entities; it

is not true if it means that they have no impact on politics. No better
proof is required than the attention paid by all regimes, especially
authoritarian ones, to the establishment of controls over the working
class. O'Donnell makes this point explicitly, and Chalmers himself
recognizes the fact. It is paradoxical but true that class effects upon
politics are most salient precisely where classes are in greater disarray.
In these cases they can only operate through the influence of prestigious individuals, and influence is much more unevenly distributed
than capacity to organize. That is, entrepreneurs can be heard either
through their organs or through the voices of particular men; workers
or peasants are heard through their organizations or not at all. The
politicized state is then compatible not only with different kinds of
regimes, but also with particular versions of class and interest-group
politics. What these particular versions consist of remains an open field
for investigation.

It should be equally recognized that certain institutions play a
greater role in Latin American politics *as institutions* than Chalmers
apparently believes. The example of the military immediately comes to
mind. Military takeovers of the last decade have been promoted by
groups of individuals who are extremely aware of the institutional
setting to which they belong, and whose particular goals are tied to
institutional ones; this is evident in the case of Brazil as analyzed by
Alfred Stepan.[2]

In short, while concentrating on the continuity of a political pattern
in Latin American societies, Chalmers disregards extrapolitical factors
and their influence upon politics. Consequently, he is unable to account
for the reasons for such continuity, as remarked before; nor is he
capable of assessing the effect of the growing importance of institutions, classes, and interest groups on the persistence of politicization.
Finally, his assertion that power struggles in Latin America have no
defined boundaries is true only in the sense that they have no explicit
limits in commitments to procedures and institutions. Politics, however,
is also shaped by the extrapolitical constraints which he ignores, and by
their transformations. Some of these transformations have been quite
dramatic during the last fifty years: the acceleration of industrial
growth; the need for a "rational," predictable social environment to
sustain this growth and the increasing role of the state in promoting
such "rationality"; and the emergence of the urban working classes
onto the political scene. Ignoring these factors, Chalmers cannot go
further than asserting that Latin American states are politicized. Beyond this (true) statement, it is necessary to understand the changing
character of this politicization. This is what the approach that we called
"structuralist" tries (implicitly) to accomplish.

This approach leads us to the first of the two final questions asked above. In answering it, authors make evident the intricacy of state-society relations in Latin America. A paradox soon becomes clear: When associated with authoritarian regimes, corporatist features operate not only as a means of control, but also as a channel (perhaps the only one) of communication between state organs and social groups. When associated with open, competitive regimes, however, corporatist arrangements become an effective tool to limit the autonomous expression of social forces. Authors have concentrated primarily on analyzing corporatism as an instrument of control; we will briefly review their positions on the subject.

One troublesome feature of the analysis of corporatism as a control device is the lack of care in distinguishing between operative corporatist arrangements and corporatist ideologies. Most authors focus primarily on institutional arrangements, while the only discussions of ideologies are concerned with the role of the "Iberian tradition" in the origins of corporatist devices in contemporary Latin America. Equally relevant, however, is the role of ideologies in the *continuity* of corporatist institutions, as attempts to provide them with a legitimate basis. This line of research is not pursued in most of this volume—except for Malloy's brief excursion into populism and Stevens's account of the institutionalization of corporatist ideology in the PRI—despite its obvious importance in establishing the nature of state control over society (that is, the relative roles of coercion and ideological loyalty in maintaining these controls).

A second troublesome feature of this analysis is that for some, Malloy among them, corporatism is a type of state or authoritarian regime, while for others, like O'Donnell, it is just one kind of link between state and society. Instead of looking at these positions as qualitatively different, we think it is better to consider them as differing in degree. In the first place, Malloy, for instance, is at least ambiguous when talking about corporatism; it is a type of authoritarian regime, but at the same time strong corporatist elements are present in competitive situations, like populist ones. This suggests that at least some of its important characteristics are independent of regime type. Second, O'Donnell himself shows how certain aspects of the state, such as its public character or its monopoly of force, have nothing to do with its corporatist or noncorporatist nature. Therefore, a corporate state is simply one whose relations with society are organized along corporatist lines. In this sense, differences among authors are here only a result of accentuating different aspects in defining the state. Third, one of the central questions of this book, as pointed out before, has to do with the relations between corporatism and authoritarianism. If we take Malloy and some others literally, the question is meaningless, since corporatism is by definition one type of authoritarianism.

Thinking about corporatism, then, as one type of link between state and society, differences among authors run along two basic dimensions, one having to do with the degree to which existing corporatist arrangements are actually institutionalized as well as operative in Latin American societies, and the other concerned with the extent of their application (that is, to which social groups they are applied).

Distinctions along the first dimension seem to be very much related to the specific case studied by each author, as well as to personal preferences regarding what aspects to emphasize. Malloy, clearly impressed by the military takeovers of the last decade, stresses corporatism as the typical way through which Latin American governments seek to enforce a limited pluralism upon their societies; David Scott Palmer—who studies Peru—follows the same line of argument. At the other extreme John J. Bailey, who analyzes Colombia, sees there only the presence of corporatist features within a pattern of interest representation which is basically pluralist. Given this diversity of views, a pragmatic approach seems to be the best one: the degree to which a case approaches the corporatist image is an empirical problem. The relevant question is, then, what factors affect the form that interest representation takes in different societies (that is, the degree to which such representation is corporatist or pluralist). Robert Kaufman's is the only paper which presents suggestions in this regard: Among other things, he argues, it is important to consider whether the formation of a political center precedes or follows intensive industrialization and the social dislocations produced by it. A center which is shaped prior to industrialization, in his view, will have a better chance to establish its dominance over social groups through corporatist or other devices.

There seem to be two basic positions regarding the application of corporatist arrangements. John and Susan Purcell, for instance, do not think that there are differences between controls applied to business and to labor (at least they never emphasize these differences), while O'Donnell, Kenneth Sharpe, and Kenneth Mericle point to the class character of these controls. The divergence can be partly explained through O'Donnell's distinction between two forms of corporatism: On the one hand, it can be an interpenetration of official and private organizations for purposes of opening channels of information and securing political support. On the other hand, it can be an active domination of social groups by state agencies. Purcell and Purcell concentrate primarily on the first aspect of corporatism, which explains to a certain extent their disregard of the class issue. The problem with this easy solution is that each form of corporatism, in O'Donnell's view, applies to distinct social classes—the first one to the entrepreneurial group, the second one to labor and peasants. As he very aptly remarks, interpenetration is possible only if private groups control resources which are independent of the state. This is not the case with labor and peasants: Once their organizational activity is curtailed they cannot effectively oppose public agencies, and corporatism becomes merely a means of social control.

The final question raised above concerns the relationship between corporatism and authoritarianism. As indicated earlier, the problem is eliminated rather than solved if corporatism is defined as a type of authoritarian regime. If it is not so defined, there clearly is no necessary relation between them, since corporatist devices can be found during the democratic interludes of Latin American societies. Also, there are authoritarian situations in which these devices are not present, such as cases of autocratic rule by strongmen (like caudillos).

The real issue is then the following : Under what conditions do authoritarian regimes need corporatist devices? O'Donnell and Malloy provide an answer: under conditions of high mobilization, in which the demands of the popular sector cannot be kept in bounds simply by indiscriminate use of coercion. This perspective is certainly the one taken by Sharpe, Mericle, Palmer, and Thomas Skidmore in their empirical analyses. The next step for most authors is to examine the origins of contemporary Latin American authoritarianism. Again, the answer has to do with the need to control the demands of workers and peasants. Skidmore points out how curbing such demands allows investment in economic infrastructure; he also emphasizes that authoritarian regimes are more capable of stabilizing inflation than open-system regimes. O'Donnell points to the unique characteristics of contemporary authoritarianism, which has its roots in the modernizing projects of the military associated with civilian experts (especially in the areas of economic planning and administration) and both domestic and foreign economic interests. Authoritarianism is a consequence of the need to introduce stability and especially predictability in social relations, so that economic growth can take place; this implies the exclusion of workers and peasants from the political arena, and their close surveillance. The bureaucratic-authoritarian state assumes the leadership of economic development: It invests in infrastructure, provides legislation facilitating credit and long-term investments, and attracts foreign capital. The role of international interests is limited by the nationalist component of governments, which protects local enterprises; the alliance with these interests is profitable but also uneasy. The basic agreement of the partners is on the necessity of controlling popular elements.

Beyond this point, arguments break down. We know that at high levels of mobilization, authoritarian regimes require corporatist arrangements or some functional equivalent. However, this does not close the debate on the nature of corporatism and authoritarianism. Regarding corporatism, the most interesting question is perhaps the one which has not been asked: What is its relation to democratic arrangements? Several authors remark that open regimes have not dismantled corporatist devices but use them in less blatant fashion than authoritarian ones. Chalmers goes so far as to suggest that the former might be as efficient as the latter in curbing popular demands. A close examination of the use of corporatist arrangements by these regimes can help to extend our notions of open politics to include competitive regimes within politicized states, as Chalmers proposes. A more inclusive question has also to be asked: Why have corporatist arrangements survived regime changes? Chalmers provides the only argument that approaches an answer. He points out that Latin American states are politicized and participate in a great number of decisions directly affecting social life. In a word, they are the prize of a political game which has no rules. Redefinition of political institutions in democratic or authoritarian terms does not affect the need of incumbents to rebuild constantly their political bases. Corporatist arrangements survive regime changes because they are one of the mechanisms used by governments of any regime to guarantee and extend their support.

Chalmers can help us once more on the issue of authoritarianism. As pointed out above, he ignores the question of the changing character of the politicization of the state; however, his basic insight into the instability of both authoritarianism and democracy in Latin America remains true. His observation on the disregard of procedure (constitutional, legal, and administrative) in these societies introduces an element which is consistently ignored by other authors: the importance of the symbolic component in politics. This is precisely the key weakness of most authoritarian governments in Latin America—their almost complete inability to institutionalize themselves, or, in Chalmers's words, to depoliticize certain issues so that a framework for politics might be created. Juan Linz has illustrated the problems faced by the Brazilian military government, especially its difficulty in finding a legitimacy formula.[3] These considerations are relevant, because most authors in this volume seem to find in the effectiveness of authoritarian regimes a solution for problems generated by modernization. Leaving aside reasonable doubts regarding this effectiveness, it should be noted that these regimes have their own difficulties, among them a remarkable awkwardness in solving questions of institutionalization. O'Donnell's coined expression—"bureaucratic-authoritarian state"—illustrates well the disregard of the potential instability of authoritarian governments in Latin America: It mixes a trend which is inherent in modernization—bureaucratic growth—with a regime type whose eventual disappearance will not reverse such a trend. It is true that authoritarian governments might last indefinitely despite their illegitimate character; however, they cannot be fully understood simply in terms of their effectiveness in economic and administrative areas. The instability of Latin American regimes, authoritarian or not, makes it necessary to attend to their problems of institutionalization. We owe it to Chalmers to bring these problems to the center of the debate on Latin American politics.

We would like to complete these considerations by casting a look at this volume from a different vantage point. A remarkable characteristic of students of Latin America—the reviewers included—is how comfortable we feel in making statements about the whole continent (or at least single countries). One cannot help but notice the contrast with scholars working on Europe, who are often afraid of generalizing beyond one village! Our goal here is not to argue the merits of either extreme. We only want to point out the conspicuous absence of the second kind of work within Latin America. The implications of this absence are clear: Who knows what a study of crowd composition would reveal about supporters of populism in different countries? What would patient monographs on the evolution of systems of taxation reveal on the relations between state and society? It will be no surprise if future work of this kind completely overturns our current wisdom on politics and societies of the region. Meanwhile, we hope we share with all authors the feeling that scholarly studies on Latin America are just beginning.

NOTES

We thank James Malloy and Guillermo O'Donnell for destroying the first version of this paper. In the second version, we looked for support elsewhere: Luis Abugattas, German Garrido-Pinto, Joy A. Grune, and John Markoff. However, the authors alone share equal responsibility for the final result.

1. Immanuel Wallerstein, *Africa: The Politics of Independence* (New York: Random House, 1971), pp. 157–59.

2. Alfred Stepan, *The Military in Politics* (Princeton: Princeton University Press, 1971).

3. Juan J. Linz, "The Future of an Authoritarian Situation or the Institutionalization of an Authoritarian Regime: The Case of Brazil," in *Authoritarian Brazil*, ed. Alfred Stepan (New Haven: Yale University Press, 1973), pp. 233–54.

Biographical Notes

Selected Bibliography

Index

Biographical Notes

JOHN J BAILEY, Assistant Professor of Government at Georgetown University, is a graduate of Indiana University and the University of Wisconsin. He is a contributing editor to the *Handbook of Latin American Studies* and has published articles in *Estudios Andinos* and the *Public Administration Review.*

DOUGLAS A. CHALMERS is Professor of Political Science at Columbia University and was Director of its Institute of Latin American Studies from 1972 to 1974. He has written on European and Latin American politics.

DAVID COLLIER is Associate Professor of Political Science at Indiana University. He is the author of *Squatters and Oligarchs: Authoritarian Rule and Policy Change in Peru* and of articles on the sequence and timing of economic, social, and political change.

RUTH BERINS COLLIER is Assistant Professor of Political Science at Indiana University. In addition to her work on labor politics and state-labor relations in Latin America, she is engaged in research on political participation and authoritarian rule in tropical Africa.

HENRY A. DIETZ is Assistant Professor of Government at the University of Texas in Austin. His interests include comparative urban politics, poverty and politics in the Third World, and the politics of Latin America, especially Peru.

HELEN E. DOUGLASS is Assistant Professor of Political Science at Boston University. She is at present completing a study of politics in the Netherlands.

SILVIO DUNCAN BARETTA, a native of Brazil, is a Ph.D. candidate in sociology at the University of Pittsburgh. He is at present preparing a study of violence and politics in the Brazilian state of Rio Grande Do Sul.

ROBERT R. KAUFMAN is Associate Professor of Political Science at Douglass College, Rutgers University, and is currently a Research Associate at the Center for International Affairs, Harvard University. He is the author of *The Politics of Land Reform in Chile* and *Transitions to Stable Authoritarian-Corporate Regimes.*

JAMES M. MALLOY is Associate Professor of Political Science at the University of Pittsburgh. He is the author of *Bolivia: The Uncompleted Revolution* and other works on Latin American politics.

KENNETH S. MERICLE is Assistant Professor of Industrial Relations at the Sloan School of Management, Massachusetts Institute of Technology. He is currently working on a book on the Brazilian wage policy and industrial relations system.

GUILLERMO A. O'DONNELL is Director of the Centro de Estudios de Estado y Sociedad (CEDES) in Buenos Aires. He is the author of *Modernization and Bureaucratic-Authoritarianism: Studies in Latin American Politics* and other works on Latin American politics.

DAVID SCOTT PALMER teaches government at Bowdoin College.

JOHN F. H. PURCELL is Associate Professor of Political Science at California State University, Fullerton, and has written on both Mexican politics and South African politics. SUSAN KAUFMAN PURCELL is a member of the Department of Political Science at U.C.L.A. and an associate of the Latin American Center. She is the author of *The Mexican Profit-Sharing Decision: Politics in an Authoritarian Regime*. The Purcells are currently in Mexico collaborating on a study of business-government relations, supported by grants from the Joint Committee of the American Council of Learned Societies and the Social Science Research Council.

SIMON SCHWARTZMAN, a Brazilian sociologist and political scientist, is Associate Professor at the Brazilian School of Public Administration and Instituto Universitário de Pesquisas do Rio de Janeiro, where he is also the editor of *Dados*. He is the author of *São Paulo e o estado nacional*.

KENNETH E. SHARPE is Assistant Professor of Political Science at Swarthmore College. He is a graduate of Yale University, where his Ph.D. dissertation was entitled, "From Consciousness to Control: The Politics of a Dominican Peasant Movement."His present research focuses on the impact of multinational corporations in Mexico and the policies of the state in regulating such direct foreign investment.

THOMAS E. SKIDMORE is Professor of Latin American History at the University of Wisconsin and a past president of the Latin American Studies Association. He is the author of *Politics in Brazil, 1930–1964* and *Black Into White: Race and Nationality in Brazilian Thought*.

EVELYN P. STEVENS is the author of *Protest and Response in Mexico*, as well as numerous scholarly articles on Mexican politics. She is Samuel B. Knight Professor in the Humanities at Case Western Reserve University.

Selected Bibliography

Academia de Ciencias Economicas. *Las cláusulas económica-sociales en las constitu- ciones de América.* 2 vols. Buenos Aires: Editorial Losada, 1947–1948.

Adelman, Irma, and Morris, Cynthia Taft. *Economic Growth and Social Equity in Developing Countries.* Stanford: Stanford University Press, 1973.

Alemán, José Luis. "La reforma agraria y la doctrina social de la Iglesia." *Estudios Sociales*, 1 (1968):126–27.

Anderson, Bo, and Cockroft, James D. "Control and Co-optation in Mexican Politics." *International Journal of Comparative Sociology*, 7 (March 1966): 19–28.

Anderson, Charles W. "Central American Political Parties: A Functional Approach." *Western Political Quarterly*, 15 (March 1962):125–39.

——. *The Political Economy of Modern Spain: Policy-Making in an Authoritarian System.* Madison: University of Wisconsin Press, 1970.

——. *Politics and Economic Change in Latin America.* Princeton: Van Nostrand, 1967.

Astiz, Carlos A. "The Military Establishment as a Political Elite: The Peruvian Case." In *Latin American Prospects for the 1970's: What Kinds of Revolutions?* edited by David H. Pollock and Arch R. M. Ritter, pp. 203–29. New York: Praeger, 1973.

——. *Pressure Groups and Power Elites in Peruvian Politics.* Ithaca: Cornell University Press, 1969.

Bachrach, Peter, and Baratz, Morton S. *Power and Poverty: Theory and Practice.* New York: Oxford University Press, 1970.

Baer, Werner. "The Economics of Prebisch and ECLA." *Economic Development and Cultural Change*, 10 (January 1962):169–82.

——. "The World Bank Group and the Process of Socio-Economic Development in the Third World." *World Development*, 2 (June 1974):1–10.

Bailey, David C. *Viva Cristo Rey!* Austin: University of Texas Press, 1973.

Bailey, John J. "Public Budgeting in Colombia: Disjoined Incrementalism in a Dependent Polity." LADAC Occasional Paper, ser. 2. Austin: University of Texas, 1974.

Banks, Arthur. *Cross-Polity Time-Series Data.* Cambridge: MIT Press, 1971.

Barkin, David, and King, Timothy. *Regional Economic Development: The River Basin Approach in Mexico.* Cambridge: Cambridge University Press, 1970.

Bernstein, Harry. "The Concept of the Nation-State in the Caribbean." In *The Caribbean: Its Political Problems*, edited by A. Curtis Wilgus. Gainesville: University of Florida Press, 1956.

Bonilla, Heraclio. *La independencia en el Perú*. Lima: Instituto de Estudios Peruanos, Campodónico, 1972.

Bourricaud, François. "Los militares: por qué y para qué?" *Aportes*, 16 (April 1970):13–55

——. "Voluntarismo y experimentación: los militares peruanos mano a la obra." *Aportes*, 18 (October 1970).

Bowen, Ralph H. *German Theories of the Corporative State*. New York: Columbia University Press, 1947.

Brandenburg, Frank. *The Making of Modern Mexico*. Englewood Cliffs, N.J.: Prentice-Hall, 1964.

——. "Mexico: An Experiment in One-Party Democracy." Ph.D. dissertation, University of Pennsylvania, 1956.

——. "Organized Business in Mexico." *Inter-American Economic Affairs*, 12 (1958):26–50.

Braun, Oscar. *Desarrollo del capital monopolista en Argentina*. Buenos Aires: Ed. Tiempo Contemporáneo, 1970.

Brill, William. "Military Civil Action in Bolivia." Ph.D. dissertation, University of Pennsylvania, 1965.

Buira, Ariel. "Development and Price Stability in Mexico." *Weltwirtschaftliches Archiv*, 101 (1968):49–69.

Burke, Melvin, and Malloy, James. "From National Populism to National Corporatism: Bolivia, 1952–1970." *Studies in Comparative International Development*, 9 (1974):49–73.

Campos, Judith Talbot, and McCamant, John F. *Cleavage Shift in Colombia: Analysis of the 1970 Elections*. Beverly Hills: Sage Publications, 1970.

Cardoso, Fernando Henrique, and Reyna, José Luis. "Industrialization, Occupational Structure, and Social Structure in Latin America." In *Constructive Change in Latin America*, edited by Cole Blasier, pp. 19–55. Pittsburgh: University of Pittsburgh Press, 1968.

Carmona, Fernando, et al. *El milagro Mexicano*. Mexico: Ed. Nuestro Tiempo, 1970.

Casanova, Pablo González. *Democracy in Mexico*. New York: Oxford University Press, 1970.

Centro de Estudios Colombianos. *Una política conservadora para Colombia: bases para la nueva plataforma social del partido*. Bogota: Centro de Estudios Colombianos, 1969.

Centro de Investigación y Acción Social. *Estructuras políticas de Colombia*. Bogota: CIAS, 1969.

Cepeda, Fernando, et al. *Los grupos de presión en Colombia: mesas redondas de "AEXANDES."* Bogota: Tercer Mundo, 1962.

Chalmers, Douglas A. "Parties and Society in Latin America." *Studies in Comparative International Development*, 7 (Summer 1972):102–30.

Chaplin, David, ed. *Peruvian Nationalism: A Corporatist Revolution?* New Brunswick, N.J.: Transaction Books, 1976.

Clausner, Martin. *Rural Santo Domingo: Settled, Unsettled, and Resettled*. Philadelphia: Temple University Press, 1973.

Cockroft, James D.; Frank, André Gunder; and Johnson, Dale L., eds. *Dependence and Underdevelopment*. Garden City, N.Y.: Doubleday, 1972.

Cole, William E. *Steel and Economic Growth in Mexico*. Austin: University of Texas Press, 1967.

Collier, David. *Squatters and Oligarchs: Urbanization and Public Policy in Peru.* Baltimore: Johns Hopkins University Press, 1976.

Converse, Philip E. "Of Time and Partisan Stability." *Comparative Political Studies,* 2 (July 1969):139–72.

Córdova, Arnoldo. *La ideología de la Revolución Mexicana: la formación del nuevo régimen.* Mexico: Instituto de Investigaciones Sociales de la Universidad Nacional Autónoma de México, 1973.

———. "La transformación del PMR al PRM. El triunfo del corporativismo en México." Paper read at the fourth international Congress of Mexican Studies, Santa Monica, California, October 1973.

Cornelius, Wayne. "Nation Building, Participation, and Distribution: The Politics of Social Reform Under Cárdenas." In *Crisis, Choice, and Change: Historical Studies of Political Development,* edited by Gabriel A. Almond et al., pp. 392–498. Boston: Little, Brown, 1973.

———, and Dietz, Henry. "Urbanization, Demand-Making, and Political System Overload: Political Participation Among the Migrant Poor in Latin American Cities." In *Frontiers of Urban Research,* edited by Rodney Stiefbold. Coral Gables: University of Miami Press, 1975.

Corr, Edwin G. *The Political Process in Colombia.* Denver: University of Denver, Social Science Foundation, 1971–1972.

Cotler, Julio. "The Mechanics of Internal Domination and Social Change in Peru." In *Masses in Latin America,* edited by Irving Louis Horowitz, pp. 407–45. New York: Oxford University Press, 1970.

———. "Political Crisis and Military Populism in Peru." *Studies in Comparative International Development,* 6 (1970–1971):95–113.

Cunningham, Charles H. *The Audiencia in the Spanish Colonies.* New York: Gordian, 1971.

Dealy, Glen. "Prolegomena on the Spanish American Political Tradition." *Hispanic American Historical Review,* 48 (February 1968):37–58.

Dent, David W. "Oligarchy and Power Structure in Urban Colombia: The Case of Cali." *Journal of Latin American Studies,* 6 (May 1974):113–33.

Derossi, Flavia. *The Mexican Entrepreneur.* Paris: OECD, 1970.

Deutsch, Karl. "Social Mobilization and Political Development." *American Political Science Review,* 55 (1961):493–514.

Diamand, Marcelo. *Doctrinas económicas, desarrollo e independencia.* Buenos Aires: Paidos, 1973.

Díaz Alejandro, Carlos F. *Essays on the Economic History of the Argentine Republic.* New Haven: Yale University Press, 1970.

———. *Exchange-Rate Devaluation in a Semi-Industrialized Country: The Experience of Argentina, 1955–1961.* Cambridge: MIT Press, 1965.

Dix, Robert, H. *Colombia: The Political Dimensions of Change.* New Haven: Yale University Press, 1967.

Ebel, Roland H. "Governing the City-State: Notes on the Politics of the Small Latin American Countries." *Journal of Inter-American Studies and World Affairs,* 14 (August 1972):325–46.

ECLA. *Development Problems in Latin America: An Analysis by the United Nations Economic Commission for Latin America.* Austin: University of Texas Press, 1970.

Eder, George. *Inflation and Development in Latin America: A Case Study of Inflation and Stabilization in Bolivia.* Ann Arbor: University of Michigan, School of Business, 1968.

Einaudi, Luigi. "The Military and Government in Peru." In *Development Adminis-tration in Latin America*, edited by Clarence Thurber and Laurence Graham, pp. 294–313. Durham, N.C.: Duke University Press, 1973.

——, and Stepan, Alfred. *Latin American Institutional Development: Changing Military Perspectives in Peru and Brazil.* Santa Monica, Calif.: Rand Corporation, 1971.

Elbow, Matthew H. *French Corporative Theory.* New York: Columbia University Press, 1953.

Erickson, Kenneth P. "Labor in the Political Process in Brazil: Corporatism in a Modernizing Nation." Ph.D. dissertation, Columbia University, 1970.

——, and Peppe, Patrick V. "The Dynamics of Dependency: Industrial Modernization and Tightening Controls Over the Working Class in Brazil and Chile." Paper read at the fifth national meeting of the Latin American Studies Association, San Francisco, November 1974.

Evers, Tilman Tönnies. *Militärregierung in Argentinien: das politische system der "Argentinischen Revolution."* Hamburg: Alfred Metzner Verlag, 1972.

Ezcurdia, Mario. *Análisis teórico del Partido Revolucionario Institucional.* Mexico: B. Costa-Amic, Editores, 1968.

Fann, K. T., and Hodges, Donald C. *Readings in U.S. Imperialism.* Boston: Sargent, 1971.

Fayt, Carlos S. *El político armando: dinámica del proceso político argentino, 1960–1971.* Buenos Aires: Ed. Rannedile, 1971.

Ferrer, Aldo, et al. *Los planes de establización en la Argentina.* Buenos Aires: Paidos, 1969.

Ferrero, César. "Los sindicatos obreros colombianos." *Estudios sindicales y co-operativos*, 4 (1970):32–78.

Field, G. Lowell. *The Syndical and Corporative Institutions of Italian Fascism.* New York: AMS Press, 1968.

Fitzgibbon, Russell H. "The Party Potpourri in Latin America." *Western Political Quarterly*, 10 (March 1957):3–22.

Fluharty, V. L. *Dance of the Millions: Military Rule and the Social Revolution in Colombia, 1930–1956.* Pittsburgh: University of Pittsburgh Press, 1957.

Frank, André Gunder. *Capitalism and Underdevelopment in Latin America.* New York: AMS Press, 1968.

Gallo, Manuel López. *Economía y política en la historia de México.* Mexico: Ediciones Solidaridad, 1965.

García, José Z. "The 1968 Velasco Coup in Peru: Causes and Policy Conse-quences." Ph.D. dissertation, University of New Mexico, 1974.

Gil, Federico G. *Genesis and Modernization of Political Parties in Chile.* Gainesville: University of Florida Press, 1962.

Glade, William P., and Anderson, Charles W. *The Political Economy of Mexico.* Madison: University of Wisconsin Press, 1963.

Goldrich, Daniel. "Political Organization and the Politicization of the Poblador." *Comparative Political Studies*, 3 (July 1970):176–203.

Goncalves de Freitas, Ivan. *Mão-de-obra industrial na Guanabara.* Rio de Janeiro: Instituto de Ciências Sociais, 1967.

Gonzalez, Nancie. "Patron-Client Relationships at the International Level." In *Structure and Process in Latin America: Patronage, Clientage and Power Systems*, edited by Arnold Strickon and Sidney M. Greenfield, pp. 179–209. Albuquerque: University of New Mexico Press, 1972.

González, Santiago Senen. *El sindicalismo después de Perón*. Buenos Aires: Ed. Galerna, 1971.

Gravil, Roger. "State Intervention in Argentina's Export Trade Between the Wars." *Journal of Latin American Studies*, 2 (November 1970):147–73.

Grayson, George. "Peru's Revolutionary Government." *Current History*, 64 (1973): 661–66.

Greenberg, Martin Harry. *Bureaucracy and Development: A Mexican Case Study*. Lexington, Mass.: D. C. Heath and Company, 1970.

Griffiths, B. *Mexican Monetary Policy and Economic Development*. New York: Praeger, 1972.

Groves, Roderick. "The Colombian National Front and Administrative Reform." *Administration and Society*, 6 (November 1974):324.

Guillen Martínez, Fernando. *La nueva forma del estado*. Bogota: Universidad Nacional de Colombia, 1974.

Hansen, Roger D. *The Politics of Mexican Development*. Baltimore: Johns Hopkins Press, 1971.

Haring, C. H. *The Spanish Empire in America*. New York: Harcourt, Brace and World, 1947.

Heath, Dwight, and Adams, Richard, eds. *Contemporary Culture and Societies of Latin America*. New York: Random House, 1965.

Heisler, Martin O., and Kuavik, Robert B. "Patterns of European Politics: The 'European Polity' Model." In *Politics in Europe*, edited by Martin O. Heisler. New York: David McKay Co., 1974.

Helguera, J. Leon. "The Problem of Liberalism Versus Conservatism in Colombia: 1849–85." In *Latin American History: Select Problems*, edited by Frederick B. Pike, pp. 224–59. New York: Harcourt, Brace and World, 1969.

Hennessy, Alistair. "América Latina." In *Populismo*, edited by Ghita Ionesui and Ernest Gellner. Buenos Aires: Amorrotu, 1969.

Hernández, Salvador. *El PRI y el movimiento estudiantil de 1968*. Mexico: Ediciones "El Caballito," 1971.

Herring, Hubert. *A History of Latin America*. New York: Knopf, 1955.

Hirschman, Albert O. *Exit, Voice and Loyalty*. Cambridge: Harvard University Press, 1970.

_____. *Journeys Toward Progress: Studies of Economic Policy-Making in Latin America*. New York: Twentieth Century Fund, 1963.

Horowitz, Irving Louis. "Political Legitimacy and the Institutionalization of Crisis in Latin America." *Comparative Political Studies*, 1 (April 1968):1–45.

Huntington, Samuel P. "Political Development and Political Decay." *World Politics*, 17 (1965):386–430.

_____. *Political Order in Changing Societies*. New Haven: Yale University Press, 1968.

Jaguaribe, Helio. *Political Development: A General Theory and a Latin American Case Study*. New York: Harper and Row, 1973.

Jaquette, Jane S. *The Politics of Development in Peru*. Ithaca: Cornell University, Latin American Studies Program, 1971.

_____. "Revolution by Fiat: The Context of Policy-Making in Peru." *Western Political Quarterly*, 25 (December 1972):648–66.

Johnson, Charles W. "Perú: los militares como un agente de cambio económico." *Revista Mexicana de Sociología*, 34 (1972):293–316.

Johnson, Kenneth F. *Mexican Democracy: A Critical View.* Boston: Allyn and Bacon, 1971.

Kahil, Raouf. *Inflation and Economic Development in Brazil, 1946–1963.* Oxford: Oxford University Press, 1973.

Kantor, Harry. *The Ideology and Program of the Peruvian Aprista Movement.* Berkeley: University of California Press, 1953.

Kaufman, Herbert. "Administrative Decentralization and Political Power." *Public Administration Review,* 29 (1969):3–15.

Kaufman, Robert R. "The Patron-Client Concept and Macro-Politics: Prospects and Problems." *Comparative Studies in Society and History,* 16 (1974):284–308.

_____. *The Politics of Land Reform in Chile, 1950–1970.* Cambridge: Harvard University Press, 1972.

_____. *Transitions to Stable Authoritarian-Corporate Regimes: The Chilean Case?* Beverly Hills: Sage Professional Papers in Comparative Politics, 1976.

_____; Geller, Daniel S.; and Chernotsky, Harry I. "A Preliminary Test of the Theory of Dependency." *Comparative Politics,* 7 (1975):303–30.

Kenworthy, Eldon. "Coalitions in the Political Development of Latin America." In *The Study of Coalition Behavior,* edited by Sven Groennings et al., pp. 103–33. New York: Holt, Rinehart and Winston, 1970.

King, Timothy. *Mexico: Industrialization and Trade Policies Since 1940.* London: Oxford University Press, 1970.

Kirkpatrick, Jeane. *Leader and Vanguard in Mass Society: A Study of Peronist Argentina.* Cambridge: MIT Press, 1971.

Klarén, Paul. *Modernization, Dislocation, and Aprismo.* Austin: University of Texas Press, 1973.

Klein, Herbert S. *Parties and Political Change in Bolivia, 1880–1952.* Cambridge: Cambridge University Press, 1969.

Kline, Harvey F. "Interest Groups in the Colombian Congress: Group Behavior in a Centralized, Patrimonial Political System." *Journal of Inter-American Studies and World Affairs,* 16 (August 1974):274–300.

Kling, Merle. *A Mexican Interest Group in Action.* Englewood Cliffs, N.J.: Prentice-Hall, 1961.

Koffman, Bennett E. "The National Federation of Coffee-Growers of Colombia." Ph.D. dissertation, University of Virginia, 1969.

König, Wolfgang. "International Financial Institutions and Latin American Development." In *Latin America in the International Economy,* edited by Victor L. Urquidi and Rosemary Thorp, pp. 116–63. New York: John Wiley, 1973.

Kornhauser, William. *The Politics of Mass Society.* Glencoe, Ill.: Free Press, 1960.

Lafer, Celso. "El sistema político Brasileño: algunas características e perspectivas." *Desarrollo Economico,* 14 (1975):641–76.

Landsberger, Henry A. "The Labor Elite: Is It Revolutionary?" In *Elites in Latin America,* edited by Seymour Lipset and Aldo Solari, pp. 256–301. New York: Oxford University Press, 1967.

Leal de Araujo, Lucila. *Aspectos económicos del Instituto Mexicano del Seguro Social.* Mexico: Cuadernos Americanos, 1966.

Leff, Nathaniel H. *Economic Policy-Making and Development in Brazil, 1947–1964.* New York: John Wiley and Sons, 1968.

Lemarchand, Rene, and Legg, Keith. "Political Clientelism and Development: Preliminary Analysis." *Comparative Politics,* 4 (January 1972):148–70.

Linz, Juan. "An Authoritarian Regime: Spain." In *Cleavages, Ideologies, and*

Party Systems, edited by Erik Allardt and Y. Littunen. Helsinki: Westermarck Society, 1964.

———. "Opposition to and Under an Authoritarian Regime: The Case of Spain." In *Regimes and Oppositions*, edited by Robert Dahl, pp. 171–259. New Haven: Yale University Press, 1973.

Lipset, Seymour M., and Rokkan, Stein, eds. *Party Systems and Voter Alignments*. New York: The Free Press, 1967.

Little, Walter. "Electoral Aspects of Peronism, 1946–1954." *Journal of Inter-American Studies*, 3 (August 1973):267–84.

Losada Lora, Rodrigo. *Los institutos descentralizados de carácter financiero: aspectos del caso colombiano*. Bogota: Fundación para la Educación Superior y el Desarrollo, 1973.

Lowenthal, Abraham F., ed. *The Peruvian Experiment: Continuity and Change Under Military Rule*. Princeton: Princeton University Press, 1975.

Lowi, Theodore. *The End of Liberalism*. New York: W. W. Norton, 1969.

Mabry, Donald J. *Mexico's Acción Nacional: A Catholic Alternative to Revolution*. Syracuse: Syracuse University Press, 1973.

McDonald, Ronald H. *Party Systems and Elections in Latin America*. Chicago: Markham, 1971.

Mackenzie, Leslie. "The Political Ideas of the Opus Dei in Spain." *Government and Opposition*, 8 (1973):72–92.

Mallon, Richard, and Surrouille, Juan. *Economic Policymaking in a Conflict Society: The Argentine Case* (Cambridge: Harvard University Press, forthcoming).

Malloy, James. *Bolivia: The Uncompleted Revolution*. Pittsburgh: University of Pittsburgh Press, 1970.

———. "Dissecting the Peruvian Military: A Review Essay." *Journal of Inter-American and World Affairs*, 15 (1973):375–82.

———. "Populismo militar en el Perú y Bolivia: antecedentes y posibilidades." *Estudios Andinos*, 2 (1971–1972):114–34.

———, and Thorn, Richard, eds. *Beyond the Revolution: Bolivia Since 1952*. Pittsburgh: University of Pittsburgh Press, 1971.

Mangin, William. "Latin American Squatter Settlements: A Problem and a Solution." *Latin American Research Review*, 2 (1967):65–97.

———, ed. *Peasants in Cities*. Boston: Houghton Mifflin, 1970.

Marshall, Dale Rogers. *The Politics of Participation in Poverty*. Berkeley: University of California Press, 1970.

Martz, John D. *Acción Democrática: Evolution of a Political Party in Venezuela*. Princeton: Princeton University Press, 1966.

———. *Colombia: A Contemporary Political Survey*. Chapel Hill: University of North Carolina Press, 1962.

———. "Dilemmas in the Study of Latin American Political Parties." *Journal of Politics*, 26 (August 1964):509–31.

———. "Political Parties in Colombia and Venezuela: Contrasts in Substance and Style." *Western Political Quarterly*, 18 (June 1965):318–33.

Mathiason, John R., and Powell, John D. "Political Participation and Political Attitudes: Attitude Change of Peasants Involved in Political Mobilization." Paper read at American Political Science Association, New York, September 1969.

Menges, Constantine C. "Public Policy and Organized Business in Chile: A Preliminary Analysis." *Journal of International Affairs*, 20 (1966):343–65.

Merkx, Gilbert W. "Sectoral Clashes and Political Change: The Argentine Experience." *Latin American Research Review*, 4 (Fall 1969):89–114.

Mesa-Lago, Carmelo. "La estratificación de la seguridad social y el efecto de desigualidad en América Latina: El caso peruano." *Estudios Andinos*, 8 (1973):17–48.

_____. "Social Security Stratification and Inequality in Chile." Pittsburgh: University of Pittsburgh, Center for Latin American Studies, 1973.

_____. "Social Security Stratification and Inequality in Mexico." Mimeographed. Santa Monica: Fourth International Congress of Mexican Studies, 1973.

Meyer, Lorenzo. "El estado mexicano contemporáneo." *Historia Mexicana*, 23 (1974):722–52.

_____. *México y Estados Unidos en el conflicto petrolero, 1917–1942.* Mexico: El Colegio de México, Centro de Estudios Internacionales, 1968.

Michaels, Albert L. "Fascism and Sinarquismo: Popular Nationalism Against the Mexican Revolution." *Journal of Church and State*, 8 (1966):234–50.

Miglioli, Jorge. *Como São Feitas as greves no Brasil.* Rio de Janeiro: Civilização Brasiliera, 1963.

Milbrath, Lester. *Political Participation.* Chicago: Rand McNally, 1965.

Mitchel, Christopher. "Reformers as Revolutionaries: The Tragedy of Bolivia's Movimiento Revolucionario 1952–1964." Ph.D. dissertation, Harvard University, 1971.

de Moraes, Evaristo, Filho. *O problema do sindicato único no Brasil.* Rio de Janeiro: Editôra a Noite, 1952.

Morris, James O. *Elites, Intellectuals, and Consensus: A Study of the Social Question and the Industrial Relations System in Chile.* Ithaca: New York State School of Industrial and Labor Relations, Cornell University, 1966.

Morse, Richard M. "The Heritage of Latin America." In *The Founding of New Societies*, edited by Louis Hartz. New York: Harcourt, Brace and World, 1964.

_____. *The Urban Development of Latin America.* Stanford: Stanford University Press, 1971.

Navarrete, Alfredo. "Mexico's Balance of Payments and External Financing." *Weltwirtschaftliches Archiv*, 101 (1968):70–85.

de Navarrete, Ifigenia. *La distribución del engreso y el desarrollo económico de México.* Mexico: Universidad Nacional Autónoma de México, 1960.

Needler, Martin C. *Latin American Politics in Perspective.* Princeton: Van Nostrand, 1963.

Nelson, Joan. *Migrants, Urban Poverty, and Instability in Developing Nations.* Cambridge: Harvard University, Center for International Affairs, 1969.

Nettl, J. P. "The State as a Conceptual Variable." *World Politics*, 20 (1968):559–92.

Newton, Ronald C. "On 'Functional Groups,' 'Fragmentation,' and 'Pluralism' in Spanish American Political Society." *Hispanic American Historical Review*, 50 (February 1970):1–29.

Nordlinger, Eric. "Soldiers in Mufti: The Impact of Military Rule Upon Economic and Social Change in the Non-Western States." *American Political Science Review*, 64 (December 1970):1131–48.

North, Liisa. *Civil-Military Relations in Argentina, Chile, and Peru.* Berkeley: University of California Press, 1966.

Oclander, Jorge I. "Córdoba, May 1969: Modernization, Grass-Roots Demands, and Political Instability." In *New Perspectives on Modern Argentina*, edited by Alberto Ciria, et al., pp. 83–91. Bloomington: Latin American Studies Program, Indiana University, 1972.

O'Donnell, Guillermo A. *Modernization and Bureaucratic-Authoritarianism: Studies in South American Politics.* Berkeley: University of California, Institute of International Studies, 1973.

Ortega y Gasset, José. *Invertebrate Spain.* New York: W. W. Norton, 1937.

Padgett, Vincent L. *The Mexican Political System.* Boston: Houghton Mifflin, 1966.

Palmer, David Scott. *"Revolution from Above": Military Government and Popular Participation in Peru, 1968–1972.* Ithaca: Cornell University, Latin American Studies Program, 1973.

Partantiero, Juan C. "Dominant Classes and Political Crisis in Argentina Today." *Latin American Perspectives*, 1 (1974):93–120.

Payne, James L. *Patterns of Conflict in Colombia.* New Haven: Yale University Press, 1968.

Pazos, Felipe. *Chronic Inflation in Latin America.* New York: Praeger, 1972.

Pereira, Luis. *Trabalho e desenvolvimento no Brasil.* São Paulo: Difusão Européia do Livro, 1965.

Petras, James. "Chile: Nationalization, Socioeconomic Change, and Popular Participation." Paper read at the 1972 meetings of the American Political Science Association, Washington, D.C.

_____. *Politics and Social Forces in Chilean Development.* Berkeley: University of California Press, 1969.

Pike, Frederick. *The Modern History of Peru.* New York: Praeger, 1967.

_____, ed. "The New Corporatism: Social and Political Structures in the Iberian World." *Review of Politics*, 36, no. 1 (special edition, January 1974).

_____, and Stritch, Thomas, eds. *The New Corporatism.* Notre Dame: University of Notre Dame Press, 1974.

Poblete Troncoso, Moises, and Burnett, Ben G. *The Rise of the Latin American Labor Movement.* New Haven: College and University Press, 1960.

Ponte, Víctor Manuel Durand. "Reformismo burgués y reformismo obrero: un análisis de la realidad mexicana." *Revista Mexicana de Sociología*, 44 (1972).

Portes, Alejandro. "Modernity and Development: A Critique." *Studies in Comparative International Development*, 8 (Fall 1973):247–79.

_____. "Rationality in the Slum: An Essay on Interpretive Sociology." *Comparative Studies in Society and History*, 14 (June 1970):286.

Potter, Jack, et al. *Peasant Society: A Reader.* Boston: Little, Brown, 1967.

Powell, John Duncan. "Peasant Society and Clientelistic Politics." *American Political Science Review*, 64 (June 1970):411–26.

_____. *Political Mobilization of the Venezuelan Peasant.* Cambridge: Harvard University Press, 1971.

Powell, Sandra. "Political Participation in the Barriadas: A Case Study." *Comparative Political Studies*, 2 (1969):195–215.

Pratt, Raymond. "Community Political Organization and Lower Class Politicization in Two Latin American Cities." *Journal of Developing Areas*, 5 (July 1971): 523–42.

_____. "Parties, Neighborhood Associations, and the Politicization of the Urban Poor in Latin America." *Midwest Journal of Political Science*, 15 (August 1971):495–524.

Purcell, Susan Kaufman. "Authoritarianism." *Comparative Politics*, 5 (January 1973):301–12.

_____. "Decision-making in an Authoritarian Regime: Theoretical Implications from a Mexican Case Study," *World Politics*, 26 (October 1973):28–54.

_____. *The Mexican Profit-Sharing Decision: Politics in an Authoritarian Regime.* Berkeley: University of California Press, 1975.

Putnam, Robert D. "Toward Explaining Military Intervention in Latin American Politics." *World Politics*, 19 (1967):83–110.

Quirk, Robert E. *The Mexican Revolution and the Catholic Church, 1910–1929.* Bloomington: Indiana University Press, 1973.

Rabello, Ophelina. *A rêde sindical parilista.* São Paulo: Institute Cultural do Trabalho, 1965.

Rabinowitz, Francine, and Trueblood, Felicity, eds. *Latin American Urban Research.* Beverly Hills: Sage Publications, 1971.

Ranis, Paul. "A Two-Dimensional Typology of Latin American Political Parties." *Journal of Politics*, 30 (August 1968):798–832.

Reyna, José Luis. *Control político, estabilidad y desarrollo en México.* Mexico: Centro de Estudios Sociológicos, El Colegio de México, 1974.

_____. "An Empirical Analysis of Political Mobilization: The Case of Mexico." Ph.D. dissertation, Cornell University, 1971.

Reyna, Manuel; Palomares, Laura; and Cortez, Guadalupe. "El control del movimiento obrero como una necesidad del estado en México. (1917–1936)." *Revista Mexicana de Sociología*, 34 (1972):785–814.

Reynolds, Clark W. *The Mexican Economy: Twentieth-Century Structure and Growth.* New Haven: Yale University Press, 1970.

Riano, Alcibiades. *Actualidad del corporativismo: ensayo político-económico.* Bogota: Editorial y Litografía "CAHOR," 1950.

Roberts, Bryan. *Organizing Strangers.* Austin: University of Texas Press, 1973.

Rodrigues, J. A. *Sindicato e desenvolvimento no Brasil.* São Paulo: Difusão Européia do Livro, 1968.

Rodrigues, Leôncio M. *Conflito indústrial e sindicalisimo no Brasil.* São Paulo: Difusão Européia do Livro, 1966.

_____. *Industrialização e atitudes operárias.* São Paulo: Editôra Brasiliense, 1970.

Roett, Riordan, ed. *Brazil in the Sixties.* Nashville: Vanderbilt University Press, 1972.

Roth, Guenther. "Personal Rulership, Patrimonialism, and Empire-Building in the New States." *World Politics*, 20 (1968):196.

Rothenberg, Irene Fraser. "Centralization Patterns and Policy Outcomes in Colombia." Ph.D. dissertation, University of Illinois, 1973.

Ruddle, Kenneth, and Gillete, Phillip, eds. *Latin American Political Statistics.* Los Angeles: U.C.L.A. Latin American Center, 1972.

Ruiz, Alberto. "El control de los establecimientos públicos." *Economía Colombiana*, 13 (1955):253–54.

Sánchez, Manuel Moreno. *México: 1968–1972, crisis y perspectiva.* Austin: University of Texas, Institute of Latin American Studies, 1973.

Sanclamente, Fernando. "Grupos de presión." Ph.D. dissertation, Universidad Javeriana, Bogota, 1965.

Santa, Eduardo. *Sociología política de Colombia.* Bogota: Ediciones Tercer Mundo, 1964.

Schapiro, Leonard, ed. *Political Opposition in One-Party States.* London: Macmillan Press, Ltd., 1972.

Schattschneider, E. E. *The Semi-Sovereign People.* New York: Holt, Rinehart and Winston, 1960.

Schmitt, Karl M. *Communism in Mexico.* Austin: University of Texas Press, 1965.

Schmitter, Philippe C. *Interest Conflict and Political Change in Brazil.* Stanford: Stanford University Press, 1971.

_____. "Paths to Political Development in Latin America." In *Changing Latin America: New Interpretations of Its Politics and Society*, edited by Douglas A. Chalmers, pp. 83–109. New York: Academy of Political Science, 1972.

Schneider, Ronald. *The Political System of Brazil.* New York: Columbia University Press, 1971.

Schwartzman, Simon. "Regional Contrasts Within a Continental Scale Nation: Brazil." In *Building States and Nations*, edited by S. Rokkan and S. M. Eisenstadt, vol. 2. Los Angeles: Sage Publications, 1973.

_____. "Representacão e cooptacão politica no Brasil." *Dados*, 7 (1970):9–41.

_____. *São Paulo e o estado nacional.* São Paulo: Difusão Européia do Livro, 1975.

Scott, James C. "Corruption, Machine Politics, and Political Change." *American Political Science Review*, 63 (December 1969):1142–59.

_____. "Patron-Client Politics and Political Change in Southeast Asia." *American Political Science Review*, 65 (March 1972):91–114.

Scott, Robert. *Mexican Government in Transition.* Urbana: University of Illinois Press, 1964.

_____. "Political Parties and Policy-Making in Latin America." In *Political Parties and Political Development*, edited by Joseph La Palombara and Myron Weiner, pp. 331–69. Princeton: Princeton University Press, 1966.

Serra, José. *El "milagro" económico brasileño: ¿realidad o mito?* Buenos Aires: Ed. Periferia, 1972.

Shafer, Robert Jones. *Mexican Business Organizations: History and Analysis.* Syracuse: Syracuse University Press, 1973.

_____. *Mexico: Mutual Adjustment Planning.* Syracuse: Syracuse University Press, 1966.

Sigal, Bertha Lerner. "Partido Revolucionario Institucional." In *México: la realidad política de sus partidos*, edited by Antonio Delhumeau. Mexico: Instituto Mexicano de Estudios Políticos A.C., 1970.

Silvert, Kalman, ed. *Expectant Peoples.* New York: Random House, 1963.

Skidmore, Thomas E. *Politics in Brazil, 1930–1964: An Experiment in Democracy.* New York: Oxford University Press, 1967.

Smith, Peter. "Social Mobilization, Political Participation, and the Rise of Juan Perón." *Political Science Quarterly*, 84 (March 1969):30–49.

Solís, Leopoldo. "Mexican Economic Policy in the Post-War Period: The Views of Mexican Economists." *American Economic Review*, 61 (June 1971):1–67.

Stepan, Alfred C., III. *The Military in Politics: Changing Patterns in Brazil.* Princeton: Princeton University Press, 1971.

_____. "Political Development Theory: The Latin American Experience." *Journal of International Affairs*, 20 (1966):223–35.

_____, ed. *Authoritarian Brazil: Origins, Policies, and Future.* New Haven: Yale University Press, 1973.

Stevens, Evelyn P. "Legality and Extra-legality in Mexico." *Journal of Interamerican Studies and World Affairs*, 12 (1970):62–75.

_____. *Protest and Response in Mexico.* Cambridge: MIT Press, 1974.

_____. "Protest Movement in an Authoritarian Regime: The Mexican Case." *Comparative Politics*, 7 (1975):361–82.

Sunkel, Oswaldo. "National Development Policy and External Dependence in Latin America." In *Contemporary Inter-American Relations*, edited by Yale H. Ferguson, pp. 465–92. Englewood Cliffs, N.J.: Prentice-Hall, 1972.

Syvrud, Donald E. *Foundations of Brazilian Economic Growth*. Stanford: Hoover Institution Press, 1974.

Tavares, Maria da Conceição. *Da substituição de importações ao capitalismo financeiro: ensaios sôbre economia brasileira*. Rio de Janeiro: Zahar, 1973.

Taylor, Philip B., Jr. *Government and Politics of Uruguay*. New Orleans: Tulane University Press, 1960.

_____. "Interests and Institutional Dysfunction in Uruguay." *American Political Science Review*, 43 (March 1963):62–74.

di Tella, Torcuato. "Populism and Reform in Latin America." In *Obstacles to Change in Latin America*, edited by Claudio Veliz, pp. 47–74. New York: Oxford University Press, 1970.

Thorp, Rosemary. "Inflation and the Financing of Economic Development." In *Financing Development in Latin America*, edited by Keith Griffin, pp. 182–224. London: Macmillan, 1971.

United States, Department of Labor. *Labor Law and Practice in Brazil*. Washington, D.C.: Government Printing Office, 1967.

Urrutia, Miguel. *The Development of the Colombian Labor Movement*. New Haven: Yale University Press, 1969.

Vanderschueren, Franz. "Political Significance of Neighborhood Committees in the Settlements of Santiago." In *The Chilean Road to Socialism*, edited by Dale Johnson, pp. 256–83. New York: Doubleday-Anchor, 1973.

Verba, Sidney, et al. "The Modes of Participation: Continuities in Research." *Comparative Political Studies*, 6 (July 1973):235–50.

Vernon, Raymond. *The Dilemma of Mexico's Development*. Cambridge: Harvard University Press, 1963.

_____, ed. *Public Policy and Private Enterprise in Mexico*. Cambridge: Harvard University Press, 1964.

Villanueva, Javier. *The Inflationary Process in Argentina, 1943–60*. 2d ed. Buenos Aires: Instituto Torcuato di Tella, 1966.

Villanueva, Víctor. *El CAEM y la revolucion de la fuerza armada*. Lima: Instituto de Estudios Peruanos, 1972.

_____. *Ejército Peruano*. Lima: Mejía Baca, 1973.

_____. *¿ Nueva mentalidad militar en el Perú?* Lima: Mejía Baca, 1969.

Walton, John. "Political Development and Economic Development: A Regional Assessment of Contemporary Theories." *Studies in Comparative International Development*, 7 (1972):39–63.

Warren, Harris G. *Paraguay*. Norman: University of Oklahoma Press, 1949.

Weiner, Myron. "Political Participation: Crisis of the Political Process." In *Crises and Sequences in Political Development*, by Leonard Binder et al. Princeton: Princeton University Press, 1971.

Weingrod, Alex. "Patrons, Patronage, and Political Parties." *Comparative Studies in Society and History*, 10 (1968):382.

Whitaker, Arthur P. *Argentina*. Englewood Cliffs, N.J.: Prentice-Hall, 1964.

Whitehead, Laurence. "The State and Sectoral Interests." Mimeograph. Oxford, 1974.

Wiarda, Howard J. "Corporatist Theory and Ideology: The Latin American Development Paradigm." Mimeograph.

_____. "Toward a Framework for the Study of Political Change in the Iberic-Latin

Tradition: The Corporative Model." *World Politics*, 25 (January 1973):206–36.

——, ed. *Politics and Social Change in Latin America: The Distinct Tradition.* Amherst: University of Massachusetts Press, 1974.

Wilgus, A. Curtis. *The Development of Hispanic America.* New York: Farrar and Rinehart, 1941.

Wilkie, James. *The Mexican Revolution: Federal Expenditure and Social Change.* Berkeley: University of California Press, 1967.

Wolf, Eric. "Kinship, Friendship, and Patron-Client Relations in Complex Societies." In *The Social Anthropology of Complex Societies*, edited by Michael Banton, pp. 1–21. New York: Barnes and Noble, 1966.

——. "The Power Seekers." In *Conflict and Violence in Latin American Politics*, edited by Francisco José Moreno and Barbara Mitrani. New York: Thomas Y. Crowell Co., 1971.

——, and Hansen, E. C. "Caudillo Politics: A Structural Analysis." *Comparative Studies of Society and History*, 9 (January 1967):168–79.

Worcester, Donald E. "The Spanish American Past—Enemy of Change." *Journal of Inter-American Studies*, 11 (January 1969):66–75.

Wynia, Gary W. "Economic Policy-Making Under Stress: Conflict and Exchange in Argentina." LADAC Occasional Papers, ser. 2, no. 11. Austin: Institute of Latin American Studies, 1974.

Yepes del Castillo, Ernesto. *Perú, 1820–1920: un siglo de desarrollo capitalista.* Lima: Instituto de Estudios Peruanos, Campodónico, 1972.

Index